W9-BWE-552

Copyright © 1973
The Bureau of National Affairs, Inc.
Washington, D.C. 20037

International Standard Book Number: ISBN 0-87179-171-4
Library of Congress Catalog Card Number: 72-93800
Printed in the United States of America

THE EQUAL EMPLOYMENT OPPORTUNIT
ACT OF 1972

Editorial Analysis

Discussion of Court Decision under 1964 Act

Text of Amended Act

Congressional Reports

Legislative History

Prepared by the Editorial Staff of
The Bureau of National Affairs, Inc.

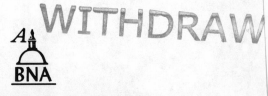

OPERATIONS MANUAL

Published by The Bureau of National Affairs, Inc.

Washington, D.C.

Table of Contents

Introduction

Immediately after Congress adopted the Civil Rights Act of 1964, pressure began building to give the Equal Employment Opportunity Commission the enforcement powers denied it by the compromise that cleared the way for passage of the Act.

For several years, the principal proposals would have given the Commission authority to issue cease-and-desist orders enforceable in the federal courts of appeals—an authority akin to that exercised by the National Labor Relations Board under the Taft-Hartley Act. These proposals regularly died in one or the other of the Houses of Congress.

In 1970, for example, the Senate passed a bill giving the Commission cease-and-desist powers. The bill was bottled up in the House by the Rules Committee.

But there was a change in strategy. The Nixon Administration proposed a measure that did not include cease-and-desist powers. Instead, it provided for giving the Commission power, after it had exhausted efforts to conciliate a meritorious claim of discrimination, to file a civil action in federal district court and to represent the charging party in the action. The remedies included injunctions against further violations, plus reinstatement and back pay for victims of unlawful discrimination.

The House acted first in 1972, approving a measure early in the session. The Senate then approved a stronger bill after a petition for cloture had been adopted on February 22, 1972. The House-Senate conferees then agreed to take the Senate bill. President Nixon signed the bill on March 24, 1972, and it became effective immediately.

It is the purpose of this volume to provide a guide to the changes made in the 1964 Act by the 1972 amendments. In addition to an editorial analysis, the volume includes the text of the Act as amended and pertinent excerpts from the legislative history.

Chapter 1

The Law in Brief

When Congress began to consider amendments to Title VII of the Civil Rights Act of 1964, the primary objective was to give the Equal Employment Opportunity Commission enforcement powers.

The amendments adopted in 1972 went much further. In addition to giving the Commission authority to institute court proceedings to enforce the prohibition against employment discrimination based on race, color, religion, sex, or national origin, the new Act made significant changes relating to coverage and exemptions, record keeping, administration, government contracts, and time for filing charges.

THE CHANGES IN COVERAGE

By a series of amendments, the coverage of Title VII is extended to millions of employees and union members. Here are the major changes:

• Prior to the amendments, Title VII applied only to employers with 25 or more employees and unions with 25 or more members. The amendments reduce the number of employees and union members required for coverage to 15. This change, however, does not become effective until one year after the adoption of the amendments. The new Act was signed by the President on March 24, 1972. It became effective immediately.

• Under the original Act, state and local governments and their employees were excluded from coverage. The amendments extend coverage to all state and local governments, governmental agencies, political subdivisions, and departments and agencies of the District of Columbia. There are some exemptions, discussed below.

• Federal employees are not within the jurisdiction of the Equal Employment Opportunity Commission. But the 1972 amendments added a new section that makes clear the obligation of the Federal Government to make all personnel actions without discrimination based on race, color, sex, religion, or national origin. Authority to enforce equal employment opportunity in federal agencies is assigned to the Civil Service Commission. If a federal employee or applicant for employment is dissatisfied with the government's handling of his complaint of discrimination, he may file an action in a federal district court.

• The 1972 amendments expand coverage to include discrimination in notices or advertising by joint labor-management committees that control apprenticeship or other training or retraining programs, including on-the-

1

job training. The basic prohibition bans discrimination both in administering the program and in admission to the program. Retaliation against persons seeking to enforce their rights is banned.

THE CHANGES IN EXEMPTIONS

Under the 1964 Act, there was an exemption for educational institutions with respect to individuals whose work involves educational activities. The amendments eliminate this exemption.

This change will bring under Title VII an estimated 120,000 educational institutions, with about 2.8 million teachers and professional staff members and another 1.5 million nonprofessional staff members.

But there is another exemption that was broadened. Under the original Title VII, there was an exemption for religious corporations, associations, or societies with respect to individuals whose work involves the religious aspects of the employing organization. The 1972 amendments broaden the exemption to include all activities of such organizations, not merely their religious activities. It should be noted, however, that the exemption permits the organization to discriminate solely on the basis of religion. It may not discriminate on the basis of race, color, sex, or national origin.

The amendment extending coverage to state and local governments and their employees provides an exemption for elected officials, their personal assistants, and their immediate advisers. It was stressed in the legislative history that this exemption "is intended to be construed very narrowly and is in no way intended to establish an over-all narrowing of the expanded coverage of state and local governmental employees."

ENFORCEMENT

The most fundamental changes made by the 1972 amendments relate to enforcement. As part of the compromise that led to the adoption of the 1964 Act, the Equal Employment Opportunity Commission was given virtually no enforcement powers. It could receive and investigate charges, and if it found reasonable cause to believe that the charges were true, it could attempt to eliminate the alleged unlawful employment practices by the informal methods of conference, conciliation, and persuasion. If these efforts failed, it notified the aggrieved, who then could file a suit in a federal district court. The period for filing a charge is extended from 90 to 180 days.

Under the 1972 amendments, if it is unable to obtain an acceptable conciliation agreement within 30 days after the filing of the charge or after the expiration of the state agency deferral period, the Commission may bring a civil suit in a federal district court for an injunction and other remedies against the charged employer, union, employment agency, or joint labor-management committee. In cases involving a state or local government, the Attorney General is authorized to bring the action.

If the Commission is not able to process a complaint with satisfactory speed or enters into a conciliation agreement that is not acceptable to the aggrieved party or parties, the aggrieved then may seek his own court remedy. Moreover, if the Commission dismisses a charge, or if, within 180 days of the filing of the charge, it has neither issued a complaint nor entered into a conciliation or settlement agreement acceptable to both the aggrieved party and the Commission, the Commission is required to notify the aggrieved party to permit him to bring an action on his own within the next 90 days. A charge may be filed within 180 days of the alleged violation; it formerly was 90 days.

In another enforcement change, the Commission is given concurrent jurisdiction with the Justice Department for a period of two years to bring actions to eliminate patterns or practices of unlawful employment discrimination. At the end of the two years, the Commission will have exclusive jurisdiction over such actions.

A new Section 7(f)(2) permits the Commission or the Attorney General, the latter in a case involving a state or local government, to bring an action for temporary or preliminary relief pending final disposition of the charge where it appears on the basis of a preliminary investigation that prompt judicial action is necessary to carry out the purposes of the Act.

In a move to expedite the trial of cases, a judge assigned to try a case is given authority to appoint a master to hear the case if the judge has not scheduled the case for trial within 120 days after the issue is joined. Another change permits a charge to be filed on behalf of an aggrieved person.

ADMINISTRATIVE CHANGES

The broadening of its jurisdiction and enforcement powers poses many problems for the Equal Employment Opportunity Commission. In the current fiscal year, the Commission already has had a case intake of about 33,000. It was 22,000 in the 1971 fiscal year. The Commission is about 22 months behind in its processing of cases.

With the Commission's new enforcement powers, these problems will be compounded. It will be necessary to hire and train new attorneys to handle the litigation in the federal courts. And it will be necessary to have competent and trained investigators to prepare cases for trial in the courts.

As part of the change in the administrative organization, the amendments provide for making the General Counsel of the Commission a Presidential appointee, subject to Senate confirmation. Five regional legal offices were to be established immediately.

During the deliberations of the Conference Committee, there was a significant deletion of a provision included in the House bill. The provision would have made the EEOC the sole federal authority to police employment discrimination of the types forbidden by the Act. The deletion has been construed as permitting an aggrieved individual to seek relief in several forums—the EEOC, OFCC, NLRB, state or local agencies, and arbitration, although there have been court decisions to the contrary.

With respect to federal contractors, the new Act provides that no contract, whether subject to Executive Order 11246 or to any other equal employment law or order, may be terminated, denied, or withheld without a full hearing where the employer had an affirmative action plan accepted within the preceding 12 months.

Another change affecting administration, which is included in a new Section 715, establishes an Equal Employment Opportunity Coordinating Council. Members of the Council will be the Secretary of Labor, the Chairman of the EEOC, the Attorney General, the Chairman of the U.S. Civil Service Commission, and the Chairman of the U.S. Civil Rights Commission or their respective designees. The objective is to coordinate the activities of all branches of the government that have responsibility for equal employment opportunity.

WHAT THE ACT MEANS TO EMPLOYERS

The basic obligations imposed on employers under the 1972 Act are virtually the same as those imposed under Title VII of the 1964 Act. Under Section 703(a), it is an unlawful employment practice for an employer to do the following:

• Fail or refuse to hire, or discharge, any individual or otherwise discriminate against any individual with respect to his compensation, terms, conditions, or privileges of employment because of his race, color, religion, sex, or national origin. This now applies to applicants for employment, as well as employees.

• Limit, segregate, or classify employees in any way that would deprive or tend to deprive any individual of employment opportunities or otherwise adversely affect his status as an employee because of his race, color, religion, sex, or national origin.

These are the basic unlawful employment practices that employers are forbidden to commit. Their scope and application have been delineated in numerous court decisions handed down under the 1964 Act. In the *Griggs* case, for example, the Supreme Court upheld the position of the EEOC that a test used in hiring or promotion must be related to the job involved; it may not be a general intelligence or aptitude test. (*Griggs* v. *Duke Power Co.*, US SupCt, 1971, 3 FEP Cases 175)

Another leading case illustrates the extent of the steps the courts will require an employer to take to eradicate the present effects of past discrimination. The court ordered the company to permit bidding for jobs across craft lines on the basis of seniority in the terminal, even though more than 20 unions were involved. (*U.S.* v. *Jacksonville Terminal Co.*, CA 5, 1971, 3 FEP Cases 862)

As a result of the 1972 amendments, many more employers will be subject to these prohibitions. State and local governments now are covered, and the elimination of an exemption for educational institutions with respect to individuals whose work involves educational activities brings about 2.8 million teachers and professional staff members and another 1.5 million nonprofessional staff members within the Act's coverage. Then, on March 24, 1973, employers with 15 or more employees will be covered. This will replace a requirement that an employer have 25 or more employees to be covered.

There are, however, a number of exemptions or exceptions. The prohibitions do not apply, for example, where:

• Religion, sex, or national origin is a bona fide occupational qualification reasonably necessary to the normal operation of the business or enterprise.

• The employer is a religious corporation, association, or society. Prior to the 1972 amendments, this exemption applied only to the religious activities of such groups. But it permits discrimination only on the basis of religion.

• The persons discriminated against are members of the Communist Party or a Communist-front organization.

• The employer is subject to a government security program, and the persons involved do not have security clearance.

• A business operating on or near an Indian reservation accords preferential treatment to Indians.

• The different standards of compensation or terms and conditions of employment are applied pursuant to a bona fide seniority system, a merit system, or a system that measures earnings by quantity or quality of production, or they result from the fact that the employees work in different locations.

• The employer acts upon the results of a professionally developed ability test that is not designed or intended to be used to discriminate. Under the *Griggs* v. *Duke Power* decision discussed above, however, the test must be related to the job to be filled.

• Differentiations in pay based on sex are authorized under the provisions of the Equal Pay Act of 1963 where the jobs performed are not equal. Under the *Wheaton Glass* decision, however, an appeals court applied a strict concept of inequality in comparing jobs performed by male and female employees. The court rejected the argument that the jobs were different because of certain additional tasks performed by the male employees. (*Shultz* v. *Wheaton Glass Co.*, CA 3, 1970, 19 WH Cases 336)

Training Programs

The 1964 Act made it an unlawful employment practice for an employer, a union, or a joint labor-management committee to discriminate against any individual because of his race, color, religion, sex, or national origin in admission to or employment in any apprenticeship, training, or retraining program, including on-the-job training.

The prohibition was expanded by the 1972 amendments to include the publication of advertising or printing of notices relating to such training or retraining programs indicating any preference, limitation, specification, or discrimination based on race, color, religion, sex, or national origin.

There is an exception, however. A notice or advertisement may indicate a preference, limitation, specification, or discrimination based on religion, sex, or national origin when religion, sex, or national origin is a bona fide occupational qualification for employment.

The same prohibitions relating to advertising already applied to employers, unions, and employment agencies. Another unfair employment practice prohibition applies across the board to employers, unions, employment agencies, and joint labor-management committees. It is unlawful for any of them to discriminate against any employee, job applicant, or union member because he has opposed any unlawful practice under the Act or because he has made a charge, testified, assisted, or participated in an investigation, proceeding, or hearing.

Employment Imbalance

Although the law forbids employers to discriminate in employment on the basis of race, color, religion, sex, or national origin, it does not require them to take affirmative steps to rectify an already-existing imbalance in the work force. Nothing in the law, it is stated, shall be interpreted to require an employer or training program to grant preferential treatment to any individual or group because of an imbalance that may exist with respect to the total number or percentage of persons of any race, color, religion, sex, or national origin already employed.

In framing remedies for affirmative relief to eradicate the effects of past discrimination, however, some courts have said that the ban on "preferential treatment" solely because of racial imbalance must be read in conjunction with the fundamental purposes of the Act and the provision for affirmative relief. So Section 703(j) "cannot be construed as a ban on affirmative relief against continuation of effects of past discrimination resulting from present practices (neutral on their face) which have the practical effect of continuing past injustices." (See *U.S.* v. *IBEW, Local 38*, CA 6, 1970, 2 FEP Cases 716.)

Affirmative action plans for government construction and manufacturing contractors, moreover, often require the establishment of goals for employment of certain percentages of minority-group employees. Such a plan was upheld in a case involving the *Contractors Ass'n of Eastern Pa.* v. *Hodgson*, CA 3, 1971, 3 FEP Cases 395; *cert. denied* by US SupCt, 1971, 3 FEP Cases 1030.

Notices, Records

The law imposes on employers an obligation to post notices prepared by the EEOC and to make and keep such records as the Commission prescribes. To avoid duplication, however, employers who are subject to a state fair employment practice law or to an executive order prescribing fair employment practices for government contractors will not be required to maintain two sets of records. Employers subject to the executive orders need not keep any additional records or file any additional reports under the law. But the Commission may require employers subject to state laws to make such notations on the records as may be necessary because of differences in the state and federal laws.

The 1972 amendments make an important change relating to the record-keeping obligation. Under the 1964 Act, a party required to keep records could seek an exemption from these requirements on the ground of undue hardship either by applying to the Commission or by bringing a civil action in a district court. The amendments require the party seeking such an exemption first to apply to the Commission. He may bring a court action only if the Commission denies his request.

The amendments also authorize the Commission to apply for a court order compelling compliance with the record-keeping and reporting requirements of the Act.

WHAT THE ACT MEANS TO EMPLOYMENT AGENCIES

There are two specific unlawful employment practices for employment agencies. As set out in Section 703(b), they are:

- To fail or refuse to refer for employment, or otherwise to discriminate against, any individual because of his race, color, religion, sex, or national origin.
- To classify or refer any individual for employment on the basis of his race, color, religion, sex, or national origin.

The prohibitions against retaliation against those who invoke the law's processes and advertising that indicates a preference or discrimination based on race, color, religion, sex, or national origin apply to employment agencies. The exceptions relating to jobs in which religion, sex, or national origin is an occupational qualification, members of the Communist Party or Communist organizations, and employees denied security clearance also apply to actions taken by employment agencies.

Definition of 'Agency'

An "employment agency" is defined broadly to include "any person regularly undertaking with or without compensation to procure employees for an employer or to procure for employees opportunities to work for an employer." The term also embraces the United States Employment Service and state and local employment services that receive federal assistance. It does not, however, include other federal agencies or agencies of a state or political subdivision of a state.

Employment agencies, like employers, are not required by the law to take affirmative steps to rectify any existing imbalance in the number or percentage of minority-group persons employed by any employer. They must make and keep the records prescribed by the Commission, subject to the same exceptions noted above for employers.

WHAT THE ACT MEANS TO UNIONS

The 1972 amendments made two principal changes relating to the obligations of unions. First, they provide for reducing the number of union members required for coverage from 25 to 15 on March 24, 1973. Second, they impose the same prohibition that is imposed on employers with respect to notices or advertising involving joint labor-management apprenticeship, training, retraining, or on-the-job training programs. The notices or advertising may not indicate any preference, limitation, specification, or discrimination based on race, color, religion, sex, or national origin.

Section 703(c) proscribes three unlawful employment practices by unions. They are:

• To exclude or to expel from membership, or otherwise to discriminate against, any individual because of his race, color, religion, sex, or national origin.

• To limit, segregate, or classify membership or to classify or fail or refuse to refer an individual for employment in any way that would deprive or tend to deprive him of employment opportunities or would limit such employment opportunities or otherwise adversely affect his status as an employee or as an applicant for employment because of his race, color, religion, sex, or national origin. This now applies to applicants for membership as well as to members.

• To cause or attempt to cause an employer to unlawfully discriminate against an individual.

Unions also are subject to the prohibitions against retaliating against those who invoke the law's processes, discrimination in the operation of

apprenticeship and training programs, and advertising that indicates a preference or discrimination based on race, color, religion, sex, or national
origin. The exceptions relating to members of the Communist Party or its
organizations, employees denied security clearance, and jobs in which
religion, sex, or national origin is an occupational qualification apply to
unions as well as to employers and employment agencies.

Definition of 'Union'

Title VII contains a long and involved definition of a "labor organization." It essentially is the same definition used in the 1959 Landrum-
Griffin Act, except that state and local central bodies are covered in the
same way other labor organizations are. A "state or local central body" is
excepted from the definition in the Landrum-Griffin Act. So the Title VII
definition is a broad one covering national or international labor organizations and their subordinate bodies, independent unions, employee representation committees, and so forth.

To be subject to Title VII, however, a union must be engaged in an
industry "affecting commerce." It so qualifies if:

- It maintains or operates a hiring hall or hiring office that obtains
employees for employers or jobs for employees; or
- It has 25 or more members (15 or more members after March 24,
1973). It also must be a certified bargaining representative or a recognized
or acting bargaining representative of employees in an industry affecting
commerce or a parent or subordinate body of a bargaining representative.

A union is not required to take affirmative steps to rectify an existing
imbalance in the number or percentage of minority-group persons in its
membership. But in pattern-or-practice actions brought against both
employers and unions under Title VII and in actions brought under the
executive orders applicable to government contractors, unions have been
required to take such action as merging seniority lines, abolishing segregated locals, and permitting job bidding on a company-wide basis. (See
Local 189, Papermakers & Paperworkers v. *U.S.*, CA 5, 1969, 1 FEP Cases
875; *U.S.* v. *Jacksonville Terminal Co.*, CA 5, 1971, 3 FEP Cases 862.)

WHAT THE ACT MEANS TO EMPLOYEES

The purpose of Title VII is to protect employees against any discrimination involving the employment relationship that is based on race, color,
religion, sex, or national origin. The protection extends far beyond the
mere act of hiring. Subject to the exceptions already noted above,
employees and applicants for employment are protected against the following where the action is based on race, color, religion, sex, or national
origin:

- A refusal by an employer to hire or a refusal by an employment
agency or labor union to refer for employment.

- Discrimination with respect to compensation, terms, conditions, or privileges of employment.
- Limitation, segregation, or classification by an employer in such a way as to deprive or tend to deprive them of employment opportunities or otherwise adversely to affect their status as employees.
- Discrimination by employers, labor unions, or joint labor-management committees in admission to or employment in apprenticeship, training, or retraining programs.
- Discriminatory classifications or referrals by employment agencies.
- Exclusion or expulsion from membership or other discriminatory treatment by a labor union.
- Limitation, segregation, classification of membership, or classification or failure or refusal to refer for jobs by a labor union in any way that would deprive or tend to deprive them of employment opportunities, limit their employment opportunities, or otherwise adversely affect their status as employees or applicants for employment.

Enforcement of Rights

Under the 1964 Act, the aggrieved employee or union member was left almost on his own in enforcing his rights. The EEOC had no authority to file an action. The only situation in which the government actively could pursue charges of violation was where there was an alleged pattern or practice of violation. In such a situation, the Justice Department could bring an action. Under the amendments, a charge may be filed on behalf of an aggrieved individual by another organization, such as the NAACP.

Now the EEOC may file an action in a federal district court if it is unable to eliminate the alleged unlawful employment practices by the informal methods of conference, conciliation, and persuasion. But the aggrieved individual is not deprived of a right to seek a remedy on his own. He still may bring an action in any of the following circumstances:

- The Commission is not able to process a complaint with satisfactory speed.
- The Commission enters into a conciliation agreement that is not acceptable to the aggrieved party or parties.
- The Commission dismisses the charge.
- Within 180 days of the filing of the charge, the Commission has neither issued a complaint nor entered into a conciliation or settlement agreement acceptable to both the aggrieved party and the Commission.

The employee also is protected against retaliation for invoking the processes of the Act.

WHAT THE ACT MEANS TO THE STATES

At the time Title VII of the federal Civil Rights Act of 1964 was adopted, 25 of the states already had similar laws. Moreover, several cities had fair employment practice ordinances. The 1964 Act made it clear that there was no intent to undercut or preempt these laws. In fact, the provisions in the federal Act for deferral to the procedures under the state laws led to the adoption of several new state laws.

The 1972 amendments to the federal Act made major changes affecting state and local governments. First, they brought state and local governments within the coverage of the Federal Act. The Justice Department was given the assignment of enforcing the Act in this area. Second, the amendments made changes in the enforcement procedures (1) where there is no state law and (2) where there is a state law. Here are the procedures:

Where There Is No State Law

Under the 1972 amendments, the following procedures apply where no state equal employment opportunity law exists:

- A charge must be filed within 180 days after the occurrence of an alleged unlawful employment practice. (The time limitation had been 90 days under the 1964 law.)

Court decisions under the 1964 law showed an inclination to interpret this time limitation to give the aggrieved person the maximum benefit of the law. In adopting the 1972 amendments, the legislators indicated that it was not intended that such court decisions should be circumscribed. Continued validity was specified for existing case law that certain types of violations are continuing in nature.

- After a charge is filed, the Commission must serve a notice of the charge on the respondent within 10 days. This is new.
- The Commission then must investigate the charge, after which it must determine whether there is reasonable cause to believe that the charge is true. The Commission shall make its determination of reasonable cause as promptly as possible and, so far as practicable, within 120 days. No time limit was specified in the 1964 law.
- If it finds no reasonable cause, the Commission must dismiss the charge; if it finds reasonable cause, it will attempt to conciliate the case.
- If the Commission is unable to obtain a conciliation agreement that is acceptable to the Commission, it may bring a civil action against the respondent in an appropriate federal district court. In the case of a government, a governmental agency, or a political subdivision, the Commission notifies the Attorney General, who may bring a civil action. A special master may be appointed if the district court has not assigned the case for trial within 120 days.
- If the court finds that a respondent is engaging in an unlawful employment practice charged in the complaint, the court may enjoin the respondent from engaging in the unlawful employment practice and grant such affirmative relief as it may deem appropriate, including, but not limited to, reinstatement with or without back pay. Back pay is limited,

however, to no more than that accrued during the two years prior to the filing of a charge with the Commission.

• In the event that the Commission dismisses a charge, or if, within 180 days from the filing of the charge, the Commission or the Attorney General has not filed a civil action or entered into a conciliation agreement to which the aggrieved person is a party, the Commission or the Attorney General will notify the aggrieved party. Within 90 days after the receipt of such notice, the aggrieved person may bring a civil action against the respondent. Should such a private action be brought, the Commission or the Attorney General (where a government agency is involved) may seek to intervene in the action.

Where There Is A State Law

Where a state equal employment opportunity law exists, the 1972 amendments specify this procedure:

• A charge must be filed within 180 days after the occurrence of an alleged unlawful employment practice. It was 90 days under the 1964 law.

• If a charge is initially filed with a state or local agency, such charge must be filed with the Commission within 300 days after the alleged unlawful practice has occurred or within 30 days after receipt of notice that the state or local agency has terminated its proceedings. Under the old law, the time limitations were 210 days after occurrence and 30 days after notice of termination of state proceedings.

• Where a state or local EEO statute exists, the EEOC must wait 60 days after state or local proceedings have been commenced, unless those proceedings are terminated sooner, before it can act on a charge. The deferral period is extended to 120 days during the first year after enactment of a state or local law.

• Once the deferral is concluded, the Commission must serve a notice of the charge on the respondent within 10 days.

• The Commission then must investigate the charge, after which it must determine whether there is reasonable cause to believe that the charge is true. The Commission shall make its determination of reasonable cause as promptly as possible and, so far as practicable, within 120 days. It is required to accord substantial weight to the decision of state or local authorities. The 120-day period is new, as is the provision on the weight to be accorded the state or local decision.

The procedure from this point forward is the same as that followed in cases where there is no state or local EEO law.

In leaving the deferral provisions basically unchanged, the legislators indicated that no change was deemed necessary in view of the Supreme Court decision holding that the EEOC may receive and defer a charge to a state agency and begin to process the charge upon lapse of the 60-day deferral, even though the language provides that no charge can be filed before the expiration of 60 days after proceedings have been commenced under the state or local law. (*Love* v. *Pullman Co.*, US SupCt, 1972, 4 FEP Cases 150) Similarly cited with approval was the decision of the U.S. Court of Appeals at Denver holding that in order to protect the aggrieved individual's right to file with the EEOC within the specified time periods, a charge filed with a state or local agency also may be filed with the EEOC during the 60-day deferral period. (*Vigil* v. *AT&T*, CA 10, 1972, 4 FEP Cases 345)

At the time the 1972 Act was adopted, 40 states had FEP laws of general application, although their provisions varied widely.

Chapter 2

Background of the FEP Law

Like much of our social legislation, Title VII of the Civil Rights Act of 1964 and the 1972 amendments have roots extending deep into the past. But until the New Deal period of the 1930s, governmental action was largely confined to government employees.

The Civil Service Act of 1883, for example, sought to establish the principle of "merit employment," and one of the first regulations issued under the law outlawed religious discrimination in federal employment. (The Pendleton Act [Civil Service Act], 22 Stat. 403, 1883, 5 U.S.C. ch. 12, 1958; U.S. Civil Service Commission, Rule VIII, 1883)

In 1940, a Civil Service rule forbade racial, as well as religious, discrimination. (Executive Order 8587, 5 Fed. Reg. 445, 1940) Then, when Congress adopted the Ramspeck Act, extending the coverage of the Civil Service Act and amending the Classification Act of 1923, the philosophy of "equal rights for all" in classified federal employment was established. The Act declared:

"In carrying out the provisions of this title, and the provisions of the Classification Act of 1923, as amended, there shall be no discrimination against any person, or with respect to the position held by any person, on account of race, creed, or color." (Ramspeck Act, 54 Stat. 1211, 1940, Title I, 5 U.S.C. sec. 631a, 1958)

Action Under New Deal

In the early New Deal period, a policy of equal opportunity in employment and training created through federal funds was established by congressional and executive action. The policy extended not only to direct federal employment and employment by government contractors, but to employment and training opportunities provided by grant-in-aid programs as well.

The first enunciation by Congress of the principle of equal job opportunity was in the Unemployment Relief Act of 1933. It provided:

"That in employing citizens for the purpose of the Act no discrimination shall be made on account of race, color, or creed." (Unemployment Relief Act of 1933, 48 Stat. 22)

Similar provisions were included in many of the laws passed during the New Deal period. Where the laws themselves did not bar such discrimination, the policy of nondiscrimination was enunciated by the executive branch. Regulations issued under the National Industrial Recovery Act

14

and the laws providing for public low-rent housing and defense housing programs, for example, forbade discrimination based on race, color, or religion. (National Industrial Recovery Act of 1933, Title II, 48 Stat. 200; 44 C.F.R. sec. 265-33, 1938)

Although these amounted to unequivocal declarations by the legislative and executive branches, they were of limited effect in most instances. They amounted to little more than expressions of policy. There were no standards by which discrimination could be determined, and machinery and sanctions for enforcement were rare.

THE WORLD WAR II FEPC

The practice of including nondiscrimination provisions in laws providing for federally financed training programs continued after the outbreak of World War II. But leaders of the Negro community contended that, despite these provisions, Negroes still were being denied federally financed training for defense jobs.

Following the threat of a Negro march on Washington, President Roosevelt on June 25, 1941, issued Executive Order 8802 establishing a five-man Fair Employment Practice Committee. The Committee was set up as an independent agency responsible solely to the President.

The executive order declared the following to be the policy of the Government:

"To encourage full participation in the national defense program by all citizens of the United States, regardless of race, creed, color, or national origin, in the firm belief that the democratic way of life within the nation can be defended successfully only with the help and support of all groups within its borders." (6 Fed. Reg. 3109, 1941)

Scope of Order

The order was broad in scope. It applied to all defense contracts, to employment by the Federal Government, and to vocational and training programs administered by federal agencies. For its part, the FEPC was authorized to receive and investigate complaints of discrimination, to take "appropriate steps" to redress valid grievances, and to recommend to federal agencies and to the President whatever measures it deemed necessary and proper to carry out the purposes of the order.

But the FEPC had its weaknesses. It had a staff of only eight members, and it lacked direct enforcement powers. So it concentrated on drafting policies and conducting public hearings throughout the country.

The FEPC later lost its autonomy by being transferred to the War Manpower Commission, and a dispute with the Chairman of the Commission led to the resignation of several members of the FEPC. The Committee, in effect, suspended operations early in 1943.

The Second FEPC

A few months later, President Roosevelt issued Executive Order 9346, establishing a new Fair Employment Practice Committee and declaring it to be the policy of the Government to promote the fullest utilization of manpower and to eliminate employment discrimination. (8 Fed. Reg. 7183, 1943)

The jurisdiction of the new FEPC was broader than that of its predecessor. It extended to all employment by government contractors (not merely in defense industries), recruitment and training for war production, and employment by the Federal Government. Moreover, its authority with respect to labor unions was extended to include discrimination in membership as well as in employment.

When it came to staff, the new FEPC was much better taken care of than was its predecessor. It was given a budget that enabled it to employ a staff of nearly 120 and to open 15 field offices. In the three years of its existence, the FEPC processed approximately 8,000 complaints and conducted 30 public hearings. But it still lacked power to enforce its decisions except by negotiation, moral suasion, and the pressure of public opinion. Its authority expired at the end of June 1946.

THE GOVERNMENT CONTRACTS COMMITTEES

Although the Government continued to insert nondiscrimination clauses in some contracts, the termination of the FEPC ended coordinated, government-wide efforts to effectuate a policy of equal employment opportunity. In 1951, however, President Truman sought to revitalize the policy of nondiscrimination on government contracts.

First, Truman issued a series of executive orders directing certain government agencies to include nondiscrimination clauses in their contracts. Then, on December 3, 1951, he issued Executive Order 10308 creating the Committee on Government Contract Compliance. It was an 11-member group composed of representatives of industry, the public, and the five principal government contracting agencies. (16 Fed. Reg. 12303, 1951)

Charged primarily with studying and appraising the effectiveness of the existing program, the Committee issued a report drawing these conclusions, among others (31 LRRM 186):

• The nondiscrimination clause is almost "forgotten, dead, and buried" under thousands of standard legal and technical words in contracts.

• Government contracting is so far-reaching that nondiscriminatory employment would be practically assured if every contractor were made to live up to the letter of the nondiscrimination clause in his contract.

• There is no effective enforcement of the nondiscrimination clause.

The Committee then made more than 20 specific recommendations, many of which were aimed at the establishment of effective enforcement procedures for the nondiscrimination clause.

Eisenhower Committee

On August 13, 1953, President Eisenhower replaced the Truman Committee with the President's Committee on Government Contracts. This was a 15-member group composed of representatives of industry, labor, government, and the public. (Executive Order 10479, 18 Fed. Reg. 4899, 1953)

The new committee was given these duties:

• To make recommendations to contracting agencies for improving nondiscrimination provisions in government contracts.

• To serve as a clearing house for complaints alleging violation of the nondiscrimination clauses.

• To encourage and assist with educational programs by nongovernmental groups.

Like its predecessor, the Eisenhower Committee had no power to enforce its recommendations. It had to rely on the procurement agencies to adjust complaints, although a report on the disposition of each complaint had to be made to the Committee.

Kennedy-Johnson Committee

It was under the Kennedy Administration that the policy of nondiscrimination by government contractors was given teeth. In a sweeping Executive Order 10925, issued on March 6, 1961, Kennedy created a new President's Committee on Equal Employment Opportunity charged with the responsibility of effectuating equal employment opportunity both in government and in employment on government contracts. (26 Fed. Reg. 1977, 1961)

The new executive order made a dramatic break with those issued under previous Administrations with respect to the obligations imposed on government contractors. While the earlier orders imposed an obligation on contractors not to discriminate on the basis of race, creed, color, or national origin, the Kennedy Order also required the contractors to take affirmative action to make the policy effective.

The order required government contractors to do the following:

• Not to discriminate against any employee or job applicant because of race, creed, color or national origin.

• To take affirmative action to ensure that applicants are employed and employees are treated during their employment without regard to race, creed, color, or national origin.

• To state in all solicitations or advertisements for employees that all qualified applicants will receive consideration without regard to race, creed, color, or national origin.

- To advise each labor union with which they deal of their commitments under the order.
- To include the obligations under the order in every subcontract or purchase order, unless specifically exempted.
- To comply with all provisions of the order and the rules and regulations issued by the Committee; to furnish all information and reports required by the Committee; to permit access to books, records, and accounts for the purpose of investigation to ascertain compliance.
- To file regular compliance reports describing hiring and employment practices.

Enforcement Powers

In addition to requiring the compliance reports, the Kennedy Order gave the Committee specific enforcement powers. To assure compliance, the Committee could do the following: (1) publish the names of noncomplying contractors and unions; (2) recommend suits by the Justice Department to compel compliance; (3) recommend criminal actions by the Justice Department for furnishing false information; (4) terminate the contract of a noncomplying employer; and (5) forbid the contracting agencies to enter into new contracts with a contractor who discriminates unless he demonstrates that his policy has changed.

But the most effective method of achieving compliance was the "plan for progress," which the Committee described as a procedure for effecting compliance through cooperation. Essentially, it required the contractor to set up effective recruiting programs to give members of minority groups equal opportunity of employment.

Extension of Program

The scope of Executive Order 10925 was extended by two orders subsequently issued, one by President Kennedy and the other by President Johnson. On June 22, 1963, Kennedy issued Executive Order 11114 extending the nondiscrimination requirement for federally assisted construction contracts. (28 Fed. Reg. 6485) Then, on February 13, 1964, President Johnson issued Executive Order 11141 broadening the nondiscrimination clause to forbid discrimination on the basis of age, except upon the basis of a bona fide occupational qualification, retirement plan, or statutory requirement. (29 Fed. Reg. 2477)

Union Discrimination—The President's Committee was directed to use its best efforts to get unions to cooperate with and comply in the implementation of the orders, and the Committee was authorized to hold public hearings on the policies and practices of unions and submit reports and recommendations to the President on discriminatory practices of unions. But the Committee had no direct means of compelling compliance by unions; the obligation ran from the contractor to the Government.

Shortly after Title VII was adopted, however, the Committee provided for adoption for government-contract work of the Secretary of Labor's standards for nondiscrimination in apprenticeship and training. The standards thus apply to any registered or unregistered apprenticeship program that includes apprentices employed by a government contractor during performance of government contract work or work on a federally assisted construction project. So the Government may blacklist a government supply or construction contractor whose apprenticeship standards are out of line with the federal standards.

The standards and compliance procedures for federal programs were issued in December 1963. They require selection of apprentices on the basis of qualifications other than race, creed, color, or national origin. They make clear, however, that nothing in them requires or supports a quota system for minorities in apprenticeship programs.

OFFICE OF FEDERAL CONTRACT COMPLIANCE

During the late 1960s, responsibility for administering and enforcing nondiscrimination provisions in government contracts was placed in the Labor Department. An Office of Federal Contract Compliance was set up to handle the job. This was done by Executive Order 11246 signed by President Johnson on September 24, 1965. It was amended by Executive Order 11375 on October 13, 1967. Part I of this Order was superseded by Executive Order 11478; Part II was amended to add sex as a prohibited basis of discrimination, effective October 13, 1968.

Executive Order 11246 now is enforced by the Department of Labor and its Office of Federal Contract Compliance, with the cooperation of the contracting agencies and departments within the Federal Government.

Under the Executive Order, the Secretary of Labor or the appropriate contracting agency is given the power to do the following:

- Publish the names of noncomplying contractors or unions.
- Recommend suits by the Justice Department to compel compliance.
- Recommend action by the EEOC or the Justice Department under Title VII as amended by the 1972 Act giving the EEOC authority to file suit in a federal district court.
- Cancel the contract of a noncomplying employer.
- Blacklist a noncomplying employer from participating in future government contracts until the employer has shown a willingness to comply.

The threat of contract cancellation or the loss of future government contract work is the government's major weapon. It has, however, been rarely used.

In enforcing the Executive Order, the OFCC has placed primary emphasis on compliance reviews and pre-award programs that cover the entire program of a contractor or subcontractor, rather than on encouraging individual complaints. Although it has machinery for processing complaints, the OFCC is concerned primarily with broader compliance efforts.

The specific enforcement procedures of the OFCC are discussed in Chapter 6.

STATE LAWS, MUNICIPAL ORDINANCES

As an outgrowth of the World War II Fair Employment Practice Committees, several of the states adopted laws forbidding racial and religious discrimination in employment. In addition, a number of cities adopted ordinances forbidding discrimination in employment by private employers and, in some cases, by municipal agencies and contractors.

Ordinarily such a state law superseded municipal ordinances that had been adopted in the state. But this was not always the case. Section 12 of the Pennsylvania FEP law, for example, provides for the continuing validity of the previously enacted municipal ordinances. Once the state agency's enforcement procedures are invoked, however, they are exclusive.

By now most states, except in the Deep South, have enforceable fair employment practice laws. The provisions of the state laws are discussed in detail in Chapter 7.

TAFT-HARTLEY, RAILWAY LABOR ACTS

While employer discrimination against employees on the basis of race or religion was being dealt with by state laws and executive orders of the Federal Government, union discrimination for the same reasons was being handled under a new doctrine of "fair representation" enunciated by the courts and the National Labor Relations Board.

The duty of a statutory bargaining agent to represent all employees in the bargaining unit without arbitrary discrimination was first established in cases arising under the Railway Labor Act. In a case decided in 1945, the U.S. Supreme Court declared that the Act requires the bargaining agent "in collective bargaining and in making contracts with the carrier, to represent nonunion or minority union members of the craft without hostile discrimination, fairly, impartially, and in good faith." (*Steele* v. *Louisville & Nashville R.R. Co.*, U.S. SupCt, 1944, 15 LRRM 708)

The Supreme Court later held that a union which discriminates by contract against a minority group may be enjoined from enforcing its contract in this respect. (*Railroad Trainmen* v. *Howard*, U.S. SupCt, 1952, 30 LRRM 2258)

Policy of NLRB

Applying the same principle under the Wagner Act, the NLRB established a corresponding duty of certified unions to represent the members in their bargaining unit equally and without discrimination. It indicated that it would have revoked the certification of a union that placed Negro members in a segregated local except for the fact that the union offered to give up its discriminatory practices during the proceeding before the Board. (*Larus and Bros.*, NLRB, 1945, 16 LRRM 242)

Several years later, the Board repeated that execution of a contract which discriminates on the basis of race would endanger the union's certification, and added that such a contract would not bar an election sought by a rival union. (*Pioneer Bus Co.*, NLRB, 1962, 51 LRRM 1546)

Then in December of 1962, the Board broadened the doctrine of fair representation in a dramatic way. It ruled that:

• The Taft-Hartley Act gives employees the right to be free from "unfair or irrelevant or invidious treatment by their bargaining agent."

• If the union treats any worker it represents in this manner, it unlawfully restrains employees in the exercise of their rights and thereby violates the unfair practice provisions of the law. The employer also commits an unfair labor practice if he participates in such arbitrary action by the union against an employee. (*Miranda Fuel Co.* NLRB, 1962, 51 LRRM 1585)

The *Miranda* holding was denied enforcement by the U.S. Court of Appeals at New York in a two-to-one decision in which there was no majority opinion. All three judges wrote opinions (54 LRRM 2715). The future of the holding, therefore, is in question, particularly in view of the fact that Congress in the Civil Rights Act has dealt directly with the type of discrimination with which NLRB's *Miranda* decision dealt indirectly.

Nevertheless, on the same day that President Johnson signed the Civil Rights Act, the NLRB issued a decision finding a union guilty of unfair labor practices and stripping it of its certification as bargaining agent because of its racially discriminatory practices. The union maintained segregated locals, and the white local refused to process a grievance for a Negro employee because of his race. (*Independent Metal Workers Union, Local Nos. 1 and 2* [*Hughes Tool Co.*], NLRB, 1964, 56 LRRM 1289)

Employer Practices

The role of the NLRB in policing racial discrimination in employment could have been greatly expanded by a decision handed down by the U.S. Court of Appeals for the District of Columbia. The court held that racial discrimination by an employer in employment practices was a violation of Section 8(a)(1) of the Taft-Hartley Act. It remanded the case to the NLRB for a finding on whether the employer engaged in discriminatory practices. (*Packinghouse Workers* v. *NLRB*, CA DC, 1969, 70 LRRM 2489)

On remand, however, the Board found that the employer had not discriminated in employment on the basis of race. Member Jenkins dissented vigorously. (*Farmers' Cooperative Compress*, NLRB, 1971, 78 LRRM 1465)

There is another issue involving racial discrimination in employment that has arisen under the Taft-Hartley Act. It is whether employees who picket an employer because of the employer's allegedly racial discriminatory employment practices are engaged in protected activity under the Act. The U.S. Court of Appeals for the Ninth Circuit remanded the case to the NLRB to determine the question whether the employees who picketed had acted in derogation of their contractual bargaining representative by not first proceeding under the grievance-arbitration procedure under the union contract.

By a three-to-two decision, the NLRB held that the pickets lost their protection under the Taft-Hartley Act when they picketed without first exhausting the grievance-arbitration procedure negotiated by their union representative. Members Jenkins and Brown dissented. (*The Emporium*, NLRB, 1971, 77 LRRM 1669)

Chapter 3

How the Law Evolved

Many years elapsed between the initial proposals to establish equal employment opportunity without regard to race, color, religion, sex, or national origin and the adoption first of Title VII of the Civil Rights Act of 1964 and second of the Equal Employment Opportunity Act of 1972.

One of the first equal employment opportunity bills was introduced in February 1943 by Congressman Vito Marcantonio (ALP, N.Y.). Between 1943 and 1963, bills were introduced in each house of each Congress to regulate or at least to conciliate matters involving alleged discrimination for reasons involving race, creed, color, religion, sex, age, or national origin. The scope, the method of administration, and the power of enforcement to be established varied widely.

The Dawson-Scanlon House bill of 1954 proposed an agency with authority and power of enforcement similar to those of the National Labor Relations Board. A Senate bill by Senator Robert A. Taft (R., Ohio) in 1945 proposed to resolve disputes over such discrimination by voluntary methods. A number of bills over the years would have added racial, religious, or other forms of discrimination to the unfair labor practices policed by the Labor Board. In fact, the last of these was proposed as an amendment to the Civil Rights Act of 1964 by Senator Prouty (R., Vt.). It was rejected.

In the period between 1943 and 1964, only one bill was passed by either house; two others were killed by Senate filibuster. Other propositions met burial earlier in the legislative process, running sometimes into the opposition of the chairman of the committee within whose purview the matter resided. The Senate had less trouble than the House with committee approval, but the problem of bringing legislation to a floor vote was an even greater obstruction than that posed by House rules.

McConnell Bill

The single piece of legislation dealing with "fair employment practices" was the bill by Congressman Samuel K. McConnell, Jr. (R., Pa.) in 1950. In an all-night session running over Washington's Birthday to 3 a.m. the next morning, February 23, the House voted to substitute McConnell's bill for one introduced by Congressman Adam C. Powell (D., N.Y.). The vote to substitute was 221 to 178, and the substitute passed 240 to 177. The Powell bill provided for enforcement of orders based on findings of illegal discrimination; the McConnell bill would have set up a Fair Employment Practices Commission with power to study the matter of dis-

23

crimination on the basis of race, creed, or color; to recommend procedures for its elimination, and to seek to create employment opportunities for minority groups without the use of compulsion. Discrimination on account of sex, physical disability, and political affiliation were added on the House floor as matters for concern before the substitute was adopted. Apparently the only power McConnell's FEPC would have had was that of subpoena, to compel the attendance of witnesses. Congressman Powell called the bill "nothing but good advice."

Proposal in Senate

In the same year (1950), FEP legislation floundered in the Senate. It was not the McConnell bill at issue; the legislation provided administrative enforcement, backed up by court review. Opponents charged, in echo of similar charges brought against the National Labor Relations Board, that it would substitute the judgment of a single individual for a jury; a hearing officer would serve as ex parte judge and jury; no rules of evidence were prescribed, and court review would be limited to administrative findings of fact. The legislation never came to vote; the effort was abandoned after the Senate refused to vote cloture by a margin of 55 to 33. A vote of 64 "aye" was required.

This was the second time that "extended debate" had blocked consideration of FEP legislation in the Senate. A bill introduced by Senator Chavez (D., N. Mex.) reached the Senate floor in 1946 but a cloture motion failed and no vote on the merits of the legislation was taken.

Except for these times, no bill reached the floor of either House. This is not to say that bills were not introduced and supported by legislators of both parties. For instance, the Chavez bill which had failed to survive the filibuster in 1946 was—with some modifications—co-sponsored by Senator Ives (R., N.Y.) the following year, and was reported to the Senate by the Labor Committee. President Truman's challenge to the Republicans to enact FEP legislation in his famous "turnip day" session following the party conventions in 1948 was not accepted.

The ensuing years saw committees of one house or the other, and sometimes both, considering legislation and conducting hearings, without issue except in 1950.

ACTION IN THE 88th CONGRESS

As usually had happened in a Presidential election year, the out-going Administration made proposals with respect to Fair Employment Practices for the consideration of Congress in 1960, this time to write the principle of equal employment opportunity into the Civil Rights Act of 1960—an Act dealing principally with voting rights. Congress did not see fit to act on the proposal, although it did enact a Civil Rights bill.

With the election of President Kennedy and the change of Administration, some efforts were made at the outset—and were successful to an important degree—to change the composition of the Rules Committee of the House and Rule XXII of the Senate. Efforts had been made before. The House Rules Committee, as traffic cop for legislation coming before the House for vote, had been uniformly unfriendly to FEPC legislation for two decades and on several occasions had blocked its consideration on the floor. By adding sufficient members appointed by a Speaker friendly to the Administration, the power balance, with respect to this legislation at least, was shifted from the iron rule of Chairman Howard W. Smith (D., Va.).

In the Senate, several extended debates had been held from year to year at the beginning of new Congresses over proposals to alter the requirement for putting an end to debate; the end result was that a two-thirds vote of those present and voting would be necessary to impose eventual silence after one hour per Senator, instead of two-thirds of all Senators. The difference may be unimportant; all Senators voted on the Civil Rights Act of 1964, including one in a wheel-chair.

Proposals in 87th Congress

President Kennedy made no proposal for FEP legislation during the 87th Congress, and he was not without criticism from proponents of such legislation for his oversight. Bills had been introduced: Congressman Powell, then Chairman of the House Labor Committee, had a bill and declared that Fair Employment Practice legislation was a target for 1962. Congressman Griffin (R., Mich.) offered another bill to make discrimination for race, creed, color, etc., an unfair labor practice.

It may be significant that two things happened during House committee consideration of H.R. 10144, which it eventually reported. One is that the principal point of dispute was over the question of the enforcing agency: an administrative body or the courts. The other was the title: The name of the legislation was changed to the "Equal Opportunity Act of 1962." But H.R. 10144 did not get by Chairman Smith's Rules Committee.

Kennedy Proposal

Having been accused of dragging anchor on FEP for half of his first term, President Kennedy announced in a televised conference on June 11, 1963, that he would seek Civil Rights legislation from the 88th Congress. On June 19, 1963, a draft of his proposed legislation went to Congress. It was a year later, to the day, that the Senate passed a compromise bill acceptable to the House without further change. The last roadblocks had been removed; the House passed the legislation on July 2, 1964, and President Johnson signed it into law at about 6:55 p.m., EST, the same day.

So related, the matter sounds simple.

But in between, there had to be the resolution of differences; the fracture of a more-than-occasional alliance between some Republicans and Southern Democrats; agreement on common objectives of enough Democrats and Republicans in both Houses to ensure that (1) the legislation could not be blocked or defeated in the House, and (2) then could not be postponed indefinitely in the Senate.

The matter was accomplished. A bit of the congressional maneuvering involved tentative approval by the House Labor Committee of H.R. 405, an Equal Employment Opportunities bill, providing for enforcement through suits in the federal district courts. When this enforcement channel drew no approval, if not disapproval, from the Administration, the Committee took another look and set its sights on a procedure similar to that of the National Labor Relations Board. Republicans objected vigorously.

Senate Measure

Meanwhile, in the Senate a bill (S. 1937) introduced by Senator Humphrey (D., Minn.) was approved in committee to place enforcement of equal employment opportunities in an administrator to be appointed in the Department of Labor. The administrator was to prosecute complaints before an independent Equal Employment Opportunity Board. The Board was to issue cease-and-desist orders enforceable in the federal courts of appeals.

In an ordinary year, this might have been sufficient divergence to assure that no legislation on the matter would be agreeable, even though H.R. 7152, produced by the House Judiciary Committee under Chairman Emanuel Celler (D., N.Y.) and its senior Republican, William M. McCulloch of Ohio, had bipartisan support. Despite objections of opponents of the legislation that the Judiciary Committee had been remiss in failing to hold hearings on the legislation (an accusation denied by Celler and, so far as FEP was concerned, by a 20-year file of the Labor Committee), the legislation was reported by the Judiciary Committee as ready for consideration. The dispute with respect to the method of enforcing the Equal Employment Opportunity section had been resolved: There would be an Equal Employment Opportunity Commission, bipartisan in character, without enforcement power; that detail would be handled by trial of the matter in a federal district court.

Action by House

The assassination of President Kennedy put a spotlight on the unfinished legislative business of his program. Succeeding him, President Johnson gave civil rights legislation a position equal with the 1964 tax cut. House Rules Committee Chairman Smith said he would not clear H.R. 7152 for action before the New Year, but immediately after the New Year of 1964 he did so, and the bill passed, with his own amendment adding discrimination for reasons of sex to the list of proscribed "unlawful employment practices."

The supporters of the legislation short-stopped H.R. 7152 as it came from the House, preventing its referral to the Senate Judiciary Committee, which was viewed as hostile to the bill.

Then the Senate's debate began. It was the early hope of supporters of the legislation that the House bill, H.R. 7152, would be accepted by the Senate verbatim, in order to by-pass a conference between the two houses to reconcile differences between bills; such a reconciliation might take as long a time as the original bills, or longer.

Compromise Bill

It did not turn out that way. While the extended debate in the Senate was going—it lasted 534 hours, 1 minute and 37 seconds—bipartisan negotiations among the bill's supporters, principally Senators Dirksen (R., Ill.) and Humphrey, in consultation with Attorney General Kennedy, hammered out a version that would be acceptable to enough Senators to vote to bring the debate to a close.

Their judgment proved correct. The Senate voted 71 to 29 to close debate, and 76 to 18 to pass the bill.

On return to the House, H.R. 7152 again got unusual treatment. Instead of the usual procedure of setting it up for a conference with the Senate on points of disagreement, a shortened procedure was adopted whereby the question was on accepting the measure as amended by the Senate. Chairman Smith of the Rules Committee understood that he could not delay action by pocketing the bill. He also learned, when the Rules Committee met to clear the Senate substitute bill to the House for action, that his Committee did not wish him to present the rule to the House, which could have involved more delay. Chairman Smith said this was the first time in his 32 years on the Committee that such a thing had occurred.

Final House Action

After an hour of debate on July 2, 1964, the House passed H.R. 7152, as amended, by a vote of 289 to 126.

So far as Title VII is concerned, the principal change in the original House bill provided an increased resort to state anti-discrimination agencies where they exist, giving the states first opportunity at solving issues. It also undertook to avoid duplication of records already required by state laws or federal executive orders.

After more than 20 years an FEP bill, under another name, became law with President Johnson's signature.

EQUAL EMPLOYMENT OPPORTUNITY ACT OF 1972

Like the 1964 Act, the Equal Employment Opportunity Act of 1972 was the result of a compromise. The compromise was worked out in the conference committee in early 1972.

Three times before there had been action in either the House or the Senate on amendments giving the EEOC enforcement power. On April 27, 1966, the House passed the Roosevelt-Hawkins bill to give the EEOC cease-and-desist powers similar to those exercised by the National Labor Relations Board. There was no Senate action.

Then on April 25, 1968, the Senate Labor Committee reported the Clark bill to give the EEOC cease-and-desist powers and the power to seek pre-decision injunctions. No action was taken on the measure.

In November 1970, the Senate approved the Williams bill, a measure very similar to one already approved by the House Labor Committee. The vote was 47 to 24. Reportedly, passage was not hampered by extended debate because it was believed that the House Rules Committee would bottle up the bill. This happened, and the bill died at the end of the 91st Congress.

In the 92nd Congress, the House Labor Committee reported a measure that would give the EEOC power to issue cease-and-desist orders enforceable in the federal courts of appeals. The House, however, approved a substitute measure favored by the Administration. This authorized the EEOC to sue directly in a federal district court where it found reasonable cause to believe a violation had been committed.

The Senate Labor Committee also reported a bill giving the EEOC cease-and-desist powers. This measure was faced with the prospect of extended debate until Senators Williams (D., N.J.) and Javits (R., N.Y.) introduced an amendment embodying the direct court enforcement procedures. The Senate approved the bill late in February 1972, after a petition for cloture was adopted on February 22.

When the bills went to conference, the House conferees agreed to accept the Senate measure, which was the stronger of the two. It was approved by the conference committee on March 1. The Senate approved the conference measure by a vote of 62 to 10; the House approved it by a vote of 303 to 110.

President Nixon signed the measure on March 24, 1972.

Chapter 4

Who Is Covered by the Law

The coverage of Title VII of the Civil Rights Act of 1964 was broad. It is still broader because of the changes made by the Equal Employment Opportunity Act of 1972.

Coverage depends on a series of definitions in Section 701, certain express exemptions in Section 702, and certain provisos or definitions in Section 703. Coverage is grounded on the power given to Congress to regulate commerce by the Commerce Clause of the U.S. Constitution. A key definition is that of the term "industry affecting commerce."

Industry 'Affecting Commerce'

There are two definitions that determine the scope of the term "industry affecting commerce." First, there is the definition of "commerce." Second, there is the definition of "industry affecting commerce."

The term "commerce" is defined to include "trade, traffic, commerce, transportation, transmission, or communication among the several states; or between a state and any place outside thereof; or within the District of Columbia or a possession of the United States; or between points in the same state but through a point outside thereof."

The term "industry affecting commerce" is defined as "any activity, business, or industry in commerce or in which a labor dispute would hinder or obstruct commerce or the free flow of commerce and includes any activity or industry 'affecting commerce' within the meaning of the Labor-Management Reporting and Disclosure Act of 1959, and further includes any governmental industry, business, or activity."

Except for the limitations on the size of the organization and the explicit exemptions, the coverage of the Act apparently is intended to reach as far as the power of Congress to regulate commerce.

A memorandum from the Department of Labor that was introduced into the record by Senator Clark (D., Pa.) (110 Cong. Rec., pp. 7207-7212, April 8, 1964) said the following:

"It can therefore be authoritatively said that it is now well settled that the constitutional power extends to activities affecting commerce in any amount or volume not so minimal or sporadic as to fall within the doctrine of *de minimis non curat lex.* As the Supreme Court said in a National Labor Relations Act case, *NLRB* v. *Fainblatt*, 306 U.S. 601, 59 SCt 668, 4 LRRM 535, the 'power of Congress to regulate interstate commerce is plenary and extends to all such commerce be it great or small,' because 'commerce may be affected in the same manner and to the same extent in proportion to its volume, whether it be great or small.' See also *NLRB* v. *Denver Bldg. & Constr. Tr. Council*, 341 U.S. 675, 71 SCt 943, 28 LRRM 2108; *Carpenter's Union* v. *NLRB*, 341 U.S. 947, 71 SCt 1011, 28 LRRM 2121. And in *NLRB* v. *Stoller*, 207 F.2d 305, 32 LRRM 2742 (CA 9), *cert. denied*, 347 U.S. 919, 74 SCt 517, 33 LRRM 2589, the National Labor Relations Act was held applicable to a local dry cleaner who purchased $12,000 worth of supplies from outside the state, the Court holding that this amount 'was not so insignificant as to come within the rule *de minimis non curat lex.'*"

So the reach of Title VII is greater than that provided in the Fair Labor Standards Act of 1938, as amended, which speaks of being engaged "in commerce" or "the production of goods for commerce." The ultimate grasp of Title VII is more nearly that of the National Labor Relations Act, in which the statutory boundary is activity "affecting commerce." The farthest limit of the term "affecting commerce" has yet to be delineated by the courts under the NLRA in any quantitative term. As a practical matter, the National Labor Relations Board, with approval of the courts and Congress, has set for itself some lower limits in terms of volume of business below which it will not assert jurisdiction.

But the scope of Title VII may not stop where NLRB stays its hand.

Section 701(h) includes everything defined as affecting commerce in the Landrum-Griffin Act, which includes NLRA, But this statement appears to be only explanatory, rather than limiting. The full sweep of the definition of "industry affecting commerce" remains as broad as the courts may be willing to make it before invoking the maxim *de minimis non curat lex*. And while this maxim has been invoked from time to time in administration of federal labor legislation, a matter usually has to be trivial indeed to escape the care of the courts.

COVERAGE OF EMPLOYERS

An already broad coverage of employers under Title VII of the Civil Rights Act of 1964 was extended still further by the 1972 amendments. The coverage of employers is governed by three sections of the Act.

• *First*, there is Section 701(a), which defines "person." This definition was enlarged by the 1972 amendments to include state and local governments, governmental agencies, and political subdivisions.

• *Second*, there is Section 701(b), which defines an "employer." This definition also was expanded to include state and local government, governmental agencies, and political subdivisions. But it does not include the U.S. Government, corporations wholly owned by the Government, or departments of the District of Columbia who are subject to competitive service under 5 U.S.C., Sec. 2102.

• *Third*, there is Section (h), which defines "industry affecting commerce."

Under Section 701(b), an employer is a "person engaged in an industry affecting commerce." This is not limited to a person with flesh and blood. It also includes, by explicit listing, the usual organization that people establish to further a common purpose—corporations, associations, labor unions, mutual companies, joint-stock companies, trusts, and unincorporated associations. Moreover, legal representatives are "persons" and so are other persons having certain legal responsibilities, such as trustees, trustees in bankruptcy, and receivers.

Number of Employees

Under the 1964 Act, coverage was extended to employers on the basis of the number of employees, with the number being reduced each year. This was the schedule:

- From July 2, 1965, to July 1, 1966, the required number of employees was 100.
- From July 2, 1966, to July 1, 1967, the number was 75.
- From July 2, 1967, to July 1, 1968, the number was 50.
- From July 2, 1968, until the change made by the 1972 amendments, the number was 25.

The 1972 amendments provide for reducing the number of employees required for coverage to 15 on March 24, 1973. (See Appendix F-6 for congressional debate on this change.)

To be covered under this test, an employer must have the required number of employees on each working day in each of 20 or more calendar weeks in the current or preceding calendar year. This test could be important to seasonal employers. If coverage is continuous, the seasonal employer would be subject to the law's requirements during the slack season even though at the time he had fewer than the required number of employees as long as he had the required number for 20 or more weeks. Once this requirement is met it is satisfied for two calendar years.

Multiple Establishments

When nominally separate business entities meet the jurisdictional requirements of Title VII when combined but not when treated separately, the EEOC will apply the criteria used by the NLRB in determining coverage. The controlling criteria used by the NLRB are "interrelation of operations, common management, centralized control of labor relations, and common ownership." (EEOC General Counsel's Opinion, July 27, 1966)

The U.S. Court of Appeals for the Fifth Circuit, however, held that a district court did not have jurisdiction of an action under Title VII brought by a black employee against an employer who had fewer than 25 employees, even though the employer was a wholly owned subsidiary of another company. The court reasoned that the two did not have the "substantial identity" necessary to qualify them as a single employer. It noted, among other things, that the affairs of the two companies generally were handled separately, that the one was not liable for the debts of the other, and that the subsidiary was recognized as a separate entity for tax purposes. (*Hassell* v. *Harmon Foods, Inc.*, CA 5, 1971, 4 FEP Cases 163)

State, Local Governments

One of the major changes in coverage made by the 1972 amendments was the broadening of the definition of "employer" to bring within the Act's coverage state and local governments, governmental agencies, political subdivisions, and departments and agencies of the District of Columbia, except those subject to competitive service under 5 U.S.C. Sec. 2102.

But there was an exemption from this coverage extension. Senators Ervin (D., N.C.) and Allen (D., Ala.) introduced an amendment that, as later modified, provided an exemption for elected officials, their personal assistants, and their immediate advisers. The amendment was adopted in the Senate by a vote of 69 to 2. It was included in the bill as enacted.

During the legislative history, it was stressed that this exemption was "intended to be construed very narrowly and is in no way intended to establish an over-all narrowing of the expanded coverage of state and local governmental employees" (For a discussion of the debate preceding the adoption of this amendment see Appendix F-9 and F-10.)

Federal Employees

Under the 1964 Act, federal employees were not within the jurisdiction of the EEOC. But the 1972 amendments added a new section that makes clear the obligation of the Federal Government to make all personnel actions without discrimination based on race, color, sex, religion, or national origin. The authority to enforce equal employment opportunity in federal agencies is assigned to the Civil Service Commission. If a federal employee or applicant is dissatisfied with the government's handling of his complaint of discrimination, he may file an action in a federal district court.

WHO IS AN EMPLOYEE

An "employee" is defined in Section 701(f) as an individual employed by an employer. The definition by its terms does not include applicants for employment. The omission may be of no particular significance, since Section 703(a)(1) makes it unlawful to refuse to hire "any individual" on account of race, color, religion, sex, or national origin.

But it should be observed that to be an "employee" for the purposes of Title VII, the individual must be employed by an employer; that is, by someone or something which is itself subject to Title VII as described above.

Other than this, it does not appear to matter what sort of work the employee does. Supervisors are not excluded from the definition, as they are in the NLRA. Nor, indeed, are company presidents, confidential secretaries, guards, or management personnel generally, even though these are given special status either by law or by policy under the NLRA.

On the other hand, the Civil Rights Act does not make employees out of members of a corporation's board of directors, nor does it make employers out of stockholders. (110 Cong. Rec. pp. 7215-7218, April 8, 1964) But an employee who owns stock or serves as a director does not thereby lose his status as an employee.

In other words, in totting up the number of employees for the purpose of the numerical yardstick of coverage, the whole work force is counted from the executive suite to the sweeper—inclusively. And so also would they be protected from discrimination.

LABOR ORGANIZATION

A labor organization may be covered by Title VII, as amended in 1972, on two bases.

First, it may be covered as an employer, and as such it must meet the same requirements as any other employer, including that relating to number of employees—25 until March 24, 1973, and 15 thereafter.

Second, it may be covered as a labor union, and as such it must meet a variety of criteria, including that relating to number of members—25 until March 24, 1973, and 15 thereafter.

The definition of a "labor organization" is lifted practically verbatim from the Landrum-Griffin Act and includes "any organization in which employees participate" in order to deal with their employer on the usual subjects of collective bargaining. National and international unions, intermediate and collateral bodies such as councils, joint boards, and the like, are included in the definition as well as local unions. The only difference between the Title VII definition and that in the Landrum-Griffin Act is that Title VII covers state or local central bodies, while Landrum-Griffin does not.

The definition does not, however, cite the Landrum-Griffin Act as its source, and the use of the term "employee," therefore, probably should be read as the word is defined in Section 701(f) of Title VII. Thus it could include organizations of supervisors, confidential secretaries, or agricultural workers. It conceivably could include, say, an association of bank vice-presidents, with a purpose, among others, of improving the wages, hours, working conditions, and expense accounts of its members—if there were enough of these.

The labor organization will be considered "engaged in an industry affecting commerce" on either of two bases:

- If it maintains a hiring hall or hiring office that brings "employers" and employees together, or
- If it has an aggregate number of members —25 until March 24, 1973, and 15 thereafter.

The numbers apply to the aggregate membership of constituent bodies for the purpose of determining the status of national, international, and intermediate or collateral organizations.

If it has the numerical strength, the organization is covered if it (1) is certified as a bargaining representative under the National Labor Relations Act or the Railway Labor Act, or (2) is recognized by an employer covered by Title VII, or (3) has some formal relationship with a labor organization which is covered by Title VII, as a chartered, chartering, or joint-interest organization.

HIRING HALLS

The provision explicitly making union hiring halls subject to the Act without regard to the criteria of membership did not appear in the bill as it passed the House in 1964. According to Senator Humphrey, the amendment provides "that wherever a labor organization maintains a hiring hall which supplies workers for employers covered by the Title, that labor organization is deemed to affect commerce and is covered by the Title." (110 Cong. Rec., pp. 12721-12725, June 4, 1964)

The thrust of this provision may be found in the following excerpt from the Q & A with Senator Dirksen inserted in the Record by Senator Clark (110 Cong. Rec., pp. 7215-7218, April 8, 1964):

QUESTION: "If an employer obtains his employees from a union hiring hall through operation of his labor contract, is he in fact the true employer from the standpoint of discrimination because of race, color, religion, or national origin when he exercises no choice in their selection? If the hiring hall sends only white males is the employer guilty of discrimination within the meaning of this title? If he is not, then further safeguards must be provided to protect him from endless prosecution under the authority of this title."

ANSWER: "An employer who obtains his employees from a union hiring hall through operation of a labor contract is still an employer. If the hiring hall discriminates against blacks, and sends him only whites, he is not guilty of discrimination but the union hiring hall would be."

Joint labor-management committees that control apprenticeship or other training or retraining programs were subject to the basic ban on discrimination under the 1964 Act. But the obligations of such committees were expanded by the 1972 amendments to make it unlawful for them to retaliate against any person for enforcing his rights under the Act or to advertise or post a notice that indicates any preference, limitation, specification, or discrimination based on religion, sex, or national origin, except where religion, sex, or national origin is a bona fide occupational qualification for employment.

EMPLOYMENT AGENCIES

In the 1964 Act, the term "employment agency" was defined as "any person undertaking with or without compensation to procure for an employer or to procure for employees opportunities to work for an employer and includes an agent of such a person; but shall not include an agency of the United States, or an agency of a state or political subdivision of a state, except that such term shall include the United States Employment Service and the system of state and local employment services receiving federal assistance."

The 1972 amendments modified the definition to reflect the changes made in the definition of a "person" and an "employer," including the broader coverage in the area of state and local governmental employment. The new definition follows:

"The term "employment agency" means any person regularly undertaking with or without compensation to procure employees for an employer or to procure for employees opportunities to work for an employer and includes an agent of such a person."

So the coverage of employment agencies is tied to the definitions of "employer" and "employee." The definition also embraces the United States Employment Service and state and local employment services that receive federal assistance.

EXEMPTIONS FROM THE LAW

There were some important changes in exemptions under the 1972 amendments. Moreover, there were some exemptions to the extension of coverage. Here are the changes:

• Under the 1964 Act, there was an exemption for educational institutions with respect to individuals whose work involves educational activities. This exemption is eliminated. The result will be to bring under Title VII an estimated 120,000 educational institutions, with about 2.8 million teachers and professional staff members and another 1.5 million nonprofessional staff members.

• Under the original Title VII, there was an exemption for religious corporations, associations, or societies with respect to individuals whose work involves the religious aspects of the employing organization. The 1972 amendments broaden the exemption to include all activities of such organizations, not merely their religious activities. The provision, however, permits the organization to discriminate solely on the basis of religion. It may not discriminate on the basis of race, color, sex, or national origin.

• The new coverage of state and local governments contains an exemption for elected officials, their personal assistants, and their immediate advisers. But it was emphasized during the congressional debate that this exemption was "to be construed very narrowly and is in no way intended to establish an over-all narrowing of the expanded coverage of state and local governmental employees." (See Appendix F-10 for the text of debate on this issue.)

Continued Exemptions

There were a number of exemptions that were contained in the 1964 Act and were not changed by the 1972 amendments. Included in this group were the following:

• Indians living on or near a reservation may be given preference in employment by businesses on or near the reservation. This does not mean that they are excluded from the protection of Title VII; they are employees, just like anyone else. But they are entitled to preferential treatment.

• There is an exemption for bona fide, tax-exempt private clubs, the exemption being based on the exclusion of such clubs from the definition of "an employer" under the Act. But Congress apparently did not intend to permit such clubs to be used as a cover for operation of businesses that otherwise would be covered by Title VII.

• Employers who otherwise are covered are exempt with respect to aliens they employ in lands other than those described as "states" of the United States (the 50 states, Puerto Rico, Virgin Islands, District of Columbia, American Samoa, Guam, Wake Island, Canal Zone, and Continental Shelf Lands). Overseas employment of "indigenous personnel," as they are known, may be subject to special agreements with, or laws of, the host countries and may be beyond U.S. jurisdiction.

• There is an exemption for employees where the employer is subject to a government security program, and the individuals involved do not have security clearance. Such employees are not protected by Title VII.

• There is a similar exemption for any individual who "is a member of the Communist Party of the United States or of any other organization required to register as a Communist-action or Communist-front organization by final order of the Subversive Activities Control Board pursuant to the Subversive Activities Control Act of 1959. Such an employee is not protected by Title VII. A similar exemption to permit discrimination against atheists was deleted during the debate on the 1964 Act because of "doubtful constitutionality."

• Perhaps the broadest of the exemptions is that provided by Section 703(e)(1). Under this section, there is an exemption to the prohibitions "where religion, sex, or national origin is a bona fide occupational qualification reasonably necessary to the normal operation of that particular business or enterprise." This and some of the other exemptions are discussed in more detail in the next chapter. The changes in the exemptions for religious and educational organizations are discussed above.

Chapter 5

What Discrimination Is Forbidden

The anti-discrimination provisions of Title VII are broad. They forbid employers, employment agencies, and labor organizations to take certain discriminatory actions where they are based on race, color, religion, sex, or national origin. Thus, there are five proscribed bases of discrimination.

The prohibitions also apply to a joint labor-management committee that controls an apprenticeship or training or retraining program. Finally, there is a prohibition against retaliatory action directed at a person who files a charge or otherwise participates in enforcement of the Act. All these prohibitions are discussed in more detail below.

CHANGES MADE BY 1972 AMENDMENTS

The provisions of Title VII relating to discrimination in employment were not changed substantially by the Equal Employment Opportunity Act of 1972. But there were a few changes, some resulting from modification of coverage and exemptions. Following is a summary of the statutory changes affecting the obligation not to discriminate:

• Under the 1964 Act, joint labor-management committees that control apprenticeship or other training or retraining programs, including on-the-job training, were forbidden to discriminate on the basis of race, color, religion, sex, or national origin in the administration of such programs. The 1972 amendments broadened the obligations of such committees in two ways. First, an amendment made it unlawful for such a committee to discriminate in advertising or job notices. Second, another amendment made it unlawful for such a committee to discriminate against persons for enforcing their rights under Title VII.

• The 1964 Act exempted educational institutions with respect to individuals whose work involves educational activities. The 1972 amendments deleted this exemption, thus bringing within the Title VII prohibitions an estimated 120,000 educational institutions with respect to about 2.8 million teachers and professional staff members and another 1.5 million non-professional staff members. (See Appendix F-11 for congressional debate on this change.)

• The amendments also extended coverage to state and local governments and their employees. But there is an exemption for elected officials and their personal assistants and immediate advisers. (See Appendix F-9 for congressional debate on this change.)

ion was broadened. Under the original Title VII,
n for religious corporations, associations, or socie-
viduals whose work involves the religious aspects
ganization. The amendments broaden the exemption
activities of such organizations, not merely their religious
but the exemption permits discrimination only on the basis of
on; it does not apply to discrimination based on race, color, sex, or
national origin. (See Appendix F-11 for congressional debate on this
change.)

Equal Pay Act Amendment

In 1963, Congress adopted the Equal Pay Act as an amendment to
Section 6 (the minimum-wage section) of the Fair Labor Standards Act.
In brief, the amendment required equal pay for equal work without regard
to sex. But as part of Section 6, it was subject to all the exemptions under
Section 6.

One of the most important of these exemptions was that applicable to
employees who are employed in bona fide executive, administrative, or
professional capacities or as outside salesmen. Included in the 1972
amendments to the Higher Education Act, however, is a Section 906(b)
that eliminates the exemption from the equal-pay requirement for executive, administrative, and professional employees, and outside salesmen. So
the Act now forbids any discrimination in pay among such employees on
the basis of sex.

Under Title VII of the Civil Rights Act, there is no exemption for
executive, administrative, or professional employees or outside salesmen.
So any discrimination in employment, including salaries, among such employees would be a violation of Title VII, as well as Section 6 of the Fair
Labor Standards Act, where it is based on sex.

DISCRIMINATION BY EMPLOYERS

As amended in 1972, Title VII still will have its greatest impact on
employers. Section 703(a) describes a number of actions by employers
that will be unlawful employment practices if they are based on race,
color, religion, sex, or national origin. In addition, Section 703(d) makes
it unlawful to discriminate on any of the five bases in apprenticeship,
training, or retraining programs. Section 704(b) makes it unlawful to indicate a preference or a discrimination based on race, color, religion, sex, or
national origin in notices or advertisements relating to employment. All
these prohibitions, however, are subject to some important exceptions, as
discussed later.

Hiring, Firing

Just as the National Labor Relations Act makes it unlawful to discriminate with respect to hiring or discharge on the basis of union membership

or union activities, Title VII makes it an unlawful employment practice for an employer to fail or refuse to hire or to discharge any individual because of his race, color, religion, sex, or national origin.

Proof of such discrimination will be different under the 1972 amendments. Under the 1964 Act, the function of the EEOC normally ended with the finding of reasonable cause to believe a violation of the Act had been committed. The Commission then would notify the parties of the finding and that it had been unable to obtain voluntary compliance. This would clear the way for an action in a federal district court by the aggrieved party or parties. The EEOC has intervened in some of these actions, but there have been decisions denying intervention, the courts stating that EEOC had only a permissive, not an unconditional, right to intervene in Title VII proceedings. (See *Thornton* v. *East Texas Motor Freight*, CA 6, 1972, 4 FEP Cases 205; *Stewards and Stewardesses* v. *American Airlines, Inc.*, CA 7, 1972, 4 FEP Cases 152.)

The 1972 amendments authorize the EEOC to file a suit on its own if it finds reasonable cause to believe a violation has occurred and it is unable to settle the case by voluntary methods.

Employment Conditions

It also is an unlawful employment practice for an employer to discriminate against an individual because of his race, color, religion, sex, or national origin with respect to compensation, terms, conditions, or privileges of employment.

This is a broad prohibition and would appear to embrace virtually all aspects of the employer-employee relationship. So far as compensation is concerned, some guidance as to the scope of the term may be obtained from interpretations under the Equal Pay Act of 1963. Guidance as to the scope of terms and conditions of employment, as well as wages, may be found under the National Labor Relations Act.

In the Interpretative Bulletin on Equal Pay for Equal Work, "wages" are defined to include "all payments made to or on behalf of the employee as remuneration for employment." This includes overtime, as well as straight-time, rates. (Part 800, C.F.R.—Equal Pay for Equal Work under the Fair Labor Standards Act; WHM [BNA] 95:571)

Under the National Labor Relations Act, an employer is obligated to bargain with the union representing his employees concerning "wages, hours, and other terms and conditions of employment." The phrase "wages, hours, and other terms and conditions of employment" has been construed to include a variety of subjects, including various fringe benefits, bonuses, company housing, employee stock purchase plans, group insurance, lunch and rest periods, individual merit raises, and employee discounts. Discrimination with respect to any of such matters would appear to come within the scope of Title VII.

In applying the executive orders applicable to government contracts and federally assisted construction, the Office of Federal Contract Compliance has taken the position that the obligation not to discriminate extends to the physical environment in which an employee works. So unequal treatment with respect to such facilities as rest rooms, lunch rooms, and drinking fountains could be the basis for a charge of discrimination. The same rule, presumably, would apply under the Act.

Segregation, Classification

It also is an unlawful employment practice for an employer to limit, segregate, or classify employees in any way that would deprive or tend to deprive any individual of employment opportunities or otherwise adversely affect his status as an employee because of his race, color, religion, sex, or national origin.

Under this provision, such practices as separate seniority rosters for male and female or white and Negro employees have been held to be violations. (See *Griggs* v. *Duke Power Co.*, U.S. SupCt, 1971, 3 FEP Cases 175; *U.S.* v. *Jacksonville Terminal Co.*, CA 5, 1971, 3 FEP Cases 862.)

The district court in the *Jacksonville Terminal* case had held that the union's maintenance of segregated locals did not violate the Act, but the Fifth Circuit reversed the holding. But another district court had held in the *Crown Zellerbach* case that the maintenance of separate white and black locals was a *per se* violation of the Act. (*Hicks* v. *Crown Zellerbach Corp.*, USDC ELa, 1971, 3 FEP Cases 90)

The 1972 Amendments broadened Section 703 to make it unlawful to limit, segregate, or classify applicants for employment or union membership, as well as present employees or members, on the basis of race, color, religion, or national origin. Courts had so held under the 1964 law. (See *Phillips* v. *Martin-Marietta Corp.*, U.S. SupCt, 1971, 3 FEP Cases 40.)

Advertising, Job Notices

Under Section 704(b), it is an unlawful employment practice to indicate a preference, limitation, specification, or discrimination based on race, color, religion, sex, or national origin in printing or publishing any employment notices or advertising. This unlawful practice applied to employers, employment agencies, and labor unions under the 1964 Act. The 1972 amendments extended it to joint labor-management committees operating apprenticeship and other training programs.

Subject to some exceptions discussed later, this provision would appear to bar any mention of race, color, religion, sex, or national origin in employment notices or advertising. The report of the House Judiciary Committee on the 1964 Act, however, stressed that this does not require newspapers and other publications to exercise any control or supervision over, or to do any screening of, the advertisements and notices published by them. (House Report No. 914, 88th Congress, 1st Session, p. 28)

After considering the matter, the EEOC concluded that advertising in "male" and "female" help-wanted columns is unlawful, unless sex is a bona fide occupational qualification.

Employment Testing

Under an amendment sponsored by Senator Tower (R., Tex.), the 1964 Act provided that it would not be an unlawful employment practice "for an employer to give and to act upon the results of any professionally developed ability test provided that such test, its administration or action upon the results is not designed, intended, or used to discriminate because of race, color, religion, sex, or national origin."

This amendment has been the subject of considerable controversy. During the period between 1964 and 1972, several bills were introduced to limit the employer's use of ability tests. But none was adopted.

Meanwhile, the EEOC had issued guidelines for employment tests. The major principle to be followed under the guidelines is that the test be related to the job sought by the applicant or employee. Its current guidelines require validation of any paper-and-pencil or performance test used as a basis for an employment or promotion decision. But its job-related test is subject to the following qualifications under the guidelines:

Tests based on an expectation of promotion, such as those designed to determine an applicant's ability to perform a higher than entry-level job, may be validated against the requirements of the higher-level job—but only if the new employee "will probably, within a reasonable period of time and in a great majority of cases, progress to a higher level."

Where the same test is used in different units or locations in a multiplant company, the employer need validate a test at just one location where "no significant differences exist between units, jobs, and applicant populations."

In cases where required validation is in effect "technically impossible," such as where the size of the test group is inadequate, the employer may rely on validity studies conducted by other organizations, such as those reported in test manuals and professional literature, if the jobs are comparable and there are no major differences in "contextual variables or sample composition."

The general reputation of a test will not be accepted in lieu of evidence of validity, nor will professional supervision of testing activities serve as a substitute for validation. (See Fair Employment Practice Manual [BNA], p. 421:451.)

Supreme Court Decision—The EEOC's requirement that tests be job-related was upheld by the Supreme Court in *Griggs* v. *Duke Power Co.* An employer who uses a test or an educational requirement, such as possession of a high-school diploma, the Court said, must show that the requirement is "demonstrably a reasonable measure of job performance." It added that an employment practice that operates to exclude blacks is

_less it can be shown to be related to job performance. But _t open the question whether an employer may use tests or _g requirements that take into account capability for future promouons. (*Griggs* v. *Duke Power Co.*, US SupCt, 1971, 3 FEP Cases 175)

The decision of the Supreme Court in the *Duke Power* case was discussed in the Report of the House Committee on Education and Labor. The bill reported by the Committee contained a provision on testing, but it did not appear in the bill finally adopted. The Committee's Report, however, had this to say about the Court's *Duke Power* decision:

"The provisions of the bill are fully in accord with the decision of the Court and with the testing guidelines established by the Commission. The addition of the requirement for a bona fide occupational qualification which is reasonably necessary to perform the normal duties of the position to which it is applied requires that employers, who use employment tests as standards for qualifications of employees for a particular job, must determine whether the test is necessary to the particular position to which it is applied. Even if after such determination, if the use of the test acts to maintain existing or past discriminatory imbalances in the job, or tends to discriminate against applicants on the basis of race, color, religion, sex, or national origin, the employer must show an overriding business necessity to justify use of the test." (See Appendix D for the text of the Committee's Report.)

Discrimination Based on Age

During the debate in the House on the 1964 Act, Congressman Dowdy (D., Tex.) introduced an amendment to add "age" to the proscribed bases of employment discrimination. Dowdy contended that discrimination based on age was the "worst kind of discrimination." The amendment was defeated by a vote of 123 to 94, after some members had stated that they agreed with the objective of the amendment, but did not regard this as the way to achieve that objective.

Three years later, however, Congress adopted the Age Discrimination in Employment Act of 1967. Effective June 12, 1968, discrimination in employment against persons between the ages of 40 and 65 was forbidden. The administration and enforcement of the Act was assigned to the Department of Labor.

In the bill sent to the House Judiciary Committee by its subcommittee, discrimination based on ancestry was forbidden. But the full Judiciary Committee dropped "ancestry" as a prohibited basis of employment discrimination, and it did not appear in the 1964 Act.

Discrimination Based on Race or Color

Because of the bitterness of the debate that preceded the adoption of Title VII in 1964, considerable confusion developed as to what the Act did and did not require. Some of its opponents viewed it as a drastic measure—one that would change the mix of the work force radically by virtually requiring the employment of quotas of minority group members. Some of its proponents, on the other hand, looked upon Title VII as little more than a voluntary program—a starting point for more effective steps to be taken later. This conflict of views was very acute where charges of employment discrimination based on race or color was involved.

As finally adopted by Congress, Title VII did not conform to either of these views. The obligations it imposed on employers, employment agencies, and unions were primarily negative in character. They were prohibited from engaging in specified unlawful employment practices. And Section 703(j) stated that the law does not require that preferential treatment be given any individual or group on account of an imbalance that may exist with respect to the total number or percentage of persons of any race, color, religion, sex, or national origin employed in comparison with the total number or percentage of persons in that or any other area. (110 Cong. Rec. pp. 12721-12725, June 4, 1964)

As a practical matter, however, the courts have not been reluctant in Title VII actions, as pointed out in the 1971 Report of the American Bar Association's Committee on Equal Employment Opportunity Law, "to order a broad spectrum of affirmative action, including an extensive revamping of established seniority and referral systems and more recently reinstatement and back pay." There are also increasing indications, the report pointed out, that the courts will not be satisfied that compliance has been achieved until an employment census discloses that blacks especially have substantially accelerated their advancement into higher paying jobs at all levels.

Although the *Duke Power* case, for example, was concerned directly with the issue of ability tests, the Supreme Court made clear that it approved the rationale of circuit court decisions requiring affirmative action to remedy the present consequences of past, pre-Act discrimination. The Court said:

"Under the Act, practices, procedures, or tests neutral on their face, and even neutral in terms of intent, cannot be maintained if they operate to 'freeze' the status quo of prior discriminatory employment practices." (*Griggs* v. *Duke Power Co.*, US SupCt, 1971, 3 FEP Cases 175)

In cases involving charges of discrimination based on race or color, some courts have used "goals" or a "statistical test" in finding a violation of the Act. In a case involving the Southwestern Bell Telephone Company, for example, a circuit court utilized "statistics" to find employment discrimination as a matter of law. It said:

"We hold as a matter of law that these statistics, which revealed an extraordinarily small number of black employees, except for the most part as menial laborers, established a violation of Title VII of the Civil

Rights Act of 1964." (*Parham* v. *Southwestern Bell Telephone Co.*, CA 8, 1970, 2 FEP Cases 1017)

In *Hicks* v. *Crown Zellerbach*, a federal district court decree required that blacks be given preference over all other employees in filling vacancies at every entry-level job in formerly all-white lines of progression. (*Hicks* v. *Crown Zellerbach Corp.*, USDC, ELa, 2 FEP Cases 1059)

Then in a craft union pattern-or-practice case, a circuit court reversed a federal district court's refusal to order affirmative relief. It held, in line with other circuit courts, that Section 703(j) of Title VII, which forbids "preferential treatment" solely because of racial imbalance, must be read in conjunction with the fundamental purpose of the Act and the provisions for affirmative relief. (*U.S.* v. *IBEW, Local 38*, CA 6, 1970, 2 FEP Cases 716; *cert. denied* by US SupCt, 1970, 2 FEP Cases 1121)

These decisions become increasingly important with the new enforcement powers given to the EEOC by the 1972 amendments.

In early 1973, the U.S. Court of Appeals for the Ninth Circuit upheld a district court decision that an employer violated Title VII of the Civil Rights Act of 1964 by refusing to hire a black job applicant because of his arrest record. The court's theory was that blacks are arrested substantially more frequently than whites; so a hiring policy that takes into account arrests is discriminatory against blacks. The same rule would not apply to convictions. (*Gregory* v. *Litton Systems, Inc.*, CA 9, 1972, 5 FEP Cases 267)

The same federal district court that handed down the ruling in the *Litton* case on arrest records later ruled that an employer may violate Title VII by discharging a minority-group employee for incurring a number of wage garnishments, stating that such employees are more subject to garnishments than white employees. (*Johnson* v. *Pike Corporation*, USDC CenCalif, 1971, 3 FEP Cases 1025)

Discrimination Based on Religion

Under Title VII as originally enacted, the impact of the prohibition against employment discrimination based on religion was somewhat confused. It was assumed by many that the intent of Congress was simply that no person should be discriminated against in being hired, promoted, etc., or in being accepted for union membership merely because of his religious affiliation.

But the major legal issue that developed under this prohibition was the extent to which employers were required to accommodate their operations to particular aspects of religious beliefs, such as wearing beards or refusing to work on certain religious holidays.

In its original Religious Discrimination Guidelines issued in 1966, the EEOC permitted employers to require performance of work on Saturdays or Sundays, even in the face of good-faith religious beliefs to the contrary.

But in the amended guidelines issued in 1967, the EEOC changed its position. It placed the burden on the employer to prove that the making of "reasonable accommodations to the religious needs of employees" would cause "undue hardship on the conduct of the employer's business."

Both federal and state courts, however, generally have agreed that an employer need not accommodate to specific religious beliefs. In the leading *Dewey* v. *Reynolds Metals* case, the U.S. Court of Appeals for the Sixth Circuit upheld the discharge of an employee who refused to work on Sunday because of his religious beliefs. It said that the employer had no intent to discriminate on account of religion and had no obligation to accommodate the work schedule to the religious beliefs of an employee. (*Dewey* v. *Reynolds Metals Co.*, CA 6, 1970, 2 FEP Cases 869)

The Dewey case was carried to the Supreme Court, but unfortunately, the Court divided four-to-four, with Justice Harlan disqualifying himself. So the decision merely affirmed that of the Sixth Circuit and is not binding on the courts below. (*Dewey* v. *Reynolds Metals Co.*, US SupCt, 1971, 3 FEP Cases 508)

Other holdings by courts in cases involving religious discrimination included the following:

• In a case involving the New York Act, a court affirmed the discharge of an employee who refused to get rid of a beard he wore because of his religious belief as a Muslim. (*Eastern Greyhound Lines* v. *New York State Division of Human Rights*, NY SupCt, 1970, 2 FEP Cases 710)

• A Seventh Day Adventist was properly treated as having quit by the California Government when he refused to perform needed work on Saturdays. The court rejected a claim that the State's action violated the First and Fourteenth Amendments to the U.S. Constitution. (*Stimpel* v. *State Personnel Board*, Calif CtApp, 1970, 2 FEP Cases 1125; petition for hearing denied by Calif SupCt, 1970, 2 FEP Cases 1126; *cert. denied* by US SupCt, 1970, 2 FEP Cases 1121)

• An employee's religious objections to paying dues to a union were rejected and the employee was held properly discharged for his failure to pay dues under a union-shop agreement. (*Linscott* v. *Millers Falls Co.*, USDC Mass, 1970, 75 LRRM 2216)

• A petition by a mail carrier to enjoin the Post Office from discharging him for excessive absenteeism resulting from his refusal, as a Seventh Day Adventist, to work his scheduled Saturdays. Finding no violation of the Constitution, the court refused to accept the employee's contention that the Department could excuse him from Saturday work without any undue hardship. It added: "The burden on this agency of the government to accommodate its pattern of work to the special requirements of each individual's religion would result in a chaotic and impossible situation." (*Dawson* v. *Mitchell*, USDC EVa, 1971, 3 FEP Cases 313)

• In another case holding that an employer need not accommodate to specific religious beliefs and practices, the court observed: "If such an affirmative duty (accommodation) were intended to be imposed, Congress could easily have so provided." (*Kettell* v. *Johnson & Johnson*, USDC EArk, 1972, 4 FEP Cases 294)

1972 Amendment—In the 1972 Amendments, Congress does so provide. Section 701(7)(j) now states:

"The term 'religion' includes all aspects of religious observance and practice, as well as belief, unless an employer demonstrates that he is unable to reasonably accommodate to an employee's or prospective employee's religious observance or practice without undue hardship on the conduct of the employer's business."

This amendment provides a statutory basis for the EEOC's guidelines on religious discrimination. It may, however, raise questions of constitutionality.

Discrimination Based on Sex

The amendment to bar discrimination in employment based on sex was inserted in the 1964 Act on the floor of the House by Congressman Smith (D., Va.), who stated that he wanted to prevent discrimination against the "minority sex." (110 Cong. Rec., pp. 2577-2584, Feb. 8, 1964)

The amendment was opposed by Congressman Celler (D., N.Y.), Chairman of the House Judiciary Committee. In support of his position, Celler put into the record a letter from the Labor Department stating that the President's Commission on the Status of Women had concluded that "discrimination based on sex involves problems sufficiently different from discrimination based on other factors listed to make separate treatment preferable." (110 Cong. Rec., p. 2584, Feb. 8, 1964)

It also was pointed out that executive orders applicable to government contractors and federally assisted construction, while forbidding discrimination based on age, do not prohibit discrimination based on sex. Notwithstanding this opposition, the amendment was adopted by a vote of 168 to 133. (110 Cong. Rec., p. 2584, Feb. 8, 1964)

The 1972 amendments made no change relating specifically to employment discrimination based on sex. But the scope of the prohibition will be affected by the changes in coverage and exemptions. Also, the equal-pay provisions of the Fair Labor Standards Act were broadened to include outside salesmen and executive, administrative, and professional employees.

Meanwhile, the courts have handed down a number of decisions involving the sex-discrimination provisions of Title VII. Here are some of the leading ones:

• *Parents of Pre-School Age Children*—In the first case involving an issue of alleged sex discrimination to be reviewed by the Supreme Court, the Court vacated a decision of the U.S. Court of Appeals for the Fifth Circuit. The Fifth Circuit had upheld a summary judgment for the company, which had refused to hire women with pre-school age children. The Supreme Court remanded the case for further development of the record and further consideration of whether the case came within the "bona fide occupational qualification" exception to the general rules on nondiscrimination. (*Phillips* v. *Martin Marietta Corp.*, US SupCt, 1971, 3 FEP Cases 40.)

• *Flight Cabin Attendants*—Hiring policies followed by airlines were the subject of two important decisions. In the first, the U.S. Court of Appeals for the Fifth Circuit held that female sex is not a "bona fide occupational qualification" for the job of flight cabin attendant. So the airline violated the Act by refusing solely on the basis of sex to hire a male applicant for the position of flight cabin attendant. (*Diaz* v. *Pan American World Airways, Inc.*, CA 5, 1971, 3 FEP Cases 337)

• *Marriage and Pregnancy*—An airline's policy that stewardesses must be unmarried was held unlawful where no other female employees were subject to the policy and there was no policy or rule restricting employment to single male stewards. The policy was illegal, the court said, since it applied one standard to male stewards and another to female stewardesses. (*Sprogis* v. *United Air Lines,* CA 7, 1971, 3 FEP Cases 621) In another case, an employer was held to have violated the Act by discharging a female employee because she was pregnant and unmarried. The court held that the discharge was illegal, since it was for a condition peculiar to the female physiology and such condition did not affect her job performance adversely. (*Doe* v. *Osteopathic Hospital of Wichita, Inc.*, USDC Kan., 1971, 3 FEP Cases 1128)

In two cases brought under the equal-protection-of-the-laws provisions of Section 41 of U.S. Code, Section 1983, two city school boards were held to have violated the Section when they compelled female teachers to take maternity leave after five months of pregnancy. (*Cohen* v. *Chesterfield County School Board*, CA 4, 1972, 4 FEP Cases 1237; *LaFleur* v. *Cleveland Board of Education*, CA 6, 1972, 4 FEP Cases 1070) At the time these actions were brought, municipal employees were not covered by Title VII. They were brought within its coverage by the 1972 Act.

• *State Protective Statutes*—There have been a number of decisions by both state and federal courts holding that state protective statutes for women are in direct conflict with Title VII and, therefore, under the Supremacy Clause of the U.S. Constitution are invalid. A few examples follow:

A railroad company violated the Act by refusing to assign a woman to a position of agent telegrapher. The railroad gave two reasons: (1) the arduous nature of the work rendered a woman physically unsuited for the job; and (2) appointing a woman to the position would result in a violation of California labor laws and regulations that limit hours of work for women and restrict the weight they are permitted to lift. The court held that the company could not reject women on the basis of general assumptions regarding the physical capabilities of female employees. Women must be judged as individuals and may be excluded from the job only upon a showing of individual incapacity. The court also held that the state laws were in direct conflict with Title VII and so invalid. (*Rosenfeld* v. *Southern Pacific Co.*, CA 9, 1971, 3 FEP Cases 604)

Ohio statutes excluding women from working more than 48 hours a week, lifting more than 25 pounds, and not being furnished seats when not engaged in active work were held contrary to Title VII and invalid under the Supremacy Clause. (*Manning* v. *General Motors Corp.*, USDC NOhio, 1971, 3 FEP Cases 968; *Rinehart* v. *Westinghouse Electric Corp.*, USDC NOhio, 1971, 3 FEP Cases 851)

The Massachusetts law limiting female employees to employment of more than 48 hours in one week is unenforceable as in direct conflict with Title VII of the Federal Act. It must yield under the Supremacy Clause of the U.S. Constitution. (*Garneau* v. *Raytheon Co.*, USDC Mass., 1971, 3 FEP Cases 18)

These are just a few of the cases dealing with the issue, but they represent the majority view.

Discrimination Based on National Origin

Except for the changes in coverage and exemptions that affect all forbidden bases of employment discrimination, the 1972 amendments made no change in the ban on discrimination based on national origin.

In its guidelines on discrimination based on national origin, the EEOC noted a number of cases that have come to its attention involving covert, as well as overt, discrimination based on national origin. They included the following:

• The use of tests in the English language where the individual tested came from circumstances where English was not the mother tongue and where skill in the English language is not a requirement of the work to be performed.

• The denial of equal opportunity to persons married to or associated with persons of a specific national origin or because of seeking to promote the interests of national groups.

• Denial of equal opportunity because the name reflects a certain national origin.

• Denial of equal opportunity to persons who, as a class, tend to fall outside national norms for height and weight where such height and weight specifications are not necessary for the performance of the work involved.

• Denial of equal opportunity to a lawfully immigrated alien on the basis of his citizenship, although under Section 703(g) an employer may refuse to employ such a person who does not meet the requirements in the interests of national security. (See Fair Employment Practice Manual [BNA], p. 401: 34.)

Occupational Qualification

The most important of the exceptions to the discrimination provisions is that permitting an employer to discriminate where the job involves a bona fide occupational qualification, provided it is "reasonably necessary to the normal operation" of the enterprise. The exception, however, applies only to discrimination based on religion, sex, or national origin. It does not recognize an exception for race or color.

No change in this exception was made by the 1972 amendments, but there have been a number of court decisions construing it. If applicable, the exception generally permits:

• Employers to "hire and employ" on the basis of an occupational qualification tied to religion, sex, or national origin.

• Unions to classify their memberships or to classify or refer individuals on these bases.

• Employment agencies to classify or refer individuals on these bases.

• Apprenticement and training programs to admit or employ individuals on these bases.

In addition, employers, unions, and employment agencies may indicate in advertising or job notices a preference, limitation, or discrimination based on sex, religion, or national origin when this is a bona fide occupational qualification for employment.

In one of the leading cases on this issue, an air line contended that a rule requiring stewardesses to be unmarried reflected a bona fide occupational qualification for the position, although it did not require that male stewards be unmarried. In holding the rule to be a violation of the law, the court stated: "The marital status of a stewardess cannot be said to affect the individual woman's ability to create the proper psychological climate of comfort, safety, and security for passengers. Nor does any passenger preference for single stewardesses provide a valid reason for involving the rule." (*Sprogis* v. *United Air Lines,* CA 7, 1971, 3 FEP Cases 621)

Security Exception

Another exception that has broad application operates where the employer is subject to a government security program, and the individual involved does not have security clearance. In discussing this exemption during the Senate debate, Senator Humphrey (D., Minn.) said:

"A new Section 703(g) provides that it shall not be an unlawful employment practice for a job to be denied, or a person to be fired, because of his inability to obtain a security clearance when the position involved requires such a clearance. Of course, this provision may not be used as a pretense for denying employment on the basis of race, religion, sex, or national origin. Thus, if employers normally require their employees to apply for clearances only after they are hired, such employers may not refuse all Negro job applicants on the ground that they lack a security clearance at the time they apply for a job. Actually, this provision is intended to cover the obvious situation where a person, for one reason or another, is simply not able to obtain a required security clearance. In such cases, the employer should not be liable under this title if he refuses to hire or discharges such a person for that reason." (110 Cong. Rec., pp. 12721-12725, June 4, 1964)

Communist Party Membership

Closely related to the security exception is one that excludes from "unlawful employment practices" any employment discrimination against an individual who "is a member of the Communist Party of the United States or of any other organization required to register as a Communist-action or Communist-front organization by final order of the Subversive Activities Control Board pursuant to the Subversive Activities Control Act of 1950." (110 Cong. Rec., pp. 2719-2720, Feb. 10, 1964)

A similar exception to permit discrimination against atheists was deleted in the Senate because it was, as Senator Humphrey explained, of "doubtful constitutionality." (110 Cong. Rec., pp. 12721-12725, June 4, 1964)

Seniority, Merit Systems

There is another exception, broadly applicable, that applies where the different standards or compensation or terms and conditions of employment are applied pursuant to a bona fide seniority system, a merit system, or a system that measures earnings by quantity or quality of production. This same exception was included in the Equal Pay Act of 1963. In his interpretation of the Equal Pay Act exception, the Wage and Hour Administrator said that the exception is not restricted to formal systems or systems or plans that are reduced to writing, although formal or written systems or plans may provide better evidence of the actual factors that provide a basis for a wage differential. (Part 800 C.F.R.—Equal Pay for Equal Work under the Fair Labor Standards Act, WHM 95:571)

It was pointed out by Senator Clark (D., Pa.) during the Senate debate that any differences in treatment based on established seniority rights would not be based on any of the forbidden factors and thus would not be unlawful. (110 Cong. Rec., pp. 7215-7218, April 8, 1964)

Differences in treatment also may be justified under this exception by virtue of the fact that the employees work in different locations. Discussing this point, Senator Humphrey said:

"For example, if an employer has two plants in different locations, and one of the plants employs substantially more Negroes than the other, it is not unlawful if the pay, conditions, or facilities are better at one plant than at the other unless it is shown that the employer was intending to discriminate for or against one of the racial groups." (110 Cong. Rec., pp. 12721-12725, June 4, 1964)

Other Exceptions

There are other exceptions to the discrimination provisions that are narrower. These include:

• Employment by a religious corporation, association, or society, including all aspects of observance and practice. Prior to the 1972 amendments, this exemption was limited to the religious aspects of such an organization. Another exemption in the 1964 Act was deleted entirely by the 1972 amendments. The deleted exemption was for educational institutions with respect to individuals whose work involved educational activities. (See Appendix F-11 for congressional debate on the changes in these exemptions.)

• Preferential treatment in employment accorded to Indians by a business operating on or near an Indian reservation. The 1972 amendments made no change in this exemption.

• Reliance and action by an employer on the results of a professionally developed ability test that is not designed or intended to be used to discriminate. Bills to modify this exemption were introduced, but no change was adopted. In a leading case, however, the Supreme Court upheld the position of the EEOC that a test must be related to the job to be filled. (*Griggs* v. *Duke Power Co., supra*)

• Differences in pay based on sex that are authorized under the provisions of the Equal Pay Act of 1963. An amendment to provide such an exemption was introduced by Senator Bennett (R., Utah) and was included in the 1964 Act. But in a decision handed down in 1970, an appeals court applied a strict concept of inequality in comparing jobs performed by male and female employees. The court rejected the contention that the jobs were different because of certain additional tasks performed by the male employees. (*Shultz* v. *Wheaton Glass Co.*, CA 3, 1970, 19 WH Cases 336)

DISCRIMINATION BY EMPLOYMENT AGENCIES

Because of their key position in the hiring process, employment agencies are singled out for specific attention in Title VII. Under Section 703(b), it is an unlawful employment practice for an employment agency to (1) fail or refuse to refer for employment, or otherwise discriminate against, any individual because of his race, color, religion, sex, or national origin, or (2) classify or refer any individual for employment on the basis of his race, color, religion, sex, or national origin. The 1972 amendments made no change in these provisions.

These prohibitions apply not only to private employment agencies, but also to the United States Employment Service and state and local employment services that receive federal assistance.

Under the state fair employment practice laws, lists of lawful and unlawful questions that may be put to job applicants have been issued for the guidance of both employment agencies and employers. In one New York case an employment agency was held to have violated the law when it asked an applicant questions concerning a previous change of name, the national origin of his name, and the nation of schooling and religion of a former employer and his wife. (*Holland* v. *Edwards,* NY CtApp, 1954, 34 LRRM 2018)

DISCRIMINATION BY LABOR UNIONS

The obligation not to discriminate imposed on labor unions by Title VII is two-pronged. First, where the union is acting as an employer, it must not violate any of the prohibitions imposed on employers generally. Second, a union has additional obligations not to discriminate as an organization representing employees in their relationships with employers.

In its capacity as a labor organization, rather than as an employer, a union may not do any of the following:

• Exclude or expel from membership, or otherwise discriminate against, any individual because of his race, color, religion, sex, or national origin.

• Limit, segregate, or classify membership or classify or fail or refuse to refer an individual for employment in any way that would deprive or tend to deprive him of employment opportunities or would limit such employment opportunities or otherwise adversely affect his status as an employee or as an applicant for employment because of his race, color, religion, sex, or national origin.

• Cause or attempt to cause an employer to discriminate against an individual because of his race, color, religion, sex, or national origin.

Subject to the exceptions discussed below, these provisions would appear to outlaw union membership requirements that are in any way tied to race, color, religion, sex, or national origin. They also would appear to bar segregated locals and discriminatory union action toward applicants or members where based on any of the five factors.

Taft-Hartley Rules

In this connection, there may be some overlapping of the Title VII prohibitions and those laid down by the NLRB under its Taft-Hartley doctrine of fair representation. It is the position of a majority of the NLRB that a union that discriminates against a member of the bargaining unit it represents on the basis of race commits an unfair labor practice under the National Labor Relations Act.

In the *Hughes Tool* case, for example, the Board held a union guilty of unfair labor practices and stripped it of its certification where it maintained racially segregated locals and refused to process a grievance of a member of the bargaining unit because of his race. (*Independent Metal Workers Union, Locals Nos. 1 and 2* [*Hughes Tool Co.*] NLRB, 1964, 56 LRRM 1289)

Commenting on this question during the Senate debate, Senator Clark (D. Pa.) said that nothing in Title VII affects rights and duties under the Taft-Hartley or Railway Labor Acts. Although the procedures of Title VII are the exclusive means of relief against practices forbidden by Title VII, he added, they do not deny the individual any rights he may have under other statutes.

Causing Discrimination

The prohibition against a union's causing or attempting to cause an employer to discriminate against individuals because of race, color, religion, sex, or national origin is akin to the Section 8(b)(2) unfair labor practice under the Taft-Hartley Act of causing an employer to discriminate against individuals because of union membership or activities.

Decisions under Section 8(b)(2) of the Taft Act thus would provide some guidance to interpretation of the Title VII prohibition. It was stated by the NLRB in one 8(b)(2) case that the test of a violation is not whether the pressure exerted on the employer is direct or indirect, but whether it is intended to cause the unlawful discrimination and is reasonably calculated to bring about that result. (*Plumbers & Pipefitters* [*Carrier Corp.*], NLRB, 1955, 36 LRRM 1218)

As a result of the 1972 amendments to Title VII, there may be less inclination by the NLRB and the courts to seek to police racial discrimination in employment under the Taft-Hartley Act. In a major case remanded to it by the US Court of Appeals for the District of Columbia for a determination of whether a company had engaged in invidious racial discrimination, the NLRB avoided the basic issue—whether such discrimination is a violation of the Taft-Hartley Act—by finding that there was no invidious discrimination. (*Farmers' Cooperative Compress*, NLRB, 1971, 78 LRRM 1465)

Earlier, the Board had held that a company did not violate the Taft-Hartley Act by discharging two employees who, on their own time, had picketed the company's department store and distributed handbills characterizing the store as "racist" and calling for a boycott. In finding that the picketing was unprotected, a majority of the Board stated that the employees, who were represented by a union, abandoned the contractual grievance procedure and sought direct negotiations with the employer. (*The Emporium*, NLRB, 1971, 77 LRRM 1669)

PROTECTION FOR COMPLAINANTS

Following precedents under the National Labor Relations and Fair Labor Standards Acts, Title VII protects those who seek to invoke or participate in the law's enforcement processes against retaliation.

Under Section 704(a), it is an unlawful employment practice for an employer, an employment agency, or a labor union to discriminate against any employee or job applicant because he has done the following:

• Opposed any unlawful practice under the Act; or

• Made a charge, testified, assisted, or participated in an investigation, proceeding, or hearing under the Act.

This unlawful employment practice is subject to the same remedies as other unlawful employment practices under Title VII, including reinstatement or hiring, with or without back pay.

Chapter 6

How the Law is Administered and Enforced

Prior to the 1972 amendments, the five-member Equal Employment Opportunity Commission was given the task of administering Title VII of the Civil Rights Act of 1964, but it was given virtually no enforcement powers.

The Commission could receive charges of unlawful employment discrimination based on race, color, religion, sex, or national origin, or any member of the Commission could initiate such a charge. If a charge appeared to have merit, the Commission then could seek to obtain voluntary compliance through conference, conciliation, or persuasion.

If the Commission did not succeed in its efforts, it then could notify the aggrieved person or persons that it found reasonable cause to believe a violation had been committed. The aggrieved then could file a suit against the charged party or parties in a federal district court. If it was found that there was a "pattern or practice" of unlawful employment discrimination, the Department of Justice was permitted to file an action against the employer, the union, the employment agency, or all three.

If an aggrieved individual filed a suit, the EEOC was permitted to intervene as *amicus curiae,* but it could not initiate an action on its own. Nevertheless, there was a substantial volume of litigation under the 1964 Act.

The 1972 Amendments

From the time the law was adopted in 1964, bills were introduced in Congress to give the EEOC enforcement powers. The most common proposal was to permit the EEOC to operate in much the same way as the NLRB—to hold hearings before trial examiners (now administrative law judges), to have the report and recommendations reviewed by the Board, and to have the Board issue a cease-and-desist order which could be enforced or reviewed by a federal court of appeals. These bills regularly failed of passage.

In the 1972 Congress, the deadlock was broken. Instead of giving the EEOC power to issue cease-and-desist orders, the Administration proposed to give the Commission authority to file an action directly in a federal court whenever it was unable to resolve a charge by conference, conciliation, or persuasion. This is the procedure used to enforce the Age Discrimination in Employment Act and much the same as the enforcement procedure under the Fair Labor Standards Act. It is direct, rather than indirect, enforcement by the courts. There is no preliminary administrative cease-and-desist order.

ADMINISTRATIVE CHANGES

The enlargement of its jurisdiction and its enforcement powers created many problems for the Equal Employment Opportunity Commission. At the time the amendments were passed the Commission's intake of charges of violation was in excess of 33,000 a year, and it was about 22 months behind in its processing of charges.

As part of the change in the administrative organization of the EEOC, the amendments provide for making the General Counsel of the EEOC a Presidential appointee, subject to Senate confirmation, rather than permitting the Commission to hire its own General Counsel. (See Appendix F-24 for congressional debate on this change.)

Differences in the House and Senate bills were resolved on this point in the Conference Committee. The Senate bill provided for establishing the office of General Counsel to be appointed by the President for a term of four years with the advice and consent of the Senate. The General Counsel would be given the responsibility for filing complaints and conducting all litigation for the Commission. The Senate conferees receded to a change reserving to the Attorney General the conduct of all litigation to which the Commission is a party in the Supreme Court.

In another change, the General Counsel is given responsibility for litigation, other than in the Supreme Court, and concurrence with the Chairman of the EEOC in the appointment and supervision of regional attorneys. The Commission is establishing regional legal offices in Philadelphia, Atlanta, Chicago, Denver, and San Francisco; it plans to hire about 150 additional attorneys.

Other changes affecting the administration of Title VII include:

• An amendment adopted by the Senate and agreed to by the House conferees to place the position of the General Counsel in the executive pay scale and to raise the pay level of the Chairman and other members of the Commission. The purpose was to give them parity with officials in comparable positions in such agencies as the NLRB, the Federal Trade Commission, and the Federal Power Commission.

• There is an amendment permitting a member of the Commission to serve until his successor is appointed. But it adds that a member may serve no longer than (1) 60 days when Congress is in session, unless a nomination has been submitted to the Senate; or (2) after adjournment *sine die* of the session of the Senate in which the nomination was submitted.

• The 1964 Act provided for a study by the Secretary of Labor on discrimination because of age. In 1967, Congress passed the Age Discrimination in Employment Act forbidding employers, employment agencies, or labor unions to discriminate against persons between the ages of 40 and 65 with respect to employment or union membership because of their age. (See Labor Relations Expediter [BNA], p. 1815.) Section 715 of the 1964 Act, which provided for the study by the Secretary of Labor, was replaced in the 1972 Act by a provision establishing an Equal Employment Opportunity Coordinating Council. Members of the Council are the Secretary of Labor, the Chairman of the Equal Employment Opportunity Commission, the Attorney General, the Chairman of the Civil Service Commission, and the Chairman of the Civil Rights Commission, or their respective designees. The Council is given the responsibility for enforcing equal employment opportunity legislation and is required to make an annual report to Congress on its activities, as well as recommendations for legislative or administrative changes. (See Appendix F-34 for congressional debate on the establishment of the Coordinating Council.)

• A new Section 717 in the Act provides that all "personnel actions involving employees of the Federal Government be free from discrimination based on race, color, sex, religion, or national origin." The administration and enforcement of this provision is assigned to the Civil Service Commission with regard to all government employees except those of the Library of Congress. The Librarian of Congress will administer and enforce the rights of employees of the Library.

• Another change made by Section 717 requires the Civil Service Commission to create and annually review an equal employment opportunity plan for all agencies within Section 717(a)—the military departments, the executive agencies, the General Accounting Office, the U.S. Postal Service, the Postal Rate Commission, and competitive service positions in the District of Columbia government. The Librarian of Congress has a similar responsibility for employees of the Library.

• The Civil Service Commission also is required by Section 717 to publish, on a semiannual basis, progress reports from departments or agencies on implementation of such equal opportunity plans.

No Centralized Power

When the 1972 bill went to the Conference Committee, there was a provision in the House bill that would have made the EEOC the sole federal authority to combat employment discrimination of the type forbidden by the Act. This provision was deleted by the Conference Committee. It has been construed by some as permitting allegedly aggrieved individuals to seek relief in several forums—the EEOC, OFCC, NLRB, state and municipal FEP agencies, and arbitration.

Regarding federal contractors, however, the new Act provides that no contract, whether subject to Executive Order 11246 or any other equal employment opportunity law, may be terminated, denied, or withheld without a full hearing where the employer has had an affirmative action plan accepted within the past 12 months.

The question of multiple and overlapping remedies is discussed in detail below.

THE NEW ENFORCEMENT POWERS

As had been anticipated, the most far-reaching changes relating to equal employment opportunity made by the 1972 amendments to the Civil Rights Act of 1964 related to enforcement of the prohibition against discrimination in employment based on race, color, sex, religion, or national origin. The amendments, however, were not related solely to the EEOC. Here are the changes made:

• Under the 1964 Act, the EEOC had virtually no enforcement power.

The amendments give the Commission authority to bring civil suits in federal district courts for injunctions and other remedies for unlawful employment practices on the part of employers, unions, employment agencies, and joint labor-management committees. In the Senate, there were a number of proponents of a measure to give the EEOC power, akin to that of the NLRB, to issue cease-and-desist orders enforceable in the federal courts of appeals. To curtail extended debate and obtain a favorable vote on the entire bill, the Senate agreed to accept the Administration proposal for direct enforcement by the EEOC in the federal district courts. (See Appendices F-5 and F-13 through F-18 for congressional debate on this issue.)

• Under the 1964 Act, the Justice Department had sole jurisdiction to prosecute actions involving an alleged "pattern or practice" of unlawful employment discrimination. The 1972 amendments give the EEOC concurrent jurisdiction with the Justice Department to bring such actions for a period of two years. Thereafter, the EEOC will have exclusive jurisdiction to bring "pattern or practice" actions. (See Appendix F-20 for congressional debate on this issue.)

• One of the amendments extends the coverage of Title VII to state and local governments. But jurisdiction to prosecute alleged employment discrimination violations by state and local governments is given to the Justice Department, instead of to the EEOC. (See Appendices F-20 and F-26 for debate on this and related changes.)

• Under the 1964 Act, an aggrieved could sue on his own for an injunction, reinstatement, hiring, and back pay if the EEOC found "reasonable cause" to believe a violation had been committed and was unable to settle the case by conference, conciliation, or persuasion. Although the 1972 amendments authorize the EEOC to file actions when it cannot settle cases, the aggrieved individuals may still file suits of their own if the EEOC fails to sue. (See Appendix F-26 for congressional debate on this and related changes.)

• The 1964 Act did not permit other groups or individuals to file charges on behalf of allegedly aggrieved individuals. This was changed by the amendments. So now such organizations as the NAACP may file charges on behalf of persons who allegedly are victims of employment discrimination because of race, color, sex, religion, or national origin. A provision to permit other groups or individuals to file charges on behalf of allegedly aggrieved individuals was deleted in the Dirksen-Mansfield substitute in the 1964 legislation. The 1972 amendments permit other groups or individuals to file charges on behalf of allegedly aggrieved individuals, but there is no language indicating that the other groups or individuals may bring an action in court on behalf of such individuals if the EEOC fails to resolve the dispute by conference, conciliation, or persuasion. This is an issue that is likely to be litigated.

PROCEDURAL ISSUES

By the time the 1972 amendments were adopted, many of the procedural issues under Title VII had been resolved. The courts, for example, made the following rulings:

Attorneys' Fees—If the Justice Department brings a pattern-or-practice suit against a company, union, or both, Title VII specifically provides for payments to the defendants by the government of attorneys' fees if it loses the suit. In a case decided by a federal district court in Florida, the court pointed out that the general statutory prohibition upon the award of attorney's fees against the United States was not applicable, since Title VII specifically states that such an award may be made in the discretion of the court. (*U.S.* v. *Jacksonville Terminal Co.*, USDC MFla, 1970, 2 FEP Cases 611) The case later was remanded by the Court of Appeals for the Fifth Circuit, which told the district court to consider, among other things, the total employment picture at the terminal. (*U.S.* v. *Jacksonville Terminal Co.*, CA 5, 1971, 3 FEP Cases 862) The appeals court reversed the lower court on almost all points and ordered sweeping relief.

In other cases in which aggrieved employees sued employers and unions and won, they were awarded substantial attorneys' fees. In one class action, for example, the court gave the successful employees costs plus $20,000 in attorneys' fees. (*Clark* v. *American Marine Corp.*, USDC ELa, 1970, 2 FEP Cases 670)

The court in the *Clark* case gave consideration to the time and work required by the attorneys and the novelty of the action.

In an unusual action, the U.S. Court of Appeals for the Fourth Circuit reversed a district court's refusal to allow attorney's fees in a case filed by black females who were not really interested in employment but merely in attacking the employer's employment policies and practices. (*Lea* v. *Cone Mills Corp.*, CA 4, 1971, 3 FEP Cases 137)

Class Actions—The use of class actions in Title VII suits under the 1964 Act appeared to have been firmly established prior to the amendments. In the leading *Crown Zellerbach* case, the U.S. Court of Appeals for the Fifth Circuit held that it was not necessary for each member of the class to have filed a charge with the EEOC. On this ground, the court reinstated as plaintiffs several blacks who had been eliminated from the action because they had not sought relief through the EEOC. The court added, however, that participation by the members of the class was limited to the issues raised by the employees who did file a charge with the EEOC. (*Oatis* v. *Crown Zellerbach Corp.*, CA 5, 1968, 1 FEP Cases 328)

But there were cases in which courts refused to permit an applicant for employment to represent a class that included present employees. (See for example, *Johnson* v. *Georgia Highway Express, Inc.*, USDC NGa, 1968, 1 FEP Cases 637; *Russell* v. *Alpha Portland Cement Corp.*, USDC WAla, 1968, 1 FEP Cases 386.) There also was a decision upholding the right of white employees to joinder in a class action brought by black employees that could affect the seniority of the white employees. (*English* v. *Seaboard Coastline R.R. Co.*, CA 5, 1972, 4 FEP Cases 1125)

When the 1972 amendments were being considered, some employer groups supported a change that would bar class actions under Title VII. No change was made, however.

Conciliation by EEOC—In a number of cases handed down before the 1972 amendments, several federal courts of appeals held that conciliation efforts by the Commission were not a jurisdictional prerequisite to the maintenance of a Title VII suit by an individual. The courts said that the 1964 Act merely required that the Commission have an opportunity to persuade the employer or union before the action could be brought. (See *Gaston County Dyeing Machine Co.* v. *Brown*, CA 4, 1968, 1 FEP Cases 699, *cert. denied* by US SupCt, 1969, 1 FEP Cases 699; *Observer Transportation Co.* v. *Lee*, CA 4, 1968, 1 FEP Cases 702, *cert. denied* by US SupCt, 1969, 1 FEP Cases 699; *Pilot Freight Carriers, Inc.* v. *Walker*, CA 4, 1968, 1 FEP Cases 456, *cert. denied* by US SupCt, 1969, 2 FEP Cases 699, *Electrical Workers, IBEW* v. *EEOC*, CA 3, 1968, 1 FEP Cases 335; *Dent* v. *St. Louis-San Francisco Ry.*, CA 5, 1969, 1 FEP Cases 583; *Choate* v. *Caterpillar Tractor Co.*, CA 7, 1968, 1 FEP Cases 431.)

Filing of Charge—There were, on the other hand, cases in which federal courts of appeals held that the filing of a charge with the EEOC was a prerequisite to the filing of a suit in court by an allegedly aggrieved individual. (See *Stebbins* v. *Nationwide Mutual Insurance Co.*, CA 4, 1967, 1 FEP Case 235, *cert. denied* by US SupCt, 1968, 68 LRRM 2889; *Mickel* v. *South Carolina State Employment Service*, CA 4, 1967, 1 FEP Cases 182, *cert. denied* by US SupCt, 1967, 1 FEP Cases 300.)

Although lower courts had divided on the issue, the U.S. Court of Appeals for the Third Circuit held that a finding by the EEOC of "reasonable cause" to believe a violation of Title VII had been committed was not a prerequisite to the filing of a court action by an alleged victim of unlawful discrimination. After examining the legislative history of the

1964 Act, the court found that "good reason and fealty to the spirit and purpose of the Act command that we do not require an affirmative finding by the Commission, as a passport for judicial review." (*Fekete* v. *U.S. Steel Corp.*, CA 3, 1970, 2 FEP Cases 540) See below under "Exhaustion of Procedures" for a holding that the EEOC must go through all the procedural steps before filing an action in court under the 1972 Act.

Suits Under 19th Century Acts

The procedural and technical difficulties posed by Title VII were avoided by some plaintiffs by using Civil Rights Acts adopted after the Civil War as an alternative way of obtaining a remedy for alleged racial discrimination in employment. The actions were brought under 29 U.S.C. Sec. 1981 *et seq.*

The issue was whether the jurisdiction to sue under the 19th Century laws was preempted by Title VII of the Civil Rights Act of 1964. But there was a second issue—whether the allegedly aggrieved individual could bypass the EEOC and sue directly under the earlier laws.

Jurisdiction to sue for alleged racial discrimination in employment under the earlier laws was upheld by three federal courts of appeals. (See *Waters* v. *Wisconsin Steel Works of International Harvester Co.*, CA 7, 1970, 2 FEP Cases 574, *cert. denied* by US SupCt, 1971, 2 FEP Cases 911; *Sanders* v. *Dobbs Houses, Inc.*, CA 5, 1970, 2 FEP Cases 942, *cert. denied* by US SupCt, 1971, 2 FEP 942; *Young* v. *International Telephone & Telegraph Co.*, CA 3, 1971, 3 FEP Cases 146.)

Courts have held, however, that the use of these earlier laws is limited to cases based on alleged racial discrimination. They may not be used where the charge is one of discrimination based on sex, religion, or national origin. (See *Fitzgerald* v. *United Methodist Community Center*, USDC Neb, 1972, 4 FEP Cases 167.)

Statute of Limitations

Under the 1964 Act, a court that found that a violation of Title VII had or was being committed had authority to enjoin the unlawful conduct and to award appropriate affirmative relief, such as reinstatement with back pay less interim earnings obtained by the employee, who should exercise reasonable diligence to obtain other work. There was no specified limitation on the time for suing and obtaining redress. If the employee sued under the 19th Century Act, however, the statute of limitations could be as long as 10 years. In a key case, the U.S. Court of Appeals for the Fifth Circuit held that action brought under that Act was a contract action and so was subject to the 10-year limitation period applicable to contract claims, rather than to the one-year period applicable to tort claims. (*Boudreaux* v. *Baton Rouge Marine Contracting Co.*, CA 5, 1971, 3 FEP Cases 99)

An amendment introduced by Senator Beall (R., Md.) and included in the 1972 Act provides that back-pay liability under Title VII shall not exceed that accruing from a date more than two years prior to the filing of the charge.

According to a section-by-section analysis placed in the Congressional Record by Senator Williams (D., N.J.), Section 706(g) in which the two-year limitation on back pay was inserted, "is intended to give the court wide discretion, as has been generally exercised by the courts under existing law, in fashioning the most complete relief possible." (See Appendix F-5.)

Exhaustion of Procedures

An amendment to Title VII sponsored by Senator Javits (R., N.Y.) made the provisions of the 1972 Act applicable to pending suits. This amendment was given effect in a decision handed down by a federal district court in late 1972. The court held that the EEOC was required to go through all the procedures specified in the Act before filing a suit in a federal district court. It must do the following:

• If a charge is filed with or by the Commission, notice must be served on the offending employer or union, and the Commission must investigate the charge.

• If the Commission determines that no "reasonable cause" exists to support the charge, the respondent must be so notified and the charge dismissed.

• But if the Commission finds "reasonable cause" to believe a violation has been committed, it must notify the respondent and attempt to eliminate the problem through conference, conciliation, or persuasion.

• If the Commission is unable to obtain satisfactory results within 30 days, it may bring an action in a federal district court.

• Finally, if the Commission does not bring an action within 180 days, it must notify the aggrieved party, who then has 90 days to file a suit on his own behalf. (*Equal Employment Opportunity Commission* v. *Container Corp.*, USDC MFla, 1972, 5 FEP Cases 108)

Under the reasoning of the court, earlier decisions permitting aggrieved individuals to sue before the Commission completed the specified procedural steps involved different considerations. Aggrieved individuals, the court observed, should not be penalized by the delays of the Commission, but when the Commission files a suit, it should be required to exhaust the administrative procedures first.

MULTIPLE REMEDIES AND FORUMS

During the consideration of the 1972 amendments, the House adopted a provision that would have made the EEOC the sole federal agency to police the types of discrimination forbidden by the Act. But this provision was deleted during the deliberations of the Conference Committee. As a result, enforcement of bans on discrimination based on race, color, sex, religion, or national origin continues to be split among a number of agencies, public and private.

The EEOC has the broadest jurisdiction. But under the 1972 amendments, the Justice Department will enforce the Act with respect to the newly covered state and local government employees—and until April 24, 1974, it will have concurrent jurisdiction with EEOC over "pattern or practice" actions; the Office of Federal Contract Compliance in the Labor Department retains jurisdiction to police discriminatory practices by government contractors; and the Civil Service Commission has jurisdiction over federal employees, except those of the Library of Congress, the Librarian of Congress having jurisdiction over them. The amendments did, however, provide for establishment of an Equal Employment Opportunity Coordinating Council consisting of the Secretary of Labor, the Chairman of the EEOC, the Attorney General, the Chairman of the U.S. Civil Service Commission, and the Chairman of the Civil Rights Commission, or their respective designees.

Then there is still the question of the overlapping federal and state and local jurisdictions where states or municipalities have fair employment practice acts or human relations commissions. The rules governing deferral by the EEOC to such state or local agencies are discussed in Chapter 1.

In some areas, there is also overlapping of jurisdiction between the EEOC and the Wage and Hour Division of the Labor Department and the NLRB. The Wage and Hour Division enforces the equal-pay amendment to Section 6 of the Fair Labor Standards Act, which requires that there be no discrimination in pay on the basis of sex. Such discrimination also would be a violation of Title VII, but Section 703(h) of the 1964 Act, which was not changed by the 1972 amendments, specifies that "it shall not be an unlawful employment practice under this title for any employer to differentiate upon the basis of sex in determining the amount of the wages or compensation paid or to be paid to employees of such employer if such differentiation is authorized by the provisions of Section 6(d) of the Fair Labor Standards Act of 1938, as amended (29 U.S.C. 206(d))."

The NLRB moved into the area of racial discrimination when it ruled that a union that discriminated against a member of the bargaining unit on the basis of race violated its duty of fair representation and so was subject not only to the loss of its certification, but also to an unfair-labor-practice charge. Some of the decisions were upheld by federal courts of appeals. (See *NLRB* v. *Local 1367, International Longshoremen's Assn.* [*Galveston Maritime Assn.*], CA 5, 1966, *cert. denied* by US SupCt, 1967, 66 LRRM 2307; Local 12, *United Rubber Workers* v. *NLRB*, CA 5, 1966, 63 LRRM 2395, *cert. denied* by US SupCt, 1967, 66 LRRM 2306.)

In a decision handed down in 1969, the U.S. Court of Appeals for the District of Columbia decided that employment discrimination by an employer on the basis of race was a violation of Section 8(a)(1) of the Taft-Hartley Act. (*Packinghouse Workers* v. *NLRB* [*Farmers Cooperative Compress*], CA DC, 1969, 70 LRRM 2489)

The court remanded the case to the NLRB for a determination of whether the particular employer had engaged in invidious discrimination on the basis of race. The Board decided on remand that the employer had not engaged in such discrimination and thus avoided the basic issue of whether such discrimination is a violation of the Taft-Hartley Act. (*Farmers Cooperative Compress*, NLRB, 1971, 78 LRRM 1465)

Title VII and Arbitration

If an employee or a union member pursues a claim of discrimination based on race, color, sex, religion, or national origin through the grievance-arbitration machinery of a collective bargaining contract and loses, may he then file a suit in court under Title VII based on the same claim?

There have been several cases in which federal appeals courts have attempted to balance the national policy favoring resolution of labor disputes by arbitration with the antidiscrimination policy of Title VII. In one key case, the U.S. Court of Appeals for the Sixth Circuit held that an employee who claimed to have been discriminated against on religious grounds could not bring a Title VII action after an arbitrator had issued an award adverse to the employee. The arbitrator's award, the court said, was "as binding as a judgment." (*Dewey* v. *Reynolds Metals Co.*, CA 6, 1970, 2 FEP Cases 678)

When the case was taken to the Supreme Court, Justice Harlan disqualified himself during the oral argument, and the decision below was affirmed by an equally divided Court. It never will be known whether the division was on the religious or the arbitration issue. (*Dewey* v. *Reynolds Metals Co.*, US SupCt, 1971, 3 FEP Cases 509)

In a later case, however, the Sixth Circuit held that an employee could maintain a Title VII action against an employer and a union even though his claim of racial discrimination had been rejected by an arbitrator. Distinguishing the case from the *Dewey* case, the court noted that the employee did not have a "clearly voluntary choice" as to whether to submit his grievance to arbitration, that his Title VII action challenged the fairness and impartiality of the arbitration proceeding, and that there was grave doubt whether the collective bargaining contract gave the arbitrator the right to consider the discrimination claim. (*Newman* v. *Avco Corp.*, CA 6, 1971, 3 FEP Cases 1137)

Another appeals court held that employees claiming to have been discriminated against on the basis of sex could maintain an action under Title VII while pursuing the remedies available to them under the grievance-arbitration provisions of their collective bargaining contract. But the court held that after an adjudication had been made, the employees must make an election of remedies so as to preclude duplicate relief and a "windfall" to the employees. (*Bowe* v. *Colgate-Palmolive Co.*, CA 7, 1969, 2 FEP Cases 121)

There was a further refinement in a Title VII action brought by a black employee who alleged that his discharge was racially motivated. In deciding that the employee was bound by an arbitrator's award rejecting his claim of discrimination, the appeals court adopted as conclusive the lower court's opinion stating "we hold that where an employee voluntarily submits a claim of discrimination to arbitration under a union contract grievance procedure—a submission which is binding on the employer no matter what the result—the employee is bound by the arbitration award just as is the employer." (*Alexander* v. *Gardner-Denver Co.*, CA 10, 1972, 4 FEP Cases 1210, *affirming* USDC Colo, 1971, 4 FEP Cases 1205)

Finally, the U.S. Court of Appeals for the Fifth Circuit, in effect, adopted the rules developed by the NLRB in the 1955 *Spielberg Manufacturing Co.* case (36 LRRM 1152) and later cases for honoring arbitration awards in cases involving issues under the Taft-Hartley Act. An arbitration award may be deferred to, the Fifth Circuit said, if "the contractual right coincides with rights under Title VII" and if it is "plain that the arbitrator's decision is in no way violative of the private rights guaranteed by Title VII." Moreover, the court added, before deferring, the district court must find that:

• The factual issues before it are identical to those decided by the arbitrator.

• The arbitrator had power under the collective bargaining contract to decide the ultimate issue of discrimination.

• The evidence presented at the arbitration hearing dealt adequately with all factual issues.

• The arbitrator actually decided the factual issues presented to the court.

• The arbitration proceeding was fair and regular and free of procedural infirmities.

The appeals court thus put the burden of proof in establishing "these conditions of limitation" on the defendant, rather than the plaintiff, and it remanded the case to the district court for further proceedings. (*Rios* v. *Reynolds Metals Co.*, CA 5, 1972, 5 FEP Cases 1)

In view of the differing views of the appeals courts, this issue of deferral to arbitration in Title VII suits will not be resolved until the Supreme Court hands down a decision.

Chapter 7

How State Laws Deal With Discrimination

One of the purposes of the Civil Rights Act of 1964 was to encourage more states to adopt fair employment practice laws; another purpose was to stimulate increased activity under laws already in existence. There had been a dearth of activity under those laws in the years immediately preceding 1964.

At the time the 1964 Federal Act was adopted, 25 states had fair employment practice laws, although they varied considerably in their form. The first fair employment practice law was adopted by New York in 1945. It was a broad law, applying to employers, employment agencies, and labor unions.

By the time Congress passed the Civil Rights Act of 1964, more than 49 percent of the nonwhite population was covered by state fair employment practice laws. (Report 867, Senate Labor Committee, Feb. 4, 1964)

The state laws were applied to all employers, unions, and employment agencies located within a state. They were not restricted to those engaged solely in intrastate operations. This application of the state laws to interstate employers was upheld by the Supreme Court. Such laws do not place an unconstitutional burden on interstate commerce, the Court held, and federal law does not prevent the states from enacting fair employment practice legislation. (*Colorado Antidiscrimination Commission* v. *Continental Air Lines*, US SupCt, 52 LRRM 2889 (1963).)

In addition to the state laws, several cities had fair employment practice ordinances, including some in states that did not have state-wide laws.

Effect of 1972 Amendments

Much happened in the states during the interval between the 1964 and 1972 Federal Acts. Forty states had adopted fair employment practice laws of general application, including Florida. Prior to October 1, 1972, the Florida Act was limited to public employees.

North Carolina still has a law limited to public employment. Tennessee and South Dakota have no fair employment practice laws, but they have commissions to promote equal employment opportunity. Both South and North Dakota have laws forbidding discrimination against female jockeys, and North Dakota has a law prohibiting employment discrimination based on age.

The state laws vary widely. Some have more limited coverage than others. Some provide for any type of administrative agency or enforcement of orders, but make employment discrimination of a forbidden type a misdemeanor. Still others are strictly voluntary. Section 706(c) of Title VII, as amended, permits the EEOC to defer to a state agency in the handling of charges of discrimination, provided the law of the state meets specified requirements.

Questions of coverage, forbidden discrimination, enforcement, and deferral to state agencies are discussed in more detail below. There also are charts, from BNA's Fair Employment Practice Manual, showing the differences in the provisions of the laws of the various states. These are reproduced later in this chapter. (See Appendix F-1 for a discussion of the Conference Committee Report of the differences in procedures where state FEP laws exist and where there are no state FEP laws.)

FORBIDDEN DISCRIMINATION

State fair employment practice laws generally are aimed at employers, employment agencies, and labor unions. The usual law forbids an employer to engage in employment discrimination, such as hiring, firing, promotion, or other change in employment status, on the basis of race, religion, or national origin. Employment agencies may not discriminate on these bases in employment referrals, and unions may not discriminate in accepting a person for membership, referring him for a job, or otherwise adversely affecting his union membership or employment. Such laws usually include national origin in the proscribed bases of discrimination.

The laws of some states also forbid employment discrimination based on sex or age. In the case of sex, there is a conflict between the Federal Act and state protective laws for female employees, such as those limiting the number of hours that females may work or the number of pounds they may lift. There have been a number of court decisions on whether Title VII supersedes these state laws. The holdings are discussed later in this chapter.

Racial Discrimination

The majority of the cases involving charges of discrimination under both the federal and the state laws have involved race or color, although there has been a marked increase in charges of discrimination based on sex.

The prohibitions based on race, color, religion, sex, or national origin generally are subject to an exception incorporated in the federal law. Discrimination is permitted if based on a "bona fide occupational qualification." How this exception has been construed under the Federal Act is discussed in Chapter 5 at page 49.

Age Discrimination

Fair employment practice agencies in 32 states have been given the responsibility of preventing employment discrimination based on age. The states and the citations to their laws in Fair Employment Practice Manual (BNA) are as follows:

Alaska, 451:51; California, 451:169; Colorado, 451:182; Connecticut, 451:201; Delaware, 451:225; Georgia, 451:277; Hawaii, 451:285; Idaho, 455:311; Illinois, 451:332; Indiana, 451:385; Iowa, 451:401; Kentucky, 451:451; Louisiana, 451:491; Maine, 451:501; Maryland, 451:531; Massachusetts, 451:559; Michigan, 451:577; Montana, 451:701; Nebraska, 451:745; New Hampshire, 451:775; New Jersey, 451:801; New Mexico, 451:851; New York, 451:875; North Dakota, 451:921; Ohio, 451:932; Oregon, 451:975; Pennsylvania, 451:1001; Puerto Rico, 451:1051; Rhode Island, 451:1101; Washington, 451:1225; West Virginia, 451:1251; Wisconsin, 451:1275.

The Montana and Texas laws, however, only declare a "general public policy" against discrimination in employment on the basis of age. The Federal Government also has an Age Discrimination Act. It is administered and enforced by the Labor Department.

Sex Discrimination

Like the Federal Act, many of the state laws include a prohibition on discrimination in employment on the basis of sex. But there is a major problem. They often collide with other state laws designed to protect female employees, such as those limiting the number of hours a female employee may work or the number of pounds she may lift.

In addition, a number of states have laws requiring equal pay for female employees for equal work. The Federal Government also has such a law, and it was amended this year to apply to executive, administrative, and professional employees, and outside salesmen. Such employees already were subject to the provisions of Title VII of the Civil Rights Act forbidding discrimination in matters of employment, including compensation, on the basis of sex.

States with equal-pay laws are Alaska, Arizona, Arkansas, California, Colorado, Connecticut, Florida, Georgia, Hawaii, Idaho, Illinois, Indiana, Kansas, Kentucky, Maine, Massachusetts, Michigan, Minnesota, Missouri, Montana, Nebraska, Nevada, New Hampshire, New Jersey, New York, North Dakota, Ohio, Oklahoma, Oregon, Pennsylvania, Rhode Island, South Dakota, Washington, West Virginia, and Wyoming.

In addition to the states that have specific equal-pay laws, discrimination in compensation also is barred, either specifically or by implication, in the states that include sex bias in their fair employment practice laws.

ADMINISTRATION AND ENFORCEMENT OF STATE LAWS

The enforceable state FEP laws share a common pattern. They rely upon civil, rather than criminal, proceedings and vest responsibility for enforcement in an administrative agency. They stress education and conciliation, using public hearings and court proceedings as a last resort.

Under the state FEP laws, an individual may file a complaint with the commission. If the commission, after investigating, finds no probable cause to support the complaint, it dismisses the complaint. Most commissions, however, still may study the employer's general employment pattern and attempt to eliminate any discriminatory practice found.

If the commission finds probable cause to believe the complaint, or finds evidence of other discriminatory practices, it attempts to adjust the matter through conciliation. If conciliation fails, the dispute becomes public for the first time, and a hearing is held. This results either in dismissal of the complaint or issuance of an order requiring the accused to cease and desist from discriminating and to take affirmative remedial action. Such orders may be enforced or reviewed in the courts.

Filing of Complaints

In most states, the complaint must be filed by the aggrieved individual. Some states allow private groups to file complaints on behalf of an individual, but this privilege has been seldom used. Some states also allow the commission to initiate an investigation without the submission of a complaint, but this authority usually is employed for educational and exhortatory purposes.

Thus the state laws rely primarily upon the injured individual to initiate the complaint proceedings and bring the commission to action. How has this worked?

An examination of the annual reports makes it clear that the state commissions, prior to Title VII, received considerably fewer complaints than had been expected.

Since the establishment of EEOC and its deferral policy, the number of complaints received by the state agencies appears to have increased considerably, although accurate statistics are not available at present.

Probable Cause

A large proportion of the complaints filed are dismissed at the outset because the commission's preliminary investigation indicates that the complaint is not supported by probable cause. When they dismiss a specific complaint but find other discriminatory practices, many commissions list the case under a "violation found" heading without distinguishing these cases from those in which probable cause is found to credit the particular complaint.

New York is one of the few states to make this distinction in its statistics. Its reports suggest that the individual who files a complaint has his charge sustained in only about one case out of every three or four. Other discriminatory practices are found in about the same proportion of cases, but no discrimination of any sort is found in one third to one half of the cases.

Absolute proof of discrimination is next to impossible, except in the clear-cut case where an employer runs a "whites only" help-wanted advertisement or inquires as to race or religion in an employment application. Presumptions of discrimination may arise from the refusal to hire a qualified minority-group applicant by an employer who doesn't employ any member of the minority group or employs them only in certain jobs. But even these presumptions are of little help where an employer hires a token number of minority-group members and decides "this far and no farther."

The difficulties in proving job discrimination were stated by the New York Court of Appeals:

"One intent on violating the Law Against Discrimination cannot be expected to declare or announce his purpose. Far more likely is it that he will pursue his discriminatory practices in ways that are devious, by methods subtle and elusive—for we deal with an area in which 'subtleties of conduct . . . play no small part.' . . . All of which amply justifies the legislature's grant of broad power to the commission to appraise, correlate, and evaluate the facts uncovered." (*Holland* v. *Edwards,* NY Ct App, 1954, 34 LRRM 2018, 1 FEP Cases 9)

After finding that probable cause exists, the commission tries to eliminate the discriminatory practices by conciliation. The commission reports indicate that a very large proportion of the complaints filed are settled by this technique and never reach the stage of public hearing.

A 1963 study by the Senate Labor Committee showed that the more than 19,000 complaints resulted in only 62 hearings, 26 cease-and-desist orders, and 18 court actions. Thus, only one out of every 313 complaints resulted in a hearing, only one out of every 747 produced a cease-and-desist order, and only one out of 1,080 resulted in a court action.

The state agencies say so few cases reach the public hearing or court action stage because of the commissions' efforts and the respondents' cooperation in the conciliation process. All agree, however, that the threat of a public hearing or court action is needed for effective conciliation.

In explaining why it seeks as much voluntary compliance as possible, the New York Commission has said: "It would be of little avail if compulsive action on the basis of individual complaints resulted in temporary compliance which could only be maintained by a policing operation. . . ."

The commissions generally take the position that they can insist during the conciliation stage that the accused take any action which the commission could order after a hearing. As previously noted, they also assume jurisdiction to go beyond the immediate complaint and eliminate all the discriminatory practices found.

The statutory basis for this is not exactly clear. The New York law, for example, directs the commission to "eliminate the unlawful discriminatory practice complained of . . ." but goes on to provide that the commission may issue an order where it finds that the accused "has engaged in *any* unlawful discriminatory practices" (emphasis added). The New York Court of Appeals has upheld, at least by implication, the commission's authority to eliminate all unlawful discriminatory practices, not just the one cited in the complaint. (*Holland* v. *Edwards,* NY Ct App, 1954, 34 LRRM 2018, 1 FEP Cases 9)

During the conciliation stage the accused usually is in no position to challenge the commission's authority to delve into all of his employment practices. He has no right to seek judicial review at this stage and may challenge the commission only by risking a public hearing.

Similarly, the state laws do not give the complainant any right to seek judicial review of the commission's acts during the conciliation process or even of the conciliation agreement itself. There is some authority, however, for the proposition that the complainant can go into court if his complaint is dismissed during the conciliation process. (*Jeanpierre* v. *Arbury*, NY Ct App, 1958, 41 LRRM 2849, 1 FEP Cases 13)

The conciliation process as practiced by the state commissions has been described as follows:

"The process of conciliation is necessarily an adjustment of differences. It demands the ability to know when to give way and when to stand firm. It demands the courage to stand firm. It demands the courage to stand absolutely firm on points which matter and to give way with good grace on points which do not. The essence of the conciliation process is compromise. Compromise does not signify retreat because one is too timid to press one's convictions, nor does it signify moral inertia. Compromise is an essential requirement of the law, necessitated, among other things, by the difficulty of proving discrimination even when one has found probable cause to credit the allegations of a complaint." (Spitz, *Patterns of Conciliation Discrimination,* 125 N.Y. L.J. No. 71, 1951)

The commission usually tries to follow up on its conciliation agreements. If it finds renewed violation it reopens the proceedings and again attempts to obtain compliance. It may insist upon more extensive supervisory powers over the employment practices of a two-time loser. (Note, *The Operation of State FEPC,* 68 Harv. L. Rev. 685, 694)

Hearing and Order

If no agreement is reached at the conciliation stage, the commission holds a public hearing, makes findings of fact, and either issues a cease-and-desist order or dismisses the case. Both the complainant and the accused are given the right to appeal from this decision.

A single finding of a discriminatory incident may form the basis for a broad order against the accused. For example, the New York commission found that an employment agency had questioned a job applicant about her change of name and her national origin. On the basis of this finding, the commission ordered the agency to cease and desist from making any inquiry respecting race, creed, color, or national origin when interviewing job applicants; from giving consideration to such factors when evaluating applicants; and from using an application form which includes any inquiry concerning the applicant's change of name unless the form is approved by the commission.

The agency also was directed not to furnish any information to prospective employers concerning an applicant's race, creed, color, or national origin and not to accept job orders containing limitations of specifications on that score. The agency also was required to maintain and make available for one year records of the action taken on all job applications and orders and to make available to the commission all other records relating to the agency's business until such time as the commission should determine that the agency was complying with the statute.

Only on the last part of the order was any doubt expressed by the courts as to the commission's authority and then only because of the absence of a time limit on the commission's supervision of the agency's business. (*Holland* v. *Edwards,* NY CtApp, 1954, 307 N.Y. 38, 1 19 NE 2d 581, 34 LRRM 2018, 1 FEP Cases 9)

Judicial Review

Since the primary purpose of the commissions is to employ conciliation and persuasion to achieve compliance with the law, there has been little litigation in the state courts.

In the few cases brought, the courts have followed the rules generally applicable to judicial review of actions by an administrative agency. The judicial function has been held to be exhausted when a rational basis is found for the conclusions approved by the commission. (*In re Delaney,* NY SupCt, 1963, 39 Misc. 2d 499, 53 LRRM 2530, 1 FEP Cases 32)

A finding of discriminatory intent and motive has been held necessary to sustain a complaint, but the commission's determination on this score is not reviewable by the courts unless its conclusion is one which cannot reasonably be reached. (*Electrical Workers, IBEW, Local 35* v. *Commission on Civil Rights,* Conn SupCtErr, 1953, 140 Conn 537, 102A.2d 366, 33 LRRM 2307, 1 FEP Cases 5)

Most of the state laws provide judicial review of orders made by the commission only after a formal hearing. It has been argued that, in the absence of extraordinary circumstances, the courts may not review other actions taken by the commission.

This theory was rejected by the New York Court of Appeals in holding that a commission decision to dismiss a complaint is subject to judicial review and will be disturbed if the dismissal is found to be arbitrary or capricious. (*Jeanpierre* v. *Arbury,* NY CtApp, 1958, 149 NE 2d 882, 41 LRRM 2849, 1 FEP Cases 13)

Subsequently the court reversed the commission's dismissal of a complaint, basing its reversal not upon the ground that the commission's action was arbitrary or capricious, but rather upon the court's own determination that probable cause existed for crediting the allegations of the complaint. (*American Jewish Congress* v. *Carter,* NY CtApp, 1961, 173 NE 2d 788, 47 LRRM 2949, 1 FEP Cases 17)

Municipal Ordinances

In addition to the state FEP laws, a number of cities have ordinances forbidding discrimination in employment by private employers within their jurisdiction or by municipal agencies or municipal contractors.

Municipal activity in this field is subject to attack on two grounds. First, it may be contended that the municipality has no power to act in the absence of specific state sanction. Second, if the state has legislated in the field, local authority may be held to have been preempted by the state law.

Several states (*e.g.*, California, Pennsylvania, Minnesota) expressly provide in their FEP laws for the continued effectiveness of local ordinances.

EEOC POLICY ON DEFERENCE TO STATE AGENCIES

In Section 706(c) of Title VII, as amended, the Equal Opportunity Commission is directed to defer processing of charges of alleged employment discrimination to states or political subdivisions of states that have a state or local law prohibiting the alleged discriminatory practice and establishing or authorizing a state or local entity to grant or seek relief from such practice, or to institute criminal proceedings with respect thereto. Additionally, the same section prohibits EEOC from processing any charge it receives, before the expiration of 60 days after proceedings on the charge have been commenced under the state or local FEP law, unless such proceedings have been earlier terminated. The 60-day period is extended to 120 days during the first year after the effective date of such state or local law.

The 1972 amendments to Title VII extended EEOC coverage to employees of state and local governments, governmental agencies, political subdivisions, and educational institutions. In an effort to carry out its broadened responsibilities, EEOC has revamped its deferral policy with respect to the manner and conditions under which it will defer charges filed with it to agencies. Agencies that presently are recognized as appropriate deferral agencies have been given provisional deferral status until July 1, 1973, after which they must apply to EEOC for deferral status. The application must be accompanied by a copy of the state or local FEP law, rules, regulations, etc., and EEOC will designate as appropriate deferral agencies only those whose laws prohibit essentially all the practices prohibited by Title VII, by essentially all of the persons by whom such practices are illegal under Title VII, and on essentially all of the grounds covered by Title VII. Therefore, EEOC will not accord substantial weight to the findings of these provisional agencies vis-à-vis its own findings until the agencies are accorded formal deferral status, confirmation to be indicated by publication in the FEDERAL REGISTER at the appropriate time.

The first two charts below, which appeared in the FEDERAL REGISTER for May 6, 1972, show the states and state agencies which EEOC has designated as (1) Provisional 706 Agencies and (2) Provisional Notice Agencies until July 1, 1973. These are followed by BNA charts providing data on state laws dealing with discrimination based on race or religion, sex, and age and on state protective laws for women.

I–PROVISIONAL 706 AGENCIES

State	State FEP law appears to provide enforceable sanctions against discrimination on account of race, color, religion, and national origin, and charges alleging violations on these grounds will be deferred to the agency listed below	State FEP law also appears to bar sex discrimination	State FEP law appears to provide enforceable sanctions against discrimination by State or local governments, government agencies, and political subdivisions	State has failed to enact legislation with enforceable sanctions against any practice prohibited by title VII	Comments
A	B	C	D	E	F
Alabama				X	
Alaska	Commission for Human Rights.	X	X		
Arizona				See chart II	
Arkansas				Chart II	
California	Fair Employment Practices Commission.	X	X		
Colorado	Civil Rights Commission.	X	X		
Connecticut	Commission on Human Rights and Opportunities.	X	X		
Delaware	Department of Labor.				All charges will be deferred for 120 days until July 15, 1972.

I–PROVISIONAL 706 AGENCIES

State	Provisional 706 Agency relationships			No Provisional 706 Agency relationship	Comments
	State FEP law appears to provide enforceable sanctions against discrimination on account of race, color, religion, and national origin, and charges alleging violations on these grounds will be deferred to the agency listed below	State FEP law also appears to bar sex discrimination	State FEP law appears to provide enforceable sanctions against discrimination by State or local governments, government agencies, and political subdivisions	State has failed to enact legislation with enforceable sanctions against any practice prohibited by title VII	
A	B	C	D	E	F
District of Columbia.	Office of Human Rights	X	X		
Florida				X	
Georgia				See chart II	
Hawaii	Department of Labor and Industrial Relations.	X			
Idaho	Commission on Human Rights.	X	X		
Illinois	Fair Employment Practices Commission.	X	X		Charges alleging sex discrimination will be deferred for 120 days until Aug. 27, 1972.
Indiana	Civil Rights Commission.	X	X		Charges alleging sex discrimination will be deferred for 120 days until Sept. 3, 1972.
Iowa	Civil Rights Commission.	X	X		

I—PROVISIONAL 706 AGENCIES

State	Provisional 706 Agency relationships			No Provisional 706 Agency relationship	Comments
	State FEP law appears to provide enforceable sanctions against discrimination on account of race, color, religion, and national origin, and charges alleging violations on these grounds will be deferred to the agency listed below	State FEP law also appears to bar sex discrimination	State FEP law appears to provide enforceable sanctions against discrimination by State or local governments, government agencies, and political subdivisions	State has failed to enact legislation with enforceable sanctions against any practice prohibited by title VII	
A	B	C	D	E	F
Kansas____	Commission on Civil Rights.	See chart II ____	X_____		When a charge is received alleging violations of jurisdictional areas covered by both the Commissioner of Labor and the Commission on Civil Rights a copy of the charge will be deferred to the Commission on Civil Rights and an information copy of the charge will be forwarded to the Labor Commissioner's office and each agency will be notified of the action taken with respect to the other.
Kentucky__	Commission on Human Rights.		X_____		
Louisiana _____				X _____	

I–PROVISIONAL 706 AGENCIES

State	Provisional 706 Agency relationships			No provisional 706 Agency relationship	Comments
	State FEP law appears to provide enforceable sanctions against discrimination on account of race, color, religion, and national origin, and charges alleging violations on these grounds will be deferred to the agency listed below	State FEP law also appears to bar sex discrimination	State FEP law appears to provide enforceable sanctions against discrimination by State or local governments, government agencies, and political subdivisions	State has failed to enact legislation with enforceable sanctions against any practice prohibited by title VII	
A	B	C	D	E	F
Maine	Human Rights Commission after July 1, 1972.			See Chart II	Maine has passed a new FEP statute with enforceable sanctions effective July 1, 1972; for 1 yr. following that date, the EEOC will defer all appropriate charges for 120 days until the expiration date of the Provisional 706 Agency designation.
Maryland	Commission on Human Relations.	X	X		
Massachusetts	Commission Against Discrimination.	X	X		
Michigan	Civil Rights Commission.	X	X		
Minnesota	Department of Human Rights.	X	X		
Mississippi				X	
Missouri	Commission on Human Rights.	X	X		
Montana				See chart II	
Nebraska	Equal Employment Opportunity Commission.	X	X		

I—PROVISIONAL 706 AGENCIES

State	Provisional 706 Agency relationships			No Provisional 706 Agency relationship	Comments
	State FEP law appears to provide enforceable sanctions against discrimination on account of race, color, religion, and national origin, and charges alleging violations on these grounds will be deferred to the agency listed below	State FEP law also appears to bar sex discrimination	State FEP law appears to provide enforceable sanctions against discrimination by State or local governments, government agencies, and political subdivisions	State has failed to enact legislation with enforceable sanctions against any practice prohibited by title VII	
A	B	C	D	E	F
Nevada	Commission on Equal Rights of Citizens.	Commissioner of Labor (but see comments).	X		Although the Commissioner of labor is responsible for processing complaints alleging sex discrimination by agreement among the EEOC and the 2 Nevada agencies, all complaints will be deferred to the Commission on Equal Rights of Citizens, which will transfer appropriate charge to the Commissioner of Labor.
New Hampshire	Commission for Human Rights.	X	X		Charges alleging sex discrimination will be deferred for 120 days until Sept. 5, 1972.
New Jersey	Division on Civil Rights, Department of Law and Public Safety.	X	X		Charges alleging sex discrimination will be deferred for 120 days until Sept. 5, 1972.

I—PROVISIONAL 706 AGENCIES

State	State FEP law appears to provide enforceable sanctions against discrimination on account of race, color, religion, and national origin, and charges alleging violations on these grounds will be deferred to the agency listed below	State FEP law also appears to bar sex discrimination	State FEP law appears to provide enforceable sanctions against discrimination by State or local governments, government agencies, and political subdivisions	State has failed to enact legislation with enforceable sanctions against any practice prohibited by title VII	Comments
A	B	C	D	E	F
New Mexico	Human Rights Commission.	X	X		
New York	Division of Human Rights.	X	X		
North Carolina				X	
North Dakota				See chart II	
Ohio	Civil Rights Commission.	Dayton Human Relations Council (only those violations which occur within city limits).	X		
Oklahoma	Human Rights Commission.	X	X		
Oregon	Bureau of Labor.	X	X		
Pennsylvania	Human Relations Commission.	X	X		
Puerto Rico	Department of Labor.		X		
Rhode Island	Commission for Human Rights.	X			Charges alleging sex discrimination will be deferred for 120 days until May 13, 1972.
South Carolina				X	
South Dakota				See chart II	

I–PROVISIONAL 706 AGENCIES

State	Provisional 706 Agency relationships			No Provisional 706 Agency relationship	Comments
	State FEP law appears to provide enforceable sanctions against discrimination on account of race, color, religion, and national origin, and charges alleging violations on these grounds will be deferred to the agency listed below	State FEP law also appears to bar sex discrimination	State FEP law appears to provide enforceable sanctions against discrimination by State or local governments, government agencies, and political subdivisions	State has failed to enact legislation with enforceable sanctions against any practice prohibited by title VII	
A	B	C	D	E	F
Tennessee				X	
Texas				X	
Utah	Industrial Commission.	X	X		
Vermont				See chart II	
Virginia				X	
Virgin Islands	Commissioner of Public Safety.	Department of Labor.			
Washington	Human Rights Commission.	X	X		Charges alleging sex discrimination will be deferred for 120 days until July 1, 1972.
West Virginia	Human Rights Commission.	X	X		Charges alleging sex discrimination will be deferred for 120 days until June 3, 1972.
Wisconsin	Department of Industry, Labor and Human Relations.	X	X		
Wyoming	Fair Employment Commission.	X	X		

II—PROVISIONAL NOTICE AGENCIES

State	State law prohibits discrimination on account of race, color, religion, and national origin, and charges alleging violations on these grounds will be forwarded to the agency listed below	State law bars sex discrimination	State has enacted a (sex) equal pay statute and agency (or title of person) listed below will be forwarded charges filed alleging violations on those grounds	State FEP law appears to prohibit discrimination by State or local governments, government agencies, and political subdivisions
A	B	C	D	E
Arkansas			Commissioner of Labor.	
Arizona	Civil Rights Commission.	X		X
Georgia			Commissioner of Labor.	
Kansas		Commissioner of Labor.	Commissioner of Labor.	
Kentucky			Commissioner of Labor.	
Maine	Commission of Labor and Industry (but see chart I for action after July 1, 1972).			
Montana	Attorney General.	X		X
North Dakota			Commissioner of Agriculture and Labor.	
Ohio			Director of Industrial Relations.	
South Dakota			Department of Labor and Management Relation.	
Vermont	Attorney General.	X		

STATE LAWS ON RACIAL & RELIGIOUS DISCRIMINATION

	FEP Law	COVERAGE			ENFORCEMENT		
		Ers.*	Unions	Empl. Agencies	Comm. or Dept.	Fine and/or Jail	Volun- tary
Ala.	...	...	...	...	...	...	...
Alas.	X	X(1)	X	X	X	...	...
Ariz.	X	X(20)	X	X	X	X	X(a)
Ark.	...	...	...	...	...	...	...
Calif.	X	X(5)	X	X	X	X	...
Colo.	X	X(6)	X	X	X	...	...
Conn.	X	X(3)	X	X	X	...	...
Del.	X	X(4)	X	X	X	X	...
D.C.	X	X(1)	X	X	X	X	...
Fla.	X(c)	...	...	...	...	...	...
Ga.	...	...	...	...	...	...	...
Haw.	X	X(1)	X	X	X	X	...
Ida.	X	X(4)	X	X	X	X	...
Ill.	X	X(25)	X	X	X	...	...
Ind.	X	X(6)	X	X	X	...	...
Iowa	X	X(4)	X	X	X	...	...
Kan.	X	X(4)	X	X	X	X	...
Ky.	X	X(8)	X	X	X	X	...
La.	...	...	...	...	...	...	...
Me.	X	X(b)	X	X	...	X	...
Md.	X	X(25)	X	X	X	...	...
Mass.	X	X(6)	X	X	X	X	...
Mich.	X	X(8)	X	X	X	...	...
Minn.	X	X(8)	X	X	X	X	...
Miss.	...	...	...	...	...	...	...
Mo.	X	X(6)	X	X	X	X	...
Mont.	X	X(b)	X	X	...	X	...
Neb.	X	X(25)	X	X	X	X	...
Nev.	X	X(15)	X	X	X	...	...

* The numbers in parentheses indicate the minimum number of employees an employer must have to be covered by the law.
(a) First offense only.
(b) No minimum number of employees specified.
(c) Public employment only until Oct. 1, 1972, when law of general application became effective.
(d) No FEP law but a commission to promote equal opportunity.
(e) Also prohibits discrimination because of handicap.

STATE LAWS ON RACIAL & RELIGIOUS DISCRIMINATION

		COVERAGE			ENFORCEMENT		
	FEP Law	Ers.*	Unions	Empl. Agencies	Comm. or Dept.	Fine and/or Jail	Voluntary
N.H.	X	X(6)	X	X	X	X	...
N.J.	X	X(b)	X	X	X	X	...
N. Mex.	X	X(4)	X	X	X	...	...
N.Y.	X	X(4)	X	X	X	X	...
N.C.	X(c)	...	...	...	...	...	...
N. Dak.	...	...	...	...	...	...	...
Ohio	X	X(4)	X	X	X	X	...
Okla.	X	X(25)	X	X	X	...	...
Ore.	X	X(1)	X	X	X	X	...
Pa.	X	X(4)	X	X	X	X	...
P.R.	X	X(b)	X	...	X	X	...
R.I.	X	X(4)	X	X	X	...	...
S.C.	...	...	...	...	...	...	...
S. Dak.	X	X(b)	X	X	X	...	...
Tenn.	...	...	...	...	X(d)	...	X
Tex.	X(c)	...	...	...	...	...	X
Utah	X	X(25)	X	X	X	...	...
Vt.	X	X(b)	X	X	...	X	...
Va.	...	...	...	...	...	...	...
Wash.	X	X(8)	X	X	X	X	...
W.Va.	X	X(25)	X	X	X	X	...
Wis.	X	X(b)	X	X	X	X	...
Wyo.	X	X(2)	X	X	X	...	...

* The numbers in parentheses indicate the minimum number of employees an employer must have to be covered by the law.
(a) First offense only.
(b) No minimum number of employees specified.
(c) Public employment only.
(d) No FEP law but a commission to promote equal opportunity.
(e) Also prohibits discrimination because of handicap.

State Age Discrimination Laws

Alaska (451:51)
California (451:169)
Colorado (451:182)
Connecticut (451:201)
Delaware (451:225)
Georgia (451:277)
Hawaii (451:285)
Idaho (451:311)
Illinois (451:332)
Indiana (451:385)
Iowa (451:401)

Kentucky (451:451)
Louisiana (451:491)
Maine (451:501)
Maryland (451:525)
Massachusetts (451:551)
Michigan (451:577)
Montana (451:701)
Nebraska (451:745)
New Hampshire (451:775)
New Jersey (451:801)
New Mexico (451:851)

New York (451:871)
North Dakota (451:921)
Ohio (451:933)
Oregon (451:975)
Pennsylvania (451:1001)
Puerto Rico (451:1051)
Rhode Island (451:1101)
Washington (451:1225)
West Virginia (451:1251)
Wisconsin (451:1275)

STATE LAWS ON SEX DISCRIMINATION

	Ban on Sex Discrim.	COVERAGE			ENFORCEMENT		
		Ers.*	Unions	Empl. Agencies	Comm. or Dept.	Fine and/or Jail	Voluntary
Ala.	...	...	...	...	...	...	...
Alas.	X	X(1)	X	X	X	X	...
Ariz.	X	X(20)	X	X	X	X	X(a)
Ark.	...	...	...	...	...	...	...
Calif.	X	X(5)	X	X	X	X	...
Colo.	X	X(6)	X	X	X	...	...
Conn.	X	X(3)	X	X	X	...	...
Del.	X	X(4)	X	X	X	X	...
D.C.	X	X(1)	X	X	X	X	...
Fla.	X	X(c)	X	...	X	...	...
Ga.	...	...	...	...	...	...	...
Haw.	X	X(1)	X	X	X	X	...
Ida.	X	X(4)	X	X	X	X	...
Ill.	X	X(25)	X	X	X	...	...
Ind.	X	X(6)	X	X	X	...	...
Iowa	X	X(4)	X	X	X	...	...
Kan.	X	X(c)	...	...	X	X	...
Ky.	X	X(8)	X	X	X	X	...
La.	...	...	...	...	...	...	...
Me.	...	...	...	...	...	...	...
Md.	X	X(25)	X	X	X	...	...
Mass.	X	X(6)	X	X	X	X	...
Mich.	X	X(8)	X	X	X	...	...
Minn.	X	X(8)	X	X	X	X	...
Miss.	...	...	...	...	...	...	...
Mo.	X	X(6)	X	X	X	X	...
Mont.	X	X(c)	X	X	...	X	...
Neb.	X	X(25)	X	X	X	X	...
Nev.	X	X(15)	X	X	X	...	...

* The numbers in parentheses indicate the minimum number of employees an employer must have to be covered by the law.

(a) First offense only.

(b) Public employment only.

(c) No minimum number of employees specified.

STATE LAWS ON SEX DISCRIMINATION

	Ban on Sex Discrim.	COVERAGE			ENFORCEMENT		
		Ers.*	Unions	Empl. Agencies	Comm. or Dept.	Fine and/or Jail	Volun- tary
N.H.	X	X(6)	X	X	X	X	...
N.J.	X	X(c)	X	X	X	X	...
N. Mex.	X	X(4)	X	X	X	...	...
N.Y.	X	X(4)	X	X	X	X	...
N.C.	X(b)	...	...	...	...	...	...
N. Dak.	...	...	...	...	...	...	...
Ohio	...	...	...	...	...	...	...
Okla.	X	X(25)	X	X	X	...	...
Ore.	X	X(1)	X	X	X	X	...
Pa.	X	X(4)	X	X	X	X	...
P.R.	...	...	...	...	...	...	...
R.I.	X	X(4)	X	X	X	...	...
S.C.	...	...	...	...	...	...	...
S. Dak.	X	X	X	X	X	...	...
Tenn.	...	...	...	...	...	...	...
Tex.	X(b)	...	...	...	...	...	...
Utah	X	X(25)	X	X	X	...	...
Vt.	X	X(c)	X	X	...	X	...
Va.	...	...	...	...	...	...	...
Wash.	X	X(8)	X	X	X	X	...
W. Va.	X	X(25)	X	X	X	X	...
Wis.	X	X(c)	X	X	X	X	...
Wyo.	X	X(2)	X	X	X	...	...

* The numbers in parentheses indicate the minimum number of employees an employer must have to be covered by the law.

(a) First offense only.

(b) Public employment only.

(c) No minimum number of employees specified.

STATE PROTECTIVE LAWS FOR

In the early 1900s, many states adopted laws
women from the hazards of industrial life by restric
might work, the weights they might lift, the types
handle, etc. EEOC and the federal courts general
position that these laws conflict with the ban on sex
Title VII of the Civil Rights Act insofar as they exclude women as a
group from holding certain jobs.

The checklist that follows indicates the states that have protective
laws for women in the designated areas. In addition to the subject matters noted, other state laws may require that certain benefits be provided for female employees, such as minimum wages, premium pay for
overtime, rest periods, and physical facilities.

State Protective Laws for Women

STATE	WEIGHT LIFTING	HOURS PER DAY OR WEEK	NIGHT WORK	BARS, ETC.	OTHER INDUS- TRIES
Alabama	—	—	—	—	Coal Mine
Alaska	Yes	—	—	Yes	—
Arizona	—	—	—	—	Yes
Arkansas	—	Yes	—	—	Yes
California	Yes 1	Yes 1	—	Yes 2	—
Colorado	—	—	—	—	—
Connecticut	—	Yes 3	Yes	—	—
Delaware	—	—	—	—	—
District of Columbia	—	Yes 4	(Messen- gers) Yes	—	—
Florida	—	—	—	—	—
Georgia	—	—	—	—	—
Hawaii	—	—	—	—	—
Idaho	—	Yes	—	—	—
Illinois	—	Yes 5	—	—	—
Indiana	—	—	—	—	—
Iowa	—	—	—	—	—

1 Declared invalid by U.S. Court of Appeals. (Rosenfeld v. Southern Pacific, CA 9, 1971, 3 FEP Cases 604)
2 Declared invalid by ruling of California Supreme Court. (Sail'er Inn, Inc. v. Kirby, Cal SupCt, 1971, 3 FEP Cases 550)
3 Ruled in conflict with, and therefore held preempted by, Title VII of the Civil Rights Act of 1964. (Attorney General Opinion, issued September 27, 1972)
4 Ruled "inconsistent with Title VII" by EEOC (Decision 70382, Case No. DC 7-6-255, Decem- ber 16, 1969, 2 FEP Cases 338) and by DC Corporation Counsel, April 1970.
5 Ruled in conflict with Title VII of the 1964 Civil Rights Act and therefore held invalid. (Caterpillar Tractor Co. v. Grabiec, USDC SIll, 2 FEP Cases 945)

STATE PROTECTIVE LAWS FOR WOMEN

STATE	WEIGHT LIFTING	HOURS PER DAY OR WEEK	NIGHT WORK	BARS, ETC.	OTHER INDUS- TRIES
Kansas	—	Yes 6	Yes	—	—
Kentucky	—	Yes 7	—	Yes †	—
Louisiana	—	Yes 8	—	—	—
Maine	—	Yes	—	—	—
Maryland	—	Yes 9	—	—	Mines
Massachusetts	Yes	Yes 10	Yes	—	—
Michigan	Yes	Yes 11	—	—	Yes 12
Minnesota	—	Yes	—	—	—
Mississippi	—	Yes	—	—	—
Missouri	—	Yes 13	—	—	—
Montana	—	—	—	—	—
Nebraska	—	—	—	—	—
Nevada	—	Yes	—	—	—
New Hampshire	—	Yes	Yes	—	—
New Jersey	—	—	—	—	—
New Mexico	—	Yes 14	—	—	—
New York	Yes	Yes 15	Yes 15	—	—
North Carolina	—	Yes 16	—	—	—
North Dakota	—	Yes 17	Elevator Operators	—	Yes 18

6 Not applicable to employers covered under Title VII, Commissioner of Labor's Opinion 1969.

7 Ruled in conflict with Title VII. (General Electric v. Young, USDC WKy, 1971, 3 FEP Cases 560) Ruled to have been preempted by Title VII for employers covered by such Title VII and by those fact situations in which there is a necessary conflict between state and federal law. (Attorney General Opinion No. 72-361, 1972)

8 Ruled unenforceable under the Supremacy Clause of the U.S. Constitution since the Louisiana state law conflicts with Title VII of the 1964 Civil Rights Act. (LeBlanc v. Southern Bell T & T, USDC ELa, 1971, 3 FEP Cases 1083)

9 Repealed by Ch. 211, L. 1972, effective July 1, 1972.

10 Ruled unenforceable under the Supremacy Clause of the U.S. Constitution since the Massachusetts state law conflicts with Title VII of the 1964 Civil Rights Act. (Garneau v. Raytheon Co., USDC Mass, 1971, 3 FEP Cases 251)

11 Ruled invalid and in conflict with Title VII in Attorney General's Opinion, December, 1969.

12 "Any place detrimental to morals, health or potential capacity for motherhood." (Sec. 750.556, Michigan Revised Statutes)

13 Ruled in conflict with Title VII in Attorney General's Opinion, November 11, 1971, and held invalid insofar as such provision "would compel [employer] to uniformly deny women employees the right to work in excess of 54 hours weekly. . . ." (Vogel v. Trans World Airlines, USDC, WMo, 5 FEP Cases 378)

14 Ruled invalid and unenforceable to employees covered by Title VII of the Civil Rights Act of 1964. (Attorney General's Opinion No. 72-22, issued May 3, 1972)

15 Ruled unenforceable under the Supremacy Clause of the U.S. Constitution, since the provisions conflict with Title VII. (Attorney General's Opinion No. 228, issued November 13, 1972)

16 Applies only to those not covered by Fair Labor Standards Act.

17 Attorney General held that EEOC guidelines "may prevent prosecution for violation of statutory provisions limiting hours of work for women."

18 "Surrounding or conditions, sanitary or otherwise which may be detrimental to their health or morals." (Secs. 34-06-05 and 34-06-19, North Dakota Code)

† Ruled unconstitutional under the Equal Protection Clause of the Fourteenth Amendment. (Commonwealth v. Burke, 4 FEP Cases 756, Ky CtApp, May 12, 1972)

STATE PROTECTIVE LAWS FOR WOMEN

STATE	WEIGHT LIFTING	HOURS PER DAY OR WEEK	NIGHT WORK	BARS, ETC.	OTHER INDUS- TRIES
Ohio	Yes [19]	Yes [19]	Yes [19]	Yes	Yes
Oklahoma	—	Yes [20]	—	—	Yes
Oregon	Yes [21]	—	—	—	—
Pennsylvania	—	Yes [22]	Yes [22]	Yes	Yes
Puerto Rico	Yes	Yes	Yes	—	—
Rhode Island	—	Yes *	—	Yes	—
South Carolina	—	—	—	—	—
South Dakota	—	Yes [23]	—	—	—
Tennessee	—	Yes [24]	—	—	—
Texas	—	Yes [25]	—	—	—
Utah	Yes	Yes	—	—	Smelters Mines
Vermont	—	—	—	—	—
Virginia	—	Yes	—	—	—
Washington	Yes	Yes [26]	—	—	—
West Virginia	—	—	—	—	—
Wisconsin	—	—	—	—	—
Wyoming	—	Yes	—	—	—

----

[19] Ruled in conflict with Title VII by the Ohio Supreme Court. (Jones Metal Products Co. v. Walker, Ohio SupCt, 1972, 4 FEP Cases 483; *reversing* Ohio CtApp, 1971, 3 FEP Cases 253)

[20] Applies only to those not covered by federal Fair Labor Standards Act; "because of the Supremacy Clause of the U.S. Constitution, the federal regulation barring sex discrimination must take precedence over the state law." (Okla Attorney General's Opinion, December 5, 1969)

[21] A U.S. district court has ruled that the weight lifting restrictions may not be used to deny a female employee "rights given her under Title VII." (Richards v. Griffith Rubber Mills, USDC Ore. 1969, 71 LRRM 2755, 1 FEP Cases 837)

[22] Ruled in conflict with Title VII of 1964 Civil Rights Act. (Kober v. Westinghouse Electric Corp., USDC WPa, 1971, 3 FEP Cases 326)

[23] Ruled in conflict with Title VII. (Attorney General's Opinion, February 27, 1969)

[24] Applies only to those not covered by federal Fair Labor Standards Act. Ruled in conflict with Title VII by EEOC. (Decision No. 71-865, 1970, 3 FEP Cases 268)

[25] Unless a written agreement is signed to work for more than eight hours a day or 40 hours a week. (Sec. 1 of Art. 5172a, RCS)

[26] Ruled in conflict with Title VII by EEOC (Decision 70471, Case No. AU68-5-708E, 1970, 2 FEP Cases 412), and by Washington Attorney General's Opinion issued May 26, 1970.

* Amended to exempt women in executive, administrative capacities. (Ch. 44, L. 1071, effective May 20, 1971)

Appendix A

Text of Title VII of the Civil Rights Act of 1964 as Amended by the Equal Employment Opportunity Act of 1972

DEFINITIONS

Sec. 701. For the purposes of this title—

(a) The term "person" includes one or more individuals, governments, governmental agencies, political subdivisions, labor unions, partnerships, associations, corporations, legal representatives, mutual companies, joint-stock companies, trusts, unincorporated organizations, trustees, trustees in bankruptcy, or receivers. (As amended by P.L. No. 92-261, eff. March 24, 1972.)

(b The term 'employer' means a person engaged in an industry affecting commerce who has fifteen or more employees for each working day in each of twenty or more calendar weeks in the current or preceding calendar year, and any agent of such a person, but such term does not include (1) the United States, a corporation wholly owned by the Government of the United States, an Indian tribe, or any department or agency of the District of Columbia subject by statute to procedures of the competitive service (as defined in section 2102 of title 5 of the United States Code), or (2) a bona fide private membership club (other than a labor organization) which is exempt from taxation under section 501(c) of the Internal Revenue Code of 1954, except that during the first year after the date of enactment of the Equal Employment Opportunity Act of 1972, persons having fewer than twenty-five employees (and their agents) shall not be considered employers. (As amended by P.L. No. 92-261, eff. March 24, 1972.)

(c) The term "employment agency" means any person regularly undertaking with or without compensation to procure employees for an employer or to procure for employees opportunities to work for an employer and includes an agent of such a person. (As amended by P.L. No. 92-261, eff. March 24, 1972.)

(d) The term "labor organization" means a labor organization engaged in an industry affecting commerce, and any agent of such an organization, and includes any organization of any kind, any agency, or employee representation committee, group, association, or plan so engaged in which employees participate and which exists for the purpose, in whole or in part, of dealing with employers concerning grievances, labor disputes, wages, rates of pay, hours, or other terms or conditions of employment, and any conference, general committee, joint or system board, or joint council so engaged which is subordinate to a national or international labor organization.

(e) A labor organization shall be deemed to be engaged in an industry affecting commerce if (1) it maintains or operates a hiring hall or hiring office which procures employees for an employer or procures for employees opportunities to work for an employer, or (2) the number of its members (or, where it is a labor organization composed of other labor organizations or their representatives, if the aggregate number of the members of of such labor organization) is (A) twenty-five or more during the first year after the date of enactment of the Equal Employment Opportunity Act of 1972, or (B) fifteen or more thereafter. (As amended by P.L. No. 92-261, eff. March 24, 1972)

(1) is the certified representative of employees under the provisions of the National Labor Relations Act, as amended, or the Railway Labor Act, as amended;

(2) although not certified, is a national or international labor organization or a local labor organization recognized or acting as the representative of employees of an employer or employers engaged in an industry affecting commerce; or

(3) has chartered a local labor organization or subsidiary body which is representing or actively seeking to represent employees of employers within the meaning of paragraph (1) or (2); or

(4) has been chartered by a labor organization representing or actively seeking to represent employees within the meaning of paragraph (1) or (2) as the local or subordinate body through which such employees may enjoy membership or become affiliated with such labor organization; or

(5) is a conference, general committee, joint or system board, or joint council subordinate to a national or international labor organization, which includes a labor organization engaged in an industry affecting commerce within the meaning of any of the preceding paragraphs of this subsection.

(f) The term "employee" means an individual employed by an employer, except that the term "employee" shall not include any person elected to public office in any State or political subdivision of any State by the qualified voters thereof, or any person chosen by such officer to be on such officer's personal staff, or an appointee on the policy making level or an immediate adviser with respect to the exercise of the constitutional or legal powers of the office. The exemption set forth in the preceding sentence shall not include employees subject to the civil service laws of a State government, governmental agency or political subdivision. (As amended by P.L. 92-161, eff. March 24, 1972)

(g) The term "commerce" means trade, traffic, commerce, transportation, transmission, or communication among the several States; or between a State and any place outside thereof; or within the District of Columbia, or a possession of the United States; or between points in the same State but through a point outside thereof.

(h) The term "industry affecting commerce" means any activity, business, or industry in commerce or in which a labor dispute would hinder or obstruct commerce or the free flow of commerce and includes any activity or industry "affecting commerce" within the meaning of the Labor-Management Reporting and Disclosure Act of 1959, and further includes any governmental industry, business, or activity. (As amended by P.L. No. 92-261, eff. March 24, 1972)

(i) The term "State" includes a State of the United States, the District of Columbia, Puerto Rico, the Virgin Island, American Samoa, Guam, Wake Island, the Canal Zone, and Outer Continental Shelf lands defined in the Outer Continental Shelf Lands Act.

(j) The term 'religion' includes all aspects of religious observance and practice, as well as belief, unless an employer demonstrates that he is unable to reasonably accommodate to an employee's or prospective employee's religious observance or practice without undue hardship on the conduct of the employer's business. (As amended by P.L. 92-261, eff. March 24, 1972)

EXEMPTION

Sec. 702. This title shall not apply to an employer with respect to the employment of aliens outside any State, or to a religious corporation, association, educational institution, or society with respect to the employment of individuals of a particular religion to perform work connected with the carrying on by such corporation, association, educational insititution, or society of its activities. (As amended by P.L. 92-261, eff. March 24, 1972)

DISCRIMINATION BECAUSE OF RACE, COLOR, RELIGION, SEX, OR NATIONAL ORIGIN

Sec. 703. (a) It shall be an unlawful employment practice for an employer—

(1) to fail or refuse to hire or to discharge any individual, or otherwise to discriminate against any individual with respect to his compensation, terms, conditions, or privileges of employment, because of such individual's race, color, religion, sex, or national origin; or

(2) to limit, segregate, or classify his employees or applicants for employment in any way which would deprive or tend to deprive any individual of employment opportunities or otherwise adversely affect his status as an employee, because of such individual's race, color, religion, sex, or national origin. (As amended by P.L. 92-261, eff. March 24, 1972)

(b) It shall be an unlawful employment practice for an employment agency to fail or refuse to refer for employment, or otherwise to discriminate against, any individual because of his race, color, religion, sex, or national origin, or to classify or refer for employment any individual on the basis of his race, color, religion, sex or national origin.

(c) It shall be an unlawful employment practice for a labor organization—

(1) to exclude or to expel from its membership, or otherwise to discriminate against, any individual because of his race, color, religion, sex, or national origin;

(2) to limit, segregate, or classify its membership or applicants for membership or to classify or fail or refuse to refer for employment any individual, in any way which would deprive or tend to deprive any

individual of employment opportunities, or would limit such employment opportunities or otherwise adversely affect his status as an employee or as an applicant for employment, because of such individual's race, color, religion, sex, or national origin; or

(3) to cause or attempt to cause an employer to discriminate against an individual in violation of this section.

(d) It shall be an unlawful employment practice for any employer, labor organization, or joint labor-management committee controlling apprenticeship or other training or retraining, including on-the-job training programs to discriminate against any individual because of his race, color, religion, sex, or national origin in admission to, or employment in, any program established to provide apprenticeship or other training.

(e) Notwithstanding any other provision of this title, (1) it shall not be an unlawful employment practice for an employer to hire and employ employees, for an employment agency to classify, or refer for employment any individual, for a labor organization to classify its membership or to classify or refer for employment any individual, or for an employer, labor organization, or joint labor-management committee controlling apprenticeship or other training or retraining programs to admit or employ any individual in any such program, on the basis of his religion, sex, or national origin in those certain instances where religion, sex, or national origin is a bona fide occupational qualification reasonably necessary to the normal operation of that particular business or enterprise, and (2) it shall not be an unlawful employment practice for a school, college, university, or other educational institution or institution of learning to hire and employ employees of a particular religion if such school, college, university, or other educational institution or institution of learning is, in whole or in substantial part, owned, supported, controlled, or managed by a particular religion or by a particular religious corporation, association, or society, or if the curriculum of such school, college, university, or other educational institution or institution of learning is directed toward the propagation of a particular religion.

(f) As used in this title, the phrase "unlawful employment practice" shall not be deemed to include any action or measure taken by an employer, labor organization, joint labor-management committee, or employment agency with respect to an individual who is a member of the Communist Party of the United States or of any other organization required to register as a Communist-action or Communist-front organization by final order of the Subversive Activities Control Board pursuant to the Subversive Activities Control Act of 1950.

(g) Notwithstanding any other provision of this title, it shall not be an unlawful employment practice for an employer to fail or refuse to hire and employ any individual for any position, for an employer to discharge an individual from any position, or for an employment agency to fail or refuse to refer any individual for employment in any position, or for a labor organization to fail or refuse to refer any individual for employment in any position, if—

(1) the occupancy of such position, or access to the premises in or upon which any part of the duties of such position is performed or is to be performed, is subject to any requirement imposed in the interest of the national security of the United States under any security program in effect pursuant to or administered under any statute of the United States or any Executive order of the President; and

(2) such individual has not fulfilled or has ceased to fulfill that requirement.

(h) Notwithstanding any other provision of this title, it shall not be an unlawful employment practice for an employer to apply different standards of compensation, or different terms, conditions, or privileges of employment pursuant to a bona fide seniority or merit system, or a system which measures earnings by quantity or quality of production or to employees who work in different

locations, provided that such differences are not the result of an intention to discriminate because of race, color, religion, sex, or national origin; nor shall it be an unlawful employment practice for an employer to give and to act upon the results of any professionally developed ability test provided that such test, its administration or action upon the results is not designed, intended, or used to discriminate because of race, color, religion, sex, or national origin. It shall not be an unlawful employment practice under this title for any employer to differentiate upon the basis of sex in determining the amount of the wages or compensation paid to employees of such employer if such differentiation is authorized by the provisions of Section 6(d) of the Fair Labor Standards Act of 1938 as amended (29 USC 206(d)).

(i) Nothing contained in this title shall apply to any business or enterprise on or near an Indian reservation with respect to any publicly announced employment practice of such business or enterprise under which a preferential treatment is given to any individual because he is an Indian living on or near a reservation.

(j) Nothing contained in this title shall be interpreted to require any employer, employment agency, labor organization, or joint labor-management committee subject to this title to grant preferential treatment to any individual or to any group because of the race, color, religion, sex, or national origin of such individual or group on account of an imbalance which may exist with respect to the total number or precentage of persons of any race, color, religion, sex, or national origin employed by any employer, referred or classified for employment by any employment agency or labor organization, admitted to membership or classified by any labor organization, or admitted to, or employed in, any apprenticeship or other training program, in comparison with the total number or percentage of persons of such race, color, religion, sex, or national origin in any community, State, section, or other area, or in the available work force in any community, State, section, or other area. (As amended by P.L. 92-261, eff. March 24, 1972)

OTHER UNLAWFUL EMPLOYMENT PRACTICES

Sec. 704. (a) It shall be an unlawful employment practice for an employer to discriminate against any of his employees or applicants for employment, for an employment agency or joint labor-management committee controlling apprenticeship or other training or retraining, including on-the-job training programs, to discriminate against any individual, or for a labor organization to discriminate against any member thereof or applicant for membership, because he has opposed any practice, made an unlawful employment practice by this title, or because he has made a charge, testified, assisted, or participated in any manner in an investigation, proceeding, or hearing under this title. (As amended by P.L. No. 92-261, eff. March 24, 1972)

(b) It shall be an unlawful employment practice for an employer, labor organization, employment agency, or joint labor-management committee controlling apprenticeship or other training or retraining, including on-the-job training programs, to print or cause to be printed or published any notice or advertisement relating to employment by such an employer or membership in or any classification or referral for employment by such a labor organization, or relating to any classification or referral for employment by such an employment agency, or relating to admission to, or employment in, any program established to provide apprenticeship or other training by such a joint labor-management committee indicating any preference, limitation, specification, or discrimination, based on race, color religion sex or national origin, except that such a notice or advertisement may indicate a preference, limitation, specification, or discrimination based on religion, sex or national origin when religion, sex, or national origin

is a bona fide occupational qualification for employment. (As amended by P.L. No. 92-216, eff. March 24, 1972)

EQUAL EMPLOYMENT OPPORTUNITY COMMISSION

Sec. 705 (a) There is hereby created a Commission to be known as the Equal Employment Opportunity Commission, which shall be composed of five members, not more than three of whom shall be members of the same political party. Members of the Commission shall be appointed by the President by and with the advice and consent of the Senate for a term of five years. Any individual chosen to fill a vacancy shall be appointed only for the unexpired term of the member whom he shall succeed, and all members of the Commission shall continue to serve until their successors are appointed and qualified, except that no such member of the Commission shall continue to serve (1) for more than sixty days when the Congress is in session unless a nomination to fill such vacancy shall have been submitted to the Senate, or (2) after the adjournment sine die of the session of the Senate in which such nomination was submitted. The President shall designate one member to serve as Chairman of the Commission, and one member to serve as Vice Chairman. The Chairman shall be responsible on behalf of the Commission for the administrative operations of the Commission, and, except as provided in subsection (b), shall appoint, in accordance with the provisions of title 5, United States Code, governing appointments in the competitive service, such officers, agents, attorneys, hearing examiners, and employees as he deems necessary to assist it in the performance of its functions and to fix their compensation in accordance with the provisions of chapter 51 and subchnapter III of chapter 53 of title 5, United States Code, relating to classification and General Schedule pay rates: Provided, That assignment, removal, and compensation of hearing examiners shall be in accordance with sections 3105, 3344, 5362, and 7521 of title 5, United States Code.

(b)(1) There shall be a General Counsel of the Commission appointed by the President, by and with the advice and consent of the Senate, for a term of four years. The General Counsel shall have responsibility for the conduct of litigation as provided in sections 706 and 707 of this title. The General Counsel shall have such other duties as the Commission may prescribe or as may be provided by law and shall concur with the Chairman of the Commission on the appointment and supervision of regional attorneys. The General Counsel of the Commission on the effective date of this Act shall continue in such position and perform the functions specified in this subsection until a successor is appointed and qualified.

(2) Attorneys appointed under this section may, at the direction of the Commission, appear for and represent the Commission in any case in court, provided that the Attorney General shall conduct all litigation to which the Commission is a party in the Supreme Court pursuant to this title. (As amended by P.L. No. 92-261, eff. March 24, 1972)

(c) A vacancy in the Commission shall not impair the right of the remaining members to exercise all the powers of the Commission and three members thereof shall constitute a quorum.

(d) The Commission shall have an official seal which shall be judicially noticed.

(e) The Commission shall at the middle and at the close of each fiscal year report to the Congress and to the President concerning the action it has taken; the names, salaries, and duties of all individuals in its employ and the moneys it has disbursed; and shall make such further reports on the cause of and means of eliminating discrimination and such recommendations for further legislation as may appear desirable.

(f) The principal office of the Commission shall be in or near the District of Columbia, but it may meet or exercise any or all its powers at any other place. The Commission may establish such regional or State offices as it deems necessary to accomplish the purpose of this title.

(g) The Commission shall have power—

(1) to cooperate with and, with their consent, utilize regional, State, local, and other agencies, both public and private, and individuals;

(2) to pay to witnesses whose depositions are taken or who are summoned before the Commission or any of its agents the same witness and mileage fees as are paid to witnesses in the courts of the United States;

(3) to furnish to persons subject to this title such technical assistance as they may request to further their compliance with this title or an order issued thereunder;

(4) upon the request of (i) any employer, whose employees or some of them, or (ii) any labor organization, whose members or some of them, refuse or threaten to refuse to cooperate in effectuating the provisions of this title, to assist in such effectuation by conciliation or such other remedial action as is provided by this title:

(5) to make such technical studies as are appropriate to effectuate the purposes and policies of this title and to make the results of such studies available to the public;

(6) to intervene in a civil action brought under section 706 by an aggrieved party against a respondent other than a government, governmental agency or political subdivision. (As amended by P.L. No. 92-261, eff. March 24, 1972)

(h) The Commission shall, in any of its educational or promotional activities, cooperate with other departments and agencies in the performance of such educational and promotional activities.

(i) All officers, agents, attorneys and employees of the Commission, including the members of the Commission, shall be subject to the provisions of section 9 of the act of August 2, 1939, as amended (Hatch Act), notwithstanding any exemption contained in such section.

PREVENTION OF UNLAWFUL EMPLOYMENT PRACTICES

Sec. 706. (a) The Commission is empowered, as hereinafter provided, to prevent any person from engaging in any unlawawful employment practice as set forth in section 703 or 704 of this title.

(b) Whenever a charge is filed by or on behalf of a person claiming to be aggrieved, or by a member of the Commission, alleging that an employer, employment agency, labor organization, or joint labor-management committee controlling apprenticeship or other training or retraining including on-the-job training programs, has engaged in an unlawful employment practice, the Commission shall serve a notice of the charge (including the date, place and circumstances of the alleged unlawful employment practice) on such employer, employment agency, labor organization, or joint labor-management committee (hereinafter referred to as the 'respondent') within ten days and shall make an investigation thereof. Charges shall be in writing under oath or affirmation and shall contain such information and be in such form as the Commission requires. Charges shall not be made public by the Commission. If the Commission determines after such investigation that there is not reasonable cause to believe that the charge is true, it shall dismiss the charge and promptly notify the person claiming to be aggrieved and the respondent of its action. In determining whether reasonable cause exists, the Commission shall accord substantial weight to final findings and orders made by State or local authorities in proceedings commenced under State or local law pursuant to the requirements of subsections (c) and (d). If the Commission determines after such investigation that there is reasonable cause to believe that the charge is true, the Commission shall endeavor to eliminate any such alleged unlawful employment practice by informal methods of conference, conciliation, and persuasion. Nothing said or done during and as a part of such informal endeavors may be made public by the

Commission, its officers or employees, or used as evidence in a subsequent proceeding without the written consent of the persons concerned. Any person who makes public information in violation of this subsection shall be fined not more than $1,000 or imprisoned for not more than one year, or both. The Commission shall make its determination on reasonable cause as promptly as possible and, so far as practicable, not later than one hundred and twenty days from the filing of the charge or, where applicable under subsection (c) or (d), from the date upon which the Commission is authorized to take action with respect to the charge.

(c) In the case of an alleged unlawful employment practice occurring in a State, or political subdivision of a State, which has a State or local law prohibiting the unlawful employment practice alleged and establishing or authorizing a State or local authority to grant or seek relief from such practice or to institute criminal proceedings with respect thereto upon receiving notice thereof, no charge may be filed under subsection (a) by the person aggrieved before the expiration of sixty days after proceedings have been commenced under the State or local law, unless such proceedings have been earlier terminated, provided that such sixty-day period shall be extended to one hundred and twenty days during the first year after the effective date of such State or local law. If any requirement for the commencement of such proceedings is imposed by a State or local authority other than a requirement of the filing of a written and signed statement of the facts upon which the proceeding is based, the proceeding shall be deemed to have been commenced for the purposes of this subsection at the time such statement is sent by registered mail to the appropriate State or local authority.

(d) In the case of any charge filed by a member of the Commission alleging an unlawful employment practice occurring in a State or political subdivision of a State which has a State or local law prohibiting the practice alleged and establishing or authorizing a State or local authority to grant or seek relief from such practice or to institute criminal proceedings with respect thereto upon receiving notice thereof, the Commission shall, before taking any action with respect to such charge, notify the appropriate State or local officials and, upon request, afford them a reasonable time, but not less than sixty days (provided that such sixty-day period shall be extended to one hundred and twenty days during the first year after the effective day of such State or local law), unless a shorter period is requested, to act under such State or local law to remedy the practice alleged.

(e) A charge under this section shall be filed within one hundred and eighty days after the alleged unlawful employment practice occurred and notice of the charge (including the date, place and circumstances of the alleged unlawful employment practice) shall be served upon the person against whom such charge is made within ten days thereafter, except that in a case of an unlawful employment practice with respect to which the person aggrieved has initially instituted proceedings with a State or local agency with authority to grant or seek relief from such practice or to institute criminal proceedings with respect thereto upon receiving notice thereof, such charge shall be filed by or on behalf of the person aggrieved within three hundred days after the alleged unlawful employment practice occurred, or within thirty days after receiving notice that the State or local agency has terminated the proceedings under the State or local law, whichever is earlier, and a copy of such charge shall be filed by the Commission with the State or local agency.

(f)(1) If within thirty days after a charge is filed with the Commission or within thirty days after expiration of any period of reference under subsection (c) or (d), the Commission has been unable to secure from the respondent a conciliation agreement acceptable to the Commission, the Commission may bring a civil action against any respondent not a government, governmental agency, or political subdivision named in the charge. In the case of a respondent which is a government, governmental agency, or political subdivision, if the Commission has been unable to secure from the respondent a conciliation agreement acceptable to the Commission, the Commission shall take no further action and shall refer the case to the Attorney General who may bring a civil action against such respondent in the appropriate United States district court. The person or persons aggrieved shall have the right to intervene in a civil action brought by the Commission or the Attorney General in a case involving a government, governmental agency, or political subdivision. If a charge filed with the Commission pursuant to subsection (b) is dismissed by the Commission, or if within one hundred and eighty days from the filing of such charge or the expiration of any period of reference under subsection (c) or (d), whichever is later, the Commission has not filed a civil action under this section or the Attorney General has not filed a civil action in a case involving a government, governmental agency, or political subdivision, or the Commission has not entered into a conciliation agreement to which the person aggrieved is a party, the Commission, or the Attorney General in a case involving a government, governmental agency, or political subdivision, shall so notify the person aggrieved and within ninety days after the giving of such notice a civil action may be brought against the respondent named in the charge (A) by the person claiming to be aggrieved or (B) if such charge was filed by a member of the Commission, by any person whom the charge alleges was aggrieved by the alleged unlawful employment practice. Upon application by the complainant and in such circumstances as the court may deem just, the court may appoint an attorney for such complainant and may authorize the commencement of the action without the payment of fees, costs, or security. Upon timely application, the court may, in its discretion, permit the Commission, or the Attorney General in a case involving a government, governmental agency, or political subdivision, to intervene in such civil action upon certification that the case is of general public importance. Upon request, the court may, in its discretion, stay further proceedings for not more than sixty days pending the termination of State or local proceedings described in subsections (c) or (d) of this section or further efforts of the Commission to obtain voluntary compliance.

(2) Whenever a charge is filed with the Commission and the Commission concludes on the basis of a preliminary investigation that prompt judicial action is necessary to carry out the purpose of this Act, the Commission, or the Attorney General in a case involving a government, governmental agency, or political subdivision, may bring an action for appropriate temporary or preliminary relief pending final disposition of such charge. Any temporary restraining order or other order granting preliminary or temporary relief shall be issued in accordance with rule 65 of the Federal Rules of Civil Procedure. It shall be the duty of a court having jurisdiction over proceedings under this section to assign cases for hearing at the earliest practicable date and to cause such cases to be in every way expedited.

(3) Each United States district court and each United States court of a place subject to the jurisdiction of the United States shall have jurisdiction of actions brought under this title. Such an action may be brought in any judicial district in the State in which the unlawful employment practice is alleged to have been committed, in the judicial district in which the employment records relevant to such practice are maintained and administered, or in the judicial district in which the aggrieved person would have worked but for the alleged unlawful employment practice, but if the respondent is not found within any such district,

such an action may be brought within the judicial district in which the respondent has his principal office. For purposes of sections 1404 and 1406 of title 28 of the United States Code, the judicial district in which the respondent has his principal office shall in all cases be considered a district in which the action might have been brought.

(4) It shall be the duty of the chief judge of the district (or in his absence, the acting chief judge) in which the case is pending immediately to designate a judge in such district to hear and determine the case. In the event that no judge in the district is available to hear and determine the case, the chief judge of the district, or the acting chief judge, as the case may be, shall certify this fact to the chief judge of the circuit (or in his absence, the acting chief judge) who shall then designate a district or circuit judge of the circuit to hear and determine the case.

(5) It shall be the duty of the judge designated pursuant to this subsection to assign the case for hearing at the earliest practicable date and to cause the case to be in every way expedited. If such judge has not scheduled the case for trial within one hundred and twenty days after issue has been joined that judge may appoint a master pursuant to rule 53 of the Federal Rules of Civil Procedure

(g) If the court finds that the respondent has intentionally engaged in or is intentionally engaging in an unlawful employment practice charged in the complaint, the court may enjoin the respondent from engaging in such unlawful employment practice, and order such affirmative action as may be appropriate, which may include, but is not limited to, reinstatement or hiring of employees, with or without back pay (payable by the employer, employment agency, or labor organization, as the case may be, responsible for the unlawful employment practice), or any other equitable relief as the court deems appropriate. Back pay liability shall not accrue from a date more than two years prior to the filing of a charge with the Commission. Interim earnings or amounts earnable with reasonable diligence by the person or persons discriminated against shall operate to reduce the back pay otherwise allowable. No order of the court shall require the admission or reinstatement of an individual as a member of a union, or the hiring, reinstatement, or promotion of an individual as an employee, or the payment to him of any back pay, if such individual was refused admission, suspended, or expelled, or was refused employment or advancement or was suspended or discharged for any reason other than discrimination on account of race, color, religion, sex, or national origin or in violation of section 704(a). (As amended by P.L. No. 92-261, eff. March 24, 1972)

(h) The provisions of the Act entitled "An Act to amend the Judicial Code and to define and limit the jurisdiction of courts sitting in equity, and for other purposes," approved March 23, 1932 (29 U.S.C. 101-115), shall not apply with respect to civil actions brought under this section.

(i) In any case in which an employer, employment agency, or labor organization fails to comply with an order of a court issued in a civil action brought under this section the Commission may commence proceedings to compel compliance with such order. (As amended)

(j) Any civil action brought under this section and any proceedings brought under subsection (j) shall be subject to appeal as provided in sections 1291 and 1292, title 28, United States Code. (As amended by P.L. 92-261, eff. March 24, 1972)

(k) In any action or proceeding under this title the court, in its discretion, may allow the prevailing party, other than the Commission or the United States, a reasonable attorney's fee as part of the costs, and the Commission and the United States shall be liable for costs the same as a private person.

Sec. 707. (a) Whenever the Attorney General has reasonable cause to believe that any person or group of persons is engaged in a pattern or practice of resistance to the full enjoyment of any of the rights secured by this title, and that the pattern or practice is of such a nature and is intended to deny the full exercise of the rights herein described, the Attorney General may bring a civil action in the appropriate district court of the United States by filing with it a complaint (1) signed by him (or in his absence the Acting Attorney General), (2) setting forth facts pertaining to such pattern or practice, and (3) requesting such relief, including an application for a permanent or temporary injunction, restraining order or other order against the person or persons responsible for such pattern or practice, as he deems necessary to insure the full enjoyment of the rights herein described.

(b) The district courts of the United States shall have and shall exercise jurisdiction of proceedings instituted pursuant to this section, and in any such proceeding the Attorney General may file with the clerk of such court a request that a court of three judges be convened to hear and determine the case. Such request by the Attorney General shall be accompanied by a certificate that, in his opinion, the case is of general public importance. A copy of the certificate and request for a three-judge court shall be immediately furnished by such clerk to the chief judge of the circuit (or in his absence, the presiding circuit judge of the circuit) in which the case is pending. Upon receipt of such request it shall be the duty of the chief judge of the circuit or the presiding circuit judge, as the case may be, to designate immediately three judges in such circuit, of whom at least one shall be a circuit judge and another of whom shall be a district judge of the court in which the proceeding was instituted, to hear and determine such case, and it shall be the duty of the judges so designated to assign the case for hearing at the earliest practicable date, to participate in the hearing and determination thereof, and to cause the case to be in every way expedited. An appeal from the final judgment of such court will lie to the Supreme Court.

In the event the Attorney General fails to file such a request in any such proceeding, it shall be the duty of the chief judge of the district (or in his absence, the acting chief judge) in which the case is pending immediately to designate a judge in such district to hear and determine the case. In the event that no judge in the district is available to hear and determine the case, the chief judge of the district, or the acting chief judge, as the case may be, shall certify this fact to the chief judge of the circuit (or in his absence, the acting chief judge) who shall then designate a district or circuit judge of the circuit to hear and determine the case.

It shall be the duty of the judge designated pursuant to this section to assign the case for hearing at the earliest practicable date and to cause the case to be in every way expedited.

(c) Effective two years after the date of enactment of the Equal Employment Opportunity Act of 1972, the functions of the Attorney General under this section shall be transferred to the Commission, together with such personnel, property, records, and unexpended balances of appropriations, allocations, and other funds employed, used, held, available, or to be made available in connection with such functions unless the President submits, and neither House of Congress vetoes, a reorganization plan pursuant to chapter 9 of title 5, United States Code, inconsistent with the provisions of this subsection. The Commission shall carry out such functions in accordance with subsections (d) and (e) of this section.

(d) Upon the transfer of functions provided for in subsection (c) of this section, in all suits commenced pursuant to this section prior to the date of such transfer, proceedings shall continue without abatement, all court orders and decrees shall remain in effect, and the Commission shall be substituted as a party for the United States of America, the Attorney General, or the Acting Attorney General, as appropriate.

(e) Subsequent to the date of enactment of the Equal Employment Opportunity Act of 1972, the Commission shall have authority to investigate and act on a charge of a pattern or practice of discrimination, whether filed by or on behalf of a person claiming to be aggrieved or by a member of the Commission. All such actions shall be conducted in accordance with the procedures set forth in section 706 of this Act. (As last amended by P.L. No. 92-261, eff. March 24, 1972)

EFFECT OF STATE LAWS

Sec. 708. Nothing in this title shall be deemed to exempt or relieve any person from any liability, duty, penalty, or punishment provided by any present or future law of any State or political subdivision of a State, other than any such law which purports to require or permit the doing of any act which would be an unlawful employment practice under this title.

INVESTIGATIONS, INSPECTIONS, RECORDS, STATE AGENCIES

Sec. 709. (a) In connection with any investigation of a charge filed under section 706, the Commission or its designated representative shall at all reasonable times have access to, for the purposes of examination, and the right to copy any evidence of any person being investigated or proceeded against that relates to unlawful employment practices covered by this title and is relevant to the charge under investigation.

(b) The Commission may cooperate with State and local agencies charged with the administration of State fair employment practices laws and, with the consent of such agencies, may, for the purpose of carrying out its functions and duties under this title and within the limitation of funds appropriated specifically for such purpose, engage in and contribute to the cost of research and other projects of mutual interest undertaken by such agencies, and utilize the services of such agencies and their employees, and, notwithstanding any other provision of law, pay by advance or reimbursement such agencies and their employees for services rendered to assist the Commisssion in carrying out this title. In furtherance of such cooperative efforts, the Commission may enter into written agreements with such State or local agencies and such agreements may include provisions under which the Commission shall refrain from processing a charge in any cases or class of cases specified in such agreements or under which the Commission shall relieve any person or class of persons in such State of locality from requirements imposed under this section. The Commission shall rescind any such agreement whenever it determines that the agreement no longer serves the interest of effective enforcement of this title.

(c) Every employer, employment agency, and labor organization subject to this title shall (1) make and keep such records relevant to the determinations of whether unlawful employment practices have been or are being committed, (2) preserve such records for such periods, and (3) make such reports therefrom as the Commission shall prescribe by regulation or order, after public hearing, as reasonable, necessary, or appropriate for the enforcement of this title or the regulations or orders thereunder. The Commission shall, by regulation, require each employer, labor organization, and joint labor-management committee subject to this title which controls an apprenticeship or other training program to maintain such records as are reasonably necessary to carry out the purposes of this title, including, but not limited to, a list of applicants who wish to participate in such program, including the chronological order in which applications were received, and to furnish to the Commission upon request, a detailed description of the manner in which persons are selected to participate in the apprenticeship or other training program. Any employer, employment agency, labor organization, or joint labor-management committee which believes that the application to it of any regulation or order issued under this section would result in undue hardship

may apply to the Commission for an exemption from the application of such regulation or order, and, if such application for an exemption is denied, bring a civil action in the United States district court for the district where such records are kept. If the Commission or the court, as the case may be, finds that the application of the regulation or order to the employer, employment agency, or labor organization in question would impose an undue hardship, the Commission or the court, as the case may be, may grant appropriate relief. If any person required to comply with the provisions of this subsection fails or refuses to do so, the United States district court for the district in which such person is found, resides, or transacts business, shall, upon application of the Commission, or the Attorney General in a 'case involving a governmental agency or political subdivision, have jurisdiction to issue to such person an order requring him to comply.

(d) In prescribing requirements pursuant to subsection (c) of this section, the Commission shall consult with other interested State and Federal agencies and shall endeavor to coordinate its requirements with those adopted by such agencies. The Commission shall furnish upon request and without cost to any State or local agency charged with the administration of a fair employment practice law information obtained pursuant to subsection (c) of this section from any employer, employment agency, labor organization, or joint labor-management committee subject to the jurisdiction of such agency. Such information shall be furnished on condition that it not be made public by the recipient agency prior to the institution of a proceeding under State or local law involving such information. If this condition is violated by a recipient agency, the Commission may decline to honor subsequent requests pursuant to this subsection. (As amended by P.L. 92-261, eff. March 24, 1972)

(e) It shall be unlawful for any officer or employee of the Commission to make public in any manner whatever any information obtained by the Commission this section prior to the institution of any proceeding under this title involving such information. Any officer or employee of the Commission who shall make public in any manner whatever any information in violation of this subsection shall be guilty of a misdemeanor and upon conviction thereof, shall be fined not more than $1,000, or imprisoned not more than one year.

INVESTIGATORY POWERS

Sec. 710. For the purpose of all hearings and investigations conducted by the Commission or its duly authorized agents or agencies, section 11 of the National Labor Relations Act (49 Stat. 455; 29 U.S.C. 161) shall apply. (As amended by P.L. 92-261, eff. March 24, 1972)

NOTICES TO BE POSTED

Sec. 711. (a) Every employer, employment agency and labor organization, as the case may be, shall post and keep posted in conspicuous places upon its premises where notices to employees, applicants for employment and members are customarily posted a notice to be prepared or approved by the Commission setting forth excerpts from or, summaries of, the pertinent provisions of this title and information pertinent to the filing of a complaint.

(b) A willful violation of this section shall be punishable by a fine of not more than $100 for each separate offense.

VETERANS' PREFERENCE

Sec. 712. Nothing contained in this title shall be construed to repeal or modify any Federal, State, territorial, or local law creating special rights or preference for veterans.

RULES AND REGULATIONS

Sec. 713. (a) The Commission shall have authority from time to time to issue, amend, or rescind suitable procedural regulations to carry out the provisions of this title. Regulations issued under this section shall be in conformity with the standards and limitations of the Administrative Procedure Act.

(b) In any action or proceeding based on any alleged unlawful employment practice, no person shall be subject to any liability or punishment for or on account of (1) the commission by such person of an unlawful employment practice if he pleads and proves that the act or omission complained of was in good faith, in conformity with, and in reliance on any written interpretation or opinion of the Commission, or (2) the failure of such person to publish and file any information required by any provision of this title if he pleads and proves that he failed to publish and file such information in good faith, in conformity with the instructions of the Commission issued under this title regarding the filing of such information. Such a defense, if established, shall be a bar to the action or proceeding, notwithstanding that (A) after such act or omission, such interpretation or opinion is modified or rescinded or is determined by judicial authority to be invalid or of no legal effect, or (B) after publishing or filing the description and annual reports, such publication or filing is determined by judicial authority not to be in conformity with the requirements of this title.

FORCIBLY RESISTING THE COMMISSION OR ITS REPRESENTATIVES

Sec. 714. The provisions of sections 111 and 1114, title 18, United States Code, shall apply to officers, agents, and employees of the Commission in the performance of their official duties. Notwithstanding the provisions of sections 111 and 1114 of title 18, United States Code, whoever in violation of the provisions of section 1114 of such title kills a person while engaged in or on account of the performance of his official functions under this Act shall be punished by imprisonment for any term of years or for life. (As amended by P.L. 92-261, eff. March 24, 1972)

SPECIAL STUDY BY SECRETARY OF LABOR

Sec. 715. There shall be established an Equal Employment Opportunity Coordinating Council (hereinafter referred to in this section as the Council) composed of the Secretary of Labor, the Chairman of the Equal Employment Opportunity Commission, the Attorney General, the Chairman of the United States Civil Service Commission, and the Chairman of the United States Civil Rights Commission, or their respective delegates. The Council shall have the responsibility for developing and implementing agreements, policies and practices designed to maximize effort, promote efficiency, and eliminate conflict, competition, duplication and inconsistency among the operations, functions and jurisdictions of the various departments, agencies and branches of the Federal Government responsible for the implementation and enforcement of equal employment opportunity legislation, orders, and policies. On or before July 1 of each year, the Council shall transmit to the President and to the Congress a report of its activities, together with such recommendations for legislative or administrative changes as it concludes are desirable to further promote the purposes of this section. (As amended by P.L. No. 92-261, eff. March 24, 1972)

EFFECTIVE DATE

Sec. 716. (a) This title shall become effective one year after the date of its enactment. (The effective date thus is July 2, 1965.)

(b) Notwithstanding subsection (a), sections of this title other than sections 703, 704, 706, and 707 shall become effective immediately.

(c) The President shall, as soon as feasible after the enactment of this title, convene one or more conferences for the purpose of enabling the leaders of groups whose members will be affected by this title to become familiar with the rights afforded and obligations imposed by its provisions, and for the purpose of making plans which will result in the fair and effective administration of this title when all of its provisions become effective. The President shall invite the participation in such conference or conferences of (1) the members of the President's Committee on Equal Employment Opportunity, (2) the members of the Commission on Civil Rights, (3) representatives of State and local agencies engaged in furthering equal employment opportunity, (4) representatives of private agencies engaged in furthering equal employment opportunity, and (5) representatives of employers, labor organizations, and employment agencies who will be subject to this title.

NON DISCRIMINATION IN FEDERAL GOVERNMENT EMPLOYMENT

Sec. 717. (a) All personnel actions affecting employees or applicants for employment (except with regard to aliens employed outside the limits of the United States) in military departments as defined in section 102 of title 5, United States Code in executive agencies (other than the General Accounting Office) as defined in section 105 of title 5, United States Code (including employees and applicants for employment who are paid from nonappropriated funds), in the United States Postal Service and the Postal Rate Commission, in those units of the Government of the District of Columbia having positions in the competitive service, and in those units of the legislative and judicial branches of the Federal Government having positions in the competitive service, and in the Library of Congress shall be made free from any discrimination based on race, color, religion, sex, or national origin.

(b) Except as otherwise provided in this subsection, the Civil Service Commission shall have authority to enforce the provisions of subsection (a) through appropriate remedies, including reinstatement or hiring of employees with or without back pay, as will effectuate the policies of this section, and shall issue such rules, regulations, orders and instructions as it deems necessary and appropriate to carry out its responsibilities under this section. The Civil Service Commission shall—

(1) be responsible for the annual review and approval of a national and regional equal employment opportunity plan which each department and agency and each appropriate unit referred to in subsection (a) of this section shall submit in order to maintain an affirmative program of equal employment opportunity for all such employees and applicants for employment;

(2) be responsible for the review and evaluation of the operation of all agency equal employment opportunity programs, periodically obtaining and publishing (on at least a semi-annual basis) progress reports from each such department, agency, or unit; and

(3) consult with and solicit the recommendations of interested individuals, groups, and organizations relating to equal employment opportunity.

The head of each such department, agency, or unit shall comply with such rules, regulations, orders, and instructions which shall include a provision that an employee or applicant for employment shall be notified of any final action taken on any complant of discrimination filed by him thereunder. The plan submitted by each department, agency, and unit shall include, but not be limited to—

(1) provision for the establishment of training and education programs designed to provide a maximum opportunity for employees to advance so as to perform at their highest potential; and

(2) a description of the qualifications in terms of training and experience relating to equal employment opportunity for the principal and operating officials of each such department, agency, or unit responsible for carrying out the equal employment opportunity program and of the allocation of personnel and resources proposed by such department, agency, or unit to carry out its equal employment opportunity program.

With respect to employment in the Library of Congress, authorities granted in this subsection to the Civil Service Commission shall be exercised by the Librarian of Congress.

(c) Within thirty days of receipt of notice of final action taken by a department, agency, or unit referred to in subsection 717(a), or by the Civil Service Commission upon an appeal from a decision or order of such department, agency, or unit on a complaint of discrimination based on race, color, religion, sex or national origin, brought pursuant to subsection (a) of this section, Executive Order 11478 or any succeeding executive orders, or after one hundred and eighty days from the filing of the initial charge with the department, agency, or unit or with the Civil Service Commission on appeal from a decision or order of such department, agency, or unit until such time as final action may be taken by a department, agency, or unit, an employee or applicant for employment, if aggrieved by the final disposition of his complaint, or by the failure to take final action on his complaint, may file a civil action as provided in section 706, in which civil action the head of the department, agency, or unit, as appropriate, shall be the defendant.

(d) The provisions of section 706 (f) through (k), as applicable, shall govern civil actions brought hereunder.

(e) Nothing contained in this Act shall relieve any Government agency or official of its or his primary responsibility to assure nondiscrimination in employment as required by the Constitution and statutes or of its or his responsibilities under Executive Order 11478 relating to equal employment opportunity in the Federal Government. (As amended by 92-261, eff. March 24, 1972)

SPECIAL PROVISION WITH RESPECT TO DENIAL, TERMINATION AND SUSPENSION OF GOVERNMENT CONTRACTS

Sec. 718. No Government contract, or portion thereof, with any employer, shall be denied, withheld, terminated, or suspended, by any agency or officer of the United States under any equal employment opportunity law or order, where such employer has an affirmative action plan which has previously been accepted by the Government for the same facility within the past twelve months without first according such employer full hearing and adjudication under the provisions of title 5, United States Code, section 554, and the following pertinent sections: Provided, That if such employer has deviated substantially from such previously agreed to affirmative action plan, this section shall not apply: Provided further, That for the purposes of this section an affirmative action plan shall be deemed to have been accepted by the Government at the time the appropriate compliance agency has accepted such plan unless within forty-five days thereafter the Office of Federal Contract Compliance has disapproved such plan. (As added by P.L. 92-261, eff. March 24, 1972)

1. Conference Report on H.R. 1746
2. Joint Explanatory Statement of Managers

EQUAL EMPLOYMENT OPPORTUNITY ACT OF 1972

MARCH 2, 1972.—Ordered to be printed

Mr. WILLIAMS, from the committee of conference,
submitted the following

CONFERENCE REPORT

[To accompany H.R. 1746]

The committee of conference on the disagreeing votes of the two
Houses on the amendment of the Senate to the bill (H.R. 1746) An
Act to further promote equal employment opportunities for American
workers, having met, after full and free conference, have agreed to
recommend and do recommend to their respective Houses as follows:

That the House recede from its disagreement to the amendment
of the Senate and agree to the same with an amendment as follows:

In lieu of the matter proposed to be inserted by the Senate amendment insert the following:

*That this Act may be cited as the "Equal Employment Opportunity
Act of 1972".*

*SEC. 2. Section 701 of the Civil Rights Act of 1964 (78 Stat. 253; 42
U.S.C. 2000e) is amended as follows:*

*(1) In subsection (a) insert "governments, governmental agencies,
political subdivisions," after the word "individuals".*

(2) Subsection (b) is amended to read as follows:

*"(b) The term 'employer' means a person engaged in an industry
affecting commerce who has fifteen or more employees for each working
day in each of twenty or more calendar weeks in the current or preceding
calendar year, and any agent of such a person, but such term does not
include (1) the United States, a corporation wholly owned by the Government of the United States, an Indian tribe, or any department or agency
of the District of Columbia subject by statute to procedures of the competitive
service (as defined in section 2102 of title 5 of the United States Code), or
(2) a bona fide private membership club (other than a labor organization)
which is exempt from taxation under section 501(c) of the Internal
Revenue Code of 1954, except that during the first year after the date of*

enactment of the Equal Employment Opportunity Act of 1972, persons having fewer than twenty-five employees (and their agents) shall not be considered employers."

(3) In subsection (c) beginning with the semicolon strike out through the word "assistance".

(4) In subsection (e) strike out between "(A)" and "and such labor organization", and insert in lieu thereof "twenty-five or more during the first year after the date of enactment of the Equal Employment Opportunity Act of 1972, or (B) fifteen or more thereafter,".

(5) In subsection (f), insert before the period a comma and the following: "except that the term 'employee' shall not include any person elected to public office in any State or political subdivision of any State by the qualified voters thereof, or any person chosen by such officer to be on such officer's personal staff, or an appointee on the policy making level or an immediate adviser with respect to the exercise of the constitutional or legal powers of the office. The exemption set forth in the preceding sentence shall not include employees subject to the civil service laws of a State government, governmental agency or political subdivision."

(6) At the end of subsection (h) insert before the period a comma and the following: "and further includes any governmental industry, business, or activity".

(7) After subsection (i) insert the following new subsection (j):

"(j) The term 'religion' includes all aspects of religious observance and practice, as well as belief, unless an employer demonstrates that he is unable to reasonably accommodate to an employee's or prospective employee's religious observance or practice without undue hardship on the conduct of the employer's business."

SEC. 3. Section 702 of the Civil Rights Act of 1964 (78 Stat. 255; 42 U.S.C. 2000e–1) is amended to read as follows:

"EXEMPTION

"SEC. 702. This title shall not apply to an employer with respect to the employment of aliens outside any State, or to a religious corporation, association, educational institution, or society with respect to the employment of individuals of a particular religion to perform work connected with the carrying on by such corporation, association, educational institution, or society of its activities."

SEC. 4. (a) Subsections (a) through (g) of section 706 of the Civil Rights Act of 1964 (78 Stat. 259; 42 U.S.C. 2000e–5(a)–(g)) are amended to read as follows:

"SEC. 705. (a) The Commission is empowered, as hereinafter provided, to prevent any person from engaging in any unlawful employment practice as set forth in section 703 or 704 of this title.

"(b) Whenever a charge is filed by or on behalf of a person claiming to be aggrieved, or by a member of the Commission, alleging that an employer, employment agency, labor organization, or joint labor-management committee controlling apprenticeship or other training or retraining, including on-the-job training programs, has engaged in an unlawful employment practice, the Commission shall serve a notice of the charge (including the date, place and circumstances of the alleged unlawful employment practice) on such employer, employment agency, labor organization, or joint labor-management committee (hereinafter referred to as the

'respondent') within ten days, and shall make an investigation thereof. Charges shall be in writing under oath or affirmation and shall contain such information and be in such form as the Commission requires. Charges shall not be made public by the Commission. If the Commission determines after such investigation that there is not reasonable cause to believe that the charge is true, it shall dismiss the charge and promptly notify the person claiming to be aggrieved and the respondent of its action. In determining whether reasonable cause exists, the Commission shall accord substantial weight to final findings and orders made by State or local authorities in proceedings commenced under State or local law pursuant to the requirements of subsections (c) and (d). If the Commission determines after such investigation that there is reasonable cause to believe that the charge is true, the Commission shall endeavor to eliminate any such alleged unlawful employment practice by informal methods of conference, conciliation, and persuasion. Nothing said or done during and as a part of such informal endeavors may be made public by the Commission, its officers or employees, or used as evidence in a subsequent proceeding without the written consent of the persons concerned. Any person who makes public information in violation of this subsection shall be fined not more than $1,000 or imprisoned for not more than one year, or both. The Commission shall make its determination on reasonable cause as promptly as possible and, so far as practicable, not later than one hundred and twenty days from the filing of the charge or, where applicable under subsection (c) or (d), from the date upon which the Commission is authorized to take action with respect to the charge.

"(c) In the case of an alleged unlawful employment practice occurring in a State, or political subdivision of a State, which has a State or local law prohibiting the unlawful employment practice alleged and establishing or authorizing a State or local authority to grant or seek relief from such practice or to institute criminal proceedings with respect thereto upon receiving notice thereof, no charge may be filed under subsection (a) by the person aggrieved before the expiration of sixty days after proceedings have been commenced under the State or local law, unless such proceedings have been earlier terminated, provided that such sixty-day period shall be extended to one hundred and twenty days during the first year after the effective date of such State or local law. If any requirement for the commencement of such proceedings is imposed by a State or local authority other than a requirement of the filing of a written and signed statement of the facts upon which the proceeding is based, the proceeding shall be deemed to have been commenced for the purposes of this subsection at the time such statement is sent by registered mail to the appropriate State or local authority.

"(d) In the case of any charge filed by a member of the Commission alleging an unlawful employment practice occurring in a State or political subdivision of a State which has a State or local law prohibiting the practice alleged and establishing or authorizing a State or local authority to grant or seek relief from such practice or to institute criminal proceedings with respect thereto upon receiving notice thereof, the Commission shall, before taking any action with respect to such charge, notify the appropriate State or local officials and, upon request, afford them a reasonable time, but not less than sixty days (provided that such sixty-day period shall be extended to one hundred and twenty days during *the first year after the effective day of such State or local law), unless a shorter period is requested, to act under such State or local law to remedy the practice alleged.*

"(e) A charge under this section shall be filed within one hundred and eighty days after the alleged unlawful employment practice occurred and notice of the charge (including the date, place and circumstances of the alleged unlawful employment practice) shall be served upon the person against whom such charge is made within ten days thereafter, except that in a case of an unlawful employment practice with respect to which the person aggrieved has initially instituted proceedings with a State or local agency with authority to grant or seek relief from such practice or to institute criminal proceedings with respect thereto upon receiving notice thereof, such charge shall be filed by or on behalf of the person aggrieved within three hundred days after the alleged unlawful employment practice occurred, or within thirty days after receiving notice that the State or local agency has terminated the proceedings under the State or local law, whichever is earlier, and a copy of such charge shall be filed by the Commission with the State or local agency.

"(f) (1) If within thirty days after a charge is filed with the Commission or within thirty days after expiration of any period of reference under subsection (c) or (d), the Commission has been unable to secure from the respondent a conciliation agreement acceptable to the Commission, the Commission may bring a civil action against any respondent not a government, governmental agency, or political subdivision named in the charge. In the case of a respondent which is a government, governmental agency, or political subdivision, if the Commission has been unable to secure from the respondent a conciliation agreement acceptable to the Commission, the Commission shall take no further action and shall refer the case to the Attorney General who may bring a civil action against such respondent in the appropriate United States district court. The person or persons aggrieved shall have the right to intervene in a civil action brought by the Commission or the Attorney General in a case involving a government, governmental agency, or political subdivision. If a charge filed with the Commission pursuant to subsection (b) is dismissed by the Commission, or if within one hundred and eighty days from the filing of such charge or the expiration of any period of reference under subsection (c) or (d), whichever is later, the Commission has not filed a civil action under this section or the Attorney General has not filed a civil action in a case involving a government, governmental agency, or political subdivision, or the Commission has not entered into a conciliation agreement to which the person aggrieved is a party, the Commission, or the Attorney General in a case involving a government, governmental agency, or political subdivision, shall so notify the person aggrieved and within ninety days after the giving of such notice a civil action may be brought against the respondent named in the charge (A) by the person claiming to be aggrieved or (B) if such charge was filed by a member of the Commission, by any person whom the charge alleges was aggrieved by the alleged unlawful employment practice. Upon application by the complainant and in such circumstances as the court may deem just, the court may appoint an attorney for such complainant and may authorize the commencement of the action without the payment of fees, costs, or security. Upon timely application, the court may, in its discretion, permit the Commission, or the Attorney General in a case involving a government, governmental agency, or political subdivision,

to intervene in such civil action upon certification that the case is of general public importance. Upon request, the court may, in its discretion, stay further proceedings for not more than sixty days pending the termination of State or local proceedings described in subsections (c) or (d) of this section or further efforts of the Commission to obtain voluntary compliance.

"(2) Whenever a charge is filed with the Commission and the Commission concludes on the basis of a preliminary investigation that prompt judicial action is necessary to carry out the purposes of this Act, the Commission, or the Attorney General in a case involving a government, governmental agency, or political subdivision, may bring an action for appropriate temporary or preliminary relief pending final disposition of such charge. Any temporary restraining order or other order granting preliminary or temporary relief shall be issued in accordance with rule 65 of the Federal Rules of Civil Procedure. It shall be the duty of a court having jurisdiction over proceedings under this section to assign cases for hearing at the earliest practicable date and to cause such cases to be in every way expedited.

"(3) Each United States district court and each United States court of a place subject to the jurisdiction of the United States shall have jurisdiction of actions brought under this title. Such an action may be brought in any judicial district in the State in which the unlawful employment practice is alleged to have been committed, in the judicial district in which the employment records relevant to such practice are maintained and administered, or in the judicial district in which the aggrieved person would have worked but for the alleged unlawful employment practice, but if the respondent is not found within any such district, such an action may be brought within the judicial district in which the respondent has his principal office. For purposes of sections 1404 and 1406 of title 28 of the United States Code, the judicial district in which the respondent has his principal office shall in all cases be considered a district in which the action might have been brought.

"(4) It shall be the duty of the chief judge of the district (or in his absence, the acting chief judge) in which the case is pending immediately to designate a judge in such district to hear and determine the case. In the event that no judge in the district is available to hear and determine the case, the chief judge of the district, or the acting chief judge, as the case may be, shall certify this fact to the chief judge of the circuit (or in his absence, the acting chief judge) who shall then designate a district or circuit judge of the circuit to hear and determine the case.

"(5) It shall be the duty of the judge designated pursuant to this subsection to assign the case for hearing at the earliest practicable date and to cause the case to be in every way expedited. If such judge has not scheduled the case for trial within one hundred and twenty days after issue has been joined, that judge may appoint a master pursuant to rule 53 of the Federal Rules of Civil Procedure.

"(g) If the court finds that the respondent has intentionally engaged in or is intentionally engaging in an unlawful employment practice charged in the complaint, the court may enjoin the respondent from engaging in such unlawful employment practice, and order such affirmative action as may be appropriate, which may include, but is not limited to, reinstatement or hiring of employees, with or without back pay (payable by the employer, employment agency, or labor organization, as the case may be, responsible for the unlawful employment practice), or any other equitable *relief as the court deems appropriate. Back pay liability shall not accrue from a date more than two years prior to the filing of a charge with the Commission. Interim earnings or amounts earnable with reasonable diligence by the person or persons discriminated against shall operate to reduce the back pay otherwise allowable. No order of the court shall require the admission or reinstatement of an individual as a member of a union, or the hiring, reinstatement, or promotion of an individual as an employee, or the payment to him of any back pay, if such individual was refused admission, suspended, or expelled, or was refused employment or advancement or was suspended or discharged for any reason other than discrimination on account of race, color, religion, sex, or national origin or in violation of section 704(a)."*

(b)(1) Subsection (i) of section 706 of such Act is amended by striking out "subsection (e)" and inserting in lieu thereof "this section".

(2) Subsection (j) of such section is amended by striking out "subsection (e)" and inserting in lieu thereof "this section".

Sec. 5. *Section 707 of the Civil Rights Act of 1964 is amended by adding at the end thereof the following new subsection:*

"(c) Effective two years after the date of enactment of the Equal Employment Opportunity Act of 1972, the functions of the Attorney General under this section shall be transferred to the Commission, together with such personnel, property, records, and unexpended balances of appropriations, allocations, and other funds employed, used, held, available, or to be made available in connection with such functions unless the President submits, and neither House of Congress vetoes, a reorganization plan pursuant to chapter 9 of title 5, United States Code, inconsistent with the provisions of this subsection. The Commission shall carry out such functions in accordance with subsections (d) and (e) of this section.

"(d) Upon the transfer of functions provided for in subsection (c) of this section, in all suits commenced pursuant to this section prior to the date of such transfer, proceedings shall continue without abatement, all court orders and decrees shall remain in effect, and the Commission shall be substituted as a party for the United States of America, the Attorney General, or the Acting Attorney General, as appropriate.

"(e) Subsequent to the date of enactment of the Equal Employment Opportunity Act of 1972, the Commission shall have authority to investigate and act on a charge of a pattern or practice of discrimination, whether filed by or on behalf of a person claiming to be aggrieved or by a member of the Commission. All such actions shall be conducted in accordance with the procedures set forth in section 706 of this Act."

Sec. 6. *Subsections (b), (c), and (d) of section 709 of the Civil Rights Act of 1964 (78 Stat. 263; 42 U.S.C. 2000e-8(b)-(d)) are amended to read as follows:*

"(b) The Commission may cooperate with State and local agencies charged with the administration of State fair employment practices laws and, with the consent of such agencies, may, for the purpose of carrying out its functions and duties under this title and within the limitation of funds appropriated specifically for such purpose, engage in and contribute to the cost of research and other projects of mutual interest undertaken by such agencies, and utilize the services of such agencies and their employees, and, notwithstanding any other provision of law, pay by advance or reimbursement such agencies and their employees for services rendered to assist the Commission in carrying out this title. In

furtherance of such cooperative efforts, the Commission may enter into written agreements with such State or local agencies and such agreements may include provisions under which the Commission shall refrain from processing a charge in any cases or class of cases specified in such agreements or under which the Commission shall relieve any person or class of persons in such State or locality from requirements imposed under this section. The Commission shall rescind any such agreement whenever it determines that the agreement no longer serves the interest of effective enforcement of this title.

"(c) Every employer, employment agency, and labor organization subject to this title shall (1) make and keep such records relevant to the determinations of whether unlawful employment practices have been or are being committed, (2) preserve such records for such periods, and (3) make such reports therefrom as the Commission shall prescribe by regulation or order, after public hearing, as reasonable, necessary, or appropriate for the enforcement of this title or the regulations or orders thereunder. The Commission shall, by regulation, require each employer, labor organization, and joint labor-management committee subject to this title which controls an apprenticeship or other training program to maintain such records as are reasonably necessary to carry out the purposes of this title, including, but not limited to, a list of applicants who wish to participate in such program, including the chronological order in which applications were received, and to furnish to the Commission upon request, a detailed description of the manner in which persons are selected to participate in the apprenticeship or other training program. Any employer, employment agency, labor organization, or joint labor-management committee which believes that the application to it of any regulation or order issued under this section would result in undue hardship may apply to the Commission for an exemption from the application of such regulation or order, and, if such application for an exemption is denied, bring a civil action in the United States district court for the district where such records are kept. If the Commission or the court, as the case may be, finds that the application of the regulation or order to the employer, employment agency, or labor organization in question would impose an undue hardship, the Commission or the court, as the case may be, may grant appropriate relief. If any person required to comply with the provisions of this subsection fails or refuses to do so, the United States district court for the district in which such person is found, resides, or transacts business, shall, upon application of the Commission, or the Attorney General in a case involving a government, governmental agency or political subdivision, have jurisdiction to issue to such person an order requiring him to comply.

"(d) In prescribing requirements pursuant to subsection (c) of this section, the Commission shall consult with other interested State and Federal agencies and shall endeavor to coordinate its requirements with those adopted by such agencies. The Commission shall furnish upon request and without cost to any State or local agency charged with the administration of a fair employment practice law information obtained pursuant to subsection (c) of this section from any employer, employment agency, labor organization, or joint labor-management committee subject to the jurisdiction of such agency. Such information shall be furnished on condition that it not be made public by the recipient agency prior to the institution of a proceeding under State or local law involving such information. If this condition is violated by a recipient agency, the Commission may decline to honor subsequent requests pursuant to this subsection."

SEC. 7. *Section 710 of the Civil Rights Act of 1964 (78 Stat. 264; 42 U.S.C. 2000e–9) is amended to read as follows:*

"INVESTIGATORY POWERS"

"SEC. 710. *For the purpose of all hearings and investigations conducted by the Commission or its duly authorized agents or agencies, section 11 of the National Labor Relations Act (49 Stat. 455; 29 U.S.C. 161) shall apply."*

SEC. 8. (a) *Section 703(a)(2) of the Civil Rights Act of 1964 (78 Stat. 255; 42 U.S.C. 2000e–2(a)(2)) is amended by inserting the words "or applicants for employment" after the words "his employees".*

(b) *Section 703(c)(2) of such Act is amended by inserting the words "or applicants for membership" after the word "membership".*

(c)(1) *Section 704(a) of such Act is amended by inserting a comma and the following: "or joint labor-management committee controlling apprenticeship or other training or retraining, including on-the-job training programs," after "employment agency".*

(2) *Section 704(b) of such Act is amended by (A) striking out "or employment agency" and inserting in lieu thereof "employment agency, or joint labor-management committee controlling apprenticeship or other training or retraining, including on-the-job training programs,", and (B) inserting a comma and the words "or relating to admission to, or employment in, any program established to provide apprenticeship or other training by such a joint labor-management committee" before the word "indicating".*

(d) *Section 705(a) of the Civil Rights Act of 1964 (78 Stat. 258; 42 U.S.C. 2000e–4(a)) is amended to read as follows:*

"SEC. 705. (a) *There is hereby created a Commission to be known as the Equal Employment Opportunity Commission, which shall be composed of five members, not more than three of whom shall be members of the same political party. Members of the Commission shall be appointed by the President by and with the advice and consent of the Senate for a term of five years. Any individual chosen to fill a vacancy shall be appointed only for the unexpired term of the member whom he shall succeed, and all members of the Commission shall continue to serve until their successors are appointed and qualified, except that no such member of the Commission shall continue to serve (1) for more than sixty days when the Congress is in session unless a nomination to fill such vacancy shall have been submitted to the Senate, or (2) after the adjournment sine die of the session of the Senate in which such nomination was submitted. The President shall designate one member to serve as Chairman of the Commission, and one member to serve as Vice Chairman. The Chairman shall be responsible on behalf of the Commission for the administrative operations of the Commission, and, except as provided in subsection (b), shall appoint, in accordance with the provisions of title 5, United States Code, governing appointments in the competitive service, such officers, agents, attorneys, hearing examiners, and employees as he deems necessary to assist it in the performance of its functions and to fix their compensation in accordance with the provisions of chapter 51 and subchapter III of chapter 53 of title 5, United States Code, relating to classification and General Schedule pay rates: Provided, That assignment, removal, and compensation of hearing examiners shall be in accordance with sections 3105, 3344, 5362, and 7521 of title 5, United States Code."*

(e)(1) Section 705 of such Act is amended by inserting after subsection (a) the following new subsection (b):

"(b)(1) There shall be a General Counsel of the Commission appointed by the President, by and with the advice and consent of the Senate, for a term of four years. The General Counsel shall have responsibility for the conduct of litigation as provided in sections 706 and 707 of this title. The General Counsel shall have such other duties as the Commission may prescribe or as may be provided by law and shall concur with the Chairman of the Commission on the appointment and supervision of regional attorneys. The General Counsel of the Commission on the effective date of this Act shall continue in such position and perform the functions specified in this subsection until a successor is appointed and qualified.

"(2) Attorneys appointed under this section may, at the direction of the Commission, appear for and represent the Commission in any case in court, provided that the Attorney General shall conduct all litigation to which the Commission is a party in the Supreme Court pursuant to this title."

(2) Subsections (e) and (h) of such section 705 are repealed.

(3) Subsections (b), (c), (d), (i), and (j) of such section 705, and all references thereto, are redesignated as subsections (c), (d), (e), (h), and (i), respectively.

(f) Section 705(g)(6) of such Act, is amended to read as follows:

"(6) to intervene in a civil action brought under section 706 by an aggrieved party against a respondent other than a government, governmental agency or political subdivision."

(g) Section 714 of such Act is amended to read as follows:

"FORCIBLY RESISTING THE COMMISSION OR ITS REPRESENTATIVES

"SEC. 714. The provisions of sections 111 and 1114, title 18, United States Code, shall apply to officers, agents, and employees of the Commission in the performance of their official duties. Notwithstanding the provisions of sections 111 and 1114 of title 18, United States Code, whoever in violation of the provisions of section 1114 of such title kills a person while engaged in or on account of the performance of his official functions under this Act shall be punished by imprisonment for any term of years or for life."

SEC. 9. (a) Section 5314 of title 5 of the United States Code is amended by adding at the end thereof the following new clause:

"(58) Chairman, Equal Employment Opportunity Commission."

(b) Clause (72) of section 5315 of such title is amended to read as follows:

"(72) Members, Equal Employment Opportunity Commission (4)."

(c) Clause (111) of section 5316 of such title is repealed.

(d) Section 5316 of such title is amended by adding at the end thereof the following new clause:

"(131) General Counsel of the Equal Employment Opportunity Commission."

SEC. 10. Section 715 of the Civil Rights Act of 1964 is amended to read as follows:

"EQUAL EMPLOYMENT OPPORTUNITY COORDINATING COUNCIL

"SEC. 715. There shall be established an Equal Employment Opportunity Coordinating Council (hereinafter referred to in this section as the Council) composed of the Secretary of Labor, the Chairman of the Equal Employment Opportunity Commission, the Attorney General, the Chairman of the United States Civil Service Commission, and the Chairman of the United States Civil Rights Commission, or their respective delegates. The Council shall have the responsibility for developing and implementing agreements, policies and practices designed to maximize effort, promote efficiency, and eliminate conflict, competition, duplication and inconsistency among the operations, functions and jurisdictions of the various departments, agencies and branches of the Federal Government responsible for the implementation and enforcement of equal employment opportunity legislation, orders, and policies. On or before July 1 of each year, the Council shall transmit to the President and to the Congress a report of its activities, together with such recommendations for legislative or administrative changes as it concludes are desirable to further promote the purposes of this section."

SEC. 11. Title VII of the Civil Rights Act of 1964 (78 Stat. 253; 42 U.S.C. 2000e et seq.) is amended by adding at the end thereof the following new section:

"NONDISCRIMINATION IN FEDERAL GOVERNMENT EMPLOYMENT

"SEC. 717. (a) All personnel actions affecting employees or applicants for employment (except with regard to aliens employed outside the limits of the United States) in military departments as defined in section 102 of title 5, United States Code, in executive agencies (other than the General Accounting Office) as defined in section 105 of title 5, United States Code (including employees and applicants for employment who are paid from nonappropriated funds), in the United States Postal Service and the Postal Rate Commission, in those units of the Government of the District of Columbia having positions in the competitive service, and in those units of the legislative and judicial branches of the Federal Government having positions in the competitive service, and in the Library of Congress shall be made free from any discrimination based on race, color, religion, sex, or national origin.

"(b) Except as otherwise provided in this subsection, the Civil Service Commission shall have authority to enforce the provisions of subsection (a) through appropriate remedies, including reinstatement or hiring of employees with or without back pay, as will effectuate the policies of this section, and shall issue such rules, regulations, orders and instructions as it deems necessary and appropriate to carry out its responsibilities under this section. The Civil Service Commission shall—

"(1) be responsible for the annual review and approval of a national and regional equal employment opportunity plan which each department and agency and each appropriate unit referred to in subsection (a) of this section shall submit in order to maintain an affirmative program of equal employment opportunity for all such employees and applicants for employment;

"(2) be responsible for the review and evaluation of the operation of all agency equal employment opportunity programs, periodically

*obtaining and publishing (on at least a semiannual basis) progress
reports from each such department, agency, or unit; and*

*"(3) consult with and solicit the recommendations of interested
individuals, groups, and organizations relating to equal employment
opportunity.*

*The head of each such department, agency, or unit shall comply with such
rules, regulations, orders, and instructions which shall include a provision
that an employee or applicant for employment shall be notified of any final
action taken on any complaint of discrimination filed by him thereunder.
The plan submitted by each department, agency, and unit shall include,
but not be limited to—*

*"(1) provision for the establishment of training and education
programs designed to provide a maximum opportunity for employees
to advance so as to perform at their highest potential; and*

*"(2) a description of the qualifications in terms of training and
experience relating to equal employment opportunity for the principal
and operating officials of each such department, agency, or unit
responsible for carrying out the equal employment opportunity program and of the allocation of personnel and resources proposed by
such department, agency, or unit to carry out its equal employment
opportunity program.*

*With respect to employment in the Library of Congress, authorities
granted in this subsection to the Civil Service Commission shall be exercised
by the Librarian of Congress.*

*"(c) Within thirty days of receipt of notice of final action taken by a
department, agency, or unit referred to in subsection 717(a), or by the
Civil Service Commission upon an appeal from a decision or order of such
department, agency, or unit on a complaint of discrimination based on
race, color, religion, sex or national origin, brought pursuant to subsection
(a) of this section, Executive Order 11478 or any succeeding Executive
orders, or after one hundred and eighty days from the filing of the initial
charge with the department, agency, or unit or with the Civil Service Commission on appeal from a decision or order of such department, agency, or
unit until such time as final action may be taken by a department, agency,
or unit, an employee or applicant for employment, if aggrieved by the final
disposition of his complaint, or by the failure to take final action on his
complaint, may file a civil action as provided in section 706, in which
civil action the head of the department, agency, or unit, as appropriate,
shall be the defendant.*

*"(d) The provisions of section 706 (f) through (k), as applicable, shall
govern civil actions brought hereunder.*

*"(e) Nothing contained in this Act shall relieve any Government agency
or official of its or his primary responsibility to assure nondiscrimination
in employment as required by the Constitution and statutes or of its or his
responsibilities under Executive Order 11478 relating to equal employment opportunity in the Federal Government."*

SEC. 12. *Section 5108(c) of title 5, United States Code, is amended by—*

(1) striking out the word "and" at the end of paragraph (9);

*(2) striking out the period at the end of paragraph (10) and in-
serting in lieu thereof a semicolon and the word "and"; and*

*(3) by adding immediately after paragraph (10) the last time it
appears therein in the following new paragraph:*

"(11) the Chairman of the Equal Employment Opportunity Commission, subject to the standards and procedures prescribed by this chapter, may place an additional ten positions in the Equal Employment Opportunity Commission in GS–16, GS–17, and GS–18 for the purposes of carrying out title VII of the Civil Rights Act of 1964."

SEC. 13. Title VII of the Civil Rights Act of 1964 (78 Stat. 253; 42 U.S.C. 2000e et seq.) is further amended by adding at the end thereof the following new section:

"SPECIAL PROVISION WITH RESPECT TO DENIAL, TERMINATION, AND SUSPENSION OF GOVERNMENT CONTRACTS

"SEC. 718. No Government contract, or portion thereof, with any employer, shall be denied, withheld, terminated, or suspended, by any agency or officer of the United States under any equal employment opportunity law or order, where such employer has an affirmative action plan which has previously been accepted by the Government for the same facility within the past twelve months without first according such employer full hearing and adjudication under the provisions of title 5, United States Code, section 554, and the following pertinent sections: Provided, That if such employer has deviated substantially from such previously agreed to affirmative action plan, this section shall not apply: Provided further, That for the purposes of this section an affirmative action plan shall be deemed to have been accepted by the Government at the time the appropriate compliance agency has accepted such plan unless within forty-five days thereafter the Office of Federal Contract Compliance has disapproved such plan."

SEC. 14. The amendments made by this Act to section 706 of the Civil Rights Act of 1964 shall be applicable with respect to charges pending with the Commission on the date of enactment of this Act and all charges filed thereafter.

And the Senate agree to the same.

H. A. WILLIAMS,	CARL D. PERKINS,
JENNINGS RANDOLPH,	JOHN H. DENT,
CLAIBORNE PELL,	AUGUSTUS F. HAWKINS,
GAYLORD NELSON,	PATSY T. MINK,
THOMAS F. EAGLETON,	PHILLIP BURTON,
ADLAI E. STEVENSON III,	WM. L. (BILL) CLAY,
HAROLD E. HUGHES,	JOSEPH M. GAYDOS,
JACOB JAVITS,	WILLIAM D. FORD,
RICHARD S. SCHWEIKER,	MARIO BIAGGI,
BOB PACKWOOD,	ROMANO L. MAZZOLI,
ROBERT TAFT, Jr.,	ROMAN C. PUCINSKI,
ROBERT T. STAFFORD,	JOHN BRADEMAS,
Managers on the Part of the Senate.	ALBERT H. QUIE,
	JOHN N. ERLENBORN,
	ALPHONZO BELL,
	MARVIN L. ESCH,
	EARL F. LANDGREBE,
	ORVAL HANSEN,
	WILLIAM A. STEIGER,
	JACK KEMP,
	Managers on the Part of the House.

JOINT EXPLANATORY STATEMENT OF MANAGERS AT THE CONFERENCE ON H.R. 1746 TO FURTHER PROMOTE EQUAL EMPLOYMENT OPPORTUNITIES FOR AMERICAN WORKERS

The managers on the part of the House and Senate at the conference on the disagreeing votes of the two Houses on the amendment of the Senate to the bill (H.R. 1746) an Act to further promote equal employment opportunities for American workers, submit the following joint statement to the House and Senate in explanation of the effect of the action agreed upon by the managers and recommended in the accompanying conference report.

The points in disagreement and the conference resolution of them are as follows:

The House bill provided the short title "Equal Employment Opportunity Act of 1971". The Senate amendment provided the short title "Equal Employment Opportunities Enforcement Act of 1972". The Senate receded with an amendment changing the date in the House provision to 1972.

Under the House bill, there was no provision for an expansion of coverage of Title VII.

The Senate amendment expanded coverage to include:

(1) State and local governments, governmental agencies, political subdivisions (except for elected officials, their personal assistants and immediate advisors) and the District of Columbia departments and agencies (except where such are subject by law to the Federal competitive service). State agencies previously covered by reference to the United States Employment Service continue to be covered; and

(2) employers who employ 15 or more full-time employees and labor organizations with 15 or more members beginning one year after enactment.

In addition, the Senate amendment included a new definition of "religion" to include all aspects of religious observance and practice, as well as belief, unless an employer demonstrates that he is unable to reasonably accommodate to an employee's or prospective employee's religious observance or practice without undue hardship on the conduct of the employer's business.

The House receded with an amendment exempting, in addition to State and local government elected officials, persons chosen by such officials to be on their personal staffs, appointees of such officials on a policymaking level or immediate advisors of such elected officials. The exemption does not include civil service employees.

It is the intention of the conferees to exempt elected officials and members of their personal staffs, and persons appointed by such elected officials as advisors or to policymaking positions at the highest levels of the departments or agencies of State or local governments, such as cabinet officers, and persons with comparable responsibilities at the local level. It is the conferees intent that this exemption shall be construed narrowly. Also, all employees subject to State or local civil service laws are not exempted.

The Senate amendment eliminated the present exemption from Title VII for educational institutions. Also, the Senate provision expanded the exemption for religious organizations from coverage under this title with respect to the employment of individuals of a particular religion in all their activities instead of the present limitation to religious activities. The House bill did not change the existing exemptions. The House receded.

Both the House bill and Senate amendment contained procedures for filing of charges. The Senate amendment provided for charges to be filed by or on behalf of a person claiming to be aggrieved, or by an officer or employee of the Commission upon request of any person claiming to be aggrieved. Charges were to be in writing under oath or affirmation and in the specific form required by the Commission. The Senate amendment further provided that the Commission serve a notice of the charge including the date, place and circumstances of the alleged unlawful employment practice on the respondent within 10 days. Under the Senate amendment, the Commission would dismiss the charge if it determined after investigation that there was not reasonable cause to believe the charge was true and would be required to accord substantial weight to the decision of state and local authorities under state and local equal employment opportunity laws in making such reasonable cause determination. The Senate amendment also required the Commission to make its determination so far as practicable not later than 120 days from the date the Commission was authorized to act on the charge.

The House bill provided for charges to be filed by the person claiming to be aggrieved or by a member of the Commission if he had reasonable cause to believe a violation occurred. The Commissioner's charge had to set forth the facts upon which it was based and the person or persons aggrieved. The House bill also provided that the Commission furnish the respondent with a copy of the charge within five days. Both the House bill and the Senate amendment prohibited disclosure of anything said or done during informal conciliation efforts without the consent of the parties.

The Senate receded with an amendment providing that charges be filed by or on behalf of the person claiming to be aggrieved or by a member of the Commission, alleging that an unlawful employment practice occurred. Charges are to be in writing under oath or affirmation and in such form as the Commission requires. A notice of a charge including the date, place and circumstances of the alleged unlawful employment practice is to be served on the respondent within 10 days. If the Commission determines after investigation that there is not reasonable cause to believe the charge is true, it shall dismiss the charge and notify the parties. The Commission is required to accord substantial weight to the decision of state or local authorities under state or local equal employment opportunity laws and to make the determination on reasonable cause as promptly as possible and so far as practicable not later than 120 days from the date the Commission was authorized to act on the charge. If the Commission determines that there is reasonable cause to believe the charge is true, it shall attempt conciliation in conformity with the requirements of existing law. Nothing said or done during conciliation may be disclosed without the consent of the parties.

The Senate amendment contained two provisions allowing the Commission to defer to state and local equal employment opportunity agencies. It deleted the language of existing law providing that no charge may be filed during the 60-day period allowed for the deferral and substituted a provision prohibiting the Commission from acting on such a charge until the expiration of the 60-day period. The House bill made no change in existing law. The Senate receded with an amendment that would re-state the existing law on the deferral of charges to state agencies. The conferees left existing law intact with the understanding that the decision in *Love* v. *Pullman,* — *U.S.* —— (February 7, 1972) interpreting the existing law to allow the Commission to receive a charge (but not act on it) during such deferral period is controlling.

Both the House bill and the Senate amendment provided that charges be filed within 180 days. The Senate allowed an additional 120 days if a charge is deferred to a state agency and the House allowed only 30 additional days. The Senate amendment required that notice of the charge be served in 10 days. The House bill provided that charges under Title VII are the exclusive remedy for unlawful employment practices. The House receded.

Both the House bill and the Senate amendment authorized the bringing of civil actions in Federal district courts in cases involving unlawful employment practices.

The Senate amendment provided that the Attorney General bring actions against state and local governments. As to other respondents, suits were to be brought by the Commission. The Senate amendment permitted suits by the Commission or the Attorney General if the Commission was unable to secure from the respondent "a conciliation agreement acceptable to the Commission" while the House bill permitted the Commission to sue if it is unable to obtain "voluntary compliance." The Senate amendment permitted aggrieved persons to intervene in suits and allowed a private action if no case is brought by the Commission or Attorney General within 150 days. The House bill permitted a private action after 180 days. The Senate amendment allowed the General Counsel or Attorney General to intervene in private actions; the House bill permitted only the Attorney General to intervene. The Senate amendment permitted a private action in a case where the Commission entered into a conciliation agreement to which the aggrieved person was not a party (i.e. a signatory).

The conferees adopted a provision allowing the Commission, or the Attorney General in a case against a state or local government agency, to bring an action in Federal district courts if the Commission is unable to secure from the respondent "a conciliation agreement acceptable to the Commission." Aggrieved parties are permitted to intervene. They may bring a private action if the Commission or Attorney General has not brought suit within 180 days or the Commission has entered into a conciliation agreement to which such aggrieved party is not a signatory. The Commission, or the Attorney General in a case involving state and local governments, may intervene in such private action.

The Senate amendment provided for the appointment of a three judge district court in cases certified to be of general public importance, provided for the immediate designation of a single judge if no three judge court was requested, and required cases to be assigned for hearing at the earliest practicable date and to be expedited in every way. The House bill contained no such provision. The Senate receded with an amendment which provides that the chief judge of the district in which a case is filed designate the judge to hear the case which is to be assigned for hearing at the earliest practicable date and expedited in every way. The amendment deleted the provision for the three judge district court. Such a court is now provided for in "pattern or practice" cases.

The Senate amendment authorized the Commission or the Attorney General to seek preliminary injunctive relief. The House bill authorized the Commission to seek preliminary relief and required a showing that substantial and irreparable injury to the aggrieved party would be unavoidable. The Senate receded with an amendment that authorizes the Commission or the Attorney General to seek preliminary injunctive relief and a provision that Rule 65 of the Federal Rules of Civil Procedure should govern all actions brought under this subsection.

The Senate amendment restated existing law as to venue for civil actions except that the term "aggrieved person" was substituted for the word "plaintiff." The House bill left existing law intact. The House receded.

The House bill and the Senate amendment provided for the scope of relief that could be granted by the district courts. The differences were as follows:

1. The Senate amendment required a finding that the respondent engaged in an unlawful employment practice and the House bill required a finding that respondent "intentionally" engaged in such unlawful employment practice.

2. The Senate amendment added the phrase "or any other equitable relief that the court deems appropriate" to the description of the relief available from the court.

3. The Senate amendment limited back pay liability to that which accrues from a date not more than two years prior to the filing of a charge with the Commission; the House bill limited back pay liability to that which accrues not more than two years before the filing of a complaint with the court. Both the House bill and the Senate amendment provided that interim earnings shall operate to reduce the back pay otherwise allowable.

4. The House bill restated the provisions of existing law prohibiting court ordered remedies based on any adverse action except unlawful employment practices prohibited under Title VII.

5. The House bill prohibited class action lawsuits.

The Senate receded with an amendment that provides the following:

1. A finding that the respondent has intentionally engaged or is intentionally engaging in an unlawful employment practice, as the language of the current law reads.

2. Authority for the court to enjoin the respondent from such practices, order such affirmative action as may be appropriate and any other equitable relief that the court deems appropriate.

3. The court is authorized to award back pay except that such back pay liability is limited to that which accrues from the date not

more than two years prior to the filing of a charge with the Commission. Interim earnings shall operate to reduce the back pay otherwise allowable.

4. The provisions of existing law prohibiting court ordered remedies based on any adverse action except unlawful employment practices under Title VII are retained.

The Senate amendment permitted payment of costs and counsel fees to small employers or labor organizations if they prevailed in actions brought against them by the Commission or the United States. An employer or union with 25 or fewer employees or members would have been entitled to up to $5000, and an employer or labor organization with from 25 to 100 employees or members whose average income from such employment was less than $7500, would have been entitled to one-half the cost of its defense up to $2500. The House bill had no comparable provisions. The Senate receded.

The Senate amendment authorized the courts to appoint a special master if the district court had not assigned a case for trial within 120 days after issue had been joined. There was no comparable House provision. The House receded.

The Senate amendment provided for a transfer of the Attorney General's "pattern or practice" jurisdiction to the Commission two years after enactment. In the interim period there would be concurrent jurisdiction. The transfer would be subject to change in accordance with a presidential reorganization plan if not vetoed by Congress. The House bill left pattern or practice jurisdiction with the Attorney General. The House receded.

The Senate amendment revised the Commission's procedures for cooperating with State and local agencies and in its record keeping requirements and provided procedures for compelling compliance with such requirements. The House bill did not amend the provisions of the current law. The House receded.

The Senate amendment simplified procedures for subpoenaing witnesses or records by providing the same investigative authority as is contained in the National Labor Relations Act. The House bill made no changes in existing authority. The House receded.

The Senate amendment provided for the appointment, with the advice and consent of the Senate, of up to four new commission members at any time after one year from the effective date of the act. The proportion of commissioners of one political party to another would remain the same. Regional Directors were to be appointed by the Chairman of the Commission with the concurrence of the General Counsel. The Senate amendment also placed a limit on the time that a Commissioner may serve after the appointment expires and the Senate has not acted. The House bill contained no such provisions. The Senate receded with an amendment limiting the time that a Commissioner may serve after the appointment expires and the Senate has not acted.

The Senate amendment established the office of General Counsel to be appointed by the President for a term of four years with the advice and consent of the Senate. The General Counsel was given the responsibility for filing complaints and the conduct of all litigation for the Commission. Also the General Counsel was given authority to appoint regional attorneys, with the concurrence of the Chairman, and other necessary employees. The House bill did not establish a General Counsel, and required that the Attorney General conduct all litigation to which the Commission is a party in the Supreme Court or in the United States Court of Appeals. All other litigation in which the Commission was a party was to be conducted by the Commission. The Senate receded with an amendment establishing the Office of General Counsel to be appointed by the President for a term of four years with the advice and consent of the Senate giving the General Counsel responsibility for litigation and concurrence with the Chairman in the appointment and supervision of regional attorneys but reserving to the Attorney General the conduct of all litigation to which the Commission is a party in the Supreme Court.

The Senate amendment permitted the Commission to accept uncompensated services for the limited purpose of publicizing in the media the Commission and its activities. The House bill did not provide such authority. The Senate receded.

The Senate amendment permitted the Commission to delegate certain functions, except for rulemaking and the power to make agreements with States. The House bill did not contain such a provision. The Senate receded.

The Senate amendment afforded additional protection to officers and employees of the Commission in the performance of their official duties by including them within section 1114 of Title 18, U.S.C. The House bill contained no such provision. The Senate receded with an amendment affording this new protection but excluding capital punishment for offenders.

The Senate amendment raised the level of the position of the Chairman and members of the Commission and established the position of General Counsel in the executive pay scale. The House bill made no provision for such change. The House receded.

The Senate amendment established an Equal Employment Opportunity Coordinating Council. The House bill had no such provision. The House receded.

The Commitee of Conference believes that there are instances in which more than one agency may have legitimate interests in the employment standards applicable to a number of employees. So for example, the merit system standards of the Civil Service Commission should be considered by the Coordinating Council in relation to their effect on the conciliation and enforcement efforts of the Equal Employment Opportunity Commission and the Attorney General with respect to employees of governments, governmental agencies or political subdivisions.

The Senate amendment provided that all personnel actions involving Federal employees be free from discrimination. This policy was to be enforced by the United States Civil Service Commission. Each agency of the Federal Government would be responsible for establishing an internal grievance procedure and programs to train personnel so as to enable them to advance under the supervision of the Civil Service Commission. If final action had been taken by an agency or the Civil Service Commission, an aggrieved party could bring a civil action under the provisions of section 706. The House bill did not cover Federal employees. The House receded. In providing the statutory basis for such appeal or court access, it is not the intent of the

Committee to subordinate any discretionary authority or final judgment now reposed in agency heads by, or under, statute for national security reasons in the interests of the United States.

The Senate amendment required consultation among the Executive branch agencies on Equal Employment matters. The House bill had no similar provision. The Senate receded in light of the action of the Conferees in establishing the Equal Employment Opportunity Coordinating Council.

The Senate amendment provided the Commission with authorization for an additional 10 positions at GS–16, GS–17, and GS–18 level. The House bill had no such provision. The House receded.

The Senate amendment provided that the new enforcement provisions of section 706 apply to charges pending before the Commission on enactment. The House bill was silent. The House receded.

The Senate amendment provided that no Government contract, whether subject to Executive Order 11246 or any other equal employment opportunity law such as section 3 of the Housing and Urban Development Act of 1968, as amended, could be terminated, denied, or withheld without a full hearing, where the employer had an affirmative action plan previously accepted within the past twelve months. The House bill had no such provision. The House receded.

CARL D. PERKINS,
JOHN H. DENT,
AUGUSTUS F. HAWKINS,
PATSY T. MINK,
PHILLIP BURTON,
WM. L. (BILL) CLAY,
JOSEPH M. GAYDOS,
WILLIAM D. FORD,
MARIO BIAGGI,
ROMANO L. MAZZOLI,
ROMAN C. PUCINSKI,
JOHN BRADEMAS,
ALBERT H. QUIE,
JOHN N. ERLENBORN,
ALPHONZO BELL,
MARVIN L. ESCH,
EARL F. LANDGREBE,
ORVAL HANSEN,
WILLIAM A. STEIGER,
JACK KEMP,
Managers on the Part of the House.

H. A. WILLIAMS,
JENNINGS RANDOLPH,
CLAIBORNE PELL,
GAYLORD NELSON,
THOMAS F. EAGLETON,
ADLAI E. STEVENSON III,
HAROLD E. HUGHES,
JACOB JAVITS,
RICHARD S. SCHWEIKER,
BOB PACKWOOD,
ROBERT TAFT, Jr.,
ROBERT T. STAFFORD,
Managers on the Part of the Senate.

Appendix C
Section-by-Section Analysis

Following is full text of an analysis of the Equal Employment Opportunity Act of 1972 as it appeared in the Congressional Record, March 6, 1972.

This analysis explains the major provisions of H.R. 1746, the Equal Employment Opportunity Act of 1972, as agreed to by the Conference Committee of the House and Senate on February 29, 1972. The explanation reflects the enforcement provisions of Title VII, as amended by the procedural and jurisdictional provisions of H.R. 1746, recommended by the Conference Committee.

In any area where the new law does not address itself, or in any areas where a specific contrary intention is not indicated, it was assumed that the present case law as developed by the courts would continue to govern the applicability and construction of Title VII.

SECTION 2

This section amends certain definitions contained in section 701 of the Civil Rights Act of 1964.

Section 701(a)—This subsection defines "person" as used in Title VII. Under the provisions of H.R. 1746, the term is now expanded to include State and local governments, governmental agencies, and political subdivisions.

Section 701(b)—This subsection defines the term "employer" as used in Title VII. This subsection would now include, within the meaning of the term "employer," all State and local governments, governmental agencies, and political subdivisions, and the District of Columbia departments or agencies (except those subject by statute to the procedures of the Federal competitive service as defined in 5 U.S.C. § 2102, who along with all other Federal employees would now be covered by section 717 of the Act.)

This subsection would extend coverage of the term "employer," one year after enactment, to those employers with 15 or more employees. The present standard for determining the number of employees of an employer, i.e., "employees for each working day in each of 20 or more calendar weeks in the current or preceding calendar year," presently applicable to all employers of 25 or more employees would apply to the expanded coverage of employers of 15 or more employees.

Section 701(c)—This subsection eliminates the present language that provides a partial exemption for agencies of the United States, States or the political subdivisions of States from the definition of "employment agency" to reflect the provisions of section 701(a) and (b) above. States agencies, previously covered by reference to the United States Employment Service, continue to be covered as employment agencies under this section.

Section 701(e)—This subsection is revised to include labor organizations with 15 or more members within the coverage of Title VII, one year after enactment.

Section 701(f)—This subsection is intended to exclude from the definition of "Employee" as used in Title VII those persons elected to public office in any State or political subdivision. The exemption extends to persons chosen by such officials to be on their personal staffs, appointees of such officials to be on their personal staff, appointees of such officials on the highest policymaking levels such as cabinet members or other immediate advisors of such elected officials with respect to the exercise of the Constitutional or legal powers of the office held by such elected officer.

The exemption does not include civil service employees. This exemption is intended to be construed very narrowly and is in no way intended to establish an overall narrowing of the expanded coverage of State and local governmental employees as set forth in section 701(a) and (b) above.

Section 701(j)—This s u b s e c t i o n, which is new, defines "religion" to include all aspects of religious observance, practice and belief, so as to require employers to make reasonable accommodations for employees whose "religion" may include observances, practices and beliefs such as sabbath observance, which differ from the employer's or potential employer's requirements regarding standards, schedules, or other business-related employment conditions.

Failure to make such accommodation would be unlawful unless an employer can demonstrate that he cannot reasonably accommodate such beliefs, practices, or observances without undue hardship on the conduct of his business.

The purpose of this subsection is to provide the statutory basis for EEOC to formulate guidelines on discrimination because of religion such as those challenged in Dewey v. Reynolds Metals Company, 429 F.2d 325 (6th Cir. 1970), Affirmed by an equally divided court, 402 U.S. 689 (1971).

SECTION 3

This section amends the exemptions allowed in section 702 of the Civil Rights Act of 1964.

Section 702 — This s e c t i o n is amended to eliminate the exemption for employees of educational institutions. Under the provisions of this section, all private and public educational institutions would be covered under the provisions of Title VII. The special provision relating to religious educational institutions in Section 703(e)(2) is not disturbed.

The limited exemption from coverage in this section for religious corporations, associations, educational institutions or societies has been broadened to allow such entities to employ individuals of a particular re-

ligion in all their activities instead of the present limitation to religious activities. Such organizations remain subject to the provisions of Title VII with regard to race, color, sex or national origin.

SECTION 4

This section establishes the enforcement powers and functions of the EEOC and the Attorney General to aid in the prevention of unlawful employment practices proscribed by Title VII of the Civil Rights Act of 1964.

H.R. 1746 retains the general scheme of the present law which enables the EEOC to process a charge of employment discrimination through the investigation and conciliation stages. In addition, H.R. 1746 now authorizes the EEOC, in cases where the respondent is not a government, governmental agency or political subdivision to file a civil action against the respondent in an appropriate Federal District Court, if it has been unable to eliminate an alleged unlawful employment practice by informal methods of conference, conciliation, and persuasion. The Attorney General is authorized to file civil actions against respondents that are governments, governmental agencies or political subdivisions if the EEOC is unable to achieve a successful conciliation.

Accordingly, section 4 of H.R. 1746, amends section 706(a) through (g) of the present act to accomplish the stated national purpose of achieving equal employment opportunity as follows:

Section 706(a)—This subsection empowers the Commission to prevent persons from engaging in unlawful employment practices under sections 703 and 704 of Title VII of the Civil Rights Act of 1964. The unlawful employment practices encompassed by sections 703 and 704, which were enumerated in 1964 in the original Act, and as defined and expanded by the courts remain in effect.

Section 706(b)—This subsection sets out the procedures to be followed when a charge of an unlawful employment practice is filed with the Commission.

Under present law, a charge may be filed by a person aggrieved under oath or by a member of the Commission. As amended, this subsection now also permits a charge to be filed by or on behalf of a person aggrieved or by a member of the Commission. Among other things, this provision would enable aggrieved persons to have charges processed under circumstances where they are unwilling to come forward publicly for fear of economic or physical reprisals.

Charges (whether by or on behalf of an aggrieved person or a member of the Commission) must be in writing and under oath or affirmation and in such form as the Commission requires.

The Commission is to serve a notice of the charge on the respondent within ten days. It is not intended, however, that failure to give notice of the charge to the respondent within ten days would prejudice the rights of the aggrieved party. The Commission would be expected to investigate the charge as quickly as possible and to make its determination on whether there is reasonable cause to believe that the charge is true. If it finds that there is not reasonable cause to believe that the charge is true, it shall dismiss the charge and notify the complainant and the respondent of its decision.

If the Commission finds reasonable cause, it will attempt to conciliate the case. Nothing said or done during the Commission's informal endeavors may be made public or used as evidence in a subsequent proceeding without the written consent of the parties covered.

The Commission would be required to make its determination on reasonable cause as promptly as possible and, "so far as practicable," within 120 days from the filing of the charge or from the date upon which the Commission is authorized to act on the charge under section 706(c) or (d). The Commission, where appropriate, would be required in making its determination of reasonable cause to accord substantial weight to final findings and orders made by State or local authorities under State and local laws.

This subsection and section 9(a)-(d) of the bill clarifies existing law to carry out the intent of the present statute to provide full coverage for joint labor-management committees controlling apprenticeship or other training or retraining, including on-the-job training programs as reflected in Rios v. Enterprise Assn., Steamfitters Local No. 638, 326 F.Supp. 198 (S.D.N.Y. 1971).

Sections 706(c) and (d)—These subsections, dealing with deferral to appropriate State and local equal employment opportunity agencies, are identical to sections 706(b) and (c) of the Civil Rights Act of 1964. No change in these provisions was deemed necessary in view of the recent Supreme Court decision of Love v. Pullman Co., U.S. , 92 S.Ct. 616 (1972) which approved the present EEOC deferral procedures as fully in compliance with the intent of the Act. That case held that the EEOC may receive and defer a charge to a State agency on behalf of a complainant and begin to process the charge in the EEOC upon lapse of the 60-day deferral period, even though the language provides that no charge can be filed under section 706 (a) by the person aggrieved before the expiration of sixty days after proceedings have been commenced under the State or local law. Similarly, the recent circuit court decision in Vigil v. AT&T, F.2d , 4 FEP cases 345 (10th Cir. 1972), which provided that in order to protect the aggrieved person's right to file with a State or local agency may also be filed with the EEOC during the 60-day deferral period, is within the intent of this Act.

Section 706(e)—This subsection sets forth the time limitations for filing charges with the Commission.

Under the present law, charges must be filed within 90 days after an alleged unlawful employment practice has occurred. In cases where the Commission defers to a State or local agency under the provisions of section 706(c) or (d), the charge must be filed within 30 days after the person aggrieved receives notice that the State or local agency has terminated its proceedings, or within 210 days after the alleged unlawful employment practice occurred, whichever is earlier.

This subsection as amended provides that charges be filed within 180 days of the alleged unlawful employment practice. Court decisions under the present law have shown an inclination to interpret this time limitation so as to give the aggrieved person the maximum benefit of the law; it is not intended that such court decisions should be in any way circumscribed by the extension of the time limitations in this subsection. Existing case law which has determined that certain types of violations are continuing in nature, thereby measuring the running of the required time period from the last occurrence of the discrimination and not from the first occurrence is continued, and other interpretations of the courts maximizing the coverage of the law are not affected. It is intended by expanding the time period for filing charges in this subsection that aggrieved individuals, who frequently are untrained laymen and who are not always aware of the discrimination which is practiced against them, should be given a greater opportunity to prepare their charges and file their complaints and that existant but undiscovered acts of discrimination should not escape the effect of the law through a procedural oversight. Moreover, wide latitude should be given individuals in such cases to avoid any prejudice to their rights as a result of government inadvertence, delay or error.

The time period for filing a charge where deferral is required to a State or local antidiscrimination agency has been extended to 300 days after the alleged unlawful employment practice occurred or to 30 days after the State or local agency has terminated proceedings under the State or local law, whichever is earlier. This subsection also restates the provision of Section 706(b) requiring a notice of the charge to the respondent within ten days after its having been filed.

Section 706(f) — This subsection, which is new, sets forth the enforcement procedures which may be followed in those cases where the Commission has been unable to achieve voluntary compliance with the provisions of the Act.

Section 706(f)(1)—Under this subsection, if the respondent is not a government, governmental agency, or political subdivision and if the Commission is unable to secure a conciliation agreement that is acceptable to the Commission within 30 days from the filing of the charge or within 30 days after subsection (c) or (d) it may thereafter bring a civil action against the respondent in an appropriate district court. In cases involving a government, governmental agency, or political subdivision, the Commission will not bring the case before a Federal District Court. After the Commission has had an opportunity to complete its investigation, and to attempt conciliation, the Commission shall then refer the case to the Attorney General who may bring the case to court. The aggrieved party is permitted to intervene in any case brought by the Commission or the Attorney General under this subsection.

With respect to cases arising under this subsection, if the Commission: (a) has dismissed the charge, or (b) 180 days have elapsed from the filing of the charge without the Commission, or the Attorney General, as the case may be, having filed a complaint under section 706(f), or without the Commission having entered into a conciliation agreement to which the person aggrieved is a party (i.e. a signatory) the person aggrieved may bring an action in an appropriate district court within 90 days after receiving notification. The retention of the private right of action, as amended, is intended to make clear that an individual aggrieved by a violation of Title VII should not be forced to abandon the claim merely because of a decision by the Commission or the Attorney General as the case may be, that there are insufficient grounds for the Government to file a complaint. Moreover, it is designed to make sure that the person aggrieved does not have to endure lengthy delays if the Commission or Attorney General does not act with due diligence and speed. Accordingly, the provisions described above allow the person aggrieved to elect to pursue his or her own remedy under this title in the courts where there is agency inaction, dalliance or dismissal of the charge, or unsatisfactory resolution.

It is hoped that recourse to the private lawsuit will be the exception and not the rule, and that the vast majority of complaints will be handled through the offices of the EEOC or the Attorney General, as appropriate. However, as the individual's rights to redress are paramount under the provisions of Title VII it is necessary that all avenues be left open for quick and effective relief.

In any civil action brought by an aggrieved person, or in the case of a charge filed by a member of the Commission, by any person whom the charge alleges was aggrieved, the court may upon timely application of the complainant, appoint an attorney and authorize the commencement of the action without the payment of fees, costs, or security in such circumstances as it deems just. The Commission, or the Attorney General in case involving a governmental entity, upon timely application and subject to the court's discretion, may intervene in such a private action if it is certified that the private action is of general public importance. In addition, the court is given discretion to stay proceedings for not more than 60 days pending the termination of State or local proceedings or efforts by the Commission to obtain voluntary compliance.

In establishing the enforcement provisions under this subsection and subsection 706(f) generally, it is not intended that any of the provisions contained therein shall affect the present use of class action lawsuits under Title VII in conjunction with Rule 23 of the Federal Rules of Civil Procedure. The courts have been particularly cognizant of the fact that claims under Title VII involve the vindication of a major public interest, and that any action under the Act involves considerations beyond those raised by the individual claimant. As a consequence, the leading cases in this area to date have recognized that many Title VII claims are necessarily class action complaints and that, accordingly, it is not necessary that each individual entitled to relief be named in the original charge or in the claim for relief. A provision limiting class actions was contained in the House bill and specifically rejected by the Conference Committee.

Section 706(f)(2)—This subsection authorizes the Commission or the Attorney General, in a case involving a government, a governmental agency or political subdivision, based upon a preliminary investigation of a charge filed, to bring an action for appropriate temporary or preliminary relief, pending the final disposition of the charge. Such actions are to be assigned for hearing at the earliest possible date and expedited in every way. The provisions of Rule 65 of the Federal Rules of Civil Procedure shall apply to actions brought under this subsection.

The importance of preliminary relief in actions involving violations of Title VII is central to ensuring that persons aggrieved under this title are adequately protected and that the provisions of this Act are being followed. Where violations become apparent and prompt judicial action is necessary to insure these provisions, the Commission or the Attorney General, as the case may be, should not hesitate to invoke the provisions of this subsection.

Section 706(f)(3)—This subsection, which is similar to the present section 706(f) of the Act, grants the district courts jurisdiction over actions brought by the EEOC, the Attorney General or aggrieved persons under this title and provides the venue requirements. Such jurisdiction includes the power to grant such temporary or preliminary relief as the court deems just and proper.

Section 706(f)(4) and (5)—Under these paragraphs, the chief judge is required to designate a district judge to hear the case. If no judge is available, then the chief judge of the circuit assigns the judge. Cases are to be heard at the earliest practicable date and expedited in every way. If the judge has not scheduled the case for trial within 120 days after issue has been joined he may appoint a master to hear the case under Rule 53 of the Federal Rules of Civil Procedure. The purpose of this provision is to relax the very strongest requirements of Rule 53 which preclude appointment of a master except in extremely unusual cases.

Section 706(g)—This subsection is similar to the present section 706(g) of the Act. It authorizes the court, upon a finding that the respondent has engaged in or is engaging in an unlawful employment practice, to enjoin the respondent from such unlawful conduct and order such affirmative relief as may be appropriate including, but not limited to, reinstatement or hiring, with or without back pay, as will effectuate the policies of the Act. Backpay is limited to that which accrues from a date not more than two years prior to the filing of a charge with the Commission. Interim earnings or amounts earnable with reasonable diligence by the aggrieved person(s) would operate to reduce the backpay otherwise allowable.

The provisions of this subsection are intended to give the courts wide discretion exercising their equitable powers to fashion the most complete relief possible. In dealing with the present section 706(g) the courts have stressed that the scope of relief under that section of the Act is intended to make the victims of unlawful discrimination whole, and that the attainment of this objective rests not only upon the elimination of the particular unlawful employment practice complained of, but also requires that persons aggrieved by the consequences

and effects of the unlawful employment practice be, so far as possible, restored to a position where they would have been were it not for the unlawful discrimination.

SECTION 5

This section amends section 707, concerning the Attorney General's "pattern or practice" authority to provide for a transfer of the "pattern or practice" jurisdiction to the Commission two years after the enactment of the bill. The bill further provides the Commission with concurrent jurisdiction in this area from the date of enactment until the transfer is complete. The transfer is subject to change in accordance with a Presidential reorganization plan if not vetoed by Congress. The section would provide that currently pending proceedings would continue without abatement, that all court orders and decrees remain in effect, and that upon the transfer the Commission would be substituted as a party for the United States of America or the Attorney General as appropriate.

Under the provisions of this section, the Commission's present powers to investigate charges of discrimination remain. In addition, it now has jurisdiction to initiate court action to correct any pattern or practice violations.

SECTION 6

This section amends section 709 of the Civil Rights Act of 1964, entitled "Investigations, Inspections, Records, State Agencies."

Section 709(a)—This subsection, which gives the Commission the right to examine and copy documents in connection with its investigation of a charge, would remain unchanged.

Section 709(b)—This subsection would authorize the Commission to corporate with State and local fair employment practice agencies in order to carry out the purposes of the title, and to enter into agreements with such agencies under which the Commission would refrain from processing certain types of charges or relieve persons from the record keeping requirements. This subsection would make two changes in the present statute. Under this subsection, the Commission could, within the limitations of funds appropriated for the purpose, also engaged in and contribute to the cost of research and other projects undertaken by these State and local agencies and pay these agencies in advance for services rendered to the Commission. The subsection also deletes the reference to private civil actions under section 706(e) of the present statute.

Section 709(c)—This subsection, like the present statute, would require employers, employment agencies, labor organizations, and joint labor-management apprenticeship committees subject to the title to make and keep certain records and to make reports to the Commission. Under the present statute, a party required to keep records could seek an exemption from these requirements on the ground of undue hardship either by applying to the Commission or bringing a civil action in the district court. This subsection would require the party seeking the exemption first to make an application to the Commission and only if the Commission denies the request could the party bring an action in the disctrit court. This subsection would also authorize the Commission to apply for a court order compelling compliance with the record keeping and reporting obligations set forth in the subsection.

Section 709(d)—This subsection would eliminate the present exemption from record keeping requirements for those employers in States and political subdivisions with equal employment opportunity laws or for employers subject to Federal executive order or agency record keeping requirements. Under this subsection, the Commission would consult with interested State and other Federal agencies in order to coordinate the Federal record keeping requirement under section 709(c) with those adopted by such agencies. The subsection further provides that the Commission

furnish to such agencies information pertaining to State and local fair employment agencies, on condition that the information would not be made public prior to the institution of State or local proceedings.

SECTION 7

This section amends section 710 of the Civil Rights Act of 1964 by deleting the present section 710 and substituting therefor and to the extent appropriate the provisions of section 11 of the National Labor Relations Act (29 U.S.C. § 161). By making this substitution, the Commission's present demand power with respect to witnesses and evidence is repealed, and the power to subpoena witnesses and evidence, and to allow any of its designated agents, agencies or members to issue such subpoenas, as necessary for the conduct of any investigation, and to take testimony under oath is substituted.

SECTIONS 8 (a) and (b)

These subsections would amend sections 703(a) and 703(c)(2) of the present statute to make it clear that discrimination against applicants for employment and applicants for membership in labor organizations is an unlawful employment practice. This subsection is merely declaratory of present laws as contained in the decisions in Phillips v. Martin-Marietta Corp., 400 U.S. 542 (1971); U.S. v. Sheet Metal Workers International Assn., Local 36, 416 F.2d 123 (8th Cir. 1969); Asbestos Workers, Local 53 v. Vogler, 407 F.2d 1047 (5th Cir. 1969).

SECTIONS 8(c)(1) and (2)

These subsections would amend section 704(a) and (b) of the present statute to make clear that joint labor-management apprenticeship committees are covered by those provisions which relate to discriminatory advertising and retaliation against individuals participating in Commission proceedings.

SECTION 8(d)

This subsection would amend section 705(a) of the present statute to permit a member of the Commission to serve until his successor is appointed but not for more than 60 days when Congress is in session unless the successor has been nominated and the nomination submitted to the Senate, or after the adjournment sine die of the session of the Senate in which such nomination was submitted.

The rest of the subsection provides that the Chairman of the Commission on behalf of the Commission, would be responsible, except as provided in section 705(b), for the administrative operations of the Commission and for the appointment of such officers, agents, attorneys, hearing examiners, and other employees of the Commission, in accordance with Federal law, as he deems necessary.

SECTION 8(e)

This subsection would provide a new section 705(b) of the Act which establishes a General Counsel appointed by the President, with the advice and consent of the Senate for a four (4) year term. The responsibilities of the General Counsel would include, in addition to those the Commission may prescribe and as provided by law, the conduct of all litigation as provided in sections 706 and 707 of the Act. The concurrence of the General Counsel with the Chairman is required, on the reappointment and supervision of regional attorneys.

This subsection would also continue the General Counsel on the effective date of the Act in that position until a successor has been appointed and qualified.

The Commission's attorneys may at the Commission's direction appear for and represent the Commission in any case in court, except that the Attorney General shall conduct all litigation to which the Commission is a party to in the Supreme Court pursuant to this title.

SECTION 8(f)

This subsection would eliminate the provision in present section 705(g) authorizing the Commission to request the Attorney General to intervene in private civil actions. Instead, this subsection permits the Commission itself to intervene in such civil actions as provided in section 706. Where the respondent is a government, governmental agency or political subdivision, the Attorney General should be authorized to seek intervention.

SECTION 8(g)

This section amends section 714 of Title VII of the Civil Rights Act of 1964 by making the provisions of sections 111 and 1114 of Title 18, United States Code, applicable to officers, agents and employees of the Commission in performance of their official duties. This section also specifically prohibits the imposition of the death penalty on any person who might be convicted of killing an officer, agent or employee of the Commission while on his official duties.

SECTION 9(a), (b), (c), and (d)

These subsections would raise the executive level of the Chairman of the Commission (from Level 4 to level 3) and the members of the Commission (from Level 5 to Level 4) and include the General Counsel (Level 5) in the executive pay scale, so as to place them in a position of parity with officials in comparable positions in agencies having substantially equivalent powers such as the National Labor Relations Board, the Federal Trade Commission and the Federal Power Commission.

SECTION 10

Section 715—This section, which is new, establishes an Equal Employment Opportunity Coordinating Council composed of the Secretary of Labor, the Chairman of the Equal Employment Opportunity Commission, the Attorney General, the Chairman of the United States Civil Service Commission and the Chairman of the United States Civil Rights Commission or their respective designees. The Council will have the responsibility to co-ordinate the activities of all the various branches of government with responsibility for equal employment opportunity. The Council will submit an annual report to the President and Congress including a summary of its activities and recommendations as to legislative or administrative changes which it considers desirable.

SECTION 11

Section 717(a)—This subsection provides that all personnel actions of the U.S. Government affecting employees or applicants for employment shall be free from discrimination based on race, color, religion, sex or national origin. Included within this coverage are executive agencies, the United States Postal Service, the Postal Rate Commission, certain departments of the District of Columbia Government, the General Accounting Office, Government Printing Office and the Library of Congress.

Section 717(b)—Under this subsection, the Civil Service Commission is given the authority to enforce the provisions of subsection (a), except with respect to Library of Congress employees. The Civil Service Commission would be authorized to grant appropriate remedies which may include, but are not limited to, back pay for aggrieved applicants or employees. Any remedy needed to fully recompense the employee for his loss, both financial and professional, is considered appropriate under this subsection. The Civil Service Commission is also granted authority to issue rules and regulations necessary to carry out its responsibilities under this section. The Civil Service Commission shall also annually review national and regional equal employment opportunity plans and be responsible for review and evaluation of all agency equal employment opportunity programs. Agency and executive department heads and officers of the District of Columbia shall comply with such rules and regulations, submit an annual equal employment opportunity plan

and notify any employee or applicant of any final action taken on any complaint of discrimination filed.

Section 717(c) and (d)—The provisions of sections 706(f) through (k), concerning private civil actions by aggrieved persons, are made applicable to aggrieved Federal employees or applicants for employment. Such persons would be permitted to file a civil action within 30 days of notice of final action by an agency or by the Civil Service Commission or an appeal from the agency's decision or after 180 days from the filing of an initial charge with the agency, or the Civil Service Commission.

Section 717(e)—This subsection provides that nothing in this Act relieves any Government agency or official of his or its existing equal employment opportunity obligations under the Constitution, other statutes, or under any Executive Order relating to equal employment opportunity in the Federal Government.

SECTION 12

This section allows the Chairman of the Commission to establish ten additional positions at the GS-16, GS-17 and GS-18 levels, as needed to carry out the purposes of this Act.

SECTION 13

A new Section 718 is added which provides that no government contract, or portion thereof, can be denied, withheld, terminated, or superseded by a government agency under Executive Order 11246 or any other order of law without according the respective employer a full hearing and adjudication pursuant to 5 U.S.C. § 554 et. seq where such employer has an affirmative action program for the same facility which had been accepted by the Government within the previous twelve months. Such plan shall be deemed to be accepted by the Government if the appropriate compliance agency has accepted such plan and the Office of Federal Contract Compliance has not disapproved of such plan within 45 days. However, an employer who substantially deviates from any such previously accepted plan is excluded from the protection afforded by this section.

SECTION 14

This section provides that the amended provisions of section 706 would apply to charges filed with the Commission prior to the effective date of this Act.

Tabular Analysis of Changes in Title VII

The following tables were produced by the law firm of Kothe and Eagleton, Inc., Suite 2-4, Philtower Building, Tulsa, Oklahoma, 74103. They are reproduced in this volume with the permission of the firm.

Provisions of 1964 Act	Changes Made by 1972 Act	Comments
Sec. 701	Section 2	
	Sec. 701	
(a) The term "person" includes one or more individuals, labor unions, partnerships, associations, corporations, legal representatives, mutual companies, joint stock companies, trusts, unincorporated organizations, trustees in bankruptcy or receivers.	(a) Same as in 1964 Act, but expanded to include governments, governmental agencies, and political subdivisions.	"Governments" mean state and local governments. The Federal Government is not included in this part of the Act, but is separately covered by Section 11 of this Act, which adds a new Sec. 717 to the 1964 Civil Rights Act.
(b) The term "employer" means a person engaged in an industry affecting commerce who has 25 or more employees for each working day in each of 20 calendar weeks in the current or preceding calendar year, and any agent of such person, but such term does not include: (1) United States (2) Corporations wholly owned by U.S. Government	(b) "Employer" now includes all state and local governments, governmental agencies, and political subdivisions. Does not include departments or agencies of the District of Columbia who are subject to competitive service under 5 U.S.C. §2102. One year after the effective date of this Act, an "employer" will be a person who employs 15 or more employees.	The change to 15 employees in one year is a definitional change only. All of this section will continue to apply except the numerical term, which will change from 25 to 15, effective March 24, 1973. The new Act amends and supplements the 1964 Civil Rights Act. All sections which are not changed by this Act are intended to continue in full force and effect. In addition, in all areas where a specific contrary intention is not indicated, it is assumed that the present

Provisions of 1964 Act	Changes Made by 1972 Act	Comments
	Section 2	case law developed by the courts will continue to govern the applicability and construction of Title VII.
Sec. 701	Sec. 701	
(3) Indian tribe		
(4) State or political subdivision thereof		
(5) Bona fide private membership clubs (other than labor unions) which are tax-exempt under Sec. 501(c) of I.R.C. of 1954.		Amended so as to reflect the changes made in Sec. 701(a) and (b).
(c) "Employment agency" means any person regularly undertaking with or without compensation, to procure employees for an employer or to procure for employees opportunities to work for an employer. Also includes agents of such person. Includes U.S. Employment Service, and those state and local employment services getting Federal aid. Excludes agencies of U.S. states or political subdivisions thereof.	(c) The term "employment agency" means any person regularly undertaking, with or without compensation, to procure for employees opportunities to work for an employer and includes an agent of such a person.	
(e) A labor organization shall be deemed to be engaged in an industry affecting commerce if it has 25 or more members, and satisfies the other requirements of this subsection.	(e) Effective one year after enactment, a labor organization which has 15 or more members, and meets other requirements of this subsection, will be deemed to be engaged in an industry affecting commerce.	
(f) The term "employee" means an individual employed by an employer.	(f) Excludes from term "employee" the following people:	This provision is to be narrowly construed, and does not include any employees subject

(j) No similar provision in 1964 Act.

Sec. 702

Exempts the following persons from effects of this Title:

(1) Employer employing aliens outside any state;
(2) Religious association employing those of a particular religion to carry on its religious activities;
(3) Educational institutions employing individuals to perform education-connected activities.

---

to the civil service laws of any state or political subdivision.

(1) Persons elected to public office in any state or political subdivision;
(2) Personal staff of such elected official;
(3) Appointees of such elected official who are on the policy-making level;
(4) Intermediate advisors of such elected official who advise on exercise of the constitutional or legal powers of the office.

(j) The term "religion" includes all aspects of religious observance and practice, as well as belief, unless an employer demonstrates that he is unable to reasonably accommodate to an employee's or prospective employee's religious observance or practice without undue hardship on the conduct of the employer's business.

Section 3

Sec. 702

Exempts the following persons from the effects of this Title:

(1) Employer employing aliens outside any state;
(2) Religious corporation, association, educational institution or society with respect to employing those of a particular religion to perform work connected with the carrying on of its activities.

Purpose of this provision was to create statutory basis for EEOC to make guidelines on religion-based discrimination, thus resolving questions such as those raised in *Dewey v. Reynolds Metal Co.,* U.S. SupCt, 1971, 402 U.S. 689, 3 FEP Cases 508.

Note that religious educational institutions are the only educational institutions still exempt from charges of religion-based discrimination. Remember that religious organizations are subject to provisions of Title VII as to discrimination on other than religious bases, but may now discriminate on a religious basis in *all* their activities, not just religious activities.

Provisions of 1964 Act	Changes Made by 1972 Act	Comments
Sec. 703	**Section 8** **Sec. 703**	
(a)(2) Unlawful employment practice to limit, segregate or classify employees so as to adversely affect employment opportunities.	(a)(2) Amended to state that it is unlawful to limit, segregate or classify employees or *applicants for employment*	This new phrase is merely declarative of present case law. (See *Phillips* v. *Martin-Marietta Corp.*, U.S. SupCt, 1971, 400 U.S. 542, 3 FEP Cases 40.)
(c)(2) Unlawful employment practice for a labor organization to limit, segregate or classify membership so as to adversely affect employment opportunities.	(c)(2) Unlawful employment practice to limit, segregate or classify membership or *applicants for membership*	This new phrase is declarative of present case law. (See *Asbestos Workers, Local 53* v. *Vogler*, CA5, 1969, 407 F.2d 1047, 1 FEP Cases 577.)
Sec. 704	**Sec. 704**	
(a) Unlawful employment practice to discriminate against those enforcing their rights under this title. Applies to employees, employment agencies and labor organizations.	(c)(1) Now applies to joint labor-management committees controlling apprenticeship or other training or retraining programs, as well as to those persons covered by 1964 Act.	
(b) Employer, labor organizations or employment agency may not advertise or cause to be advertised any ad related to employment which indicates a preference based on race, color, religion, sex or national origin, except where such preference is a bona fide occupational qualification.	(c)(2) Employer, labor organization, employment agency or *joint labor management committee controlling apprenticeship or other training or retraining*, may not advertise. . . .	

	Section 8(d)
Sec. 705	Sec. 705
(a) Provides for the make-up of the five-member Equal Employment Opportunity Commission.	Amends (a) to permit a member of the Commission to serve until his successor is appointed, but may serve no longer than:
	(1) Sixty days when Congress is in session, unless a nomination to fill such vacancy has been submitted to the Senate; or
	(2) After adjournment sine die of session of the Senate in which such nomination was submitted.
	Provides also that the Chairman of EEOC is responsible for administration and the appointment of officers, agents, attorneys, etc., in accordance with Federal law, except as provided in Sec. 705(b).
	Section 8(e)
(b) Quorum provisions for exercising powers of Commission.	Sec. 705
	(b) This provision is renumbered in the new Act, and is now 705(c).
No similar provision to new subsection (b) in the 1964 Act.	Sec. 705
	The new subsection (b) provides for:
	(1) Appointment of a General Counsel by the President, with Senate confirmation, for four-year term. General Counsel will be responsible for conducting litigation under Sec. 706 and 707 of this Act, and shall concur with the Chairman of the Commis-

Provisions of 1964 Act	Changes Made by 1972 Act	Comments
Sec. 705	Section 8(e)	
(g)(6) Provides for referral to Attorney General with recommendations for intervention in civil actions brought under Sec. 706, or recommending institution of actions under Sec. 707.	Sec. 705 sion in the appointment of regional attorneys. (2) Representation by the Commission's attorneys in all cases to which the Commission is a party, except that Attorney General shall conduct all litigation to which the EEOC is a party in the Supreme Court. Section 8(f) Sec. 705 (g)(6) EEOC is now empowered to intervene itself in all civil actions except those against a government, government agency or political subdivision.	
Sec. 706	Section 4	Section 14 of the new Act provides that the amended provisions of Sec. 706 will apply to charges filed prior to the effective date of this Act.
(a) Procedure to be followed in filing and processing charges. No similar provision to the new subsection (a) in the 1964 Act.	Sec. 706 (a) Procedure now appears in § 706(b). The new subsection (a) empowers the EEOC to prevent any person from engaging in any unlawful employment practice described in Sec. 703 or 704 of this title.	

(b) Procedure (through conciliation)

(1) Charge made by aggrieved party in writing and under oath or by a written charge filed by a member of the Commission which states facts upon which the Commission finds reasonable cause to believe a violation has occurred.

(2) Commission shall furnish respondent in the charge a *copy* of this charge, then make a non-public investigation as to reasonable cause.

(Note: No time period for notification of the charge.)

(3) No similar provision in the 1964 Act.

(4) Provisions relating to conciliation, non-disclosure of such proceedings by EEOC, and penalties for disclosure.

(5) No similar provision in 1964 Act.

(b) Procedure (through conciliation):

(1) Charge may be filed by or on behalf of an aggrieved person or by the EEOC. *All* charges must be in writing, under oath or affirmation, contain such information as the EEOC requires, and be in such form as the EEOC establishes.

(2) Commission shall serve a *notice* of the charge (stating date, place, and circumstances of the alleged violation) upon the respondent within 10 days after filing of the charge, then make a non-public investigation as to reasonable cause.

(3) Determination as to reasonable cause should be made, so far as is practicable, within 120 days after filing of the charge or 120 days after the EEOC is authorized to act on the charge under subsection (c) and (d) of this section.

(4) These provisions remain unchanged by the new Act.

(5) Where the Commission finds no reasonable cause to believe the charge is true, it shall dismiss the charge, notifying the complainant and respondent of its decision.

The provision for filing charges on behalf of an aggrieved party is hoped to facilitate filing of charges where there is fear of economic or physical reprisals.

Failure to give notice of the charge within 10 days is not intended to prejudice the rights of the aggrieved party. Where there have been prior state or local proceedings involving the charge, the EEOC shall give weight to their findings in determining probable cause.

Provisions of 1964 Act	Changes Made by 1972 Act	Comments
Sec. 706	Section 4	No change was deemed necessary in subsections (b) and (c) of the 1964 Act in light of *Love* v. *Pullman Co.*, U.S. SupCt, 1972, 404 U.S. 522, 4 FEP Cases 150 (approving present EEOC deferral procedures), and *Vigil* v. *AT&T*, CA10, 1972, 455 F.2d 1222, 4 FEP Cases 345, which approved the filing of a complaint with the EEOC during the 60-day deferral period after filing with state or local agencies.
(b) Procedure by EEOC on *charges filed by aggrieved person* where there is a state or local law authorizing an agency of such state or local government to seek or grant relief for unlawful employment practices.	Sec. 706	
	(c) Subsection (b) of 1964 Act was renumbered (c) in the new Act, but was otherwise unchanged.	
(c) Procedure by EEOC on *charges filed by a member of the Commission* where there is a state or local law authorizing an agency of such state or local government to seek or grant relief for unlawful employment practices.	(d) Subsection (c) of the 1964 Act was renumbered (d) in the 1972 Act, but was otherwise unchanged.	(Note: No provision is expressly made for deferral by EEOC on charges filed *on behalf of* an aggrieved person.)
(d) Charges must be filed with the EEOC within 90 days after the alleged violation occurred, except that those charges filed by an aggrieved person with a state or local agency under subsection (b) must be filed with the EEOC within 30 days after notice of termination or 210 days after the alleged violation, whichever is earlier.	(e) Subsection (d) of the 1964 Act is renumbered (e) in the 1972 Act. Charges must be filed with the EEOC within *180* days after the alleged violation occurred, except that those charges filed by an aggrieved person with a state or local agency (under subsection (c)) must be filed with the EEOC within 30 days after notice of termination or 210 days after the alleged violation, whichever is earlier.	These time limitations will continue to be liberally construed, in accordance with present case law.

(f) Enforcement procedures where no voluntary compliance.

Provisions of this subsection relating to jurisdiction and venue are found in subsection f(3) of Sec. 706.

(f) Enforcement Procedures Where No Voluntary Compliance.

(1)(a) When An Action May Be Brought By U.S. Govt.

(1) Where the respondent is *not* a government, govt. agency, or political subdivision, and no conciliation agreement acceptable to the EEOC has been secured within 30 days after the charge, the EEOC may file a civil action against the respondent in an appropriate district court.

(2) Where the respondent is a government, govt. agency, or political subdivision and the EEOC has obtained no acceptable conciliation agreement, such charge shall be referred to the Attorney General, who may then bring an action in the appropriate district court.

(f)(1)(a) When An Action May Be Brought By U.S. Govt.

(3) The aggrieved party may intervene in cases brought by the EEOC or the Attorney General.

It is not intended that any provision of Sec. 706(f) shall affect the present use of class actions under Title VII. A provision limiting class actions was expressly rejected by the Conference Committee.

Provisions of 1964 Act	Changes Made by 1972 Act	Comments
Sec. 706	Sec. 706	
(e) Where the EEOC notifies complainant that it has been unable to obtain voluntary compliance, the complainant may bring a civil action against respondent within 30 days after such notice. The Court may, at its discretion, appoint an attorney, excuse payment of fees and costs, etc., for the complainant, and may allow the Attorney General to intervene where the case is certified to be of general public importance. May stay proceedings for up to 60 days pending termination of related state or local proceedings or further EEOC efforts for voluntary compliance.	(f)(1)(b) Section 4 When An Action May Be Brought By Aggrieved Party. (1) The aggrieved party may bring a civil action in the appropriate district court within 90 days after notice that the EEOC has discharged the complaint; or, (2) Where 180 days have elapsed since the EEOC could act on the charge without a civil action being filed by the EEOC (or, in appropriate cases, the Attorney General) and a conciliation agreement to which the aggrieved is a signatory has not been obtained, the aggrieved may file a civil action within 90 days thereafter in appropriate district court. (3) In actions brought privately by an aggrieved, the court may, upon application of the Complainant, appoint an attorney for complainant, and excuse payment of fees, costs or security.	May be brought by anyone named as an aggrieved in the charge, no matter whether the charge made by an individual, on his behalf, or by the Commission.
(See related section 706(e) of 1964 Act.)		

(4) Upon timely application, the court may allow the EEOC (or Attorney General, in appropriate cases) to intervene in such private action upon certification that the case is of general public importance.

(5) Upon request, the court may, in its discretion, stay proceedings for up to 60 days pending termination of local proceedings under subsections (c) or (d) of this section, or further efforts by the EEOC to obtain voluntary compliance.

The Congressional intent regarding this section appears to be that it should be liberally construed, enabling the Commission or Attorney General to seek such preliminary relief as they deem proper under the circumstances.

No similar provision to Sec. 706(f)(2) in 1964 Act.

(f)(2) Where the Commission or, in an appropriate case, the Attorney General, finds in their preliminary investigation that there is a violation, they may bring an action for temporary relief where necessary to adequately protect the aggrieved party pending final disposition of the case. Such actions are to be expedited in every way, subject to Rule 65 of Fed. Rules of Civil Procedure.

(f)(3) Identical to subsection (f) of the 1964 Act.

(f)(4) Chief judge of the district is required to immediately designate a judge of

---

(f) Empowers U.S. district courts with jurisdiction to hear actions brought under this Title, and to grant such preliminary relief as they see fit. Also sets up venue provisions.

(f)(4) and (f)(5) No similar provisions in 1964 Act.

Provisions of 1964 Act	Changes Made by 1972 Act	Comments
Sec. 706	**Section 4** Sec. 706 the district to hear actions brought under this section. Where no judge available, the chief judge of the district will certify this to the chief judge of the circuit, who shall assign a district or circuit judge to hear the case.	
	(f)(5) Cases brought under this Act are to be expedited in every possible way. Where a judge has not scheduled a case for trial within 120 days after issue has been joined, he may appoint a master to hear the case pursuant to Rule 53 of Federal Rules of Civil Procedure.	The provision for appointment of a master is intended to relax Rule 53, which has precluded appointment of a master except in unusual cases.
(g) Authorizes court, upon finding violation of the Act, to: (1) Enjoin unlawful conduct, (2) Give appropriate affirmative relief, such as reinstatement, back pay, etc. Interim earnings or amounts earnable with reasonable diligence operate to reduce back pay allowable.	(g) Same as present section, except that back pay recoverable is limited to that accruing from a date not more than two years prior to the filing of a charge with the Commission.	Courts are to be allowed wide discretion in exercise of equitable powers in order to effectuate complete relief for the aggrieved party.
Sec. 707 (a) and (b) This section authorizes the Attorney General to seek injunctions, re-	**Section 5** Sec. 707 Subsections (a) and (b) of the 1964 Act are unchanged by the 1972 Act. To this section,	

straining orders or other relief where he believes that any person or group is engaged in a pattern or practice of discrimination prohibited by this Title. This section gives district courts, or, in appropriate cases, three-judge courts, jurisdiction to hear such actions and grant the necessary relief.

however, the following subsections were added.

(c) Two years after the date of enactment of this Act, the EEOC will assume the Attorney General's functions under this section.

(d) Upon transfer of functions, the EEOC will be substituted as a party in all actions brought under this section, and all proceedings will continue without abatement.

(e) Upon passage of this Act, the EEOC will exercise concurrent jurisdiction with the Attorney General in charges of a pattern or practice of discrimination.

Title of this section is *"Investigations, Inspections, Records, State Agencies."*

Section 6

Sec. 709

(a) Investigative powers of EEOC.

(b) Cooperation with, and reimbursement of, state agencies.

(c) Keeping of records; remedies in cases of undue hardship.

(d) Exemptions from record-keeping requirements of subsection (c).

Sec. 709

(a) No change.

(b) No change.

(c) Same as in 1964 Act, with added provision that, where employer fails or refuses to keep such records as are required, the EEOC (or Attorney General, where state or political subdivision) may bring an action in the district court where such person is found, resides or transacts business, and such district court shall have jurisdiction to order compliance.

(d) Completely rewritten. Provides that EEOC shall endeavor to coordinate it's

Provisions of 1964 Act	Changes Made by 1972 Act	Comments
Sec. 709	Section 6	
	Sec. 709	
	record-keeping requirements with those of other state and Federal agencies. The Commission shall furnish to any state or local agency, without charge, such information as it has obtained, pursuant to subsection (c), about any persons over which such agency has jurisdiction. This information is furnished on the condition that it remain confidential until such time as the agency institutes proceedings involving such information. The Commission may refuse to furnish further information to an agency breaching this confidentiality.	
(e) Sanctions for disclosure by EEOC employees of information obtained under this section.	(e) Sanctions remain the same.	
Sec. 710	Section 7	
Investigatory powers of the EEOC.	Sec. 710	
	Repealed former section.	
	New provision empowers Commission to conduct all hearings and investigations under Sec. 11 of the National Labor Relations Act (49 Stat. 455, 29 U.S.C. 161). Thus, now have power to issue subpoenas for witnesses and evidence, and to take testimony under oath.	

Section 8(g)

Sec. 714

The provisions of Sec. 111, Title 18, U.S.C. shall apply to officers, agents and employees of the Commission in the performance of their official duties.

Sec. 714

Amends this section so that both Sec. 111 and Sec. 1114 of Title 18, U.S.C. apply, with the provision that the punishment for killing an agent of the EEOC while such agent was engaged in his official duties shall be imprisonment for any term of years or for life.

Section 10

Sec. 715

Provided for a study by Secretary of Labor on discrimination because of age.

Sec. 715

Deletes section 715 of 1964 Act, and replaces it with a provision establishing an Equal Employment Opportunity Coordinating Council composed of Secretary of Labor, Chairman of EEOC, Attorney General, Chairman of U.S. Civil Service Commission and Chairman of U.S. Civil Rights Commission, or their respective designees. This Council shall coordinate government activity in enforcing equal employment opportunity legislation. The Council will give President and Congress an annual report on their activities, as well as recommendations for legislative or administrative changes.

Provisions of 1964 Act	Changes Made by 1972 Act	Comments
Sec. 717	Section 11	
	Sec. 717	
(a) No such section in 1964 Act.	This new section provides:	
	(a) That all personnel actions affecting employees or applicants for employment in military departments, executive agencies, the General Accounting Office, U.S. Postal Service, Postal Rate Commission, competitive service positions in District of Columbia government, units of legislative and judicial branches of Federal Government in competitive service positions, and in the Library of Congress shall be free from discrimination based on race, color, religion, sex or national origin.	Military departments are defined in Sec. 102, Title 5, U.S.C.; executive agencies are defined in Sec. 105, Title 5, U.S.C.
(b) No such provision in 1964 Act. (Some similar provisions in Executive Order 11478, relating to duty of officials to insure non-discrimination.)	(b) Gives Civil Service Commission authority to enforce § 717(a) as to all government employees except those of the Library of Congress, whose rights will be enforced by the Librarian of Congress. Remedies which may be given include reinstatement, back pay, and other appropriate relief. In addition, Civil Service Commission shall: (1) Create, and annually review, an equal employment opportunity plan for all agencies covered by Sec. 717(a).	All authority given to the Civil Service Commission applies equally to the Librarian of Congress.

(2) Publish, on semi-annual basis, progress reports from departments or agencies on implementation of plan.	
(c) An employee of any agency or department in Sec. 717(a) may file a civil action, as provided in Sec. 706, upon complaint based on race, color, religion, sex or national origin.	(c) No such provision in 1964 Act.
(1) Within 30 days after receipt of notice of final action taken by a department, agency, etc. on the complaint;	
(2) Within 30 days after receipt of notice of final action by the Civil Service Commission on an appeal from a departmental order brought pursuant to Sec. 717(a) or an executive order; or	
(3) Within 180 days after Complaint filed with Department, or appeal filed with the Civil Service Commission.	
(d) The provisions of Sec. 706(f) through (k) shall govern civil actions brought under Sec. 717(c).	(d) No similar provision in 1964 Act.
(e) Nothing in this Act shall relieve any government agency or official from existing equal employment opportunity obligations under the Constitution, other statutes, or any Executive Orders.	(e) No similar provision in 1964 Act.

Appendix D

Report of House Committee

on Education and Labor

EQUAL EMPLOYMENT OPPORTUNITIES
ENFORCEMENT ACT OF 1971

JUNE 2, 1971.—Committed to the Committee of the Whole House on the
State of the Union and ordered to be printed

Mr. HAWKINS, from the Committee on Education and Labor,
submitted the following

REPORT

together with

MINORITY AND SEPARATE VIEWS

[To accompany H.R. 1746]

The Committee on Education and Labor, to whom was referred the
bill (H.R. 1746) to further promote equal employment opportunities
for American workers, having considered the same, report favorably
thereon without amendment and recommend that the bill do pass.

PURPOSE OF LEGISLATION

The basic purpose of H.R. 1746 is to grant the Equal Employment
Opportunity Commission authority to issue, through well established
procedures, judicially enforceable cease and desist orders. The bill
would transfer the functions and responsibilities of the Office of Federal Contract Compliance (now in the Department of Labor—pursuant to Executive Order 11246) to the Equal Employment Opportunity
Commission; and transfer the Attorney General's authority in practice or pattern discrimination suits to the Equal Employment Opportunity Commission. The bill would broaden jurisdictional coverage by
deleting the existing exemptions of State and local government employees and of certain employees connected with educational institutions. The bill would extend some protection to Federal employees. One
year after enactment, coverage is extended to employers and labor
unions with eight or more employees or members, a reduction from the
present requirement of 25 employees or members.

BACKGROUND OF LEGISLATION

The Equal Employment Opportunity Commission was established under the authority of Title VII of the Civil Rights Act of 1964. Under that authority the Commission is not given the power to issue judicially enforceable orders but is limited essentially to the function of conciliation. In 1965 the Committee recommended passage of a bill supporting cease and desist authority. That bill (H.R. 10065) was acted on favorably in the House of Representatives but was not taken up by the Senate.

In the 91st Congress the Senate succeeded in passing S. 2453, a bill granting the Equal Employment Opportunity Commission self-enforcing cease and desist authority. This Committee, during the second half of the 91st Congress, favorably reported H.R. 17555, identical, with two exceptions, to H.R. 1746. Neither S. 2453 nor H.R. 17555 reached the House floor for debate.

Provisions in H.R. 1746 not found in H.R. 17555 relate to the transfer of the functions and responsibilities of the Office of Federal Contract Compliance (pursuant to Executive Order 11246) to the Equal Employment Opportunity Commission; and the transfer of the Attorney General's authority in "pattern or practice" discrimination suits to the Equal Employment Opportunity Commission.

Time and experience have re-enforced this Committee's strongly held view of the necessity of establishing the Equal Employment Opportunity Commission as a quasi-judicial agency with authority to obtain enforcement of orders. H.R. 1746 is an effort to implement in a meaningful way the national policy of equal employment opportunity for employees without discrimination because of race, color, religion, national origin, or sex.

SUBCOMMITTEE HEARINGS

The General Subcommittee on Labor held six days of public hearings on H.R. 17555 and related bills during the 91st Congress. The principal witnesses were: Honorable William H. Brown, III, Chairman, Equal Employment Opportunity Commission; Deputy Attorney General Richard G. Kleindienst; a panel representing the Leadership Conference on Civil Rights, headed by Clarence Mitchell, Washington Bureau, NAACP, including Thomas C. Harris, Associate Counsel, AFL–CIO; former Commission Chairman Clifford L. Alexander, Jr.; and Irving Kator, Director, Federal Equal Employment Opportunity, U.S. Civil Service Commission.

The subcommittee held hearings on H.R. 1746 on March 3, 4, and 18, 1971. These hearings were primarily concerned with the transfer of the Office of Federal Contract Compliance and the transfer of the Attorney General's practice or pattern discrimination authority to the Equal Employment Opportunity Commission. Witnesses, however, were free to and did submit statements and discuss other significant aspects of the proposed legislation. The principal witnesses were: Deputy Assistant Attorney General David L. Norman; Under Secretary of Labor Laurence Silberman; Assistant Secretary of Labor Arthur Fletcher; OFCC Director John Wilks; Commission Chairman

William H. Brown, III; Howard Glickstein, Staff Director, U.S. Commission on Civil Rights; U.S. Representative Shirley Chisholm; U.S. Representative Bella Abzug; Thomas C. Harris, Associate General Counsel, AFL–CIO; Clarence Mitchell, NAACP; Irving Kator, Assistant Executive Director, U.S. Civil Service Commission; Don White, American Retail Federation; Lucille Shriver, National Federation of Business and Professional Woman; Robert Nystrom, Motorola, Inc.; and Warren Anderson, The Black Committee, Maywood, Illinois.

The subcommittee concluded its consideration of the bill in executive session on April 7, 1971, voting to report the bill to the full Committee without amendment. The Committee on Education and Labor ordered H.R. 1746 by a rollcall vote of 21 to 12 on May 4, 1971.

NEED FOR THE BILL

A little more than 6 years ago, Congress enacted Title VII of the Civil Rights Act of 1964, Public Law 88–352, 42 U.S.C. 2000(e)– 2000(e–15). That act recognized the prevalence of discriminatory employment practices in the United States and the need for Federal legislation to deal with the problem. Title VII of that Act, created the Equal Employment Opportunity Commission which became effective July 2, 1965. In the intervening 6 years, the Commission made an heroic effort to reduce discrimination in employment which was found to pervade our system.

Despite the commitment of Congress to the goal of equal employment opportunity for all our citizens, the machinery created by the Civil Rights Act of 1964 is not adequate.

Despite the progress which has been made since passage of the Civil Rights Act of 1964, discrimination against minorities and women continues. The persistence of discrimination, and its detrimental effects require a reaffirmation of our national policy of equal opportunity in employment. It is essential that seven years after the passage of the Civil Rights Act of 1964, effective enforcement procedures be provided the Equal Employment Opportunity Commission to strengthen its efforts to reduce discrimination in employment.

An examination of the statistics with respect to the progress of equal employment opportunities clearly shows that the voluntary approach currently applied has failed to eliminate employment discrimination. During the first 5 years of its existence, the Commission has received more than 52,000 charges. Of these, 35,445 were recommended for investigation. Of this number approximately 56% involved complaints of discrimination because of race, 23% discrimination on sex, and the remainder involved charges of discrimination because of national origin or religion.

The number of charges is increasing. The incidence of discrimination does not appear to be waning. In Fiscal Year 1969, the Commission received 12,148 charges; in Fiscal Year 1970, the Commission received 14,129 charges. In testimony before this Committee, William H. Brown, III, Chairman of the Equal Employment Opportunity Commission, stated that during the first seven and a half months of the current fiscal year, the Commission has received 14,644 charges, a greater number than the total charges received for all of last year.

With the steady growth in the number of cases filed with the Commission, an effective and suitable procedure and remedy become increasingly important. Effective remedies have not resulted from present practice. Of the 35,445 charges that were recommended for investigation, reasonable cause was found in over 63% of the cases, but in less than half of these cases was the Commission able to achieve a totally or even partially successful conciliation.

There is nothing that would lead anyone to expect that with the limited authority currently available to it the Commission might produce any higher degree of compliance in the future. With the increasing number of complaints it now receives, and in the absence of adequate cease and desist enforcement procedures, the Commission can only be expected to catalog an increasing number of complaints for which there is no reasonable expectation of an adequate remedy.

The impact of the Commission's inability to obtain relief from employment discrimination is reflected in an examination of statistics showing the distribution of minorities in occupational groups. While the tables show some improvement since 1964, minority groups are not obtaining their rightful place in our society.

PERCENT DISTRIBUTION OF TOTAL WORK FORCE BY OCCUPATIONAL GROUPS

Occupation	Nonwhites employed			White employed	
	1964	1969	1970	1969	1970
Professional technician	6.7	8.3	9.1	14.5	14.8
Farmer, farm manager	1.9	1.0	1.0	2.5	2.4
Managers, proprietors	2.6	3.0	3.5	11.1	11.4
Clerical	7.6	12.9	13.2	17.7	18.0
Sales	1.8	2.0	2.1	6.5	6.7
Craftsmen	7.0	8.5	8.2	13.6	13.5
Operatives	20.3	23.9	23.7	17.8	17.0
Private household	13.6	8.5	7.7	1.3	1.3
Service workers	18.7	18.2	18.3	9.2	9.4
Farmworkers	6.8	3.2	2.9	1.7	1.6
Laborers (nonfarm)	13.0	10.5	10.3	4.0	4.1

The situation of the working women is no less serious. Women currently comprise approximately 38% of the total work force of the Nation. There are approximately 30 million employed women.

Recent statistics released from the U.S. Department of Labor indicate that there exists a profound economic discrimination against women workers. Ten years ago, women made 60.8% of the average salaries made by men in the same year; in 1968, women's earnings still only represented 58.2% of the salaries made by men in that year. Similarly, in that same year, 60% of women, but only 20% of men earned less than $5,000. At the other end of the scale, only 3% of women, but 28% of men had earnings of $10,000 or more.

Women are subject to economic deprivation as a class. Their self-fulfillment and development is frustrated because of their sex. Numerous studies have shown that women are placed in the less challenging, the less responsible and the less remunerative positions on the basis of their sex alone.

Such blatantly disparate treatment is particularly objectionable in view of the fact that Title VII has specifically prohibited sex discrimination since its enactment in 1964. The Equal Employment Opportunity Commission has progressively involved itself in the problems posed by sex discrimination, but its efforts here, as in the area of racial discrimination, have been ineffective due directly to its inability to enforce its findings.

In recent years, the courts have done much to create a body of law clearly disapproving of sex discrimination in employment.[1] Despite the efforts of the courts and the Commission, discrimination against women continues to be widespread, and is regarded by many as either morally or physiologically justifiable.

This Committee believes that women's rights are not judicial divertissements. Discrimination against women is no less serious than other forms of prohibited employment practices and is to be accorded the same degree of social concern given to any type of unlawful discrimination.

Enactment of this bill will not automatically end employment discrimination in this country. The bill offers no panaceas or guarantees of success. The experiences of the last 6 years under Title VII, while in many respects reflecting major advancements in securing equal opportunity for all Americans, nonetheless are disappointing in terms of what minorities and women in this country have a right to expect.

The time has come to bring an end to job discrimination once and for all, and to insure every citizen the opportunity for the decent self-respect that accompanies a job commensurate with one's abilities. The hopeful prospects that Title VII offered millions of Americans in 1964 must be revived.

ESTIMATE OF COSTS

In an effort to secure an accurate estimate of the projected costs of this legislation to satisfy the requirements of clause 7 of rule XIII the General Subcommittee on Labor, through its chairman, the Honorable John H. Dent, sought the views of the Equal Employment Opportunity Commission. The response of the Commission to that inquiry is contained in the following letter:

EQUAL EMPLOYMENT OPPORTUNITY COMMISSION,
Washington, D.C., April 22, 1971.

Hon. JOHN H. DENT,
*Chairman, General Subcommittee on Labor, Committee on Education and Labor,
House of Representatives, Washington, D.C.*

DEAR MR. CHAIRMAN: Thank you for your letter of March 26, 1971, requesting this Commission, pursuant to Rule XIII, clause 7 of the Rules of the House of Representatives, to submit to the Subcommittee estimated costs for carrying out the provisions of H.R. 1746. I have set out below our cost projections with respect to H.R. 1746, based upon available data and workload approximations for FY 1971 through FY 1976.

It is the Commission's view that the accompanying figures represent a reasonable estimate of minimum additional budgetary requirements for administration of the three new areas of the application of Title VII of the Civil Rights Act of 1964 heretofore not discharged by any Federal agency:

---

[1] See e.g., *Weeks* v. *Southern Bell Telephone Co..* 408 F. 2d 228 (5th Cir. 1969) ; *Bowe* v. *Colgate Palmolive Co.,* 416 F. 2d 711 (7th Cir. 1969) ; *Philips* v. *Martin Marietta Corp.,* ——— U.S. ———, ——— S. Ct. ———. 3 FEP Cases 40 (S. Ct. 1971) ; *Diaz* v. *Pan American,* ——— F. 2d ———, 3 EPD 8166 (C.A. 5, 1971) and cases cited therein.

COST PROJECTIONS FOR H.R. 1746

[Figures in thousands]

	Fiscal year—					
	1971	1972	1973	1974	1975	1976
Cease and desist operations	501	9, 431	11, 912	12, 081	12, 123	12, 151
Federal, State, county, and municipal jurisdiction		2, 600	3, 900	3, 900	3, 900	3, 900
Extended jurisdiction to 8 or more employees		685	4, 034	4, 213	4, 223	4, 243
Total	501	12, 716	19, 846	20, 194	20, 246	20, 294

In preparing the above figures, several assumptions have been made which are, I feel, extremely important for consideration of these projections. In the first instance, despite the Commission's desire to commence operations under its own enforcement powers, it is unlikely that any of the operations proposed in H.R. 1746 could be implemented in any significant manner in FY 1971. It will be necessary to develop administrative procedures to implement the bill, and this will require some time. For example, the writing and approval of rules to establish operating procedures and personnel recruitment to meet the additional operational requirements in H.R. 1746 will require several months. It is, therefore, realistic to assume that implementation of the cease and desist operations as well as the other aspects of enforcement contained in the bill would not begin until FY 1972, and that the first full year of operation would not be until FY 1973. Accordingly, the cost projections for FY 1971, and also for FY 1972, based upon a full year's operation as requested by the Subcommittee, are hypothetical, insofar as they assume that operations under H.R. 1746 will begin immediately upon its passage.

The cost projections for the cease and desist operations as proposed by H.R. 1746 have been derived from Commission caseload projections. Using these figures as a base, the staffing requirements for implementation of the hearing procedures encompassed by the cease and desist powers have been projected on the basis of an adjudication of 15 cases per year for each hearing examiner and the preparation and presentation of 20 cases per year for each trial attorney. From these figures, allowances have also been made for a *minimum* of supporting staff and expenses which will be involved in maintaining the hearing process. It is difficult for me to say at this time whether the cease and desist cost projections contained herein are accurate. The assumptions regarding the number of cases that a hearing examiner and a trial attorney will handle per year are based upon approximations of the average length of an adjudication of a Title VII violation based upon the estimated degree of complexity involved in such cases. It may well evolve that these approximations are not realistic; the estimates that each hearing examiner will be able to hear 15 cases per year and that each trial attorney can prepare 20 cases per year are derived from NLRB experience and may not hold true for Title VII litigation.

The extension of Title VII jurisdiction to include Federal, State, county and municipal employees will bring an additional 12,880,000 employees within the provisions of the Act. As there is currently no uniform Federal law which applies in this area, it is difficult to project, with any degree of accuracy, the impact of this extension of jurisdiction. However, due to the large number of employees which this will bring within the provisions of the Act, it can be safely assumed that this new availability of a Federal administrative forum, where none has been available, will generate a substantial number of complaints. The figures projected in the table above for this area of enforcement have been derived from existant Civil Service Commission estimates regarding Federal EEO complaint adjudication, and upon an approximation, based upon the number of employees involved, for enforcement of complaints against State and local agencies.

The figures projected for the extension of Title VII jurisdiction to include all persons employed in establishments which employ eight or more full time employees have been derived from a projected 25% increase in the Commission's workload due to the extended coverage. The cost projections for this extended jurisdiction for FY 1972 assume that the jurisdictional expansion will only operate for the last few months of that year and will not be operational in FY 1971, as H.R. 1746 provides that this power will not become effective until one year after the Act is passed. Similarly, the cost projection for the extended jurisdiction to Federal, State, county and municipal employees in FY 1972 is based upon less than a full year's operation, as the Act provides for a six-month's delay in instituting this function.

The other two areas of enforcement to be assigned to the Commission by H.R. 1746, transfer of OFCC functions and enforcement of pattern or practice suits, are currently administered by other Federal agencies, and do not, therefore, represent areas of Federal enforcement where new funds will be needed. As regards both the transfer of OFCC functions and the enforcement of pattern or practice suits by the EEOC, H.R. 1746 specifically provides that the functions of the respective agency currently administering these operations, together with "such personnel, property, records, and *unexpended balances of appropriations, allocations, and other funds employed, used, held, available, or to be made available in connection with the functions transferred . . .*" (emphasis added) shall be transferred to the Commission. Accordingly, in projecting requirements for these operations, the Commission restricted its projections to using only the appropriation requirements proposed by these agencies, as set forth below:

[In thousands]

	Fiscal year—					
	1971	1972	1973	1974	1975	1976
OFCC functions	262	2,594	2,600	2,600	2,600	2,600
Pattern or practice enforcement	300	1,800	1,800	1,800	1,800	1,800

Once the above referenced operations have been transferred to the Commission, however, it may subsequently be necessary to modify these figures, dependent upon any change in the enforcement patterns which may become apparent after the consolidation of the enforcement of employment discrimination as proposed by H.R. 1746.

If I can be of any further assistance to you on this matter, please feel free to call on me.

Sincerely,

WILLIAM H. BROWN, III.

The estimate by the General Subcommittee on Labor of the costs of implementing H.R. 1746 vary somewhat from the views of the Commission and are contained in the following chart:

ESTIMATE BY THE GENERAL SUBCOMMITTEE ON LABOR OF THE COST OF IMPLEMENTING H.R. 1746

[In thousands]

	Fiscal year—					
	1971	1972	1973	1974	1975	1976
Cease and desist operations	300	7,431	9,912	10,081	11,123	11,151
Extension of jurisdiction to Federal employees		900	900	900	900	900
Extension of jurisdiction to State, county, and municipal employees		1,600	2,034	3,000	3,000	4,000
Transfer of OFCC functions	262	2,594	2,600	2,600	2,600	2,600
Transfer of pattern or practice functions	300	1,800	1,800	1,800	1,800	1,800
Extension of jurisdiction to 8 or more employees		3,034	3,213	3,223	3,223	4,243

It will be noted that the subcommittee estimates, in most cases, are lower than those of the Commission. With all due respect to the Commission, it is felt that staff recruitment and preparation of applicable implementing rules and regulations will require more time than anticipated by the Commission. Further, the mere existence of a law with enforcement authority will be a deterring factor; therefore it is highly speculative how many new cases will arise as a result of the extension of coverage. The subcommittee does not anticipate any significant costs based on this factor; though a large number of small employers would be covered. Also, the law would not usurp the State agencies, and undoubtedly a large number of cases would still be settled at the State level.

The transfer of functions from OFCC, CSC, and Justice, will not require additional Federal expenditures because the transfers will also involve the conveyance of "unexpended balances of appropriations, allocations, and other funds employed, used, held, available, or to be made available in connection with the functions transferred . . ."

Major Provisions of the Bill

Cease and Desist Enforcement Powers

During the preparation and presentation of Title VII of the Civil Rights Act of 1964, employment discrimination tended to be viewed as a series of isolated and distinguishable events, due, for the most part, to ill-will on the part of some identifiable individual or organization. It was thought that a scheme which stressed conciliation rather than compulsory processes would be more appropriate for the resolution of this essentially "human" problem. Litigation, it was thought, would be necessary only on an occasional basis in the event of determined recalcitrance. Experience, however, has shown this to be an oversimplified expectation, incorrect in its conclusions.

Employment discrimination, as we know today, is a far more complex and pervasive phenomenon. Experts familiar with the subject generally describe the problem in terms of "systems" and "effects" rather than simply intentional wrongs. The literature on the subject is replete with discussions of the mechanics of seniority and lines of progression, perpetuation of the present effects of earlier discriminatory practices through various institutional devices, and testing and validation requirements.[2] The forms and incidents of discrimination which the Commission is required to treat are increasingly complex. Particularly to the untrained observer, their discriminatory nature may not appear obvious at first glance. A recent striking example was provided by the U.S. Supreme Court in its decision in *Griggs* v. *Duke Power Co.*, —— U.S. ——, 91 S.Ct. 849, 3 FEP Cases 175 (S.Ct. 1971), where the Court held that the use of employment tests as determinants of an applicant's job qualification, even when nondiscriminatory and applied in good faith by the employer, was in violation of Title VII if such tests work a discriminatory effect in hiring patterns and there is no showing of an overriding business necessity for the use of such criteria.

It is increasingly obvious that the entire area of employment discrimination is one whose resolution requires not only expert assistance, but also the technical perception that a problem exists in the first place, and that the system complained of is unlawful.

---

[2] See, e.g., Note.—80 Harv. L. Rev. 1260 (1967) ; Cooper and Sobol, "Seniority and Testing Under Fair Employment Laws: A General Approach To Objective Criteria of Hiring and Promotion," 82 Harv. L. Rev. 1623 (1969) ; Blumrosen, "The Duty of Fair Recruitment Under the Civil Rights Act of 1964," 22 Rutgers Law Review 465 (1968) ; Sovern, "Legal Restraints on Racial Discrimination in Employment" (1966) ; "Bonfield, the Substance of American Fair Employment Practices Legislation I and II," 61 and 62 Northwestern Law Review 707 and 19 (1967). See also *Quarles* v. *Phillip Morris*, 279 F. Supp. 505 (E.D. Va., 1968) ; *United States* v. *Local 189, United Papermakers* 282 F. Supp. 39 (E.D. La., 1968), 416 F. 2d 980 (C.A. 5, 1969) ; *Asbestos Workers, Local 53* v. *Vogler*, 407 F. 2d. 1047 (C.A. 5 1969) and cases cited therein.

This kind of expertise normally does not reside in either the personnel or legal arms of employers, and the result in terms of conciliation is often an impasse, with the respondent unwilling or unable to understand the problem in the way the Commission perceives it. As we have already noted, the Commission has been able to achieve successful conciliation in less than half of the cases in which reasonable cause was determined. It has been the emphasis on voluntariness that has proven to be most detrimental to the successful operation of Title VII. In cases posing the most profound consequences, respondents have more often than not shrugged off the Commission's entreaties and relied upon the unlikelihood of the parties suing them.

Facts, statistical evidence and experience demonstrate that employers, labor organizations, employment agencies and joint labor-management committees continue to engage in conduct which contravenes the provisions of Title VII. The existence of such practices demonstrates the immediate need to effectuate the purposes of the Civil Rights Act of 1964.

H.R. 1746 remedies the failure to include effective enforcement powers in Title VII by enacting a new section 706 (section 4 of the bill) which empowers the Commission, after it has exhausted the procedures for achieving voluntary compliance, to issue complaints and hold hearings, to issue cease and desist orders against discriminatory practices, and to seek enforcement of its orders in the Federal Courts. Comparable powers are now exercised by most Federal regulatory agencies, the Federal Communications Commission, the Federal Trade Commission, and the National Labor Relations Board, to name a few, as well as the vast majority of State Fair Employment Practice Commissions. By providing this expansion of Title VII authority, we will remove present shortcoming of the act and provide a quick and effective remedy against employment discrimination.

Under the new section 706, in the event of a violation of Title VII the Commission would proceed in the following manner:

1. Upon the filing of a charge, the Commission would serve a copy of the charge on the respondent and would investigate. If, after investigation, the Commission decides that there is no reasonable cause to believe that the charge is true, it would dismiss the charge and notify both the person claiming to be aggrieved and the respondent (sec. 706 706(b)).

2. If the Commission finds reasonable cause, it would seek to eliminate the unlawful practice by informal methods of conference, conciliation, and persuasion (sec. 706(b)). An agreement for the elimination of the alleged unlawful practice may be entered into by the Commission any time between the filing of the charge and until the record is filed with the Court of Appeals (sec. 706(i)).

3. Existing law relating to actions filed under State or local law has been retained. In such cases, the Commission will not assume jurisdiction for sixty days after the commencement of the action under the State or local authority (sec. 706(c)).

4. If the Commission determines that it is unable to secure an acceptable agreement, the Commission will then issue and serve upon the respondent a complaint setting forth the facts upon which the allegation is based and a notice of hearing (sec. 706(f)). The respondent

and the party claiming to be aggrieved shall be the primary parties to the proceeding, but the Commission may grant any other persons the right to intervene, file briefs, or appear as amicus curiae (sec. 706(g)).

5. After completion of a hearing, if an unlawful employment practice is found to have occurred, the Commission is empowered to issue an order requiring the respondent to cease and desist from continuing such practices. The Commission may also prescribe such relief as the case may require (sec. 706(h)). Hearings conducted pursuant to this section will be governed by the Administrative Procedure Act, 5 U.S.C. § 551, et. seq.

6. Any person who has been affected by a decision of the Commission may petition for a review of such order in the appropriate United States court of appeals (sec. 706(l)). All litigation to which the Commission is a party or affecting the Commission, except litigation in the Supreme Court, shall be conducted by the Commission's attorneys; litigation in the Supreme Court will be conducted by the Attorney General (sec. 706(n)).

7. Where the Commission feels that, as a result of its preliminary investigation, prompt judicial action is necessary, it may petition the appropriate United States district court for a preliminary injunction or temporary restraining order, pending its final disposition of the charge (sec. 706(o)).

The Committee has considered various enforcement mechanisms. Experience demonstrates that of the enforcement mechanisms available, cease-and-desist authority will achieve the fairest and most expeditious results.[3]

Administrative tribunals are better equipped to handle the complicated issues involved in employment discrimination cases. In employment discrimination litigation the District Courts increasingly have found themselves grappling with difficult problems of discriminatory practices inherent in employers' basic methods of recruitment, hiring, placement or promotions. Issues that have perplexed courts include plant-wide restructuring of pay scales and progression lines, seniority rosters and testing.

The sorting out of the complexities surrounding employment discrimination can give rise to enormous expenditure of judicial resources in already heavily overburdened Federal district courts. For example, Judge Allgood of the Federal District Court for the Northeastern District of Alabama, wrote an opinion 157 pages in length in *U.S.* v. *H.K.*

---

[3] The committee's view regarding the benefits of cease and desist authority for the Commission has received support from public interest groups. Typical is a letter to the General Subcommittee on Labor, from David A. Brody, Director of the Washington, D.C. Office of the Anti-Defamation League, stating: "In our view, authority to issue cease and desist orders after an administrative hearing will be more effective in bringing about compliance with the law than will the court enforcement approach. It is only through the administrative hearing procedure that regulatory agencies are able to handle expeditiously, and dispose of, the multitude of cases coming before them. The administrative agency is better suited and better geared than the courts for carrying out the public rights which Congress has enacted into law. As the late Justice Frankfurter has stated: "Unlike courts, which are concerned primarily with the enforcement of private rights although public interests may thereby be implicated, administrative agencies are predominantly concerned with enforcing public rights although private interests may thereby be affected. To no small degree administrative agencies for the enforcement of public rights were established by Congress because more flexible and less traditional procedures were called for than those evolved by the courts. It is therefore essential to the vitality of the administrative process that the procedural powers given to these administrative agencies not be confined within the conventional modes by which business is done in courts." Dissenting opinion, *Federal Communications Commission* v. *National Broadcasting Co., Inc.*, 319 U.S. 239,248 (1943).

Porter, a Title VII suit alleging employment discrimination in a single steel plant. Judge Allgood stated in his opinion that enough use was made of pre-trail discovery in that case to "fill several court files".

Administrative tribunals are better suited to rapid resolution of such complex issues than are Courts. Efficiency and predicability will be enhanced if the necessarily detailed case by case findings of fact and fashioning of remedy is performed by experts in the subject matter. Moreover, administrative tribunals are less subject to technical rules governing such matters as pleadings and motion practice—which afford opportunities for dilatory tactics—and are less constrained by formal rules of evidence—which give rise to a lengthier (and more costly) process of proof.

Further, congested Court calendars necessitate inordinate delays in bringing cases to trial. In fiscal 1970, in the Southern District of New York, the average wait from the time a case was ready for trial until nonjury trial was 38 months. In the Eastern District of Louisiana the delay was 24 months. While delays also are encountered in administrative proceedings, the average amount of time from the filing of a charge until the issuance of the trial examiner's decision in an unfair labor practice case before the National Labor Relations Board is less than 7½ months. Approximately 95% of unfair labor practice cases are disposed of without further proceedings beyond this stage.

In addition, past experience with administrative hearings and court enforcement indicates that cease-and-desist would be more effective. Experience has shown that one of the main advantages of granting enforcement power to a regulatory agency is that the existence of the sanction encourages settlement of complaints before the enforcement stage is reached.

The NLRB disposes of approximately 95% of its cases at the administrative level. Information on State fair employment practice commissions indicates this is similarly effective cease-and-desist authority. For example, through 1969, the Pennsylvania Human Relations Commission pointed to the fact that while 47 cease-and-desist orders were issued in equal employment cases before the State agency, another 3,838 complaints were processed successfully and adjusted without the need for such order.

Cease and desist authority will assure greater consistency in the development of equal employment law since decisions will be rendered by one agency rather than by several hundred district court judges. The uniformity and predictability of rules and decisions are of significant importance to employers who must look to the Federal Government for guidance in equal employment practices and to individuals who look to the Federal Government for leadership and assurance that employment opportunity exists without regard to race, color, religion, sex or national origin.

PRIVATE ACTIONS

The bill retains the right of an individual to bring a civil suit under the Act in Section 715 (Section 6(j) of the bill). Section 715 provides that if the Commission finds no reasonable cause, fails to make a finding of reasonable cause, or takes no action in respect to a charge, or has not within 180 days issued a complaint nor entered into a conciliation or settlement agreement which is acceptable to the person aggrieved, it shall notify the person aggrieved. Within 60 days after such notification the person aggrieved shall then have the right to commence an action under the provisions of the Act against the respondent in the proper United States district court. Provision for the individual's right to sue is presently contained in Section 706(e) of Title VII. Section 715 in the bill retains this right and extends both the period of Commission action and the time period allowed for filing an action in the appropriate court.

In recent years regulatory agencies have been submerged with increasing workloads which strain their resources to the breaking point. The Commission has stated, in testimony before this committee, that its caseload has increased even more rapidly than its projections had anticipated. The result of this increasing use of many of the Federal regulatory agencies has frequently affected those agencies' abilities to remain current on all of the matters for which they are responsible. This has led to lengthy delays in the administrative process and has frequently frustrated the remedial role of the agency. In the case of the Commission, the burgeoning workload, accompanied by insufficient funds and a shortage of staff, has, in many instances, forced a party to wait 2 to 3 years before final conciliation procedures can be instituted. This situation leads the committee to believe that the private right of action, both under the present Act and in the bill, provides the aggrieved party a means by which he may be able to escape from the administrative quagmire which occasionally surrounds a case caught in an overloaded administrative process.

In this respect, it is important to note that subsection 715(a) in the bill provides that where the individual has elected to pursue his action in the court, the court may, in such circumstances as it deems just, appoint an attorney for the complainant and authorize the commencement of the action without the payment of fees, costs or security. By including this provision in the bill, the committee emphasizes that the nature of Title VII actions more often than not pits parties of unequal strength and resources against each other. The complainant, who is usually a member of a disadvantaged class, is opposed by an employer who not infrequently is one of the nation's major producers, and who has at his disposal a vast array of resources and legal talent.

The committee was concerned about the interrelationship between the newly created cease and desist enforcement powers of the Commission and the existing right of private action. It concluded that duplication of proceedings should be avoided. The bill, therefore, contains a provision for termination of Commission jurisdiction once a private action has been filed (except for the power of the Commission to intervene in the private actions). It contains as well a provision for termination of the right of private action once the Commission issues a complaint or enters into a conciliation or settlement agreement which is satisfactory to the Commission and to the person aggrieved. If such an agreement is not acceptable to the aggrieved party, his private right of action is preserved.

The bill provides that an aggrieved person's right to institute a private action should be reactivated under certain circumstances where the Commission does not act promptly after issuing a complaint.

Section 715(a) provides that an aggrieved person may bring an independent action against the respondent if the Commission has not issued its order within 180 days. The committee believes that aggrieved persons are entitled to have their cases processed promptly and that the Commission should develop its capacity to proceed rapidly to hearing and decision once the complaint is issued. The committee recognizes that it will not be possible to render a decision in all cases within the time limit prescribed. The complexity of many of the charges, and the time required to develop the cases, is well recognized by the committee. It is assumed that individual complainants, who are apprised of the need for the proper preparation of a complex complaint involving multiple issues and extensive discovery procedures, would not cut short the administrative process merely to encounter the same kind of delays in a court proceeding. It would, however, be appropriate for the individual to institute a court action where the delay is occasioned by administrative inefficiencies. The primary concern must be protection of the aggrieved person's option to seek a prompt remedy in the best manner available. It should be noted, however, that it is not the intention of the committee to permit an aggrieved party a chance to retry his case merely because he is dissatisfied with the Commission's action. Once the Commission has issued an order, further proceedings must be in the courts of appeals pursuant to subsection 706(1) of the bill.

"PATTERN OR PRACTICE" SUITS

Section 707 of the act has been amended by transferring the "pattern or practice" suit authority from the Department of Justice to the Commission.

"Pattern or practice" discrimination suits are currently handled in the Civil Rights Division of the Department of Justice. This Division, established some 15 years ago, and has had its responsibilities greatly increased by virtue of the civil rights legislation enacted in 1964, 1965, and 1968. It has been given authority to prosecute suits in a variety of areas including public accommodations, public facilities, schools, housing, and discrimination in Federally assisted programs. It has also received authority to deal with voting discrimination and to act against persons who interfere with the civil rights of others.

Unfortunately, the size of the Division has not kept pace with its vastly increased responsibilities. As a consequence the Division has been highly selective and very limited in the number and the nature of suits which it has filed. It has been unable to pursue title VII suits with the vigor and intensity needed to reduce the wide-spread prevalence of systemic discrimination. Indeed, for several years it has accorded the lowest priority to employment discrimination cases.

Those selected suits which the Division has been able to bring, however, have contributed significantly to the Federal effort to combat employment discrimination.[4]

---

[4] See e.g. *U.S.* v. *Local 189 United Papermakers & Paperworkers*, 282 F. Supp. 39 (E.D. La. 1968), *affirmed* 416 F. 2d 980 (5th Cir. 1969), *cert. denied* 397 U.S. 919 (1970); *U.S.* v. *Hayes International Corp.*, 415 F. 2d 1038, 1045 (5th Cir. 1969); *U.S.* v. *Hayes International Corp.*, 415 F. 2d 1038, 1045 (5th Cir. 1969); *U.S.* v. *Sheet Metal Workers International Association, Local 36*, 416 F. 2d (8th Cir. 1969); *U.S.* v. *Georgia Power Co.*, 301 F. Supp. 538 (N.D. Ga. 1969).

Unrelenting broad-scale action against patterns or practices of discrimination is, however, critical in combatting employment discrimination. The Committee believes these powers should be exercised by
the Commission as an integral and coordinated part of the overall
enforcement effort.

Pattern or practice discrimination is a pervasive and deeply im-
bedded form of discrimination. Specific acts or incidents of discrimination within the Commission's jurisdiction are frequently sympto-
matic of a pattern or practice which Title VII seeks to eradicate. The
Commission has the basic responsibility to achieve the objectives of
Title VII. Since the Commission is being vested with cease and desist
enforcement authority, it is imperative that it be empowered also to
deal with "pattern or practice" discrimination in order to deal compre-
hensively with systemic discrimination.

The Committee feels that the transfer of the "pattern or practice"
jurisdiction to the Equal Employment Opportunity Commission
would eliminate overlapping jurisdictions and unnecessary duplication of functions. It would promote uniformity in development of law,
goals, policies, and procedures and promote economic use of governmental resources. "Pattern or practice" jurisdiction in the Department
of Justice was justified at a time when the Commission did not have
its own enforcement powers. However, with the acquisition of cease
and desist powers, the Commission's operations are sufficiently broad
to encompass "pattern or practice" violations as well as individual
complaints of discrimination.

The Commission is best able to determine where "pattern or practice"
litigation is warranted. It has access to the most current statistical com-
putations and analyses regarding employment patterns and has the
most extensive expertise in dealing with employment discrimination.

Most importantly, persons charged with unfair employment practices should not be answerable to several Federal agencies pursuing
separate policies. Multifarious remedies cause undue burden and harassment by a multiplicity of simultaneous or successive procedures.
An example is the *Crown Zellerbach Corp.* vs. *U.S.* (Supra. 5th cir.
cuit, 1969) where the union and employer after negotiating a compliance agreement with the Commission were nevertheless subjected to
litigation in the Federal court. Next the Office of Federal Contract
Compliance entered the picture. Ultimately the Department of Justice filed suit. Such duplication and overlapping proceedings are burdensome and harassing and should be avoided.

TRANSFER OF THE OFFICE OF FEDERAL CONTRACT COMPLIANCE

Approximately one third of the Nation's labor force is employed by
government contractors. Not infrequently these employers are
the Nation's largest and most prestigious firms. Because of their size
and standing in the business community, these employers are leaders
in the employment practices of their respective industries. The policies
they adopt, therefore, are frequently prototypes for the industry at
large.

Section 717(f) of the H.R. 1746 transfers all the authority, functions, and responsibilities of the Secretary of Labor pursuant to Ex-

ecutive Order 11246 relating to contract compliance to the Equal Employment Opportunity Commission.

Pursuant to Executive Order 11246, the Secretary of Labor is responsible for the administration of the Federal Government's contract compliance program as prescribed by the executive order. He is responsible for adopting such rules and regulations and issuing such orders as he deems necessary and appropriate to achieve the purposes of the order. The Secretary of Labor through OFCC monitors, coordinates and evaluates the Government-wide contract compliance program and supervises the activities of the 15 Federal contracting agencies which have responsibility for contract compliance in their respective areas.

Despite the increasingly strong Presidential commitment to the goals of equal employment opportunity, despite the strength of the sanctions available to secure this goal, and despite the potential effectiveness of the Federal monitoring mechanisms, the contract compliance program has not been successful.

The Committee believes that the transfer will benefit both the administration of the contract compliance program and the Title VII program. The two programs are addressed to the same basic mission—the elimination of discrimination in employment.

The obligations imposed on the government contractor by the Executive Order would reinforce the obligations imposed by Title VII. The transfer would promote the centralized enforcement of all Federal employment non-discrimination programs. It would reduce administrative overlap and encourage coordination. Clarity, uniformity, and predictability in policy and practice are aided by having the definition of discrimination and the shaping of remedies developed by a single agency. More significantly, it will authorize a single agency with a full complement of enforcement mechanisms that can be coordinated in the attack on employment discrimination.

Studies have shown that current jurisdictional overlap between the Office of Federal Contract Compliance and the Equal Employment Opportunity Commission have contributed to confusion, duplication and a general lack of coordination of equal employment opportunity enforcement programs.

Although administrative efforts have been made to coordinate the overlapping legal jurisdictions of the Commission and OFCC, such as the memorandum of understanding agreed to in May 1970, they have not been effective. Each agency has continued independently to develop its goals, policies and programs. As a result, the entire Federal effort to end employment discrimination in the private sector has suffered.

The U.S. Commission on Civil Rights in its report, *Federal Civil Rights Enforcement Effort* noted that OFCC has established industry-wide hiring goals without full consultation with the Commission which possesses substantial knowledge and expertise in this area. The Commission on the other hand, has held hearings to examine the patterns of industry-wide discrimination without consultation or effective participation of OFCC. Cases continue to be referred between the Commission and OFCC on an *ad hoc* basis.

The report concluded that "until an effective procedure is developed to assure that the Commission and OFCC act in coordination, progress in achieving the goal of equal employment opportunity will continue to be impeded." To achieve this end the report recommends that the contract compliance responsibilities of the Office of Federal Contract Compliance be transferred to the Equal Employment Opportunity Commission.

This conclusion corresponds with the recommendations made in an earlier publication of the U.S. Commission on Civil Rights, *Jobs and Civil Rights*, prepared by Richard P. Nathan, Associate Director of the Office of Management and Budget, then with the Brookings Institute. Mr. Nathan recommended that the contract compliance function of OFCC be transferred to the Equal Employment Opportunity Commission. The report underscored the fact that Title VII and the Executive Order 11246 are addressed to the same problem—identifying and remedying employment discrimination—and that there is not reasonable basis for continuing to have two duplicating mechanisms dealing with the same problem.

The Committee believes that the transfer would substantially increase the effectiveness of both the contract compliance and Title VII enforcement programs. Affirmative action is relevant not only to the enforcement of Executive Order 11246 but is equally essential for more effective enforcement of Title VII in remedying employment discrimination. H.R. 1746 would confer, cease-and-desist authority as well as contract termination and debarment authority on the Equal Employment Opportunity Commission. The availability of these complementary sanctions will enhance the administration of the Federal equal employment programs.

The Federal contract compliance program always has suffered from the great reluctance of administrators to use debarment and contract termination sanction.

Although contract termination could become an effective sanction if used properly, it is clear that the compliance program could be strength considerably if alternative remedies were made available. An effective way to accomplish this is to transfer the contract compliance effort to the Equal Employment Opportunity Commission while at the same time giving the Commission power to issue cease-and-desist orders to prevent unlawful employment practices. Cease-and-desist power exercised by the Equal Employment Opportunity Commission would prove to be an effective sanction supplementary or alternative to termination of a contract. Conversely, having the authority to direct that contracts be terminated and contractors debarred would enhance the Equal Employment Opportunity Commission's ability to ensure that its cease and desist orders are obeyed.

The transfer of OFCC's contract compliance program to the Equal Employment Opportunity Commission will not impair the procurement function of the Executive branch of the government nor will it interfere with the government's internal functions. Primary responsibility for compliance with still rest with the various compliance agencies. The Equal Employment Opportunity Commission will be responsible, however, for issuing basic guidelines to coordinate and give guidance to the compliance program. In addition, the Commision will provide an additional independent source of review and resource if the compliance agencies fail to meet their obligations.

STATE AND LOCAL GOVERNMENT EMPLOYEES

Presently approximately 10.1 million persons are employed by State and local governmental units. This figure represents an increase of over 2 million employees since 1964. Indications are that the number of employees in State and local government will continue to increase, perhaps even more rapidly. Few of these employees, however, are afforded the protection of an effective forum to assure equal employment. The bill amends section 701 of the Civil Rights Act of 1964 (section 2 of the bill) to include State and local governments, governmental agencies and political subdivisions within the definition of an "employer" under Title VII. All State and local government employees would under the bill have access to the remedies available under the Act.

In a report released in 1969, the U.S. Commission on Civil Rights examined equal employment opportunity in public employment in seven urban areas located throughout the country—North as well as South. The report's findings indicate that widespread discrimination against minorities exists in State and local government employment, and that the existence of this discrimination is perpetuated by the presence of both institutional and overt discriminatory practices. The report cites widespread perpetuation of past discriminatory practices through *de facto* segregated job ladders, invalid selection techniques, and stereotyped misconceptions by supervisors regarding minority group capabilities. The study also indicates that employment discrimination in State and local governments is more pervasive than in the private sector. The report found that in six of the seven areas studied, Negroes constitute over 70 percent of the common laborers, but that most white-collar jobs were found to be largely inaccessible to minority persons. For example, in Atlanta and Baton Rouge, there were no blacks in city managerial positions.

In another report issued by the U.S. Commission on Civil Rights in 1970, *Mexican Americans and the Administration of Justice in the Southwest*, the Commission found, on the basis of a 1968 survey, that in the law enforcement agencies and district attorneys' offices in the five Southwestern States, Mexican Americans were generally underrepresented in proportion to their demographic distribution. The statistics in this report show that in the Southwestern States Mexican Americans, who constitute approximately 12 percent of the population, account for only 5.2 percent of police officers and 6.11 percent of civilian employers with law enforcement agencies.

The problem of employment discrimination is particularly acute and has the most deleterious effect in these governmental activities which are most visible to the minority communities (notably education, law enforcement, and the administration of justice) with the result that the credibility of the government's claim to represent all the people equally is negated.

This widespread discrimination is evidence that State and local governmental units have not instituted equal employment opportunity required by the national policy to eliminate discrimination in employment. In its 1969 report, *For All the People ... By All the People*, the U.S. Civil Rights Commission concludes that:

The basic finding of this report is that State and local governments have failed to fulfill their obligation to assure equal job opportunity. . . . Not only do State and local governments consciously and overtly discriminate in hiring and promoting minority group members, but they do not foster positive programs to deal with discriminatory treatment on the job.

The Constitution is as imperative in its prohibition of discrimination in state and local government employment as it is in barring discrimination in Federal jobs. The courts have consistently held that discrimination by state and local governments, including job discrimination, violates the Fourteenth Amendment and is prohibited.[5]

While an individual has a right of action in the appropriate court if he has been discriminated against, the adequacy of protection against employment discrimination by state and local governments has been severely impeded by the failure of the Congress to provide Federal administrative machinery to assist the aggrieved employee. There are two exceptions. Federal Merit Standards provisions are applied to approximately 250,000 state employees where the Federal and state governments participate jointly in furnishing government services, and there are nondiscrimination requirements Department of Housing and Urban Development (HUD) contracts which are applicable to approximately 900 local urban renewal agencies and 2,000 local public housing authorities.

Otherwise, state and local governments constitute the only large group of employees in the nation who are almost entirely exempt from Federal nondiscrimination protections. Although the aggrieved individual may enforce his rights directly in the Federal district courts, this remedy, as already noted, is frequently an empty promise due to the expense and time involved in pursuing a Federal court suit. It is unrealistic to expect disadvantaged individuals to bear the burden.

The Committee feels that it is an injustice to provide employees in the private sector with an administrative forum in which to redress their grievances while at the same time, denying a similar protection to the increasing number of state and local employees. Accordingly, H.R. 1746 provides the administrative remedies available to employees in the private sector should also be extended to state and local employees.

In establishing the applicability of Title VII to State and local employees, the Committee wishes to emphasize that the individual's right to file a civil action in his own behalf, pursuant to the Civil Rights Act of 1870 and 1871, 42 U.S.C. §§ 1981 and 1983, is in no way affected. During the floor debate surrounding the passage of Title VII of the Civil Rights Act of 1964, it was made clear that the Act was not intended to preempt existing rights under the National Labor Relations Act or the Railway Labor Act. Title VII was envisioned as an independent statutory authority meant to provide an aggrieved individual with an additional remedy to redress employment dis-

---

[5] See e.g., *Shelly* v. *Kraemer,* 334 U.S. 1 (1948) ; *Burton* v. *Wilmington Parking Authority,* 365 U.S. 715 (1961).

crimination. Two recent court decisions, *Young* v. *International Telephone and Telegraph Co.*, ——F. 2d ——, 3 FEP Cases 145 (3rd Cir. 1971) and *Saunders* v. *Dobbs House*, 431 F. 2d 1097 (5th Cir. 1970), have affirmed this Committee's belief that the remedies available to the individual under Title VII are co-extensive with the indivdual's right to sue under the provisions of the Civil Rights Act of 1866, 42 U.S.C. § 1981, and that the two procedures augment each other and are not mutually exclusive. The bill, therefore, by extending jurisdiction to State and local government employees does not affect existing rights that such individuals have already been granted by previous legislation.

The expansion of Title VII coverage to State and local government employment is firmly embodied in the principles of the Constitution of the United States. The Constitution has recognized that it is inimical to the democratic form of government to allow the existence of discrimination in those bureaucratic systems which most directly affect the daily interactions of this Nation's citizens. The clear intention of the Constitution, embodied in the Thirteenth and Fourteenth Amendments, is to prohibit all forms of discrimination.

Legislation to implement this aspect of the Fourteenth Amendment is long overdue, and the committee believes that an appropriate remedy has been fashioned in the bill. Inclusion of state and local employees among those enjoying the protection of Title VII provides an alternate administrative remedy to the existing prohibition against discrimination perpetuated "under color of state law" as embodied in the Civil Rights Act of 1871, 42 U.S.C. § 1983. In extending Title VII coverage, the Committee recognizes that States frequently can best deal with violations which occur within their boundaries and has, accordingly, retained the provisions of Section 706(b) of the present Act (706(c) under the bill) whereby the Commission will defer to appropriate State agencies cases where the State or local agency can grant the complainant relief similar to that which he can obtain with the Commission under the provisions of this bill.

EDUCATIONAL INSTITUTION EMPLOYEES

The present Section 702 of Title VII exempts educational institution employees connected with educational activities ·from the equal employment requirements. The bill removes this exemption (Section 3 of the bill).

There is nothing in the legislative background of Title VII, nor does any national policy suggest itself to support the exemption of these educational institution employees—primarily teachers—from Title VII coverage. Discrimination against minorities and women in the field of education is as pervasive as discrimination in any other area of employment. In the field of higher education, the fact that black scholars have been generally relegated to all-black institutions, or have been restricted to lesser academic positions when they have been permitted entry into white institutions is common knowledge. Similarly, in the area of sex discrimination, women have long been invited to participate as students in the academic process, but without the prospect of gaining employment as serious scholars.

When they have been hired into educational institutions, particularly in institutions of higher education, women have been relegated to positions of lesser standing than their male counterparts. In a study conducted by Theodore Kaplow and Reece J. McGee, it was found that the primary factors determining the hiring of male faculty members were prestige and compatability, but that women were generally considered to be outside of the prestige system altogether.[6]

The committee feels that discrimination in educational institutions is especially critical. The committee can not imagine a more sensitive area than educational institutions where the Nation's youth are exposed to a multitude of ideas that will strongly influence their fuure development. To permit discrimination here would, more than in any other area, tend to promote misconceptions leading to future patterns of discrimination. Accordingly, the committee feels that educational institutions, like other employers in the Nation, should report their activities to the Commission and should be subject to the provisions of the Act.

EMPLOYERS AND LABOR UNIONS WITH EIGHT OR MORE EMPLOYEES OR MEMBERS

The bill amends section 701 of the Act, by changing the jurisdictional reach of Title VII to include all employers and labor unions with eight or more employees or members, effective one year after enactment (section 2 of the bill). The present coverage is 25 or more employees or members.

The committee feels that discrimination in employment is contrary to the national policy and equally invidious whether practiced by small or large employers. Because of the existing limitation in the bill proscribing the coverage of Title VII to 25 or more employees or members, a large segment of the Nation's work force is excluded from an effective Federal remedy to redress employment discrimination. For the reasons already stated in earlier sections of this report, the committee feels that the Commission's remedial power should also be available to all segments of the work force. With the amendment proposed by the bill, Federal equal employment protection will be assured to virtually every segment of the Nation's work force.

TESTING

Section 8 of the bill amends subsection 703(h) of the Act and perfects the Title VII provisions dealing with testing and apprenticeship training. Tests, while they are a useful and necessary selection device for management purposes, often operate unreasonably and unnecessarily to the disadvantage of minority individuals. General intelligence tests commonly used by employers as selection devices for hiring and promotion deprive minority group members of equal employment opportunities.[7] Culturally disadvantaged groups—groups

---

[6] See generally, Kaplow and McGee, *The Academic Marketplace,* Anchor Edition (Garden City : 1965).

[7] See e.g., M. Culhane, "Testing the Disadvantaged," *The Journal of Social Issues* (April, 1965) ; D. Goslin, *The Search for Ability: Standarized Testing on Social Perspective,* (New York : Russell Sage Foundation (1963)) ; R. Krug, "The Problem of Cultural Bias in Selection," *Selecting and Training Negroes for Management Positions,* Princeton : Educational Testing Service (1965).

which because of low incomes, substandard housing, poor education, and other "atypical" environmental experiences—perform less well on these types of tests on the average than do applicants from middle class environments. The net result is that members from culturally disadvantaged groups are screened out of employment and training programs merely because of their failure to score well on such tests. Such tests are often irrelevant to the job to be performed by the individual being tested and uncritical reliance on test results may not aid management decisions and selection of personnel, but will screen out the disadvantaged minority individual.

In a report issued in 1970, *Personnel Testing and Employment Opportunity*, the Commission describes the ways in which employment tests can discriminate against minority groups. An aptitude test that fails to predict job performance in the same way for both minorities and whites, or fails to predict job performance at all is an invalid test. If such a test is weighted to differentiate between blacks and whites, it is similarly discriminatory. Tests may discriminate in the social sense if they deny equal opportunity for consideration. A test which tends to discriminate generally operates in the following manner: (a) when scores on it tend to differentiate between identifiable sub-groups where sub-grouping itself is not a relevant factor, and either (b) scores for the lower group underpredict performance on the job when the standards of the upper group are applied, or (c) scores on the test do not predict job performance of either group.

The Supreme Court recently examined the problem of employment testing and its relationship to employment discrimination in its decision in *Griggs* v. *Duke Power Co.*, —— U.S. ——, 91 S. Ct. 849 (1971). In its decision, the court held that employment tests, even if valid on their face and applied in a non-discriminatory manner, were invalid if they tended to discriminate against minorities and the company could not show an overriding reason why such tests were necessary. At page 5 of its opinion, the Court stated:

> The objective of Congress in the enactment of Title VII is plain from the language of the statute. It was to achieve equality of employment opportunities and remove barriers that have operated in the past to favor an identifiable group of white employees over other employees. Under the Act, practices, procedures, or tests neutral on their face, and even neutral in terms of intent cannot be maintained if they operate to "freeze" the status quo of prior discriminatory practices.

The Court stated further, on page 6 of its opinion, that:

> Congress has now provided that tests or criteria for employment or promotion may not provide equality of opportunity only in the sense of the fabled offer of milk for the stork and the fox. On the contrary, Congress has now required that the posture and condition of the job seeker be taken into account . . . . The Act proscribes not only overt discrimination but also practices that are fair in form but discriminatory in operation. The touchstone is business neces-

sity. If an employment practice which excludes Negroes cannot be shown to be related to job performance, the practice is prohibited.

The provisions of the bill are fully in accord with the decision of the Court and with the testing guidelines established by the Commission. The addition of the requirement for a bona fide occupational qualification which is reasonably necessary to perform the normal duties of the position to which it is applied requires that employers, who use employment tests as determinants for qualifications of employees for a particular job, must determine whether the test is necessary for the particular position to which it is applied. Even after such determination, if the use of the test acts to maintain existing or past discriminatory imbalances in the job, or tends to discriminate against applicants on the basis of race, color, religion, sex or national origin, the employer must show an overriding business necessity to justify use of the test.

Section 8 perfects Title VII's provisions with respect to testing and apprenticeship training. With regard to testing, the amendment is limited to tests for particular positions; it is not intended to apply to tests given to ascertain potential ability to undertake apprenticeship or other learning capacities. Of course, tests given for apprenticeship and related status must satisfy the requirement that the test, its administration or action upon the results, is not designed, intended, used, or have the effect of discriminating because of race, color, religion, sex or national origin.

FEDERAL EMPLOYMENT

The bill adds a new section 717 (section 11 of the bill) which, in paragraphs (a) and (b), gives the Equal Employment Opportunity Commission the authority to enforce the obligations of equal employment opportunity in Federal employment.

The Federal service is an area where equal employment opportunity is of paramount significance. Americans rely upon the maxim, "government of the people," and traditionally measure the quality of their democracy by the opportunity they have to participate in governmental processes. It is therefore imperative that equal opportunity be the touchstone of the Federal system.

The prohibition against discrimination by the Federal Government, based upon the due process clause of the fifth amendment to the Constitution, was judicially recognized long before the enactment of the Civil Rights Act of 1964.[8] And Congress itself has specifically provided that it is "the policy of the United States to insure equal employment opportunities for Federal employees without discrimination because of race, color, religion, sex, or national origin. . . ." (5 U.S.C. § 7151 (Supp. II 1965, 1966)).

The primary responsibility for implementing this stated national policy has rested with the Civil Service Commission, pursuant to Executive Order 11246 (1964) as clarified by Executive Order 11748.

In his memorandum accompanying Executive Order 11478, President Nixon stated that "discrimination of any kind based on factors

---

[8] See *Bolling* v. *Sharpe,* 347 U.S. 497, 74 S. Ct. 693 (1954), and cases cited therein.

not relevant to job performance must be eradicated completely from Federal employment." Accordingly there can exist no justification for anything but a vigorous effort to accord Federal employees the same rights and impartial treatment which the law seeks to afford employees in the private sector.

Despite some progress that has been made in this area, the record is far from satisfactory. Statistical evidence shows that minorities and women continue to be excluded from large numbers of government jobs, particularly at the higher grade levels. According to statistics released by the Civil Service Commission, as of May 31, 1970, minorities accounted for 19.4 percent of the total number of government employees and 14.4 percent of general schedule employees. An examination of the distribution of employees within the various levels of the Federal system shows that the majority of these employees are at the lower levels of government employment. Approximately 80% of the minority employees on the general schedule are in grades 1 through 8. In grades GS-1 through 4 minorities account for 27.3 percent of all employees, and in grades GS-5 through 8 they represent 17.2 percent of all employees. On the other end of the scale, in grades GS-14 through 15, minorities represent only 3.3 percent of all employees, and at grades GS-16 through 18 minorities account for 2.0 percent of all employees. These figures represent little improvement over the statistics from the previous study done by the Civil Service Commission in November, 1969. In fact comparison of the two sets of figures shows no perceptible change in the proportion of minorities in the Federal service during the 6 month period. Although minority representation in positions above GS-14 has increased slightly the minority concentration in the lower level positions (GS-1-4) has also increased by .6% from 26.7%.

The figures for Spanish-surnamed employees reflect a similar pattern. For example, according to the 1970 statistics, only 2.9% of the Federal employees were Spanish-surnamed (this was an increase from 2.8% in November, 1969). Only .63% of the government executives (GS-14—18) were Spanish-surnamed. Over 72% of the Spanish-surnamed employees on the General Schedule were in positions of GS-8 and below.

Moreover, figures show different levels of minority representation within the different agencies. For example, although 15% of Federal employees are Negro, only 5.2% of the Department of Interior's employees are Negro and 2.9% of NASA's employees are Negro. According to 1967 figures, fewer than 550 of the Federal Aviation Administration's air traffic controllers out of a total of over 20,000 were minority. Only 13 out of the Administration's 1,612 supervisory and administrative personnel (GS-14 to 18) were Negro.

This disproportionatte distribution of minorities and women throughout the Federal bureaucracy and their exclusion from higher level policy-making and supervisory positions indicates the government's failure to pursue its policy of equal opportunity.

A critical defect of the Federal equal employment program has been the failure of the complaint process. That process has impeded rather than advanced the goal of the elimination of discrimination in

Federal employment. The defect, which existed under the old complaint procedure, was not corrected by the new complaint process. The new procedure, intended to provide for the informal resolution of complaints, has, in practice, denied employees adequate opportunity for impartial investigation and resolution of complaints.

Under the revised procedure, effective July 1, 1969, the agency is still responsible for investigating and judging itself. Although the procedure provides for the appointment of a hearing examiner from an outside agency, the examiner does not have the authority to conduct an independent investigation. Further, the conclusions and findings of the examiner are in the nature of recommendations to the agency head who makes the final agency determination as to whether discrimination exists. Although the complaint procedure provides for an appeal to the Board of Appeals and Review in the Civil Service Commission, the record shows that the Board rarely reverses the agency decision.

The system, which permits the Civil Service Commission to sit in judgment over its own practices and procedures which themselves may raise questions of systemic discrimination, creates a built-in conflict-of-interest.

Testimony reflected a general lack of confidence in the effectiveness of the complaint procedure on the part of Federal employees. Complainants were skeptical of the Civil Service Commission's record in obtaining just resolutions of complaints and adequate remedies. This has discouraged persons from filing complaints with the Commission for fear that it will only result in antagonizing their supervisors and impairing any hope of future advancement.

Aside from the inherent structural defects the Civil Service Commission has been plagued by a general lack of expertise in recognizing and isolating the various forms of discrimination which exist in the system. The revised directives to Federal agencies which the Civil Service Commission has issued are inadequate to meet the challenge of eliminating systemic discrimination. The Civil Service Commission seems to assume that employment discrimination is primarily a problem of malicious intent on the part of individuals. It apparently has not recognized that the general rules and procedures it has promulgated may actually operate to the disadvantage of minorities and women in systemic fashion. All too frequently policies established at the policy level of the Civil Service Commission do not penetrate to lower administrative levels. The result is little or no action in areas where unlawful practices are most pronounced. Civil Service selection and promotion requirements are replete with artificial selection and promotion requirements that place a premium on "paper" credentials which frequently prove of questionable value as a means of predicting actual job performance. The problem is further aggravated by the agency's use of general ability tests which are not aimed at any direct relationship to specific jobs. The inevitable consequence of this, as demonstrated by similar practices in the private sector, and, found unlawful by the Supreme Court, is that classes of persons who are culturally or educationally disadvantaged are subjected to a heavier burden in seeking employment.

To correct this entrenched discrimination in the Federal service, it is necessary to insure the effective application of uniform, fair and strongly enforced policies. The present law and the proposed statute do not permit industry and labor organizations to be the judges of their own conduct in the area of employment discrimination. There is no reason why government agencies should not be treated similarly. Indeed, the government itself should set the example by permitting its conduct to be reviewed by an impartial tribunal. Because the Equal Employment Opportunity Commission is the expert agency in the field of employment discrimination and because it is an independent agency removed from the administration of Federal employment, it is the most logical place for the enforcement power to be vested.

Despite the series of executive and administrative directives on equal employment opportunity, Federal employees, unlike those in the private sector to whom Title VII is applicable, face legal obstacles in obtaining meaningful remedies. There is serious doubt that court review is available to the aggrieved Federal employee. Monetary restitution or back pay is not attainable. In promotion situations, a critical area of discrimination, the promotion is often no longer available. Information and documents contained in Government files are not obtainable since the Freedom of Information Act exempts internal personnel rules. Under the proposed law, court review, back pay, promotions, reinstatement, and appropriate affirmative relief is available to employees in the private sector; also the Commission has broad powers to conduct an intensive investigation and obtain access to all pertinent records.

The Commission is established as a government administrative agency to protect employees against discrimination. This agency under the proposed law assumes the burden and expense of litigation to obtain adequate redress for the employee. These substantial benefits and protections are not presently available to the Federal employee. Presently the Federal employee is entirely dependent on his own resources and does not have recourse to an impartial governmental agency with developed expertise.

The transfer of the civil rights enforcement function from the Civil Service Commission to the Equal Employment Opportunity commission does not preclude the Civil Service Commission from maintaining its internal equal employment programs. Consistent with Federal law it is expected that the Civil Service Commission and the Federal agencies will continue their commitment to affirmative measures such as recruiting and training, specialized hiring programs, the training of compliance personnel and supervisory Federal personnel in equal employment, and the appointment of EEO officers. In all these cases, the primary responsibility shall rest with the Civil Service Commission and the other Federal agencies. The Equal Employment Opportunity Commission will work closely with these agencies to aid the development and maintenance of programs which will best serve the needs for equal employment in the government. It is expected that the expertise of the Equal Employment Opportunities Commission will be utilized to review existing programs, to evaluate new systems which will be established, and to issue guidelines and standards where appropriate. The Equal Employment Opportunity Commission will be authorized by the statute to hear complaints of discrimination in Federal employment and establish appropriate procedures for an impartial adjudication of the complaints.

An employee of a Federal agency may have recourse to a civil action, as provided in section 715 (discussed infra), if he is not satisfied with the disposition of his complaint.

SECTION-BY-SECTION ANALYSIS

Section 1

This section contains the enacting clause and style of the Act.

Section 2, Jurisdiction

Section 701 (a).—This subsection defines "person" to include State and local governments, governmental agencies and political subdivisions.

Section 701 (b).—This subsection would extend coverage of employers to those with eight or more employees at the end of the first year. This subsection would broaden the meaning of "employer" to include State and local governments and the District of Columbia departments or agencies (except those subject by statute to procedures of the Federal competitive service as defined in 5 USC 2102).

Section 701 (c).—This subsection eliminates the exemption for agencies of the States or of political subdivisions of States from the definition of "employment agency" in order to conform with the expanded coverage of State and local governments in section 701(a) and (b).

Section 701 (e).—This subsection is revised to include coverage of labor organizations with eight or more members after the first year.

Section 701 (h).—This subsection is revised to include "any governmental industry, business, or activity" in the definition of "industry affecting commerce."

Section 3. Educational Institutions

Section 702.—Comparable to present Section 702. The exemption currently provided to certain employees (primarily teachers) of educational institutions is deleted.

Section 4. Employment

Section 706 (a).—New Section. The Commission is empowered to prevent any person from engaging in any unlawful employment practice as set forth in Sections 703 or 704.

Section 706 (b).—Comparable to present Section 706 (a). The requirement that aggrieved person's charges be made under oath is deleted. Charges shall contain such information as the Commission requires. Charges may also be filed on behalf of persons aggrieved. The Commission shall make its finding as to reasonable cause as promptly as possible, and so far as is practicable, not later than 120 days from the filing of the charge, or when deferral is applicable under subsection (c) or (d), from the date on which the Commission is authorized to take action with respect to the charge. If reasonable cause is not found, the Commission shall dismiss the charge, giving prompt notification to the parties. The conciliation and confidentiality provisions are retained.

Section 706 (c).—Comparable to present Section 706 (b). Charges of persons in FEPC States may be filed with the Commission, but the latter may take no action until 60 days after commencement of proceedings in the appropriate State or local agency (120 days if a new agency). The latter proceeding shall be deemed to have commenced at the time a written statement of the facts is sent to such agency by certified mail.

Section 706(d).—Comparable to present Section 706(c).

Section 706(e).—Comparable to present Section 706(d). The 90 day filing period is expanded to 180 days, and the 210 day period to 300 days (or 30 days after receiving notice of termination of proceedings, whichever comes earlier). Provision is added requiring that a copy of the charge be served on the respondent as soon as practicable after filing.

Section 706(f).—Comparable to present Section 706(e). After attempting to secure voluntary compliance under subsection (b), if the Commission determines (which determination is not reviewable in any court) that it is unable to secure from the respondent a conciliation agreement acceptable to the Commission and the person aggrieved, the Commission shall issue and cause to be served upon the respondent a complaint stating the facts upon which the allegation of the unlawful employment practice is based, together with a notice of hearing before the Commission, or a member or agent of it, at a specified place not less than 5 days after service of the complaint and notice. Any member of the Commission who filed a charge in any case shall not participate in a hearing on any complaint arising out of such charge, except as a witness.

Section 706(g).—New Section. Respondent has the right to file an answer to the complaint and with the Commission's permission, may amend his answer at any time if deemed reasonable. Respondent and the person aggrieved shall be parties and may appear at any stage of the proceedings with or without counsel. The Commission may grant others the right to intervene or file briefs or make oral arguments as amicus curiae, or for other purposes as it considers appropriate. All testimony shall be taken under oath and shall be reduced to writing.

Section 706(h).—New Section. If the Commission finds that respondent has engaged in an unlawful employment practice, the Commission shall state its findings of fact and shall issue and cause to be served upon the respondent and aggrieved person an order requiring the respondent to cease and desist from such unlawful employment practice and take such affirmative action (including reinstatement or hiring with or without back pay) as will effectuate the policies of the Act. Interim earnings or amounts earnable with reasonable diligence operate to reduce the backpay otherwise allowable. Such order may further require the respondent to make reports from time to time showing the extent to which he has complied with the order. If the Commission finding is that no unlawful employment practice occurred, it shall state its findings of fact and so notify the respondent and complainant of an order dismissing the complaint.

Section 706(i).—New Section. After a charge has been filed and until the record has been filed in court, the proceedings may at any time be ended by agreement between the Commission and the parties and the Commission may at any time, upon reasonable notice, modify or set aside, in whole or in part, any order or finding issued or made by it. An agreement approved by the Commission shall be enforceable under subsection (k).

Section 706(j).—New Section. Findings of fact or orders made or issued under subsection (b) or (i) shall be determined on the record.

Section 706(k).—New Section. The Commission may petition any U.S. Court of Appeals wherein whose circuit the unlawful employment practice occurred or wherein respondent resides or transacts business, for enforcement of its order and for appropriate temporary relief or restraining order. The Commission shall file in the court the record of its proceedings as provided in section 2112 of title 28 of the U.S. Code. Upon serving notice on the parties, the court shall have jurisdiction and the power to grant such temporary relief, restraining order, or other order as it deems just and proper and enter upon the record a decree enforcing, modifying, and enforcing as so modified or setting aside in whole or in part the order of the Commission. No objection that has not been urged before the Commission, its member, or its agent shall be considered by the court except under extraordinary circumstances. The findings of the Commission with respect to questions of fact shall be conclusive if supported by substantial evidence on the record considered as a whole. The court may order additional evidence to be taken by the Commission, which may then modify its fact findings. Upon the filing of the record with it, the jurisdiction of the court shall be exclusive and its judgment and decree final, subject only to review by the Supreme Court.

Section 706(l).—New Section. Any party aggrieved by a final order of the Commission may obtain review of such order in any U.S. Court of Appeals in the circuit wherein the unlawful employment practice was alleged to have been engaged in or wherein such person resides or transacts business, or in the D.C. Court of Appeals. Upon receiving a copy of such petition, the Commission shall file in the court the record of its proceedings, and the court shall then proceed in the same manner as in the case of a petition by the Commission under subsection (k). Commencement of proceedings under this subsection or subsection (k) shall not operate as a stay of the Commission's order.

Section 706(m).—New Section. The provisions of 29 U.S.C. 101–115 with respect to preliminary injunctions are made inapplicable to judicial proceedings under the Title.

Section 706(n).—New Section. The general counsel of the Commission shall conduct all litigation affecting it, or to which it is a party, except that the Attorney General shall conduct all litigation to which the Commission is a party in the Supreme Court.

Section 706(o).—New Section. When after the filling of a charge, the Commission concludes on the basis of a preliminary investigation that prompt judicial action is necessary to preserve the power of the Commission to grant effective relief, it may bring an action for appropriate temporary or preliminary relief in the district court for the district where the unlawful employment practice is alleged to have been committed, or in the district where the aggrieved person would have been employed, or if the respondent cannot be found in these districts, in the district where the respondent has his principal office. Upon the bringing of such action, the district court may grant such injunctive relief or temporary restraining order as it deems just and proper, as governed by Rule 65 of the Federal Rules of Civil Procedures.

Section 5. Records Required To Be Kept and Investigations

Section 707(c).—New Section. Any record or paper required by section 709(c) shall be made available to the Commission on written demand, for purposes of inspection and copying, but unless otherwise ordered by a court of the United States, the Commission shall not disclose any information thus obtained except to Congress or any committee thereof, a governmental agency, or in the presentation of any case or preceding before any court or grand jury. The appropriate district court may compel the production of such records or papers.

Section 707(d).—Transfers the function of the Attorney General with respect to patterns or practice of resistance to the full enjoyment of the rights secured by Title VII, together with personnel, property, records and funds, to the Commission.

Section 707(e).—Provides for continuation by the Commission of pending proceedings brought by the Attorney General under Section 707.

Section 707(f).—Assimilates procedures for new proceedings brought under Section 707 to those now provided for under Section 706 so that the Commission may provide an administrative procedure to be the counterpart of the present Section 707 action.

Section G. State and Local Agencies, Recordkeeping

Section 709(b).—Comparable to present Section 709(b). The contracts to State and local agencies language is enlarged to include Commission contributions to research and other projects of mutual interest, and payment to State and local agencies may be made in advance as well as in reimbursement. The provisions concerning agreements whereby no civil actions may be brought is omitted. The power of the Commission to rescind any agreement no longer serving the interest of effective enforcement is retained.

Section 709(c).—The Section 709(d) reporting exemption is deleted, and the hardship language is changed to require that persons or organizations alleging hardship must exhaust the relief processes provided by the Commission before applying for relief in the district court.

Section 709(d).—Deletes the present subsection, and in its place provides that the Commission shall consult with other interested State and Federal agencies and shall endeavor to coordinate its requirements with those of such other agencies. The Commission shall furnish information obtained pursuant to subsection (c) of this section without cost to any State or local FEPC on request, except that public disclosure of such information provided on the part of such State or local agency prior to the institution of a proceeding under State or local law shall be grounds for declining to honor subsequent requests pursuant to this subsection.

Section 7. Commission Investigations

Section 710.—Comparable to present Section 710. Incorporates the provisions of section 11 of the NLRA (29 U.S.C. 161). The Commission shall have access to and the right to copy evidence of a person being investigated or proceeded against that relates to the matter under investigation or in question. It shall issue subpenas to parties on application requiring the presence and testimony of witnesses and the production of evidence as specified in such application. Within 5 days of service, the person served may petition the Commission to revoke its subpena on grounds that the evidence sought is not relevant to the matter in question. Attendance of witnesses and the production of evidence may be required from any place in the United States or its possessions, and any Federal court with jurisdiction may enforce such subpenas by order. Witnesses may not refuse to answer questions on grounds of self incrimination, but may not be subsequently proceeded against on the basis of information thus gained. Complaints, orders and other processes may be served personally or by registered mail or telegraph, or by leaving a copy at the principal office of the person to be served. No subpena shall be issued to any party to a proceeding before the Commission until after the respondent has been served a copy of the complaint and notice of hearing under section 706(f). Witnesses and persons making depositions shall receive the same mileage and fees as witnesses and persons making depositions in the district courts.

Section 8. Selection Procedures, Apprenticeship Programs, Commission Organization

Section 703(a)(2).—Comparable to present Section 703(a)(2). Adds "or applicants for employment" after "employees."

Section 703(c)(2).—Comparable to present Section 703(c)(2). Adds "or applicants for membership" after "membership."

Section 703(h).—Comparable to present Section 703(h). Retains the seniority and merit system language, but changes the testing provisions to stipulate that such tests must be directly related to the determination of bona fide occupational qualifications reasonably necessary to perform the normal duties of the particular position concerned. The provision prohibiting tests designed or used to discriminate on the basis of race, color, religion, national origin, or sex is retained.

Section 704(a) and (b).—Comparable to present Section 704(a) and (b). Adds 'or joint labor-management committee controlling apprenticeship or other training or retraining, including on-the-job training programs"; after "employment agency."

Section 705(a).—Comparable to present Section 705(a). Amends the Section to include "members of the Commission shall continue to serve until their successors are appointed and qualified," provided that no such member shall continue to serve for more than 60 days when the Congress is in session unless a nomination to fill the vacancy has been submitted to the Senate, or after the adjournment sine die of the session of the Senate in which such nomination was submitted. The section also adds "hearing examiners" to the appointments the Chairman may make in accordance with title 5, U.S.C. on behalf of the Commission, and provides that assignment, removal and compensation of such hearing examiners shall be in accordance with sections 3105, 3344, 5362, and 7521 of title 5, U.S.C. Section 3105 provides for the appointment of the necessary number of hearing examiners, requires that they be assigned to cases in rotation, and stipulates that they may not be assigned duties that are inconsistent with their position as hearing examiners. Section 3344 authorizes an agency's use of hearing examiners from other agencies as selected by the Civil Service Commission if the borrowing agency is short staffed. Section 5362 states that such hearing examiners are entitled to the pay prescribed by the Civil Service Commission for them independently of agency recommendations or ratings, in accordance with subchapter III and chapter 51 of title 5, U.S.C. Section 7521 allows removal of hearing examiners only for good cause established and determined by the Civil Service Commission on the record after hearing.

Section 705(g)(1).—Comparable to present Section 705(g)(1). Adds "and to accept voluntary and uncompensated services, notwithstanding that provisions of section 3679(b) of the Revised Statutes" after the word "individuals."

Section 705(g)(6).—Comparable to present Section 706(g)(6). Substitutes Section "715" for Section "706."

Section 713(c) and (d).—New subsections. Authorizes the Commission to delegate its powers with respect to investigating, conciliating, hearing, determining, ordering, certifying, reporting, or otherwise acting to such persons as the Commission may designate by regulation, with certain exceptions. The exceptions concern the power to issue cease and desist orders, the power to modify or set aside findings under subsections (i) and (k) of Section 706, certain aspects of the rulemaking powers, and the power to enter into or rescind agreements with State and local agencies as provided in subsection (b) of Section 709. The Commission is specifically not authorized to provide for persons other than those referred to in section 556, subsection (b), clauses (2) and (3) of title 5, U.S.C. to conduct any hearing to which that section applies. New subsection (d) authorizes the Commission to delegate to any group of three or more of its members any or all of the powers which it may itself exercise.

Section 714.—Comparable to present Section 714. Adds section 1114 of title 18, U.S.C. (murder of Commission employees).

Section 715.—New Section, comparable in part to present Section 706. Deletes the provisions of the present Section 715, which called for a 1965 study of discrimination because of age, provides that if the Commission dismisses a charge after a preliminary investigation indicates no cause, or on grounds of lack of jurisdiction, or if after 180 days from the filing of a charge the Commission has not made a finding of no reasonable cause or entered into a conciliation agreement acceptable to the Commission and to the person aggrieved, the Commission shall notify the aggrieved party, and within 60 days of such notification such party may bring a civil action against the respondent named in the charge. The court may upon application appoint an attorney for such complainant, and may dispense with the payment of fees, costs, or security. It may also permit the Commission to intervene if it certifies that the cause is of general public importance. Upon the commencement of such action the Commission is divested of jurisdiction over the proceeding and may take no further action, except that the court may in its discretion stay further proceedings for not longer than 60 days pending termination of State or local proceedings, or the efforts of the Commission to obtain voluntary compliance. Subsections (b) and (c) retain the procedural provisions of present Section 706, subsections (f) and (g), while subsections (d), (e), and (f) duplicate Section 706, subsections (i), (j) and (k), the latter subsection modified to delete the exceptions of the Commission and the

United States in regard to attorney's fees and to change the words "prevailing party" to "prevailing plaintiff." Present subsection (h) excepting such proceedings from the provisions of 29 U.S.C. 101–115 is retained with modified language at Section 706(m).

Section 9. Commissioner's Compensation.

Title 5, U.S.C. Add "Chairman, Equal Employment Opportunity Commission" at the end of section 5314 (Level III Positions). Add "Members, Equal Employment Opportunity Commission" to clause (72) of section 5315 (Level IV Positions). Repeal clause (III) of section 5316 (the Level V slot presently occuped by Members of the Commission).

Section 10. Pending Cases

Sections 706 and 710 of the Civil Rights Act of 1964, as amended by this Act, shall not be applicable to charges filed with the Commission prior to the effective date of this Act.

Section 11. Federal Employees, Federal Contractors

Section 717(a) and (b).—New Section. All personnel actions affecting employees of applicants for employment in the competitive service of the United States or in positions of the District of Columbia Government covered by the Civil Service Retirement Act shall be made free from any discrimination based on race, color, religion, sex, or national origin.

The Equal Employment Opportunity Commission shall enforce the nondiscrimination provisions of subsection (a), and shall issue appropriate rules, regulations, orders, and instructions. The responsibilities of the Civil Service Commission with regard to nondiscrimination in Federal employment are transferred to the Equal Employment Opportunity Commission. This, of course, will not relieve the Civil Service Commission, the Federal agencies, or the District of Columbia, of their affirmative responsibilities to assure equal opportunity in government employment, nor transfer any functions relating thereto (as distinguished from enforcement functions).

Section 717(c).—Persons aggrieved by the final disposition of complaints may, within thirty days of receipt of notice, file a civil action in the same manner as in Section 715, in which action the head of the executive department or agency, or the District of Columbia, as appropriate, shall be the respondent.

Section 717(f).—With respect to employment discrimination by government contractors and subcontractors and federally assisted construction contractors and subcontractors, this subsection, effectively, transfers those functions of the Secretary of Labor, established pursuant to Executive Order 11246, to the Equal Employment Opportunity Commission. Under the provisions of this bill the Commission is given the statutory responsibility to carry out all such authority, functions, and responsibilities in order to enforce and implement the substantive requirements.

Section 718.—New Section. Reiterates the individual obligation of all Government agencies or officials to assure nondiscrimination in employment.

Section 12. Effective Date of Section 11

New Section 717, added by Section 11 of the Act shall become effective six months after the effective date of the Act.

CHANGES IN EXISTING LAW MADE BY THE BILL, AS REPORTED

In compliance with clause 3 of rule XIII of the Rules of the House of Representatives, changes in existing law made by the bill, as reported, are shown as follows (existing law proposed to be omitted is enclosed in black brackets, new matter is printed in italic, existing law in which no change is proposed is shown in roman) :

TITLE VII OF THE CIVIL RIGHTS ACT OF 1964

TITLE VII—EQUAL EMPLOYMENT OPPORTUNITY

DEFINITIONS

SEC. 701. For the purposes of this title—

(a) The term "person" includes one or more individuals, *governments, governmental agencies, political subdivisions*, labor unions, partnerships, associations, corporations, legal representatives, mutual companies, joint-stock companies, trusts, unincorporated organizations, trustees, trustees in bankruptcy, or receivers.

(b) The term "employer" means a person engaged in an industry affecting commerce who has [twenty-five] *eight* or more employees for each working day in each of twenty or more calendar weeks in the current or preceding calendar year, and any agent of such a person, but such term does not include (1) the United States, a corporation wholly owned by the Government of the United States, an Indian tribe or [a State or political subdivision thereof] *the District of Columbia*, (2) a bona fide private membership club (other than a labor organization) which is exempt from taxation under section 501(e) of the Internal Revenue Code of 1954: *Provided*, That during the first year after the effective date prescribed in subsection (a) of section 716, persons having fewer than one hundred employees (and their agents) shall not be considered employers, and, during the second year after such date, persons having fewer than seventy-five employees (and their agents) shall not be considered employers, and, during the third year after such date, persons having fewer than fifty employees (and their agents) shall not be considered employers.

(c) The term "employment agency" means any person regularly undertaking with or without compensation to procure employees for an employer or to procure for employees opportunities to work for an employer and includes an agent of such a person; but shall not include an agency of the United States, [or an agency of a State or political subdivision of a State,] except that such term shall include the United States Employment Service and the system of State and local employment services receiving Federal assistance.

(d) The term "labor organization" means a labor organization engaged in an industry affecting commerce, and any agent of such an organization, and includes any organization of any kind, any agency, or employee representation committee, group, association, or plan so engaged in which employees participate and which exists for the purpose, in whole or in part, of dealing with employers concerning grievances, labor disputes, wages, rates of pay, hours, or other terms or conditions of employment, and any conference, general committee, joint or system board, or joint council so engaged which is subordinate to a national or international labor organization.

(e) A labor organization shall be deemed to be engaged in an industry affecting commerce if (1) it maintains or operates a hiring hall or hiring office which procures employees for an employer or procures for employees opportunities to work for an employer, or (2) the number of its members (or, where it is a labor organization composed of other labor organizations or their representatives, if the aggregate number of the members of such other labor organization) is (A) one hundred or more during the first year after the effective date prescribed in subsection (a) of section 716, (B) seventy-five or more during the second year after such date or fifty or more during the third year, or (C) [twenty-five] *eight* or more thereafter, and such labor organization—

(1) is the certified representative of employees under the provision of the National Labor Relations Act, as amended, or the Railway Labor Act, as amended:

(2) although not certified, is a national or international labor organization or a local labor organization recognized or acting as the representative of employees of an employer or employers engaged in an industry affecting commerce; or

(3) has chartered a local labor organization or subsidiary body which is representing or actively seeking to represent employees of employers within the meaning of paragraph (1) or (2); or

(4) has been chartered by a labor organization representing or actively seeking to represent employees within the meaning of paragraph (1) or (2) as the local or subordinate body through which such employees may enjoy membership or become affiliated with such labor organization; or

(5) is a conference, general committee, joint or system board, or joint council subordinate to a national or international labor organization, which includes a labor organization engaged in an industry affecting commerce within the meaning of any of the preceding paragraphs of this subsection.

(f) The term "employee" means an individual employed by an employer.

(g) The term "commerce" means trade, traffic, commerce, transportation, transmission, or communication among the several States; or between a State and any place outside thereof; or within the District of Columbia, or a possession of the United States; or between points in the same State but through a point outside thereof.

(h) The term "industry affecting commerce" means any activity, business, or industry in commerce or in which a labor dispute would hinder or obstruct commerce or the free flow of commerce and includes any activity or industry "affecting commerce" within the meaning of the Labor-Management Reporting and Disclosure Act of 1959, *and further includes any governmental industry, business, or activity.*

(i) The term "State" includes a State of the United States, the District of Columbia, Puerto Rico, the Virgin Islands, American Samoa, Guam, Wake Island, the Canal Zone, and Outer Continental Shelf lands defined in the Outer Continental Shelf Lands Act.

EXEMPTION

SEC. 702. This title shall not apply to an employer with respect to the employment of aliens outside any State, or to a religious corporation, association, or society with respect to the employment of individuals of a particular religion to perform work connected with the carrying on by such corporation, association, or society of its religious activities [or to an educational institution with respect to the employment of individuals to perform work connected with the educational activities of such institution].

DISCRIMINATION BECAUSE OF RACE, COLOR, RELIGION, SEX, OR NATIONAL ORIGIN

SEC. 703. (a) It shall be an unlawful employment practice for an employer—

(1) to fail or refuse to hire or to discharge any individual, or otherwise to discriminate against any individual with respect to his compensation, terms, conditions, or privileges of employment, because of such individual's race, color, religion, sex, or national origin; or

(2) to limit, segregate, or classify his employees *or applicants for employment* in any way which would deprive or tend to deprive any individual of employment opportunities or otherwise adversely affect his status as an employee, because of such individual's race, color, religion, sex, or national origin.

(b) It shall be an unlawful employment practice for an employment agency to fail or refuse to refer for employment, or otherwise to discriminate against, any individual because of his race, color, religion, sex, or national origin, or to classify or refer for employment any individual on the basis of his race, color, religion, sex, or national origin.

(c) It shall be an unlawful employment practice for a labor organization—

(1) to exclude or to expel from its membership, or otherwise to discriminate against, any individual because of his race, color, religion, sex, or national origin;

(2) to limit, segregate, or classify its membership *or applicants for membership*, or to classify or fail or refuse to refer for employment any individual, in any way which would deprive or tend to deprive any individual of employment opportunities, or would limit such employment opportunities or otherwise adversely affect his status as an employee or as an applicant for employment, because of such individual's race, color, religion, sex, or national origin; or

(3) to cause or attempt to cause an employer to discriminate against an individual in violation of this section.

(d) It shall be an unlawful employment practice for any employer, labor organization, or joint labor-management committee controlling apprenticeship or other training or retraining, including on-the-job training programs to discriminate against any individual because of his race, color, religion, sex, or national origin in admission to, or employment in, any program established to provide apprenticeship or other training.

(e) Notwithstanding any other provision of this title, (1) it shall not be an unlawful employment practice for an employer to hire and employ employees, for an employment agency to classify, or refer for employment any individual, for a labor organization to classify its membership or to classify or refer for employment any individual, or for an employer, labor organization, or joint labor-management committee controlling apprenticeship or other training or retraining programs to admit or employ any individual in any such program, on the basis of his religion, sex, or national origin in these certain instances where religion, sex, or national origin is a bona fide occupational qualification reasonably necessary to the normal opeartion of that particular business or enterprise, and (2) it shall not be an unlawful employment practice for a school, college, university, or other educational institution or institution of learning to hire and employ employees of a particular religion if such school, college, university, or other educational institution or institution of learning is, in whole or in substantial part, owned, supported, controlled, or managed by a particular religion or by a particular religious corporation, association, or society, or if the curriculum of such school, college, university, or other educational institution or institution of learning is directed toward the propagation of a particular religion.

(f) As used in this title, the phrase "unlawful employment practice" shall not be deemed to include any action or measure taken by an employer, labor organization, joint labor-management committee, or employment agency with respect to an individual who is a member of the Communist Party of the United States or of any other organization required to register as a Communist-action or Communist-front organization by final order of the Subversive Activities Control Board pursuant to the Subversive Activities Control Act of 1950.

(g) Notwithstanding any other provision of this title, it shall not be an unlawful employment practice for an employer to fail or refuse to hire and employ any individual for any position, for an employer to discharge any individual from any position, or for an employment agency to fail or refuse to refer any individual for employment in any position, or for a labor organization to fail or refuse to refer any individual for employment in any position, if—

(1) the occupancy of such position, or access to the premises in or upon which any part of the duties of such position is performed or is to be performed, is subject to any requirement imposed in the interest of the national security of the United States under any security program in effect pursuant to or administered under any statute of the United States or any Executive order of the President; and

(2) such individual has not fulfilled or has ceased to fulfill that requirement.

(h) Notwithstanding any other provision of this title, it shall not be an unlawful employment practice for an employer to apply different standards of compensation, or different terms, conditions, or privileges of employment pursuant to a bona fide seniority or merit system, or a system which measures earnings by quantity or quality of production or to employees who work in different locations, provided that such differences are not the result of an intention to discriminate because of race, color, religion, sex, or national origin, nor shall it be an unlawful employment practice for an employer to give and to act upon the results of any professionally developed ability test [provided that] *which is directly related to the determination of bona fide occupational qualifications reasonably necessary to perform the normal duties of the particular position concerned: Provided, That* such test, its administration or action upon the results is not designed, intended, or used to discriminate because of race, color, religion, sex, or national origin. It shall not be an unlawful employment practice under this title for any employer to differentiate upon the basis of sex in determining the amount of the wages or compensation paid or to be paid to employees of such employer if such differentiation is authorized by the provisions of section 6(d) of the Fair Labor Standards Act of 1938, as amended (29 U.S.C. 206(d)).

(i) Nothing contained in this title shall apply to any business or enterprise on or near an Indian reservation with respect to any publicly announced employment practice of such business or enterprise under which a preferential treatment is given to any individual because he is an Indian living on or near a reservation.

(j) Nothing contained in this title shall be interpreted to require any employer, employment agency, labor organization, or joint labor-management committee subject to this title to grant preferential treatment to any individual or to any group because of the race, color, religion, sex, or national origin of such individual or group on account of an imbalance which may exist with respect to the total number or percentage of persons of any race, color, religion, sex, or national origin employed by any employer, referred or classified for employment by any employment agency or labor organization, admitted to membership or classified by any labor organization, or admitted to, or employed in, any apprenticeship or other training program, in comparison with the total number or percentage of persons of such race, color, religion, sex, or national origin in any community, State, section, or other area, or in the available work force in any community, State, section, or other area.

OTHER UNLAWFUL EMPLOYMENT PRACTICES

SEC. 704. (a) It shall be an unlawful employment practice for an employer to discriminate against any of his employees or applicants for employment, for an employment agency *or joint labor-management committee controlling apprenticeship or other training or retraining, including on-the-job training programs.* to discriminate against any individual, or for a labor organization to discriminate against any member thereof or applicant for membership, because he has opposed any practice made an unlawful employment practice by this title, or because he has made a charge, testified, assisted, or participated in any manner in an investigation, proceeding, or hearing under this title.

(b) It shall be an unlawful employment practice for an employer, labor organization, [or employment agency] *employment agency, or joint labor-management committee controlling apprenticeship or other training or retraining, including on-the-job training programs,* to print or publish or cause to be printed or published any notice or advertisement relating to employment by such an employer or membership in or any classification or referral for employment by such a labor organization, or relating to any classification or referral for employment by such an employment agency, *or relating to admission to, or employment in, any program established to provide apprenticeship or other training by such a joint labor-management committee* indicating any preference, limitation, specification, or discrimination, based on race, color, religion, sex, or national origin, except that such a notice or advertisement may indicate a preference, limitation, specification, or discrimination based on religion, sex, or national origin when religion, sex, or national origin is a bona fide occupational qualification for employment.

EQUAL EMPLOYMENT OPPORTUNITY COMMISSION

SEC. 705. (a) There is hereby created a Commission to be known as the Equal Employment Opportunity Commission, which shall be composed of five members, not more than three of whom shall be members of the same political party, who shall be appointed by the President by and with the advice and consent of the Senate. One of the original members shall be appointed for a term of one year, one for a term of two years, one for a term of three years, one for a term of four years, and one for a term of five years, beginning from the date of enactment of this title, but their successors shall be appointed for terms of five years each, except that any individual chosen to fill a vacancy shall be appointed only for the unexpired term of the member whom he shall succeed, *and all members of the Commission shall continue to serve until their successors are appointed and qualified : Provided, That no such member of the Commission shall continue to serve (1) for more than sixty days when the Congress is in session unless a nomination to fill such vacancy shall have been submitted to the Senate, or (2) after the adjournment sine die of the session of the Senate in which such nomination was submitted.* The President shall designate one member to serve as Chairman of the Commission, and one member to serve as Vice Chairman. The Chairman shall be responsible on behalf of the Commission for the administrative operations of the Commission, and shall appoint, in accordance with the [civil service laws, such officers, agents, attorneys, and employees as it deems necessary to assist it in the performance of its functions and to fix their compensation in accordance with the Classification Act of 1949, as amended] *provisions of title 5, United States Code, governing appointments in the competitive service, such officers, agents, attorneys, hearing examiners, and employees as he deems necessary to assist it in the performance of its functions and to fix their compensation in accordance with the provisions of chapter 51 and subchapter III of chapter 53 of title 5, United States Code, relating to classification and General Schedule pay rates: Provided, That assignment, removal, and compensation of hearing examiners shall be in accordance with sections 3105, 3344, 5362, and 7521 of title 5, United States Code.* The Vice Chairman shall act as Chairman in the absence or disability of the Chairman or in the event of a vacancy in that office.

(b) A vacancy in the Commission shall not impair the right of the remaining members to exercise all the powers of the Commission and three members thereof shall constitute a quorum.

(c) The Commission shall have an official seal which shall be judicially noticed.

(d) The Commission shall at the close of each fiscal year report to the Congress and to the President concerning the action it has taken; the names, salaries, and duties of all individuals in its employ and the moneys it has disbursed; and shall make such further reports on the cause of and means of eliminating discrimination and such recommendations for further legislation as may appear desirable.

(e) The Federal Executive Pay Act of 1956, as amended (5 U.S.C. 2201–2209), is further amended—

(1) by adding to section 105 thereof (5 U.S.C. 2204) the following clause:

"(32) Chairman, Equal Employment Opportunity Commission"; and

(2) by adding to clause (45) of section 106(a) thereof (5 U.S.C. 2205(a)) the following: "Equal Employment Opportunity Commission (4)."

(f) The principal office of the Commission shall be in or near the District of Columbia, but it may meet or exercise any or all its powers at any other place. The Commission may establish such regional or State offices as it deems necessary to accomplish the purpose of this title.

(g) The Commission shall have power—

(1) to cooperate with and, with their consent, utilize regional, State, local, and other agencies, both public and private, and individuals *and to accept voluntary and uncompensated services, notwithstanding the provisions of section 3679(b) of the Revised Statutes (31 U.S.C. 665(b))*;

(2) to pay to witnesses whose depositions are taken or who are summoned before the Commission or any of its agents the same witness and mileage fees as are paid to witnesses in the courts of the United States;

(3) to furnish to persons subject to this title such technical assistance as they may request to further their compliance with this title or an order issued thereunder;

(4) upon the request of (i) any employer, whose employees or some of them, or (ii) any labor organization, whose members or some of them, refuse or threaten to refuse to cooperate in effectuating the provisions of this title, to assist in such effectua-

tion by conciliation or such other remedial action as is provided by this title;

(5) to make such technical studies as are appropriate to effectuate the purposes and policies of this title and to make the results of such studies available to the public;

(6) to refer matters to the Attorney General with recommendations for intervention in a civil action brought by an aggrieved party under section [706] *715*, or for the institution of a civil action by the Attorney General under section 707, and to advise, consult, and assist the Attorney General on such matters.

(h) Attorneys appointed under this section may, at the direction of the Commission, appear for and represent the Commission in any case in court.

(i) The Commission shall, in any of its educational or promotional activities, cooperate with other departments and agencies in the performance of such educational and promotional activities.

(j) All officers, agents, attorneys, and employees of the Commission shall be subject to the provisions of section 9 of the Act of August 2, 1939, as amended (the Hatch Act), notwithstanding any exemption contained in such section.

[PREVENTION OF UNLAWFUL EMPLOYMENT PRACTICES

[SEC. 706. (a) Whenever it is charged in writing under oath by a person claiming to be aggrieved, or a written charge has been filed by a member of the Commission where he has reasonable cause to believe a violation of this title has occurred (and such charge sets forth the facts upon which it is based) that an employer, employment agency, or labor organization has engaged in an unlawful employment practice, the Commission shall furnish such employer, employment agency, or labor organization (hereinafter referred to as the "respondent") with a copy of such charge and shall make an investigation of such charge, provided that such charge shall not be made public by the Commission. If the Commission shall determine, after such investigation, that there is reasonable cause to believe that the charge is true, the Commission shall endeavor to eliminate any such alleged unlawful employment practice by informal methods of conference, conciliation, and persuasion. Nothing said or done during and as a part of such endeavors may be made public by the Commission without the written consent of the parties, or used as evidence in a subsequent proceeding. Any officer or employee of the Commission, who shall make public in any manner whatever any information in violation of this subsection shall be deemed guilty of a misdeameanor and upon conviction thereof shall be fined not more than $1,000 or imprisoned not more than one year.

[(b) In the case of an alleged unlawful employment practice occurring in a State, or political subdivision of a State, which has a State or local law prohibiting the unlawful employment practice alleged and establishing or authorizing a State or local authority to grant or seek relief from such practice or to institute criminal proceedings with respect thereto upon receiving notice thereof, no charge may be filed under subsection (a) by the person aggrieved before the expiration of sixty days after proceedings have been commenced under the

State or local law, unless such proceedings have been earlier terminated, provided that such sixty-day period shall be extended to one hundred and twenty days during the first year after the effective date of such State or local law. If any requirement for the commencement of such proceedings is imposed by a State or local authority other than a requirement of the filing of a written and signed statement of the facts upon which the proceeding is based, the proceeding shall be deemed to have been commenced for the purposes of this subjection at the time such statement is sent by registered mail to the appropriate State or local authority.

[(c) In the case of any charge filed by a member of the Commission alleging an unlawful employment practice occurring in a State or political subdivision of a State, which has a State or local law prohibiting the practice alleged and establishing or authorizing a State or local authority to grant or seek relief from such practice or to institute criminal proceedings with respect thereto upon receiving notice thereof, the Commission shall, before taking any action with respect to such charge, notify the appropriate State or local officials and, upon request, afford them a reasonable time, but not less than sixty days (provided that such sixty-day period shall be extended to one hundred and twenty days during the first year after the effective day of such State or local law), unless a shorter period is requested, to act under such State or local law to remedy the practice alleged.

[(d) A charge under subsection (a) shall be filed within ninety days after the alleged unlawful employment practice occurred, except that in the case of an unlawful employment practice with respect to which the person aggrieved has followed the procedure set out in subsection (b), such charge shall be filed by the person aggrieved within two hundred and ten days after the alleged unlawful employment practice occurred, or within thirty days after receiving notice that the State or local agency has terminated the proceedings under the State or local law, whichever is earlier, and a copy of such charge shall be filed by the Commission with the State or local agency.

[(e) If within thirty days after a charge is filed with the Commission or within thirty days after expiration of any period of reference under subsection (c) (except that in either case such period may be extended to not more than sixty days upon a determination by the Commission that further efforts to secure voluntary compliance are warranted), the Commission has been unable to obtain voluntary compliance with this title, the Commission shall so notify the person aggrieved and a civil action may, within thirty days thereafter, be brought against the respondent named in the charge (1) by the person claiming to be aggrieved, or (2) if such change was filed by a member of the Commission, by any person whom the charge alleges was aggrieved by the alleged unlawful employment practice. Upon application by the complainant and in such circumstances as the court may deem just, the court may appoint an attorney for such complainant and may authorize the commencement of the action without the payment of fees, costs, or security. Upon timely application, the court may, in its discretion, permit the Attorney General to intervene in such civil action if he certifies that the case is of general public importance. Upon request, the court may, in its discretion, stay further proceedings for not more than sixty days pending the termination of State or local proceedings described in subsection (b) or the efforts of the Commission to obtain voluntary compliance.

[(f) Each United States district court and each United States court of a place subject to the jurisdiction of the United States shall have jurisdiction of actions brought under this title. Such an action may be brought in any judicial district in the State in which the unlawful employment practice is alleged to have been committed, in the judicial district in which the employment records relevant to such practice are maintained and administered, or in the judicial district in which the plaintiff would have worked but for the alleged unlawful employment practice, but if the respondent is not found within any such district, such an action may be brought within the judicial district in which the respondent has his principal office. For purposes of sections 1404 and 1406 of title 28 of the United States Code, the judicial district in which the respondent has his principal office shall in all cases be considered a district in which the action might have been brought.

[(g) If the court finds that the respondent has intentionally engaged in or is intentionally engaging in an unlawful employment practice charged in the complaint, the court may enjoin the respondent from engaging in such unlawful employment practice, and order such affirmative action as may be appropriate, which may include reinstatement or hiring of employees, with or without back pay (payable by the employer, employment agency, or labor organization, as the case may be, responsible for the unlawful employment practice). Interim earnings or amounts earnable with reasonable dilligence by the person or persons discriminated against shall operate to reduce the back pay otherwise allowable. No order of the court shall require the admission or reinstatement of an individual as a member of a union or the hiring, reinstatement, or promotion of an individual as an employee, or the payment to him of any back pay, if such individual was refused admission, suspended, or expelled or was refused employment or advancement or was suspended or discharged for any reason other than discrimination on account of race, color, religion, sex or national origin or in violation of section 704(a).

[(h) The provisions of the Act entitled "An Act to amend the Judicial Code and to define and limit the jurisdiction of courts sitting in equity, and for other purposes," approved March 23, 1932 (29 U.S.C. 101–115), shall not apply with respect to civil actions brought under this section.

[(i) In any case in which an employer, employment agency, or labor organization fails to comply with an order of a court issued in a civil action brought under subsection (e), the Commission may commence proceedings to compel compliance with such order.

[(j) Any civil action brought under subsection (e) and any proceedings brought under subsection (i) shall be subject to appeal as provided in sections 1291 and 1292, title 28, United States Code.

[(k) In any action or proceeding under this title the court, in its discretion, may allow the prevailing party, other than the Commission or the United States, a reasonable attorney's fee as part of the costs, and the Commission and the United States shall be liable for costs the same as a private person.]

PREVENTION OF UNLAWFUL EMPLOYMENT PRACTICES

SEC. 706. (a) *The Commission is empowered, as hereinafter provided, to prevent any person from engaging in any unlawful employment practice as set forth in section 703 or 704 of this title.*

(b) Whenever a charge is filed by or on behalf of a person claiming to be aggrieved, or by a member of the Commission, alleging that an employer, employment agency, labor organization, or joint labor-management committee controlling apprenticeship or other training or retraining, including on-the-job training programs has engaged in an unlawful employment practice, the Commission shall serve a copy of the charge on such employer, employment agency, labor organization, or joint labor-management committee (hereinafter referred to as the "respondent") and shall make an investigation thereof. Charges shall be in writing and shall contain such information and be in such form as the Commission requires. Charges shall not be made public by the Commission. If the Commission determines after such investigation that there is no reason to believe that the charge is true, it shall dismiss the charge and promptly notify the person claiming to be aggrieved and the respondent of its action. If the Commission determines after such investigation that there is reasonable cause to believe that the charge is true, the Commission shall endeavor to eliminate any such alleged unlawful employment practice by informal methods of conference, conciliation, and persuasion. Nothing said or done during and as a part of such informal endeavors may be made public by the Commission, its officers or employees, or used as evidence in a subsequent proceeding without the written consent of the persons concerned. Any person who makes public information in violation of this subsection shall be fined not more than $1,000 or imprisoned not more than one year, or both. The Commission shall make its determination on reasonable cause as promptly as possible and, so far as practicable, not later than one hundred and twenty days from the filing of the charge or, where applicable under subsection (c) or (d), from the date upon which the Commission is authorized to take action with respect to the charge.

(c) In the case of a charge filed by or on behalf of a person claiming to be aggrieved alleging an unlawful employment practice occurring in a State, or political subdivision of a State, which has a State or local law prohibiting the unlawful employment practice alleged and establishing or authorizing a State or local authority to grant or seek relief from such practice or to institute criminal proceedings with respect thereto upon receiving notice thereof, the Commission shall take no action with respect to the investigation of such charge before the expiration of sixty days after proceedings have been commenced under the State or local law: Provided, That such sixty-day period shall be extended to one hundred and twenty days during the first year after the effective date of such State or local law. If any requirement for the commencement of such proceedings is imposed by a State or local authority other than a requirement of the filing of a written and signed statement of the facts upon which the

proceeding is based, the proceeding shall be deemed to have been commenced for the purposes of this subsection at the time such statement is sent by certified mail to the appropriate State or local authority.

(d) In the case of any charge filed by a member of the Commission alleging an unlawful employment practice occurring in a State or political subdivision of a State which has a State or local law prohibiting the practice alleged and establishing or authorizing a State or local authority to grant or seek relief from such practice or to institute criminal proceedings with respect thereto upon receiving notice thereof the Commission shall, before taking any action with respect to such charge, notify the appropriate State or local officials and, upon request, afford them a reasonable time, but not less than sixty days: Provided, That such sixty-day period shall be extended to one hundred and twenty days during the first year after the effective date of such State or local law, unless a shorter period is requested, to act under such State or local law to remedy the practice alleged.

(e) A charge shall be filed within one hundred eighty days after the alleged unlawful employment practice occurred and a copy shall be served upon the person against whom such charge is made as soon as practicable thereafter, except that in a case of an unlawful employment practice with respect to which the person aggrieved has initially instituted proceedings with a State or local agency with authority to grant or seek relief from such practice or to institute criminal proceedings with respect thereto upon receiving notice thereof, such charge shall be filed by the person aggrieved within three hundred days after the alleged unlawful employment practice occurred, or within thirty days after receiving notice that the State or local agency has terminated the proceedings under the State or local law, whichever is earlier, and a copy of such charge shall be filed by the Commission with the State or local agency.

(f) If the Commission determines after attempting to secure voluntary compliance under subsection (b) that it is unable to secure from the respondent a conciliation agreement acceptable to the Commission and to the person aggrieved, which determination shall not be reviewable in any court, the Commission shall issue and cause to be served upon the respondent a complaint stating the facts upon which the allegation of the unlawful employment practice is based, together with a notice of hearing before the Commission, or a member or agent thereof, at a place therein fixed not less than five days after the serving of such complaint. Related proceedings may be consolidated for hearing. Any member of the Commission who filed a charge in any case shall not participate in a hearing on any complaint arising out of such charge, except as a witness.

(g) A respondent shall have the right to file an answer to the complaint against him and with the leave of the Commission, which shall be granted whenever it is reasonable and fair to do so, may amend his answer at any time. Respondents and the person aggrieved shall be parties and may appear at any stage of the proceedings, with or without counsel. The Commission may grant such other persons a right to intervene or to file briefs or make oral arguments as amicus curiae or for other purposes, as it considers appropriate. All testimony shall be taken under oath and shall be reduced to writing.

(h) If the Commission finds that the respondent has engaged in an unlawful employment practice, the Commission shall state its findings of fact and shall issue and cause to be served on the respondent and the person or persons aggrieved by such unlawful employment practice an order requiring the respondent to cease and desist from such unlawful employment practice and to take such affirmative action, including reinstatement or hiring of employees, with or without backpay (payable by the employer, employment agency, or labor organization, as the case may be, responsible for the unlawful employment practice), as will effectuate the policies of this title: Provided, That interim earnings or amounts earnable with reasonable diligence by the aggrieved person or persons shall operate to reduce the backpay otherwise allowable. Such order may further require such respondent to make reports from time to time showing the extent to which he has complied with the order. If the Commission finds that the respondent has not engaged in any unlawful employment practice, the Commission shall state its findings of fact and shall issue and cause to be served on the respondent and the person or persons alleged in the complaint to be aggrieved an order dismissing the complaint.

(i) After a charge has been filed and until the record has been filed in court as hereinafter provided, the proceeding may at any time be ended by agreement between the Commission and the parties for the elimination of the alleged unlawful employment practice, approved by the Commission, and the Commission may at any time, upon reasonable notice, modify or set aside, in whole or in part, any finding or order made or issued by it. An agreement approved by the Commission shall be enforceable under subsection (k) and the provisions of that subsection shall be applicable to the extent appropriate to a proceeding to enforce an agreement.

(j) Findings of fact and orders made or issued under subsection (h) or (i) of this section shall be determined on the record.

(k) The Commission may petition any United States court of appeals within any circuit wherein the unlawful employment practice in question occurred or wherein the respondent resides or transacts business for the enforcement of its order and for appropriate temporary relief or restraining order, and shall file in the court the record in the proceedings as provided in section 2112 of title 28, United States Code. Upon such filing, the court shall cause notice thereof to be served upon the parties to the proceeding before the Commission, and thereupon shall have jurisdiction of the proceeding and of the question determined therein and shall have power to grant such temporary relief, restraining order, or other order as it deems just and proper, and to make and enter a decree enforcing, modifying and enforcing as so modified, or setting aside in whole or in part the order of the Commission. No objection that has not been urged before the Commission, its member, or agent, shall be considered by the court, unless the failure or neglect to urge such objection shall be excused because of extraordinary circumstances. The findings of the Commission with respect to questions of fact if supported by substantial evidence on the record considered as a whole shall be conclusive. If any party shall apply to the court for leave to adduce additional evidence and shall show to the satisfaction of the court that such additional evidence is material

and that there were reasonable grounds for the failure to adduce such evidence in the hearing before the Commission, its member, or its agent, the court may order such additional evidence to be taken before the Commission, its member, or its agent, and to be made a part of the record. The Commission may modify its findings as to the facts, or make new findings, by reason of additional evidence so taken and filed, and it shall file such modified or new findings, which findings with respect to question of fact if supported by substantial evidence on the record considered as a whole shall be conclusive, and its recommendatons, if any, for the modification or setting aside of its original order. Upon the filing of the record with it the jurisdiction of the court shall be exclusive and its judgment and decree shall be final, except that the same shall be subject to review by the Supreme Court of the United States as provided in section 1254 of title 28, United States Code. Petitions filed under this subsection shall be heard expeditiously.

(l) Any party aggrieved by a final order of the Commission granting or denying, in whole or in part, the relief sought may obtain a review of such order in any United States court of appeals in the circuit in which the unlawful employment practice in question is alleged to have occurred or in which such party resides or transacts business, or in the United States Court of Appeals for the District of Columbia, by filing in such court a written petition praying that the order of the Commission be modified or set aside. A copy of such petition shall be forthwith transmitted by the clerk of the Court to the Commission (and to the other parties to the proceeding before the Commission) and thereupon the Commission shall file in the court the certified record in the proceeding as provided in section 2112 of title 28, United States Code. Upon the filing of such petition, the court shall proceed in the same manner as in the case of an application by the Commission under subsection (k), the findings of the Commission with respect to questions of fact if supported by substantial evidence on the record considered as a whole shall be conclusive, and the court shall have the same jurisdiction to grant such temporary relief or restraining order as it deems just and proper, and in like manner to make and enter a decree enforcing, modifying, and enforcing as so modified, or setting aside in whole or in part the order of the Commission. The commencement of proceedings under this subsection or subsection (k) shall not, unless ordered by the court, operate as a stay of the order of the Commission.

(m) The provisions of the Act entitled "An Act to amend the Judicial Code and to define and limit the jurisdiction of courts sitting in equity, and for other purposes", approved March 23, 1932 (47 Stat. 70 et seq.; 29 U.S.C. 101–115), shall not apply with respect to (1) proceedings under subsection (k), (l), or (o) of this section, (2) proceedings under section 707 of this title, or (3) proceedings under section 715 of this title.

(n) The Attorney General shall conduct all litigation to which the Commission is a party in the Supreme Court of the United States pursuant to this title. All other litigation affecting the Commission, or to which it is a party, shall be conducted by the General Counsel of the Commission.

(o) Whenever a charge is filed with the Commission pursuant to sub-section (b) and the Commission concludes on the basis of a preliminary investigation that prompt judicial action is necessary to preserve the power of the Commission to grant effective relief in the proceeding the Commission may bring an action for appropriate temporary or preliminary relief pending its final disposition of such charge, in the United States district court for any judicial district in the State in which the unlawful employment practice concerned is alleged to have been committed, or the judicial district in which the aggrieved person would have been employed but for the alleged unlawful employment practice, but, if the respondent is not found within any such judicial district, such an action may be brought in the judicial district in which the respondent has his principal office. For purposes of sections 1404 and 1406 of title 28, United States Code, the judicial district in which the respondent has his principal office shall in all cases be considered a judicial district in which such an action might have been brought. Upon the bringing of any such action, the district court shall have jurisdiction to grant such injunctive relief or temporary restraining order as it deems just and proper, notwithstanding any other provision of law. Rule 65 of the Federal Rules of Civil Procedure, except paragraph (a)(2) thereof, shall govern proceedings under this subsection.

SEC. 707. (a) Whenever the Attorney General has reasonable cause to believe that any person or group of persons is engaged in a pattern or practice of resistance to the full enjoyment of any of the rights secured by this title, and that the pattern or practice is of such a nature and is intended to deny the full exercise of the rights herein described, the Attorney General may bring a civil action in the appropriate district court of the United States by filing with it a complaint (1) signed by him (or in his absence the Acting Attorney General), (2) setting forth facts pertaining to such pattern or practice, and (3) requesting such relief, including an application for a permanent or temporary injunction, restraining order or other order against the person or persons responsible for such pattern or practice, as he deems necessary to insure the full enjoyment of the rights herein described.

(b) The district courts of the United States shall have and shall exercise jurisdiction of proceedings instituted pursuant to this section, and in any such proceeding the Attorney General may file with the clerk of such court a request that a court of three judges be convened to hear and determine the case. Such request by the Attorney General shall be accompanied by a certificate that, in his opinion, the case is of general public importance. A copy of the certificate and request for a three-judge court shall be immediately furnished by such clerk to the chief judge of the circuit (or in his absence, the presiding circuit judge of the circuit) in which the case is pending. Upon receipt of such request it shall be the duty of the chief judge of the circuit or the presiding circuit judge, as the case may be, to designate immediately three judges in such circuit, of whom at least one shall be a circuit judge and another of whom shall be a district judge of the court in which the proceeding was instituted, to hear and determine such case, and it shall be the duty of the judges so designated to assign the case for hearing at the earliest practicable date, to participate in the hearing and determination thereof, and to cause the case to be in every way expedited. An appeal from the final judgment of such court will lie to the Supreme Court.

In the event the Attorney General fails to file such a request in any such proceeding, it shall be the duty of the chief judge of the district (or in his absence, the acting chief judge) in which the case is pending immediately to designate a judge in such district to hear and determine the case. In the event that no judge in the district is available to hear and determine the case, the chief judge of the district, or the acting chief judge, as the case may be, shall certify this fact to the chief judge of the circuit (or in his absence, the acting chief judge) who shall then designate a district or circuit judge of the circuit to hear and determine the case.

It shall be the duty of the judge designated pursuant to this section to assign the case for hearing at the earliest practicable date and to cause the case to be in every way expedited.

(c) *Any record or paper required by section 709(c) of this title to be preserved or maintained shall be made available for inspection, reproduction, and copying by the Commission, the Attorney General, or his representative, upon demand in writing directed to the person having custody, possession, or control of such record or paper. Unless otherwise ordered by a court of the United States, neither the Commission, the Attorney General, nor his representative shall disclose any record or paper produced pursuant to this title, or any reproduction or copy, except to Congress or any committee thereof, or to a governmental agency, or in the presentation of any case or proceeding before any court or grand jury. The United States district court for the district in which a demand is made or in which a record or paper so demanded is located, shall have jurisdiction to compel by appropriate process the production of such record or paper.*

(d) *Effective on the date of enactment of the Equal Employment Opportunities Enforcement Act, the functions of the Attorney General and the Acting Attorney General, as the case may be, under this section shall be transferred to the Commission, together with such personnel, property records, and unexpended balances of appropriations, allocations, and other funds employed, used, held, available, or to be made available in connection with the functions transferred to the Commission hereby as may be necessary to enable the Commission to carry out its functions pursuant to this subsection, and the Commission shall thereafter carry out such functions in the manner set forth in subsections (e) and (f) of this section.*

(e) *In all suits commenced pursuant to this section prior to the date of enactment of the Equal Employment Opportunities Enforcement Act of 1971, proceedings shall continue without abatement, all court orders and decrees shall remain in effect, and the Commission shall be substituted as a party for the United States of America or the Attorney General or Acting Attorney General, as appropriate.*

(f) *Subsequent to the date of enactment of the Equal Employment Opportunities Enforcement Act of 1971, the Commission shall have authority to investigate and act on a charge of a pattern or practice of discrimination, whether filed by or on behalf of a person claiming to be aggrieved or by a member of the Commission: Provided, That all such actions shall be in accordance with the procedures set forth in section 706, including the provisions for enforcement and appellate review contained in subsections (k), (l), (m), and (n) thereof.*

EFFECT ON STATE LAWS

SEC. 708. Nothing in this title shall be deemed to exempt or relieve any person from any liability, duty, penalty, or punishment provided by any present or future law of any State or political subdivision of a State, other than any such law which purports to require or permit the doing of any act which would be an unlawful employment practice under this title.

INVESTIGATIONS, INSPECTIONS, RECORDS, STATE AGENCIES

SEC. 709. (a) In connection with any investigation of a charge filed under section 706, the Commission or its designated representative shall at all reasonable times have access to, for the purposes of examination, and the right to copy any evidence of any person being investigated or proceeded against that relates to unlawful employment practices covered by this title and is relevant to the charge under investigation.

(b) The Commission may cooperate with State and local agencies charged with the administration of State fair employment practices laws and, with the consent of such agencies, may, for the purpose of carrying out its functions and duties under this title and within the limitation of funds appropriated specifically for such purpose, *engage in and contribute to the cost of research and other projects of mutual interest undertaken by such agencies, and* utilize the services of such agencies and their employees and, notwithstanding any other provision of law, may [reimburse] *pay by advance or reimbursement* such agencies and their employees for services rendered to assist the Commission in carrying out this title. In furtherance of such cooperative efforts, the Commission may enter into written agreements with such State or local agencies and such agreements may include provisions under which the Commission shall refrain from processing a charge in any cases or class of cases specified in such agreements [and under which no person may bring a civil action under section 706 in any cases or class of cases so specified,] or under which the Commission shall relieve any person or class of persons in such State or locality from requirements imposed under this section. The Commission shall rescind any such agreement whenever it determines that the agreement no longer serves the interest of effective enforcement of this title.

[(c) Except as provided in subsection (d), every employer, employment agency, and labor organization subject to this title shall (1) make and keep such records relevant to the determinations of whether unlawful employment practices have been or are being committed, (2) preserve such records for such periods, and (3) make such reports therefrom, as the Commission shall prescribe by regulation or order, after public hearing, as reasonable, necessary, or appropriate for the enforcement of this title or the regulations or orders thereunder. The Commission shall, by regulation, require each employer, labor organization, and joint labor-management committee subject to this title which controls an apprenticeship or other training program to maintain such records as are reasonably necessary to carry out the purpose of this title, including, but not limited to, a list of applicants who wish to participate in such program, including the chronological order in which such applications were received, and shall furnish to the Commission, upon request, a detailed description of the manner in which persons are selected to participate in the apprenticeship or other training program. Any employer, employment agency, labor organization, or joint labor-management committee which believes that the application to it of any regulation or order issued under this section would result in undue hardship may (1) apply to the Commission for an exemption from the application of such regulation or order, or (2) bring a civil action in the United States district court for the district where such records are kept. If the Commission or the court, as the case may be, finds that the application of the regulation or order to the employer, employment agency, or labor organization in question would impose an undue hardship, the Commission or the court, as the case may be, may grant appropriate relief.]

(c) *Every employer, employment agency, and labor organization subject to this title shall (1) make and keep such records relevant to the determinations of whether unlawful employment practices have been or are being committed, (2) preserve such records for such periods, and (3) make such reports therefrom as the Commission shall prescribe by regulation or order, after public hearing, as reasonable, necessary, or appropriate for the enforcement of this title or the regulation or orders thereunder. The Commission shall, by regulation, require each employer, labor organization, and joint labor-management committee subject to this title which controls an apprenticeship or other training program to maintain such records as are reasonably necessary to carry out the purpose of this title, including, but not limited to, a list of applicants who wish to participate in such program, including the chronological order in which such applicants were received, and to furnish to the Commission upon request, a detailed description of the manner in which persons are selected to participate in the apprenticeship or other training program. Any employer, employment agency, labor organization, or joint labor-management committee which believes that the application to it of any regulation or order issued under this section would result in undue hardship may apply to the Commission for an exemption from the application of such regulation or order, and, if such application for an exemption is denied, bring a civil action in the United States district court for the district where such records are kept. If the Commission or the court, as the case may be, finds that the application of the regulation or order to the employer, employment agency, or labor organization in question would impose an undue hardship, the Commission or the court, as the case may be, may grant appropriate relief. If any person required to comply with the provisions of this subsection fails or refuses to do so, the United States district court for the district in which such person is found, resides or transacts business, shall, upon application of the Commission, have jurisdiction to issue to such person an order requiring him to comply.*

[(d) The provisions of subsection (c) shall not apply to any employer, employment agency, labor organization, or joint labor-management committee with respect to matters occurring in any State or political subdivision thereof which has a fair employment practice law during any period in which such employer, employment agency, labor organization, or joint labor-management committee is subject to such law, except that the Commission may require such notations on records which such employer, employment agency, labor organization, or joint labor-management committee keeps or is required to keep as are necessary because of differences in coverage or methods of enforcement between the State or local law and the provisions of this title. Where an employer is required by Executive Order 10925, issued March 6, 1961, or by any other Executive order prescribing fair employment practices for Government contractors and subcontractors, or by rules or regulations issued thereunder, to file reports relating to his employment practices with any Federal agency or committee, and he is substantially in compliance with such requirements, the Commission shall not require him to file additional reports pursuant to subsection (c) of this section.]

(*d*) *In prescribing requirements pursuant to subsection (c) of this section, the Commission shall consult with other interested State and Federal agencies and shall endeavor to coordinate its requirements with those adopted by such agencies. The Commission shall furnish, upon request and without cost to any State or local agency charged with the administration of a fair employment practice law, information obtained pursuant to subsection (c) of this section from any employer, employment agency, labor organization, or joint labor-management committee subject to the jurisdiction of such agency. Such information shall be furnished on condition that it not be made public by the recipient agency prior to the institution of a proceeding under State or local law involving such information. If this condition is violated by a recipient agency, the Commission may decline to honor subsequent requests pursuant to this subsection.*

(e) It shall be unlawful for any officer or employee of the Commission to make public in any manner whatever any information obtained by the Commission pursuant to its authority under this section prior to the institution of any proceeding under this title involving such information. Any officer or employee of the Commission who shall make public in any manner whatever any information in violation of this subsection shall be guilty of a misdemeanor and upon conviction thereof, shall be fined not more than $1,000, or imprisoned not more than one year.

[INVESTIGATORY POWERS

[SEC. 710. (a) For the purposes of any investigation of a charge filed under the authority contained in section 706, the Commission shall have authority to examine witnesses under oath and to require the production of documentary evidence relevant or material to the charge under investigation.

[(b) If the respondent named in a charge filed under section 706 fails or refuses to comply with a demand of the Commission for permission to examine or to copy evidence in conformity with the provisions of section 709(a), or if any person required to comply with the provisions of section 709 (c) or (d) fails or refuses to do so, or if any person fails or refuses to comply with a demand by the Commission to give testimony under oath, the United States district court for the district in which such person is found, resides, or transacts business, shall, upon application of the Commission, have jurisdiction to issue to such person an order requiring him to comply with the provisions of section 709 (c) or (d) or to comply with the demand of the Commission, but the attendance of a witness may not be required outside the State where he is found, resides, or transacts business and the production of evidence may not be required outside the State where such evidence is kept.

[(c) Within twenty days after the service upon any person charged under section 706 of a demand by the Commission for the production of documentary evidence or for permission to examine or to copy evidence in conformity with the provisions of section 709(a), such person may file in the district court of the United States for the judicial district in which he resides, is found, or transacts business, and serve upon the Commission a petition for an order of such court modifying or setting aside such demand. The time allowed for compliance with the demand in whole or in part as deemed proper and ordered by the court shall not run during the pendency of such petition in the court. Such petition shall specify each ground upon which the petitioner relies in seeking such relief, and may be based upon any failure of such demand to comply with the provisions of this title or with the limitations generally applicable to compulsory process or upon any constitutional or other legal right or privilege of such person. No objection which is not raised by such a petition may be urged in the defense to proceeding initiated by the Commission under subsection (b) for enforcement of such a demand unless such proceeding is commenced by the Commission prior to the expiration of the twenty-day period, or unless the court determines that the defendant could not reasonably have been aware of the availability of such ground of objection.

[(d) In any proceeding brought by the Commission under subsection (b), except as provided in subsection (c) of this section, the defendant may petition the court for an order modifying or setting aside the demand of the Commission.]

INVESTIGATORY POWERS

Sec. 710. For the purpose of all hearings and investigations conducted by the Commission or its duly authorized agents or agencies, section 11 of the National Labor Relations Act (49 Stat. 455; 29 U.S.C. 161) shall apply: Provided, That no subpena shall be issued on the application of any party to proceedings before the Commission until after the Commission has issued and caused to be served upon the respondent a complaint and notice of hearing under subsection (f) of section 706.

NOTICES TO BE POSTED

SEC. 711. (a) Every employer, employment agency, and labor organization, as the case may be, shall post and keep posted in conspicuous places upon its premises where notices to employees, applicants for employment, and members are customarily posted a notice to be prepared or approved by the Commission setting forth excerpts from or, summaries of, the pertinent provisions of this title and information pertinent to the filing of a complaint.

(b) A willful violation of this section shall be punishable by a fine of not more than $100 for each separate offense.

VETERANS' PREFERENCE

SEC. 712. Nothing contained in this title shall be construed to repeal or modify any Federal, State, territorial, or local law creating special rights or preference for veterans.

RULES AND REGULATIONS

SEC. 713. (a) The Commission shall have authority from time to time to issue, amend, or rescind suitable procedural regulations to carry out the provisions of this title. Regulations issued under this section shall be in conformity with the standards and limitations of the Administrative Procedure Act.

(b) In any action or proceeding based on any alleged unlawful employment practice, no person shall be subject to any liability or punishment for or on account of (1) the commission by such person of an unlawful employment practice if he pleads and proves that the act or omission complained of was in good faith, in conformity with, and in reliance on any written interpretation or opinion of the Commission, or (2) the failure of such person to publish and file any information required by any provision of this title if he pleads and proves that he failed to publish and file such information in good faith, in conformity with the instructions of the Commission issued under this title regarding the filing of such information. Such a defense, if established, shall be a bar to the action or proceeding, notwithstanding that (A) after such act or omission, such interpretation or opinion is modified or rescinded or is determined by judicial authority to be invalid or of no legal effect, or (B) after publishing or filing the description and annual reports, such publication or filing is determined by judicial authority not to be in conformity with the requirements of this title.

(c) *Except for the powers granted to the Commission under subsection (h) of section 706, the power to modify or set aside its findings, or make new findings, under subsections (i) and (k) of section 706, the rulemaking power as defined in subchapter II of chapter 5 of title 5, United States Code, with reference to general rule as distinguished from rules of specific applicability, and the power to enter into or rescind agreements with State and local agencies, as provided in subsection (b) of section 709, under which the Commission agrees to refrain from processing a charge in any cases or class of cases or under which the Commission agrees to relieve any person or class of persons in such State or locality from requirements imposed by section 709, the Commission may delegate any of its functions, duties, and powers to such person or persons as the Commission may designate by regulation, including functions, duties, and powers with respect to investigating, conciliating, hearing, determining, ordering, certifying, reporting or otherwise acting as to any work, business, or matter: Provided, That nothing in this subsection authorizes the Commission to provide for persons other than those referred to in clauses (2) and (3) of subsection (b) of section 556 of title 5 of the United States Code to conduct any hearing to which that section applies.*

(d) The Commission is authorized to delegate to any group of three or more members of the Commission any or all of the powers which it may itself exercise.

FORCIBLY RESISTING THE COMMISSION OR ITS REPRESENTATIVES

Sec. 714. The provisions of [section 111] *sections 111 and 1114* title 18, United States Code, shall apply to officers, agents, and employees of the Commission in the performance of their official duties.

[SPECIAL STUDY BY SECRETARY OF LABOR

[Sec. 715. The Secretary of Labor shall make a full and complete study of the factors which might tend to result in discrimination in employment because of age and the consequences of such discrimination on the economy and individuals affected. The Secretary of Labor shall make a report to the Congress not later than June 30, 1965, containing the results of such study and shall include in such report such recommendations for legislation to prevent arbitrary discrimination in employment because of age as he determines advisable.]

CIVIL ACTIONS BY PERSONS AGGRIEVED

Sec. 715. (a) If (1) the Commission determines that there is no reasonable cause to believe the charge is true and dismisses the charge in accordance with section 706(b), (2) finds no probable jurisdiction and dismisses the charge, or (3) within one hundred and eighty days after a charge is filed with the Commission, or within one hundred and eighty days after expiration of any period of reference under section 706 (c) or (d), the Commission has not either (i) issued a complaint in accordance with section 706(f), (ii) determined that there is not reasonable cause to believe the charge is true and dismissed the charge in accordance with section 706(b) or found no probable jurisdiction and dismissed the charge, or (iii) entered into a conciliation agreement acceptable to the Commission and to the person aggrieved in accordance with section 706(f) or an agreement with the parties in accordance with section 706(i), the Commission shall so notify the person aggrieved and within sixty days after the giving of such notice a civil action may be brought against the respondent named in the charge (1) by the person claiming to be aggrieved, or (2) if such charge was filed by a member of the Commission, by any person whom the charge alleges was aggrieved by the alleged unlawful employment practice. Upon application by the complaintant and in such circumstances as the court may deem just, the court may appoint an attorney for such complaintant and may authorize the commencement of the action without the payment of fees, costs, or security. Upon timely application, the court may, in its discretion, permit the Commission to intervene in such civil action if it certifies that the case is of general public importance. Upon the commencement of such civil action, the Commission shall be divested of jurisdiction over the proceeding and shall take no further action with respect thereof: Provided, That, upon request, the court may, in its discretion, stay further proceedings for not more than sixty days pending termination of State or local proceedings described in subsection (c) or (d) or the efforts of the Commission to obtain voluntary compliance.

(b) Each United States district court and each United States court of a place subject to the jurisdiction of the United States shall have jurisdiction of actions brought under this section. Such an action may be brought in any judicial district in the State in which the unlawful employment practice is alleged to have been committeed, or in the judicial district in which the plaintiff would have been employed but for the alleged unlawful employment practice, but if the respondent is not found within any such district, such an action may be brought within the judicial district in which the respondent has his principal office. For purposes of sections 1404 and 1406 of title 28 of the United States Code, the judicial district in which the respondent has his principal office shall in all cases be considered a district in which the action might have been brought. Upon the bringing of any such action, the district court shall have jurisdiction to grant such temporary or preliminary relief as it deems just and proper.

(c) If the court finds that the respondent has intentionally engaged in or is intentionally engaging in an unlawful employment practice charged in the complaint, the court may enjoin the respondent from engaging in such unlawful employment practice, and order such affirmative action as may be appropriate, which may include reinstatement or hiring of employees, with or without backpay (payable by the employer, employment agency, or labor organization, as the case may be, responsible for the unlawful employment practice). Interim earnings or amounts earnable with reasonable diligence by the person or persons discriminated against shall operate to reduce the backpay otherwise allowable. No order of the court shall require the admission or reinstatement of an individual as a member of a union or the hiring, reinstatement, or promotion of an individual as an employee, or the payment to him of any backpay, if such individual was refused admission, suspended, or expelled or was refused employment or advancement or was suspended or discharged for any reason other than discrimination on account of race, color, religion, sex, or national origin or in violation of section 704(a).

(d) In any case in which an employer, employment agency, or labor organization fails to comply with an order of a court issued in a civil action brought under subsection (a), the Commission may commence proceedings to compel compliance with such order.

(*e*) *Any civil action brought under subsection (a) and any proceedings brought under subsection (d) shall be subject to appeal as provided in sections 1291 and 1292, title 28, United States Code.*

(*f*) *In any action or proceeding under this section, the court, in its discretion, may allow the prevailing plaintiff a reasonable attorney's fee as part of the costs.*

EFFECTIVE DATE

SEC. 716. (a) This title shall become effective one year after the date of its enactment.

(b) Notwithstanding subsection (a), sections of this title other than sections 703, 704, 706, and 707 shall become effective immediately.

(c) The President shall, as soon as feasible after the enactment of this title, convene one or more conferences for the purpose of enabling the leaders of groups whose members will be affected by this title to become familiar with the rights afforded and obligations imposed by its provisions, and for the purpose of making plans which will result in the fair and effective administration of this title when all of its provisions become effective. The President shall invite the participation in such conference or conferences of (1) the members of the President's Committee on Equal Employment Opportunity, (2) the members of the Commission on Civil Rights, (3) representatives of State and local agencies engaged in furthering equal employment opportunity, (4) representatives of private agencies engaged in furthering equal employment opportunity, and (5) representatives of employers, labor organizations, and employment agencies who will be subject to the title.

NONDISCRIMINATION IN FEDERAL GOVERNMENT EMPLOYMENT

SEC. 717.[1] (*a*) *All personnel actions affecting employees or applicants for employment in the competitive service (as defined in section 2102 of title 5 of the United States Code) or employees or applicants for employment in positions with the District of Columbia government covered by the Civil Service Retirement Act shall be made free from any discrimination based on race, color, religion, sex, or national origin.*

(*b*) *The Equal Employment Opportunity Commission shall have authority to enforce the provision of subsection (a) and shall issue such rules, regulations, orders, and instructions as it deems necessary and appropriate to carry out its responsibilities hereunder, and the head of each executive department and agency and the appropriate officers of the District of Columbia shall comply with such rules, regulations, orders, and instructions: Provided, That such rules and regulations shall provide that an employee or applicant for employment shall be notified of any final action taken on any complaint filed by him thereunder.*

(*c*) *Within thirty days of receipt of notice given under subsection (b), the employee or applicant for employment, if aggrieved by the final disposition of his complaint, may file a civil action as provided in section 715, in which civil action the head of the executive department or agency, or the District of Columbia, as appropriate, shall be respondent.*

---

[1] Effective 6 months after date of enactment.

(*d*) *The provisions of section 715 shall govern civil actions brought hereunder.*

(*e*) *All functions of the Civil Service Commission which the Director of the Bureau of the Budget determines relate to nondiscrimination in government employment are transferred to the Equal Employment Opportunity Commission.*

(*f*) *All authority, functions, and responsibilities vested in the Secretary of Labor pursuant to Executive Order 11246 relating to nondiscrimination in employment by Government contractors and subcontractors and nondiscrimination in federally assisted costruction contracts are transferred to the Equal Employment Opportunity Commission, together with such personnel, property, records, and unexpended balances of appropriations, allocations, and other funds employed, used, held, available or to be made available in connection with the functions transferred to the Commission hereby as may be necessary to enable the Commission to carry out its functions pursuant to this subsection, and the Commission shall hereafter carry out all such authority, functions, and responsibilities pursuant to such order.*

EFFECT UPON OTHER LAW

S EC. *718. Nothing contained in this Act shall relieve any government agency or official of its or his primary responsibility to assure nondiscrimination in employment as required by the Constitution, statutes, and Executive orders.*

§ 5316. Positions at level V.

Level V of the Executive Schedule applies to the following positions, for which the annual rate of basic pay is $36,000:

*   *   *   *   *   *   *

[(111) Members, Equal Employment Opportunity Commission (4).]

*   *   *   *   *   *   *

MINORITY VIEWS ON H.R. 1746

We all agree that, if equal employment opportunity for all Americans is to become a reality, the Equal Employment Opportunity Commission should be given enforcement powers. We are convinced, however, that H.R. 1746 will not accomplish this goal, and thus we must oppose it.

First and foremost, on the premise that anyone charged with violating the law is innocent until proven guilty, we believe that enforcement of our laws can best be effectuated through our courts.

Additionally, we fear that, in view of the estimated 18-month to two-year backlog that currently exists at the EEOC, the intent of H.R. 1746 to expand the EEOC's jurisdiction will serve only to retard and frustrate the purposes and objectives of the Equal Employment Opportunity Act.

Under the procedures of the Committee bill, upon receipt of a charge, the Commission is required to investigate and to find reasonable cause before issuing a formal complaint. In effect, this finding is a presumption of the guilt of the defendant, which subtly shifts the burden of proof from the plaintiff to the defendant. Thus, in practice, if not by law, the defendant is faced with the burden of proving his innocence.

During Committee sessions, we offered amendments to assure that title VII of the Civil Rights Act would be enforced, and that enforcement would be fair and impartial. Our amendments, which were rejected, would permit the EEOC attorneys, if they are unsuccessful in their conciliation and if they found reasonable cause to believe that a violation of the law has taken place, to seek enforcement in Federal district courts.

I. The Major Issue

As indicated above, the most significant issue that separates the majority of the committee from the minority is not whether the EEOC should be given enforcement authority. Rather, the issue is: What procedures will insure the most effective enforcement of the substantive provisions of title VII of the Civil Rights Act of 1964.

By providing the EEOC with authority to issue cease and desist and other remedial orders, the Committee bill would transform this agency into a quasi-judicial body very similar to the National Labor Relations Board.

In the next section we explain and justify our belief that the court approach will be more effective and more expeditious than the administrative approach. We are compelled, however, to point out as well that the authority provided in H.R. 1746 ignores and denies basic American principles.

Under our system of justice, a person charged with violating the law is presumed innocent until proved guilty. In practical effect the Committee bill creates a system that presumes persons charged with certain law violations are guilty until proved innocent. We contend that the EEOC has attained an image as an advocate of civil rights, and properly so. For this very reason, we submit that it cannot be an impartial arbiter of the law. An advocate, by nature, represents one side of an issue. How can he then be asked to apply the law without prejudice?

THE JUDICIAL APPROACH

The direct judicial approach offers greater advantages than the administrative cease and desist approach. While both methods would involve an adversary proceeding before a finder of fact, in the judicial approach the original finder of fact would be the federal district court judge as compared to a hearing officer who is a civil service employee, under the administrative approach.

There are substantial reasons for supporting direct resort to the courts. They include:

A. Timeliness of Relief and Remedy

Contrary to the proponents of the "cease and desist" approach, the district court approach is clearly preferable because relief can be more quickly granted. The pertinent yardstick is the amount of time an aggrieved person must wait before he is afforded relief. Empowering the EEOC to bring court suits will greatly facilitate its ability to implement the law without delay and to bring effective relief to victims of discrimination. If the EEOC prevails before the court, it is entitled to an immediate injunction and other relief to bring about a rapid end to the discriminatory practices. In many instances a relatively simple proof would allow the EEOC to obtain a preliminary injunction pending a full trial of the case.

A close examination of the time factors involved in processing charges before the National Labor Relations Board (which was the model for formulating the enforcement powers given to the EEOC by the Committee bill) and the district courts conclusively establishes that quicker relief can be achieved when the direct court approach is utilized.

It is significant that the Special Subcommittee on Labor opened hearings on May 6, 1971, on a bill (H.R. 7152) to expedite the processes of the National Labor Relations Board, and in the explanatory sheet it distributed it discussed the delay incurred in the six stages of the administrative process which culminated in a court enforced order in the Court of Appeals. The delay was summarized as follows:

> In sum, it can easily take 2½ years from the time a worker walks into a regional Labor Board office with a charge that he has been discharged illegally until the time a court of appeals finally issues an order that he be reinstated to his job with back pay.

Even the 2½ year figure cited appears unduly optimistic in light of recent testimony given before the Special Subcommittee on Labor on H.R. 7152, on May 12, 1971, by Frank W. McCulloch, former Chairman of the NLRB, about the length of delay between the issuance of a Board decision and a court order. He stated:

> In operation, the lack of such a provision [referring to a self-enforcing provision] has resulted in the build-up of a median time interval of 630 days in enforcement cases, as previously noted, from Board decision to a Court order which for the first time applies the sanctions of the law to a non-complying respondent.

When these time factors are added up, the 18–24 month backlog currently existing at EEOC, the time needed for an administrative proceeding and review by the Commission, plus the 630 day figure currently required to get court enforcement (using the NLRB figure), 3½ to 4 years would appear to be a more correct approximation of the time involved in getting enforcement through the administrative cease and desist approach.

In striking contrast, the 1970 Annual Report of the Director of the Administrative Office of the United States Courts states that ten months was the median time interval from issue to trial for non-jury trials completed in United States District Courts in 1970. Even assuming time for issuance of a decision such forum would clearly be quicker. Moreover, the district courts located in those states which have most of the charges of employment discrimination often have better time records in case handling.

An examination of the Fourth Annual Report of the Equal Employment Opportunity Commission, submitted on July 30, 1970, shows that the top ten states in terms of the number of charges of employment discrimination recommended for investigation are: Texas (1232 charges), Louisiana (1007), Florida (1000), Alabama (734), Tennessee (672), California (546), Georgia (519), Pennsylvania (501), Illinois (334) and New Jersey (306). As federal district courts in such metropolitan areas as New York City and Philadelphia would obviously be much busier than those in less populolus areas, the case handling time factor should therefore, be correlated with the areas where most charges originate.

The median time interval in months for non-jury trials in such states discloses the following:

Texas:
    Northern District, 4 months, Dallas.
    Eastern District, 5 months, Beaumont.
    Southern District, 12 months, Houston.
    Western District, 3 months, San Antonio.
Louisiana:
    Eastern District, 13 months, New Orleans.
    Western District, 13 months, Shreveport.
Florida:
    Northern District, 8 months [1], Tallahassee.
    Middle District, 12 months, Jacksonville.
    Southern District, 9 months, Miami.
Alabama:
    Northern District, 8 months, Birmingham.
    Middle District, 3 months,[1] Montgomery.
    Southern District, 11 months, Mobile.
Tennessee:
    Eastern District, 4 months, Knoxville.
    Middle District [2], Nashville.
    Western District, 8 months, Memphis.
California:
    Northern District, 23 months, San Francisco.
    Eastern District, 21 months,[1] Sacramento.
    Central District, 10 months, Los Angeles.
    Southern District [3], San Diego.
Georgia:
    Northern District, 4 months, Atlanta.
    Middle District, 4 months, Macon.
    Southern District, 1 month, Savannah.
Pennsylvania:
    Eastern District, 36 months, Philadelphia.
    Middle District, 21 months [1], Scranton.
    Western District, 12 months, Pittsburgh.

---

[1] Jury and non-jury trials—total.
[2] No figure given: only one jury trial reported completed in fiscal year 1970.
[3] No figure given: only one jury trial reported completed in fiscal year 1970.

Illinois:
> Northern District, 11 months, Chicago.
> Eastern District, 12 months [1] East St. Louis.
> Southern District, 11 months [1], Peoria.

New Jersey: 1 month, Newark.

Of the 29 district courts represented in the above statistics, 21 courts had a median time of 12 months or less; 8 courts had median trial completion times of 6 months or less.

In hearings last April before the House Committee on Appropriations, discussing the EEOC budget request for FY 1971, Chairman Brown noted that EEOC's backlog "now means an average delay of 18 months to 2 years before the Commission can complete action on a complaint." How much longer would this interval be extended if at the end thereof, the Commission then had to begin its administrative proceedings followed by resort to the appellate courts? In his testimony before the General Subcommittee on Labor recently, Chairman Brown noted that "during the first seven and a half months of this Fiscal Year, 14,644 charges were filed with the Commission, *a number greater than the number received in all of last Fiscal Year.*" (Emphasis supplied.) He also stated that as of February 20, 1971, the backlog of charges pending before the Commission numbered 25,195.

The increased caseload and backlog of EEOC alone not only undermines but clearly refutes the contention that the administrative process would bring quicker relief. Add to this backlog the increased workload that would be generated by the additional jurisdiction bestowed on EEOC by the Committee bill (jurisdiction over state and local employees, transfer of the Office of Federal Contract Compliance to EEOC, transfer of pattern and practice suits to EEOC from the Justice Department, transfer of authority over discrimination among federal employees to EEOC from the Civil Service Commission, jurisdiction extended to employers with 8 employees as compared to the present 25 employee limitation) conclusively establishes that claims of quicker remedies through the administrative "cease and desist" process are more fiction than fact.

Finally, we suggest that a further impediment to timely action is presented by virtue of the fact that under the administrative approach the decision to grant relief can be made only by the Commission. An EEOC attorney in the field could investigate, and he could attempt conciliation; but there would be only one facility available to issue a cease and desist order—the Commission in Washington. Through the judicial approach, EEOC attorneys would have access to our 93 Federal district courts for enforcement.

It seems eminently more sensible to us to proceed in a forum where not only can preliminary relief be made available at the outset, but, if circumstances warrant, further relief can be obtained as the case proceeds, with *permanent relief* embodied in a self-enforcing decree issuing at the culmination of trial. Thus we will have avoided the multiplicity of opportunities for delay that are inherent in the cease-and-desist approach, and aggrieved parties will have their remedy at the earliest possible moment.

---

[1] Jury and non-jury trials total.

This alternative saves the best features of the independent agency approach—expertise and political autonomy—while avoiding the problems that arise when an active enforcement stance must be accommodated within a structure that contemplates quasi-judicial neutrality. The problem title VII seeks to correct is not one susceptible to the kind of policy balancing that is usual in the administration of law regulating utilities or other situations involving competing interests. Racial discrimination does not occupy the status of an "interest" under our system of law. It is a grave injustice which should be eliminated in as quick and efficient a manner as possible.

B. *Greater Prestige of Federal Judges*

The appropriate forum to resolve civil rights questions, questions of employment discrimination as well as such matters as public accommodations, school desegregation, fair housing, and voting rights, is a court. Civil rights issues usually arouse strong emotions. United States district court proceedings provide procedural safeguards; Federal judges are well known in their areas and enjoy great respect; the forum is convenient for the litigants and is impartial; the proceedings are public, and the judge has power to resolve the problem and fashion a complete remedy.

C. *Evidentiary Matters*

The district court approach has a great advantage over an administrative hearing procedure in securing the needed evidence. The Federal Rules of Civil Procedure, with respect to discovery, would greatly facilitate the collection of evidence for trial. Under a cease-and-desist approach, the rather cumbersome method of enforcing subpoenas severely inhibits the acquisition of evidence for trial, making the hearing very dependent upon the investigation. Experience has shown that investigations, which are aimed simply at developing enough evidence to find reasonable cause, fall short of providing adequate evidence for obtaining a decision where the standard, as it is in the courts, is a preponderance of evidence on the record. Discovery procedures take less time than administrative fact-gathering techniques, and the contempt powers of the court operate to inhibit any intimidation of witnesses, which is a rather difficult problem that is often real, but seldom apparent.

II. Detrimental Provisions and Critical Omissions in the Committee Bill

A. As elaborated or hereafter, we .conclude that those provisions in the Committee bill dealing with the transfer of the Office of Federal Contract Compliance (OFCC), the extension of EEOC jurisdiction to state and local employees, and the transfer of pattern and practice suits from the Justice Department to the EEOC are detrimental to the major objective of this bill, which is to provide an enforcement power to effectuate appropriate and timely remedies for discriminatory employment conditions.

1. Section 11 of the Committee bill would transfer the function of the Office of Federal Contract Compliance under Executive Order

11246 from the Department of Labor to the Equal Employment Opportunity Commission. We oppose this transfer because: OFCC has made commendable progress in achieving the Executive Order's goal of equal employment opportunity by government contractors; the transfer would create a hiatus in the administration of these crucial programs and add an insurmountable administrative burden to an already overburdened agency; and the administration of the programs will prove unworkable because the EEOC would be assuming a dual role of contract compliance and the regulatory function of processing complaints of employment discrimination.

OFCC is charged with the administration of the nondiscrimination and affirmative action provisions of the Executive Order which relate to Federal contractors and Federally-assisted construction contractors. We feel that this function falls logically within the Department of Labor. The present location of OFCC permits it to benefit directly from the experience gained by the Labor Department in the administration of other workplace standards and anti-discrimination programs which are enforced by similar sanctions as well as its general expertise in labor-management relations. The Department also includes the Manpower Administration, thus making it possible for OFCC to include job training efficiently in the development of useful affirmative action programs.

While OFCC and EEOC share the goal of promoting the civil rights of minority workers, the programs they are presently administering are considerably different. EEOC acts, following an individual complaint, to redress instances of actual job discrimination. OFCC works with Government contractors to insure equal employment opportunity. The merging of these two distinct functions in a single agency will create serious problems, and such combination will undoubtedly work to the detriment of both programs. Incidentally, it should be pointed out, that once EEOC is given enforcement powers, federal contractors will be, just as other employers, subject to the processes and remedies of the EEOC in addition to those exercised by OFCC.

The EEOC presently has a tremendous backlog of pending charges. The addition of some form of enforcement powers will greatly increase its administrative responsibilities. We feel that it is simply unrealistic to expect EEOC simultaneously to shoulder the burden of OFCC's program. If the Committee's bill is enacted, we foresee a significant disruption of the compliance program. Regarding such transfer Chairman Brown of the EEOC appeared before the General Subcommittee on Labor and stated:

> Given the tremendous backlog of charges pending now with the Commission—25,195 as of February 20, 1971—the additioanl work which would have to be undertaken by the Commission if it gets enforcement powers, the difficulty of obtaining adequate funding for the Commission, and finally, the tremendous administrative difficulties embodied in such a transfer, I am doubtful as to the desirability of transferring OFCC at this time. Specifically, the administrative difficulties are by far the greatest in my view; almost insurmountable.

The primary responsibility for the implementation of the Executive Order as it relates to government procurement rests and must remain, with the individual Executive agencies. The coordination of the goals of equal employment opportunity with the needs of these agencies to obtain goods and services can be most effectively accomplished from within the Executive Branch of Government. Indeed, the experience of the various Presidential Committees formerly charged with the compliance program indicates the inherent difficulties in placing the operations of the agencies under the control of a separate body, such as the EEOC.

2. The Extension of Coverage to State and Local Employees. Apart from adding to the EEOC's already swollen workload which is treated in more detail in other portions of this report, we believe this area helps substantiate our earlier conclusion that the Federal courts are the proper forum. If its jurisdiction is thus extended, we will have the anomaly of a federal administrative agency interposing itself in the internal administration of state and local government. The NLRB does not have such jurisdiction over employees of state and local governments in matters involving discrimination in employment and we see no justification for extending such jurisdiction to the EEOC. It would be inconsistent with our system of division of governmental powers to subject state and local authorities to the cease-and-desist power of a federal commission.

3. Transfer of Pattern and Practice Suits to EEOC. We oppose the provisions of the Committee bill which would transfer from the Department of Justice to the EEOC the authority to try pattern and practice suits because it involves not only the transfer of authority from one agency to another, but also the elimination of the judicial remedies now provided by Section 707 of the Civil Rights Act. It will unquestionably hinder the achievement of equal employment opportunity. In effect, the Committee bill, will merely delay the achievement of any remedy to groups of discriminatees by interposing yet another obstacle, the additional forum of the EEOC, which after reaching its conclusion in such matters, under its hearing and cease and desist procedures, must ultimately petition a Federal Circuit Court of Appeals for enforcement. Certainly, it is in this area, that suits are frequently initiated as class actions because of the numbers of employees involved and the amounts of backpay due, which will usually require the authority of a Court enforced decree.

Between July, 1965, when title VII took effect and April 2, 1971, the Civil Rights Division of the Department of Justice filed some 60 suits on the basis of Section 707. The Division has had a high degree of success in litigating these cases, and principles established in them, at the trial or appellate level, have been useful to complaining private litigants and to other federal agencies. Six Circuit Courts have rendered decisions favorable to the Division's position and to date the Division has prevailed in each pattern and practice suit that has come to final decision. Such a record warrants a retention of pattern and practice suits in the Department of Justice. Some of the reasons for its success are the fact that it has access to the investigative resources of the Federal Bureau of Investigation—resources which have proved invaluable in ascertaining the facts and marshaling them for evidence in pattern or practice suits. Moreover, the United States Attorneys, who are the Department's field representatives located in every judicial district in the nation, have a thorough knowledge of local situations and are in a position to render valuable counsel and assistance.

4. Recovery of Court Costs Limited to "Prevailing Plaintiff." Under existing law, the Court has the discretion to allow the "prevailing party" a reasonable attorney's fee as part of the costs for litigation proceeding under this title. The Committee bill eliminated the term "prevailing party" and substitutes the term "prevailing plaintiff". No justification for such change was presented in hearings on the bill; it is contrary to the rule in most jurisdictions; and it may constitute an incentive for harassment suits and a "disincentive" to respondents not to resist ill-founded claims.

B. Critical Omissions of the Committee Bill. At the subcommittee and committee levels, we attempted to amend the Committee bill because it lacked certain procedural and due process safeguards. These deficiencies include: failure to provide for a reasonable statute of limitations on backpay; failure to provide for service of a charge on the named respondent within a reasonable time; failure to provide that title VII, as amended, shall be the exclusive remedy. We believe these omissions are critical and should be called to the attention of the House for we expect to make further attempts on the House floor to provide minimal due process standards in the Committee bill.

1. Statute of Limitations. Under the Committee bill, the time period in which individual charges of employment discrimination must be filed has been extended from 90 days to 180 days from the date of the alleged discriminatory conduct; this is identical to the statute of limitations under the National Labor Relations Act. We concur in such extension. However, testimony in the hearings indicates that pattern or practice suits now brought by the Justice Department are not subject to such limitation. Civil suits in most jurisdiction are subject to statutes of limitations ranging usually between two or three years. Under existing law, recovery of backpay in such pattern or practice suits can extend back to 1965, the effective date of enactment of the Civil Rights Act of 1964. Thus potential respondents whether they be employers, labor organizations or employment agencies may be subject to enormous monetary penalties in the absence of a definite limitation. To avoid the litigation of stale charges and to preclude respondents from being subject to indefinite liabilities, it is clear that a precise statute of limitations is needed. In view of the tremendous backlog currently existing at the EEOC, and the failure to require a prompt serving of the charge on named respondents as discussed hereafter, equitable principles require a limitation on liability.

Our amendment, which failed by a tie vote, inserted language which provided that no order shall include backpay or liability which accrued more than two years prior to the filing of a charge with the Commission. In view of the equitable principles on which such amendment is based, it is deserving of bipartisan support.

2. Service of the Charge. At the hearings of this bill, it was brought out that in most cases, employers were not notified about the filing of a charge until months later, not uncommonly a year or more. As the Committee bill failed to remedy this problem, we sought to amend it to require service on the named respondent within 5 days after the filing of a charge. In the discussion that ensued it was emphasized that

the 5 day figure was not a magic number and that any reasonable time period would be acceptable. Nevertheless, the Committee rejected the 5 day requirement and no reasonable alternative was offered.

It seems patent that failure to require timely notice violates all concepts of due process. Under the National Labor Relations Act, a charge is not deemed effectively filed for purposes of the 6 months statute of limitation *until* service of a copy of the charge on the respondent. In view of specific abuses regarding service of charges under title VII. a specific requirement for service on the respondent within a specified time period (5 to 7 days) is a prerequisite to maintaining minimum standards of due process.

3. Failure to Make Title VII an Exclusive Federal Remedy. Despite the enactment of title VII of the Civil Rights Act, charges of discriminatory employment conditions may still be brought under prior existing federal statutes such as the National Labor Relations Act and the Civil Rights Act of 1866. In view of the comprehensive prohibitions against discrimination contained in title VII, and the intent of the Committee bill to consolidate procedures and remedies under one agency, it would be consistent to make title VII the exclusive remedy. No public interest is served in continuing to permit a multiplicity of statutes or forums to deal with discrimination in employment. However, our attempt to amend the Committee bill to make title VII an exclusive remedy (except for pattern or practice suits) was rejected. In our view, the failure to make this an exclusive remedy merely encourages an individual who has lost his case in one forum under one statute to relitigate his case in still another forum under another federal statute. Under NLRB procedures and the proposed EEOC procedures, the burden as well as the cost of prosecuting charges is borne by the respective agencies, and therefore, the taxpayer.

CONCLUSIONS

In essence, the Committee bill will result in interposing an additional obstacle in the nature of an administrative forum, between the aggrieved party and the effective judicial relief which can be achieved by a court enforced order. For the reasons previously documented, direct judicial relief can be obtained more quickly and thus more effectively through the federal district courts.

Secondly, and equally as important, the massive expansion of jurisdiction and the transferring of various programs to the EEOC at a time when the agency is struggling to control a burgeoning backlog of cases, will further hamstring efforts to bring meaningful and timely relief to persons aggrieved by discriminatory employment conditions. At a time when Congress should be directing its efforts solely to helping the EEOC become a more effective agency by giving it access to judicial enforcement, the committee bill represents a step backward and will thrust the EEOC into an administrative quagmire which can only delay the attainment of a reasonable standard of operational efficiency that Congress should expect and demand.

Lastly, the failure of the committee bill to include such minimal due process requirements as the prompt notification to named respondents, a reasonable statute of limitations as to backpay and other liability, and failure to make this an exclusive remedy, are critical omissions whose inclusion we deem vital to meet due process standards.

ALBERT H. QUIE.
JOHN N. ERLENBORN.
JOHN DELLENBACK.
MARVIN L. ESCH.
EDWIN D. ESHLEMAN.
WILLIAM A. STEIGER.
ORVAL HANSEN.
EARL B. RUTH.
EDWIN B. FORSYTHE.
VICTOR V. VEYSEY.
JACK F. KEMP.

SEPARATE VIEWS OF REPRESENTATIVE GREEN OF OREGON

I should like to dissent to one provision in the bill.

The new section 717(f), in connection with the transfer of the Office of Federal Contract Compliance to the EEOC, provides that all authority, functions and responsibilities vested in the Secretary of Labor pursuant to Executive Order 11246 relating to nondiscrimination in employment by government contractors and subcontractors and nondiscrimination in federally assisted construction contracts are transferred to the EEOC . . . and the Commissioner shall hereafter carry out all such authority, functions, and responsibilities pursuant to such order.

The EEOC will operate under two authorities—Executive Order 11246 as adopted by subsection (f), and Congressional enactments amended title VII of the Civil Rights Act. Those authorities are divergent in important ways. For example:

(1) Under title VII an individual may sue the offending party after his complaint has been with the EEOC for 60 days.

Under the Executive Order an individual may not sue but may seek debarment of the contract.

(2) Under title VII, EEOC can initiate an investigation only after the filing of a discrimination complaint. The company is entitled to judicial review if it should feel that the investigation is unwarranted.

Under the Executive Order contract review can be conducted at will. A decision to investigate is not subject to judicial review.

(3) Under Title VII EEOC is specifically prohibited from public disclosure of a complaint.

Under the Executive Order there is authority to publish the names of persons accused of discrimination.

(4) Under title VII (Sec. 703(j)) EEOC is expressly prohibited from imposing racial quota requirements.

Under the Executive Order there is authority to require an affirmative action plan including the imposition of racial quotas. In my view, the Philadelphia plan is such a quota plan.

These contradictions place the EEOC in the intolerable situation of being compelled to select between contradictory expressions of

Congressional intent. It is unreasonable to ask the EEOC to decide which intention we really mean.

I am particularly concerned that the EEOC may decide that it can, under the Executive Order authority, impose racial quotas which it is forbidden to do under direct Congressional statute. Such artificial quotas, unrelated to competence, are a distortion of civil rights and a disservice to our working people. Personal rights are individual rights, and the imposition of quotas infringes on them.

In our committee consideration of the bill, I offered an amendment for the single purpose of removing the contradiction. It would have made the present authority of title VII of the Civil Rights Act take precedence in any conflict situation. The EEOC deserves such guidance.

EDITH GREEN.

INDIVIDUAL VIEWS OF REPRESENTATIVE MAZZOLI

I favor equal employment opportunity for all Americans and support all realistic legislative measures directed toward this goal. However, because of significant provisions contained in, and omitted from, the Committee version of H.R. 1746, I cannot support this legislation in the form in which it has been reported. It requires major amendment in order to become, in my opinion, realistic and appropriate legislation to end job discrimination.

My objections to H.R. 1746 conform generally to the objections raised in the Minority Views printed in this Report.

Basically, I prefer the stability, expedition and protection to plaintiff and defendant alike offered by judicial enforcement of equal employment rights over the administrative cease and desist approach contained in H.R. 1746.

I also prefer that a choice of remedies be incorporated into this legislation. A multiplicity of remedies and of forums, except in pattern and practice suits, is inconsistent with the intent of this legislation which is to consolidate and coordinate all efforts to eliminate discrimination in employment.

There ought also, in my opinion, to be a two-year statute of limitations incorporated into H.R. 1746. I concur with the Minority Views on this matter as set forth elsewhere in this Report.

Likewise, I concur in the conclusion and the reasoning of the minority in opposing the shift of the Office of Federal Contract Compliance to the Equal Employment Opportunities Commission.

On these groups and on others, most of which are discussed in the Minority Views printed in this Report, I cannot support the Committee version of H.R. 1746, and will support amendments or substitutes thereto.

ROMANO L. MAZZOLI.

SUPPLEMENTAL VIEWS OF REPRESENTATIVES JOHN M. ASHBROOK AND EARL F. LANDGREBE

We generally agree with the views expressed in the Minority report.

However, we do not conclude as they do that the EEOC should be given enforcement authority.

JOHN M. ASHBROOK.
EARL F. LANDGREBE.

INDIVIDUAL VIEWS OF REPRESENTATIVE REID OF NEW YORK

Since 1965, I have authored, supported, and fought for legislation to strengthen the Equal Employment Opportunity Commission by giving it cease and desist powers. In 1965, such a bill passed the House and in 1970 a similar measure was approved by the Senate. I very much hope that in 1971 both houses of the Congress will agree that the right to equal employment opportunity is dependent upon a strong EEOC with judicially enforceable cease and desist powers.

The Commission's powers under present law are limited to conciliation and it is apparent that this authority is grossly inadequate to obtain meaningful action in the cases before it. Reasonable cause has been found in 63 percent of the 27,000 cases brought before the EEOC and recommended for investigation between 1965 and 1970. But in only less than half of these cases was the Commission able to achieve a totally or even partially successful conciliation.

Based on my experience as Chairman of the New York State Commission for Human Rights in 1961 and 1962, I deeply believe that only cease and desist powers will give the EEOC the strength it needs to be effective. Redress through the courts, instead of cease and desist powers, will not be as effective, will not be as expeditious, and will not result in prompt equal employment opportunity for all Americans.

H.R. 1746 also expands the jurisdiction of EEOC to cover state and local government employees and to cover employers and labor unions with 8 or more employees or members instead of the present 25, and transfers equal employment functions of the Civil Service Commission to the EEOC. These amendments fill a critical need and they will make the protection of a strong Federal law available to government workers in almost 20 states which lack meaningful legislation in this field.

Transfers of authority to the EEOC from the Civil Service Commission, the Department of Labor (in the case of Federal contract compliance) and the Department of Justice (in the case of pattern or practice discrimination suits) will centralize the equal employment functions of the Federal government. Hopefully, this will result in a more vigorous pursuit of these rights than now is the case by certain of these agencies. In particular, adequate staff and resources must be provided to the EEOC to handle its increased responsibilities. Otherwise, these transfers of authority will have the effect of reduced, rather than strengthened, compliance. This is especially important with regard to the transfer of Federal Contract Compliance pursuant to Executive Order 11246 from the Department of Labor to EEOC.

Equal employment opportunity legislation with effective enforcement is now the law in over 30 states. Support for this bill is nationwide among educational, religious, civic, labor, and civil rights groups. I know of no black, Spanish-American, Chicano, American Indian, or women's organization that does not totally support cease and desist powers. Indeed, the most persistent opposition to cease and desist comes from those who do not really want the Federal government to enforce effectively the right of all Americans to equal employment opportunity now.

The plain hard fact of the matter is that we should have enacted this bill in 1965, instead of wasting six years conjuring up legal niceties to evade our constitutional responsibilities. To delay still longer the enactment of cease and desist powers for the EEOC would be a grave dereliction of duty by the Congress. To dilute this legislation by the substitution of authority weaker and less effective than cease and desist would be a callous and empty gesture and a cynical failure to fulfill a right due all Americans regardless of color or sex.

Finally, I hope that the Rules Committee, unlike its past performance, will grant a rule for H.R. 1746 promptly so that Members will have a chance to debate and vote on the bill. Amendments will doubtless be offered on the Floor to weaken this legislation, and I hope that all Members will join in defeating them. Justice demands nothing less.

OGDEN R. REID.

Report of Senate Committee
on Labor and Public Welfare

EQUAL EMPLOYMENT OPPORTUNITIES
ENFORCEMENT ACT OF 1971

OCTOBER 28, 1971.—Ordered to be printed

Mr. WILLIAMS, from the Committee on Labor and Public Welfare,
submitted the following

REPORT

together with

INDIVIDUAL AND SUPPLEMENTAL VIEWS

[To accompany S. 2515]

The Committee on Labor and Public Welfare, to which was referred
the bill (S. 2515) to further promote equal employment opportunities
for American workers, having considered the same, reports favorably
thereon with an amendment (in the nature of a substitute) and recommends that the bill as amended do pass.

SUMMARY

The principal purpose of S. 2515 is to amend title VII of the Civil
Rights Act of 1964 to provide the Equal Employment Opportunity
Commission with a method for enforcing the rights of those workers
who have been subjected to unlawful employment practices.

The enforcement procedures provided for in S. 2515 include the
issuance of a complaint by the Commission after an investigation and
efforts to conciliate, followed by a full administrative hearing on the
record, the issuance of a cease and desist order by the Commission, and
an opportunity for review by an appropriate court of appeals.

The bill confers upon the Commission the authority to proceed with
pattern and practice cases of discrimination, and phases out the Attorney General's existing authority in such cases over a 2-year period.
The Secretary of Labor's enforcement functions under Executive
Order 11246 as amended relating to nondiscrimination in employment
by Government contractors and Federally assisted construction contractors are transferred to the Commission.

In addition, S. 2515 expands coverage of Title VII, from those employers and labor organizations having 25 or more employees or members to those having eight or more employees or members one year after the date of enactment. The bill also includes coverage of employees of State and local governments with a provision that complaints involving these employees will be litigated by the Attorney General in U.S. district courts, and eliminates the exemption for employees of educational institutions.

The Civil Service Commission is given expanded authority to eliminate discrimination in Federal employment, and individual Federal employees are expressly granted a right of private action to obtain relief from such discrimination.

The time limitations on filing charges are expanded from 90 to 180 days for a direct charge to the Commission and from 210 to 300 days for a charge which is first brought under a State or local law. Back pay awards are limited to two years prior to the date a charge is filed with the Commission. The bill also authorize the appointment of up to four additional members of the Commission.

As a result of six years experience with title VII, and in order to accommodate the enforcement power provided for in this bill, a number of administrative changes are contained in S. 2515. They include expanded record-keeping requirements and subpoena power, authority for the Commission to conduct its own litigation, and additional protections for aggrieved persons.

BACKGROUND

During the 90th Congress, a bill to provide the Equal Employment Opportunity Commission with power to issue cease and desist orders, S. 3465, was reported by the Committee on Labor and Public Welfare, but was not acted upon by the Senate. A closely comparable measure, S. 2453, was reported by the Committee during the 91st Congress, and was passed by the Senate on October 1, 1970, by a vote of 47 to 24. This measure was not brought to a vote in the House of Representatives, however.

On September 14, 1971, a bill with similar cease and desist provisions, S. 2515, was introduced by Senator Byrd of West Virginia, for Senator Williams and for 32 other Senators. Subsequently, on September 16, 1971, the House of Representatives passed H.R. 1746, a bill which would authorize the Equal Employment Opportunity Commission to go into United States district courts on charges of discrimination, rather than to issue its own cease and desist orders. An identical bill to H.R. 1746, S. 2617, was introduced by Senator Dominick on September 30, 1971.

The Subcommittee on Labor held hearings on these three bills on October 4, 6 and 7, 1971. S. 2515 was reported favorably by that Subcommittee on October 14, 1971, and was considered by the full Committee on Labor and Public Welfare on October 19, 20, and 21, 1971, when it was unanimously ordered reported to the Senate.

Testimony was received from a number of Federal Government officials on these bills. The Chairman of the United States Commission on Civil Rights, Reverend Theodore Hesburgh, testified in support of all of the provisions of S. 2515, including cease and desist enforcement powers, consolidation of Federal equal employment opportunity functions, and expansion of coverage to state and local government employees. William Brown III, Chairman of the Equal Employment Opportunity Commission testified in support of S. 2515's cease and desist authority with the reservation that it should also contain court enforcement for pending cases. He endorsed expanded coverage, although he was not in favor of consolidation of EEOC functions. David Norman, Assistant Attorney General, Civil Rights Division, Department of Justice testified in support of a court enforcement approach, and against consolidation of functions. Laurence Silberman, Under Secretary of Labor testified against the transfer of the Executive Order program to the Commission, and Irving Kator, Assistant Executive Director of the Civil Service Commission presented testimony in opposition to the transfer of that Commission's equal employment opportunity functions to the Equal Employment Opportunity Commission.

Congressman Erlenborn of Illinois testified in behalf of a court enforcement approach and Congressman Walter Fauntroy testified on behalf of transferring the Civil Service equal employment opportunity functions to the Equal Employment Opportunity Commission.

Clarence Mitchell of the Leadership Conference on Civil Rights and the NAACP, Ken Meiklejohn on behalf of the AFL–CIO, Jack Greenberg of the NAACP Legal Defense and Education Fund., Inc., Joseph Rauh of the Leadership Conference on Civil Rights, Lucille Shriver of the National Federation of Business and Professional Women's Clubs, Olga Madar, Vice President, United Auto Workers, Esther Lawton and Daisy Fields of the Federally Employed Women and Doris Meissner of the National Women's Political Caucus testified in support of S. 2515, including its cease and desist enforcement functions, expanded coverage, and consolidation of functions.

Statements in support of S. 2515 were also received from: Donald E. Morrison, President, National Education Association; Reverend Dr. Ralph David Abernathy, President, Southern Christian Leadership Conference; Paul J. Minarchenko, Legislative Representative, American Federation of State, County and Municipal Employees—AFL–CIO; Hope Eastman, Acting Director, Washington Office, American Civil Liberties Union; William G. Lunsford, on behalf of Friends Committee on National Legislation; David A. Brody, Director, Washington Office, Anti-Defamation League of B'nai B'rith; National Council of Jewish Women; Ann Scott, Vice President—Legislation, The National Organization for Women; Mary Jean Collins-Robson, President, Chicago Chapter, NOW; The League of Women Voters; Mrs. Sherman Ross, Chairman, Legislative Program Committee, American Association of University Women; Germaine Krettek, Director, American Library Association; Edward Taylor Anderson, Legislative Associate, Common Cause; and Julius W. Hobson, Washington, D.C.

Testimony in support of a court enforcement bill, S. 2617 or H.R. 1746, was also received from Gerard Smetana on behalf of the American Retail Federation and William Dunn on behalf of the Associated General Contractors. In addition, statements in support of those bills were submitted by the National Association of Manufacturers, Chamber of Commerce of the United States and the American Protestant Hospital Association.

NEED FOR THE BILL

Seven years ago, in response to compelling national need and concern, Congress enacted Title VII of the Civil Rights Act of 1964 (Public Law 88–352). By its action, Congress acknowledged the prevalence of employment discrimination in the United States and the need for Federal legislation to deal with the problem of such discrimination. The Act also established the Equal Employment Opportunity Commission (EEOC), whose operations were initiated on July 2, 1965. It was the intention of Congress that the EEOC should be the primary Federal agency responsible for eliminating discriminatory employment practices in the United States.

During the 6 years since its inception, the EEOC has made an heroic attempt to reduce the incidence of employment discrimination in the Nation, and to ameliorate the conditions which have led to the persistence of these practices. During this period, however, it has been demonstrated that employment discrimination is even more pervasive and tenacious than the Congress had assumed it to be at the time it passed the Act. It affects employees in both the private and the public sectors as well as those working in large and small establishments. It has also become clear that despite the national commitment of Congress to the goal of assuring equal employment opportunity for all our citizens, the machinery created by the Civil Rights Act of 1964 is not in all respects equal to that commitment.

The most striking deficiency of the 1964 Act is that the EEOC does not have the authority to issue judicially enforceable orders to back up its findings of discrimination. In prohibiting discrimination in employment based on race, religion, color, sex or national origin, the 1964 Act limited the Commission's enforcement authority to "informal methods of conference, conciliation and persuasion."

As a consequence, unless the Department of Justice concludes that a pattern or practice of resistance to Title VII is involved, the burden of obtaining enforceable relief rests upon each individual victim of discrimination, who must go into court as a private party, with the delay and expense that entails, in order to secure the rights promised him under the law. Thus, those persons whose economic disadvantage was a prime reason for enactment of equal employment opportunity provisions find that their only recourse in the face of unyielding discrimination is one that is time consuming, burdensome, and all too often, financially prohibitive.

This failure to grant the EEOC meaningful enforcement powers has proven to be a major flaw in the operation of Title VII. While the statutes dealing with discrimination in housing and in education provide appropriate enforcement powers for the agencies responsible for the elimination of discrimination in those areas of the law, Title VII, as it now stands, is little more than a declaration of national policy. Regretably, the practices and policies of discrimination in employment are so deeply ingrained that the voluntary conciliation approach has not succeeded in adequately combating the existence of such practices.

In 1964, employment discrimination tended to be viewed as a series of isolated and distinguishable events, for the most part due to ill-will on the part of some identifiable individual or organization. It was thought that a scheme that stressed conciliation rather than compulsory processes would be most appropriate for the resolution of this essentially "human" problem, and that litigation would be necessary only on an occasional basis. Experience has shown this view to be false.

Employment discrimination as viewed today is a far more complex and pervasive phenomenon. Experts familiar with the subject now generally describe the problem in terms of "systems" and "effects" rather than simply intentional wrongs, and the literature on the subject is replete with discussions of, for example, the mechanics of seniority and lines of progression, perpetuation of the present effect of pre-act discriminatory practices through various institutional devices, and testing and validation requirements.[1] In short, the problem is one whose resolution in many instances requires not only expert assistance, but also the technical perception that the problem exists in the first instance, and that the system complained of is unlawful. This kind of expertise normally is not found in either the personnel or legal arms of corporations, and the result in terms of conciliations is often an impasse, with the respondent unwilling or unable to understand the problem in the same way that the Commission perceives it.

The resulting impasse between EEOC and the employer has played a large part in the present failure of Title VII. The employer realizes that any attack on its policies by the EEOC presents largely an ineffectual threat. To comply with the Commission's interpretation of a problem, and to accord the appropriate relief, is a purely voluntary matter with the respondent with no direct legal sanctions available to EEOC. This absolute discretion available to respondents has not proven conducive to the success of Title VII objectives. In cases posing the most profound consequences, respondents have frequently ignored the EEOC's findings, preferring rather to chance the unlikelihood that the complainant will pursue his claim further through the costly and time-consuming process of court enforcement. The social consequences have been extreme.

The failure of the voluntary conciliation approach is reflected in the present EEOC workload statistics presented by its Chairman, William H. Brown, III. Since its inception, the Commission has received 81,000 charges. Of this number, the Commission has been able to achieve a totally, or even partially satisfactory conciliation in less than half. This means that in a significant number of cases the aggrieved individual was not able to achieve any satisfactory settlement of his claim through the EEOC, and was forced to either give up his or her claim or, if the necessary funds and time were available, to pursue the case through the Federal courts.

---

[1] See e.g. "Developments in the Law—Employment Discrimination and Title VII of the Civil Rights Act of 1964" 84 Harv. L. Rev. 1109 (1971) ; Cooper and Sobol, "Seniority and Testing Under Fair Employment Laws : A General Approach To Objective Criteria of Hiring and Promotion," 82 Harv. L. Rev. 1623 (1969) ; Blumrosen, "The Duty of Fair Recruitment Under the Civil Rights Act of 1964," 22 Rutgers L. Rev. 465 (1968). See also M. Sovern, Legal Restraints on Racial Discrimination in Employment (1966), and decisions in *Griggs* v. *Duke Power Co.,* 401 U.S. 424 (1971) ; *Asbestos Workers, Local 53* v. *Vogler,* 407 F. 2d 1047 (C.A. 5 1969) ; *Quarles* v. *Phillip Morris,* 279 F. Supp. 505 (E.D. Va., 1968) ; *United States* v. *Local 189, United Papermakers,* 282 F. Supp. 39 (E.D. La., 1968) and cases cited therein.

While the above-noted number of charges is disturbing by its very size, it becomes even more significant when considered in light of the fact that each year the number of charges filed with the Commission continues to increase. For example, in FY 1970, 14,129 charges were filed with EEOC; in FY 1971, this number increased to 22,920 charges; and current estimates submitted by the Commission indicate that more than 32,000 charges will be filed this year. It is obvious that without effective enforcement powers, the EEOC will become little more than a receptacle for charges of violations of Title VII, and that an ever-increasing number of aggrieved individuals will be left without an adequate remedy for violations which are clearly prohibited by the law.

The impact of this inability to obtain relief from employment discrimination surfaces in another, more indicative set of facts—the economic disparities which presently affect this Nation's minorities and women.

In a special report released this year by the Bureau of the Census, "The Social and Economic Status of Negroes in the United States," the evidence is clear that while some progress has been made toward bettering the economic position of the Nation's black population, the avowed goal of social and economic equality is not yet anywhere near a reality. For example, the report shows that the median family income for Negroes in 1970 was $6,279, while the median income for whites during the same period was $10,236. This earnings gap shows that Negroes are still far from reaching their rightful place in society.

Support for the above statement is provided by statistics in the Census Bureau report which show that Negroes are concentrated in the lower-paying, less prestigious positions in industry and are largely precluded from advancement to the higher paid, more prestigious positions. For example, while Negroes constitute about 10% of the labor force, they account for only 3% of all jobs in the high-paying professional, technical, and managerial positions. In the nine industries with the highest earning capabilities (printing and publishing, chemicals, primary metals, fabricated metals, nonelectrical machinery, transportation equipment, air transportation, and instruments manufacture), Negroes hold only 1% of professional and managerial positions. On the other hand, in the lowest paying laborer and service worker categories, Negroes account for 24% of all jobs.

This economic disparity is further reinforced by statistics which show that the unemployment rate for Negroes is considerably higher than that for whites. Figures available for 1970 show that while 4.0% of white males were unemployed, and the unemployment rate for all whites was 5.4%, 9.3% of all Negroes were unemployed. Even in the managerial and professional positions, the area with the lowest unemployment rate, Negro unemployment was 2.1% while white unemployment was 1.7%.

While statistics on Spanish-speaking Americans are not nearly as current or as complete, available data indicates that this, the second-largest ethnic minority group in the Nation, with approximately 7.5 million members, is in a similar situation. In 1969, the median family income for Spanish-speaking American families was $5,641. About 17% of these families had incomes of less than $3,000. Both male and female Spanish-speaking workers, as has already been shown to be the case with Negroes, are also concentrated in the lower-paying occupations. Only 25% of employed Spanish-speaking males are in white-collar jobs, compared to 41% of men for all other origins. On the other hand, 58.8% of Spanish-speaking males are concentrated in blue-collar occupations. The statistics for Spanish-speaking women workers indicates a similar disparate distribution. Also, as with Negroes, Spanish-speaking workers suffer a higher unemployment rate when compared to the white population. In 1969, 6.0% of Spanish-speaking Americans were unemployed, compared to 3.5% for the rest of the Nation.

The situation for working women is no less serious. The disparate treatment of women in this country has been shown in a series of studies undertaken by the Women's Bureau of the U.S. Department of Labor. [2] These studies show that there are aproximately 30 million employed women in the Nation, constituting about 38% of the total work force. The number of working women has also increased very rapidly during the last two decades—between 1947 and 1968 the number of women in the civilian labor force increased by 75% while the number of men during the same period increased only 16%. Despite this large increase in the numbers of women in the work force, women continue to be relegated to low paying positions and are precluded from high-paying executive positions. Similarly, the rate of advancement for women is slower than for men in similar positions.

Information supplied by the U.S. Department of Labor's Women's Bureau shows that 70% of all employed women work in order to provide primary support for themselves or to provide a supplement to the incomes of their husbands which may be needed to meet household expenses. However, within established occupational categories, women are paid less for doing the same jobs as are done by men. For example, in 1968, the latest year for which extensive data is presently available, the median salary for all scientists was $13,200; for women scientists the median saary was $10,000. Similarly, the median salary for a full-time male factory worker was $6,738 while his female counterpart could only expect to earn $3,991. This economic disparity is further emphasized by figures which show that 60% of women but only 20% of men earned less than $5,000 per year, while only 3% of women but 28% of men earned $10,000 per year or more.

While some have looked at the entire issue of women's rights as a frivolous divertissement, this Committee believes that discrimination against women is no less serious than other prohibited forms of discrimination, and that it is to be accorded the same degree of concern given to any type of similarly unlawful conduct. As a further point, recent studies have shown that there is a close correlation between discrimination based on sex and racial discrimination, and that both possess similar characteristics. [3] Both categories involve large, natural classes, membership in which is beyond the individual's control; both

---

[2] U.S. Department of Labor, *Fact Sheet on the Earnings Gap* (1971) ; U.S. Department of Labor, *Underutilization of Women Workers* (1970) ; U.S. Department of Labor, Bulletin 294, *1969 Handbook on Women Workers* (1969) ; U.S. Department of Labor, *Changing Patterns of Women's Lives* (1970).

[3] See A. Montagu, *Man's Most Dangerous Myth* 181–4 (4th ed. 1964) : G. Myrdal, *An American Dilemma* 1073–78 (2d ed. 1962). See also "Sex Discrimination and Equal Protection : Do We Need a Constitutional Amendment?", 84 Harv. L. Rev. 1499 (1971) ; Murphy & Eastwood, "Jane Crow and the Law: Sex Discrimination and Title VII," 34 Geo. Wash. L. Rev. 232 (1965).

involve highly visible characteristics on which it has been easy to draw gross, stereotypical distinctions. The arguments justifying different treatment of the sexes were also historically used to justify different treatment of the races.

While it is true that the extreme aspects of sex-discrimination as it existed in the early part of the twentieth century have been dispelled, and women have now been granted the right to vote and may serve on juries, their status in employment is still subject to blatant discrimination. In a series of decisions in recent years, the courts have voided employment practices and policies which discriminate on the basis of sex, and have, accordingly, set the necessary legal precedents for dealing with this form of discrimination.[4] However, despite the effort by the courts and EEOC, discrimination against women continues to be widespread; and is regarded by many as either morally or physiologically justifiable.

The Committee realizes that enactment of this bill will not automatically end employment discrimination in this country. The bill offers no panaceas or guarantees of success. Despite several aspects of the operation of Title VII during these last 6 years which reflect major advancements in securing equal employment opportunity for all Americans, the results are, nonetheless, disappointing in terms of what minorities and women have a right to expect under the provisions of that law. Particularly disillusioning has been the Congressional establishment of the EEOC without adequate enforcement; it has, in most respects, proved to be a cruel joke to those complainants who have in good faith turned to the Federal government with the complaint of discrimination only to find, after a lengthy investigatory and conciliatory process, that the Government cannot compel compliance.

The accomplishment of Congress in enacting the Civil Rights Act of 1964 is further dimmed by the fact that this is the fourth effort since that time to enact suitable enforcement legislation. The time has come for Congress to correct the defects in its own legislation. The promises of equal job opportunity made in 1964 must be made realities in 1971.

Major Provisions of the Bill

Changes in Coverage Under Title VII

The bill expands the coverage of Title VII in the following respects:

1. *Eight or more employees.*—Section 701 of the Act (section 2 of the bill) is amended to expand the coverage of title VII to include employers of eight or more persons, and labor organizations with eight or more members. The Committee agrees with the Chairman of EEOC that discrimination should be attacked wherever it exists, and recognizes that small establishments have frequently been the most flagrant violators of equal employment opportunity.

At present, the jurisdiction of the EEOC extends to approximately 83% of the nation's non-agricultural work force (approximately 250,-000 employers and 37,800 labor organizations). By adding the provi-

---

[4] See e.g. *Phillips* v. *Martin-Marietta Corp.* 400 U.S. 542 (1971); *Diaz* v. *Pan American World Airways,* 442 F. 2d 385 (C.A. 5, 1971); *Weeks* v. *Southern Bell Telephone Co.,* 408 F. 2d 228 (C.A. 5, 1969); *Bowe* v. *Colgate Palmolive Co.,* 416 F. 2d 711 (C.A. 7, 1969)

sions as currently proposed, the jurisdiction of the EEOC would encompass another 8% of the present work force, or approximately 6.5 million employees and about 90,000 employers.

The need for coverage in this area is obvious. The absence of EEOC jurisdiction over these small employers and labor organizations has made it impossible for the Commission to compile sufficient information in this area to pinpoint those areas where patterns or practices of discrimination exist. As a consequence, it has not been possible to institute changes where necessary to insure compliance with the provisions of Title VII.

The Committee is not persuaded by arguments that the increased coverage will inundate EEOC with complaints and paperwork. In the first instance, the proposition that the increased coverage will overwhelm the Commission with an unmanageable number of new cases is not convincing. This argument, which has traditionally been presented whenever a new jurisdictional area is opened up, has proven to be largely false in other areas of expanded Federal jurisdiction. Also, it must be noted that although the proposed increase will result in coverage of more employers, these employers represent proportionately fewer employees, therefore mitigating against any massive influx of cases. The argument that the Commission will be overburdened by additional paperwork is similarly alarmist. All EEOC reporting procedures are now fully computerized, and once the initial reprogramming is accomplished to account for the new coverage, the Committee believes that any additional burden will not be noticeable.

However, since the Commission will be undertaking several new areas of responsibility under the proposed legislation, the Committee recognizes that the Commission may have some difficulty in handling the increased caseload immediately. Therefore, the bill provides that the expansion take place one year after enactment of the bill.

2. *State and local governments.*—The bill would amend section 701 of the Act (section 2 of the bill) to broaden the jurisdictional coverage of title VII by deleting the existing exemptions for State and local government employees. The Attorney General is given the authority to bring civil actions involving unlawful employment practices committed by State and local governmental agencies.

The Committee believes that employees of State and local governments are entitled to the same benefits and protections in equal employment as the employees in the private sector of the economy.

There are at present approximately 10.1 million persons employed by State and local governmental units. This figure represents an increase of over 2 million since 1964, and all indications are that the number of State and local employees will continue to increase more rapidly during the next few years. Few of these employees, however, are afforded the protection of an effective Federal forum for assuring equal employment opportunity. By amending the present section 701 to include State and local governmental units within the definition of an "employer" under Title VII, all State and local governmental employees would, under the provisions of the bill, have access to the remedies available under the Act.

In a report released in 1969 by the U.S. Commission on Civil Rights, "For All the People * * * By All the People," that Commission concluded that:

* * * State and local governments have failed to fulfill
their obligation to assure equal job opportunity * * * Not
only do State and local governments consciously and overtly
discriminate in hiring and promoting minority group members, but they do not foster positive programs to deal with
discriminatory treatment on the job.

The report's findings indicate that the existence of discrimination is
perpetuated by both institutional and overt discriminatory practices,
and that past discriminatory practices are maintained through *de facto*
segregated job ladders, invalid selection techniques, and stereotypical
misconceptions by supervisors regarding minority group capabilities.
The study also indicates that employment discrimination in State and
local governments is more pervasive than in the private sector.

In another report issued by the U.S. Commission on Civil Rights in
1970, "Mexican Americans and the Administration of Justice in the
Southwest," the Commission found that in the five Southwestern
states with the highest concentration of Spanish-speaking Americans,
their representation in the vital area of law enforcement was significantly disproportionate to their demographic distribution. The report
shows that in these five Southwestern states, Spanish-speaking Americans, who constitute approximately 12% of the population account for
only 5.2% of police officers and 6.11% of civilian employees associated
with law enforcement agencies.

This failure of State and local governmental agencies to accord equal
employment opportunities is particularly distressing in light of the
importance that these agencies play in the daily lives of the average
citizen. From local law enforcement to social services, each citizen in a
community is in constant contact with many local agencies. The importance of equal opportunity in these agencies is, therefore, self-evident.
In our democratic society, participatory government is a cornerstone
of good government. Discrimination by government therefore serves a
doubly destructive purpose. The exclusion of minorities from effective
participation in the bureaucracy not only promotes ignorance of minority problems in that particular community, but also creates mistrust,
alienation, and all too often hostility toward the entire process of
government.

The Constitution is imperative in its prohibition of discrimination
by State and local governments. The Fourteenth Amendment guarantees equal treatment of all citizens by States and their political subdivisions, and the Supreme Court has reinforced this directive by holding that State action which denies equal protection of the laws to any
person, even if only indirectly, is in violation of the Fourteenth
Amendment.[5] It is clear that the guarantee of equal protection
must also extend to such direct action as discriminatory employment
practices.

The Committee believes that it is an injustice to provide employees
in the private sector with the assistance of an agency of the Federal

---

[5] See, e.g., *Shelly* v. *Kraemer,* 334 U.S. 1 (1948) ; *Burton* v. *Wilmington Parking Authority,* 365 U.S. 715 (1961).

Government in redressing their grievances while at the same time denying assistance similar to State and local government employees. The last sentence of the Fourteenth Amendment, enabling Congress to enforce the Amendment's guarantees by appropriate legislation is frequently overlooked, and the plain meaning of the Constitution allowed to lapse. The inclusion of State and local government employees within the jurisdiction of Title VII guarantees and protections will fulfill the Congressional duty to enact the "appropriate legislation" to insure that all citizens are treated equally in this country.

The Supreme Court has further indicated that at least part of the extension of jurisdiction as contemplated by S. 2515 is a proper constitutional exercise of power under the Commerce Clause. In its decision in *Maryland* v. *Wirtz*, 392 U.S. 183 (1968), the Court upheld the extension of the Fair Labor Standards Act to certain classes of public employees as a legitimate exercise of congressional regulatory authority under the Commerce Clause. The Court rejected the argument that Federal regulation of the employment practices of State and local governments is an improper infringement upon the sovereignty of the States. Pointing out that the activities of State and local governments can affect commerce, it held:

> If a State is engaging in economic activities that are validly regulated by the Federal Government when engaged in by private persons, the State too may be forced to conform its activities to Federal regulation.[6]

A question was raised in the Committee concerning the application of Title VII in the case of a Governor whose cabinet appointees and close personal aides are drawn from one political party. The Committee's intention is that nothing in this bill should be interpreted to prohibit such appointments unless they are based on discrimination because of race, color, religion, sex or national origin. That intention is reflected in sections 703(h) and 706(w) of the law.

3. *Employees of educational institutions.*—The existing exemption for employees of educational institutions is eliminated by an amendment to section 702 (sec. 3 of the bill).

There are at present over 120,000 educational institutions, with approximately 2.8 million teachers and professional staff members and another 1.5 million non-professional staff members. Yet all of these employees are, in effect, without an effective Federal remedy in the area of employment discrimination.

The presence of discrimination in the Nation's educational institutions is no secret. Many of the most famous and best remembered civil rights cases have involved discrimination in education. This discrimination, however, is not limited to the students alone. Discriminatory practices against faculty, staff, and other employees is also common. The practices complained of parallel the same kinds of illegal actions which are encountered in other sectors of business, and include illegal

---

[6] In rejecting the State sovereignty argument the Court cited a long series of decisions holding that a State, when engaged in activities affecting interstate commerce, may be held subject to Federal regulations. See *United States* v. *California*, 297 U.S. 175 (1936) ; *Board of Trustees* v. *United States*, 289 U.S. 48 (1932). See also, *Parden* v. *Terminal Railroad Co.*, 371 U.S. 184 (1962).

hiring policies, testing provisions which tend to perpetuate racial imbalances, and discriminatory promotion and certification techniques.[7]

As in other areas of employment, statistics for educational institutions indicate that minorities and women are precluded from the more prestigious and higher-paying positions, and are relegated to the more menial and lower-paying jobs. While in elementary and secondary school systems Negroes accounted for approximately 10% of the total number of positior , in the higher-paying and more prestigious positions in institutions of higher learning, blacks constituted only 2.2% of all positions, most of these being found in all-black or predominantly black institutions. Women are similarly subject to discriminatory patterns. Not only are they generally under-represented in institutions of higher learning, but those few that do obtain positions are generally paid less and advanced more slowly than their male counterparts. Similarly, while women constitute 67% of elementary and secondary school teachers, out of 778,000 elementary and secondary school principals, 78% of elementary school principals are men and 94% of secondary school principals are men.

The Committee believes that it is essential that these employees be given the same opportunity to redress their grievances as are available to other employees in the other sectors of business. Accordingly, the Committee has concluded that educational institutions, like other employers in the Nation, should report their activities to the Commission and should be subject to the Act. There is nothing in the legislative background of Title VII, nor does any national policy suggest itself, to support the present exemption. In fact, the Committee believes that the existence of discrimination in educational institutions is particularly critical. It is difficult to imagine a more sensitive area than educational institutions, where the youth of the Nation are exposed to a multitude of ideas and impressions that will strongly influence their future development. To permit discrimination here would, more than in any other area, tend to promote existing misconceptions and stereotypical categorizations which in turn would lead to future patterns of discrimination.

4. *Federal employment.*—The bill adds to title VII a new section 717 (section 11 of the bill) making clear the obligation of the Federal Government to make all personnel actions free from discrimination based on race, color, sex, religion or national orgin. The Civil Service Commission, which presently has the responsibility under Executive Order 11478, is given the authority under this title to enforce equal employment opportunity in the Federal government.

The Federal government, with 2.6 million employees, is the single largest employer in the Nation. It also comprises the central policy-making and administrative network for the Nation. Consequently, its policies, actions, and programs strongly influence the activities of all other enterprises, organizations and groups. In no area is government action more important than in the area of civil rights.

The prohibition against discrimination by the Federal government, based upon the due process clause of the Fifth Amendment, was judi-

---

[7] See e.g. *Armstead* v. *Starkville School District,* 325 F. Supp. 560 (N.D. Miss. 1971) : *Singleton* v. *Jackson Municipal Separate School District,* 419 F. 2d 1211 (C.A. 5, 1969) : *Jackson* v. *Wheatley School District,* 430 F. 2d 1359 (C.A. 8, 1970) ; *Wall* v. *Stanley County Board of Education,* 378 F. 2d 275 (C.A. 4, 1967). See also "A Muncipal Corporation May be Sued Under the Civil Rights Act for Equitable Relief," 70 Colum. L. Rev. 1467 (1970).

cially recognized long before the enactment of the Civil Rights Act of 1964.[8] Congress itself has specifically provided for nondiscrimination in the Federal government by stating that it is "the policy of the United States to insure equal employment opportunities for Federal employees without discrimination because of race, color, religion, sex, or national origin . . ." (5 U.S.C. § 7151). The primary responsibility for implementing this stated National objective has been granted to the Civil Service Commision pursuant to Executive Order 11246 (1964), and more recently by Executive Order 11478 (1969). In his memorandum accompanying Executive Order 11478, President Nixon stated that "discrimination of any kind based on factors not relevant to job performance must be eradicated completely from Federal employment." This was an important step forward in the field of equal employment opportunity for Federal employees.

Progress has been made in this field, however, much remains to be done. Statistical evidence shows that minorities and women continue to be denied access to a large number of government jobs, particularly in the higher grade levels. The disparity can be clearly seen in figures presented in a recent report released by the Civil Service Commission, *Minority Group Employment in the Federal Government* (1970). On the basis of the figures presented therein, the following listing shows the percentage of minority group employees under the General Schedule by grade level:

	Negro	Spanish-surnamed	American Indian	Oriental
GS-1 through GS-4	21.8	3.0	1.8	.6
GS-5 through GS-8	13.5	2.2	.7	.8
GS-9 through GS-11	5.1	1.5	.5	1.0
GS-12 through GS-13	2.7	.8	.2	.9
GS-14 through GS-15	1.7	.7	.2	.8
GS-16 through GS-18	1.4	.3	.1	.2

Minorities represent 19.4% of the total employment in the Federal government (15.0% are Negroes, 2.9% are Spanish-surnamed, 0.7% are American Indians, and 0.8% are Oriental). Their concentration in the lower grade levels indicates that their ability to advance to the higher levels has been restricted.

In many areas, the pattern at regional levels is worse than the national pattern. For example, the committee notes with special concern the particularly low percentage of Federal jobs held by Spanish-surnamed persons in areas of high residential concentration of such persons, particularly in California and the Southwestern States, and expects the Commission to undertake a special study of this problem to develop programs to provide greater entry level and advancement employment opportunities for Spanish-surnamed persons.

The position of women in the Federal government has not fared any better. In testimony before the Senate Labor Subcommittee this year, Mrs. Daisy B. Fields, past president of Federally Employed Women (FEW), testified as to the distribution, by percent, of all women employed by the Federal government (approximately 665,000 or about 34%) as represented by the following breakdown:

Percent

GS-1 through GS-6	76.7
GS-7 through GS-12	21.7
GS-13 and above	1.1

---

[8] See *Bolling* v. *Sharpe*, 347 U.S. 497 (1954) and cases cited therein.

The inordinate concentration of women in the lower grade levels, and their conspicuous absence from the higher grades is again evident.

One feature of the present equal employment opportunity program which deserves special scrutiny by the Civil Service Commission is the complaint process. The procedure under the present system, intended to provide for the informal disposition of complaints, may have denied employees adequate opportunity for impartial investigation and resolution of complaints.

Under present procedures, in most cases, each agency is still responsible for investigating and judging itself. Although provision is made for the appointment of an outside examiner, the examiner does not have the authority to conduct an independent investigation, and his conclusions and findings are in the nature of recommendations to the agency head who makes the final agency determination on whether there is, in fact, discrimination in that particular case. The only appeal is to the Board of Appeals and Review in the Civil Service Commission.

The testimony before the Labor Subcommittee reflected a general lack of confidence in the effectiveness of the complaint procedure on the part of Federal employees. Complaints have indicated skepticism regarding the Commission's record in obtaining just resolutions of complaints and adequate remedies. This has, in turn, discouraged persons from filing complaints with the Commission for fear that doing so will only result in antagonizing their supervisors and impairing any future hope of advancement. The new authority given to the Civil Service Commission in the bill is intended to enable the Commission to reconsider its entire complaint structure and the relationships between the employee, agency and Commission in these cases.

Another task for the Civil Service Commission is to develop more expertise in recognizing and isolating the various forms of discrimination which exist in the system it administers. The Commission should be especially careful to ensure that its directives issued to Federal agencies address themselves to the various forms of systemic discrimination in the system. The Commission should not assume that employment discrimination in the Federal Government is solely a matter of malicious intent on the part of individuals. It apparently has not fully recognized that the general rules and procedures that it has promulgated may in themselves constitute systemic barriers to minorities and women. Civil Service selection and promotion techniques and requirements are replete with artificial requirements that place a premium on "paper" credentials. Similar requirements in the private sectors of business have often proven of questionable value in predicting job performance and have often resulted in perpetuating existing patterns of discrimination (see e.g. *Griggs* v. *Duke Power Co.*, supra n.1). The inevitable consequence of this kind of a technique in Federal employment, as it has been in the private sector, is that classes of persons who are socio-economically or educationally disadvantaged suffer a very heavy burden in trying to meet such artificial qualifications.

It is in these and other areas where discrimination is institutional, rather than merely a matter of bad faith, that corrective measures appear to be urgently required. For example, the Committee expects the Civil Service Commission to undertake a thorough re-examination of its entire testing and qualification program to ensure that the standards enunciated in the *Griggs* case are fully met.

The Civil Service Commission's primary responsibility over all personnel matters in the Government does create a built-in conflict of interest for examining the Government's equal employment opportunity program for structural defects which may result in a lack of true equal employment opportunity. Yet, the Committee was persuaded that the Civil Service Commission is sincere in its dedication to the principles of equal employment opportunity enunciated in Executive Order 11478 and that the Commission has the will and desire to overcome any such conflict of interest. In order to assist the Commission in accomplishing its goals and to make clear the Congressional expectation that the Commission will take those further steps which are necessary in order to satisfy the goals of Executive Order 11478, the Committee adopted in Section 707(b) of the bill specific requirements under which the Commission is to function in developing a comprehensive equal employment opportunity program.

Thus the provision in section 717(b) for applying "appropriate remedies" is intended to strengthen the enforcement powers of the Civil Service Commission by providing statutory authority and support for ordering whatever remedies or actions by Federal agencies are needed to ensure equal employment opportunity in Federal employment. Remedies may be applied as a result of individual allegations of discrimination, CSC investigation of equal employment opportunity programs in Federal agencies or their field installations, or from review of agency plans of action and progress reports. Remedies may be in terms of action required to correct a situation regarding a single employee or group of employees or broader management action to correct systemic discrimination and to improve equal employment opportunity program effectiveness to bring about needed progress. The Commission is to provide Federal agencies with necessary guidance and authority to effectuate necessary remedies in individual cases, including the award of back pay, reinstatement or hiring, and immediate promotion where appropriate.

The bill also directs the Commission to require each Federal department and agency (including appropriate units of the District of Columbia Government) to prepare an equal employment opportunity affirmative plan of action at least annually. The Commission is to review, modify, and approve each department or agency developed with full consideration of particular problems and employment opportunity needs of individual minority group populations within each geographic area. These legislative directions are, of course, not intended to limit the Commission in requiring the establishment of affirmative equal employment opportunity plans for any agency level, including local installations as needed; indeed, the Committee expects the Commission to require that agency plans include specific regional plans for particularly large Federal regional installations and other regional offices with deficient records of progress in equal employment opportunity. The Committee recognizes that this new emphasis on regional installation equal employment opportunities and action plans will require a greater commitment of both agency and Civil Service Commission personnel to planning and enforcement activities and expects the Civil Service Commission to ensure that such staffing additions will be made both at the national and regional office levels. Finally, to lend the greatest credibility to its equal employment opportunity efforts at a national and regional level, the Commission should review and revise its own equal employment action plan and implementation, particularly at its regional offices and higher grade levels, to ensure that its own record in this field is exemplary and thus a model for all other Federal agencies.

The bill requires the Commission to obtain, on at least a semi-annual basis, minority group employment and such other data as are necessary for effective evaluation by the Commission and the public of each department's, agency's or unit's record of equal employment opportunity achievement and to publish at least semi-annually full statistical and other reports (comparable to the report now published annually) of equal employment opportunity progress. In evaluating agency plans for approval, the Commission is also directed to study and determine the appropriate allocation of personnel and resources committed to, and the qualifications to be established for top equal employment opportunity officials responsible for, carrying out program responsibilities, including necessary affirmative action as well as processing of individual discrimination cases, on both a central office and regional (SMSA) basis.

The Committee wishes to emphasize the significant reservoir of expertise developed by the EEOC with respect to dealing with problems of discrimination. According, the committee strongly urges the Civil Service Commission to take advantage of this knowledge and experience and to work closely with EEOC in the development and maintenance of its equal employment opportunity programs.

An important adjunct to the strengthened Civil Service Commission responsibilities is the statutory provision of a private right of action in the courts by Federal employees who are not satisfied with the agency or Commission decision.

The testimony of the Civil Service Commission notwithstanding, the committee found that an aggrieved Federal employee does not have access to the courts. In many cases, the employee must overcome a U.S. Government defense of sovereign immunity or failure to exhaust administrative remedies with no certainty as to the steps required to exhaust such remedies. Moreover, the remedial authority of the Commission and the courts has also been in doubt. The provisions adopted by the committee will enable the Commission to grant full relief to aggrieved employees, or applicants, including back pay and immediate advancement as appropriate. Aggrieved employees or applicants will also have the full rights available in the courts as are granted to individuals in the private sector under title VII.

The bill (section 717(c)) enables the aggrieved Federal employee (or applicant for employment) to file an action in the appropriate U.S. district court after either a final order by his agency or a final order of the Civil Service Commission on an appeal from an agency decision or order in any personnel action in which the issue of discrimination on the basis of race, color, religion, sex or national origin has been raised by the aggrieved person. It is intended that the employee have the option to go to the appropriate district court or the District Court for the District of Columbia after either the final decision within his agency on his appeal from the personnel action complained of or after an appropirate appeal to the Civil Service Commission or after the elapse of 180 days from the filing of the initial complaint or appeal with the Civil Service Commission.

CHANGES IN ENFORCEMENT PROVISIONS

Section 4 of the bill revises section 706 of the act to enable the EEOC to process a charge of employment discrimination through the investigation, conciliation, administrative hearing, and judicial review stages.

The present act, which only allows the Commission to pursue charges through the informal methods of persuasion and conciliation, has, as already shown, proven to be seriously defective in providing an effective Federal remedy for violations of title VII. Since the compliance provisions of the present law, as regards the findings of the EEOC, are purely voluntary, and respondents have not generally been very agreeable to accepting EEOC decisions where discriminatory practices are found, the burden of relief has been placed upon the aggrieved individual's private right of action in the Federal courts.

This method has generally worked to the disadvantage of the aggrieved individuals. Since most title VII complainants are by the very nature of their complaint disadvantaged, the burden of going to court, initiating legal proceedings by retention of private counsel, and the attendant time delays and legal costs involved, have effectively precluded a very large percentage of valid title VII claims from ever being decided. This disparity between complainants and respondents in title VII litigation has been recognized by the courts which have characterized such litigation as a "modern day David and Goliath confrontation." [9] In such situations, the public has an overriding interest in protecting the individual from the denial of those rights which Congress has specifically provided.

To accomplish the stated purpose of title VII, the bill, while retaining the private right of action, provides, as well, for the elimination of unfair employment practices through a system of administrative hearings, Commission decisions and orders, and ultimate court review in appropriate cases—the method of enforcement which has long been utilized by other regulatory agencies.

The need to provide some form of direct enforcement power to the EEOC has been voiced since the inception of the Commission. There is disagreement whether this enforcement power should be through a Commission lawsuit in a U.S. district court, or by an administrative proceeding followed by a cease-and-desist order with review in the appropriate U.S. court of appeals.

The committee is unanimous in its view that some method of enforcement is required for title VII. An alternative measure providing for court enforcement for title VII, instead of the administrative cease-and-desist procedure, was given full and careful consideration in the hearings and in the full committee. That measure, however, was rejected, and the bill with administrative cease-and-desist procedures was adopted. Without exception, all spokesmen for the major civil

---

[9] See *Sanchez* v. *Standard Brands, Inc.,* 431 F. 2d 455 (C.A. 5, 1970); *Jenkins* v. *United Gas Corp.,* 400 F. 2d 28 (C.A. 5, 1968); *Pettway* v. *American Cast Iron Pipe Co.,* 411 F. 2d 998 (C.A. 5, 1969).

rights groups strongly supported the cease-and-desist enforcement powers.

Father Theodore Hesburgh, Chairman of the U.S. Commission on Civil Rights, testified that cease-and-desist authority is the most effective and expeditious enforcement mechanism available for use against employment discrimination and that experience has demonstrated that the existence of cease-and-desist authority encourages settlement of complaints before the enforcement state is reached.

The Committee was not persuaded that the direct court enforcement technique would be faster and more effective than traditional administrative enforcement. The present—and ever increasing overcrowded—caseloads of the Federal courts is a well-known fact, and, as repeatedly emphasized by the Judicial Conference of the United States, measures are desparately needed to expedite trials and relieve the dockets of these courts.

Statistics appearing in the 1970 Annual Report of the Director of the Administrative Office of the U.S. Courts indicate that there were 16,032 trials completed in the U.S. district courts in 1970, up 11 percent over 1969 and about 60 percent more than in 1962. There was a total of 127,240 civil and criminal cases on the dockets in 1970, and in jurisdictions where the caseloads are the heaviest, it is not uncommon for several years to elapse before a matter is reached for trial.

The Judicial Conference Report mentions specifically that civil rights cases have accounted for a good part of the overall growth in case filings. Between 1961 and 1970 there was an increase of more than 1,200 percent in civil rights cases filed and in the year 1970 itself, there were 3,985 civil rights cases filed compared to 2,453 in 1969, an increase of 63 percent.

The potential for court backlog created by requiring these cases to be handled at the initial level in the district courts is clear from these statistics. Moreover, Chief Justice Burger called attention to the problem of overburdening the courts with new cases in his address to the American Bar Association in July of 1970 when he stated:

> From time to time Congress adds more judges, but the total judicial organization never quite keeps up with the caseload Two recent statutes alone added thousands of cases relating to commitment of narcotic addicts and the mentally ill. These additions came when civil rights cases, the voting cases and prisoner petitions were expanding by the thousands.

In appraising the question of enforcement by district court trials rather than through agency hearings followed by appellate court review, the committee was thus particularly concerned with the acute problem of overcrowding of our trial court system. It recognized that to thrust this additional caseload on the district courts would not only clog the already overburdened trial dockets of the courts, but might well delay the administration of justice on a national scale unprecedented in our history. It is truly said that "Justice delayed is justice denied." Such is not our objective.

Another aspect that is involved in the enforcement of Title VII concerns the importance of administrative expertise relating to the resolution of problems of employment discrimination. Many of the Title VII proceedings involve complex labor relations and business operations issues particularly in the fashioning of the remedies for eliminating discrimination. The Equal Employment Opportunity Commission would be expected to develop an important reservoir of expertise in these matters, expertise which would not readily be available to a widespread court system. It is expected that through the administrative process the Commission will continue to define and develop the approaches to handling serious problems of discrimination that are involved in the area of employment including testing and labor relations (including seniority systems). It is incumbent upon this administrative agency to develop the necessary expertise, ingenuity, and sensitivity that will effectuate the purposes of Title VII, provide full relief to aggrieved persons, and still maintain an appropriate understanding of the problems faced by the employment sector.

It should also be noted that the administrative cease-and-desist approach encourages early settlement of claims, thereby further alleviating the courts and providing quick relief for aggrieved individuals. For example, in the Summary of Operations by the General Counsel of the National Labor Relations Board (NLRB) for fiscal year 1970 and the first 6 months of 1971, figures show that in fiscal year 1970 the NLRB received a record 33,581 cases. Of these, however, 92.4 percent were disposed of without the need for a formal hearing. Of the 2,217 cases which were heard by hearing examiners, only 420 had to be filed for review or enforcement in the courts of appeals, and only about half of these were ever set for oral argument. Experience with other Federal agencies and State fair employment agencies indicates a similar trend toward relatively few incidents of actual adjudication.

Further considerations weighing in favor of administrative cease-and-desist powers are:

(1) This is the type of authority given to many other Federal regulatory agencies.[10-11]

(2) It is the type of enforcement authority preferred by 32 of 37 States which have equal employment opportunity laws.[12]

(3) It will insure more quickly a unified approach to the problems of discrimination since decisions would be rendered by one agency rather than several hundred district court judges.

(4) It will provide the needed expertise in recognizing and solving the more subtle, institutional forms of discrimination.

Following is a comparison of the procedures which are followed when a charge is filed with the Commisson under title VII in its present form and those that would be followed under the bill:

Under existing law.—After a charge is filed alleging that an unlawful employment practice has been committed, the Commission investigates and determines whether there is reason to believe that the al-

[10-11] In addition to the NLRB, other agencies having such powers include: Atomic Energy Commission, National Transportation Board, Federal Communications Commission, Federal Power Commission, Securities and Exchange Commission, Subversive Activities Control Board, Department of Agriculture, Department of Health, Education, and Welfare, Department of Justice, Department of Transportation, Department of Defense, Department of Interior, Interstate Commerce Commission, Treasury Department, and Department of Labor.

[12] States will cease and desist authority: Alaska, Arizona, California, Colorado, Connecticut, Delaware, Hawaii, Illinois, Indiana, Iowa, Kansas, Kentucky, Maryland, Massachusetts, Michigan, Minnesota, Missouri, Nebraska, New Hampshire, New Jersey, New Mexico, New York, Oklahoma, Ohio, Oregon, Pennsylvania, Rhode Island, Utah, Washington, West Virginia, Wisconsin, and Wyoming It is interesting to note that two of the above, Delaware and New Mexico recently amended their existing enforcement laws to include cease-and-desist powers.

legations in the charge are true. If the Commisison finds no reasonable cause, it dismisses the charge, thus terminating the proceeding before the Commission. If the Commission decides that there is reasonable cause to believe that the allegation of the charge is true, it attempts to eliminate the unlawful practice by means of informal methods of conference, conciliation, and persuasion. If the Commission is unable to achieve voluntary compliance, it notifies the person claiming to be aggrieved, who then has a right to bring a private civil action against the respondent in the district court. The Commission now has no further authority to act to resolve the dispute.

Under the bill—1. Upon the filing of a charge, the Commission would investigate. If, after investigation, the Commission decides that there is no reasonable cause to believe that the charge is true, it would dismiss the charge and notify the person claiming to be aggrieved and the respondent (sec. 706(b)).

2. If the Commission finds reasonable cause, it would seek to eliminate the unlawful practice by informal methods of conference, conciliation, and persuasion (sec. 706(b)). An agreement for the elimination of the alleged unlawful practice can be entered into by the Commission (Sec. 706 (f) and (i)), any time between the filing of the charge and until the record is filed in the Court of Appeals (sec. 706(i)). (See below regarding private right of action if the aggrieved person does not enter into the conciliation agreement.)

3. If the Commission determines that it is unable to secure an acceptable agreement, it would issue and serve upon the respondent a complaint and notice of hearing (sec. 706(f)). The administrative hearing, the purpose of which is to take evidence as to whether an unlawful practice has been committed and to adjucate the claims of the parties named in the charge, or permitted to be joined, or allowed to intervene, would be conducted in accordance with the provisions of the Administrative Procedure Act, 5 U.S.C. § 551, *et seq.*, before the Commission, one of its members, or a hearing examiner appointed in accordance with Federal law (sec. 706 (g) and (j)). The rules of evidence applicable to the district courts would be followed so far as practicable.[13]

4. After completion of the administrative hearing, the Commission would issue a decision disposing of the case on the merits. The Commission could find that the respondent has engaged in an unlawful employment practice, in which case it would issue an order requiring the respondent to cease and desist from its unlawful conduct and to take such affirmative action as would effectuate the policies of the title (sec. 706(h)). In issuing its order, the Commission, in any situation involving back pay, would be limited to an award of two years prior to the date of the filing of the charge with the Commission.

The Commission's order may be enforced through entry of an appropriate decree of a United States court of appeals.

5. If, on the basis of a preliminary investigation, the Commission determines that prompt judicial action is necessary to preserve its power to grant effective relief, it would be required, following the

---

[13] See *Universal Camera Corp.* v. *NLRB*, 340 U.S. 474 (1951) ; *On Lee* v. *United States*, 343 U.S. 747 (1952) ; *United States* v. *Costello*, 221 F. 2d 668 (C.A. 2, 1955), aff'd on other grounds 350 U.S. 359 (1956) ; *American Rubber Products Corp.* v. *NLRB*, 214 F. 2d 47 (C.A. 7, 1954).

issuance of a complaint, to seek preliminary or temporary relief in Federal district court, pending the final disposition of the charge or appeal to the court of appeals (sec. 706(p)).

The intent of section 706(p) is to incorporate existing law developed in private actions and "pattern or practice" suits under title VII of the Civil Rights Act of 1964.[14-15] Courts have generally regarded petitions for preliminary relief in such cases favorably, and have granted preliminary injunctions against the continuation of unlawful employment practices in situations which would normally call for such relief in proceedings under rule 65 of the Federal Rules of Civil Procedure.

The committee believes that in determining whether or not to issue preliminary relief, the appropriate standard for the courts to apply was aptly stated by the Court of Appeals for the Fifth Circuit in *United States* v. *Hayes International Corp.*:

> Where, as here, the statutory rights of employees are involved and an injunction is authorized by statute and the statutory conditions are satisfied as in the facts presented here, the usual prerequisite of irreparable injury need not be established and the agency to whom the enforcement of the right has been entrusted is not required to show irreparable injury before obtaining an injunction. *Fleming* v. *Salem Box Co.* 38 F. Supp. 997, 998–99 (D. Ore., 1940); *Western Electric Co., Inc.* v. *Cinema Supplies, Inc.*, 80 F. 2d 106, cert. den. 297 U.S. 717. We take the position that in such a case, irreparable injury should be presumed from the very fact that the statute has been violated. Whenever a qualified Negro employee is discriminatorily denied a chance to fill a position for which he is qualified and has the seniority to obtain, he suffers irreparable injury and so does the labor force of the country as a whole.
>
> Moreover, we hold as did the court in *Vogler* v. *McCarty, Inc.*, 294 F. Supp. 368, 372 (E.D.. La. 1967) affirmed 407 F. 2d 1047 (5th Cir., 1969) that where an employer has engaged in a pattern and practice of discrimination on account of race, et cetera, in order to insure the *full* enjoyment of the rights protected by title VII of the 1954 Civil Rights Act, affirmative and mandatory preliminary relief is required. 415 F. 2d at 1045.

The Commission may not bring an action for preliminary relief until it has issued a complaint. However, in those cases where the need for preliminary relief is serious—including but in no way limited to situations where aggrieved persons are transferred, fired, or otherwise harassed for bringing other charges before the Commission—the Commission is expected to act swiftly in issuing a complaint so that the person aggrieved will not be harmed by a delay between the time his charge is filed and the issuance of the complaint by the Commission.

It is the committee's view that this authority be broadly construed with the view toward completely rooting out and eliminating employ-

---

[14-15] *Culpepper* v. *Reynolds Metals Corp.*, 421 F. 2d 888 (C.A. 5, 1970); *United States* v. *Hayes International Corp.*, 415 F. 2d 1038 (C.A. 1969); *Hicks* v. *Crown Zellerbach Corp.*, 49 FRD 184 (D.C. La. 1968). See also Note, "Developments in the Law—Injunctions", 78 Harv. L. Rev. 994 (1965).

ment discrimination. The Commission is to take whatever affirmative steps are needed to provide a full and complete remedy to the aggrieved party or class and to obtain full and immediate compliance with the Civil Rights Act of 1964.

If the Commission finds that no unlawful employment practice has been committed, it would issue an order dismissing the complaint (sec. 706(h)).

ENFORCEMENT AND REVIEW OF COMMISSION ORDERS

Review of a Commission order may be obtained in an appropriate court of appeals upon the petition of an aggrieved party within 60 days of the Commission's order (706(k)). In accordance with the provisions of the Administrative Procedure Act, and established judicial practice, the courts of appeals would review the Commission's record as a whole and would make its determination on an examination of the record to ascertain whether there is substantial evidence to support the agency's findings. In this regard, the committee notes that this is not a second hearing but a review under appellate procedure.

If no petition is filed within 60 days, the Commission's order is conclusive, and an enforcement decree may be obtained by the Commission from the clerk of the court of appeals. This automatic enforcement provision places the burden upon the respondent to seek review (as is the case in regular civil litigation before district courts). The automatic enforcement mechanism also answers the contention that administrative proceedings necessarily involve long delays before a judicial enforcement order can be obtained. It is anticipated that in the vast majority of cases no review will be sought by any party affected by an order, and that the Commission or other person will be able to obtain the enforcement decree of the court without the burden of moving forward with an entire review proceeding.

If, however, the Commission found it desirable in a particular case to seek enforcement before the expiration of the 60-day period provided for a review petition, it would be enabled to do so by section 706(l). This section would, among other things, permit the Commission to apply for a preliminary injunction enforcing its order pending the entry of a final decree.

Finally, if the respondent has not appealed, and if the Commission has not sought enforcement under section 706 (l) or (m), any person entitled to relief under the Commission's order could, after 90 days from service of the Commission's order, also obtain an enforcement decree from the clerk of the court of appeals. (Sec. 706(n).)

The court of appeals, on application of the Commission or any other party to the proceeding, would be authorized to grant preliminary or temporary relief pending disposition of the appeal. This power would exist both in the case of petitions for review by a party (sec. 706(k)) or petitions for enforcement by the Commission (sec. 706(l)).

Decisions of the court of appeals would be subject to review by the Supreme Court of the United States in accordance with 28 U.S.C. 1254 (sec. 706 (k) and (l)).

As provided by section 706(t), as redesignated by this bill, the provisions of the Norris-LaGuardia Anti-Injunction Act (29 U.S.C.

101–115) would not apply to such proceedings for review or enforcement or for preliminary or temporary relief.

The Committee is aware that in the cases of other administrative agencies with quasi-judicial functions the need for obtaining a decree of a U.S. Court of Appeals to enforce an agency order has sometimes resulted in a substantial delay in securing compliance with the order. All too frequently, many months elapse between the date an order is issued by an agency and the date a decree of a U.S. Court of Appeals is entered enforcing it.

We have had no experience with Administration cease and desist orders issued by EEOC. Therefore the Committee does not recommend, at this time, that civil penalties be imposed upon respondents who refuse to obey Commission orders prior to the entry of a decree of the Court of Appeals enforcing such orders. However, the Committee does wish to emphasize the need for prompt action by the Commission to secure enforcement of its orders. In that connection, the Committee expects the Commission will take full advantage of the availability of preliminary relief from the Courts of Appeals, of the summary procedures available in the Courts of Appeals, and the provisions of Rule 38 of the Federal Rules of Appellate Procedure which authorize the imposition of damages and double costs in the case of frivolous appeals.

PRIVATE ACTIONS

The bill contains a provision (sec. 706(q)) that if the Commission dismisses a charge, or, within 180 days of its filing has neither issued a complaint nor entered into a conciliation or settlement agreement which is acceptable to the Commission and the aggrieved party, it shall so notify the aggrieved party. Within 60 days after such notification the person aggrieved, or, in the case of a charge filed by an officer or employee of the Commission, the person or persons named in such charge, shall have the right to commence a private civil action in the appropriate U.S. district court.

The committee is aware that in recent years regulatory agencies have been submerged in increasing workloads which strain their resources to the breaking point. The EEOC is no exception to this problem. As it indicated in testimony, its caseload has increased at a rate which surpasses its own projections. The result has been increasing backlogs in making determinations, and the possibility of occasional hasty decisions, made under the press of time, which have unfairly prejudiced complaints. Accordingly, where the Commission is not able to pursue a complaint with satisfactory speed, or enters into an agreement which is not acceptable to the aggrieved party, the bill provides that the individual shall have an opportunity to seek his own remedy, even though he may have originally submitted his charge to the Commission. It is expected that recourse to this remedy will be the exception and not the rule, particularly once the Commission's enforcement procedures are fully operational. In the meantime, however, the committee believes that the aggrieved person should be given an opportunity to escape the administrative process when he feels his claim has not been given adequate attention.

The committee is concerned, however, about the interplay between the newly created enforcement powers of the Commission and the existing right of private action. It concluded that duplication of proceedings should be avoided. The bill therefore contains a provision for cutoff of the Commission's jurisdiction once the private action has been filed—except for the power to intervene—as well as a cutoff of the right of private action once the Commission issues a complaint or enters into a conciliation or settlement agreement which is satisfactory to the Commission and the aggrieved party.

If the Commission is able to reach a conciliation or settlement agreement with the respondent, but such agreement is not acceptable to the person aggrieved, the Commission need not proceed with the issuance of a complaint. In such event, the private right of action would be preserved.

The committee also concluded that the aggrieved person's right to institute a private action should be reactivated under certain circumstances if the Commission does not act promptly after issuing a complaint. The bill contains a provision, in section 706(q), that permits the aggrieved person to bring a civil action against the respondent if the Commission has not issued its order within 180 days after issuing the complaint. However, during the period from 180 days to 1 year after issuance of the Commission's complaint, the aggrieved person who files a private action must notify the Commission of such filing, and the Commission may petition the court to stay or dismiss the private action if the Commission shows that it has been acting with due diligence, that it anticipates the issuance of its order within a reasonable period of time, that the proceeding is an exceptional one, and that extension of the Commission's jurisdiction is warranted.

The committee believes that aggrieved persons are entitled to have their cases processed promptly and that the Commission should develop its capacity to proceed rapidly with the hearing and decision on charges once the complaint has issued. Six months is a sufficient period of time for the normal case to be processed from complaint to order, and the Commission should be required to explain to the satisfaction of the court why it needs additional time. Accordingly, when a private action is filed after the 180 day period has elapsed from the issuance of the Commission's complaint, the court ordered delay that is provided for by this section should be the exception rather than the rule, and would not be justified simply because backlogs and inadequate resources have slowed the Commission's work. The primary concern should be to protect the aggrieved person's option to seek a prompt remedy.

It should be noted, however, that it is not the intention of the committee to permit an aggrieved party to retry his case merely because he is dissatisfied with the Commission's action. Once the Commission has issued an order, further proceedings must be in the courts of appeals pursuant to subsections 706(k)–(n).

The committee would also note that neither the above provisions regarding the individual's right to sue under title VII, nor any of the other provisions of this bill, are meant to affect existing rights granted under other laws.

SPECIAL ENFORCEMENT PROCEDURE FOR CASES INVOLVING EMPLOYEES OF STATE AND LOCAL GOVERNMENTS

In those cases involving a respondent which is a "government, governmental agency, or political subdivision", and in which EEOC has been unable to secure voluntary compliance as provided under section 706(b) and (f), the bill provides that the Commission shall refer the case to the Attorney General for filing of a civil action against the respondent in the appropriate U.S. district court. A person aggrieved is given the right to intervene in such civil actions.

The committee has no doubt of the need for strong enforcement of equal employment opportunity at all levels of government, and believes that governmental units should lead the way in providing equal opportunity.

Accordingly, the committee bill provides for coverage of State and local government employees and for a concommitant means of enforcement to make that coverage meaningful. By placing the full weight of the U.S. Attorney General and the authority of the U.S. district courts behind equal employment opportunity at the State and local government level, the committee believes that the machinery has been provided to insure State and local leadership in the area of equal employment opportunity.

This enforcement scheme provides the necessary power to achieve results without the needless friction that might be created by a Federal executive agency issuing orders to sovereign States and their localities. In short, the committee believes that the objective of equal employment opportunity can best be achieved by providing this particular means of enforcement where State or local governmental units fail to comply with the law.

FAIRNESS AND DUE PROCESS

Recognizing the importance that the concept of due process plays in the American ideal of justice, the committee wishes to emphasize certain provisions which are included in the bill to insure that fairness and due process are part of the enforcement scheme.

(a) *Protection of rights of respondent.*—The bill contains a number of provisions designed to protect fully the rights of the person or persons against whom the charge is filed:

1. The committee retained the requirement that charges be in writing. The Commission must serve the respondent with a notice of the charge, which would advise the respondent of the nature of the alleged violation. As amended by the committee, the bill would require such notice to be served on the respondent within 10 days. (sec. 760 (b)).

2. During the Commission's investigation of the charge, the allegations would not be made public by the Commission, and it would undertake to resolve the matter by informal means before issuing a complaint (sec. 706(b)).

3. If the Commission decides to issue a complaint, it would be served upon the respondent (sec. 706(f)), who would then have a right to file an answer and to amend it with leave of the Commission.

Such leave is to be granted under normal circumstances. The respondent would be a party to the proceedings before the Commission, and he would have a right to appear at any stage of these proceedings, with or without counsel. (Sec. 706 (g).)

4. Hearings of the Commission must be on the record and under the provisions of the Administrative Procedure Act (5 U.S.C. 551, et seq.) (sec. 706(j)). Such proceedings provide the maximum protection of the rights of all parties to the proceedings.

5. The respondent would have the right to seek judicial review of a Commission decision which ruled against him, and he could petition the Supreme Court for certiorari from an unfavorable decision of the court of appeals. (Sec. 706(k).)

(b) *Separation of functions.*—The provisions of the bill and title 5 of the United States Code refered to above, would insure that the same persons would not both prosecute and decide cases for the Commission. Section 554(d) of title 5 imposes the following requirements on the operations of administrative agencies, such as the Commission, whose decisions must be made after hearing and on the record:

1. The person presiding at the reception of evidence (typically, the hearing examiner) may not be responsible to or subject to the supervision or direction of any person engaged in the performance of investigative or prosecuting functions.

2. An employee of the agency performing investigative or prosecution functions in a particular case may not participate in or advise in the decision, recommended decision, or agency review in that or a factually related case, except as a witness or as counsel in public proceedings.

The net effect of these provisions would be to prevent the intermingling of functions within the Commission.

(c) *Protection of rights of person aggrieved*—In addition to the provisions already discussed involving the individual right to sue, the rights of persons claiming to be aggrieved would be further protected by the following provisions:

1. Charges may be filed by or on behalf of an aggrieved person. The Commission is directed to make its findings on reasonable cause as promptly as possible, and so far as practicable, within 120 days of the filing of the charge. The committee, as noted above, considers prompt action on charges and complaints to be a major responsibility of the Commission in all cases. The existing 90-day time limitation on filing a charge has been extended by 90 days (sec. 706(e)).

2. If the Commission finds no reasonable cause to believe that the charge is true, or enters into a settlement which is not acceptable to the aggrieved person, the aggrieved person would still have a right of action against the respondent.

3. The aggrieved person would have a right to be a party to all proceedings before the Commission and to be represented by counsel of his choosing if he desires. Particularly at the hearing stage, the guarantees of administrative due process as provided by the Administrative Procedure Act should be scrupulously maintained. As one authority has pointed out:

> The true principle is that a party who has a sufficient interest or right at stake in a determination of govenmental action

should be entitled to an opportunity to know and to meet, with the weapons of rebuttal evidence, cross-examination, and argument, unfavorable evidence of adjudicative facts..."
1 K. Davis, *Treatise on Administrative Law* 412.

The right of a person to participate at the hearing stage through his own counsel is intended to supplement or complement, but in no way to replace, the traditional advocate role of the representatives of the Commission charged with carrying forward the complaint.

Provisions of present law requiring that the person aggrieved be notified of his rights have been retained. Especially in light of the further safeguards in this bill, the Commission is expected, at the commencement and at other appropriate stages of the proceedings, to fully notify the aggrieved person in clear and understandable fashion of the various procedural rights and steps open to him. Too often a person files a charge but then blunders along lost in the bureaucratic process. The committee believes that further steps should be taken, including perhaps followup notification, to ensure that an aggrieved person knows at apropriate times the status of the case and his rights under the law.

(d) *"Commissioner's complaint" provision*—The provision permitting a member of the Commission to file a charge of unlawful employment practice as contained in the present section 706 was amended by the committee to provide for such charges to be made by an officer or employee of the Commission upon the request of any person claiming to be aggrieved. The original bill had continued the Commissioner's charge but would have barred the Commissioner filing the charge from participating in a hearing except as a witness. The committee concluded that this provision might cause some appearance of conflict of interest if Commissioners were to hear charges placed by a colleague; moreover the Commission's caseload might not permit the routine disqualification of Commissioners who had placed charges.

Placing the authority to make a charge at a lower level of the Commission, however, would accomplish the same purposes while avoiding these problems.

The purpose of this provision is to enable aggrieved persons to have charges processed under circumstances where they are unwilling to come forward publicly for fear of economic or physical reprisals. In this connection the committee wishes to make clear that the device of a Commission charge may be used to maintain the confidential identity of the persons aggrieved and that no disclosure need be made of the identity of the person aggrieved at any stage of the proceeding unless it is voluntary or in such circumstances where the person aggrieved is required to be a witness.

This section is not intended in any way to restrict the filing of class complaints. The committee agrees with the courts that title VII actions are by their very nature class complains,[16] and that any restriction on such actions would greatly undermine the effectiveness of title VII.

---

[16] *Oatis* v. *Crown Zellerbach Corp.*, 398 F. 2d 496 (C.A.5, 1968). Cf. *Jenkins* v. *United Gas Corp.*, 400 F. 2d 28 (C.A. 5, 1968) ; *Blue Bell Boots* v. *EEOC*, 418 F. 2d 355 (C.A. 6, 1969) ; *Local 104, Sheet Metal Workers* v. *EEOC*, 303 F. Supp. 528 (N.D. Calif. 1969). Similarly, labor organizations may also petition for relief on behalf of their members. *Chemical Workers* v. *Planters Manufacturing Co.*, 259 F. Supp. 365 (N.D. Miss. 1965) ; *Pulp Sulphite and Paper Mill Workers, Local 186* v. *Minnesota Mining & Manufacturing Co.*, 304 F. Supp. 1284 (N.D. Ind. 1969).

CONSOLIDATION OF ANTI-DISCRIMINATION ENFORCEMENT ACTIVITIES

(a) *Transfer of "Pattern or Practice" Cases to EEOC.*—The authority to bring "pattern or practice" suits directly in the district courts, as provided by section 707 of the present law, is amended by section 5 of the bill which transfers the present section 707 functions from the Attorney General to the Commission.

While the broad-scale actions against any "pattern or practice" of discrimination that have been brought by the Justice Department under section 707 of the Civil Rights Act of 1964, have been an integral and important part of the overall Federal effort to combat discrimination, the committee believes that with the enactment of legislation providing the Commission with effective power to enforce title VII, the further retention of section 707 power in the Department of Justice is not necessary. With the adoption of this bill, which includes the transfer to the Commission of the functions of the Office of Federal Contract Compliance (OFCC) and the functions of the Department of Justice, the Federal Government, through the procedures of the Commission, will be able to pursue a unified program of attack upon all elements of employment discrimination.

Employees would benefit by having to look to only one agency to obtain relief; employers similarly would be free from the burden of multiple investigations examining their employment policies and personnel records in response to similar or identical complaints filed with different agencies.[17]

Similarly, the duplication of effort that would inevitably result from similar pursuits of identical complaints, with the appurtenant double expense and unnecessary waste of scarce legal talent, is something the committee wishes to avoid by effecting the transfer.

In providing for the transfer of the authority under section 707, the committee has, however, retained jurisdiction in the Department of Justice for the first 2 years after enactment of the bill to bring "pattern or practice" suits where necessary. The committee believes that this will safeguard the important "pattern or practice" power, while at the same time providing for a smooth and efficient transfer of that authority.

The committee recognizes that with the institution of the new enforcement powers, the Commission will have to undertake extensive internal reorganization, and will have to cope with its present backlog and the press of incoming cases at the same time. In light of this, the Commission may not be able to fully utilize the "pattern or practice" function immediately. It is expected, however, that the two agencies will exercise concurrent jurisdiction over "pattern or practice" enforcement during the first 2 years of operation under the new law, since the committee intends that the Commission's administrative cease-and-desist enforcement authority will not be used exclusively to resolve individual complaints but will also include the elimination of "patterns or practices" of discrimination wherever its inves-

---

[17] For an example of a situation where several Government agencies were all involved in essentially the same complaint, see *Local 189, United Papermakers and Paperworkers, AFL–CIO* v. *United States,* 416 F.2d 980 (C.A. 5 1969), *cert. denied* 397 U.S. 919 (1970), aff'g 282 F. Supp. 39 (E.D. La. 1968) and 301 F. Supp. 906 (E. D. La. 1969). In this particular case, conclusions as to the legality of a seniority system used by the respondent were reached by the EEOC, the OFCC, and the Department of Justice, with separate investigations and litigation employed by each agency independent of the other.

tigation of a charge discloses the existence of such employment situations.

In this regard, the committee believes that it is incumbent upon the Attorney General and the Commission to cooperate and consult whenever necessary to insure the maximum use of these legal tools to end employment discrimination, as well as to avoid duplication of effort and conflicting approaches to the implementation of the statute.

The committee also believes that the future transfer of the "pattern or practice" authority should not be a burden upon the already meager resources of the Commission. Accordingly, the committee has provided that along with the transfer of the functions, there would also be a transfer of the funds and personnel positions previously budgeted for this work in the Department of Justice.

(b) *Transfer of Contract Compliance activities to EEOC.*—Section 715 of the bill transfers the powers and duties of the Secretary of Labor under Executive Order 11246 (as amended by Executive Order 11375) to the Equal Employment Opportunity Commission.

Executive Order 11246 enunciates the policy of the Government of the United States ". . . to provide equal opportunity in Federal employment for all qualified persons, to prohibit discrimination in employment because of race, color, religion, sex, or natural origin, and to promote the full realization of equal employment opportunity through a positive, continuing program in each executive department and agency . . ." (E.O. 11246 § 101 as amended). The Executive order program is presently administered within the Department of Labor by the Office of Federal Contract Compliance, a division of the Employment Standards Administration. Under the Executive Order, government contractors and subcontractors are required to agree to the following contract provision:

> The contractor will not discriminate against any employee or applicant for employment because of race, color, religion, sex or national origin. The contractor will take affirmative action to ensure that applicants are employed, and that employees are treated during employment, without regard to their race, color, religion, sex, or national origin.

The Secretary of Labor has overall responsibility for administration of the Executive Order, including ultimate authority over the contracting agencies in the implementation of both the nondiscrimination and the affirmative action provisions of the contract clause.

The bill transfers all of the functions of the Secretary of Labor under the Executive Order to EEOC without modifying in any way those functions or relieving, in any way, government contracting agencies or government contractors of their obligations thereunder.

This transfer was considered by the Committee last year during its deliberation on S. 2453. In the report on S. 2453, the bases for then not transferring the program included a concern that the Commission might be overburdened and that a complete consolidation of all agencies was not necessarily appropriate at that time. The report, however, made clear that the credibility of the executive order program was very much suspect and so stated:

> However, the committee also believes that an adequate job of providing equal employment opportunity has not, and is

not, being provided through the Federal Procurement function. There has been far too much non-public discussion and negotiation and far too few understandable results. In many instances the Department's claim that something major happened, when measured against the demonstration that something actually happened, is grossly lacking in the clarity that the public and minorities can understand.

The United States Commission on Civil Rights, in October 1970, recommended transferring of "the Contract Compliance responsibilities of OFCC" to EEOC in order to achieve a consolidation of equal employment oportunity functions into a single, independent agency. This recommendation was reconfirmed by the Commission in April 1971, and again in testimony before the Committee on S. 2515, by Father Theodore Hesburgh, Chairman of the Civil Rights Commission.

During testimony on this bill, the Department of Labor vigorously opposed the transfer citing legal standards, substantive results, and procurement considerations as support of its position.

The Committee was not persuaded that any of the three reasons warrant maintenance of the programs with the Secretary of Labor. The question of whether differing legal standards apply to EEOC and OFCC has been the subject of much discussion both before and since the hearings. Suffice it to say that the courts are developing the body of case law rationalizing the relationship between Title VII and the Executive Order program.[18]

The Committee intends that the standards applicable under Title VII shall govern all proceedings under that Title. Furthermore, the Committee intends that EEOC shall exercise the same authority under the Executive Order as has governed OFCC, being limited by the standards applicable to Execctive Order 11246. The Committee believes that both these functions. though somewhat different in nature, can be fulfilled effectively by EEOC. Of course, in neither case, can an employer be required to violate Title VII.

The procurement considerations are minimal. The Secretary of Labor has acted in essentially a directive or supervisory role *vis-a-vis* the procurement agencies—no change is contemplated by this transfer. The Committee expects that the main burden of obtaining compliance with the executive order will still rest with the contracting agencies.

The question raised last year was whether the program has had sub-s^tantive results. Unfortunately, the paucity of credible achievement cited last year is still the rule. The successes described in the testimony suffer from an inability of the program managers to furnish reliable data to support their claim. The program looks good on paper, but despite many opportunities very minimal information was furnished to the Committee that would support the contention that significant results have been achieved. To the contrary, in the history of the Contract Compliance Program. until two days after introduction of this bill, no sanction had ever been imposed for violation of the

---

[18] *Contractors Ass'n. of Eastern Penna.* v. *Secretary of Labor*, 442 F.2d 1959 (3d Cir. 1971), cert. denied — U.S. — (1971). See also the cases cited at for. 17, *Supra*.

Executive Order. Since then, only one small contractor (10 employees) has been subjected to sanctions.

In 1969, then Secretary of Labor Shultz, testifying before this Committee asked for time for the new administration to get its House in order. The Department's testimony this year suggested that real success is just around the corner.

The rights of minorities and women are too important to continue this important function in an agency that has not really been able to achieve the promised results. The contract compliance program is an important and viable tool in the government's efforts to achieve equal employment opportunity. It should have a chance to operate in a fresh atmosphere with an agency that has Equal Employment Opportunities as its sole priority.

CHANGES IN RECORDKEEPING REQUIREMENTS

Section 709 is revised to provide a more effective system for requiring records to be kept, to permit the Commission to arrange for appropriate operating agreements with State and local fair employment practice agencies, to provide a scheme for avoiding duplication of records, and for agreements to share information with Federal, State, and local agencies.

The committee believes strongly that adequate records are essential to the proper and effective administration of this Title. However, it is also mindful of the increasing burdens that employers and unions are faced with under the proliferation of statutes and regulations which affect them. Therefore, the committee urges the Commission to undertake serious efforts to ease the paperwork requirements under this act consistent with maximum efforts to secure complete compliance with the law.

EXPANSION OF COMMISSION MEMBERSHIP

The bill contains two provisions (Secs. 705(a) and 713(d)) designed to help the Commission deal promptly with the huge volume of cases expected to come before it for decision upon the enactment of this bill. These provisions authorize the President, at the request of the Chairman of the Commission, to appoint up to four additional members of the Commission by and with the advice and consent of the Senate, and permit the Commission itself to sit in panels of three members.

As has already been noted in this report, the number of charges filed with the EEOC during the past several years has exceeded all expectations at the time the Civil Rights Act of 1964 was enacted. Furthermore, the volume of charges continues to increase, with over 32,000 charges expected to be filed during the current fiscal year.

While it is impossible to state with assurance at this time what the workload of the Commission will be, the Committee believes that authorization for additional Commissioners and the use of three-member panels should provide sufficient flexibility for the Commission to manage its caseload expeditiously.

EFFECTIVE DATE

The provisions of this bill would be effective upon enactment. However, under the terms of the bill's amendment to section 701 of the

Civil Rights Act of 1964, the expansion of title VII's coverage to employers with eight or more employees, and to unions with eight or more members, would not be operative until 1 year after enactment.

ESTIMATE OF COSTS

In accordance with the requirements of section 252 of the Legislative Reorganization Act of 1970, the Commission has prepared an estimate of the projected costs for the new areas of enforcement activity for which the bill provides. It is the committee's view that the accompanying figures represent a reasonable estimate of the minimum additional budgetary requirements for administration of these new undertakings:

[In thousands]

	Fiscal year—				
	1972	1973	1974	1975	1976
Cease and desist operations under present jurisdictional limits_	9, 431	11, 912	12, 081	12, 123	12, 151
Extension of jurisdiction to State and local government employees_____	2, 100	3, 000	3, 000	3, 000	3, 000
Extension of jurisdiction to 8 or more employees_____	(¹)	1, 234	2, 115	4, 034	4, 243
Total_____	12, 031	17, 046	18, 096	20, 057	20, 294

¹ Not effective.

The bill also contains provisions for the transfer of two activities presently administered by different agencies of the Government. As the transfer of these activities also involves transfer of funds and personnel positions allocated to those agencies, the cost estimates for these activities are based upon cost projections by the agencies presently administering those operations:

[In thousands]

	Fiscal year—				
	1972	1973	1974	1975	1976
OFCC functions_____	2, 594	2, 600	2, 600	2, 600	2, 600
Pattern or practice enforcement_____	1, 800	1, 800	1, 800	1, 800	1, 800

The figures provided in both the above tables are based on projections of anticipated case loads and estimates of the level of enforcement activity which will be needed. Because of the uncertain nature of these factors it is impossible to attempt any realistic projection beyond FY 1976.

TABULATION OF VOTES IN COMMITTEE

Pursuant to section 133(b) of the Legislative Reorganization Act of 1946, as amended, the following tabulation of votes in committee is provided.

1. Senator Dominick's substitute amendment to strike from the bill the transfer to EEOC of authority to bring "pattern or practice" cases (defeated 14 to 1):

YEAS—1

Mr. Dominick

NAYS—14

Mr. Williams
Mr. Randolph
Mr. Pell
Mr. Nelson
Mr. Mondale
Mr. Eagleton
Mr. Cranston
Mr. Hughes
Mr. Stevenson

Mr. Javits
Mr. Schweiker
Mr. Packwood
Mr. Taft
Mr. Stafford

2. Senator Eagleton's amendment to delay the transfer of the "pat·tern or practice" authority for two years, to provide for the concur·rent jurisdiction in the EEOC of such pattern or practice cases, and to make ·sure transfer subject to the President's exercise of authority under the Reorganization Act (adopted 13 to 2):

YEAS—13

Mr. Williams
Mr. Randolph
Mr. Pell
Mr. Nelson
Mr. Mondale
Mr. Eagleton
Mr. Cranston
Mr. Hughes
Mr. Stevenson

Mr. Javits
Mr. Schweiker
Mr. Packwood
Mr. Stafford

NAYS—2

Mr. Dominick
Mr. Taft

3. Senator Dominick's amendment to substitute court enforcement for administrative cease-and-desist authority (defeated 15 to 2):

YEAS—2

Mr. Dominick
Mr. Beall

NAYS—15

Mr. Williams
Mr. Randolph
Mr. Pell
Mr. Kennedy
Mr. Nelson
Mr. Mondale
Mr. Eagleton
Mr. Cranston
Mr. Hughes
Mr. Stevenson

Mr. Javits
Mr. Schweiker
Mr. Packwood
Mr. Taft
Mr. Stafford

4. Senator Williams' motion that the committee favorably report S. 2515, as amended (adopted 17 to 0):

YEAS—17

Mr. Williams
Mr. Randolph
Mr. Pell
Mr. Kennedy
Mr. Nelson
Mr. Mondale
Mr. Eagleton
Mr. Cranston
Mr. Hughes
Mr. Stevenson

Mr. Javits
Mr. Dominick
Mr. Schweiker
Mr. Packwood
Mr. Taft
Mr. Beall
Mr. Stafford

SECTION-BY-SECTION ANALYSIS
SECTION 2

This section amends certain definitions in section 701 of the Civil Rights Act of 1964.

Section 701(a).—This subsection defines "person" to include State and local governments, governmental agencies and political subdivisions.

Section 701(b).—This subsection would extend coverage of employers to those with 8 or more employees one year after enactment. The standard for determining the number of employees of an employer, that is, "employees for each working day in each of 20 or more calendar weeks in the current or preceding calendar year," would apply to employers of 25 or more employees during the first year as well as the final coverage of eight or more employees. This subsection would broaden the meaning of "employer" to include State and local governments and the District of Columbia departments or agencies (except those subject by statute to procedures of the Federal competitive service as defined in 5 U.S.C. 2102, who are covered by section 717, as are all Federal employees).

Section 701(c).—This subsection eliminates the exemption for agencies of the United States, States or political subdivisions of States from the definition of "employment agency" in order to conform with the expanded coverage of State and local governments in section 701(a) and (b). State employment services, previously covered by reference to the United States Employment Service, continue to be covered as part of the State or local government coverage. Employees of the United States Employment Service, as Federal employees, are covered by the new section 717 of the act.

Section 701(e).—This subsection is revised to include coverage of labor organizations with 8 or more members one year after enactment.

SECTION 3

Section 702 is amended to eliminate the exemption for employment of individuals engaged in educational activities of non-religious educational institutions. It continues the exemption for employment of aliens outside the United States and for a religious corporation, association, educational institution or society with respect to employment of individuals of a particular religion to perform work connected with religious activities.

SECTION 4(a)

This section amends sections 706 (a)–(e) of the Civil Rights Act of 1964 entitled "Prevention of Unlawful Employment Practices."

Section 706(a).—This subsection would empower the Commission to prevent persons from engaging in unlawful employment practices under sections 703 and 704 of title VII of the Civil Rights Act of 1964.

Section 706(b).—This subsection prescribes the procedures to be followed when a charge of an unlawful employment practice is filed with the Commission. The Commission must serve a notice of the charge on the respondent within ten days, investigate the charge and make its determination on whether there is reasonable cause to believe that the charge is true. It is not the intent of the committee that failure to give notice within ten days should prejudice the rights of an aggrieved party. If it finds no reasonable cause, the Commission must dismiss the charge; if it finds reasonable cause, it must attempt to conciliate the case. The subsection makes a number of changes in existing law:

1. Under present law, a charge may be filed only by a person aggrieved under oath or by a member of the Commission where he has reasonable cause to believe a violation has occurred. This subsection is amended to permit a charge to be filed by or on behalf of a person aggrieved or by an officer or employee of the Commission upon the request of a person claiming to be aggrieved.

2. The Commission would be required to make its determination on reasonable cause as promptly as possible and, "so far as practicable," within 120 days from the filing of the charge or from the date upon which the Commission is authorized to act on the charge under section 706(c) or (d). The Commission is required in its determination of reasonable cause to accord substantial weight to final findings and orders made by State or local authorities under State and local laws.

3. This subsection and section 8(c) of the bill add appropriate provisions to carry out the intent of the present statute to provide full coverage for joint labor-management committees controlling apprenticeship or other training or retraining, including on-the-job training programs. While these joint labor-management committees are prohibited under section 703(d) of the present act from discriminating, they were not expressly included in the prohibition against discriminatory advertising or retaliation against persons participating in Commission proceedings (sec. 704(a) and (b)) or in the procedures for filing charges in section 706(a).

Section 706(c).—This provision retains the present requirement that the Commission defer for a period of 60 days to State or local agencies functioning under appropriate anti-discrimination laws (or 120 days during the first year after the effective date of such law). The only change in the present law is to delete the phrase "no charge may be filed" with the Commission by an aggrieved person in such State or locality. The present statute is somewhat ambiguous respecting Commission action on charges filed prior to resort to the State or local agency. The new language clarifies the present statute by permitting the charge to be filed but prohibiting the Commission from taking action with respect thereto until the prescribed period has elapsed.

Section 706(d).—This subsection requires deferral to State or local anti-discrimination agencies in the case of charges filed by an officer or employee of the Commission.

Section 706(e).—This subsection prescribes the time limits for the filing of a charge. Under the present statute, the charge must be filed within 90 days after the alleged unlawful employment practice occurred. In cases where the Commission defers to a State or local agency, the charge must presently be filed within 210 days of the occurrence of the alleged unlawful practice, or within 30 days after the person aggrieved receives notice that the State or local agency has terminated its proceedings, whichever is earlier. This subsection would permit charges to be filed within 180 days of the alleged unlawful practice—a limitation period similar to that contained in the Labor-Management Relations Act, as amended (29 U.S.C. 160(b)). Where the Commission defers to a State or local agency, the time limit is extended to 300 days after the occurrence of the alleged unlawful practice or 30 days after receipt of notice that the State or local agency has terminated its proceedings. This subsection also requires that notice of the charge be served on the respondent within ten days after its having been filed.

Sections 706(f) through 706(p).—These subsections, which are new, set forth the procedure to be followed where the Commission, after finding reasonable cause to believe that the allegations of the charge are true, is unable to conciliate the case. The hearing and review requirements are similar to those found in most statutes governing administrative agencies.

Section 706(f).—Under this subsection, if the Commission is unable to secure a conciliation agreement pursuant to section 706(b) that is acceptable to the Commission, it would promptly issue and serve upon the respondent a complaint and notice of hearing if the respondent is not a government, governmental agency or political subdivision. In the latter case, if conciliation fails, the Commission will take no further action and refer the case to the Attorney General for filing a civil action in the district courts. Such civil actions are to be governed by sections 706 (q) through (w), as applicable. The Commission's determination that it is unable to secure such an agreement would not be reviewable in court. Conciliation agreements entered into by the Commission would be enforceable in court in accordance with the provisions of section 706(1). If an officer or employee of the Commission files a charge, he shall not participate in a hearing in any complaint arising out of such charge, except as a witness.

Section 706(g).—This subsection prescribes certain statutory procedural requirements after a complaint is issued by the Commission. The respondent would be provided an opportunity to file an answer to the complaint, and to amend its answer upon a showing of reasonableness and fairness. The respondent and the aggrieved person are full parties and are permitted to appear at any stage of the proceeding. The Commission could also, in its discretion, grant to other persons the right to intervene, to file briefs, or to make oral argument, as it deems appropriate. Testimony at hearings must be under oath and reduced to writing and proceedings shall, so far as practicable, be conducted in accordance with the rules of evidence in the district courts of the United States. This last provision is similar to that contained in the Labor-Management Relations Act (29 U.S.C. 160(b)). As specified in section 706(j), all hearings must be conducted in accordance with the Administrative Procedure Act. The only persons, in addition to members of the Commission, who may preside at hearings are hearing examiners appointed under section 3105 of title 5 of the United States Code.

Section 706(h).—The subsection provides that if the Commission, following a hearing, finds that the respondent has engaged in an unlawful employment practice, it shall state its findings of fact and issue an order to be served on the parties, requiring that the respondent cease and desist from its unlawful conduct and take such affirmative action, including reinstatement or hiring of employees, with or without back pay as will effectuate the policies of the Act. Interim earnings or amounts earnable with reasonable diligence by the aggrieved persons would operate to reduce the back pay otherwise allowable. If any event back pay liability is limited to two years prior to the filing of a charge with the Commission. The order could also require that the respondent make reports from time to time to the Commission. If the Commission finds no unlawful employment practice, it would state such findings and issue an order dismissing the complaint. The provision is intended to give the Commission wide discretion in fashioning the most complete relief possible to eliminate all of the consequences of the unlawful employment practice caused by, or attributable to, the respondent.

Section 706(i).—This subsection would make clear the authority of the Commission, any time after a charge has been filed until the record is filed in court, to end proceedings by agreement with the respondent for the elimination of the alleged unlawful employment practice. Agreements entered into under this section or section 706(f) would be enforceable in the appropriate court of appeals under section 706 (l) through (n). The Commission would also be able, upon reasonable notice, to modify or set aside, in whole or in part, any finding or order made or issued by it. The right of the aggrieved person to file a civil action is preserved in section 706(q)(2) in those cases where the aggrieved person is not a party to the agreement.

Section 706(j).—This subsection requires that findings of fact and orders made or issued under subsection (h) or (i) be on the record in accordance with the Administrative Procedure Act.

Section 706(k).—This subsection would permit a party aggrieved by a final order of the Commission—the respondent or the person or persons on whose behalf the charge was filed—to seek review of such order in a U.S. court of appeals within 60 days after the service of the Commission's order. The subsection specifies the procedures to be followed after a petition for review is filed, including:

(1) The clerk of the court transmits a copy of the petition to the Commission and to any other party to the proceeding before the Commission;

(2) The Commission files in court the record in the proceedings pursuant to 28 U.S.C. 2112 at which time the court of appeals has exclusive jurisdiction;

(3) The Court of Appeals is authorized to grant such temporary relief, restraining order, or other orders as it deems just and proper and may enter a decree enforcing, modifying and enforcing as so modified. or setting aside in whole or in part the order of the Commission. The findings of fact by the Commission are conclusive if they are supported by substantial evidence on the record considered as a whole:

(4) Any party to the proceedings before the Commission may intervene in the court of appeals and a party may apply for leave to adduce additional evidence before the Commission, which could then modify its original findings. Modified findings would also be conclusive if supported by substantial evidence on the record considered as a whole;

(5) Objections not urged before the Commission, its member, or agent, will not be considered by the court unless the failure or neglect to urge such objection is excused because of extraordinary circumstances;

(6) Commencement of proceedings under this subsection would not stay the Commission's order unless ordered by the court; and

(7) The courts of appeals are required to hear petitions expeditiously. This requirement is intended to emphasize to the courts of appeals the need for promptly acting on petitions in order to have speedy resolution of these cases.

Section 706(l).—This subsection would authorize the Commission to petition a U.S. court of appeals for enforcement of its order. The prescribed procedures in the case of petitions for enforcement under this subsection are similar to section 706(k) except that no time limit is specified for the enforcement petition other than that provided by section 706(m) regarding the self-enforcement procedure. The Commission would be authorized to seek an order from the court for temporary or preliminary enforcement of its order pending complete review by the court of appeals.

Section 706(m).—Under this subsection, if there is no petition for review filed within 60 days as provided in section 706(k), the Commission's findings of fact and order would become conclusive in connection with any petition for enforcement filed pursuant to section 706(1). If the Commission petitions for an enforcement order thereafter, the clerk of the court of appeals would enter a decree enforcing the order of the Commission and transmit copies to the Commission, the respondent, and any other parties to the proceeding before the Commission.

Section 706(n).—This subsection provides that any person entitled to relief under a Commission order could obtain enforcement of the order if within 90 days after service of the Commission's order there has been no petition for review filed under subsection (k) or no petition for enforcement filed by the Commission under subsections (l) or (m). The procedures and provisions of subsection (m) would apply to such petition for enforcement.

Section 706(o).—This subsection provides that the Attorney General would conduct all litigation to which the Commission is a party in the Supreme Court of the United States pursuant to this title. All other litigation, except that relating to governments, governmental agencies, and political subdivisions which is conducted by the Attorney

General, including litigation arising under sections 706 (k), (l), (m), (n), (p), (q), or 707, litigation arising in connection with the Commission's record-keeping requirements under section 709, the enforcement of the Commission's authority to conduct investigations under section 710, and private litigation in which the Commission is involved as amicus curiae, as well as judicial proceedings in which the Commission intervenes, shall be conducted by attorneys appointed by the Commission.

Section 706(p).—Under this subsection, if, after a charge is filed under section 706(b), the Commission concludes on the basis of a preliminary investigation that prompt judicial action is necessary to preserve its power to grant effective relief in the proceeding, it must bring an action for appropriate preliminary or temporary relief in the United States district court in the judicial district in which the unlawful employment practice is alleged to have been committed, where the person would have been employed but for the alleged unlawful practice, or if the respondent is not to be found in any of these districts, in the judicial district where the respondent has its principal office. The subsection further provides that for purposes of 28 U.S.C. 1404 and 1406 (which permit the court to transfer an action to another judicial district where the action might have been brought) the district in which the respondent has his principal office is to be considered a judicial district where the action might have been brought.

This subsection, in addition, would make rule 65 of the Federal Rules of Civil Procedure, except paragraph (a)(2) thereof, applicable to proceedings under section 706(p). Rule 65 prescribes procedural requirements for the granting of temporary restraining orders and preliminary injunctions. Paragraph (a)(2) of rule 65 permits the court to advance the trial of the merits and to consolidate the trial on the merits with the hearing on the application for injunction. This provision would be inapplicable to proceedings under section 706(p).

Any relief ordered by the court under this subsection would be permitted to run until such time as a court of appeals has assumed jurisdiction of a review or enforcement petition.

Section 706(q).—This subsection preserves the private right of action by an aggrieved person. Under this subsection, the aggrieved person may bring such an action within 60 days after being notified by the Commission that it has dismissed the charge, or when 180 days have elapsed from the filing of the charge without the Commission having issued a complaint under section 706(f) or the Attorney General having filed a civil action under section 706(f) or without the Commission having entered into an agreement under section 706 (f) or (i) to which the person aggrieved is a party.

The subsection would also divest the Commission of jurisdiction over any pending proceedings upon the filing of a private action. Conversely, the right of an aggrieved party to bring a private action would terminate once the Commission issued a complaint under subsection 706(f), or the Attorney General filed a civil action under subsection 706(f), or the Commission entered into a conciliation agreement under subsection 706 (f) or (i) to which the person aggrieved is a party. If the Commission does not issue an order within 180 days after it issues a complaint or within 60 days after receipt of notice in the case of an agreement under subsection (i) to which the person aggrieved is not a party, the aggrieved person may also institute a civil action. If such action is instituted within one year of the issuance of the Commission's complaint, the Commission may request that it be stayed or dismissed upon a showing that it has been acting with due diligence, that it anticipates issuance of an order within a reasonable time on the complaint, that the case or proceeding is exceptional and that extension of exclusive jurisdiction of the Commission is warranted.

SECTION 4 (b) AND (d)

These sections redesignate the paragraph numbers of subsections 706(e) through (k) of the Civil Rights Act of 1964 as subsections 706(q) through (w), and also redesignate other paragraph numbers to be consistent with the changes made in section 706.

Section 4(c).—This section adds a sentence to subsection 706(r) which clarifies the power of the district courts to grant temporary relief in civil actions brought under title VII.

SECTION 5

This section amends section 707, concerning the Attorney General's "pattern or practice" action, to provide for a transfer of this function to the Commission two years after the enactment of the bill. The bill further provides for concurrent "pattern or practice" jurisdiction for the Commission from the date of enactment until the transfer is complete. The transfer is subject to change in accordance with a Presidential reorganization plan if not vetoed by Congress. The section would provide that currently pending proceedings would continue without abatement, that all court orders and decrees remain in effect, and that upon the transfer the Commission would be substituted as a party for the United States of America or the Attorney General as appropriate. The Commission would have authority to investigate and act on pattern or practice charges except that any action would follow the procedures of section 706.

SECTION 6

This section amends section 709 of the Civil Rights Act of 1964, entitled "Investigations, Inspections, Records, State Agencies."

Section 709(a).—This subsection, which gives the Commission the right to examine and copy documents in connection with its investigation of a charge, would remain unchanged.

Section 709(b).—This subsection would authorize the Commission to cooperate with State and local fair employment practice agencies in order to carry out the purposes of the title, and to enter into agreements with such agencies, under which the Commission would refrain from processing certain types of charges or relieve persons from the recordkeeping requirements. This subsection would make two changes in the present statute. Under this subsection, the Commission could, within the limitations of funds appropriated for the purpose, also engage in and contribute to the cost of research and other projects undertaken by these State and local agencies and pay these agencies in advance for services rendered to the Commission. The subsection also deletes the reference to private civil actions under section 706(e) of the present statute.

Section 709(c).—This subsection, like the present statute, would require employers, employment agencies, labor organizations, and joint labor-management apprenticeship committees subject to the title to make and keep certain records and to make reports therefrom to the Commission. Under the present statute, a party required to keep records could seek an exemption from these requirements on the ground of undue hardship either by applying to the Commission or bringing a civil action in the district court. This subsection would require the party seeking the exemption first to make an application to the Commission and only if the Commission denies the request could the party bring an action in the district court. This subsection would also authorize the Commission to apply for a court order compelling compliance with the recordkeeping and reporting obligations set forth in the subsection.

Section 709(d).—This subsection would eliminate the present exemption from recordkeeping requirements for those employers in States and political subdivisions with fair employment practice laws or for employers subject to Federal executive order or agency recordkeeping requirements. Under this subsection, the Commission would consult with interested State and other Federal agencies in order to coordinate the Federal recordkeeping requirements under section 709(c) with those adopted by such agencies. The subsection further provides that the Commission furnish to such agencies information pertaining to State and local fair employment agencies, on condition that the information would not be made public prior to the institution of State or local proceedings.

Section 709(e).—Under this subsection, the Commission or the Attorney General would have the authority to direct the person having custody of any record or paper required by section 709(c) to be preserved or maintained to make such record or paper available for inspection or copying by the Commission or the Attorney General. The district court of the judicial district where the demand is made or the papers are located would have jurisdiction by appropriate process to compel the production of such record or paper. The subsection further provides that the members of the Commission and its representatives or the Attorney General and his representatives, could not, unless ordered by the court, disclose any record or paper produced except to Congress or a congressional committee, to other government agencies, or in the presentation of cases before a court or a grand jury.

SECTION 7

This section would amend section 710 of the Civil Rights Act of 1964 to make section 11 of the National Labor Relations Act (29 U.S.C. 161), except for one provision thereof, applicable to Commission investigations. This section would require the Commission or a member thereof, upon application of a party, to issue a subpoena requiring the attendance and testimony of a witness or the production of any evidence in a proceeding. The person served with the subpoena could petition the Commission to revoke the subpoena within 5 days.

On application of the Commission, an appropriate district court could order a person to obey a subpoena and failure to comply with the court order would be punishable in contempt proceedings.

Under this section, the Commission would not be authorized to issue a subpoena on the application of a private party before it issues a complaint and notice of hearing. This provision, which is in accord with the actual practice of the National Labor Relations Board, would give the Commission exclusive authority to conduct the pre-hearing investigation.

Section 11 of the National Labor Relations Act also contains provisions relating to privileges of witnesses, immunity from prosecution, fees, process, service, and return, and information and assistance from other agencies.

SECTION 8 (a) AND (b)

These subsections would amend sections 703(a)(2) and 703(c)(2) of the present statute to make it clear that discrimination against applicants for employment and applicants for membership in labor organizations is an unlawful employment practice. This subsection would merely be declaratory of present law.

SECTIONS 8(C) (1) AND (2)

These subsections would amend section 704 (a) and (b) of the present statute to make clear that joint labor-management apprenticeship committees are covered by those provisions which relate to discriminatory advertising and retaliation against individuals participating in Commission proceedings.

SECTION 8 (d)

This subsection would amend section 705(a) of the present statute to provide for the appointment of up to four new Commission members at any time after one year from the effective date of the act at the request of the Chairman, and at the discretion of the President with the advice and consent of the Senate. Not more than the least number of members sufficient to constitute a majority may be of the same political party.

Further, this subsection would amend section 705(a) of the present statute to permit a member of the Commission to serve until his successor is appointed but not for more than 60 days when Congress is in session unless the successor has been nominated and the nomination submitted to the Senate, or after the adjournment sine die of the session of the Senate in which such nomination was submitted.

The rest of the subsection is substantially the same as present section 705(a) and would make the Chairman of the Commission, on behalf of the Commission, responsible for the administrative operations of the Commission and for the appointment of officers, agents, attorneys, hearing examiners and other employees of the Commission in accordance with Federal law.

SECTION 8 (e)

This subsection would amend section 705(g)(1) of the present act to permit the Commission to accept uncompensated services. It is intended to permit the Commission to utilize these services for such purposes as education, publicity, and the collection of data. It would not be expected to accept such services in connection with the prosecution or decision of cases before it except in extraordinary situations.

SECTION 8(f)

This subsection would eliminate the provision in present section 705(g) authorizing the Commission to request the Attorney General to intervene in private civil actions and instead permit the Commission itself to intervene in such civil actions as provided in section 706(q).

SECTION 8(g)

This subsection would, subject to certain exceptions, permit the Commission to delegate any of its functions, duties and powers to such persons as it may designate by regulation. A number of other agencies have broad authority to delegate functions; for example, the Securities and Exchange Commission (15 U.S.C. 78d–1), the Interstate Commerce Commission (49 U.S.C. 17(5)), and the Federal Communications Commission (47 U.S.C. 155(d)). The exceptions are as follows:

(1) The Commission could not delegate its powers to make decisions on the merits after administrative hearings under section 706(h) or to modify or set aside its findings or make new findings under section 706(i), (k), and (l). However, like the National Labor Relations Board (29 U.S.C. 153(b)), the Commission would be authorized to delegate this power or any of its other powers to groups of three or more members of the Commission;

(2) The Commission could not delegate its authority under section 713(c) to make rules of general applicability. A similar limitation is imposed on the Securities and Exchange Commission (15 U.S.C. 78d–1(a));

(3) The Commission could not delegate its authority under section 709(b) to make agreements with States under which the Commission agrees to refrain from processing certain charges or to relieve certain persons from the recordkeeping requirements; and

(4) The Commission could not provide for the conduct of administrative hearings except by members of the Commission or by hearing officers appointed in accord with 5 U.S.C. 556.

SECTION 8(h)

This subsection would afford additional protection to officers, agents, and employees of the Commission in the performance of their official duties by making 18 U.S.C. 1114 applicable to them.

SECTION 9(a), (b), AND (c)

These subsections would make certain modifications in the position of the Chairman of the Commission and the members of the Commission in the executive pay scale, so as to place them in a position of parity with officials in comparable positions in agencies having substantially equivalent powers such as the National Labor Relations Board, the Federal Trade Commission and the Federal Power Commission.

SECTION 10

Section 715.—This section transfers all of the powers and duties of the Secretary of Labor under Executive Order 11246 (as amended by Executive order 11375) to the Equal Employment Opportunity Commission. Executive Order 11246 enunciates the policy of the Government of the United States "... to provide equal opportunity in Federal employment for all qualified persons, to prohibit discrimination in employment because of race, color, religion, sex, or national origin, and to promote the full realization of equal employment opportunity through a positive, continuing program in each executive department and agency. . ." (E.O. 11246 § 101 as amended). The Executive order program is presently administered within the Department of Labor by the Office of Federal Contract Compliance, a division of the Employment Standards Administration. The section contemplates the transfer of all of the OFCC program functions related to Executive Order 11246, as amended. This section does not relieve any of the Government procurement agencies of their responsibilities under the executive order.

The present section 715 relating to a special study by the Secretary of Labor is repealed by the substitution of the new provisions. That study has been completed and the section has no more effect.

SECTION 11

Section 717(a).—This subsection would make clear that personnel actions of the U.S. Government affecting employees or applicants for employment shall be made free from any discrimination based on race, color, religion, sex, or national origin. All employees subject to the executive branch and Civil Service Commission control or protection are covered by this section.

Section 717(b).—Under this subsection, the Civil Service Commission is given the authority to enforce the provisions of subsection (a) through appropriate remedies. These remedies may include back pay for applicants, as well as employees, denied promotion opportunities, reinstatement, hire, immediate promotion and any other remedy needed to fully recompense the employee for his loss, both financially and professionally. The Civil Service Commission is also given authority to issue rules and regulations necessary to carry out its responsibilities under this section. The Civil Service Commission also shall annually review national and regional equal employment opportunity plans and be responsible for review and evaluation of all agency equal employment opportunity programs. Finally, agency and executive department heads and officers of the District of Columbia shall comply with such rules and regulations, submit an annual equal employment opportunity plan and notify any employee or applicant of any final action taken on any complaint of discrimination filed by him.

Sections 717(c) and *(d).*—The provisions of sections 706(q) through (w) concerning private civil actions by aggrieved persons are made applicable to aggrieved Federal employees or applicants. They could file a civil action within 30 days of notice of final action on a complaint made pursuant to section 717(b), or after 180 days from the filing of an initial charge, or an appeal with the Commission. The authority given to the Commission or the limitations placed upon the Commission under sections 706(q) through (w) would apply to the Civil Service Commission or the agencies, as appropriate, in connection with a civil action brought under section 717(c). So, for example, if the Civil Service Commission or agency does not issue an order within 180 days after a complaint or appeal is filed, the aggrieved person may also institute a civil action. If such action is instituted within one year of the filing of the complaint or appeal, the Civil Service Commission or agency may request that the action be stayed or dismissed upon a showing that it has been acting with due diligence, that it anticipates issuance of an order within a reasonable time on the complaint or appeal, that the case or proceeding is exceptional and that extension of exclusive jurisdiction of the Civil Service Commission or agency is warranted.

Section 717(e).—This subsection provides that nothing in this act relieves any Government agency or official of his existing nondiscrimination obligations under the Constitution, other statutes, or his or its responsibilities under Executive Order 11478 relating to equal employment opportunity in the Federal Government.

SECTION 12

Section 716 is amended to provide for consultation of the Attorney General, the Chairman of the Civil Service Commission, and the Chairman of the Equal Employment Opportunity Commission regarding rules, regulations and policy in the performance of their responsibilities under this act. It does not in any way limit each of the officials in independently carrying out their respective obligations under this title.

SECTION 13

This section provides that the amended provisions of section 706 concerning the cease and desist enforcement powers would not apply to charges filed with the Commission prior to the effective date of this act. In addition, those new or amended sections of title VII not specifically stated in this section to be inapplicable to current charges, such as the amendments to sections 705, 707, 709, 710, 713, and 715 would cover existing charges.

CHANGES IN EXISTING LAW

In compliance with subsection 4 of rule XXIX of the Standing Rules of the Senate, changes in existing law made by the bill are shown as follows (existing law proposed to be omitted is enclosed in black brackets, new matter is printed in italic, existing law in which no change is proposed is shown in roman) :

CIVIL RIGHTS ACT OF 1964

AN ACT To enforce the constitutional right to vote, to confer jurisdiction upon the district courts of the United States to provide injunctive relief against discrimination in public accommodations, to authorize the Attorney General to institute suits to protect constitutional rights in public facilities and public educaton, to extend the Commission on Civil Rights, to prevent discrimination in federally assisted programs, to establish a Commission on Equal Employment Opportunity, and for other purposes.

Be it enacted by the Senate and House of Representatives of the United States of America in Congress assembled, That this Act may be cited as the "Civil Rights Act of 1964".

*   *   *   *   *   *   *

TITLE VII—EQUAL EMPLOYMENT OPPORTUNITY

DEFINITIONS

SEC. 701. For the purposes of this title—

(a) The term "person" includes one or more individuals, *governments, governmental agencies, political subdivisions*, labor unions, partnerships, associations, corporations, legal representatives, mutual companies, joint-stock companies, trusts, unincorporated organizations, trustees, trustees in bankruptcy, or receivers.

(b) The term "employer" means a person engaged in an industry affecting commerce who has [twenty-five] *eight* or more employees for each working day in each of twenty or more calendar weeks in the current or preceding calendar year, and any agent of such a person, but such term does not include (1) the United States, a corporation wholly owned by the Government of the United States, an Indian tribe, or [a State or political subdivision thereof.] *any department or agency of the District of Columbia subject by statute to procedures of the competitive service (as defined in section 2102 of title 5 of the United States Code), or* (2) a bona fide private membership club (other than a labor organization) which is exempt from taxation under section 501(c) of the Internal Revenue Code of [1954: *Provided,* That] *1954, except that* during the first year after the [effective date prescribed in subsection (a) of section 716, persons having fewer than one hundred employees (and their agents) shall not be considered employers, and, during the second year after such date, having fewer than seventy-five employees (and their agents) shall not be considered employers, and, during the third year after such date] *date of enactment of the Equal Employment Opportunities Enforcement Act of 1971*, persons having fewer than [fifty] *twenty-five* employees (and their agents) shall not be considered employers.

(c) The term "employment agency" means any person regularly undertaking with or without compensation to procure employees for an employer or to procure for employees opportunities to work for an employer and includes an agent of such a person [; but shall not include an agency of the United States, or an agency of a State or political subdivision of a State, except that such term shall include the United States Employment Service and the system of State and local employment services receiving Federal assistance].

(d) The term "labor organization" means a labor organization engaged in an industry affecting commerce, and any agent of such an organization, and includes any organization of any kind, any agency, or employee representation committee, group, association, or plan so engaged in which employees participate and which exists for the purpose, in whole or in part, of dealing with employers concerning grievances, labor disputes, wages, rates of pay, hours, or other terms or conditions of employment, and any conference, general committee, joint or system board or joint council so engaged which is subordinate to a national or international labor organization.

(e) A labor organization shall be deemed to be engaged in an industry affecting commerce if (1) it maintains or operates a hiring hall or hiring office which procures employees for an employer or procures for employees opportunities to work for an employer, or (2) the number of its members (or, where it is a labor organization composed of other labor organizations or their representatives, if the aggregate number of the members of such other labor organization) is (A) [one hundred] *twenty-five* or more during the first year after the [effective date prescribed in subsection (a) of section 716, (B) seventy-five or more during the second year after such date or fifty or more during the third year, or (C) twenty-five] *date of enactment of the Equal Employment Opportunities Enforcement Act of 1971, or* (B) *eight* or more thereafter, and such labor organization—

(1) is the certified representative of employees under the provisions of the National Labor Relations Act, as amended, or the Railway Labor Act, as amended;

(2) although not certified, is a national or international labor organization or a local labor organization recognized or acting as the representative of employees of an employer or employers engaged in an industry affecting commerce; or

(3) has chartered a local labor organization or subsidiary body which is representing or actively seeking to represent employees or employers within the meaning of paragraph (1) or (2); or

(4) has been chartered by a labor organization representing or actively seeking to represent employees within the meaning of paragraph (1) or (2) as the local or subordinate body through which such employees may enjoy membership or become affiliated with such labor organization; or

(5) is a conference, general committee, joint or system board, or joint council subordinate to a national or international labor organization, which includes a labor organization engaged in an industry affecting commerce within the meaning of any of the preceding paragraphs of this subsection.

(f) The term "employee" means an individual employed by an employer.

(g) The term "commerce" means trade, traffic, commerce, transportation, transmission, or communication among the several States; or between a State and any place outside thereof; or within the District of Columbia, or a possession of the United States; or between points in the same State but through a point outside thereof.

(h) The term "industry affecting commerce" means any activity, business, or industry in commerce or in which a labor dispute would hinder or obstruct commerce or the free flow of commerce and includes any activity or industry "affecting commerce" within the meaning of the Labor-Management Reporting and Disclosure Act of [1959.] *1959, and further includes any governmental industry, business, or activity.*

(i) The term "State" includes a State of the United States, the District of Columbia, Puerto Rico, the Virgin Islands, American Samoa, Guam, Wake Island, the Canal Zone, and Outer Continental Shelf lands defined in the Outer Continental Shelf Lands Act.

EXEMPTION

SEC. 702. This title shall not apply to an employer with respect to the employment of aliens outside any State, or to a religious corporation, association, *educational institution,* or society with respect to the employment of individuals of a particular religion to perform work connected with the carrying on by such corporation, association, *educational institution,* or society of its religious activities [or to an educational institution with respect to the employment of individuals to perform work connected with the educational activities of such institution].

DISCRIMINATION BECAUSE OF RACE, COLOR, RELIGION, SEX, OR NATIONAL ORIGIN

SEC. 703. (a) It shall be an unlawful employment practice for an employer—

(1) to fail or refuse to hire or to discharge any individual, or otherwise to discriminate against any individual with respect to his compensation, terms, conditions, or privileges of employment, because of such individual's race, color, religion, sex, or national origin; or

(2) to limit segregate, or classify his employees *or applicants for employment* in any way which would deprive or tend to deprive any individual of employment opportunities or otherwise adversely affect his status as an employee, because of such individual's race, color, religion, sex, or national origin.

(b) It shall be an unlawful employment practice for an employment agency to fail or refuse to refer for employment, or otherwise to discriminate against, any individual because of his race, color, religion, sex, or national origin, or to classify or refer for employment any individual on the basis of his race, color, religion, sex, or national origin.

(c) It shall be an unlawful employment practice for a labor organization—

(1) to exclude or to expel from its membership, or otherwise to discriminate against, any individual because of his race, color, religion, sex, or national origin;

(2) to limit, segregate, or classify its membership, *or applicants for membership* or to classify or fail or refuse to refer for employment any individual, in any way which would deprive or tend to deprive any individual of employment opportunities, or would

limit such employment opportunities or otherwise adversely affect his status as an employee or as an applicant for employment, because of such individual's race, color, religion, sex, or national origin; or

(3) to cause or attempt to cause an employer to discriminate against an individual in violation of this section.

(d) It shall be an unlawful employment practice for any employer, labor organization, or joint labor-management committee controlling apprenticeship or other training or retraining, including on-the-job training programs to discriminate against any individual because of his race, color, religion, sex, or national origin in admission to, or employment in, any program established to provide apprenticeship or other training.

(e) Notwithstanding any other provision of this title, (1) it shall not be an unlawful employment practice for an employer to hire and employ employees, for an employment agency to classify, or refer for employment any individual, for a labor organization to classify its membership or to classify or refer for employment any individual, or for an employer, labor organization, or joint labor-management committee controlling apprenticeship or other training or retraining programs to admit or employ an individual in any such program, on the basis of his religion, sex, or national origin in those certain instances where religion, sex, or national origin is a bona fide occupational qualification reasonably necessary to the normal operation of that particular business or enterprise, and (2) it shall not be an unlawful employment practice for a school, college, university, or other educational institution or institution of learning to hire and employ employees of a particular religion if such school, college, university, or other educational institution or institution of learning is, in whole or in substantial part, owned, supported, controlled, or managed by a particular religion or by a particular religious corporation, association, or society, or if the curriculum of such school, college, university, or other educational institution or institution of learning is directed toward the propagation of a particular religion.

(f) As used in this title, the phrase "unlawful employment practice" shall not be deemed to include any action or measure taken by an employer, labor organization, joint labor-management committee, or employment agency with respect to an individual who is a member of the Communist Party of the United States or of any other organization required to register as a Communist-action or Communist-front organization by final order of the Subversive Activities Control Board pursuant to the Subversive Activities Control Act of 1950.

(g) Notwithstanding any other provision of this title, it shall not be an unlawful employment practice for an employer to fail or refuse to hire and employ any individual for any position, for an employer to discharge any individual from any position, or for an employment agency to fail or refuse to refer any individual for employment in any position, or for a labor organization to fail or refuse to refer any individual for employment in any position, if—

(1) the occupancy of such position, or access to the premises in or upon which any part of the duties of such position is performed or is to be performed, is subject to any requirement im-

posed in the interest of the national security of the United States under any security program in effect pursuant to or administered under any statute of the United States or any Executive order of the President; and

(2) such individual has not fulfilled or has ceased to fulfill that requirement.

(h) Notwithstanding any other provision of this title, it shall not be an unlawful employment practice for an employer to apply different standards of compensation, or different terms, conditions, or privileges of employment pursuant to a bona fide seniority or merit system, or a system which measures earnings by quantity or quality of production or to employees who work in different locations, provided that such differences are not the result of an intention to discriminate because of race, color, religion, sex, or national origin, nor shall it be an unlawful employment practice for an employer to give and to act upon the results of any professionally developed ability test provided that such test, its administration or action upon the results is not designed, intended or used to discriminate because of race, color, religion, sex or national origin. It shall not be an unlawful employment practice under this title for any employer to differentiate upon the basis of sex in determining the amount of the wages or compensation paid or to be paid to employees of such employer if such differentiation is authorized by the provisions of section 6(d) of the Fair Labor Standards Act of 1938, as amended (29 U.S.C. 206(d)).

(i) Nothing contained in this title shall apply to any business or enterprise on or near an Indian reservation with respect to any publicly announced employment practice of such business or enterprise under which a preferential treatment is given to any individual because he is an Indian living on or near a reservation.

(j) Nothing contained in this title shall be interpreted to require any employer, employment agency, labor organization, or joint labor-management committee subject to this title to grant preferential treatment to any individual or to any group because of the race, color, religion, sex, or national origin of such individual or group on account of an imbalance which may exist with respect to the total number or percentage of persons of any race, color, religion, sex, or national origin employed by any employer, referred or classified for employment by any employment agency or labor organization, admitted to membership or classified by any labor organization, or admitted to, or employed in, any apprenticeship or other training program, in comparison with the total number or percentage of persons of such race, color, religion, sex, or national origin in any community, State, section, or other area, or in the available work force in any community, State, section, or other area.

OTHER UNLAWFUL EMPLOYMENT PRACTICES

SEC. 704. (a) It shall be an unlawful employment practice for an employer to discriminate against any of his employees or applicants for employment, for an employment agency *or joint labor-management committee controlling apprenticeship or other training or retraining, including on-the-job training programs,* to discriminate against any individual, or for a labor organization to discriminate against any member thereof or applicant for membership, because he has opposed any practice made an unlawful employment practice by this title, or because he has made a charge, testified, assisted, or participated in any manner in an investigation, proceeding, or hearing under this title.

(b) It shall be an unlawful employment practice for an employer, labor organization [or employment agency] *employment agency or joint labor-management committee controlling apprenticeship or other training or retraining including on-the-job training programs,* to print or publish or cause to be printed or published any notice or advertisement relating to employment by such an employee or membership in or any classification or referral for employment by such a labor organization, or relating to any classification or referral for employment by such an employment agency, *or relating to admission to, or employment in, any program established to provide apprenticeship or other training by such a joint labor-management committee* indicating any preference, limitation, specification, or discrimination, based on race, color, religion, sex, or national origin, except that such a notice or advertisement may indicate a preference, limitation, specification, or discrimination based on religion, sex, or national origin when religion, sex, or national origin, is a bona fide occupational qualification for employment.

EQUAL EMPLOYMENT OFFORTUNITY COMMISSION

SEC. 705. (a) There is hereby created a Commission to be known as the Equal Employment Opportunity Commission, which shall be composed of five members, *unless additional members are appointed as hereinafter provided in this subsection,* [not more than three of whom] *not more than the least number of members sufficient to constitute a majority of the members of the Commission* shall be members of the same political party, [who] *members of the Commission* shall be appointed by the President by and with the advice and consent of the [Senate] *Senate. Any individual chosen to fill a vacancy shall be appointed only for the unexpired term of the member whom he shall succeed, and all members of the Commission shall continue to serve until their successors are appointed and qualified, except that no such members of the Commission shall continue to serve (1) for more than sixty days when the Congress is in session unless a nomination to fill such vacancy shall have been submitted to the Senate, or (2) after the adjournment sine die of the session of the Senate in which such nomination was submitted.* [One of the original members shall be appointed for a term of one year, one for a term of two years, one for a term of three years, one for a term of four years, and one for a term of five years, beginning from the date of enactment of this title, but their successors shall be appointed for terms of five years each, except that any individual chosen to fill a vacancy shall be appointed only for the unexpired term of the member whom he shall succeed.] The President shall designate one member to serve as Chairman of the Commission, and one member to serve as Vice Chairman. The Chairman shall be responsible on behalf of the Commission for the administrative operations of the Commission, and shall appoint, in accordance with the [civil service laws, such officers, agents, attorneys,] *provisions of title 5, United States Code, governing appointments in the competitive service, such officers, agents, attorneys; hearing examiners,* and employees as [it] *he* deems necessary to assist it in the performance of its functions and to fix their compensation in accordance with the [Classification Act of 1949, as amended. The Vice Chairman shall act as Chairman in the absence or disability of the Chairman or in the event of a vacancy in that office] *provisions of chapter 51 and subchapter III of chapter 53 of title 5, United States Code, relating to classification and General Schedule pay rates: Provided, That assignment, removal, and compensation of hearing examiners shall be in accordance with sections 3105, 3344, 5362, and 7521 of title 5, United States Code. At any time after one year from the effective date of this Act, the Chairman of the Commission, if he determines that the appointment of additional members of the Commission would help to effectuate the purposes of this Act, may request the President to appoint up to four additional members of the Commission. Upon receiving such a request, the President may appoint up to four additional members of the Commission by and with the advice and consent of the Senate. Such additional members shall be appointed for a term of five years. Upon the expiration of the term of appointment of any such additional member no further appointment to the same position shall be made, and the total number of members of the Commission shall be reduced accordingly unless the Chairman of the Commission determines that the appointment of one or more additional members of the Commission continues to be necessary to better effectuate the purposes of this Act and so advises the President.*

(b) A vacancy in the Commission shall not impair the right of the remaining members to exercise all the powers of the Commission and three members thereof shall constitute a quorum.

(c) The Commission shall have an official seal which shall be judicially noticed.

(d) The Commission shall at the close of each fiscal year report to the Congress and to the President concerning the action it has taken; the names, salaries, and duties of all individuals in its employ and the moneys it has disbursed; and shall make such further reports on the cause of and means of eliminating discrimination and such recommendations for further legislation as may appear desirable.

(e) [The Federal Executive Pay Act of 1956, as amended (5 U.S.C. 2201–2209), is further amended—

[(1) by adding to section 105 thereof (5 U.S.C. 2204) the following clause:

["(32) Chairman, Equal Employment Opportunity Commission": and

[(2) by adding to clause (45) of section 106(a) thereof (5 U.S.C. 2205(a)) the following: "Equal Employment Opportunity Commission (4)."]

(1) Section 5314 of title 5 of the United States Code is amended by adding at the end thereof the following new clause.

"(58) Chairman, Equal Employment Opportunity Commission."

(2) Clause (72) of section 5315 of such title is amended to read as follows.

"(72) Members, Equal Employment Opportunity Commission (8)."

(3) Clause (111) of section 5316 of such title is repealed.

(f) The principal office of the Commission shall be in or near the District of Columbia, but it may meet or exercise any or all its powers at any other place. The Commission may establish such regional or State offices as it deems necessary to accomplish the purpose of this title.

(g) The Commission shall have power—

(1) to cooperate with and, with their consent, utilize regional, State, local, and other agencies, both public and private, and [individuals;] *individuals. and to accept voluntary and uncompensated services, notwithstanding the provisions of section 3679(b) of the Revised Statutes (31 U.S.C. 665(b)).*

(2) to pay witnesses whose depositions are taken or who are summoned before the Commission or any of its agents the same witness and mileage fees as are paid to witnesses in the courts of the United States;

(3) to furnish to persons subject to this title such technical assistance as they may request to further their compliance with this title or an order issued thereunder;

(4) upon the request of (i) any employer, whose employees or some of them, or (ii) any labor organization, whose members or some of them, refuse or threaten to refuse to cooperate in effectuating the provisions of this title, to assist in such effectuation by conciliation or such other remedial action as is provided by this title;

(5) to make such technical studies as are appropriate to effectuate the purposes and policies of this title and to make the results of such studies available to the public;

[(6) to refer matters to the Attorney General with recommendations for intervention in a civil action brought by an aggrieved party under section 706, or for the institution of a civil action by the Attorney General under section 707, and to advise, consult, and assist the Attorney General on such matters.]

(6) to intervene in a civil action brought by an aggrieved party under section 706.

(h) Attorneys appointed under this section may, at the direction of the Commission, appear for and represent the Commission in any case in court.

(i) The Commission shall, in any of its educational or promotional activities, cooperate with other departments and agencies in the performance of such educational and promotional activities.

(j) All officers, agents, attorneys, and employees of the Commission shall be subject to the provisions of section 9 of the Act of August 2, 1939, as amended (the Hatch Act), notwithstanding any exemption contained in such section.

PREVENTION OF UNLAWFUL EMPLOYMENT PRACTICES

SEC. 706. [(a) Whenever it is charged in writing under oath by a person claiming to be aggrieved, or a written charge has been filed by a member of the Commission where he has reasonable cause to believe a violation of this title has occurred (and such charge sets forth the facts upon which it is based) that an employer, employment agency, or labor organization has engaged in an unlawful employment practice, the Commission shall furnish such employer, employment agency, or labor organization (hereinafter referred to as the "respondent") with a copy of such charge and shall make an investigation of such charge, provided that such charge shall not be made public by the Commission. If the Commission shall determine, after such investigation, that there is reasonable cause to believe that the charge is true, the Commission shall endeavor to eliminate any such alleged unlawful employment practice by informal methods of conference, conciliation, and persuasion. Nothing said or done during and as a part of such endeavors may be made public by the Commission without the written consent of the parties, or used as evidence in a subsequent proceeding. Any officer or employee of the Commission, who shall make public in any manner whatever any information in violation of this subsection shall be deemed guilty of a misdemeanor and upon conviction thereof shall be fined not more than $1,000 or imprisoned not more than one year.]

SEC. 706. (a) *The Commission is empowered, as hereinafter provided, to prevent any person from engaging in any unlawful employment practice as set forth in section 703 or 704 of this title.*

[(a)] (b) Whenever [it is charged in writing under oath by a] *a charge is filed by or on behalf of a* person claiming to be aggrieved, or [a written charge has been filed] by [a member] *an officer or employee* of the Commission [where he has reasonable cause to believe a violation of this title has occurred (and such charge sets forth the facts upon which it is based)] *upon the request of any person claiming to be aggrieved, alleging* that an employer, employment agency, [or] labor [organization] *organization, or joint labor-management, committee controlling apprenticeship or other training or retraining, including on-the-job training programs,* has engaged in an unlawful employment practice, the Commission shall [furnish] *serve a notice of the charge (including the date, place and circumstances of the alleged unlawful employment practice)* on such employer, employment agency, [or] labor [organization] *organization, or joint labor-management committee* (hereinafter referred to as the "respondent") [with a copy of such charge and shall make an investigation of such charge, provided that such charge] *within ten days and shall make an investigation thereof. Charges shall be in writing and shall contain such information and be in such form as the Commission requires. Charges* shall not be made public by the Commission. If the Commission [shall determine,] *determines* after such investigation [.] that there is *not* reasonable cause to believe that the charge is true, *it shall dismiss the charge and promptly notify the person claiming to be aggrieved and the respondent of its action. In determining whether reasonable cause exists, the Commission shall accord substantial weight to final findings and orders made by State or local authorities in proceedings commenced under State or local law pursuant to the requirements of subsections (c) and (d). If the Commission determines after such investigation that there is reasonable cause to believe that the charge is true,* the Commission shall endeavor to eliminate any such alleged unlawful employment practice by informal methods of conference, conciliation, and persuasion. Nothing said or done during and as a part of such *informal* endeavors may be made public by the [Commission] *Commission, its officers or employees, or used as evidence in a subsequent proceeding* without the written consent of the [parties, or used as evidence in a subsequent proceeding] *persons concerned.* Any [officer or employee of the Commission,] *person* who [shall make] *makes* public [in any manner whatever any] information in violation of this subsection [shall be deemed guilty of a misdemeanor and upon conviction thereof] shall be fined not more than $1,000 or imprisoned *for* not more than one [year.] *year, or both. The Commission shall make its determination on reasonable cause as promptly as possible and, so far as practicable, not later than one hundred and twenty days from the filing of the charge or, where applicable under subsection (c) or (d), from the date upon which the Commission is authorized to take action with respect to the change.*

[(b)] *(c)* In the case of [an alleged] *a charge filed by or on behalf of a person claiming to be aggrieved alleging an* unlawful employment practice occurring in a [State.] *State* or political subdivision of a [State,] *State* which has a State or local law prohibiting the unlawful employment practice alleged and establishing or authorizing a State or local authority to grant or seek relief from such practice or to institute criminal proceedings with respect thereto upon receiving notice [thereof, no charge may be filed under subsection (a) by the person aggrieved] *thereof the Commission shall take no action with respect to the investigation of such charge* before the expiration of sixty days after proceedings have been commenced under the State or local law, unless such proceedings have been earlier [terminated, provided that] *terminated, except that* such sixty-day period shall be extended to one hundred and twenty days during the first year after the effective date of such State or local law. If any requirement for the commencement of such proceedings is imposed by a State or local authority other than a requirement of the filing of a written and signed statement of the facts upon which the proceeding is based, the proceeding shall be deemed to have been commenced for the purposes of this subsection at the time such statement is sent by registered *or certified* mail to the appropriate State or local authority.

[(c)] *(d)* In the case of any charged filed by [a member] *an officer or employee* of the Commission alleging an unlawful employment practice occurring in a State or political subdivision of a State[.] which has a State or local law prohibiting the practice alleged and establishing or authorizing a State or local authority to grant or seek relief from such practice or to institute criminal proceedings with respect thereto upon receiving notice thereof[.] the Commission shall, before taking any action with respect to such charge, notify the appropriate State or local officials and, upon request, afford them a reasonable time, but not less than sixty days (provided that such sixty-day period shall be extended to one hundred and twenty days during the first year after the effective [day] *date* of such State or local [law),] *law),* unless a shorter period is requested, to act under such State or local law to remedy the practice alleged.

[(d)] (e) A charge under [subsection (a)] *this section* shall be filed within [ninety] *one hundred and eighty* days after the alleged unlawful employment practice [occurred,] *occurred and notice of the charge (including the date, place and circumstances of the alleged unlawful employment practice) shall be served upon the person against whom such charge is made within ten days thereafter,* except that in [the] *a* case of an unlawful employment practice with respect to which the person aggrieved has [followed the procedure set out in subsection (b),] *initially instituted proceedings with a State or local agency with authority to grant or seek relief from such practice or to institute criminal proceedings with respect thereto upon receiving notice thereof,* such charge shall be filed by *or on behalf of* the person aggrieved within [two hundred and ten] *three hundred* days after the alleged unlawful employment practice occurred, or within thirty days after receiving notice that the State or local agency has terminated the proceedings under the State or local law, whichever is earlier, and a copy of such charge shall be filed by the Commission with the State or local agency.

[(e) If within thirty days after a charge is filed with the Commission or within thirty days after expiration of any period of reference under subsection (c) (except that in either case such period may be extended to not more than sixty days upon a determination by the Commission that further efforts to secure voluntary compliance are warranted), the Commission has been unable to obtain voluntary compliance with this title, the Commission shall so notify the person aggrieved and a civil action may, within thirty days thereafter, be brought against the respondent named in the charge (1) by the person claiming to be aggrieved, or (2) if such charge was filed by a member of the Commission, by any person whom the charge alleges was aggrieved by the alleged unlawful employment practice. Upon application by the complainant and in such circumstances as the court may deem just, the court may appoint an attorney for such complainant and may authorize the commencement of the action without the payment of fees, costs, or security. Upon timely application, the court may, in its discretion, permit the Attorney General to intervene in such civil action if he certifies that the case is of general public importance. Upon request, the court may, in its discretion, stay further proceedings for not more than sixty days pending the termination of State or local proceedings described in subsection (b) or the efforts of the Commission to obtain voluntary compliance.]

(f) If the Commission determines after attempting to secure voluntary compliance under subsection (b) that it is unable to secure from the respondent a conciliation agreement acceptable to the Commission which determination shall not be reviewable in any court, the Commission shall issue and cause to be served upon any respondent not a government, governmental agency, or political subdivision a complaint stating the facts upon which the allegation of the unlawful employment practice is based, together with a notice of hearing before the Commission, or a member or agent thereof, at a place therein fixed not less than five days after the serving of such complaint. In the case of a respondent which is a government, governmental agency, or political subdivision, the Commission shall take no further action and

shall refer the case to the Attorney General who may bring a civil action against such respondent in the appropriate United States district court. The person or persons aggrieved shall have the right to intervene in such civil action. The provisions of section 706(q) through (w), as applicable, shall govern civil actions brought hereunder. Related proceedings may be consolidated for hearing. Any officer or employee of the Commission who filed a charge in any case shall not participate in a hearing on any complaint arising out of such charge, except as a witness.

(g) A respondent shall have the right to file an answer to the complaint against him and with the leave of the Commission, which shall be granted whenever it is reasonable and fair to do so, may amend his answer at any time. Respondents and the person or persons aggrieved shall be parties and may appear at any stage of the proceedings, with or without counsel. The Commission may grant other persons a right to intervene or to file briefs or make oral arguments as amicus curiae or for other purposes, as it considers appropriate. All testimony shall be taken under oath and shall be reduced to writing. Any such proceeding shall, so far as practicable, be conducted in accordance with the rules of evidence applicable in the district courts of the United States under the Rules of Civil Procedure for the district courts of the United States.

(h) If the Commission finds that the respondent has engaged in an unlawful employment practice, the Commission shall state its findings of fact and shall issue and cause to be served on the respondent and the person or persons aggrieved by such unlawful practice an order requiring the respondent to cease and desist from such unlawful employment practice and to take such affirmative action, including reinstatement or hiring of employees, with or without back pay (payable by the employer, employment agency, or labor organizations, as the case may be, responsible for the unlawful employment practice), as will effectuate the policies of this title, except that (1) back pay liability shall not exceed that which has accrued more than two years prior to the filing of a charge with the Commission, and (2) interim earnings or amounts earnable with reasonable diligence by the aggrieved person or persons shall operate to reduce the back pay otherwise allowable. Such order may further require such respondent to make reports from time to time showing the extent to which he has complied with the order. If the Commission finds that the respondent has not engaged in any unlawful employment practice, the Commission shall state its findings of fact and shall issue and cause to be served on the respondent and the person or persons alleged in the complaint to be aggrieved an order dismissing the complaint.

(i) After a charge has been filed and until the record has been filed in court as hereinafter provided, the proceeding may at any time be ended by agreement between the commission and the respondent for the elimination of the alleged unlawful employment practice and the Commission may at any time, upon reasonable notice, modify or set aside, in whole or in part, any finding or order made or issued by it. An agreement approved by the Commission shall be enforceable under subsections (l) through (n) and the provisions of those subsections shall be applicable to the extent appropriate to a proceeding to enforce an agreement.

*(j) Findings of fact and orders made or issued under subsections
(h) or (i) of this section shall be determined on the record. Sections
554, 555, 556, and 557 of title 5 of the United States Code shall apply
to such proceedings.*

*(k) Any party aggrieved by a final order of the Commission grant-
ing or denying in whole or in part the relief sought may obtain a review
of such order in any United States court of appeals for the circuit in
which the unlawful employment practice in question is alleged to have
occurred or in which such party resides or transacts business, or in the
Court of Appeals for the District of Columbia Circuit, by filing in such
court within sixty days after the service of such order, a written petition praying that the order of the Commission be modified or set aside.
A copy of such petition shall be forthwith transmitted by the clerk of
the court to the Commission and to any other party to the proceeding
before the Commission, and thereupon the Commission shall file in the
court the record in the proceeding as provided in section 2112 of title
28, United States Code. Upon the filing of the petition the court shall
have jurisdiction of the proceeding and of the question determined
therein, and shall have power to grant to the petitioner or any other
party, including the Commission, such temporary relief or restraining
order as it deems just and proper, and to make and enter upon the
pleadings, testimony, and proceedings set forth in such record a decree
affirming, modifying, or setting aside, in whole or in part, the order of
the Commission and enforcing the same to the extent that such order
is affirmed or modified. Any party to the proceeding before the Commission shall be permitted to intervene in the court of appeals. The
commencement of proceedings under this subsection shall not, unless
ordered by the court, operate as a stay of the order of the Commission.
No objection that has not been urged before the Commission, its member, or agent shall be considered by the court, unless the failure or
neglect to urge such objection shall be excused because of extraordinary
circumstances. The findings of the Commission with respect to questions of fact, if supported by substantial evidence on the record considered as a whole, shall be conclusive. If any party shall apply to the
court for leave to adduce additional evidence and shall show to the
satisfaction of the court that such additional evidence is material and
that there were reasonable grounds for the failure to adduce such evidence in the hearing before the Commission, its member, or its agent,
the court may order such additional evidence to be taken before the
Commission, its member, or its agent, and to be made a part of the
record. The Commission may modify its findings as to the facts, or
make new findings, by reason of additional evidence so taken and filed,
and it shall file such modified or new findings, which findings with
respect to questions of fact, if supported by substantial evidence on the
record considered as a whole, shall be conclusive, and its recommendations, if any, for the modification or setting aside of its original order.
Upon the filing of the record with it, the jurisdiction of the court shall
be exclusive and its judgment and decree shall be final, except that the
same shall be subject to review by the Supreme Court of the United
States, as provided in section 1254 of title 28, United States Code.
Petitions filed under this subsection shall be heard expeditiously.*

(l) The Commission may petition any United States court of appeals

for the circuit in which the unlawful employment practice in question occurred or in which the respondent resides or transacts business, for the enforcement of its order and for appropriate temporary relief or restraining order, by filing in such court a written petition praying that its order be enforced and for appropriate temporary relief or restraining order. The Commission shall file in court with its petition the record in the proceeding as provided in section 2112 of title 28, United States Code. A copy of such petition shall be forthwith transmitted by the clerk of the court to the parties to the proceeding before the Commission. Upon the filing of such petition, the court shall have jurisdiction of the proceeding and of the question determined therein and shall have power to grant to the Commission, or any other party, such temporary relief, restraining order, or other order as it deems just and proper, and to make and enter upon the pleadings, testimony, and proceedings set forth in such record a decree affirming, modifying, or setting aside in whole or in part, the order of the Commission and enforcing the same to the extent that such order is affirmed or modified. Any party to the proceeding before the Commission shall be permitted to intervene in the court of appeals. No objection that has not been urged before the Commission, its members, or agent shall be considered by the court, unless the failure or neglect to urge such objection shall be excused because of extraordinary circumstances. The findings of the Commission with respect to questions of fact, if supported by substantial evidence on the record considered as a whole, shall be conclusive. If any party shall apply to the court for leave to adduce additional evidence and shall show to the satisfaction of the court that such additional evidence is material and that there were reasonable grounds for the failure to adduce such evidence in the hearing before the Commission, its member, or its agent, the court may order such additional evidence to be taken before the Commission, its member, or its agent, and to be made a part of the record. The Commission may modify its findings as to the facts, or make new findings, by reason of additional evidence so taken and filed, and it shall file such modified or new findings which findings with respect to questions of fact, if supported by substantial evidence on the record considered as a whole, shall be conclusive, and its recommendations, if any, for the modification or setting aside of its original order. Upon the filing of the record with it the jurisdiction of the court shall be exclusive and its judgment and decree shall be final, except that the same shall be subject to review by the Supreme Court of the United States as provided in section 1254 of title 28, United States Code. Petitions filed under this subsection shall be heard expenditiously.

(m) If no petition for review, as provided in subsection (k), is filed within sixty days after service of the Commission's order the Commission's findings of fact and order shall be conclusive in connection with any petition for enforcement which is filed by the Commission under subsection (l) after the expiration of such sixty-day period. The clerk of the court of appeals in which such petition for enforcement is filed shall forthwith enter a decree enforcing the order of the Commission and shall transmit a copy of such decree to the Commission, the respondent named in the petition, and to any other parties to the proceeding before the Commission.

(n) *If within ninety days after service of the Commission's order, no petition for review has been filed as provided in subsection (k), and the Commission has not sought enforcement of its order as provided in subsection (l), any person entitled to relief under the Commission's order may petition for a decree enforcing the order in the United States court of appeals for the circuit in which the unlawful employment practice in question occurred, or in which a respondent named in the order resides or transacts business. The provisions of subsection (m) shall apply to such petitions for enforcement.*

(o) *The Attorney General shall conduct all litigation to which the Commission is a party in the Supreme Court of the United States pursuant to this title. All other litigation affecting the Commission, or to which it is a party, shall be conducted by attorneys appointed by the Commission.*

(p) *Whenever a charge is filed with the Commission pursuant to subsection (b) and the Commission concludes on the basis of a preliminary investigation that prompt judicial action is necessary to preserve the power of the Commission to grant effective relief in the proceeding, the Commission shall, after it issues a complaint, bring an action for appropriate temporary or preliminary relief pending its final disposition of such charge, or until the filing of a petition under subsections (k), (l), (m), or (n) of this section, as the case may be, in the United States district court for any judicial district in the State in which the unlawful employment practice concerned is alleged to have been committed, or the judicial district in which the aggrieved person would have been employed but for the alleged unlawful employment practice, but, if the respondent is not found within any such judicial district, such an action may be brought in the judicial district in which the respondent has his principal office. For purposes of sections 1404 and 1406 of title 28, United States Code, the judicial district in which the respondent has his principal office shall in all cases be considered a judicial district in which such an action might have been brought. Upon the bringing of any such action, the district court shall have jurisdiction to grant such injunctive relief or temporary restraining order as it deems just and proper, notwithstanding any other provision of law. Rule 65 of the Federal Rules of Civil Procedure, except paragraph (a) (2) thereof, shall govern proceedings under his subsection.*

(q) (1) *If a charge filed with the Commission pursuant to subsection (b) is dismissed by the Commission, or if within one hundred and eighty days from the filing of such charge or the expiration of any period of reference under subsection (c) or (d), whichever is later, the Commission has not issued a complaint under subsection (f), the Attorney General has not filed a civil action under subsection (f) or the Commission entered into an agreement under subsection (f) or (i) to which the person aggrieved is a party, the Commission shall so notify the person aggrieved and within sixty days after the giving of such notice a civil action may be brought against the respondent named in the charge (1) by the person claiming to be aggrieved, or (2) if such charge was filed by an officer or employee of the Commission, by any person whom the charge alleges was aggrieved by the alleged unlawful employment practice. Upon application by the Complainant and in such circumstances as the court may deem just, the court may ap-*

point an attorney for such complainant and may authorize the commencement of the action without the payment of fees, costs, or security. Upon the commencement of such civil action, the Commission, or the Attorney General in a case involving a government, governmental agency or political subdivision, shall take no further action with respect thereto, except that, upon timely application, the court in its discretion may permit the Commission, or the Attorney General in a case involving a government, governmental agency or political subdivision, to intervene in such civil action if the Commission, or the Attorney General in a case involving a government, governmental agency or political subdivision, certifies that the case is of general public importance. Upon request, the court may, in its discretion, stay further proceedings for not more than sixty days pending termination of State or local proceedings described in subsection (c) or (d) or the efforts of the Commission to obtain voluntary compliance.

(2) The right of an aggrieved person to bring a civil action under paragraph (1) of this subsection shall terminate once the Commission has issued a complaint under subsection (f) or the Attorney General has filed a civil action under subsection (f) or the Commission has entered into an agreement under subsection (f) or (i) to which the person aggrieved is a party, except that (1) if after issuing a complaint the Commission enters into an agreement under subsection (i) without the agreement of the person aggrieved or has not issued an order under subsection (h) within a period of one hundred and eighty days of the issuance of the complaint, the Commission shall so notify the person aggrieved and a civil action may be brought against the respondent named in the charge at any time prior to the Commission's issuance of an order under subsection (h) or, in the case of an agreement under subsection (i) to which the person aggrieved is not a party, within sixty days after receiving notice thereof from the Commission, and (2) that where there has been no agreement under subsection (i), if the person aggrieved files a civil action against the respondent during the period from one hundred and eighty days to one year after the issuance of the complaint such person shall notify the Commission of such action and the Commission may petition the court not to proceed with the suit. The court may dismiss or stay any such action upon a showing that the Commission has been acting with due diligence on the complaint, that the Commission anticipates the issuance of an order under subsection (h) within a reasonable period of time, that the case is exceptional, and that extension of the Commission's jurisdiction is warranted.

[(f)](r) Each United States district court and each United States court of a place subject to the jurisdiction of the United States shall have jurisdiction of actions brought under this title. Such an action may be brought in any judicial district in the State in which the unlawful employment practice is alleged to have been committed, in the judicial district in which the employment records relevant to such practice are maintained and administered, or in the judicial district in which the plaintiff would have worked but for the alleged unlawful employment practice, but if the respondent is not found within any such district, such an action may be brought within the judicial district in which the respondent has his principal office. For purposes of sections 1404 and 1406 of title 28 of the United States Code, the judicial district in which the respondent has his principal office shall in all cases be considered a district in which the action might have been brought. *Upon the bringing of any such action, the district court shall have jurisdiction to grant such temporary or preliminary relief as it deems just and proper.*

[(g)](*s*) If the court finds that the respondent has intentionally engaged in or is intentionally engaging in an unlawful employment practice charged in the complaint, the court may enjoin the respondent from engaging in such unlawful employment practice, and order such affirmative action as may be appropriate, which may include reinstatement or hiring of employees, with or without back pay (payable by the employer, employment agency, or labor organization, as the case may be, responsible for the unlawful employment practice). Interim earnings or amounts earnable with reasonable diligence by the person or persons discriminated against shall operate to reduce the back pay otherwise allowable. No order or the court shall require the admission or reinstatement of an individual as a member of a union or the hiring, reinstatement, or promotion of an individual as an employee, or the payment to him of any back pay, if such individual was refused admission, suspended, or expelled or was refused employment or advancement or was suspended or discharged for any reason other than discrimination on account of race, color, religion, sex, or national origin or in violation of section 704(a).

[(h)] (*t*) The provisions of the Act entitled "An Act to amend the Judicial Code and to define and limit the jurisdiction of courts sitting in equity, and for other purposes," approved March 23, 1932 (29 U.S.C. 101–115), shall not apply with respect to civil actions brought under this section.

[(i)] (*u*) In any case in which an employer, employment agency, or labor organization fails to comply with an order of a court issued in a civil action brought under subsection [(e),] (*q*), the Commission may commence proceedings to compel compliance with such order.

[(j)] (*v*) Any civil action brought under subsection [(e)] (*q*) and any proceedings brought under subsection [(i)] (*u*) shall be subject to appeal as provided in sections 1291 and 1292, title 28, United States Code.

[(k)] (*w*) In any action or proceeding under this title the court, in its discretion, may allow the prevailing party, other than the Commission or the United States, a reasonable attorney's fee as part of the costs, and the Commission and the United States shall be liable for costs the same as a private person.

SEC. 707. (a) Whenever the Attorney General has reasonable cause to believe that any person or group of persons is engaged in a pattern or practice of resistance to the full enjoyment of any of the rights secured by this title, and that the pattern or practice is of such a nature and is intended to deny the full exercise of the rights herein described, the Attorney General may bring a civil action in the appropriate district court of the United States by filing with it a complaint (1) signed by him (or in his absence the Acting Attorney General), (2) setting forth facts pertaining to such pattern or practice, and (3) requesting such relief, including an application for a permanent or temporary injunction, restraining order or other order against the person or persons responsible for such pattern or pactice, as he deems necessary to insure the full enjoyment of the rights herein described.

(b) The district courts of the United States shall have and shall exercise jurisdiction of proceedings instituted pursuant to this section, and in any such proceeding the Attorney General may file with the clerk of such court a request that a court of three judges be convened to hear and determine the case. Such request by the Attorney General shall be accompanied by a certificate that, in his opinion, the case is of general public importance. A copy of the certificate and request for a three-judge court shall be immediately furnished by such clerk to the chief judge of the circuit (or in his absence, the presiding circuit judge of the circuit) in which the case is pending. Upon receipt of such request it shall be the duty of the chief judge of the circuit or the presiding circuit judge, as the case may be, to designate immediately three judges in such circuit, of whom at least one shall be a circuit judge and another of whom shall be a district judge of the court in which the proceeding was instituted, to hear and determine such case, and it shall be the duty of the judges so designated to assign the case for hearing at the earliest practicable date, to participate in the hearing and determination thereof, and to cause the case to be in every way expedited. An appeal from the final judgment of such court will lie to the Supreme Court.

In the event the Attorney General fails to file such a request in any such proceeding, it shall be the duty of the chief judge of the district (or in his absence, the acting chief judge) in which the case is pending immediately to designate a judge in such district to hear and determine the case. In the event that no judge in the district is available to hear and determine the case, the chief judge of the district, or the acting chief judge, as the case may be, shall certify this fact to the chief judge of the circuit (or in his absence, the acting chief judge) who shall then designate a district or circuit judge of the circuit to hear and determine the case.

It shall be the duty of the judge designated pursuant to this section to assign the case for hearing at the earliest practicable date and to cause the case to be in every way expedited.

(c) *Effective two years after the date of enactment of the Equal Employment Opportunities Enforcement Act of 1971, the functions of the Attorney General under this section shall be transferred to the Commission, together with such personnel, property, records, and unexpended balances of appropriations, allocations, and other funds employed, used, held, available, or to be made available in connection with such functions unless the President submits and neither House of Congress vetoes a reorganization plan submitted pursuant to chapter 9, of title 5, United States Code, inconsistent with the provisions of this subsection. The Commission shall carry out such functions in accordance with the provisions of subsections (d) and (e) of this section.*

(d) *Upon the transfer of functions provided for in subsection (c) of this section, in all suits commenced pursuant to this section prior to the date of such transfer, proceedings shall continue without abatement, all court orders and decrees shall remain in effect, and the Commission shall be substituted as a party for the United States of Amer-*

ica. The Attorney General or Acting Attorney General, as appropriate.

(e) Subsequent to the date of enactment of the Equal Employment Opportunities Enforcement Act of 1971, the Commission shall have authority to investigate and act on a charge of a pattern or practice of discrimination, whether filed by or on behalf of a person claiming to be aggrieved or by an officer or employee of the Commission. All such actions shall be conducted in accordance with the procedures set forth in section 706, including the provisions for enforcement and appellate review contained in subsections (k), (l), (m), and (n) thereof.

EFFECT ON STATE LAWS

SEC. 708. Nothing in this title shall be deemed to exempt or relieve any person from any liability, duty, penalty, or punishment provided by any present or future law of any State or political subdivision of a State, other than any such law which purports to require or permit the doing of any act which would be an unlawful employment practice under this title.

INVESTIGATIONS, INSPECTIONS, RECORDS, STATE AGENCIES

SEC. 709. (a) In connection with any investigation of a charge filed under section 706, the Commission or its designated representative shall at all reasonable times have access to, for the purposes of examination, and the right to copy any evidence of any person being investigated or proceeded against that relates to unlawful employment practices covered by this title and is relevant to the charge under investigation.

(b) The Commission may cooperate with State and local agencies charged with the administration of State fair employment practices laws and, with the consent of such agencies, may for the purpose of carrying out its functions and duties under this title and within the limitation of funds appropriated specifically for such purpose, *engage in and contribute to the cost of research and other projects of mutual interest undertaken by such agencies, and* utilize the services of such agencies and their employees and, notwithstanding any other provision of law, [may] *pay by advance or* [reimburse] *reimbursement* such agencies and their employees for services rendered to assist the Commission in carrying out this title. In furtherance of such cooperative efforts, the Commission may enter into written agreements with such State or local agencies and such agreements may include provisions under which the Commission shall refrain from processing a charge in any cases or class of cases specified in such agreement [and under which no person may bring a civil action under section 706 in any cases or class of cases so specified, or under which the Commission shall relieve any person or class of] *or under which the Commission shall relieve any person or class of* persons in such State or locality from requirements imposed under this section. The Commission shall rescind any such agreement whenever it determines that the agreement no longer serves the interest of effective enforcement of this title.

(c) [Except as provided in subsection (d), every] *Every* employer, employment agency, and labor organization subject to this title shall (1) make and keep such records relevant to the determinations of whether unlawful employment practices have been or are being committed, (2) preserve such records for such periods, and (3) make such reports therefrom, as the Commission shall prescribe by regulation or order, after public hearing, as reasonable, necessary, or appropriate for the enforcement of this title or the regulations or orders thereunder. The Commission shall, by regulation, require each employer, labor organization, and joint labor-management committee subject to this title which controls an apprenticeship or other training program to maintain such records as are reasonably necessary to carry out the purpose of this title, including, but not limited to, a list of applicants who wish to participate in such program, including the chronological order in which [such] applications were received, and [shall] *to* furnish to the Commission, upon request, a detailed description of the manner in which persons are selected to participate in the apprenticeship or other training program. Any employer, employment agency, labor organization, or joint labor-management committee which believes that the application to it of any regulation or order issued under this section would result in undue hardship may [(1)] apply to the Commission for an exemption from the application of such regulation or order, [or (2)] *and, if such application for an exemption is denied,* bring a civil action in the United States district court for the district where such records are kept. If the Commission or the court, as the case may be, finds that the application of the regulation or order to the employer, employment agency, or labor organization in question would impose an undue hardship, the Commission or the court, as the case may be, may grant appropriate relief. *If any person required to comply with the provisions of this subsection fails or refuses to do so, the United States district court for the district in which such person is found, resides, or transacts business, shall, upon application of the Commission, or the Attorney General in a case involving a government, governmental agency or political subdivision, have jurisdiction to issue to such person an order requiring him to comply.*

[(d) The provisions of subsection (c) shall not appy to any employer, employment agency, labor organization, or joint labor-management committee with respect to matters occurring in any State or political subdivision thereof which has a fair employment practice law during any period in which such employer, employment agency, labor organization, or joint labor-management committee is subject to such law, except that the Commission may require such notations on records which such employer, employment agency, labor organization, or joint labor-management committee keeps or is required to keep as are necessary because of differences in coverage or methods of enforcement between the State or local law and the provisions of this title. Where an employer is required by Executive Order 10925, issued March 6, 1961, or by any other Executive order prescribing fair employment practices for Government contractors and subcontractors, or by rules or regulations issued thereunder, to file reports relating to his employment practices with any Federal agency or committee, and he is substantially in compliance with such requirements, the Commission shall not require him to file additional reports pursuant to subsection (c) of this section.]

(d) In prescribing requirements pursuant to subsection (c) of this

section, the Commission shall consult with other interested State and Federal agencies and shall endeavor to coordinate its requirements with those adopted by such agencies. The Commission shall furnish upon request and without cost to any State or local agency charged with the administration of a fair employment practice law information obtained pursuant to subsection (c) of this section from any employer, employment agency, labor organization, or joint labor-management committee subject to the jurisdiction of such agency. Such information shall be furnished on condition that it not be made public by the recipient agency prior to the institution of a proceeding under State or local law involving such information. If this condition is violated by a recipient agency, the Commission may decline to honor subsequent requests pursuant to this subsection.

(e) Any record or paper required by section 709(c) of this title to be preserved or maintained shall be made available for inspection, reproduction, and copying by the Commission or its representative, or by the Attorney General or his representative, upon demand in writing directed to the person having custody, possession, or control of such record or paper. Unless otherwise ordered by a court of the United States, neither the members of the Commission or its representative, nor the Attorney General, or his representative shall disclose any record or paper produced pursuant to this title, or any reproduction or copy, except to Congress or any committee thereof, or to a governmental agency, or in the presentation of any case or proceeding before any court or grand jury. The United States district court for the district in which a demand is made or in which a record or paper so demanded is located, shall have jurisdiction to compel by appropriate process the production of such record or paper.

[(e)] (*f*) It shall be unlawful for any officer or employee of the Commission to make public in any manner whatever any information obtained by the Commission pursuant to its authority under this section prior to the institution of any proceeding under this title involving such information. Any officer or employee of the Commission who shall make public in any manner whatever any information in violation of this subsection shall be guilty of a misdemeanor and upon conviction thereof, shall be fined not more than $1,000, or imprisoned not more than one year.

INVESTIGATORY POWERS

[Sec. 710. (a) For the purposes of any investigation of a charge filed under the authority contained in section 706, the Commission shall have authority to examine witnesses under oath and to require the production of documentary evidence relevant or material to the charge under investigation.

[(b) If the respondent named in a charge filed under section 706 fails or refuses to comply with a demand of the Commission for permission to examine or to copy evidence in conformity with the provisions of section 709(a), or if any person required to comply with the provisions of section 709 (c) or (d) fails or refuses to do so, or if any person fails or refuses to comply with a demand by the Commission to give testimony under oath, the United States district court for the district in which such person is found, resides, or transacts business, shall, upon application of the Commission, have jurisdiction to issue to such person an order requiring him to comply with the provisions of section 709 (c) or (d) or to comply with the demand of the Commission, but the attendance of a witness may not be required outside the State where he is found, resides, or transacts business and the production of evidence may not be required outside the State where such evidence is kept.

[(c) Within twenty days after the service upon any person charged under section 706 of a demand by the Commission for the production of documentary evidence or for permission to examine or to copy evidence in conformity with the provisions of section 709(a), such person may file in the district court of the United States for the judicial district in which he resides, is found, or transacts business, and serve upon the Commission a petition for an order of such court modifying or setting aside such demand. The time allowed for compliance with the demand in whole or in part as deemed proper and ordered by the court shall not run during the pendency of such petition in the court, Such petition shall specify each ground upon which the petitioner relies in seeking such relief, and may be based upon any failure of such demand to comply with the provisions of this title or with the limitations generally applicable to compulsory process or upon any constitutional or other legal right or privilege of such person. No objection which is not raised by such a petition may be urged in the defense to a proceeding initiated by the Commission under subsection (b) for enforcement of such a demand unless such proceeding is commenced by the Commission prior to the expiration of the twenty-day period, or unless the court determines that the defendant could not reasonably have been aware of the availability of such ground of objection.

[(d) In any proceeding brought by the Commission under subsection (b), except as provided in subsection (c) of this section, the defendant may petition the court for an order modifying or setting aside the demand of the Commission.]

SEC. 710. *For the purpose of all hearings and investigations conducted by the Commission or its duly authorized agents or agencies, section 11 of the National Labor Relations Act (49 Stat. 455; 29 U.S.C. 161) shall apply. No subpoena shall be issued on the application of any party to proceedings before the Commission until after the Commission has issued and caused to be served upon the respondent a complaint and notice of hearing under subsection (f) of section 706.*

NOTICES TO BE POSTED

SEC. 711. (a) Every employer, employment agency, and labor organization, as the case may be, shall post and keep posted in conspicuous places upon its premises where notices to employees, applicants for employment, and members are customarily posted a notice to be prepared or approved by the Commission setting forth excerpts from or, summaries of, the pertinent provisions of this title and information pertinent to the filing of a complaint.

(b) A willful violation of this section shall be punishable by a fine of not more than $100 for each separate offense.

VETERANS' PREFERENCE

SEC. 712. Nothing contained in this title shall be construed to repeal or modify any Federal, State, territorial, or local law creating special rights or preference for veterans.

RULES AND REGULATIONS

SEC. 713. (a) The Commission shall have authority from time to time to issue, amend, or rescind suitable procedural regulations to carry out the provisions of this title. Regulations issued under this section shall be in conformity with the standards and limitations of the Administrative Procedure Act.

(b) In any action or proceeding based on any alleged unlawful employment practice, no person shall be subject to any liability or punishment for or on account of (1) the commission by such person of an unlawful employment practice if he pleads and proves that the act or omission complained of was in good faith, in conformity with, and in reliance on any written interpretation or opinion of the Commission, or (2) the failure of such person to publish and file any information required by any provision of this title if he pleads and proves that he failed to publish and file such information in good faith, in conformity with the instructions of the Commission issued under this title regarding the filing of such information. Such a defense, if established, shall be a bar to the action or proceeding, notwithstanding that (A) after such act or omission, such interpretation or opinion is modified or rescinded or is determined by judicial authority to be invalid or of no legal effect, or (B) after publishing or filing the description and annual reports, such publication or filing is determined by judicial authority not to be in conformity with the requirements of this title.

(c) *Except for the powers granted to the Commission under subsection (h) of section 706, the power to modify or set aside its findings, or make new findings, under subsections (i), (k), and (l) of section 706, the rulemaking power as defined in subchapter II of chapter 5 of title 5, United States Code, with reference to general rules as distinguished from rules of specific applicability, and the power to enter into or rescind agreements with State and local agencies, as provided in subsection (b) of section 709, under which the Commission agrees to refrain from processing a charge in any cases or class of cases or under which the Commission agrees to relieve any person or class of persons in such State or locality from requirements imposed by section 709, the Commission may delegate any of its functions, duties, and powers to such person or persons as the Commission may designate by regulation, including functions, duties, and powers with respect to hearing, determining, ordering, certifying, reporting or otherwise acting as to any work, business, or matter. Nothing in this subsection authorizes the Commission to provide for persons other than those referred to in clauses (2) and (3) of subsection (b) of section 556 of title 5 of the United States Code to conduct any hearing to which that section applies.*

(d) *The Commission is authorized to delegate to any group of three*

*or more members of the Commission any or all of the powers which it
may itself exercise.*

FORCIBLY RESISTING THE COMMISSION OR ITS REPRESENTATIVES

SEC. 714. The provisions of section 111, *and 1114* title 18, United
States Code, shall apply to officers, agents, and employees of the Commission in the performance of their official duties.

SPECIAL STUDY BY SECRETARY OF LABOR

[SEC. 715. The Secretary of Labor shall make a full and complete
study of the factors which might tend to result in discrimination in
employment because of age and of the consequences of such discrimination on the economy and individuals affected. The Secretary of
Labor shall make a report to the Congress not later than June 30, 1965,
containing the results of such study and shall include in such report
such recommendations for legislation to prevent arbitrary discrimination in employment because of age as he determines advisable.]

*SEC. 715. All authority, functions, and responsibilities vested in the
Secretary of Labor pursuant to Executive Order 11246, as amended,
relating to nondiscrimination in employment by Government contractors and subcontractors and nondiscrimiation in federally assisted
construction contracts are transferred to the Equal Employment Opportunity Commission, together with such personnel, property, records,
and unexpended balances of appropriations, allocations, and other
funds employed, used, held, available or to be made available in connection with the functions transferred to the Commission hereby as
may be necessary to enable the Commission to carry out its functions
pursuant to this section, and the Commission shall hereafter carry out
all such authority, functions, and responsibilities pursuant to such
order.*

EFFECTIVE DATE

SEC. 716. (a) This title shall become effective one year after the
date of its enactment.

(b) Nothwithstanding subsection (a), sections of this title other
than sections 703, 704, 706, and 707 shall become effective immediately.

(c) The President shall, as soon as feasible after the enactment of
this title, convene one or more conferences for the purpose of enabling
the leaders of groups whose members will be affected by this title to
become familiar with the rights afforded and obligations imposed by
its provisions, and for the purpose of making plans which will result
in the fair and effective administration of this title when all of its
provisions become effective. The President shall invite the participation in such conference or conferences of (1) the members of the
president's Committee on Equal Employment Opportunity, (2) the
members of the Commission on Civil Rights, (3) representatives of
State and local agencies engaged in furthering equal employment
opportunity, (4) representatives of private agencies engaged in furthering equal employment opportunity, and (5) representatives of
employers, labor organizations, and employment agencies who will be
subject to this title.

(d) In the performance of their responsibilities under this Act, the Attorney General, the Chairman of the Civil Service Commission and the Chairman of the Equal Employment Opportunity Commission shall consult regarding their rules, regulations and policies.

NONDISCRIMINATION IN FEDERAL GOVERNMENT EMPLOYMENT

SEC. 717. (a) All personnel actions affecting employees or applicants for employment (except with regard to aliens employed outside the limits of the United States) in military departments as defined in section 102 of Title 5 United States Code, in executive agencies (other than the General Accounting Office) as defined in section 105 of Title 5, United States Code (including employees and applicants for employment who are paid from non-appropriated funds), in the United States Postal Service and the Postal Rate Commission in those unit of the Government of the District of Columbia having positions in the competitive service, and in the legislative and judicial branches of the Federal Government having positions in the competitive servce, shall be made free from any discrimination based on race, color, religion, sex, or national origin.

(b) The Civil Service Commission shall have authority to enforce the provisions of subsection (a) through appropriate remedies, including reinstatement of hiring of employees with or without back pay, as will effectuate the policies of this section, and shall issue such rules, regulations, orders and instructions as it deems necessary and appropriate to carry out its responsibilities under this section. The Civil Service Commission shall—

(1) be responsible for the annual review and approval of a national and regional equal employment opportunity plan which each department and agency and each appropriate unit referred to in section 717 (a) shall submit in order to maintain an affimative program of equal employment opportunity for all such employees and applicants for employment;

(2) be responsible for the review and evaluation of the operation of all agency equal employment opportunity programs, periodically obtaining and publishing (on at least a semiannual basis) progress reports from each such department, agency, or unit; and

(3) consult with and solicit the recommendations of interested individuals, groups, and organizations relating to equal employment opportunity.

The head of each such department, agency or unit shall comply with such rules, regulations, orders, and instructions which shall include a provision that an employee or applicant for employment shall be notified of any final action taken on any complaint of discrimination filed by his thereunder. The plan submitted by each department, agency and unit shall include, but not be limited to—

(1) provision for the establishment of training and education programs designed to provide a maximum opportunity for employees to advance so as to perform at their highest potential; and

(2) a description of the qualifications in terms of training and experience relating to equal opportunity for the principal and operating officials of each such department, agency, or unit responsible for carrying out the equal employment opportunity program

and of the allocation of personnel and resources proposed by such department, agency, or unit to carry out its equal employment opportunity program.

(c) Within thirty days of receipt of notice of final action taken by a department, agency, or unit referred to in subsection 717(a), or by the Civil Service Commission upon an appeal from a decision or order of such department, agency, or unit, on a complaint of discrimination based on race, color, religion, sex or national origin, brought pursuant to subsection (a) of this section, Executive Order 11478 or any succeeding Executive orders, or after 180 days from the filing of the initial charge with the department, agency, or unit or with the Civil Service Commission on appeal from a decision or order of such department, agency, or unit until such time as final action may be taken by a department, agency or unit, an employee or applicant for employment, if aggrieved by the final disposition of his complaint, or by the failure to take final action on his complaint, may file a civil action as provided in section 706(q), in which civil action the head of the department, agency, or unit, as appropriate, shall be the defendant.

(d) The provisions of section 706(q) through (w), as applicable, shall govern civil actions brought hereunder.

(e) Nothing contained in this Act shall relieve any Government agency or official of its or his primary responsibility to assure nondiscrimination in employment as required by the Constitution and statutes or of its or his responsibilities under Executive Order 11478 relating to equal employment opportunity in the Federal Government.

Sec. 13 of S. 2515 reads as follows: The amendments made by this Act to section 706 of the Civil Rights Act of 1964 shall not be applicable to charges filed with the Commission prior to the enactment of this Act.)

Appendix F

Excerpts From the Congressional Debate

In addition to the committee and conference reports, the debate in Congress relating to a law often provides guidance in determining the legislative intent. For that reason, selected excerpts from the congressional debate are included in this section.

To facilitate reference to the statements made, citations are given to the date of the Congressional Record and the page number at which they appear. Three asterisks (* * *) indicate the omission of text.

Appendix F-1

Conference Report: Procedures

EDITORS' NOTE: *Rep. Dent (D., Pa.) placed in the Record a summary of procedures to be followed where there are no state equal employment opportunity laws and where there are such laws.*

House

3-8-72

p. 1867

PROCEDURE WHERE NO STATE EQUAL EMPLOYMENT OPPORTUNITY LAW EXISTS

(1) A charge must be filed within 180 days after the occurrence of an alleged unlawful employment practice.

(2) After a charge is filed, the Commission must serve a notice of the charge on the respondent within ten days.

(3) The Commission must then investigate the charge, after which it must make a determination whether there is reasonable cause to believe that the charge is true. The Commission shall make its determination of reasonable cause as promptly as possible and, so far as practicable, within 120 days.

(4) If it finds no reasonable cause, the Commission must dismiss the charge: if it finds reasonable cause, it will attempt to conciliate the case.

(5) If the Commission is unable to secure a conciliation agreement, that is acceptable to the Commission, it may bring a civil action against any respondent in an appropriate federal district court. In the case of a respondent which is a government, governmental agency or political subdivision, the Commission shall take no further action and notify the Attorney General who may bring a civil action.

(6) If the court finds that a respondent is engaging in an unlawful employment practice charged in the complaint, the court may enjoin the respondent from engaging in the unlawful employment practice and grant such affirmative relief as it may deem appropriate including, but not limited to, reinstatement, with or without backpay. Backpay liability is limited, however, to no more than that accrued during the two years prior to the filing of a charge with the Commission.

(7) In the event that the Commission dismisses a charge or if within 180 days from the filing of the charge the Commission or the Attorney General has not filed a civil action or entered into a conciliation agreement to which the aggrieved person is a party, the Commission or the Attorney General will notify the aggrieved party. Within ninety days after the receipt of such notice the person aggrieved may bring a civil action against the respondent. Should such a private action be brought, the Commission or the Attorney General (where a government or political subdivision was involved) may seek to intervene in the action.

PROCEDURES WHERE STATE EQUAL EMPLOYMENT OPPORTUNITY LAW EXISTS

(1) A charge must be filed within 180 days after the occurrence of an alleged unlawful employment practice.

If a charge is initially filed with a state or local agency, such charge must be filed with the Commission within 300 days after the alleged unlawful practice has occurred or within 30 days after receipt of notice that the state or local agency has terminated its proceedings.

(2) Where a state or local equal employment statute exists, the EEOC must wait 60

297

days after state or local proceedings have been commenced, unless those proceedings have been terminated sooner, before it can act on a charge. The deferral period is extended to 120 days during the first year after enactment of a state or local law.

(3) Once the deferred is concluded, the Commission must serve a notice of the charge on the respondent within ten days (presumably, this is duplicative of the state or local proceedings).

(4) The Commission must then investigate the charge, afterwhich it must make a determination whether there is reasonable cause to believe that the charge is true. The Commission shall make its determination of reasonable cause as promptly as possible and, so far as practicable within 120 days.

(5) If it finds no reasonable cause, the Commission must dismiss the charge; if it finds reasonable cause, it will attempt to conciliate the case.

(6) If the Commission is unable to secure a conciliation agreement, that is acceptable to the Commission, it may bring a civil action against any respondent in an appropriate Federal district court. In the case of a respondent which is a government, governmental agency or political subdivision, the Commission shall take no further action

and notify the Attorney General who may bring a civil action.

(7) If the court finds that a respondent is engaging in an unlawful employment practice charged in the complaint, the court may enjoin the respondent from engaging in the unlawful employment practice and grant such affirmative relief as it may deem appropriate including, but not limited to, reinstatement, with or without backpay. Backpay liability is limited, however, to no more than that accrued during the two years prior to the filing of a charge with the Commission.

(8) In the event that the Commission dismisses a charge or if within 180 days from the filing of the charge the Commission or the Attorney General has not filed a civil action or entered into a conciliation agreement to which the aggrieved person is a party, the Commission or the Attorney General will notify the aggrieved party. Within ninety days after the receipt of such notice the person aggrieved may bring a civil action against the respondent. Should such a private action be brought, the Commission or the Attorney General (where a government or .political subdivision was involved) may seek to intervene in the action.

Appendix F-2

House Bill: In General

EDITORS' NOTE: *Rep. Perkins (D., Ky.) described the provisions of the bill reported by the Committee on Education and Labor (H.R. 1746) and discussed the compromise amendments (see below), which were introduced by Rep. Dent (D., Pa.)*

House

9-15-71

pp. 8459-8461

Mr. PERKINS. Mr. Chairman, 7 years ago Congress enacted the Civil Rights Act of 1964. Title VII of that act for the first time established Federal machinery to deal with the problem of discriminatory employment practices.

Title VII provided informal methods of conciliation and persuasion as the primary mechanism for obtaining compliance. Only when a "pattern or practice" of resistance to the statutory mandate was found did it make provision for enforcement by the Government and then only by the Attorney General.

Title VII established the Equal Employment Opportunity Commission as an

independent agency charged with administration of the policy of equal opportunity but provided no effective enforcement authority. Such enforcement as an individual might require had to be secured by a private suit in the district courts. At the time it was widely felt that litigation would be necessary only on an occasional basis to meet determined resistance.

The experience of the past 6 years, however, has shown this view to be incorrect. Title VII is not a total failure but neither is it the glowing success that was expected.

Discrimination in employment continues to pervade the United States.

Only 6.9 percent of professional and technical workers; 3.6 percent of managerial employees; 6.8 percent of craftsmen and foremen; and 3.7 percent of sales personnel are minority persons. During 1970, the unemployment rate among blacks was almost twice that among whites. While these figures are improvements over those of a decade ago, it is nonetheless clear that minorities are not very rapidly reaching their rightful place in society—this despite

7 years' experience under a law which outlawed discrimination of any kind.

The situation of the working woman is just as disappointing. Over 30 million women are employed in the United States, comprising approximately 38 percent of the Nation's work force. Ten years ago. women earned 60.8 percent of the average salaries earned by men. In 1968, however, women's earnings only represented 58.2 percent of the salaries made by men. In that same year, 60 percent of women, but only 20 percent of men earned less than $5,000 while, at the other end of the scale, only 3 percent of women, but 28 percent of men had earnings of $10,000 or more.

Effective remedies for these situations have not, and it is now clear, cannot result from the present statutory scheme. During its first 5 years, the Equal Employment Opportunity Commission received more than 52,000 charges, of these 35,145 were recommended for investigation. Each year the number of charges brought before the Commission has increased. In fiscal year 1969 the Commission received 12,148 charges; in fiscal year 1970, 14,129 charges; and in fiscal year 1971, 22,920 charges. The figures for the current fiscal year are expected to show an even sharper rise.

Of the 35,145 charges that were recommended for investigation, the Commission found reasonable cause to find that a discriminatory practice existed in 63 percent of them. In less than half of these cases, however, was the Commission able to achieve a totally or even partially successful conciliation.

ENFORCEMENT AUTHORITY

To correct these deficiencies, H.R. 1746 provides for significant revisions in the primary enforcement mechanisms of title VII. The Equal Employment Opportunity Commission would continue to seek voluntary resolution of disputes, but if conciliation efforts were unsuccessful, the Commission would be authorized to issue complaints, hold hearings and, where unlawful employment practices are found, issue appropriate cease-and-desist orders. These orders would, of course, be subject to review by the courts.

The bill also makes provision for individual recourse to the Federal district courts if the Commission dismisses a charge, or if it has not issued a complaint or entered into a conciliation attempt within a specified period of time.

All members of the Committee on Education and Labor recognized the need for some method of adjudication of charges of unfair employment practices, as indeed, did all witnesses who testified at the committee hearings. The only disagreement has been whether this enforcement power should be through administrative proceedings or through litigation in the courts.

The alternative of providing court enforcement for title VII, instead of administrative cease-and-desist proceedings, was given full and careful consideration throughout the hearings and in discussions at both the subcommittee and full committee levels.

The type of enforcement chosen by the committee is the very same type of authority which has been given to virtually all other Federal regulatory agencies including the Federal Trade Commission, the Interstate Commerce Commission, the Securities and Exchange Commission, and the National Labor Relations Board. In addition, the cease and desist method of enforcement is the same as that adopted by 34 of the 38 States which have equal employment opportunity laws.

The same considerations which led to the adoption of administrative enforcement in other areas are equally applicable here. Perhaps the most important of these is the need for the development and application of expertise in the recognition and solution of employment discrimination problems—particularly as these problems are presented in their more complex, institutional forms.

The development of case law in the area of employment discrimination in recent years has made it increasingly clear that the most difficult problem encountered is not whether discrimination has occurred but what the appropriate remedy is to be. The question of remedies is further complicated when discriminatory practices are found to be inherent in basic methods of recruitment, hiring, placement, or promotion.

The very nature of the issues arising under title VII indicates that reliance upon the expertise developed by trial examiners and Commissioners is just as important for this subject matter as it is in the equally complex fields of securities regulation and deceptive trade practices.

Enforcement through an administrative proceeding will ensure a speedy adjudication of issues and will result in a more uniform and predictable body of law.

Agency litigation is less subject to technical rules governing matters such as pleadings and motions—matters which can, and very often do, provide opportunity for delaying tactics. Administration tribunals are less constrained by formal rules of evidence which give rise to a lengthier—and, therefore, a more costly—process of proof.

The experience of other agencies indicates that an additional benefit of cease and desist authority is that the mere availability of an administrative sanction encourages settlements, usually even before the trial examiner stage is reached. The NLRB, for instance, disposes of approximately 95 percent of its cases at the administrative level. Information on State Fair Employment Practice Commissions indicates similar tendencies toward settlement. For example, the Pennsylvania Human Relations Commission issued 47 cease-and-desist orders in equal employment cases through 1969. During that same period, however, 3,838 complaints were successfully disposed of without need for an order.

PRIVATE SUITS

H.R. 1746 retains the right of an individual to bring a civil suit under the act. Section 715 provides that if the Commission finds no reasonable cause, fails to make a finding of reasonable cause, takes no action in respect to a charge, or has not issued a complaint nor entered into an acceptable conciliation or settlement agreement within 180 days after a charge is filed, it shall notify the person aggrieved. That person then has the right to bring, within 60 days, an action in the proper U.S. district court. Such a provision is a necessary protection for the rights of the individual.

To prevent duplication of proceedings under title VII, H.R. 1746 makes provision for the termination of Commission jurisdiction once a private action has been filed. The Commission would, however, retain a right to intervene in private actions. Once the Commission issues a complaint or enters into a conciliation or settlement agreement which is acceptable to all parties, the right of private action would be terminated.

PATTERN OR PRACTICE CASES

Section 707 of the Civil Rights Act would be amended to transfer the "pattern or practice" suit authority which is now vested in the Attorney General to the Equal Employment Opportunity Commission. The transfer of "pattern or practice" jurisdiction to the Commission would eliminate overlapping jurisdictions and unnecessary duplication of function. This is especially important in view of the Commission's acquisition of cease and desist authority, an authority broad enough to cover most of the same viola-

tions as formerly reached through "pattern or practice" suits. Persons charged with unfair employment practices should not have to account to several Federal agencies, each of which pursue separate policies. Such duplication is not only burdensome but also harassing.

OFFICE OF CONTRACT COMPLIANCE

For this same reason, H.R. 1746 would also transfer to the Commission all authority, functions, and responsibilities of the Secretary of Labor pursuant to Executive Order 11246 relating to requirements of nondiscrimination and affirmative action for Federal contractors. Currently, the Secretary of Labor through the Office of Federal Contract Compliance—OFCC—monitors, coordinates, and evaluates the Government-wide contract compliance program and supervises the compliance enforcement activities of the 15 Federal contracting agencies. Clarity, uniformity, and predictability, in policy and practice will undoubtedly result when a single agency, rather than a multitude of them, is responsible for enforcing the National policy of equal employment opportunity.

More important, the compliance program will be greatly strengthened if alternative remedies are made available. The only remedy currently available to the OFCC is contract debarment, a penalty so drastic that it has never been used.

STATE AND LOCAL GOVERNMENT EMPLOYEES

Presently, there are more than 10 million persons employed by State and local governmental units, an increase of over 2 million in less than a decade and, by all indications, these numbers will increase significantly in the decade ahead. Very few of these employees, however, have remedies sufficient to eliminate and deal with discriminatory employment practices. H.R. 1746 amends section 701 of the act to include State and local governments, governmental agencies, and political subdivisions within the definition of "employer" under title VII. This would effectively provide the employees of America's second largest employer—the State and local governments—the full protection of title VII.

In its 1969 report on equal employment opportunity in State and local governments, the U.S. Civil Rights Commission found that minorities are frequently denied equal access to jobs through both institutional and overt discriminatory practices. In this respect, there was little difference between State and local governments as employers and the private sector. Perpetuation of past discriminatory practices through de facto segregated job ladders, invalid selection techniques, and stereotyped supervisory opinions as to the capabilities of minorities as a class were found to be widespread, and, if anything, even more pervasive than in the private sector.

PREFERENCE FOR STATE ACTION

Under H.R. 1746, every effort is made to give State fair employment practice agencies, where they exist, the first opportunity to act. The history of State FEPC activity since 1964 suggests that the backup of Federal power in the event of a failure of local action to resolve a discrimination complaint would substantially strengthen the effectiveness of the State and local agencies. Thus, the increased coverage contemplated by this bill should provide more than ample opportunity and incentive for States to resolve their own problems of discrimination, before it becomes necessary to pass them on to the Federal Government.

EDUCATIONAL INSTITUTIONS EXEMPTION

The present section 702 of title VII exempts employees of educational institutions from the protection of the act. H.R. 1746 removes this exemption—section 3 of the bill. Discrimination against minorities and women is as pervasive in the field of education as discrimination in any other area of employment. In light of our National policy of equal employment, there is no reason to perpetuate this exemption.

JURISDICTION LIMITS

H.R. 1746 expands coverage of title VII to all employers with eight or more employees and labor unions with eight or more members. Presently, the act sets a jurisdictional limit of 25 employees or members. This amendment to the act will assure Federal equal employment protection to virtually every segment of the Nation's work force.

TESTS

H.R. 1746 includes a provision requiring that all ability tests which are to be relied on be directly related to bona fide occupational qualifications. Tests, while often useful and necessary, frequently operate unreasonably to the disadvantage of minority groups. Such tests are often irrelevant to the job to be performed by the individual being tested and uncritical reliance on tests are not only of little help in management personnel decisions, but also screen out the disadvantaged minority applicant.

The Supreme Court recognized this problem in its recent decision in *Griggs* v. *Duke Power Company* (91 S. Ct. 849, 1971). The Court held in that case that employment tests, even if valid on their face and applied in a nondiscriminatory manner, were invalid if they tended to discriminate against minorities and the company could not show an overriding reason why such tests were necessary. The Court saw business necessity as the tauchstone of the issue. If an employment practice which excludes minorities cannot be shown to be related to job performance, the Court concluded, the practice is prohibited. This amendment to the act alters the language of title VII to better reflect the congressional intent as interpreted by the Court in the Griggs case.

FEDERAL EMPLOYEES

Finally, H.R. 1746 would add a new section to title VII—section 717—giving the EEOC authority to enforce the obligations of equal employment opportunity in Federal employment.

Since Americans traditionally measure the quality of their democracy by the opportunity they have to participate in governmental processes, equal employment opportunity is of critical importance in the Federal service.

Presently, responsibility for implementing the national policy of equal employment rests in the Civil Service Commission pursuant to Executive Orders 11246 and 11478. Despite some progress in this area, the record is far from satisfactory. Statistical evidence shows that minorities and women continue to be excluded from large numbers of Government jobs. They continue to be excluded from higher level policymaking, supervisory positions.

The transfer of the civil rights enforcement function from the Civil Service Commission to the Equal Employment Opportunity Commission does not preclude the Civil Service Commission from continuing its own equal employment programs. Rather, it is expected that the Civil Service Commission and the Federal agencies will continue their commitment to affirmative measures such as recruiting and training, specialized hiring programs, the training of compliance personnel and supervisory personnel in equal employment, and the appointment of EEO officers. In all cases the primary responsibility will rest with Civil Service Commission and the other Federal agencies. It is expected that the EEOC will work closely with them in the development and maintenance of their various programs. It will, however, perform a useful function in reviewing these new programs.

H.R. 1794 was reported by the Committee on Education and Labor by substantial majority. It is a bill imminently fair in its treatment of the problem. The bill has in the meantime, however, been subject to intensive and often unfair criticisms. Some opponents of the measure have charged that it lacks "due process" procedures as will be evident in the debate. H.R. 1746 contains more meaningful elements of due process than does the substitute which is being urged on the House, H.R. 9247. The committee recognizes, however, that concern exists in the minds of some Members because of the questions raised. To reduce that concern and to remove any doubts that may remain, the committee will undertake some amendments to the measure. Briefly stated, they are:

First. There will be an amendment to impose a 2-year "statute of limitations" on the liability of the employer for back pay or reinstatement.

Second. The second amendment will prohibit the EEOC from imposing quotas or requiring preferential treatment. There is no such provision in the substitute proposal.

Third. The third amendment will require notification within 10 days to the employer, union or employer agency whenever an unlawful employment practice charge is filed with the Commission.

Fourth. The fourth amendment will insure that the informal procedure under the Office of Contract Compliance authority are confidential. Giving publicity to such action will be prohibited and punishable.

These amendments substantially improve the committee bill. We can all be grateful to the distinguished chairman of the subcommittee, the gentleman from Pennsylvania (Mr. DENT), for proposing them.

I urge all my colleagues to support the committee bill as modified by these amendments and to defeat the Erlenborn substitute.

Appendix F-3

House Bill: Erlenborn Substitute Amendment

EDITOR'S NOTE: *Reps. Erlenborn (R., Ill.) and Mazzoli (D., Ky.) proposed a substitute for the committee bill. The Substitute didn't accord EEOC authority to issue cease-and-desist orders but left enforcement up to the federal courts. The substitute also required EEOC to furnish anyone charged with violating the law with a copy of the charge within five days after the filing of the complaint; made actions under the Act the exclusive federal remedy for discrimination; authorized EEOC to seek temporary or preliminary relief pending disposition of charges; limited class action cases to those who were named or who joined; restricted liability in pattern-and-practice suits to two years prior to the filing of a charge; and limited liability with respect to individuals' complainants to 180 days. The Erlenborn amendment was accepted by a vote of 202 to 197.*

House

9-15-71

pp. 8479-8481

Amendment in the nature of a substitute offered by Mr. ERLENBORN: Strike out all after the enacting clause and insert:

That this Act may be cited as the "Equal Employment Opportunity Act of 1971".

SEC. 2. (a) Paragraph (6) of subsection (g) of section 705 of the Civil Rights Act of 1964 (42 U.S.C. 2000e–4(f)(6)) is amended to read as follows:

"(6) to refer matters to the Attorney General with recommendations for intervention in a civil action brought by an aggrieved party under section 706, or for the institution of a civil action by the Attorney General under section 707, and to recommend institution of appellate proceedings in accordance with subsection (h) of this section, when in the opinion of the Commission such proceedings would be in the public interest, and to advise, consult, and assist the Attorney General in such matters.

(b) Subsection (h) of such section 705 is amended to read as follows:

"(h) Attorneys appointed under this section may, at the direction of the Commission, appear for and represent the Commission in any case in court, provided that the Attorney General shall conduct all litigation to which the Commission is a party in the Supreme Court or in the courts of appeals of the United States pursuant to this title. All other litigation affecting the Commission, or to which it is a party, shall be conducted by the Commission."

SEC. 3. (a) Subsection (a) of section 706 of the Civil Rights Act of 1964 (42 U.S.C. 2000e–5) is amended to read as follows:

"(a) Whenever it is charged in writing under oath by a person claiming to be aggrieved, or a written charge has been filed by a member of the Commission where he has reasonable cause to believe a violation of this title has occurred (and such charge sets forth the facts upon which it is based and the person or persons aggrieved) that an employer, employment agency or labor organization has engaged in an unlawful employment practice, the Commission, within five days thereafter, shall furnish such employer, employment agency, or labor organization (hereinafter referred to as the 'respondent') with a copy of such charge and shall make an investigation of such charge, provided that such charge shall not be made public by the Commission. If the Commission shall determine after such investigation, that there is reasonable cause to believe that the charge is true, the Commission shall endeavor to eliminate any such alleged unlawful employment practice by informal methods of conference, conciliation, and persuasion. Nothing said or done during and as a part of such endeavors may be made public by the Commission without the written consent of the parties, or used as evidence in a subsequent proceeding. Any officer or employee of the Commission, who shall make public in any manner whatever any information in violation of this subsection shall be deemed guilty of a misdemeanor and upon conviction thereof shall be fined not more than $1,000 or imprisoned not more than one year.

(b) Subsection (d) of section 706 of the Civil Rights Act of 1964 (42 U.S.C. 2000e–5) is amended to read as follows:

"(d) A charge under subsection (a) shall be filed within one hundred and eighty days after the alleged unlawful employment practice occurred, except that in the case of an unlawful employment practice with respect to which the person aggrieved has followed the procedure set out in subsection (b), such charge shall be filed by the person aggrieved within two hunderd and ten days after the alleged unlawful employment practice occurred, or within thirty days after receiving notice that the State or local agency has terminated the proceedings under the State or local law, whichever is earlier, and a copy of such charge shall be filed by the Commission with the State or local agency. Except as provided in subsections (a) through (d) of this section and in section 707 of this Act, a charge filed hereunder shall be the exclusive remedy of any person claiming to be aggrieved by an unlawful employment practice of an employer, employment agency, or labor organization."

(c) Subsection (e) of section 706 of the Civil Rights Act of 1964 (42 U.S.C. 2000e–5) is amended to read as follows:

"(e) If within thirty days after a charge is filed with the Commission or within thirty days after expiration of any period of reference under subsection (c), the Commission has been unable to obtain voluntary compliance with this Act, the Commission may bring a civil action against the respondent named in the charge: *Provided,* That if the Commission fails to obtain voluntary compliance and fails or refuses to institute a civil action against the respondent named in the charge within one hundred and eighty days from the date of the filing of the charge, a civil action may be brought after such failure or refusal within ninety days against the respondent named in the charge (1) by the person claiming to be aggrieved, or (2) if such charge was filed by a member of the Commission, by any person whom the charge alleges was aggrieved by the alleged unlawful employment practice. Upon application by the complainant and in such circumstances as the court may deem just, the court may appoint an attorney for such complainant and may authorize the commencement of the action without the payment of fees, costs, or security. Upon timely application, the court may, in its discretion, permit the Attorney General to intervene in such civil action if he certifies that the case is of general public importance. Upon request, the court may, in its discretion, stay further proceedings for not more than sixty days pending the termination of State or local proceedings described in subsection (b) or further efforts of the Commission to obtain voluntary compliance."

(d) Subsections (f) through (k) of section 706 of the Civil Rights Act of 1964 (42 U.S.C. 200e–5) are redesignated as subsections (g) through (l), respectively, and the following new selection is added after section 706(e) thereof:

"(f) Whenever a charge is filed with the Commission and the Commission concludes on the basis of a preliminary investigation that prompt judicial action is necessary to carry out the purposes of this Act, the Commission may bring an action for appropriate temporary or preliminary relief pending final disposition of such charge and the court having jurisdiction over such action shall have the authority to grant such temporary or preliminary relief as it deems just and proper: *Provided,* That no temporary restraining order or other preliminary or temporary relief shall be issued absent a showing that substantial and irreparable injury to the aggrieved party will be unavoidable. It shall be the duty of a court having jurisdiction over proceeding under this section to assign cases for hearing at the earliest practicable date and to cause such cases to be in every way expedited."

(e) Subsection (h) of section 706 of the Civil Rights Act of 1964 (42 U.S.C. 2000e–5) as redesignated by this section is amended to read as follows:

"(h) If the court finds that the respondent has intentionally engaged in or is intentionally engaging in an unlawful practice charged in the complaint, the court may enjoin the respondent from engaging in such unlawful employment practice, and order such affirmative action as may be appropriate, which may include reinstatement or hiring of employees, with or without back pay (payable by the employer, employment agency, or labor organization, as the case may be, responsible for the unlawful employment practice). Interim earnings or amounts earnable with reasonable diligence by the person or persons discriminated against shall operate to reduce the back pay otherwise allowable. No order of the court shall require the admission or reinstatement of an individual as a member of a union or the hiring, reinstatement, or promotion of an individual as an employee, or the payment to him of any back pay, if such individual, pursuant to section 706(a) and within the time required by section 706(d), neither filed a charge nor was named in a charge or amendment thereto, or was refused admission, suspended, or expelled or was refused employment or advancement or was suspended or discharged for any reason other than discrimination on account of race, color, religion, sex, or national origin or in violation of section 704(a). No order made hereunder shall include back pay or other liability which has accrued more than two years before the filing of a complaint with said court under this title."

* * *

Mr. ERLENBORN. Mr. Chairman, at this point I think the merits of the amendment that I have just offered as opposed to the merits of the committee bill have been thoroughly debated. I might put this in context by saying that it is probably obvious by now that, while there are other peripheral issues that have been debated today, the outstanding difference between the alternatives before us is what type of enforcement authority should be granted the EEOC. There are those who say that the cease-and-desist approach is much preferable; that the courts cannot do this job of guaranteeing equal opportunity for employment. None of them have addressed themselves to the question that I would ask now, and I hope maybe would be answered before a vote is taken between these two bills and that is: if the courts are so inefficient and unable to grant relief in this area, why is it that over the past many years great strides have been made in the civil rights field primarily through our Federal courts? Why is it that we leave to the Federal courts the right to enforce equal voting rights, the civil rights law, the questions of integration and desegregation, if the courts are so inept?

* * *

Let me explain the other parts of my amendment as I have briefly during general debate.

As to the timely "Service of charges." That is something that should have been in the law originally and, certainly, we should add it now—those who have

charges filed against them should be given timely notice.

So a person bringing an action under this cannot shop around for another forum on which to base another law suit, we would make the Equal Employment Opportunity Act the sole Federal remedy for relief from discriminatory employment practices.

The next item is "Temporary and preliminary relief."

By giving the Commission power to go into court, relief is available at the outset.

The next item is "Class action." To limit class action cases to those who are named or who join.

Limitations on liability: Testimony before the House General Labor Subcommittee by EEOC Chairman Brown established that the position of EEOC is that remedies—including backpay—for discriminatory acts may reach back to the effective date of the act, July 2, 1965. It is not clear that the courts have so held. However, to preclude the threat of enormous backpay liability which could be utilized to coerce employers and labor organizations into surrendering their fundamental rights to a fair hearing and due process, my bill offers a new subsection (h) of section 706 of the Civil Rights Act of 1964 (42 U.S.C. 2000e–5) which limits liability in pattern and practice suits to a period of 2 years prior to the filing of a complaint with said court.

With respect to individual complainants therefore, back pay and other liability is limited to the statutory period for filing, formerly 90 days and extended under this bill to 180 days. The final sentence in subsection (h) which limits back pay orders to 2 years is directed to the pattern and practice suits authorized under section 707.

It is only fair to say that liability should not go back ad infinitum but that there should be some reasonable statute of limitations.

* * *

AMENDMENT

Strike out everything after the enacting clause and insert in lieu thereof the following:

That this Act may be cited as the "Equal Employment Opportunities Enforcement Act".

SEC. 2. Section 701 of the Civil Rights Act of 1964 (78 Stat. 253; 42 U.S.C. 2000e) is amended as follows:

(a) Effective one year after the date of enactment of this Act, strike "twenty-five" wherever it appears therein and insert in lieu thereof "eight".

(b) In subsection (a) insert "governments, governmental agencies, political subdivisions," after "individuals,".

(c) In subsection (b) strike out "a State or political subdivision thereof" and insert in lieu thereof "the District of Columbia".

(d) In subsection (c) strike out "or an agency of a State or political subdivision of a State,".

(e) At the end of subsection (h) insert before the period a comma and the following: "and further includes any governmental industry, business, or activity".

SEC. 3. Section 702 of the Civil Rights Act of 1964 (42 U.S.C. 2000e-1) is amended by striking out "or to an educational institution with respect to the employment of individuals to perform work connected with the educational activities of such institution".

SEC. 4. Section 706 of the Civil Rights Act of 1964 (89 Stat. 259; 42 U.S.C. 2000e-5) is amended to read as follows:

"PREVENTION OF UNLAWFUL EMPLOYMENT PRACTICES

"SEC. 706. (a) The Commission is empowered, as hereinafter provided, to prevent any person from engaging in any unlawful employment practice as set forth in section 703 or 704 of this title.

"(b) Whenever a charge is filed by or on behalf of a person claiming to be aggrieved, or by a member of the Commission, alleging that an employer, employment agency, labor organization, or joint labor-management committee controlling apprenticeship or other training or retraining, including on-the-job training programs has engaged in an unlawful employment practice, the Commission shall serve a copy of the charge on such employer, employment agency, labor organization, or joint labor-management committee (hereinafter referred to as the 'respondent') and shall make an investigation thereof. Charges shall be in writing and shall contain such information and be in such form as the Commission requires. Charges shall not be made public by the Commission. If the Commission determines after such investigation that there is no reason to believe that the charge is true, it shall dismiss the charge and promptly notify the person claiming to be aggrieved and the respondent of its action. If the Commission determines after such investigation that there is reasonable cause to believe that the charge is true, the Commission shall endeavor to eliminate any such alleged unlawful employment practice by informal methods of conference, conciliation, and persuasion. Nothing said or done during and as a part of such informal endeavors may be made public by the Commission, its officers or employees, or used as evidence in a subsequent proceeding without the written consent of the persons concerned. Any person who makes public information in violation of this subsection shall be fined not more than $1,000 or imprisoned not more than one year, or both. The Commission shall make its determination on reasonable cause

as promptly as possible and, as far as practicable, not later than one hundred and twenty days from the filing of the charge or, where applicable under subsection (c) or (d), from the date upon which the Commission is authorized to take action with respect to the charge.

"(c) In the case of a charge filed by or on behalf of a person claiming to be aggrieved alleging an unlawful employment practice occurring in a State, or political subdivision of a State, which has a State or local law prohibiting the unlawful employment practice alleged and establishing or authorizing a State or local authority to grant or seek relief from such practice or to institute criminal proceedings with respect thereto upon receiving notice thereof, the Commission shall take no action with respect to the investigation of such charge before the expiration of sixty days after proceedings have been commenced under the State or local law: *Provided,* That such sixty-day period shall be extended to one hundred and twenty days during the first year after the effective date of such State or local law. If any requirement for the commencement of such proceedings is imposed by a State or local authority other than a requirement of the filing of a written and signed statement of the facts upon which the proceeding is based, the proceeding shall be deemed to have been commenced for the purposes of this subsection at the time such statement is sent by certified mail to the appropriate State or local authority.

"(d) In the case of any charge filed by a member of the Commission alleging an unlawful employment practice occurring in a State or political subdivision of a State which has a State or local law prohibiting the practice alleged and establishing or authorizing a State or local authority to grant or seek relief from such practice or to institute criminal proceedings with respect thereto upon receiving notice thereof the Commission shall, before taking any action with respect to such charge, notify the appropriate State or local officials and, upon request, afford them a reasonable time, but not less than sixty days: *Provided,* That such sixty-day period shall be extended to one hundred and twenty days during the first year after the effective date of such State or local law, unless a shorter period is requested, to act under such State or local law to remedy the practice alleged.

"(e) A charge shall be filed within one hundred eighty days after the alleged unlawful employment practice occurred, except that in a case of an unlawful employment practice with respect to which the person aggrieved has initially instituted proceedings with a State or local agency with authority to grant or seek relief from such practice or to institute criminal proceedings with respect thereto upon receiving notice that the State or local agency has terminated the proceedings under the State or local law, whichever is earlier, and a copy of such charge shall be filed by the Commission with the State or local agency. The Commission shall within ten days of the filing of the charge serve a copy of such charge upon the person against whom the charge is made.

"(f) If the Commission determines after attempting to secure voluntary compliance under subsection (b) that it is unable to secure from the respondent a conciliation agreement acceptable to the Commission and to the person aggrieved, which determination shall not be reviewable in any court, the Commission shall issue and cause to be served upon the respondent a complaint stating the facts upon which the allegation of the unlawful employment practice is based, together with a notice of hearing before the Commission, or a member or agent thereof, at a place therein fixed not less than five days after the serving of such complaint. Related proceedings may be consolidated for hearing. Any member of the Commission who filed a charge in any case shall not participate in a hearing on any complaint arising out of such charge, except as a witness.

"(g) A respondent shall have the right to file an answer to the complaint against him and with the leave of the Commission, which shall be granted whenever it is reasonable and fair to do so, may amend his answer at any time. Respondents and the person aggrieved shall be parties and may appear at any stage of the proceedings, with or without counsel. The Commission may grant such other persons a right to intervene or to file briefs or make oral arguments as amicus curiae of for other purposes, as it considers appropriate. All testimony shall be taken under oath and shall be reduced to writing.

"(h) If the Commission finds that the respondent has engaged in an unlawful employment practice, the Commission shall state its findings of fact and shall issue and cause to be served on the respondent and the person or persons aggrieved by such unlawful employment practice an order requiring the respondent to cease and desist from such unlawful employment practice and to take such affirmative action, including reinstatement or hiring of employees, with or without backpay (payable by the employer, employment agency, or labor organization, as the case may be, responsible for the unlawful employment practice), as will effectuate the policies of this title: *Provided,* That interim earnings or amounts earnable with reasonable diligence by the aggrieved person or persons shall operate to reduce the backpay otherwise allowable: *Provided further,* That no order made hereunder shall include backpay or reinstatement liability which has accrued more than two years before the filing of a charge with the Commission. Such order may further require such respondent to make reports from time to time showing the extent to which he has complied with the order. If the Commission finds that the respondent has not engaged in any unlawful employment practice, the Commission shall state its findings of fact and shall issue and

cause to be served on the respondent and the person or persons alleged in the complaint to be aggrieved an order dismissing the complaint.

"(i) After a charge has been filed and until the record has been filed in court as hereinafter provided, the proceeding may at any time be ended by agreement between th Commission and the parties for the elimination of the alleged unlawful employment practice, approved by the Commission, and the Commission may at any time, upon reasonable notice, modify or set aside, in whole or in part, any finding or order made or issued by it. An agreement approved by the Commission shall be enforceable under subsection (k) and the provisions of that subsection shall be applicable to the extent appropriate to a proceeding to enforce an agreement.

"(j) Findings of fact and orders made or issued under subsection (h) or (i) of this section shall be determined on the record.

"(k) The Commission may petition any United States court of appeals within any circuit wherein the unlawful employment practice in question occurred or wherein the respondent resides or transacts business for the enforcement of its order and for appropriate temporary relief or restraining order, and shall file in the court the record in the proceedings as provided in section 2112 of title 28, United States Code. Upon such filing, the court shall cause notice thereof to be served upon the parties to the proceeding before the Commission, and thereupon shall have jurisdiction of the proceeding and of the question determined therein and shall have power to grant such temporary relief, restraining order, or other order as it deems just and proper, and to make and enter a decree enforcing, modifying, and enforcing as so modified, or setting aside in whole or in part the order of the Commission. No objection that has not been urged before the Commission, its member, or agent shall be considered by the court, unless the failure or neglect to urge such objection shall be excused because of extraordinary circumstances. The findings of the Commission with respect to questions of fact if supported by substantial evidence on the record considered as a whole shall be conclusive. If any party shall apply to the court for leave to adduce additional evidence and shall show to the satisfaction of the court that such additional evidence is material and that there were reasoanble grounds for the failure to adduce such evidence in the hearing before the Commission, its member, or its agent, the court may order such additional evidence to be taken before the Commission, its member, or its agent, and to be made a part of the record. The Commission may modify its findings as to the facts, or make new findings, by reason of additional evidence so taken and filed, and it shall file such modified or new findings, which findings with respect to questions of fact if supported by substantial evidence on the record considered as a whole shall be conclusive, and its recommendations, if any, for the modification or setting aside of its original order. Upon the filing of the record with it the jurisdiction of the court shall be exclusive and its judgment and decree shall be final, except that the same shall be subject to review by the Supreme Court of the United States as provided in section 1254 of title 28, United States Code. Petitions filed under this subsection shall be heard expeditiously.

"(l) Any party aggrieved by a final order of the Commission granting or denying, in whole or in part, the relief sought may obtain a review of such order in any United States court of appeals in the circuit in which the unlawful employment practice in question is alleged to have occurred or in which such party resides or transacts business, or in the Unitd States Court of Appeals for the District of Columbia, by filing in such court a written petition praying that the order of the Commission be modified or set aside. A copy of such petition shall be forthwith transmitted by the clerk of the court to the Commission (and to the other parties to the proceeding before the Commission) and thereupon the Commission shall file in the court the certified record in the proceeding as provided in section 2112 of title 28, United States Code. Upon the filing of such petition, the court shall proceed in the same manner as in the case of an application by the Commission under subsection (k), the findings of the Commission with respect to questions of fact if supported by substantial evidence on the record considered as a whole shall be conclusive, and the court shall have the same jurisdiction to grant such temporary relief or restraining order as it deems just and proper, and in like manner to make and enter a decree enforcing, modifying, and enforcing as so modified, or setting aside in whole or in part the order of the Commission. The commencement of proceedings under this subsection or subsection (k) shall not, unless ordered by the court, operate as a stay of the order of the Commission.

"(m) The provisions of the Act entitled 'An Act to amend the Judicial Code and to define and limit the jurisdiction of courts sitting in equity, and for other purposes', approved March 23, 1932 (47 Stat. 70 et seq.; 29 U.S.C. 101–115), shall not apply with respect to (1) proceedings under subsection (k), (l), or (o) of this section, (2) proceedings under section 707 of this title, or (3) proceedings under section 715 of this title.

"(n) The Attorney General shall conduct all litigation to which the Commission is a party in the Supreme Court of the United States pursuant to this title. All other litigation affecting the Commission, or to which it is a party, shall be conducted by the General Counsel of the Commission.

"(o) Whenever a charge is filed with the Commission pursuant to subsection (b) and the Commission concludes on the basis of a preliminary investigation that prompt judicial action is necessary to preserve the power of the Commission to grant effective relief in the proceeding the Commission may bring an action for appropriate temporary or preliminary relief pending its final disposition of such charge, in the United States district court for any judicial district in the State in which the unlawful employment practice concerned is alleged to have been committed, or the judicial district in which the aggrieved person would have been employed but for the alleged unlawful employment practice, but, if the respondent is not found within any such judicial district, such an action may be brought in the judicial district in which the respondent has his principal office. For purposes of sections 1404 and 1406 of title 28, United States Code, the judicial district in which the respondent has his principal office shall in all cases be considered a judicial district in which such an action might have been brought. Upon the bringing of any such action, the district court shall have jurisdiction to grant such injunctive relief or temporary restraining order as it deems just and proper, notwithstanding any other provision of law. Rule 65 of the Federal Rules of Civil Procedure, except paragraph (a)(2) thereof, shall govern proceedings under this subsection."

SEC. 5. Section 707 of the Civil Rights Act of 1964 (78 Stat. 261; 42 U.S.C. 2000e–6) is amended by adding the following new subsections:

"(c) Any record or paper required by section 709(c) of this title to be preserved or maintained shall be made available for inspection, reproduction, and copying by the Commission, the Attorney General, or his representative, upon demand in writing directed to the person having custody, possession, or control of such record or paper. Unless otherwise ordered by a court of the United States, neither the Commission, the Attorney General, nor his representative shall disclose any record or paper produced pursuant to this title, or any reproduction or copy, except to Congress or any committee thereof, or to a governmental agency, or in the presentation of any case or proceeding before any court or grand jury. The United States district court for the district in which a demand is made or in which a record or paper so demanded is located, shall have jurisdiction to compel by appropriate process the production of such record or paper.

"(d) Effective on the date of enactment of the Equal Employment Opportunities Enforcement Act, the functions of the Attorney General and the Acting Attorney General, as the case may be, under this section shall be transferred to the Commission, together with such personnel, property, records, and unexpended balances of appropriations, allocations, and other funds employed, used, held, available, or to be made available in connection with the functions transferred to the Commission hereby as may be necessary to enable the Commission to carry out its functions pursuant to this subsection, and the Commission shall thereafter carry out such functions in the manner set forth in subsections (e) and (f) of this section.

"(e) In all suits commenced pursuant to this section prior to the date of enactment of the Equal Employment Opportunities Enforcement Act of 1971, proceedings shall continue without abatement, all court orders and decrees shall remain in effect, and the

Commission shall be substituted as a party for the United States of America or the Attorney General or Acting Attorney General, as appropriate.

"(f) Subsequent to the date of enactment of the Equal Employment Opportunities Enforcement Act of 1971, the Commission shall have authority to investigate and act on a charge of a pattern or practice of discrimination, whether filed by or on behalf of a person claiming to be aggrieved or by a member of the Commission: *Provided,* That all such actions shall be in accordance with the procedures set forth in section 706, including the provisions for enforcement and appellate review contained in subsections (k), (l), (m), and (n) thereof."

SEC. 6. Section 709 (b), (c), and (d) of the Civil Rights Act of 1964 (78 Stat. 263; 42 U.S.C. 2000e–8(b)–(b)) are amended to read as follows:

"(b) The Commission may cooperate with State and local agencies charged with the practices laws and, with the consent of such agencies, may, for the purpose of carrying out its functions and duties under this title and within the limitation of funds appropriated specifically for such purpose, engage in and contribute to the cost of research and other projects of mutual interest undertaken by such agencies, and utilize the services of such agencies and their employees and, notwithstanding any other provision of law, may pay by advance or reimbursement such agencies and their employees for services rendered to assist the Commission in carrying out this title. In furtherance of such cooperative efforts, the Commission may enter into written agreements with such State or local agencies and such agreements may include provisions under which the Commission shall refrain from processing a charge in any cases or class of cases specified in such agreements or under which the Commission shall relieve any person or class of persons in such State or locality from requirements imposed under this section. The Commission shall rescind any such agreement whenever it determines that the agreement no longer serves the interest of effective enforcement of this title.

"(c) Every employer, employment agency, and labor organization subject to this title shall (1) make and keep such records relevant to the determinations of whether unlawful employment practices have been or are being committed, (2) preserve such records for such periods, and (3) make such reports therefrom as the Commission shall prescribe by regulation or order, after public hearing, as reasonable, necessary, or appropriate for the enforcement of this title or the regulation or orders thereunder. The Commission shall, by regulations, require each employer, labor organization, and joint labor-management committee subject to this title which controls an apprenticeship or other training program to maintain such records as are reasonably necessary to carry out the purpose of this title, including, but not limited to, a list of applicants who wish to participate in such program, including the chronological order in which such appli-

cants were received, and to furnish to the Commission upon request, a detailed description of the manner in which persons are selected to participate in the apprenticeship or other training program. Any employer, employment agency, labor organization, or joint labor-management committee which believes that the application to it of any regulation or order issued under this section would result in undue hardship may apply to the Commission for an exemption from the application of such regulation or order, and, if such application for an exemption is denied, bring a civil action in the United States district court for the district where such records are kept. If the Commission or the court, as the case may be, finds that the application of the regulation or order to the employer, employment agency, or labor organization in question would impose an undue hardship, the Commission or the court, as the case may be, may grant appropriate relief. If any person required to comply with the provisions of this subsection fails or refuses to do so, the United States district court for the district in which such person is found, resides or transacts business, shall, upon application of the Commission, have jurisdiction to issue to such person an order requiring him to comply.

"(d) In prescribing requirements pursuant to subsection (c) of this section, the Commission shall consult with other interested State and Federal agencies and shall endeavor to coordinate its requirements with those adopted by such agencies. The Commission shall furnish, upon request and without cost to any State or local agency charged with the administration of a fair employment practice law, information obtained pursuant to subsection (c) of this section from any employer, employment agency, labor organization, or joint labor-management committee subject to the jurisdiction of such agency. Such information shall be furnished on condition that it not be made public by the recipient agency prior to the institution of a proceeding under State or local law involving such information. If this condition is violated by a recipient agency, the Commission may decline to honor subsequent requests pursuant to this subsection."

SEC. 7. Section 710 of the Civil Rights Act of 1964 (78 Stat. 264; 42 U.S.C. 2000e–9) is amended to read as follows:

"INVESTIGATORY POWERS

"SEC. 710. For the purpose of all hearings and investigations conducted by the Commission or its duly authorized agents or agencies, section 11 of the National Labor Relations Act (49 Stat. 455; 29 U.S.C. 161) shall apply: *Provided,* That no subpena shall be issued on the application of any party to proceedings before the Commission until after the Commission has issued and caused to be served upon the respondent a complaint and notice of hearing under subsection (f) of section 706."

SEC. 8. (a) Section 703(a)(2) of the Civil Rights Act of 1964 (78 Stat. 255; 42 U.S.C. 2000e–2(a)(2)) is amended by inserting the words "or applicants for employment" after the words "his employees".

(b) Section 703(c)(2) of such Act (78 Stat. 255; 42 U.S.C. 2000e–2(c)(2)) is amended by inserting the words "or applicants for membership" after the word "membership".

(c) Section 703(h) of such Act (78 Stat. 257; 42 U.S.C. 2000e–2(h)) is amended by striking out "to give and to act upon the results of any professionally developed ability test provided that such test, its administration or action upon the results is not designed, intended, or used to discriminate because of race, color, religion, sex, or national origin" and inserting in lieu thereof the following: "to give and to act upon the results of any professionally developed ability test which is directly related to the determination of bona fide occupational qualifications reasonably necessary to perform the normal duties of the particular position concerned: *Provided,* That such test, its administration, or action upon the results is not designed, intended, or used to discriminate because of race, color, religion, sex, or national origin."

(d)(1) Section 704(a) of such Act (78 Stat. 256; 42 U.S.C. 2000e–3(a)) is amended by inserting "or joint labor-management committee controlling apprenticeship or other training or retraining, including on-the-job training programs," after "employment agency" in section 704(a).

(2) Section 704(b) of such Act is amended by (A) striking out "or employment agency" and inserting in lieu thereof "employment agency, or joint labor-management committee controlling apprenticeship or other training or retraining, including on-the-job training programs,", and (B) inserting a comma and the words "or relating to admission to, or employment in, any program established to provide apprenticeship or other training by such a joint labor-management committee" before the word "indicating".

(e)(1) The second sentence of section 705(a) (78 Stat. 258; 42 U.S.C. 2000e–4(a)) is amended by inserting before the period at the end thereof a comma and the following: "and all members of the Commission shall continue to serve until their successors are appointed and qualified: *Provided,* That no such member of the Commission shall continue to serve (1) for more than sixty days when the Congress is in session unless a nomination to fill such vacancy shall have been submitted to the Senate, or (2) after the adjournment sine die of the session of the Senate in which such nomination was submitted".

(2) The fourth sentence of section 705(a) of such Act is amended to read as follows: "The Chairman shall be responsible on behalf of the Commission for the administrative operations of the Commission, and shall appoint, in accordance with the provisions of title 5, United States Code, governing appointments in the competitive service, such officers, agents, attorneys, hearing examiners, and employees as he deems necessary to assist it in the performance of its functions and to fix their compensation in accordance with the provisions of chapter 51 and subchapter III of chapter 53 of title 5, United States Code, relating to classification and General Schedule pay rates: *Provided,* That assignment, removal, and compensation of hearing examiners shall be in accordance with sections 3105, 3344, 5362, and 7521 of title 5, United States Code."

(f) Section 705(g)(1) of such Act (78 Stat. 258; 42 U.S.C. 2000e–4(g)(1)) is amended by inserting before the semicolon at the end thereof the following: "and to accept voluntary and uncompensated services, notwithstanding the provisions of section 3679(b) of the Revised Statutes (31 U.S.C. 665(b))".

(g) Section 705(g)(6) of such Act (78 Stat. 259; 42 U.S.C. 2000e–4(g)(6)) is amended by striking out "section 706" and inserting in lieu thereof "section 715".

(h) Section 713 of such Act (78 Stat. 265; 42 U.S.C. 2000e–12) is amended by adding at the end thereof the following new subsections:

"(c) Except for the powers granted to the Commission under subsection (h) of section 706, the power to modify or set aside its findings, or make new findings, under subsections (i) and (k) of section 706, the rule-making power as defined in subchapter II of chapter 5 of title 5, United States Code, with reference to general rules as distinguished from rules of specific applicability, and the power to enter into or rescind agreements with State and local agencies, as provided in subsection (b) of section 709, under which the Commission agrees to refrain from processing a charge in any cases or class of cases or under which the Commission agrees to relieve any person or class of persons in such State or locality from requirements imposed by section 709, the Commission may delegate any of its functions, duties, and powers to such person or persons as the Commission may designate by regulation, including functions, duties, and powers with respect to investigating, conciliating, hearing, determining, ordering, certifying, reporting, or otherwise acting as to any work, business, or matter: *Provided,* That nothing in this subsection authorizes the Commission to provide for persons other than those referred to in clauses (2) and (3) of subsection (b) of section 556 of title 5 of the United States Code to conduct any hearing to which that section applies.

"(d) The Commission is authorized to delegate to any group of three or more members of the Commission any or all of the powers which it may itself exercise."

(i) Section 714 of such Act (78 Stat. 265; 42 U.S.C. 2000e–13) is amended by striking out "section 111" and inserting in lieu thereof "sections 111 and 1114".

(j) Section 715 of such Act (78 Stat. 265; 42 U.S.C. 2000e–14) is amended to read as follows:

"CIVIL ACTIONS BY PERSONS AGGRIEVED

"SEC. 715. (a) (If (1) the Commission determines that there is no reasonable cause to believe the charge is true and dismisses the charge in accordance with section 706(b),

(2) finds no probable jurisdiction and dismisses the charge, or (3) within one hundred and eightly days after a charge is filed with the Commission, or within one hundred and eighty days after expiration of any period of reference under section 706(c) or (d), the Commission has not either (i) issued a complaint in accordance with section 706(f), (ii) determined that there is not reasonable cause to believe the charge is true and dismissed the charge in accordance with setcion 796(b) or found no probable jurisdiction and dismissed the charge, or (iii) entered into a conciliation agreement acceptable to the Commission and to the person aggrieved in accordance with section 706(f), or an agreement with the parties in accordance with section 706(i), the Commission shall so notify the person aggrieved and within sixty days after the giving of such notice a civil action may be brought against the respondent named in the charge (1) by the person claiming to be aggrieved, or (2) if such charge was filed by a member of the Commission, by any person whom the charge alleges was aggrieved by the alleged unlawful employment practice. Upon application by the complainant and in such circumstances as the court may deem just, the court may appoint an attorney for such complainant and may authorize the commencement of the action without the payment of fees, costs, or security. Upon timely application, the court may, in its discretion, permit the Commission to intervene in such civil action if it certifies that the case is of general public importance. Upon the commencement of such civil action, the Commission shall be divested of jurisdiction over the proceeding and shall take no further action with respect thereto: *Provided,* That, upon request, the court may, in its discretion, stay further proceedings for not more than sixty days pending termination of State or local proceedings described in subsection (c) or (d) or the efforts of the Commission to obtain voluntary compliance.

"(b) Each United States district court and each United States court of a place subject to the jurisdiction of the United States shall have jurisdiction of actions brought under this section. Such an action may be brought in any judicial district in the State in which the unlawful employment practice is alleged to have been committed, or in the judicial district in which the plaintiff would have been employed but for the alleged unlawful employment practice, but if the respondent is not found within any such district, such an action may be brought within the judicial district in which the respondent has his principal office. For purposes of sections 1404 and 1406 of title 28 of the United States Code, the judicial district in which the respondent has his principal office shall in all cases be considered a district in which the action might have been brought. Upon the bringing of any such action, the district court shall have jurisdiction to grant such temporary or preliminary relief as it deems just and proper.

"(c) If the court finds that the respondent has intentionally engaged in or is intentionally engaging in an unlawful employment practice charged in the complaint, the court may enjoin the respondent from engaging in such unlawful employment practice, and order such affirmative action as may be appropriate, which may include reinstatement or hiring of employees, with or without backpay (payable by the employer, employment agency, or labor organization, as the case may be, responsible for the unlawful employment practice). No order made hereunder shall include backpay or reinstatement liability which has accrued more than two years before the filing of a charge with the Commission. Interim earnings or amounts earnable with reasonable diligence by the person or persons discriminated against shall operate to reduce the backpay otherwise allowable. No order of the court shall require the admission or reinstatement of an individual as a member of a union or the hiring, reinstatement, or promotion of an individual as an employee, or the payment to him of any backpay, if such individual was refused admission, suspended, or expelled or was refused employment or advancement or was suspended or discharged for any reason other than discrimination on account of race, color, religion, sex, or national origin or in violation of section 704(a).

"(d) In any case in which an employer, employment agency, or labor organization fails to comply with an order of a court issued in a civil action brought under subsection (a), the Commission may commence proceedings to compel compliance with such order.

"(e) Any civil action brought under subsection (a) and any proceedings brought under subsection (d) shall be subject to appeal as provided in sections 1291 and 1292 of title 28, United States Code.

"(f) In any action or proceeding under this section, the court, in its discretion, may allow the prevailing plaintiff a reasonable attorney's fee as part of the costs."

SEC. 9. (a) Section 5314 of title 5 of the United States Code is amended by adding at the end thereof the following new clause:

"(55) Chairman, Equal Employment Opportunity Commission."

(b) Clause (72) of section 5315 of such title is amended to read as follows:

"(72) Members, Equal Employment Opportunity Commission (4)."

(c) Clause (111) of section 5316 of such title is repealed.

SEC. 10. Sections 706 and 710 of the Civil Rights Act of 1964, as amended by this Act, shall not be applicable to charges filed with the Commission prior to the effective date of this Act.

SEC. 11. Title VII of the Civil Rights Act of 1964 (78 Stat. 253; 42 U.S.C. 2000e et seq.) is amended by adding at the end thereof the following new sections:

"NONDISCRIMINATION IN FEDERAL GOVERNMENT EMPLOYMENT

"SEC. 717. (a) All personnel actions affecting employees or applicants for employment in the competitive service (as defined in section 2102 of title 5 of the United States Code) or employees or applicants for employment in positions with the District of Columbia government covered by the Civil Service Retirement Act shall be made free from any discrimination based on race, color, religion, sex, or national origin.

"(b) The Equal Employment Opportunity Commission shall have authority to enforce the provision of subsection (a) and shall issue such rules, regulations, orders, and instructions as it deems necessary and appropriate to carry out its responsibilities hereunder, and the head of each executive department and agency and the appropriate officers of the District of Columbia shall comply with such rules, regulations, orders, and instructions: *Provided,* That such rules and regulations shall provide that an employee or applicant for employment shall be notified of any final action taken on any complaint filed by him hereunder.

"(c) Within thirty days of receipt of notice given under subsection (b), the employee or applicant for employment, if aggrieved by the final disposition of his complaint, may file a civil action as provided in section 715, in which civil action the head of the executive department or agency, or the District of Columbia, as appropriate, shall be the respondent.

"(d) The provisions of section 715 shall govern civil actions brought hereunder.

"(e) All functions of the Civil Service Commission which the Director of the Bureau of the Budget determines relate to nondiscrimination in government employment are transferred to the Equal Employment Opportunity Commission.

"(f) All authority, functions, and responsibilities vested in the Secretary of Labor pursuant to Executive Order 11246 relating to nondiscrimination in employment by Government contractors and subcontractors and nondiscrimination in federally assisted construction contracts are transferred to the Equal Employment Opportunity Commission together with such personnel, property, records, and unexpended balances of appropriations, allocations, and other funds employed, used, held, available or to be made available in connection with the functions transferred to the Commission hereby as may be necessary to enable the Commission to carry out its functions pursuant to this subsection, and the Commission shall hereafter carry out all such authority, functions, and responsibilities pursuant to such order. The Commission shall be prohibited from imposing or requiring a quota or preferential treatment with respect to numbers of employees, or percentage of employees of any race, color, religion, sex, or national origin. The provisions of section 706(b) with respect to nondisclosure of information shall be applicable in the carrying out of this subsection.

"EFFECT UPON OTHER LAW

"SEC. 718. Nothing contained in this Act shall relieve any Government agency or official of its or his primary responsibility to assure nondiscrimination in employment as required by the Constitution, statutes, and Executive orders."

SEC. 12. New section 717, added by section 11 of this Act, shall become effective six months after the date of enactment of this Act.

Appendix F-4

Senate Bill: In General

EDITORS' NOTE: *Sen. Williams (D., N.J.) outlined the provisions of the committee bill (S. 2551) and placed in the record a comparison of Title VII as originally enacted and the changes proposed in both the House and Senate Bills.*

Senate

1-19-72

pp. 85-97

Mr. WILLIAMS. * * *

The bill, as reported by the committee, provides for significant revisions in the primary enforcement mechanisms of title VII. The Commission would continue to seek voluntary resolution of disputes, but if conciliation efforts were unsuccessful, the Commission would be authorized to issue complaints, hold hearings, and where unlawful employment practices are found, issue appropriate orders subject to review by the courts of appeal. Upon petition by either the Commission, the respondent, or the person alleged to be aggrieved, a court of appeals may enter an order enforcing, modifying, or setting aside the order of the Commission. The committee bill requires that petitions for review must be filed within 60 days of the Commission's order. This avoids the burdensome experience encountered by the NLRB, which alone among all regulatory agencies, does not possess authority to issue orders that are in some measure self-enforcing. I might note that the procedure in this bill is similar to that contained in the Occupational Health and Safety Act and last year's equal employment opportunity bill, S. 2453.

The committee has taken pains to see that the rights of all parties to EEOC proceedings are protected. The Commission has to give respondents notice of the charges within 10 days. The right to a hearing on the record before a disinterested trial examiner is specifically provided for, and all proceedings must be conducted in accordance with the Administrative Procedure Act. Interested persons may intervene or appear as amicus curiae, and all parties to proceedings before the Commission may take part in any review in the court of appeals. Finally, provision is made for review by the U.S. Supreme Court as provided in 28 U.S.C. 1254.

During the committee deliberations, the Senator from Ohio (Mr. TAFT) suggested that the administrative procedures adopted in this bill would be strengthened by the addition of a statutory general counsel to insure the maximum in independence and separation of functions.

Last year when this bill was before us in the Senate, a separation proposal was offered as an amendment. As manager of the bill, I accepted the proposal during the floor debate. When the suggestion was made by the Senator from Ohio in committee I indicated that I would be amenable to such an amendment.

It is my understanding that the amendment will be offered, and again that will be the position of the manager of the bill when it is offered. An exchange of correspondence between the Senator from Ohio and me will be included as a part of the RECORD today. I believe that request already has been made.

The bill also contains provision for individual recourse to the Federal district courts if the Commission dismisses a charge, or if it has not issued a complaint or entered into a conciliation agreement agreeable to the parties within 60 days after filing of a charge. Under certain circumstances, the private right of action would also obtain if the Commission has issued a complaint but taken no action on it for 6 months. In any event, duplication of proceedings is avoided by termination of one at the commencement of the other. For example, if an individual should perfect and exercise his title VII right of court action, the Commission would thenceforth be divested of jurisdiction over the matter. Likewise, if the Commission issued a complaint and proceeded with reasonable speed, its jurisdiction would remain exclusive prior to the institution of enforcement or review proceedings in the court of appeals. The committee concluded that this scheme would protect

aggrieved persons from undue delay, as well as prevent respondents from being subject to dual proceedings.

Several other significant changes were made in the statute's enforcement provisions. First, the authority of the Attorney General to institute court actions directed at "patterns or practices" of resistance to the act would be transferred to the Commission after 2 years, with the Commission having concurrent jurisdiction to issue such complaints during the 2-year period. The broad scale actions against any "pattern or practice" of discrimination that have been brought by the Justice Department under section 707 of the act have been an integral and important part of the overall Federal effort to combat discrimination. It is the committee's view that with the enactment of legislation providing the Commission with effective power to enforce title VII, the further retention of section 707 power in the Department of Justice is not necessary.

Moreover, employees would benefit by having to look to only one agency to obtain relief; employers similarly would be free from the burden of multiple investigations, examining their employment policies and personnel records in response to similar or identical complaints filed with different agencies. Second, the Secretary of Labor's responsibilities for Federal contract compliance under Executive Order 11246, as amended, are transferred to the Commission. As I have stated in connection with the pattern and practice transfer, the basic purpose of this consolidation is to enable the Federal Government, through the procedures of the Commission, to pursue a unified program of attack upon all elements of employment discrimination.

Unlike the Department of Justice program, however, the contract compliance effort has not been a notable success. It should be an important and viable tool in the Government's efforts to achieve equal employment opportunity. The transfer to the Commission will enable it to operate in a fresh atmosphere within an agency that has equal employment opportunity as its sole priority.

The bill also makes a number of changes in the coverage of the act. Title VII's jurisdiction is expanded after 1 year from enactment to reach employers and unions with eight or more employees and members; it is also extended to State and local governments, and educational institutions. The extension of coverage to employees of State and local governments was accompanied by a special enforcement procedure which provides that the Commission refer the case to the Attorney General for filing of a civil action against the respondent in the appropriate U.S. district court. During discussion in the committee, several members expressed concern that States and political subdivisions would be subjected to administrative hearings and orders of EEOC. This enforcement scheme was devised to provide the necessary power to achieve results without the needless friction that might be created by a Federal executive agency issuing orders to sovereign States and their localities.

The Civil Service Commission is given added responsibilities for insuring equal employment opportunities for Federal employees. These employees are also given a right to bring actions in the Federal courts if they are not satisfied with the Civil Service Commission's actions. All of these changes are intended to provide a more universal and effective application of the national policy against job discrimination.

The bill would make a number of other changes in title VII involving filing requirements for charges, Commission organization, terms and compensation of members, and revision of the recordkeeping requirements of section 709(d) to lessen the duplicatory effect of overlapping Federal and State regulations. The investigations language of section 11 of the National Labor Relations Act has also been incorporated to complement the new enforcement authority bestowed on the Commission.

The entire committee worked hard at reporting a comprehensive bill. Throughout consideration of this legislation, there was a unanimity of views that enforcement powers were needed for the Commission.

The only significant area of disagreement was whether this enforcement power should be through a Commission lawsuit in a U.S. district court, or by an administrative proceeding followed by a cease-and-desist order, with a review in the appropriate U.S. court of appeals. The committee carefully considered both of these approaches, both of these possibilities, but decided to adopt the cease-and-desist approach.

Several other constructive changes were made in the bill during committee deliberations. For example, the provisions strengthening the equal employment program for Federal Government employees represents an approach developed by the Senator from Colorado (Mr. DOMINICK), with the cooperation of the Civil Service Commission, and the special enforcement provision for State and local governments was very carefully worked out by the Senator from Missouri (Mr. EAGLETON), and, here again, the Senator from Ohio (Mr. TAFT).   * * *

Appendix F-5

Senate Bill: Section-by-Section Analysis

EDITORS' NOTE: *Sen. Williams (D., N.J.) placed in the Record a section-by-section analysis of S. 2515 as amended.*

Senate

2-22-72

pp. 2298-2302

SECTION-BY-SECTION ANALYSIS OF S. 2515, THE EQUAL EMPLOYMENT OPPORTUNITIES ACT OF 1972

The following analysis seeks to explain the major provisions of S. 2515, the Equal Employment Opportunities Act of 1972, as amended by the Senate during its debate on the bill. These explanations, which reflect the changes adopted by the Senate from the original bill as reported by the Committee, encompass the enforcement provisions of Title VII as now adopted by the Senate and the various procedural and jurisdictional changes which are also encompassed the within provisions of S. 2515.

In any area where the new law does not address itself, or in any areas where a specific contrary intention is not indicated, it is assumed that the present case law as developed by the courts shall continue to determine the applicability of Title VII. It is also the intent of this legislation to remedy deficiencies in the current law.

SECTION 2

This section amends certain definitions contained in section 701 of the Civil Rights Act of 1964.

Section 701(a)—This subsection defines "person" as used in Title VII. Under the provisions of S. 2515, the term is now expanded to include State and local governments, governmental agencies, and political subdivisions.

Section 701(b)—This subsection defines the term "employer" as used in Title VII. This subsection would now include, within the meaning of the term "employer", all State and local governments, governmental agencies, and political subdivisions, and the District of Columbia departments or agencies (except those subject by statute to the procedures of the Federal competitive service as defined in 5 U.S.C. § 2102, who along with all other Federal employees would now be covered by section 717 of the Act).

This subsection would extend coverage of the term "employer", one year after enactment, to those employers with 15 or more employees. The standard for determining the number of employees of an employer, i.e. "employees for each working day in each of 20 or more calendar weeks in the current or preceding calendar year," would apply immediately upon enactment to all employers of 25 or more employees during the first year, as well as to the final coverage of 15 or more employees thereafter.

Section 701(c)—This subsection eliminates the exemption for agencies of the United States, States, or the political subdivisions of States from the definition of "employment agency" in order to conform with the expanded coverage of State and local governments in section 701 (a) and (b) above, State agencies, previously covered by reference to the United States Employment Service, continue to be covered as employment agencies.

Section 701(e)—This subsection is revised to include labor organizations with 15 or more members within the coverage of Title VII, one year after the enactment of the present bill.

Section 701(f)—This subsection is intended to exclude from the definition of "employee" as used in Title VII those persons elected to public office in any State or political subdivision of any State by the qualified voters of such State or political subdivision. An additional exemption from the definition of "employee" is also provided for persons chosen by such officers as personal assistants or as immediate advisors in respect to the exercise of the Constitutional or legal powers of the office held by such elected officer. This exemption is intended to be read very narrowly and is in no way intended to establish an overall narrowing of the expanded coverage of State and local governmental employees as set forth in section 701(a) and (b) above.

Section 701(j)—This subsection, which is new, defines "religion" to include all aspects of religious observance, practive and belief, so as to prohibit discrimination against employees whose "religion" requires observances, practices and beliefs which differ from the employer's or potential employer's norm. Discrimination on this basis would be unlawful unless an employer can demonstrate that he cannot reasonably accomodate beliefs without undue hardship on the conduct of his business.

SECTION 3

This section amends the exemptions allowed in section 702 of the Civil Rights Act of 1964.

Section 702—This section is amended to eliminate the exemption for employees of educational institutions. Under the provisions of this section, all private and public educational institutions, which are not religious educational institutions, would now be covered under the provisions of Title VII. With the elimination of the exemption, the employment practices of such institutions most of which have previously been covered by other relevant state and federal laws, would now be expected to conform to the standards of equal employment opportunity as established under Title VII, and employment practices such as hiring, promotion, transfer, and termination would be subject to strict equal employment standards.

The exemption in this section for religious corporations, associations, educational institutions, or societies to allow such entities to employ individuals of a particular religion to perform work connected with the particular corporation, association, educational institution or society, has been broadened to allow such religious preference regardless of the particular job which the individual is being considered.

SECTION 4(a)

This section of the bill contains the major provisions for the enforcement functions which are provided to the EEOC for the prevention of unlawful employment practices. S. 2515 revises the present section 706 of Title VII of the Civil Rights Act of 1964 to enable the EEOC to process a charge of employment discrimination through the investigation and conciliation stages of voluntary compliance. In addition, however, the provisions or S. 2515 provide that if such should prove unsuccessful, then the EEOC would be empowered to file an action against the respondent in the appropriate Federal District Court.

The accomplishment of the stated purpose of Title VII, the elimination of employment discrimination in all areas of employment in this Nation, has not been accomplished under the present system of voluntary compliance through EEOC procedures or, in the alternative, the private law suit. Under the provisions of section 4 of the bill, the overriding public interest in equal employment opportunity would be asserted through direct Federal enforcement. Accordingly, this section amends sections 706(a) through (g) of the Civil Rights Act of 1964.

Section 706(a)—This subsection would empower the Commission to prevent persons from engaging in unlawful employment practices under sections 703 and 704 of Title VII of the Civil Rights Act of 1964. As these noted sections remain largely unchanged, the unlawful employment practices which were enumerated in 1964 in the original Act, and as defined and expanded by the courts in litigation since that time, and by these amendments, remain in effect.

Section 706(b)—This subsection sets out the procedures to be followed when a charge of an unlawful employment practice is filed with the Commission. The present requirement that charges must be in writing and under oath or affirmation has been retained. In order to accord respondents fair notice that charges are pending against them, this subsection provides that the Commission must serve a notice of the charge on the respondent within ten days; further, the Commission would be expected to investigate the charge as quickly as possible and to make its determination on whether there is reasonable cause to believe that the charge is true. It is not intended that failure to give notice of the charge to the respondent within ten days should prejudice the rights of the aggrieved party.

If the Commission finds no reasonable cause, it must dismiss the charge; if it finds reasonable cause, it must attempt to conciliate the case. During the Commission's investigation of the charge, the allegations would not be made public by the Commission, and if it finds that there is not reasonable cause to believe that the charge is true, it shall dismiss the charge and notify the complainant and the respondent of its decision.

This subsection also makes a number of other changes in existing law:

1. Under present law, a charge may be filed only by a person aggrieved under oath or by a member of the Commission where that member has reasonable cause to believe a violation has occurred. This subsection would permit a charge to be filed under oath or affirmation by or on behalf of a person aggrieved, or by an officer or employee of the Commission upon the request of a person claiming to be aggrieved. The purpose of this provision would enable aggrieved persons to have charges processed under circumstances where they are unwilling to come forward publicly for fear of economic or physical reprisals. In this connection, it is intended that the device of a Commission charge may be used to maintain the confidential identity of the persons aggrieved and that no disclosure need be made of the identity of person aggrieved.

2. The Commission would be required to make its determination on reasonable cause as promptly as possible and, "so far as practicable," within 120 days from the filing of the charge or from the date upon which the Commission is authorized to act on the charge under section 706(c) or (d). The Commission, where appropriate, would be required in its determination of reasonable cause to accord substantial weight to final findings and orders made by State or local authorities under State and local laws.

3. This subsection and section 8(c) of the bill add appropriate provisions to carry out the intent of the present statute to provide full coverage for joint labor-management committees controlling apprenticeship or other training or retraining, including on-the-job training programs. While these joint labor-management committees are prohibited under section 703(d) of the present act from discriminating, they were not expressly included in the prohibition against discriminatory advertising or retaliation against persons participating in Commission proceedings (sec. 704(a) and (b)) or in the procedures for filing changes in section 706(a).

Section 706(c)—This subsection retains the present requirement that the Commission defer for a period of 60 days to State or local agencies which have a State or local law prohibiting the unlawful employment practice alleged and establishing or authorizing a State or local authority to grant or seek relief from such practice or to institute criminal proceedings with respect thereto (this period for deferral is 120 days during the first year after the effective date of such law).

The present law is changed by deleting the phrase "no charge may be filed" with the Commission by an aggrieved person in such State or locality until the deferral period has expired. The present law is somewhat unclear respecting the nature of Commission action on charges filed with it prior to resort to the State or local agency. The new language clarifies the present law by permitting a charge to be filed but prohibiting the Commission from taking any action with respect thereto until the prescribed deferral period has elapsed (see a similar holding by the Supreme Court in *Love* v. *Pullman Co.* decided on January 17, 1972 (No. 70–5033), where the Court held that a complaint filed with the Commission, then orally deferred to the State agency for the required deferral period, and then reactivated automatically after the deferral period had expired was proper procedure under the provisions of § 706(b) and (d) of the present Act.

Section 706(d).—This subsection requires deferral to State or local anti-discrimination agencies, similar to provisions contained in subsection 703(c), in the case of charges filed by an officer or employee of the Commission.

Section 706(e).—This subsection sets forth the time limits controlling certain actions by the Commission under the provisions of the bill.

Under the present law, charges must be filed within 90 days after an alleged unlawful employment practice has occurred. In cases where the Commsision defers to a State or local agency under the provisions of section 706(c) or (d), the charge must presently be filed within 30 days after the person aggrieved receives notice that the State or local agency has terminated its proceedings, or within 210 days after the alleged unlawful employment practice occurred, whichever is earlier.

The amendments to this subsection would now provide that charges be filed within 180 days of the alleged unlawful employment practice, a limitation period similar to that contained in the Labor Management Relations Act, as amended (29 U.S.C. § 160(b)). In establishing the new time period for the filing of charges, it is not intended that existing law, which has shown an inclination to interpret this type of time limitation to give the aggrieved person the maximum benefit of the law, should be in any way circumscribed. Existing case law which has determined that certain types of violations are continuing in nature, thereby measuring the running of the required time period from the last occurrence of the discrimination and not from the first occurrence is continued, and other interpretations of the courts maximizing the coverage of the law are not affected. It is intended by expanding the time period for filing charges in this subsection that aggrieved individuals, who frequently are untrained laymen who are not always aware of the discrimination which is practiced against them, should be given a greater opportunity to prepare their charges and file their complaints, and that existent but undiscovered acts of discrimination should not escape the effect of the law through a procedural oversight.

Similarly, the time period allowing a determination by a State or local anti-discrimination agency has been extended to 300 days after the alleged unlawful employment practice occurred or within 30 days after the State or local agency has terminated proceedings under the State or local law, whichever is earlier.

This subsection also requires that notice of the charge be served on the respondent within 10 days after its having been filed.

Section 706(f).—This subsection, which is new, sets forth the procedures to be followed, in those cases where the Commission is unable to achieve a satisfactory conciliation after a finding of reasonable cause, for securing compliance with the provisions of Title VII. The procedures set forth in this subsection are intended to place the primary responsibility for enforcing violations of Title VII in the Commission and to shift them from the private plaintiff where they have been under the existing provisions of title VII.

Section 706(f)(1)—Under this subparagraph, if the Commission is unable to secure a conciliation agreement pursuant to section 706(b) that is acceptable to the Commission within 30 days from the filing of the charge or within 30 days after expiration of any period of reference under subsection (c) or (d), it would promptly so notify the General Counsel who may bring a civil action against the respondent in the appropriate district court, if the respondent is not a government, governmental agency, or political subdivision.

In the case of a respondent that is a government, governmental agency, or political subdivision, if conciliation fails, the Commission will take no further action and will refer the case to the Attorney General who may bring a civil action in the appropriate district court.

With respect to cases arising under this subsection, if the Commission: (a) has dismissed the charge, or (b) 150 days have elapsed from the filing of the charge or period of reference to State agencies under subsection 706 (c) or (d), whichever is later, without the General Counsel or the Attorney General, as the case may be, having issued a complaint under section 706(f), or without the Commission having entered into a conciliation agreement to which the person aggrieved is a party, the person aggrieved may bring an action in the appropriate district court within 90 days after being notified thereof. Such civil actions are to be governed by sections 706 (f) through (k) as applicable. In providing this provision, it is intended that the individual who has been aggrieved by a violation of Title VII should not be forced to abandon his claim merely because of a decision by the agency that there is insufficient grounds upon which to file a complaint in court or that the person aggrieved should have to endure lengthy delays if the agency does not act with due diligence and speed. Accordingly, the provisions described above would allow the person aggrieved to elect to pursue his or her own remedy in the courts where agency action does not prove satisfactory.

In providing this remedy, it is intended that recourse to this form of remedy will be the exception and not the rule, and that the vast majority of complaints will be handled through the offices of the EEOC. However, as the individual's rights to redress are paramount under the provisions of Title VII, it is necessary that all avenues of relief be left open for quick and effective relief.

In providing for the individual right to sue in the event that action by the Commission is unsatisfactory or unresponsive, it is not intended that duplication of proceedings should be allowed. Therefore, in any proceeding where the General Counsel or the Attorney General, as the case may be, is proceeding with due diligence within the time limits specified in this subsection, the person aggrieved would be precluded from instituting an individual action until such time as one of the specific conditions of this subsection are not met.

In any such complaint brought by the person named in the charge as claiming to be aggrieved or in the case of a charge filed by an officer or employee of the Commission, by any person whom the charge alleges was aggrieved by the alleged unlawful employment practice, the court may upon timely application of the complainant, appoint an attorney and authorize the commencement of the action without the payment of fees, costs, or security in such circumstances as it deems just. The Attorney General or the General Counsel, upon timely application and subject to the court's discretion, may intervene in such a private action if he certifies that the private action is of general public importance. In addition, the court is given discretion to stay proceedings for not more than 60 days pending the termination of State or local proceedings or efforts by the Commission to obtain voluntary compliance.

In establishing the enforcement provisions under this subsection and subsection 706(f) generally, it is not intended that any of the provisions contained therein are designed to affect the present use of class action lawsuits under Title VII in conjunction with Rule 23 of the Federal Rules of Civil Procedure. The courts have been particularly congizant of the fact that claims under Title VII involve the vindication of a major public interest, and that any action under the Act involves considerations beyond those raised by the individual claimant. As a consequence, the leading cases in this area to date have recognized that Title VII claims are necessarily class action complaints and that, accordingly, it is not necessary that each individual entitled to relief under the claim be named in the original charge or in the claim for relief.

Section 706(f)(2)—This subsection provides a procedure by which the General Counsel or the Attorney General in a case involving a government, governmental agency, or political subdivision, could secure a three-judge court to hear and determine an action brought by him under this section, if such request is accompanied by a certificate that the case is of general public importance. The chief judge of the court is responsible for appointing the three-judge court. Cases are to be expedited in every way, and appeals from the three-judge court are to be appealed directly to the Supreme Court.

Section 706(f)(3) and 706(f)(4)—Under these paragraphs, if a three-judge court is not requested, the chief judge is required to designate a district judge to hear the case. If no judge is available, then the chief judge of the circuit assigns the judge. Cases are to be heard at the earliest parcticable date and expedited in every way.

Section 706(f)(5)—This subsection authorizes the Comission or the Attorney General in a case involving a government, governmental agency or political subdivision based upon a preliminary inevstigation of a charge filed, to bring an action for appropriate temporary or preliminary relief, pending the final disposition of the charge. Such actions are to be assigned for hearing at the earliest possible date and expedited in every way.

Section 706(g)(1)—This subsection, which is the same as the present section 706(f) of the Act, grants the district courts jurisdiction over actions brought under this title and provides the venue requirements.

It is also intended that one of the fundamental jurisdictional attributes exercised by the court under any actions brought before it under this Act includes the ability to grant such temporary or preliminary relief as it deems just and proper.

Section 706(g)(2)—This subsection is similar to the present section 706(g) of the Act. It authorizes the court, upon a finding that the respondent has engaged in or is engaging in an unlawful employment practice to enjoin the respondent from such unlawful conduct and order such affirmative relief including, but not limited to, reinstatement or hiring of employees, with or without back pay as will effectuate the policies of the Act. The court's award of back pay is limited to that which accrues from a date not more than

two years prior to the filing of a charge with the Commission. Interim earnings or amounts earnable with reasonable diligence by the aggrieved person(s) would operate to reduce the back pay otherwise allowable.

The provisions of this subsection are intended to give the court wide discretion, as has been generally exercised by the courts under existing law, in fashioning the most complete relief possible. In dealing with the present section 706(g) the courts have stressed that the scope of relief under that section of the Act is intended to make the victims of unlawful discrimination whole, and that the attainment of this objective rests not only upon the elimination of the particular unlawful employment practice complained of but also requires that the consequences and effects of the unlawful employment practice be, so far as possible, restored to a position where they would have been were it not for the unlawful discrimination. This broad reading of the need for effective remedies under this subsection is intended to be preserved in this bill in order to effectively combat the presence of employment discrimination.

SECTION 4(B)

Section 706(k)—This subsection is similar to section 706(k) of the present Act allowing the award of attorney's fees. It adds a provision allowing a prevailing party, in an action brought by the General Counsel or the Attorney General, who is an employer with less than 25 employees or a labor union with less than 25 members to be indemnified by the United States Treasury upon certification of the Commission, in an amount not to exceed $5,000 for their defense, including all expenses and reasonable attorney's fees incurred subsequent to receiving notice of a charge filed against them. Any such prevailing party with 25 to 100 employees whose average income from such employment is less than $7,500, or in the case of a labor union with 25 to 100 members, would be indemnified for one-half of the cost of their defense in an amount not to exceed $2,500. Costs are to be submitted by application to the Commission evidenced by vouchers and are to be deemed reasonable so long as they are comparable to the total amount of the expenses and attorneys fees incurred by the Commission in its investigation and prosecution of the charge. Any district court with jurisdiction over the proceedings would have the authority to make the determination provided for by the subsection.

SECTION 5

This section amends section 707, concerning the Attorney General's "pattern or practice" action, to provide for a transfer of this function to the Commission two years after the enactment of the bill. The bill further provides for current "pattern or practice" jurisdiction for the commission from the date of enactment until the transfer is complete. The transfer is subject to change in accordance with a Presidential reorganization plan if not vetoed by Congress. The section would provide that currently pending proceedings would continue without abatement, that all court orders and decrees remain in effect, and that upon the transfer the Commission would be substituted as a party for the United States of America or the Attorney General as appropriate. The Commission would have authority to investigate and act on pattern or practice charges except that any action would follow the procedures of section 706.

SECTION 6

This section amends section 709 of the Civil Rights Act of 1964, entitled "Investigations, Inspections, Records, State Agencies."

Section 709(a)—This subsection, which gives the Commission the right to examine and copy documents in connection with its investigation of a charge, would remain unchanged.

Section 709(b)—This subsection would authorize the Commission to cooperate with State and local fair employment practice agencies in order to carry out the purposes of the title, and to enter into agreements with such agencies under which the Commission would refrain from processing certain types of charges or relieve persons from the record keeping requirements. This subsection would make two changes in the present statute. Under this subsection, the Commission could, within the limitations of funds appropriated for the purpose, also engaged in and contribute to the cost of research and other projects undertaken by these State and local agencies and pay these agencies in advance for services rendered to the Commission. The subsection also deletes the reference to private civil actions under section 706(e) of the present statute.

Section 709(c)—This subsection, like the present statute, would require employers, employment agencies, labor organizations, and joint labor-management apprenticeship committees subject to the title to make and keep certain records and to make reports therefrom to the Commission. Under the present statute, a party required to keep records could seek an exemption from these requirements on the ground of undue hardship either by applying to the Commission or bringing a civil action in the district court. This subsection would require the party seeking the exemption first to make an application to the Commission and only if the Commission denies the request could the party bring an action in the district court. This subsection would also authorize the Commission to apply for a court order compelling compliance with the recordkeeping and reporting obligations set forth in the subsection.

Section 709(d)—This subsection would eliminate the present exemption from recordkeeping requirements for those employers in States and political subdivisions with fair employment practice laws or for employers subject to Federal executive order or agency recordkeeping requirements. Under this subsection, the Commission would consult with interested State and other Federal agencies in order to coordinate the Federal record-

keeping requirement under section 709(c) with those adopted by such agencies. The subsection further provides that the Commission furnish to such agencies information pertaining to State and local fair employment agencies, on condition that the information would not be made public prior to the institution of State or local proceedings.

Section 709(e)—Under this subsection, the Commission or the Attorney General would have the authority to direct the person having custody of any record or paper required by section 709(c) to be preserved or maintained to make such record or paper available for inspection or copying by the Commission or the Attorney General. The district court of the judicial district where the demand is made or the papers are located would have jurisdiction by appropriate process to compel the production of such record or paper. The subsection further provides that the members of the Commission and its representatives or the Attorney General and his representatives, could not, unless ordered by the court, disclose any record or paper produced except to Congress or a congressional committee, to other government agencies, or in the presentation of cases before a court or a grand jury.

SECTION 7

This section would amend section 710 of the Civil Rights Act of 1964 to make section 11 of the National Labor Relations Act (29 U.S.C. § 161), to the extent appropriate, applicable to Commission investigations. The person served by the Commission with the subpoena could petition the Commission to revoke the subpoena within 5 days. On application of the Commission, an appropriate district court could order a person to obey a subpoena and failure to comply with the court order would be punishable in contempt proceedings. Section 11 of the National Labor Relations Act also contains provisions relating to privileges of witnesses, immunity from prosecution, fees, process, service, and return, and information and assistance from other agencies.

SECTION 8 (A) AND (B)

These subsections would amend sections 703(a) and 703(c)(2) of the present statute to make it clear that discrimination against applicants for employment and applicants for membership in labor organizations is an unlawful employment practice. This subsection would merely be declaratory of present law.

SECTION 8(C) (1) AND (2)

These subsections would amend section 704 (a) and (b) of the present statute to make clear that joint labor-management apprenticeship committees are covered by those provisions which relate to discriminatory advertising and retaliation against individuals participating in Commission proceedings.

SECTION 8 (d)

This subsection would amend section 705(a) of the present statute to permit a member of the Commission to serve until his successor is appointed but not for more than 60 days when Congress is in session unless the successor has been nominated and the nomination submitted to the Senate, or after the adjournment *sine die* of the session of the Senate in which such nomination was submitted.

The rest of the subsection provides that the Chairman of the Commission on behalf of the Commission, would be responsible, except as provided in section 705(b), for the administrative operations of the Commission and for the appointment of officers, agents, attorneys, hearing examiners, and other employees of the Commission, and Regional Directors, with the concurrence of the General Counsel, in accordance with Federal law, as he deems necessary.

SECTION 8(e)

This subsection would provide a new section 705(b) of the Act which establishes a General Counsel appointed by the President, with the advice and consent of the Senate, for a four (4) year term. The responsibilities of the General Counsel would include, in addition to those the Commission may prescribe and provided by law, the prosecution and the conduct of all litigation as so provided in sections 706 and 707 of the Act. The General Counsel would appoint regional attorneys with the concurrence of the Chairman and other employees in the Office of the General Counsel in order to effectively carry out his functions and responsibilities.

Furthermore, this subsection would continue the General Counsel on the effective date of the act in that position until a successor has been appointed and qualified. Subsections (b) through (j) of section 705 of the act are redesignated as Subsections (e) through (k), respectively.

SECTION 8(f)

This subsection would amend section 705(g)(1) of the present Act to permit the Commission to accept uncompensated services for the purpose of publicizing its activities in the media.

SECTION 8(g)

This subsection would eliminate the provision in present section 705(g) authorizing the Commission to request the Attorney General to intervene in private civil actions and instead permit the Commission itself to intervene in such civil actions as provided in section 706.

SECTION 8(h)

This subsection would, subject to one exception, permit the Commission to delegate any of its functions, duties and powers to such persons as it may designate by regulation. A number of other Federal agencies have similar broad authority to delegate functions, e.g., the Securities and Exchange Commission (15 U.S.C. § 78(d)(1)), the Interstate Commerce Commission (49 U.S.C. § 17(5)), and the Federal Communications Commission (47 U.S.C. § 155(d)). The exception is as follows:

The Commission could not delegate its authority under section 709(b) to make agreements with States under which the Commis-

sion agrees to refrain from processing certain charges or to relieve certain persons from the recordkeeping requirements. The Commission would however be authorized to delegate this power or any of its other powers to groups of three or more members of the Commission.

SECTION 8(i)

This subsection would afford additional protection to officers, agents, and employees of the Commission in the performance of their official duties by making 18 U.S.C. 1114 applicable to them.

SECTION 9 (A), (B), (C), AND (D)

These subsections would make certain modifications in the position of the Chairman of the Commission and the members of the Commission and include the General Counsel in the executive pay scale, so as to place them in a position of parity with officials in comparable positions in agencies having substantially equivalent powers such as the National Labor Relations Board, the Federal Trade Commission and the Federal Power Commission.

SECTION 10

Section 715—This section, which is new, establishes an Equal Employment Opportunity Council (Council) composed of the Secretary of Labor, the Chairman of the Equal Employment Opportunity Commission, the Attorney General, the Chairman of the United States Civil Service Commission and the Chairman of the United States Civil Rights Commission or their respective designees. The Council will have the responsibility to coordinate and implement programs to promote the efficiency of all the various branches of government with responsibility for equal employment opportunities. The Council will submit an annual report to the President and Congress including a report of its activities and recommendations as to legislative or administrative changes it considers desirable.

SECTION 11

Section 717(a)—This subsection would make clear that all personnel actions of the U.S. Government affecting employees or applicants for employment shall be made free from any discrimination based on race, color, religion, sex, or national origin. All employees of any agency, department, office or commission having positions in the competitive service are covered by this section.

Section 717(b)—Under this subsection, the Civil Service Commission is given the authority to enforce the provisions of subsection (a) through appropriate remedies. These remedies may include but are not limited to back pay for applicants as well as employees denied promotion opportunities, reinstatement, hire, and immediate promotion. Any remedy needed to fully recompense the employee for his loss, both financially and professionally is considered appropriate under this subsection. The Civil Service Commission is also given authority to issue rules and regulations necessary to carry out its responsibilities under this section. The Civil

Service Commission also shall annually review national and regional equal employment opportunity plans and be responsible for review and evaluation of all agency equal employment opportunity programs. Finally, agency and executive department heads and officers of the District of Columbia shall comply with such rules and regulations, submit an annual equal employment opportunity plan and notify any employee or applicant of any final action taken on any complaint of discrimination filed by him.

Section 717 (c) and (d)—The provisions of sections 706(f) through (k) as applicable, concerning private civil actions by aggrieved persons, are made applicable to aggrieved Federal employees or applicants. They could file a civil action within 30 days of notice of final action on a complaint made pursuant to section 717(b), or after 180 days from the filing of an initial charge, or an appeal with the Commission. The authority given to the Commission or the limitations placed upon the Commission under sections 706(f) through (k) would apply to the Civil Service Commission or the agencies, as appropriate, in connection with a civil action brought under section 707(c). So, for example, if the Civil Service Commission or agency does not issue an order within 180 days after a complaint or appeal is filed, the aggrieved person may also instiute a civil action. If such action is instituted within one year of the filing of the complaint or appeal, the Civil Service Commission or agency may request that the action be stayed or dismissed upon a showing that it has been acting with due diligence, that it anticipates issuance of an order within a reasonable time on the complaint or appeal, that the case or proceeding is exceptional and that extension of exclusive jurisdiction of the Civil Service Commission or agency is warranted.

Section 717(e)—This subsection provides that nothing in this act relieves any Government agency or official of his existing nondiscriminating obligations under the Constitution, other statutes, or his or its responsibilities under Executve Order 11478 relating to equal employment opportunity in the Federal Government.

SECTION 12

Section 716 is amended to provide for consultation of the Attorney General, the Chairman of the Civil Service Commission, and the Chairman of the Equal Employment Opportunity Commission regarding rules, regulations and policy in the performance of their responsibilities under this act. It does not in any way limit each of the officials in independently carrying out ther respective obligations under this title.

SECTION 13

Ths section provides that the amended provisions of Section 706 would apply to charges filed with the Commission prior to the effective date of this Act. In addition, those new or amended sections of Title VII not specifically made inapplicable to current charges, would be applicable to such existing charges.

SECTION 14

This section provides that no government contract, or portion thereof, can be denied, withheld, terminated, or superseded by a government agency under the Executive Order 11246 or any other order of law without according the respective employer a full hearing and adjudication pursuant to 5 U.S.C. § 554 et. seq where such employer has an affirmative action program for the same facility which had been accepted by the Government within the prior twelve months. Such plan shall be deemed to be accepted by the Government if the appropriate compliance agency has accepted such plan and the Office of Federal Contract Compliance has not disapproved of such plan within 45 days. However, an employer who substantially deviates from the previously accepted plan is excluded from the protection afforded by this section.

EDITORS' NOTE: *Sen. Cranston (D., Calif.) analyzed the major provisions of S. 2515 as amended.*

Senate

2-22-72

pp. 2287, 2289, 2290

EQUAL OPPORTUNITY IN FEDERAL GOVERNMENT EMPLOYMENT

My Federal Government EEO amendment included in the committee bill would:

First. Put the Congress on record in favor of maximum affirmative action under Civil Service Commission direction to provide Federal jobs and real advancement opportunities for minority groups in Federal service. At the present time, the CSC derives its authority to act against discrimination from Executive order.

Second. Specifically charge the Civil Service Commission with the responsibility to require all agencies to draw up affirmative action plans and see that they are carried out.

Third. Entitle an employee to back pay if discrimination has been found to exist—the Government has insisted it does not have legal authority to make such awards.

Fourth. Direct the Civil Service Commission to publish, twice a year, employment studies, agency by agency and for every large metropolitan area, to indicate progress in eliminating discrimination in Federal employment.

Fifth. For the first time, permit Federal employees to sue the Federal Government in discrimination cases—under the theory of Federal sovereign immunity, courts have not generally allowed such suits—and to bring suit either prior to or after CSC review of the agency EEO decision in the case. As with other cases brought under title VII of the Civil Rights Act of 1964, Federal district court review would be based on the agency and/or CSC record and would not be a trial de novo. * * *

My amendment, then, adds to title VII of the Civil Rights Act a new section 717 making clear the obligation of the Federal Government to insure that all personnel actions are free from discrimination based on race, color, sex, religion, or national origin. The Civil Service Commission is mandated under this title to enforce an affirmative equal employment opportunity program in the Federal Government. * * *

I would like now to discuss some of the other major provisions of S. 2515 as reported from committee.

EXTENSION OF COVERAGE

Mr. President, section 2 of the bill amends section 701 of the Civil Rights Act of 1964 to extend coverage to the following groups: First, employees of private employers with 15—eight as reported from committee—or more workers and members of unions with 15—also eight originally—or more members, to become effective 1 year after enactment of the law; the present limit is 25; second, State and local government employees; and third, teachers and other employees of educational institutions.

The committee agreed with the Chairman of the EEOC that discrimination must be attacked wherever it exists. We recognize that smaller establishments have frequently been among the most flagrant violators of equal employment opportunity. It was for this reason that coverage under S. 2515 as reported from committee was extended to groups of eight or more workers. The compromise to reduce from 25 to 15 is still a significant step forward. The delay in the effective date of this provision was included to insure that the Commission would have adequate time to prepare to assume and carry out effectively these new responsibilities.

The bill also deletes the existing exemptions for State and local government employees but provides for enforcement through civil actions brought by the Attorney General rather than through cease-and-desist orders. I believe this is a desirable compromise rather than empowering a Federal agency—the EEOC—to order sovereign units of State and local government to take particular employment actions.

Both the Constitution and Federal law prohibit job discrimination by State and local governments, but the existence of pervasive discrimination in State and local government is all too well documented. What is lacking, however, is an effective Federal administrative machinery to enforce these prohibitions. Thus, the expansion of title VII coverage to State and local governments is necessary if we are to provide a truly effective means of implementing the declared equal employment opportunity policy of our Nation.

The existing exemption for employees of educational institutions is also eliminated by S. 2515. There are at present over 120,000 educational institutions, with approximately 2.8 million teachers and professional staff members and another 1.5 million nonprofessional staff members. Yet all of these employees are, at present, without an effective Federal remedy in the area of employment discrimination. As in other areas of employment, statistics for educational institutions indicate that minorities, and particularly women, are precluded from the more prestigious and higher paying positions and are relegated to the more menial and lower paying positions. I believe it is essential that these employees be given the same opportunity to redress their grievances as are available to other employees in the private sector.

I have already discussed in great detail the provisions of section 11 of S. 2515, which mandates the Civil Service Commission to strengthen its programs to eliminate discrimination in Federal employment and job advancement and provides for civil suit remedy in Federal district court.

ENFORCEMENT

Section 4 of S. 2515 as reported from committee would have revised section 706 of the act to enable the EEOC to process a charge of employment discrimination through the investigation, conciliation, administrative hearing, and judicial review stages. The present act allows the Commission to pursue charges only through the informal methods of persuasion and conciliation, a factor which has proven to be seriously defective in providing an effective Federal remedy for violations of title VII.

The need to provide some form of direct enforcement power for the EEOC has been voiced since the inception of the Commission. Indeed, last Congress, during testimony before the Labor and Public Welfare Committee on S. 2453 and again this past year in testimony on S. 2515, EEOC Chairman William Brown concurred in the need for cease-and-desist authority.

The committee was not persuaded that the direct court enforcement technique, the method included in the House version, would be faster and more effective than cease-and-desist enforcement. The present, and ever increasing, overcrowded caseloads of the Federal courts is a well known fact, and measures are desperately needed to expedite trials and relieve the court dockets, not to increase their case responsibilities. There is ample evidence that reliance on the court enforcement approach could create an unacceptable deluge of new cases on the already previously backlogged Federal courts. In 1970 alone, for instance, there was a 63-percent increase in the filing of civil rights cases.

It was for this reason that the Labor and Public Welfare Committee, as did the House Education and Labor Committee last May, rejected the court enforcement approach. Moreover, without exception, every spokesman for the major civil rights groups who appeared before our committee strongly supported the cease-and-desist enforcement powers provided in S. 2515.

The major benefits of the cease-and-desist approach are that: First, it would encourage early settlement of claims, thereby further alleviating the courts and providing quick relief for aggrieved individuals; second, it is the type of authority given to many other Federal regulatory agencies, including the National Labor Relations Board, the Department of Justice, the Interstate Commerce Commission, the Department of Labor, and the Department of Health, Education, and Welfare, to name but a few; third, it is the type of enforcement authority preferred by 32 of the 37 States which have equal employment opportunity laws; fourth, it would insure a unified approach to the problems of discrimination since decisions would be rendered by one agency rather than several hundred district court judges; and fifth, it would provide the needed expertise in recognizing and solving the more subtle, institutional forms of discrimination.

The enforcement authority in S. 2515 as reported from committee provided that employees of private employers would have their rights enforced by the EEOC through administrative complaint and hearing after investigation and conciliation of charges. If the EEOC found an unlawful employment practice, it could have issued cease-and-desist orders subject to review in U.S. courts of appeals.

In my judgment, cease-and-desist authority was, by far the stronger and more workable enforcement mechanism. However, the Senate has voted by a narrow margin to substitute district court suits to enforce EEOC findings. This is better than no EEO enforcement mechanism at all, and I believe that civil rights groups, and the minority community generally will make the most of this new remedy.

CONSOLIDATION OF ENFORCEMENT FUNCTIONS

Mr. President, section 5 of S. 2515 would transfer from the Attorney General, as granted under section 707 of present law—to the EEOC the authority to bring "pattern or practice" suits directly in the Federal district courts. This transfer would take place over a period of 2 years, with the EEOC and the Attorney General having concurrent jurisdiction during this time. This transfer to the Commission should also help the Federal Government pursue a more unified attack upon employment discrimination.

Section 10 of S. 2515 as reported would have provided for the transfer from the Department of Labor to the Commission of the authority, functions, and responsibilities of the Office of Federal Contract Compliance—OFCC—authority, which presently rests in Executive Order 11246—as amended by Executive Order 11375. The Executive order stipulates that Government contractors and subcontractors are required to agree to the following contract provision:

The contractor will not discriminate against any employee or applicant for employment because of race, color, religion, sex or national origin. The contractor will take affirmative action to ensure that applicants are employed, and that employees are treated during employment, without regard to their race, color, religion, sex, or national origin.

During committee consideration of the equal employment opportunities enforcement bill—S. 2453—in the 91st Congress, I joined with Senator KENNEDY in moving successfully to delete the provision transferring this function from the Department of Labor to the Commission.

I believed then, and I continue to believe, that it would be a mistake to consolidate all EEO functions in one Federal agency, thereby creating a single target for those who would seek to retard advancement in this field. I recognize, at the same time, that the OFCC record of achievement in this field leaves a good deal to be desired. I just am not convinced that consolidation of this function would have the net effect of improving the EEO Federal contract compliance effort.

Although I recognize that many, as fully committed to equal employment as I am, support this OFCC/EEOC consolidation, I differ with their views and thus voted for the successful amendment to delete this transfer from the bill.

In conclusion, Mr. President, although I believe the bill as reported has been weakened by floor amendments, I urge my colleagues to support it. If we are to make progress in fulfilling our commitment to equal employment opportunity for all Americans, we must make the Equal Employment Opportunity Commission a more effective instrument for preventing discrimination in employment. To this end, the extended coverage which S. 2515 provides; its new methods of enforcement, although not optimum; and its stress on Federal Government equal employment opportunity promise real gains in this long and arduous civil rights battle.

Appendix F-6

Coverage: Number of Employees and Union Members

EDITOR'S NOTE: *Sen. Ervin (D., N.C.) introduced amendment No. 813 to the committee bill, which would have exempted employers with fewer than 25 employees—the same coverage as specified in the 1964 Act. Sen. Williams (D., N.J.) proposed an amendment to the Ervin amendment, exempting employers with fewer than 15 employees and unions with fewer than 15 members. The modified Ervin amendment was adopted by a vote of 81 to 1, and the expansion of coverage was included in the bill enacted.*

Senate

2-2-72

p. 1071

Mr. FANNIN. Mr. President, I rise in support of amendment 813 to S. 2515.

First of all, I want to state that I am opposed to this bill without the Dominick amendment, which was narrowly defeated in two earlier votes. If we are to have this legislation, however, we must try to reduce the detrimental effects and correct some of the other obvious shortcomings of the bill.

The amendment before us is a very reasonable one, and I think goes a long way in helping in this direction.

It would maintain the present law which exempts employers with fewer than 25 workers from coverage. S. 2515 would reduce the number of employees to eight.

In other words, the new, arbitrary power we are granting to the Equal Employment Opportunities Commission could be and would be used not only against small businesses and small factories, but against what are essentially family businesses.

Senate

2-8-72

p. 1457

The legislative clerk read as follows:
On line 1, in lieu of the language proposed to be inserted, insert "fifteen".
Strike out line six and insert the following on page 33. strike out lines 6, 7, 8, 9, and 10 and insert in lieu thereof: "(4) In Subsection (e) strike out between "(A)" and "and such labor organization", and insert in lieu thereof "twenty-five or more during the first year after the date of enactment of the Equal Employment Opportunities Enforcement Act of 1971, or (B) fifteen or more thereafter,".

* * *

Mr. WILLIAMS. Mr. President, I think the amendments that have been offered speak for themselves. The bill would reduce the coverage of employers to those with 8 employees and of unions to those with 8 members. This would advance it to 15.

Appendix F-7

Coverage: Definition of Religion

EDITORS' NOTE: *An amendment defining "religion" and requiring an employer to make reasonable accommodations to the religious belief of employees or prospective employees was introduced by Sen. Randolph (D., W.Va.). The amendment was agreed to by a vote of 55 to 0 and incorporated in the final legislation.*

Senate

1-21-72

pp. 228, 229

The legislative clerk read as follows:

On page 33, after line 13, insert the following:

"(6) After subsection (i) insert the following new subsection (j):

'(j) The term "religion" includes all aspects of religious observance and practice, as well as belief, unless an employer demonstrates that he is unable to reasonably accommodate to an employee's or prospective employee's, religious observance or practice without undue hardship on the conduct of the employer's business.' "

* * *

Mr. RANDOLPH. Mr. President, freedom from religious discrimination has been considered by most Americans from the days of the Founding Fathers as one of the fundamental rights of the people of the United States. Yet our courts have on occasion determined that this freedom is nebulous, at least in some ways. So in presenting this proposal to S. 2515, it is my desire and I hope the desire of my colleagues, to assure that freedom from religious discrimination in the employment of workers is for all time guaranteed by law.

I am sure that my colleagues are well aware that there are several religious bodies—we could call them religious sects; denominational in nature—not large in membership, but with certain strong convictions, that believe there should be a steadfast observance of the Sabbath and require that the observance of the day of worship, the day of the Sabbath, be other than on Sunday. On this day of worship work is prohibited whether the day would fall on Friday, or Saturday, or Sunday. There are approximately 750,000 men and women who are Orthodox Jews in the U.S. work force who fall in this category of persons I am discussing. There are an additional 425,000 men and women in the work force who are Seventh-day Adventists.

Mr. President, I am a member of a denomination which is a relatively small one, the Seventh-Day Baptists. Perhaps there are only 5,000 individuals within that denomination in the work force. I do think it is important for me to say that within the groups that I have mentioned, we think in terms of our observance of the Sabbath beginning at sundown Friday evening and ending at sundown Saturday evening, following the Biblical words, "From eve unto eve shall you celebrate your Sabbath." I make this statement only by way of explanation of the groups I have just mentioned.

I think it is important for us to realize that the persons for whom I hope I speak—and I hope I speak for all persons in this matter—are workers scattered throughout the United States of America. There is no section of the country which would not be affected, we hope constructively, by the adoption of this amendment.

I say to the distinguished chairman of the Labor and Public Welfare Committee, who manages this bill, that there has been a partial refusal at times on the part of employers to hire or to continue in employment employees whose religious practices rigidly require them to abstain from work in the nature of hire on particular days. So there has been, because of understandable pressures, such as commitments of a family nature and otherwise, a dwindling of the membership of some of the religious organizations because of the situation to which I have just directed attention.

I hold my membership in our church here in this area. We have the Washington Seventh-Day Baptist Church. We have several of those churches in my State of West Virginia. At an earlier period I held my membership in the Salem, W. Va., Seventh-Day Baptist Church.

I invite the attention of my able colleague to the fact that in the State of New Jersey there are many, many Seventh-Day Baptist churches. In places like Shiloh, Marlboro, and Plainfield—actually being the headquarters of the denomination to which I belong, located close to New York City, but actually located in the State of New Jersey.

My own pastor in this area, Rev. Delmer Van Horne, has expressed his concern and distress that there are certain faiths that are having a very difficult time, especially with the younger people, and understandably so, with reference to a possible inability of employers on some occasions to adjust work schedules to fit the requirements of the faith of some of their workers.

The term "religion" as used in the Civil Rights Act of 1964 encompasses, as I understand it, the same concepts as are included in the first amendment—not merely belief, but also conduct; the freedom to believe, and also the freedom to act.

I think in the Civil Rights Act we thus intended to protect the same rights in private employment as the Constitution protects in Federal, State, or local governments. Unfortunately, the courts have, in a sense, come down on both sides of this issue. The Supreme Court of the United States, in a case involving the observance of the Sabbath and job discrimination, divided evenly on this question.

This amendment is intended, in good purpose, to resolve by legislation—and in a way I think was originally intended by the Civil Rights Act—that which the courts apparently have not resolved. I think it is needed not only because court decisions have clouded the matter with some uncertainty; I think this is an appropriate time for the Senate, and hopefully the Congress of the United States, to go back, as it were, to what the Founding Fathers intended. The complexity of our industrial life, the transition of our whole are of employment, of course are matters that were not always understood by those who led our Nation in earlier days.   * * *

Mr. DOMINICK. I have listened very carefully to the Senator's presentation, and was impressed by it. Could the Senator tell me, whether this amendment would also affect, for example, the Amish, or some other religious sect which has a different method of conducting their lives than do most Americans?

Mr. RANDOLPH. Yes; I envisage that it would.

Mr. DOMINICK. Would it apply to the following situation? A young man I just talked to from Virginia, works 15 days on and then is off 15 days. Would the amendment require an employer to change that kind of employment ratio around, so that he would have to work a customary 5- or 6-day week?

Mr. RANDOLPH. I do not believe that an undue hardship would come to such an employer. The Senator has explained a specific case. I do not believe that there are really problems that would flow from the adoption of this amendment in connection with the employer meeting situations that he could not properly handle with employees.

Mr. DOMINICK. I thank the Senator. I think this amendment will be helpful. All of these various situations keep arising because of our pluralistic method of conducting our business in this country. It is hard to foresee far enough ahead so that each specific type of case can be anticipated.

Am I correct in understanding that the amendment allows flexibility both to the EEOC and to its investigators to determine whether or not any particular group of religious adherents are having their customary observance of their religious activities unduly interfered with? In other words, flexibility is provided so that someone could make a discretionary judgment on it?

Mr. RANDOLPH. The Senator from Colorado correctly follows me in the thinking that I have placed in the language of the amendment, that there would be such flexibility, there would be this approach of understanding, even perhaps of discretion, to a very real degree.

I agree with the Senator's feeling, and I am sure that that is what is meant and would flow from the adoption of the practice under the amendment.

* * *

Mr. WILLIAMS. I did not follow the last colloquy entirely, and perhaps this is the same question, but where the employment is such that the job has to be done on a day that a person under his faith would make his religious observations, it might be an undue hardship to close down the operation to accommodate that person. There are jobs that are Saturday and Sunday jobs, and that is all, serving resorts and other areas. Certainly the amendment would permit the employer not to hire a person who could not work on one of the 2 days of the employment; this would be an undue hardship, and the employer's situation is protected under the amendment offered by the Senator from West Virginia, is it not?

Mr. RANDOLPH. That is correct; yes. I am in agreement with the Senator's statement.

* * *

Mr. WILLIAMS. As I read the first amendment of the Constitution, there is no problem here presented by the amendment in connection with the first clause:

Congress shall make no law respecting an establishment of religion, or prohibiting the free exercise thereof.

In dealing with the free exercise thereof, really, this promotes the constitutional demand in that regard.

I certainly agree with the objective of the amendment.

Appendix F-8

Coverage: Library of Congress

EDITORS' NOTE: *The Library of Congress was brought under the nondiscrimination provisions of the Act by an amendment introduced by Sen. Cranston (D., Calif.) and cosponsored by Sen. Dominick (R., Colo.). The amendment was adopted by a voice vote and incorporated in the final bill.*

Senate

2-22-72

p. 2279

Mr. CRANSTON. Mr. President, this amendment deals with section 11 of S. 2515, relating to nondiscrimination in Federal Government employment.

Mr. President, section 11 of the bill inserts of new section 717 in title VII of the Civil Rights Act of 1964 to provide, for the first time, a clear statutory mandate with respect to equal employment opportunity in the Federal Government. This section was added in committee as a result of an amendment which I offered with the Senator from Massachusetts (Mr. KENNEDY) and in cooperation with the Senator from Colorado (Mr. DOMINICK).

This bipartisan provision has three basic purposes:

First. Subsection (a) of the new section 717 provides a statutory mandate that all personnel actions affecting employees or applicants for employment in the Federal Government, "Shall be made free from any discrimination based on race, color, religion, sex or national origin."

Second. Subsection (b) in the new section 717 empowers the Civil Service Commission to enforce the mandate in subsection (a) and to be responsible for review of evaluation of Federal agency equal employment opportunity plans and programs. The subsection also requires that certain provisions be included in each agency's plan.

Third. Subsection (c) of the new section 717 creates a remedy in Federal district court—comparable to private employment actions—for any employee who has exhausted the equal employment opportunity complaint procedure within his Federal agency.

Mr. President, unfortunately, as drafted, these provisions, which in many respects only codify requirements presently contained in Executive orders and the Constitution, would not apply to employment in the Library of Congress. That is because legislative branch coverage in the bill is limited to "positions in the competitive service." Although this would apply to both the General Accounting Office and the Government Printing Office—which are agencies of the Congress, it would not apply to the Library of Congress which does not have positions in the competitive service and is not generally bound by the Federal personnel manual.

Presently, the Library of Congress has established its own equal employment opportunity program and generally cooperates with the Civil Service Commission with respect to equal employment, although the Library is not covered by the Government-wide Executive order. Under the amendment Senator DOMINICK and I are offering, employment in the Library of Congress would be subject to the nondiscrimination mandate of subsection (a) in the new section 717. I am assured by the Library of Congress that this would do no more than codify existing practice in the Library's personnel program.

In the same way, the amendment I am offering would also include the Library of Congress within the subsection (c) provision permitting aggrieved employees to bring civil actions in Federal court after they have exhausted their agency's administrative remedies. I am also assured by the Library of Congress that such law suits have been brought in the past against the Library in discrimination cases, and have not been dismissed on jurisdictional grounds.

However, with respect to the enforcement authorities granted to the Civil Service Commission in subsection (b) of the new section 717, to include the Library of Congress would raise substantial questions about the appropriateness of the Congress delegating to an executive agency—the Civil Service Commission—the legislative function of overseeing one of its own arms in this instance, the Library of Congress. Presently, the Civil Service Commission has no authority in the area of nondiscrimination in Library of Congress personnel programs or actions.

The amendment we offer would not in any way change that situation. Our amendment would amend subsection (b) so as specifically to remove any possibility that the Civil Service Commission or

the EEOC would be empowered to exercise enforcement, review or evaluation responsibilities or authorities vis-a-vis Library of Congress equal employment opportunity programs or actions. Instead, our amendment gives to the Librarian of Congress with respect to Library of Congress employment all enforcement authorities which are given to the Civil Service Commission under subsection (b) with respect to nondiscrimination in Federal employment generally, and bestows on the Librarian of Congress, himself, the final authority—except as it continues to repose in the Congress itself with respect to one of its own agencies—for preparing and carrying out equal employment opportunity plans and programs. Thus, there would be no invasion by this amendment of the statutory authority of the Librarian to appoint employees of the Library "solely with reference to their fitness for their particular duties." (2 U.S.C. 140).

Appendix F-9

Exemptions: State and Local Governmental Officials

EDITORS' NOTE: *Senators Ervin (D., N.C.) and Allen (D., Ala.) introduced amendment No. 888 excluding from the definition of "employee" any elected public official and anyone chosen by him to advise him on the constitutional or legal powers of his office. The amendment subsequently was modified to make clear that the exemption applies only to the personal assistants and immediate advisors of elected public officials. The amendment as modified was adopted by a vote of 69 to 2 and included in the bill as enacted.*

Senate

2-16-72

pp. 1911, 1912

The assistant legislative clerk read as follows:

On page 33, insert the following between line 10 and line 11:

"(5) In subsection (f), change the period at the end cf the subsection to a colon, and add thereafter the following words:

"'Provided, however, That the term "employee" shall not include any person elected to public office in any State or political subdivision of any State by the qualified voters thereof, or any person chosen by such officer

to advise him in respect to the exercise of the constitutional or legal powers of his office.'."
         * * *

Mr. ERVIN

This is an exceedingly important amendment. The bill defines a State and a political subdivision of a State as employers for the first time in the history of legislation of this kind. It defines an employee as one who is employed by an employer. The dictionary states that any person or concern which employs another, usually for wages or a salary, is an employer. Under these provisions, no one is excepted. In other words, the bill is broad enough in its present form to cover Governors of States, State supreme court justices, State legislators, and so forth.

The report states:

A question was raised in committee concerning the application of title VII in the case of a Governor whose cabinet appointees or close personal aides are drawn from one political party. The committee's intention is that nothing in the bill shall be interpreted to prohibit such appointments on the basis of discrimination on account of race, color, religion, sex, or national origin. That intention is reflected in section 703(h) and 706(w) of the law.

In other words, this would give the Federal courts jurisdiction to inquire as to what motive a Governor had in selecting men for his cabinet who would give him advice on his constitutional and legal duties, on if a Governor was actuated in any extent in the selection of an adviser or if the people were actuated in any extent in the election of a public official, so that the Commission could come in and remove that public official from office or that adviser from office and dictate who should be employed in his place.

I respectfully submit that that is going too far, for Congress to empower an Executive agency at the Federal level to tell the Governor of his State, or the people for that matter, whom they can elect Governor, or Supreme Court Justice, or State legislator, or what officials shall be selected to advise the Governor as to his constitutional and legal duties.

Mr. President, it is absurd for a Federal agency to be able to say to a State who its Governor, State officials, or advisers shall be. I respectfully suggest that if Congress is not going to make itself ridiculous, this amendment should be agreed to.   * * *

Mr. METCALF. Once upon a time, we had a Postmaster General who was a great political adviser to the President. Jim Farley was such an example.

Today, we have in the Department of Justice an Attorney General who is leaving to run a political campaign for his President. He first becomes Attorney General and now he leaves it.

What happens in that sort of situation?

Mr. ERVIN. If that was done at the State level, and the attorney general was an appointee of the Governor, EEOC could come in and tell the Governor that he could not have that attorney general to advise him on the law, that he would have to take someone the EEOC picked out instead.

Mr. METCALF. How could we keep such an Attorney General who comes in and says, "Well, I am going to be Attorney General for awhile," but when the next election campaign comes up, he says, "I am going back into campaigning operations." How can we prevent that?

Mr. ERVIN. We cannot prevent anything at the State level. The EEOC——

Mr. METCALF. I am trying to prevent something at the Federal level.

Mr. ERVIN. In the old days, I thought that a Postmaster General was the appropriate person to advise the President, because he did not have anything else to do except to read the Postal Guide.

Mr. METCALF. We had a lot of appointments but——

Mr. ERVIN. This bill does not deal with it at the Federal level. It deals with it at the State level.

Mr. METCALF. I was wondering what happens when we have an Attorney General who comes in at the Federal level, after he has been working at a campaign level and gets appointed Attorney General, and then after 2½ or 3 years he moves it back into his campaign.

Mr. ERVIN. Mr. President, I am trying to get for the Governor of a State the same authority to pick out his attorney general as the President has to pick out his Attorney General or campaign manager.

Mr. WILLIAMS. Mr. President, I should like to ask the Senator one or two questions just to see if there is a way to describe the scope and the limits of the amendment. Certainly it is clear that an elected official at the State or municipal level should not be covered in any way by this bill as an employee.

Mr. ERVIN. The Senator is correct. However, I feel that he is covered now.

Mr. WILLIAMS. It says "as an employee." Frankly, I do not understand the terminology. It says that the term "employee" shall not include any person elected to a public office in a State or political subdivision of any State by the qualified voters thereof.

Mr. ERVIN. Mr. President, under the Civil Rights Act of 1964, an employee is defined in substance as one who is employed by an employer. This is just to put an exception to that provision and make it clear that the term employee is not to be construed as including an elected official or a person chosen by the elected official to advise him as to his constitutional and legal duties.

I think that the point the Senator is driving at is that this is narrowly drawn to make certain that the only persons covered by the bill at a State or local level are elected officials and the people who advise them as to their constitutional and legal powers. It would leave covered by the bill those people who merely carry out the directives.

It would only exclude elected officials and those who give them advice as to how they should carry out their legal and constitutional duties, and not those who actually carry them out as administrative officials.

Mr. WILLIAMS. It would certainly be the Governor's attorney general, for example.

Mr. ERVIN. The Senator is correct.

Mr. WILLIAMS. The Governor of the State of New Jersey has personal counsel. This would cover that particular officer or individual.

Mr. ERVIN. The Senator is correct. However, it would not exclude a person who merely carries out the advice which the elected official would receive from those who advise him.

Mr. WILLIAMS. Mr. President, in other words that would be the law clerks and the law assistants of the personal counsel. The Governor or mayor would not be included within this term.

Mr. ERVIN. We are getting into a rather gray area there.

Mr. WILLIAMS. I wanted to see if we could find where the clear area is and the ambiguous area.

Mr. ERVIN. They would be excluded from this exclusion or this exception, because the only person excluded besides the elected official is the person who advises him. I chose that word advisedly. It would be the person who would advise him in regard to his legal or constitutional duties. It would not just be a law clerk. The Attorney General picks his own employees.

Mr. WILLIAMS. Mr. President, I have an instinctively favorable reaction to this particular exemption or exclusion under the law. However, I am glad that we are going until tomorrow, because some of the ambiguity can be worked out before I commit myself to it.

Mr. ERVIN. Mr. President, I really think that makes a bad bill a little less obnoxious, because I do not think the author of this bill ever intended to cover elected officials, those elected by the duly qualified voters. However, I fear that they have covered them by the breadth of the language.

In my own county we have a board of commissioners appointed by the people. They run the county affairs. They choose for themselves a legal adviser, a county attorney. I think they ought to be allowed to choose that attorney without any restrictions whatsoever, because a person ought to know who he relies on for advice as to the duties of his office. This would exclude the attorney, but not any other Government or county official, such as clerks or secretaries or people like that.

Senate

2-17-72

p. 2051

Mr. WILLIAMS. * * *

Mr. President, my understanding of the amendment offered by the Senator from North Carolina leads me to the conclusion that it has merit. As I understand it, I am certain it will be acceptable, but I would like to have it clarified to make sure that my understanding is accurate. First, State and local governments are now included under the bill as employers. The amendment would provide, for the purposes of the bill and for the basic law, that an elected individual is not an employee and, threfore, the law could not cover him. The next point is that the elected official would, in his position as an employer, not be covered and would be exempt in the employment of certain individuals.

Now we get to the inquiry of the Senator from New York (Mr. JAVITS) yesterday as the ambit of that employment by the elected official. But let me back up here to say that I certainly subscribe, and for many reasons, to the exclusion of the elected official at the State and local governing level. His test comes at the polls rather than under a law of this nature. I think that is certainly sufficient test as to propriety in the undertaking of his office, in view of the people that have the opportunity to select him for elected office. For another reason, I would think he should not be in a position to have unwarranted and irresponsible charges made against him. Again, his test would be at the polls.

The second degree relates to other people who are covered. That is basically the purpose of the amendment, to exempt from coverage those who are chosen by the Governor or the mayor or the county supervisor, whatever the elected official is, and who are in a close personal relationship and an immediate relationship with him. Those who are his first line of advisers. Is that basically the purpose of the Senator's amendment?

Mr. ERVIN. I would say to my good friend from New Jersey that that is the purpose of the amendment. I feel that those elected officials who are legal advisers or who are personal assistants or legal advisers, as to how he should exercise his constitutional, legal rights and responsibilities, should also be exempt. That is the purpose of the amendment, yes.

Mr. WILLIAMS. That is my understanding. As to the degree, certainly it would cover those who are in a Governor's cabinet, his cabinet officers. They would be included in the group of personal assistants; is that not correct?

Mr. ERVIN. That is what is intended by this amendment, plus his immediate legal advisers, because no Governor today can get along and discharge the many duties imposed upon him by his office without having someone to lean on for advice, counsel, and so forth.

Mr. WILLIAMS. But it is not the intention of the Senator's amendment to go to the employees of the personal advisers to the elected officials; is that not correct?

Mr. ERVIN. This amendment would not do that. That is not its intention. I would like to do that, but I do not think I could persuade the Senate to adopt an exclusion of that kind. It is not its purpose to go to the employees of the personal assistants or to the legal advisers.

Mr. WILLIAMS. Well, I am happy to hear that that is the intention. I accept that in principle and feel it would not be at variance with or in violation of the thrust, the scope, or the purposes of this legislation.

I shall yield in a moment to the Senator from New York (Mr. JAVITS), but first would like to say to the Senator from North Carolina, in order to make crystal clear what we have been discussing, that I would like to offer an amendment to do exactly what we have just been discussing, as an amendment to the Senator's amendment.

Mr. ERVIN. The Senator from New York has shown me what he proposes to do, and I would like to modify my amendment to include his suggestion, provided I can get unanimous consent to do so, since the yeas and nays on the amendment have already been ordered.

I would propose to accept the suggestion offered by the Senator from New Jersey and the Senator from New York for a change in the phraseology of my amendment so that the amendment would read as follows:

On page 33, insert the following between line 10 and line 11:

"(5) In subsection (f), change the period at the end of the subsection to a colon, and add thereafter the following words:

" 'Provided, however, That the term "employee" shall not include any person elected to public office in any State or political subdivision of any State by the qualified voters thereof, or any person chosen by such officer to be a personal assistant, or an immediate adviser in respect to the exercise of the constitutional or legal powers of the office.' "

Renumber section (5) as (6).

If that is agreeable to the Senator from New Jersey and the Senator from New York, I should like to modify my amendment accordingly.

Mr. JAVITS. Mr. President, I trust that it will be satisfactory and I join with the Senator from New Jersey (Mr. WILLIAMS) in the proposal. However, I want to be sure that we have no difference of opinion as to what it means.

I might tell the distinguished Senator from North Carolina (Mr. ERVIN) that I was not troubled by the word "constitutional" but by "legal powers,". He would be, as a lawyer, too. Because all that means is appertaining to the functions of his office—and all his powers are legal, of course—so we wanted to be sure of the ambit of ". . . any person chosen to be a personal assistant, or an immediate adviser. . . ."

If the Senator will bear with me for a moment, I should like to say, as we understand those difficulties, that I hope I will not be construed as being didactic. I do not mean that at all. That is, eight persons only, and not one more person—anything like that. We are talking about the order of magnitude. I have no desire to argue about the fine points of some particular appointment, but generally speaking we consider a personal assistant as being a secretary or, as I have, an administrative assistant, a legislative aide, and then a mayor may have four assistants.

So that is what we would understand a personal assistant to be. "A secretary," of course, is an accurate designation. He may have two or three secretaries. Important people have more than one.

The other thing, the immediate advisers, I was thinking more in terms of a cabinet, of a Governor who would call his commissioners a cabinet, or he may have a cabinet composed of three or four executive officials, or five or six, who would do the main and important things. That is what I would define those things expressly to mean.

What troubled me yesterday was the idea of getting down to the "nitty-gritty," as I explained to the Senator the "many assistants." When I was Attorney General, I employed 500 people. Of those 500 persons, perhaps on the outside 20 would be personal assistants or immediate advisers, but the other 480 would be persons who might be assistants in charge of a particular function, or something like that.

So, if we understand each other on that score, this is entirely satisfactory to me. Do I understand correctly, then, that we agree on this?

Mr. ERVIN. Yes. In other words, I think that the change that has been made makes it clear. I recognize that language sometimes is difficult to write, so that it may properly express the ideas intended to be expressed. However, the suggested change would, I think, express our objective in accordance with what the Senator would expect.

Mr. JAVITS. I thank the Senator.

Mr. ERVIN. Mr. President, I ask unanimous consent that the Senator from Alabama and I be permitted to modify my amendment so as to conform with the change.

Appendix F-10

Exemptions: State and Local Government Employees

EDITORS' NOTE: *An amendment depriving EEOC of jurisdiction over the employment practices of the states and their political subdivisions was introduced by Sen. Ervin (D., N.C.). The amendment was rejected by a vote of 16 to 59.*

Senate

1-28-72

pp. 706, 707

Mr. ERVIN. Mr. President, this is a simple amendment. I should like to alert Senators to the fact that it is, in my judgment, one of the most crucial amendments which will be offered to the bill.

Stated simply, the amendment would completely remove from the bill all the provisions which undertake to give the EEOC jurisdiction over the employment practices of any of the States or any of the political subdivisions of the States.

EDITORS' NOTE: *Senators Ervin (D., N.C.) and Allen (D., Ala.) introduced amendment No. 890 stating that the amendments to the 1964 Act wouldn't apply to employees of states or political subdivisions as long as Congress exempted its employees and the employees of its members. The amendment was rejected by a vote of 21 to 44.*

Senate

2-17-72

pp. 2052, 2053

The amendment was read as follows:

On page 66, insert the following new section between lines 13 and 14:

"SEC. 13. The amendments made by this Act to title VII of the Civil Rights Act of 1964 shall not be applicable to the employees of States or the political subdivisions of States as long as Congress exempts its employees and the employees of its Members from them"

Renumber SEC. 13 as SEC. 14.   * * *

The purpose of this amendment is to provide that the provisions of the bill, insofar as they affect the employees of States or political subdivisions of the States, shall not become applicable until the law is made to apply alike to Members of Congress and the employees of Members of Congress.

Under the existing law, the EEOC does not have jurisdiction over the employees of States, counties, cities, and the agencies of the States, counties, and cities; but under the bill as it now stands, the coverage by EEOC is to be extended to some 10 million employees of States, counties, and city governments.

However, the authors and proponents of the bill have seen fit to provide that in the provisions of the present bill, jurisdiction by the EEOC shall not extend to the employees of the Congress or to the employees of the Members of the House of Representatives or to the employees of the Members of the Senate.

So the purpose of this amendment would be to provide that so long as the employees of the House and Senate and of the Members of the two bodies are not covered by the bill, then the employees of States, counties, and cities shall not be covered. It puts them all on the same basis. It treats the Federal employees to which I have alluded on the same basis as State, county, and city employees.

Appendix F-11

Exemptions: Religious and Educational Institutions

EDITORS' NOTE: *An attempt to exclude educational and religious institutions from the coverage of the committee bill was defeated by a vote of 25 to 55.*

Senate

2-1-72

pp. 918, 928-930

Mr. ERVIN.   *   *   *
The amendment would change the wording of section 702, as set forth in lines 8 to 24, both inclusive, at the bottom of page 33, so that it would read as follows:

SEC. 702. This title shall not apply to an employer with respect to the employment of agents outside any State or for the employment of any individuals by any educational institution or by any religious corporation, association, or society.

The amendment, if adopted, would take away the jurisdiction of this Commission over the employment practices of all religious corporations, of religious associations, of religious educational institutions, and of religious societies. In addition, it would take away the Commission's jurisdiction over educational institutions in general, both state and private.   *   *   *

Mr. WILLIAMS. Mr. President, I am opposed to the amendment offered by the distinguished Senators from North Carolina and Alabama. This amendment broadens the present exemption of section 702 of title VII in two respects. Section 702 now exempts religious organizations employing individuals of a particular religion for religious activities and provides an exemption for the educational activities of educational institutions.

This amendment would allow religious organizations and educational institutions a complete exemption from title VII coverage. A religious organization would be exempt whether or not it is engaged in religious activities; and the present authority to hire employees of a particular religion for religious activities would be expanded to include race, color, sex, or national origin for any activity. An educational institution would be made exempt from title VII whether or not it is engaged in educational activities.

As to religious organizations, it is not clear to me that the religious integrity of these institutions would be compromised by equal employment opportunities for employees in positions unrelated to religious activities of such institutions.

It should be emphasized that religious corporations and associations often provide purely secular services to the general public without regard to religious affiliation, and that most of the many thousands of persons employed by these institutions perform totally secular functions. In this regard, employees in these "religious" institutions perform jobs that are identical to jobs in comparable secular institutions. It seems appropriate, therefore, that these persons employed by religious corporations and associations should be given the same equal employment opportunities as those persons employed in comparable positions by secular employers.

For example, religious organizations in this country own and operate a substantial number of hospitals open to the public. These hospitals employ a broad range of persons to staff them. Without expounding on all of the job classifications at a hospital, I will just note that the categories of employment range from nurses and hospital administrators to dieticians and housekeeping personnel. There is no justification, in my judgment, for such hospitals to be permitted to discriminate against a janitor, for example, on any grounds.

Further, in my judgment, it might be very well unconstitutional for Congress to permit such discrimination. I recognize that the first amendment protects the free exercise of religion. I believe it is reasonable for Congress to permit an institution such as Catholic University to require its employees to be Catholic. The major function of that university is the propagation of its faith and we should not interfere with that program. However, the major purpose of hospitals and other service agencies is to provide public service. In providing this service they should not be allowed to become instruments of invidious and unreasonable discrimination in employment.

I would note for the record that at this point a similar issue has been resolved in an almost identical manner by the administration. The Occupational Safety and Health Act, passed by this Congress in 1970, provided no exemptions for employers. In defining the term "employer engaged in the business affecting commerce," for purposes of this act, the Department of Labor of necessity faced the question of coverage of churches as employers. Let me read for the RECORD a portion of the interpretation made by that agency just 2 weeks ago. It apears in the Federal Register of Friday, January 21, 1972, at page 930:

* * * Churches or religious organizations, like charitable and nonprofit organizations, are considered employers under the Act where they employ one or more persons in secular activities. As a matter of enforcement policy, the performance of, or participation in, religious services (as distinguished from secular or proprietary activities whether for charitable or religion-related purposes) will be regarded as not constituting employment unde the Act. Any person, while performing religious services or participating in them in any degree is not regarded as an employer or employee under the Act, notwithstanding the fact that such person may be regarded as an employer or employee for other purposes—for example, giving or receiving remuneration in connection with the performance of religious services.

* * * Some examples of coverage of religious organizations as employers would be: A private hospital owned or operated by a religious organization; a private school or orphanage owned or operated by a religious organization; commercial establishments of religious organizations engaged in producing or selling products such as alcoholic beverages, bakery goods, religious goods, etc.; and administrative, executive, and other office personnel employed by religious organizations. Some examples of noncoverage in the case of religious organizations would be: clergymen while performing or participating in religious services; and other participants in religious services; namely choir masters, organists, other musicians, choir members, ushers and the like.

I have read that citation from another bit of legislation that is now law to point out the analogous situation that we are dealing with here on another point of law in another department of government activity. * * *

I reiterate my judgment expressed that day—of all the institutions in this country who should be setting the example of equal employment opportunity, of equal opportunity for that matter in all aspects of life, it is America's religious institutions. I am confident that the Houses of God in this country do not shirk that responsibility nor should we.

The impact of this amendment on educational institutions is also not in keeping with our purpose to strengthen the EEOC. Broadening the exemption instead of eliminating it will serve only to continue existing discriminatory practices against the teachers and other staffs of this Nation's educational institutions.

It is our aim, Mr. President, in considering the present legislation, to strengthen the provisions of title VII and to eliminate the inconsistencies and insufficiencies which we allowed into that law in 1964. It is not our purpose to reaffirm existing loopholes.

At present, there are approximately 2,865,000 teachers and full-time faculty in 120,000 educational institutions in our Nation. There are also approximately 1.5 million nonprofessional staff employed by these institutions.

Most of the teachers and staff are public employees, the remainder are employed by private institutions. And, yet, under the present law, most of these employees are without an adequate and effective Federal remedy. But I submit, Mr. President, that these 4 million are no different from other employees in the Nation and deserve to be accorded the same protections. To continue the existing exemption for these employees would not only continue to work an injustice against this vital segment of our Nation's work force, but would also establish a class of employers who could pursue employment policies which are otherwise prohibited by the law.

The existence of discrimination in the employment practices of our Nation's educational institutions is well known, and has been adequately demonstrated by overwhelming statistical evidence as well as numerous complaints from groups and individuals. Minorities and women continue to be subject to blatant discrimination in these institutions.

As regards minorities, statistical studies show that minorities are generally underrepresented in teaching positions in educational institutions, and those that are employed are relegated to the lower paying and less prestigious positions. For example, in elementary and secondary schools, Negroes hold only about 10 percent of all available positions, Spanish-speaking Americans about 0.8 percent and all other minorities about 0.5 percent. This under representation becomes more pronounced when we look at the institutions of higher learning where Negroes account for only 2.2 percent of all faculty, Orientals 1.3 percent, and all other minorities only 0.3 percent.

Perhaps the most extensive discrimination in educational institutions, however, is found in the treatment of women. While women are generally well represented statistically in terms of numbers employed, they are generally relegated to the lowest paying and least prestigious jobs. Women account for the majority of teachers in elementary and secondary schools but they are virtually totally excluded from positions as principals and other administrative or decisionmaking positions.

In institutions of higher education women are almost totally absent in the position of academic dean, and are grossly underrepresented in all other major faculty positions. Also, I would add, that this discrimination does not only exist as regards to the acquiring of jobs, but that it is similarly prevalent in the area of salaries and promotions where studies have shown a well-established pattern of unlawful wage differentials and discriminatory promotion policies.

And yet, Mr. President, despite the existence of this obvious discrimination, this entire segment of our working population has not been provided with adequate Federal relief.

Not only have educational institutions been excluded from the protections of title VII, but teachers and other professionals have similarly been excluded from the protection of the Equal Pay Act, which has been used successfully by other employees to halt discriminatory wage differentials. What this means is that for most employees of educational institutions, the only available remedy has been an individual suit under the antidiscrimination provisions of the Constitution. However, as has been noted by the committee in reporting out S. 2515, this method of relief is very time consuming and costly, and does not guarantee complete relief in every case.

Mr. President, I cannot help but feel that we have been very remiss in allowing the employees of this Nation's educational institutions to go without an adequate Federal remedy against job discrimination for as long as we have.

The exclusion of educational institutions from the protections offered by title VII is a major factor in the discrimination which exists in our educational institutions today. There does not appear to me to be any reason, therefore, why this legislative oversight should be continued. We must correct this important defect of title VII immediately, and provide employees of edu-

cational institutions the same protections that we accord the rest of the Nation's work force.

EDITORS' NOTE: *Senators Allen (D., Ala.) and Ervin (D., N.C.) introduced amendment No. 809 restoring to educational institutions an exemption from the ban on religious discrimination. The amendment was adopted by a voice vote.*

Senate

1-24-72

pp. 391, 392

The PRESIDING OFFICER. The amendment will be stated.

The legislative clerk read as follows:

On page 33, line 24, strike out the word "religious".   * * *

Mr. ALLEN. Mr. President, I have called up amendment No. 809, which merely strikes one word out of the bill as presently before the Senate. But it does a whole lot more than knock out a word. It changes the meaning of the bill in a very important particular.

One of the most horrendous provisions of S. 2515 is section 3, which removes the existing exemption for employees of educational institutions as presently contained in section 702 of the Civil Rights Act of 1964. This over-zealous proposal attempts, first, to subvert academic freedom and, second, violates the prohibition contained in the first amendment which guarantees the free exercise of religion.

Mr. President, under the present law, is exempted from the provisions of the EEOC Act not only educational institutions of all kinds but also religious corporations, associations, or societies with respect to the employment of individuals of a particular religion to perform work connected with the carrying on by such corporation, association, or society of its religious activities. Then it goes on in the section which is deleted from the law by the present bill, this clause, and it removes this exemption: "or to an educational institution with respect to the employment of individuals to perform work connected with the educational activities of such institution."

So it removes from the exemption, from the operation of the EEOC Act, all educational institutions of any sort with respect to their educational activities; then as to societies or corporations or associations with respect to the employment of individuals of a particular religion to preform work connected with the carrying on by such corporation, association, or society of its religious activities.

So that the only exemption that is given to religious societies or associations or corporations is with respect to the employment of individuals to perform work connected with their religious activities.

In other words, Mr. President, in the case of an educational institution sponsored by a church group, the provisions of the bill now before the Senate would protect that religious association or college or school or society in the employment of people of its own religion in carrying on the religious activities of that association or corporation or school. If it were a college supported by the Catholic Church or the Baptist Church or the Episcopal Church, the bill as submitted would protect it only as to the employment of someone for enabling it to carry on its religious activity. So that in a church supported school, if the Baptist supported school wanted to employ a Baptist to teach theology or if a Catholic supported school wanted to employ a Catholic to teach theology, it would be protected.

But as to all its other activities, there would be no protection. Under the provisions of the bill, there would be nothing to prevent an atheist being forced upon a religious school to teach some subject other than theology. A religious school would not like to have an atheist or people of a different faith teaching other subjects and confining its right to be selective in the choice of its faculty only to those phases of the work carrying out its religious activities.

The present law goes on from that, though, and says that every educational institution shall be exempt from EEOC in the carrying on of its educational work, but the present bill removes that exemption. Religious schools are protected under the present law as educational institutions, so that they are exempt. But if the bill as submitted is passed and becomes law, religious schools would be exempt from the provisions of the EEOC Act only insofar as the work pertains to the carrying on of religious activities. The educational activity would not be exempt.

All this amendment would do would be to knock out the word "religious" where it appears in the bill before "activities."

The bill reads as follows:

This title shall not apply to any employer with respect to the employment of aliens outside any State—

This is in the present law and in the bill itself.

Or to a religious corporation, association, educational institution, or society with respect to the employment of individuals of a particular religion to perform work connected with the carrying on by such corporation, association, educational institution, or society of its religious activities.

The amendment would knock out the word "religious," leaving in the exemption in the carrying out of its activities. Exemption from the act would be provided by the amendment as to religious schools, as to religious societies, as to religious corporations or associations, and as to all educational institutions.

When the bill seeks out and draws under its so-called protection, active control, and domination, every school in the county, every college in the country, every church-supported school in the country, that is going a little bit too far.

The amendment by the distinguished senior Senator from North Carolina (Mr. ERVIN) and myself would preserve this exemption and would leave the present law exactly as it is. It would say to the people who want so greatly to expand the field of operations of the EEOC, "Do not touch the colleges. Do not try to take over the method by which the colleges and schools throughout the country are educating the young people of the country."

EDITORS' NOTE: *Amendment No. 860, introduced by Sen. Ervin (D., N.C.), would have exempted teachers and other faculty members of the public schools from the coverage of Title VII. The amendment was defeated in a voice vote.*

Senate

2-22-72

p. 2275

Mr. ERVIN.   * * *

This amendment, if approved by the Senate, would remove from the coverage of the bill the employment of teachers or other members of the faculties of public schools.

We already have Federal courts dealing with the subject of employment of members of faculties and teachers of public schools. We also have the HEW dealing with that same question. To my mind, it is rather ridiculous to have a third agency or department of the Federal Government have jurisdiction in exactly that same field in which the other two are acting. We have enough confusion in this field. Indeed, we have conflicts between the EEOC and the Office of Federal Contract Compliance in the Department of Labor. So that this amendment would merely make it certain that EEOC is not going to undertake to act in the same field in which the Department of Health, Education, and Welfare and the Federal courts are now acting.

We do not need to have three different Federal governmental powers to try to deal with one situation. * * *

This is simply an effort to add to the exemptions of the bill an exemption for teachers or other members of the faculties of public elementary and secondary schools. It simply removes from title VII of the Civil Rights Act of 1964 the question of discrimination regarding teachers or other members of faculties.

There has certainly been enough involvement in this question to recognize that teachers, just as much as others, are involved in the effort to desegregate schools.

EDITORS' NOTE: *Amendment No. 844, offered by Senators Ervin (D., N.C.) and Allen (D., Ala.), would have removed from the coverage of the Act employment practices of all educational institutions. The amendment was rejected by a vote of 30 to 60.*

Senate

2-22-72

pp. 2276, 2277

The assistant legislative clerk read as follows:
On page 33, strike out everything from the word "or" on line 20 through the word "activities" on line 24, and insert the following in lieu thereof: "or to the employment of any individuals by any educational institution."

Mr. ERVIN. * * *
Mr. President, this amendment would remove from the coverage of the bill all employment practices of all educational institutions. As I pointed out some days ago, when the EEOC invades the field of

education to enforce employment practices, they have to decide two things before they can take action.

Mr. ERVIN. Mr. President, the first thing they have to decide is that a man who claims he has suffered discrimination when he applied for a job at the educational institution is qualified to teach the course of study in which the vacancy occurs. The second thing they have to decide is that he was denied employment because of his race, or religion, or national origin, or his sex.

Manifestly, as I pointed out some days ago, Federal judges, and members of the EEOC are not competent to pass on the qualifications of people who teach such abstract subjects as anthropology and other subjects in institutions of higher learning. Therefore, this amendment would remove from the coverage of the act employment in educational institutions. * * *

Mr. JAVITS. Mr. President, I think this is simply rearguing the case which has been argued before in respect of this debate as to the delimitations of the employment of any individuals by any educational institutions.

I would like to point out that the exemption as it is now contained in section 702 has been considered and reconsidered five or six times. I believe as it stands now it represents the will of the Senate in what exemptions the Senate wishes to make in this particular title. Therefore, in accordance with the pledge that was made to the Senate by the Senator from New Jersey and me, the Senate has spoken and we wish to leave the matter strictly where it is.

Therefore, I urge that the amendment be rejected.

EDITOR'S NOTE: *Sen. Ervin (D., N.C.) introduced an amendment exempting religious organizations from application of the bill insofar as they wish to employ individuals of a particular religion in connection with their religious activities. The amendment was adopted by a voice vote and incorporated in the final bill.*

Senate

2-21-72

pp. 2179, 2180

Mr. WILLIAMS. Mr. President, the

amendment proposed by the Senator from Alabama broadens the present exemption found in title VII and retained in the committee bill, for a religious corporation, association, educational institution or society with respect to employment of individuals of a particular religion to perform work connected with the religious activities of such institution.

This amendment would have the effect of exempting these institutions from the operation of title VII insofar as religion is concerned whether or not their activities are religious or secular.

I do not believe that the religious integrity of these instiutions would be compromised by providing equal job opportunities for employees in positions unrelated to the religious activities of such institutions.

Mr. President, this is the second attempt to provide such an exemption. Several weeks ago, an amendment was offered that would provide a complete exemption from title VII to employees of educational and religious institutions.

That amendment, No. 815 was soundly defeated on a vote of 55 to 25 on February 1.

Now, we are faced with another such amendment. Admittedly, it is a much narrower exemption that is offered since it only applies to religion. Nonetheless, I believe it should not be adopted.

Many of these religious corporations and associations often provide purely secular services to the general public without regard to religious affiliation, and most of the many thousands of persons employed by these instittuions perform totally secular functions. In this regard, employees in these "religious" institutions perform jobs that are identical to jobs in comparable secular institutions. It is appropriate, therefore, that these persons employed by religious corporations and associations should be given the same equal employment opportunities as those persons employed in comparable positions by secular employers.

Appendix F-12

Exemptions: Physicians and Surgeons

EDITORS' NOTE: *Sen. Ervin (D., N.C.) introduced amendment No. 858 that would have exempted the employment of physicians and surgeons by hospitals from the requirements of the Act. The amendment was rejected in a voice vote.*

Senate

2-14-72

pp. 1646, 1647

Mr. WILLIAMS. * * *

The amendment offered by the distinguished Senator from North Carolina would exempt from the coverage of the law, as it would be if the bill passes, all hospitals, public and private, in the hiring of physicians and surgeons, and in doing so it would be saying affirmatively that hospitals, in their selection of physicians and surgeons, can discriminate against a person because of his race, color, religion, sex, or national origin.

This amendment, I suggest to my colleagues of the Senate, is cut from new cloth. It is different from the other amendments we have had. It goes to

some fundamental principles. When we were talking about the preponderance of evidence, when we were talking about extending coverage to State and local governments, that was one thing, but we cannot exempt hospitals, in the selection of physicians and surgeons, from the dictates of the Constitution and the basic law against discrimination. I think that we would be stepping back 100 years, and I am most strongly opposed to this amendment.

The amendment would mean that a physician, fully qualified and accredited by appropriate State and national authorities, could be denied employment with a hospital simply on the basis of race, color, religion, sex, or national origin and be unable to appeal to the Equal Employment Opportunity Commission for relief. There is no logic to this proposed amendment. It is not based on any showing of need. It is contrary to the present law and policy of this Nation with respect to equal employment opportunities. * * *

In addition, the amendment by the distinguished Senator from North Carolina is wholly in conflict with the general need recognized by both public and private groups for more female and minority doctors.

The American Medical Association and the Department of Health, Education, and Welfare have established a goal to increase the number of blacks enrolled in medical schools to 12 percent of the total medical school enrollment by 1975.

The Comprehensive Manpower Training Act—Public Law 92-157—enacted during the first session of the 92d Congress, would provide financial assistance for medical training. Title VI of the Civil Rights Act of 1964 assures that this assistance is available to all without regard to race, color, religion, or national origin. A special section added to the manpower legislation assures that no person be denied assistance because of sex.

Appendix F-13

Enforcement: Procedure Where Conciliation Fails

EDITORS' NOTE: *Amendment No. 878, introduced by Senators Javits (R., N.Y.) and Williams (D., N.J.), gave original jurisdiction to the federal district courts in issuing orders against discriminatory employment practices. A substitute for this amendment was introduced by Sen. Dominick (R., Colo.). Dominick amendment No. 884 provided that where the EEOC is unable to secure a conciliation agreement, it notifies the General Counsel, who may then bring a civil action in the appropriate federal district court against any respondent other than a government agency. The final legislation omitted reference to the General Counsel, stating simply that the Commission may bring civil action in such cases.*

Senate

2-9-72

pp. 1526, 1527

The legislative clerk read as follows:

On page 38, line 7, strike out through line 18 on page 47 and insert in lieu thereof the following:

(f)(1) In the case of a respondent not a government, governmental agency, or political subdivision, if the Commission determines after attempting to secure voluntary compliance under subsection (b) that it is unable to secure from the respondent a conciliation agreement acceptable to the Commission, which determination shall not be reviewable in any court, the Commission shall so notify the General Counsel. The General Counsel may initiate a formal hearing before the Commission by issuing and serving upon the respondent a complaint stating the facts upon which the allegation of the unlawful employment practice is based. The General Counsel, if he issues a complaint, shall also file the complaint with the United States district court for the district in which the unlawful employment practice in question is alleged to have oc-

curred or in which the respondent resides or transacts business. Except as hereinafter provided, all further pleadings shall be filed with the Commission.

The district court shall have jurisdiction during the Commission proceedings upon motion of any party to the Commission's proceedings to review, at its discretion, any action of the Commission which involves a controlling question of law, if it finds that such review would materially advance the ultimate termination of the litigation.

After the Commission has filed its findings and recommendations with the court as provided in subsection 706(h), the court shall have jurisdiction to order the elimination of unlawful employment practices and to require such affirmative action, including reinstatement or hiring of employees, with or without backpay (payable by the employer, employment agency, or labor organization, as the case may be, responsible for the unlawful employment practice), as will effectuate the policies of this title, except that (1) backpay liability shall not exceed that which accrues from a date more than two years prior to the filing of a charge with the Commission and (2) interim earnings or amounts earnable with reasonable diligence by the aggrieved person or persons shall operate to reduce the backpay otherwise allowable. Such action may further require the respondent to make reports from time to time showing the extent to which it has complied with the court's order.

(2) In the case of a respondent which is a government, governmental agency, or political subdivision, if the Commission determines after attempting to secure voluntary compliance under subsection (b) that it is unable to secure from the respondent a conciliation agreement acceptable to the Commission, which determination shall not be reviewable in any court, the Commission shall take no further action and shall refer the case to the Attorney General who may bring a civil action against such respondent in the appropriate United States district court. The person or persons aggrieved shall have the right to intervene in such civil action. The provisions of section 706 (q)

through (w), as applicable, shall govern civil actions brought hereunder. Related proceedings may be consolidated for hearing. Any officer or employee of the Commission who filed a charge in any case shall not participate in a hearing on any complaint arising out of such charge, except as a witness.

(g) The Commission, upon receipt of the General Counsel's complaint, shall issue to all parties a notice of a hearing before it or a member or agent thereof appointed in accordance with section 556 of title 5, United States Code, relating to hearing examiners, at a place therein fixed not less than five days after service of the compliant upon the respondent.

A respondent shall have the right to file an answer to the complaint against him with the Commission and, with the leave of the Commission, which shall be granted whenever it is reasonable and fair to do so, may amend his answer at any time. Respondents and the person or persons aggrieved shall be parties and may appear at any stage of the proceedings, with or without counsel. The Commission may grant other persons a right to intervene or to file briefs or make oral arguments as amicus curiae or for other purposes, as it considers appropriate. All testimony shall be taken under oath and shall be reduced to writing. Any such proceeding shall be conducted in conformity with the rules of evidence applicable in the district court of the United States under the Rules of Civil Procedure for the district courts of the United States, and under rules of procedure that conform insofar as possible with the Federal Rules of Court Procedure for the district courts of the United States. Any officer or employee of the Commission who filed a charge in any case shall not participate in a hearing on any complaint arising out of such charge, except as a witness.

(h) If the Commission finds by a preponderance of the evidence that the respondent has intentionally engaged in or is intentionally engaging in an ulawful employment practice, the Commission shall file its findings of fact and recommendations concerning appropriate relief with the United States district court having jurisdiction of the case. If the Commission finds that the respondent has not engaged in any unlawful employment practice, the Commission shall file its findings of fact with the clerk of the court and shall dismiss the complaint. Copies of such findings and recommendations shall be served by the Commission upon the parties.

(i) After a charge has been filed and until the record has been filed in court as hereinafter provided, the proceeding may at any time be ended by agreement between the Commission or, after the filing of a complaint, the General Counsel upon approval of the Commission and the respondent for the elimination of the alleged unlawful employment practice and the Commission may at any time, upon reasonable notice, modify or set aside, in whole or in part, any finding or recommendation by it. An agreement approved by the Commission shall be enforceable under subsections (1) through (n) and the provisions of those subsections shall be applicable to the extent appropriate to a proceeding to enforce an agreement.

(j) Findings of fact and recommendations concerning appropriate relief made under subsection (h) or (i) of this section shall be determined by a preponderance of the evidence on the record as a whole. Sections 554, 555, 556, and 557 of title 5 of the United States Code shall apply to such proceedings.

(k)(1) Any party aggrieved by a recommendation of the Commission may file in the United States district court having jurisdiction of the case sixty days after the receipt of such findings and recommendations a written motion proposing new findings and recommendations or seeking such other relief as may be appropriate under this title. A copy of such motion shall be forthwith transmitted by the clerk of the court to the Commission and to any other party to the proceeding before the Commission, and thereupon the General Counsel shall file in the court the record in the proceeding in the same manner as provided in section 2112 of title 28, United States Code. The court shall have power to grant to the moving party or any other party, including the Commission, such temporary relief or restraining order as it deems just and proper; and to make and enter upon the pleadings, testimony, and proceedings set forth in such record a decree granting or denying, in whole or in part, appropriate relief. Any party to the proceeding before the Commission shall be permitted to intervene in the court.

(2) No objection that has not been urged before the Commission, its member, or agent shall be considered by the court, unless the failure or neglect to urge such objection shall be excused because of extraordinary circumstances. The findings of the Commission with respect to questions of fact, if supported by substantial evidence on the record considered as a whole, shall be conclusive. If any party shall apply to the court for leave to adduce additional evidence and shall show to the satisfaction of the court that such evidence is material and that there were reasonable grounds for the failure to adduce such evidence in the hearing before the Commission, its member, or its agent, the court may order such additional evidence to be taken before the Commission, its member, or its agent, and to be made a part of the record. The Commission may modify its findings as to the facts, or make new findings, by reason of additional evidence so taken and filed, and it shall file such modified or new findings, which findings with respect to questions of fact, if supported by substantial evidence on the record considered as a whole, shall be conclusive. On the basis of such modified or new findings the Commission may modify its recommendations concerning appropriate relief. Upon the filing of the record with it, the jurisdiction of the court shall be exclusive and its judgment and decree shall be final, except that the same shall be subject to review in the court

of appeals as provided in section 1291 of title 28, United States Code. Motion filed under this subsection shall be heard expeditiously.

(l) The General Counsel, upon the recommendation of the Commission, may move in the United States district court having jurisdiction of the case for the immediate consideration of, and the entry of a decree to carry out, the Commission's recommendations concerning appropriate relief, and for appropriate temporary relief or restraining order, by filing in such court a written motion seeking the appropriate relief. The General Counsel shall file in court with his motion the record in the proceeding in the same manner as provided in section 2112 of title 28, United States Code. Subsection (k) of this section shall apply to proceedings upon motions made by the General Counsel under this subsection.

(m) If no motion for review, as provided in subsection (k) is filed within sixty days after service of the Commission's recommendations, the Commission's findings of fact and recommendation concerning appropriate relief shall be conclusive in connection with any motion for enforcement which is filed by the General Counsel under subsection (l). The district court in which such motion for an enforcement order is filed shall forthwith enter a decree enforcing the recommendations of the Commission and shall transmit a copy of such decree to the Commission, the respondent named in the petition, and to any other parties to the proceeding before the Commission.

(n) If within ninety days after service of the Commission's recommendations, no motion for review has been filed as provided in subsection (k), and the General Counsel has not sought an enforcement of the Commission's recommendations as provided in subsection (l), any person entitled to relief under the Commission's recommendations may move for a decree enforcing the recommendations in the United States district court having jurisdiction of the case. The provisions of subsection (m) shall apply to such motion for enforcement.

(o) The Attorney General shall conduct all litigation to which the Commission is a party in the Supreme Court of the United States pursuant to this title. All other litigation affecting the Commission, or to which it is a party, shall be conducted by attorneys appointed by the Commission.

(p) Whenever a charge is filed with the Commission pursuant to subsection (b) and the Commission concludes on the basis of a preliminary investigation that prompt judicial action is necessary to preserve the power of the Commission to grant effective relief in the proceeding, the General Counsel, upon the recommendation of the Commission shall, after he issues a complaint, bring an action for appropriate temporary or preliminary relief pending its final disposition of such charge, or until the filing of a petition under subsection (k), (l), (m), or (n) of this section, as the case may be, in the United States district court in which he filed the complaint pursuant to subsection

(f). Upon the bringing of any such action, the district court shall have jurisdiction to grant such injunctive relief or temporary restraining order as it deems just and proper notwithstanding any other provision of law. Rule 65 of the Federal Rules of Civil Procedure, except paragraph (a)(2) thereof, shall govern proceedings under this subsection.

Senate

2-9-72

p. 1535

Mr. JAVITS.   * * *

Mr. President, I now deal with the differences between the Williams-Javits amendment and the bill, and also the differences between the Williams-Javits amendment and the so-called Dominick amendment, in order that Members of the Senate may be able to quickly gather the situation.

Under the bill, the complaint is filed in the commission. Under our amendment No. 878, the complaint is filed in the commission and in the district court.

Item No. 2: Under the bill, there are no interlocutory appeals for motions in the courts as of right to test questions of law which might arise—so that the normal rules of procedure would apply which say that there will be no interlocutory appeals or motions except in cases of clear illegality or unconstitutionality, in which case an application for injunction would lie.

Under the amendment, interlocutory court rulings are permitted on controlling questions of law.

This is one of the things I have cited to the Senator from Colorado (Mr. DOMINICK) as being a very important point which changes substantively the provisions of the bill.

The third item is that cease-and-desist orders are issued by the EEOC under the bill, and the EEOC must petition for enforcement of the order in the court of appeals and the review of the findings is on the basis of the so-called substantial evidence test.

Under our amendment as now submitted, there is no cease-and-desist order issued. I have pointed that out. A cease-and-desist order would not issue, and the respondent's case is not terminated by the commission, but he still has the opportunity to test out the commission's findings of facts and recommendations as far as the court is concerned, so that the review, also under the substantial evidence test, comes before any order is issued.

That is very important, for this reason: Enforcement is a matter of discretion, and a respondent might very well be bound by the substantial evidence test in terms of a finding of fact, to wit, that he did or did not discriminate in employment. But as to enforcement in terms of back pay or anything of that character, I think there will be a very real opportunity for the intercession of the court in those situations.

Hence I think, Mr. President, there, too, the way we have drafted this amendment becomes a very critical aspect of the concession which we have made and the compromise which we have offered.

The last item, which I think bears repetition in terms of this comparison, is that the rules of evidence applicable in district courts apply to the EEOC hearings. That is provided by the bill now. Under our amendment, not only the rules of evidence, but the rules of civil procedure, which are applicable in the district courts, will be applicable to the EEOC procedures.

It seems to me, Mr. President, that under all of these circumstances, we are making a very sincere and a very precise offer of compromise in a really literal sense.

In general, the amendment makes substantial concessions. Also, I would like to approach this from the point of view of the quality and climate of adjudication, which are so important, and are substantially enhanced by giving the district courts a closer supervisory role over the Commission proceedings than the courts of appeal have under the bill, in the sense that they can act in an interlocutory way while the proceeding is going on, and there is nothing operative until the court actually issues the order.

Also, as I have pointed out, the question of remedy becomes very heavily a matter of consideration by the court, and there the court is not bound by the substantial evidence rule. That is only to back up the findings of fact.

So I think we have taken a really great step toward what has been contended for in leaving the freedom the courts have in shaping a decree—and they always do have that—to the court, as to what will be the remedy, what will be the recovery of wages, or rehiring, or whatever other remedy might be employed. And the courts have been rather inventive in terms of remedies in order to deal with situations of unlawful discrimination.

Senate

2-14-72

pp. 1654-1657

(Mr. DOMINICK's substitute amendment to the Williams-Javits amendment is as follows:)

Strike out the matter to be proposed and insert the following:

On page 38, beginning with line 7, strike out all through line 18 on page 47 and insert in lieu thereof:

"'(f)(1) If within thirty days after a charge is filed with the Commission or within thirty days after expiration of any period of reference under subsection (c) or (d), the Commission has been unable to secure from the respondent a conciliation agreement acceptable to the Commission, the Commission shall so notify the General Counsel who may bring a civil action against any respondent not a government, governmental agency, or political subdivision named in the charge. In the case of a respondent which is a government, governmental agency, or political subdivision, the Commission shall take no further action and shall refer the case to the Attorney General who may bring a civil action against such respondent in the appropriate United States district court. If a charge filed with the Commission pursuant to subsection (b) is dismissed by the Commission, or if within one hundred and fifty days from the filing of such charge or the expiration of any period of reference under subsection (c) or (d), whichever is later, the General Counsel has not filed a civil action under this section or the Attorney General in a case involving a government, governmental agency, or political subdivision, or the Commission has not entered into a conciliation agreement to which the person aggrieved is a party, the Commission or the Attorney General in a case involving a government, governmental agency, or political subdivision shall so notify the person aggrieved and within ninety days after the giving of such notice a civil action may be brought against the respondent named in the charge (1) by the person named in the charge as claiming to be aggrieved or (2) if such charge was filed by an officer or employee of the Commission, by any person whom the charge alleges was aggrieved by the alleged unlawful employment practice. Upon application by the complainant and in such circumstances as the court may deem just, the court may appoint an attorney for such complainant and may authorize the commencement of the action without the payment of fees, costs, or security. Upon timely application, the court may, in its discretion, permit the Attorney General to intervene in such civil action if he certifies that the case is of general public importance. Upon request, the court may, in its discretion, stay further proceedings for not more than sixty days pending the termination of State or local proceedings described in subsection (c) of this section or further efforts of the Commission to obtain voluntary compliance.

" '(2) In any such proceeding the General Counsel or the Attorney General in a case involving a government, governmental agency, or political subdivision may file with the clerk of such court a request that a court of three judges be convened to hear and determine the case. Such request by the General Counsel or the Attorney General shall be accompanied by a certificate that, in his opinion, the case is of general public importance. A copy of the certificate and request for a three-judge court shall be immediately furnished by such clerk to the chief judge of the circuit (or in his absence, the presiding circuit judge of the circuit) in which the case is pending. Upon receipt of the copy of such request it shall be the duty of the chief judge of the circuit or the presiding circuit judge, as the case may be, to designate immediately three judges in such circuit, of whom at least one shall be a circuit judge and another of whom shall be a district judge of the court in which the proceeding was instituted, to hear and determine such case, and it shall be the duty of the judges so designated to assign the case for hearing at the earliest practicable date, to participate in the hearing and determination thereof, and to cause the case to be in every way expedited. An appeal from the final judgment of such court will lie to the Supreme Court.

" '(3) In the event the General Counsel or the Attorney General fails to file such a request in any such proceeding, it shall be the duty of the chief judge of the district (or in his absence, the acting chief judge) in which the case is pending immediately to designate a judge in such district to hear and determine the case. In the event that no judge in the district is available to hear and determine the case, the chief judge of the district, or the acting chief judge, as the case may be, shall certify this fact to the chief judge of the circuit (or in his absence, the acting chief judge) who shall then designate a district or circuit judge of the circuit to hear and determine the case.

" '(4) It shall be the duty of the judge designated pursuant to this subsection to assign the case for hearing at the earliest practicable date and to cause the case to be in every way expedited.

" '(5) Whenever a charge is filed with the Commission and the Commission concludes on the basis of a preliminary investigation that prompt judicial action is necessary to carry out the purposes of this Act, the Commission may bring an action for appropriate temporary or preliminary relief pending final disposition of such charge. It shall be the duty of a court having jurisdiction over proceedings under this section to assign cases for hearing at the earliest practicable date and to cause such cases to be in every way expedited.

" '(g)(1) Each United States district court and each United States court of a place sub-

ject to the jurisdiction of the United States shall have jurisdiction of actions brought under this title. Such an action may be brought in any judicial district in the State in which the unlawful employment practice is alleged to have been committed, in the judicial district in which the employment records relevant to s uch practice are maintained and administered, or in the judicial district in which the plaintiff would have worked but for the alleged unlawful employment practice, but if the respondent is not found within any such district, such an action may be brought within the judicial district in which the respondent has his principal office. For purposes of sections 1404 and 1406 of title 28 of the United States Code, the judicial district in which the respondent has his principal office shall in all cases be considered a district in which the action might have been brought.

" '(2) If the court finds that the respondent has engaged in or is engaging in an unlawful employment practice charged in the complaint, the court may enjoin the respondent from engaging in such unlawful employment practice, and order such affirmative action as may be appropriate, which may include, but is not limited to, reinstatement or hiring of employees, with or without backpay (payable by the employer, employment agency, or labor organization, as the case may be, responsible for the unlawful employment practice), or any other equitable relief as the court deems appropriate. Backpay liability shall not exceed that which accrues from a date more than two years prior to the filing of a charge with the Commission. Interim earnings or amounts earnable with reasonable diligence by the person or persons discriminated against shall operate to reduce the backpay otherwise allowable.' "

* * *

Mr. DOMINICK. Mr. President, with great deference to my friend from West Virginia, I would like to explain the amendment at the present time before we get into any colloquy, if he does not mind. I will be done shortly.

Mr. BYRD of West Virginia. Surely.

Mr. DOMINICK. Mr. President, there has been a great deal of discussion concerning what should or should not be done with the enforcement procedures of the EEOC. Some persons have interpreted the discussion as to whether or not those who are in favor of court procedure were in fact in favor of any enforcement procedure. Having participated in the debate before the committee, having written the individual views in the report, and having debated the issue on the floor extensively, I think it is only fair to say that, from my point of view, the EEOC deserves and needs enforcement procedure. That is why I insisted on reporting the bill and why I wrote my supplemental individual views, and that is why I have been carrying forward the discussion on the court enforcement method. It is an enforcement procedure and an enforcement procedure which myself and at least 45 other Senators happen to think is best. * * *

The language of this particular amendment is concise and uncomplicated. It says that if within 30 days after a charge is filed with the Commission, or within 30 days after expiration of any period of reference under subsection (c) or (d), of this bill, the Commission has been unable to secure a conciliation agreement, the Commission shall notify the general counsel, who then can, if he so desires, bring a civil action against any respondent other than those within the category of a governmental entity.

In those cases, Senators will recall, we have already provided in the bill that with reference to disputes involving State or local governmental employees, the dispute would go to the Attorney General for the filing of a case in U.S. District Court. Federal employees would exhaust their respective agency remedies and then the employee would have a right either to go to the Civil Service Commission Board of Appeal and Review or to submit it to the Attorney General for action through the U.S. district courts.

So the bill provides governmental employees and the governmental agencies with rights to redress their grievances in court. The only ones who are not subject to such court relief are the private employers and private employees; this, in my own humble opinion, is discrimination in and of itself. I do not see why we should arbitrarily carve out one sector.

This particular amendment, which is offered as a substitute for the Williams-Javits amendment, says that the Commission shall take no further action after the general counsel files the complaint before the court. The general counsel goes before the U.S. district court judge, and if he certifies that it is in the general public interest, he can request an expedited three-judge panel, similar to the procedure we now have in connection with voting rights, public accommodations, and the "pattern or practice" cases.

The appeal from that three-judge panel then goes directly to the Supreme Court. In terms of timing this is what happens: The charge is filed before the Commission, and they review it. If they find reasonable cause and are unable to reach a conciliation agreement then the general counsel goes into court. If he thinks that it involves an issue of general public interest, he can ask for a three-judge court. If it involves individual rights, which is probably more likely, he would go into the regular district courts with the right to have the judge assign priorities and expedite the hearing of the case.

The case would be heard and it would then go, in the first instance, from a three-judge court to the Supreme Court, and in the expedited hearing would go through the regular appellate proceedings.   * * *

The procedure I have outlined would be far quicker than would the Javits-Williams amendment. Consider for a moment the delay involved with the interlocutory appeal that might occur on evidentiary issues under amendment No. 878. The respondent raises the issue with the hearing examiner hearing the case; any evidence which creates an argument concerning admissibility would have to be heard before a judge; and I can foresee a lot of cases in that category. It seems to me the impartial court system would be far better.

For the purpose of creating a record and after thinking about this issue more and more, all the while getting more concerned over the polarization of the sides, it seemed to me that we should get an opinion on the relative merits of the two amendments from the people who have been intimately involved with the enforcement of job discrimination—the Civil Rights Division of the Department of Justice. I requested them to send up such an opinion, and I shall send a copy of that opinion to every Senator late this afternoon or early tomorrow morning.

The letter from Assistant Attorney General, David L. Norman says very candidly that in his opinion the Javits-Williams amendment would be extremely difficult to administer, it would be time consuming, and it does not afford the protections available under the Dominick amendment. Mr. Norman indicates that he had already so testified in summary on the points in favor of my procedures before the committee and that he held such testimony, urging that, as between these two amendments, the Dominick amendment should be adopted.

I hope my colleagues will read Mr. Norman's letter with some care, because his opinion also deals with the Hruska "pattern or practices" amendment, and then brings up a whole new issue which has not been considered at all concerning the exclusion from either court proceedings or enforcement proceedings those cases which are presently pending before the EEOC.

But just to give Senators some idea of what the Civil Rights Division says, I shall read into the RECORD at this point a portion of the reasoning applied by the Civil Rights Division of the Department of Justice.

Amendment 878 (the Williams-Javits Amendment) carries forward the main features of S. 515 as reported by the Senate Labor Committee. Under that Amendment, EEOC will have authority to issue orders, which may become enforceable in the courts after opportunity for judicial review. Although the words "cease and desist orders" in the original bill have been deleted and the term "recommendation" substituted therefor, this change does not appear to be a substantial one, since under either version the EEOC position becomes an enforceable order unless modified by the court upon review. Like the committee bill, the Williams-Javits Amendment calls for judicial review of the EEOC order on the Administrative record. Sec. 706(k)(1), p. 6 and 7 of the Amendment. Like the Committee bill, the William-Javits Amendment makes the findings of EEOC "conclusive" on the courts if supported by "substantial evidence on the record as a whole" (Sec. 706(k)(2), p. 7 of the Amendment).

Although the Williams-Javits Amendment provides for filing of the administrative complaint with the district court, we do not perceive any substantial change resulting from that novel procedure. Also, the Williams-Javits Amendment provides for an interlocutory appeal to the district court on any "controlling question of law" if it finds that such review "would materially advance the ultimate termination of the litigation." It is doubtful that this addition is a significant one, since controlling issues of law were judicially reviewable under S. 2515, and this Department's experience under the analogous provisions for interlocutory appeal from district court decisions (28 U.S.C. 1292 (b)) indicates that such appeals are only useful on rare occasions.

The one material change which the Williams-Javits Amendment would make in S. 2515 is to transfer judicial review from the courts of appeals to the district court. This change adds another layer of review to the already lengthy process of charge, investigation, cause finding, administrative complaint, hearing before hearing examiner, review before the Commission and review in the Court of Appeals.

Amendment 871 (the Dominick Amendment) —

The substitute incorporates those same provisions—

on the other hand, authorizes the EEOC to proceed in the appropriate United States District Court to secure relief from any employment practice it deems unlawful. In such proceedings, the evidence would be heard by the District Judge and the facts found by him. In addition, under the Dominick Amendment, those judicial proceedings would be expedited and the General Counsel could require the convening of a three-judge court with direct review in the Supreme Court upon a filing of a certificate of general public importance.

As you know, when I testified before the subcommittee on Labor of the Senate Committee on Labor and Public Welfare in October last year on behalf of the Department of Justice and the Administration, I again expressed our view that the granting of authority to the Equal Employment Opportunity Commission to bring judicial proceedings is a better means of enforcing Title VII than granting that Commission administrative enforcement powers. We still adhere to that view.

In my testimony before the Senate Labor Committee I set forth four grounds for our view that judicial enforcement is preferable to administrative proceedings. (Hearings pp. 150-151.) One of those was applicable only to governmental employers and was accepted by that Committee. The other three bases for our view may be summarized as follows: (1) Federal district judges hold court throughout the country and enjoy a confidence and respect in their communities which cannot be matched by administrative officers; and their authority to issue enforceable orders enables them to resolve cases speedily;

If I may interject, Mr. President, I think this is a most important point. Under the procedures of S. 2515, and the procedures under amendment No. 878, the Williams-Javits amendment, cease-and-desist orders or recommendations can only be issued in Washington.

Under court enforcement the district courts in every State of the Union are able to provide an impartial determination—an enormously simplified procedure insofar as both the complainant and the respondent are concerned. * * *

Mr. DOMINICK. The letter continues:

(2) because of the sensitive nature of the issues to be resolved and the fact that the larger cases involve the rights and expectations of substantial numbers of people, it is inappropriate to leave the critical factual determinations and formulations of relief to hearing examiners and Commissioners sitting in Washington; and (3) the fact that Federal courts resolve the factual and legal issues in equal opportunity cases in the areas of voting, housing, and education make them a particularly appropriate forum for resolving the same kinds of issues in employment discrimination cases. In addition, I pointed out that there is a definite, although hard to measure, advantage in having the person who has heard the evidence be responsible for fashioning the relief which he must then enforce. * * *

I think the letter is extremely important, because it indicates what I have been saying—namely, that we must retain a belief in this country that the Federal district courts provide a method of impartial review of highly emotional cases which involve not only basic human rights but also basic human emotions. Additionally, you can do far better in a court proceeding which is impartial, organized, and ruled by precedent and established rules of procedure than you can from an administrative proceeding composed of a group of people who are responsible to no one except the person who appointed them—largely in the executive department—or who may have been appointed as part of the staff of the agency itself. * * *

Mr. JAVITS. Mr. President, we have been expecting this. This is the position of the administration. They prefer court litigation to the cease-and-desist order practice which is contained in the bill reported by the committee.

I have read with great interest the letter which comes now, declaring officially this position, and I most respectfully disagree.

Inherent in the Department's view is the very basis for our disagreement. First, they say that Federal district judges hold court throughout the country and enjoy a confidence and respect in their communities which cannot be matched by administrative officers. I most respectfully submit that if that is true, we had better dismantle the whole administrative machinery in Washington, which includes tens of thousands of cases not only in this field but in many other fields as well, especially the National Labor Relations Board, which includes cases exactly in this field and which does issue cease-and-desist orders.

Second, the innuendo is made—and even was made this minute by the distinguished Senator from Colorado—that "these officers are responsible to no one." They are appointed by the President, they are confirmed by the Senate, and they are surely responsible to the courts, just as the judges are. How many lower court decisions are reversed?

As we have argued time and time again, before the cease-and-desist order can be enforced, it must be the subject of a court decree by a circuit court of appeals, and under amendment No. 878,

by a district court, as well.

But the whole point comes in the next clause of the department's view:

And their authority to issue enforcible orders enables them to resolve cases speedily.

Let us take a poll of any street—Washington, Takoma, San Diego, Miami—and see who will tell you that the courts decide cases speedily. They do not, of course; especially in the major industrial centers, where the district courts are 30 and 40 months behind in their calendars, and that is where these cases are going to come up.

The second point which gives the whole thing away is "Because of the sensitive nature of the issues to be resolved." It is pretty sensitive to deal with questions involving trade unions in the National Labor Relations Board. It is pretty sensitive to deal with questions involving fraud and deceit, just what the Federal Trade Commission deals with, in terms of the issuance of cease and desist orders. And I am naming only two. Precisely because it is sensitive, we have given that jurisdiction to commissions, because we believe they develop an expertise; they develop a sensitivity to the issues. They are mandated to negotiate settlements and to try conciliation before they engage in any summary action. We expressly created this idea of commissions in this country because of the sensitive nature and the degree of specialization and expertise which is required in these measures.

Further, the fact that the courts do resolve civil rights cases in other fields—voting, housing, and education—does not make them a particularly appropriate forum for resolving job discrimination issues, simply because it is job discrimination that gets away from you the fastest.

When a man is discriminated against in employment, he loses money every day or goes on welfare, and that is where the difference comes in with respect to housing, education, and voting, where you have time to turn around and where it is not a matter of eat or starve or go on welfare.

Appendix F-14

Enforcement: Special Masters

EDITORS' NOTE: *Under amendment No. 909, cosponsored by Senators Javits (R., N.Y.) and Cooper (R., Ky.), if a designated judge hasn't assigned a case for trial within 120 days after the issue has been joined, he may appoint a master pursuant to rule 53 of the federal rules of civil procedure. The amendment was adopted and was included in the final bill as enacted.*

Senate

2-22-72

pp. 2281, 2282

Mr. ERVIN. Mr. President, as I understand, the Senator from New York has asked unanimous consent to modify the prior amendment so as to make the appointment of special masters by the judge discretionary rather than mandatory?

Mr. JAVITS. The Senator is exactly correct.　　　* * *

The legislative clerk read as follows:

On page 50, before line 20, insert the following new section:

SEC. 4A. Section 706 of the Civil Rights Act of 1964 is amended by adding at the end thereof the following new subsection:

"(l) If the judge designated pursuant to subsection (f)(3) of this section has not assigned the case for trial within one hundred and twenty days after issue has been joined, that judge may appoint a master pursuant to rule 53 of the Federal Rules of Civil Procedure.".

Mr. JAVITS. Mr. President, the pending amendment really originated with

the Senator from Kentucky (Mr. COOPER). I begged him to offer the amendment. However, with traditional modesty, he asked me to do so and allowed me to join him as cosponsor.

It arose from the Dominick amendment, on which the Senator from Kentucky (Mr. COOPER) based his position that the courts could proceed as they wished on the appointment of a master under rule 53 of the Federal Rules of Civil Procedure. The normal rule as to the ability of the court to appoint a master if it wishes under rule 53 is quite stringent—the case must be truly exceptional to qualify. All this amendment does is relax that stringency in the area of title 7 cases, where justice delayed is very often justice denied.

Mr. DOMINICK. Mr. President, on my own time I wish to engage in a colloquy with the distinguished Senator from New York.

I discussed this amendment in its original form with the Senator from New York and suggested that rather than to strike what trial judges are supposed to do, we ought to leave it discretionary with judges because of the different situations that might arise in different jurisdictions.

As I understand it, the amendment language now is simply designed to remind the judge that Congress intends that employment discrimination cases should be expedited so if the judge thinks it wise, he can turn the case over to a master. This language simply highlights Congressional concern without trying to mandate what the judge does.

Appendix F-15

Enforcement: Interventions

EDITORS' NOTE: *Sen. Williams (D., N.J.) introduced a number of technical and perfecting amendments, including one making clear that the EEOC general counsel had the right to intervene in private actions not involving governments, governmental agencies, or political subdivisions. This amendment was included in the final bill*

Senate

2-21-72

pp. 2180, 2181

The amendments are as follows:

AMENDMENT No. 896

On page 58, line 4, after "Senate" insert

the following: "for a term of five years".

On page 58, line 9, strike out the word "members" and insert in lieu thereof the word "member".

AMENDMENT NO. 897

On page 50, before line 20, insert the following:

SEC. 4A. The fifth sentence of section 706 (f) (1) of the Civil Rights Act of 1964, as amended by the previous section, is amended to read as follows: "Upon timely application, the court may, in its discretion, permit the General Counsel, or the Attorney General in a case involving a government, government agency, or political subdivision, to intervene in such civil action if he certifies that the case is of general public importance."

AMENDMENT NO. 899

On page 60, line 9, beginning with the word "powers" strike out through the word "the" on line 12.

AMENDMENT NO. 900

On page 59, in the matter to be inserted after line 22, strike out in lines 22 and 23 on page 3 of amendment numbered 797 the following: "the issuance of complaints, the prosecution of such complaints before the Commission," and insert in lieu thereof the following: "the filing of complaints".

On page 59, in the matter to be inserted after line 22, strike out beginning after the period on line 7 through the period on line 14 on page 4 of amendment numbered 797.

AMENDMENT NO. 901

On page 56, beginning with line 15, strike out through the period in line 19.

AMENDMENT NO. 902

On page 52, line 1, beginning with the comma, strike out through the word "thereof" on line 3.

Mr. WILLIAMS. Mr. President, the first amendment, No. 896, is a technical amendment to correct a typographical errr in the redrafting of section 705 concerning the number of commissioners to make clear that their term of office is 5 years. The second sentence of the amendment corrects a typographical error.

No. 897 amendment to the court enforcement provision is intended to allow the general counsel to intervene in private actions not involving governments, governmental agencies or political subdivisions and to make clear that it is the Attorney General who will intervene in cases involving governments, governmental agencies, and political subdivisions brought by private individuals. The present language of the Dominick substitute only authorizes the Attorney General to intervene in private actions. The amendment is to clear up an inconsistency whereby the general counsel of the Commission may bring a civil action for the Commission, but might not be able to protect the Commission's interest in a case where private litigant is involved.

No. 899 is a technical amendment redefining the Commission's operational authority to eliminate references to the cease-and-desist powers.

No. 900 is a technical and conforming amendment to the provision of S. 2515 that created a general counsel. It makes clear the general counsel authority is to handle the filing of complaints under the now adopted court enforcement procedures rather than the issuance and prosecution of complaints before the Commission under cease and desist.

The amendment also strikes the provision prohibiting the Commission employees engaged in prosecutorial functions from participating in other decisional functions at the Commission since there is no administrative hearing process any longer, as a result of the amendment.

Amendment No. 901 is a technical amendment concerning the investigatory powers of the Commission which eliminates a sentence relating to the use of the subpena powers in relation to cease and desist, which again has been stricken.

Amendment No. 902 is a technical amendment, eliminating the reference in the pattern and practice transfer to cease and desist procedures to make clear that the Commission's handling of pattern and practice cases is to be through the Federal district courts.

EDITORS' NOTE: *Another group of technical and perfecting amendments introduced by Sen. Williams (D., N.J.) included modifications making clear that (1) an aggrieved party has the right to intervene in a civil suit brought by the EEOC general counsel or the Attorney General; (2) private action can be filed in a case involving a governmental agency or political subdivision if the Attorney General hasn't acted in the requisite period of time; and (3) preliminary injunctions involving a governmental agency or political subdivision are to be sought by the Attorney General. These amendments were incorporated in the final bill.*

Senate

2-21-72

p. 2181

The text of the amendments is as follows:

On page 33, in the matter to be inserted by an amendment after line 13, strike out the word "religions" and insert in lieu thereof the word "religion".

On page 33, in the matter to be inserted by an amendment after line 13, strike out the word "in" and insert in lieu thereof the word "to".

On page 38, in the matter to be inserted by amendment numbered 884, insert on page 2, line 7, after the period the following: "The person or persons aggrieved shall have the right to intervene in a civil action brought by the General Counsel or the Attorney General in a case involving a government, governmental agency, or political subdivision.".

On page 38, in the matter to be inserted by amendment numbered 884, insert on page 2, line 13, after the words "Attorney General" the following: "has not filed a civil action".

On page 38, in the matter to be inserted by amendment numbered 884, on page 3, line 11, strike out "subsection (c)" and insert in lieu thereof "subsections (c) or (d)".

On page 38, in the matter to be inserted by amendment numbered 884, insert on page 5, line 6, after the word "Commission" the following: "or the Attorney General in a case involving a government, governmental agency, or political subdivision,".

On page 38, in the matter to be inserted by amendment numbered 884, on page 5, line 20, strike out the word "plaintiff" and insert in lieu thereof the words "aggrieved person".

On page 38, in the matter to be inserted by amendment numbered 884, insert on page 5, after line 11, the following:

"(6) The provisions of section 706 (f) through (k), as applicable, shall govern civil action brought hereunder."

On page 55, line 12, strike out the word "or" and insert in lieu thereof the word "as".

On page 50, line 25, strike out "1971" and insert in lieu thereof "1972".

On page 51, line 20, strike out "1971" and insert in lieu thereof "1972".

On page 59, line 6, strike out "1971" and insert in lieu thereof "1972".   * * *

Mr. WILLIAMS. Mr. President, the first amendment that I offer makes two typographical corrections in the amendment that was adopted on religious belief. The first correction makes the word "religion" singular instead of plural. The second change is a grammatical change relating to hardship of religious practice to the conduct "of" the employer's business rather than "in" the conduct of the employer's business.

Mr. ERVIN. Mr. President, I would like to ask the Senator from New Jersey if that affects the amendment which was adopted in any respect——

Mr. WILLIAMS. No. This does not deal with the amendment offered by the Senator from North Carolina. This deals with the amendment offered by the Senator from West Virginia, not the Senator's amendment.   * * *

Mr. President, the third amendment is intended to make clear the provision under which a private action may have been filed in a case involving a governmental agency and political subdivision. Private action can be filed if the Attorney General has not filed a civil action within the requisite period of time. The words "has not filed a civil action" were left out of the amendment on court enforcement.

The fourth amendment is intended to correct a typographical error which allowed for the deferral under State and local proceedings under 706(c). It should have read 706 (c) or (d), since there are two deferral procedures.

The fifth amendment is intended to make clear that preliminary injuctions invloving a governmental agency or political subdivision are to be sought by the Attorney General.

The sixth amendment is intended to conform to language in the bill relating to an "aggrieved person" rather than the term "plaintiff," since civil actions would be in the name of the commission or the United States.

The seventh amendment is in the nature of a technical amendment, to make clear the provisions under which civil actions are to be brought.

The eighth amendment is intended to correct a grammatical error in the redesignation of several subsections. This amendment, which is No. 898, is a technical amendment, intended to reflect the fact that the bill would be passed in 1972 rather than in 1971, as it is in the bill as introduced.

That concludes this group of technical amendments.

Appendix F-16

Enforcement: Reimbursement of Costs and Fees

EDITORS' NOTE: *An amendment intro-duced by Sen. Gambrell (D., Ga.) and modified by an amendment introduced by Sen. Mondale (D., Minn.) provided for payment by the Federal Government of costs and counsel fees incurred by small companies and unions that prevailed in proceedings under the Act. The modified amendment was adopted by a vote of 72 to 2 but was eliminated in conference.*

Senate

1-31-72

pp. 815-820

The assistant legislative clerk read as follows:

On page 50, line 19, add the following new section:

(e) Subsection (w) of section 706 of such Act, as redesignated by this section is amended to read as follows:

"(w) In any action or proceeding under this title the Commission or court, as the case may be, may allow the prevailing party, other than the Commission or the United States, a reasonable attorney's fee as part of the costs. Any respondent that is an employer of less than twenty-five employees or a labor organization of less than twenty-five members shall, upon application to the Commission, be indemnified by the United States for the cost of his defense against the charge in an amount not to exceed $5,000, including all reasonable expenses and attorney's fees incurred after the serving of notice on him of the charge.

"Any respondent that is an employer of twenty-five to one hundred employees whose average income from such employment is less than $7,500, or a labor organization with twenty-five to one hundred members, shall, upon application to the Commission, be indemnified by the United States for one-half of the cost of his defense against the charge not to exceed $2,500, including all reasonable expenses and attorney's fees incurred after the serving of notice on him of the charge. The costs evidenced by respondent's vouchers of his expenses and attorney's fees shall be deemed reasonable so long as they are comparable to the total amount of the expenses and attorney's fees incurred by the Commission in investigating and prosecuting the charge. Disallowance of any part of such request shall be made a part of the Commission's order in such proceedings. Any United States court before which a proceeding under this title shall be brought may upon request by the respondent make the determination provided for in this subsection.

"The Commission and the United States shall be liable for costs as provided for in this section the same as a private person. No enforcement procedure under this title may be initiated against a respondent employer or union until the costs provided for herein shall have been paid in full. No such costs shall be paid in the event that the Commission or court having jurisdiction of such proceeding shall determine that a respondent has conducted his defense in a manner inconsistent with the achievement of the purposes of this title."

Mr. GAMBRELL. Mr. President, the amendment I have offered at this time extends relief to small businesses under the pending bill. That is to say, it provides for an allowance for attorneys' fees for certain prescribed small businesses against whom enforcement proceedings are brought under this act. * * *

In specific terms, the amendment provides that a business or a union which has 25 or fewer employees or members will get its entire expense and attorney's fee reimbursed by the Federal Government through the EEOC in any proceeding against it.

Under the act, businesses and unions having from 25 up to 100 members of employees would be reimbursed up to $2,500. But in each case, the Commission or the court before which a proceeding is pending would have to determine, before the amount could be paid, that the defenses made by small businesses were put on for purposes inconsistent with the purposes of the act itself. That is to say, the court or the EEOC would have an opportunity to determine whether the union or the small business was defending itself in bad faith. If so, the payment of fees and expenses could be denied.

The amendment also provides that this compensation would have to be paid prior to any enforcement proceedings being brought against the small business or the small union. In other words, after the investigation, or after the Commission proceedings, the Commission would determine the amount of award of a fee, and that fee would have to be paid in cash before the Commission could go to court to get a restraining order.

It seems to me that this is only fair, in order to give small business or small unions an opportunity to say, "Well, up to at least $2,500 or $25,000, I can fight the matter equally with the Federal Government. I am the first, the fourth, the seventh, the 10th, or the 100th person being proceeded against under the act.

I have some genuine questions of fact or question of law that I want to litigate. I have a competent attorney who advises me that I am not obligated to do what the Government says I am supposed to do, and I should like to have that question determined.

Of course, I would prefer to have the case determined in court, but under the law I have got to go through the Commission. In any event, I do have an opportunity, within those limits, to defend myself in good faith against the overwhelming economic power at the command of the Federal Government. * * *

We make this change or this addition: We leave the amendment without change except that we provide for discretionary authority in the case of the prevailing party. We say that any respondent— that is, a labor union or an employer— who qualifies as a small business or a small union can be compensated for his expenses, or expenses and fees, even if he loses or even if he is found at fault, so long as it is not determined that he conducted his defense in a manner inconsistent with the achievement of the purposes of the act.

Our thought in offering the amendment is simple. We feel that if a small business or a small union in good faith wishes to test some of the questions that are raised, it should have a right to do so without bankrupting itself. It should not have to depend upon its ultimately prevailing, because it could be wrong in good faith about the law, or it could be wrong in good faith about the facts. It seems to me that certainly in the early stages of enforcement under the act these questions should be subject to exploration by small businesses in the same manner as they would be by large businesses.   * * *

It has been said that the amendment which I have offered will encourage litigation, will encourage small businesses in the classification referred to, to be more litigious, and to insist on a lot of unworthy defenses and that type of thing. We have tried to deal with that possibility in the act in a number of ways, although I do not conceive of it as a real difficulty, because the average businessman has much more to do than to want to go before the EEOC or a Federal court on an unfair employment practices charge.

But the limits that are built into the amendment, aside from the practical restrictions on what one will do and what he is to do, are, first, that the provision applies only to small businesses. Some-

one who employs up to 25 gets full compensation. Someone who employs between 25 and 100 gets only half of his fees and expenses taken care of. So, first, it applies only to small businesses. Second, there are limits built into that. A very small one can get only up to $5,000 in total, and the slightly small one, you might say, gets only $2,500. But there again there are some practical limits built into it. The man going into litigation can see there is no bonanza of fees and expenses with which to defend himself.

Another limitation is that the reasonableness of the charges that he submits must be comparable to those which the EEOC itself has spent in prosecuting the charges against him.

So if the EEOC has spent only $1,000 on the claim, he would be entitled to only $2,500 or $5,000.

My guess is that, in most cases, the EEOC will spend enormously more money in dealing with any of these claims than any private business could possibly afford to do. But there are limits—that he cannot receive more for defending himself as was spent against him.

Finally, a limitation which is most important is that he does not get anything if the manner in which he conducts his defense is found by the Commission or the court to be inconsistent with the purposes of the act.

In my judgment, this amendment will encourage settlement rather than discourage it. The reason for that is this: A small businessman might go into litigation thinking in good faith that he has a defense or that he has a question of fact that would be adjudicated in his favor, and then ultimately find that he was mistaken.

So, Mr. President, I think the amendment will encourage settlement, because a man, in considering whether to settle with the EEOC some claim that is under adjudication, would be entitled to be compensated if he will admit that he was in the wrong.   * * *

Mr. WILLIAMS. Mr. President, I have reservations about some of the details of the amendment, including the fact that the assessment of fees and costs in certain areas is mandatory and not discretionary, and the fact that they must be paid in advance. These are the two major reservations I have. Yet, a provision for the fair assessment of costs and fees certainly is a principle that I would like to agree to, and it should be included in this legislation.

As it stands, the fact that the fees and

the costs are mandatorily assessed, win, lose, or draw, cause me to hesitate.

* * *

Mr. GAMBRELL. First, Mr. President, I should like to clarify the interpretation that the Senator has put on the matter. I think he is mistaken in saying that it is payable in advance. In fact, I know he is, because as I understand the bill, you do not go to court and you do not have any rendering of any kind of decision until after there has been a very thorough investigation or until after the conciliation——

Mr. WILLIAMS. I said in advance of litigation, or I meant to say that.

Mr. GAMBRELL. The Senator did say before going to court, but the way the committee has insisted on doing it, in setting up a procedure, there will be a full scale, knock down and drag out fight before the Commission itself, and the court proceedings will be a simple aftermath, the court has its hands tied, and there will not be much for the law students to make of it. Under the type of cease-and-desist procedure the committee insists on, I think it should be recognized that the whole ball game is there in front of the Commission itself. This amendment is not to provide for payment prior to that, but it is a provision for payment under the order issued by the Commission in the proceeding itself.

Mr. WILLIAMS. Mr. President, if the Senator will yield, that is helpful in clarifying it. I had read the amendment, on page 2 at line 24, to mean something different than the Senator has just described it. Where the amendment says, "No enforcement procedure under this title may be initiated against a respondent employer or union until the costs provided for herein shall have been paid in full," I interpreted that to mean payment before the hearing on the complaint before the trial examiner under cease and desist, at the Commission level. Am I in error? Is this to be paid only on appeal, then, to the circuit court of appeals?

Mr. GAMBRELL. Of course, at the time we drew this, we did not know what type of enforcement procedure would be adopted; but the intention of that language is to mean an enforcement procedure in court.

In other words, I do not interpret the proceedings before the Commission to be an enforcement procedure, in my own terminology, because it is not self-executing; it has to be taken to court to be made operative. But I would certainly not object to some clarifying change being made in that language, in order to make it clear that we are talking bout at the end of the Commission proceedings, rather than in the beginning.   * * *

Mr. MONDALE. Mr. President, I send to the desk an amendment in the form of a substitute to the pending amendment, No. 833, and I ask unanimous consent that the reading of the substitute amendment be dispensed with.

The PRESIDING OFFICER. Without objection, it is so ordered; and, without objection, the substitute amendment will be printed in the RECORD.

The substitute amendment is as follows:

In lieu of the language in amendment No. 833, insert the following new section:

"(e) subsection (w) of Section 706 of such Act, as redesignated by this section is amended to read as follows:

"'(w) in any action or proceeding under this title the Commission or Court, as the case may be, may allow the prevailing party, other than the Commission or the United States, a reasonable attoney's fee as part of the costs, and the Commission and the United States shall be liable for costs the same as a private person. Any prevailing party that is an employer of less than twenty-five employees or a labor organization of less than twenty-five members shall, upon application to the Commission, be indemnified by the United States for the cost of his defense against the charge in an amount not to exceed $5,000, including all reasonable expenses and attorney's fees incurred after the serving of notice on him of the charge."

"'Any prevailing party that is an employer of twenty-five to one hundred employees whose average income from such employment is less than $7,500, or a labor organization with twenty-five to one hundred members, shall, upon application to the Commission, be indemnified by the United States for one-half of the cost of his defense against the charge not to exceed $2,500, including all reasonable expenses and attorney's fees incurred after the serving of notice on him of the charge. The costs evidenced by respondent's vouchers of his expenses and attorney's fees shall be deemed reasonable so long as they are comparable to the total amount of the expenses and attorney's fees incurred by the Commission in investigating and prosecuting the charge. Disallowance of any part of such request shall be made a part of the Commission's order in such proceedings. Any United States court before which a proceeding under this title shall be brought may upon request by the respondent make the determination provided for in this subsection. The Treasurer of the United States shall indemnify the respondent as provided for herein upon certification by the Commission.' "   * * *

Mr. MONDALE. Mr. President, the amendment offered by the Senator from Georgia, for which I wish to offer my amendment in the form of a substitute, is designed to preserve a basically valid proposition in that amendment—but seeks to substitute language which I think is essential.

The underlying law, which is unchanged by the bill, provides that in any action or proceeding under this title, the court, in its discretion, may allow the prevailing party—other than the Commission or the United States—a reasonable attorney's fee as part of the cost; and the Commission and the United States shall be liable for the costs the same as a private person.

The proposed substitute would liberalize that provision in two basic respects. First, it would add authority to award costs to the prevailing party with respect to the cost of a proceeding before the Commission. The underlying law to which I have referred does not permit the awarding of fees with respect to proceedings before the Commission. So it liberalizes the fee awarding powers in that respect.

Second, it makes awarding of such fees mandatory for small businesses and for unions, when they prevail before the Commission or before the court, rather than leaving it discretionary as it now is.

It would provide that employers having between eight to 25 employees or unions having between eight to 25 members, could receive reasonable attorneys' fees up to $5,000; and large employers and unions, those having employees or union members in a number between 25 and 100, would receive up to $2,500—if they are the prevailing party.

Principally, Mr. President, my objection to the amendment offered by the Senator from Georgia is that while I think it justifiably recognizes the question of costs that may be visited on small businesses or small unions, it has built within it an unfortunate demension—a dimension allowing Government funds to be used to finance resistance to legitimate cases; under the original amendment, it is not necessary that the small business or the union be the prevailing party. Thus, they can take a case that is without any foundation and, at Government expense and for long periods of time, hold proceedings before the Commission or hold proceedings before the courts and be awarded fees—no matter how groundless the case is.

It seems to me that this could encourage, at Government expense, resistance through the assertion of groundless claims; and it could encourage litigation in cases that should otherwise be settled. Our substitute would bring much needed relief to small business and small unions in cases where there was some hope that they would be the prevailing party. It would bring relief to that extent, and also bring relief for the cost of such proceedings before the Commission as well as before the courts.

I think that modification retains the basic validity of the amendment offered by the Senator from Georgia without risking, in addition, the problem to which I have made reference. * * *

Mr. JAVITS. These questions need to be answered. Does the amendment take into consideration where the Commission or the Attorney General is not a party to litigation, where it is strictly private litigation between a complainant and a respondent? Is it then expected that the United States will reimburse the prevailing party if he is a small business?

Mr. MONDALE. It is not contemplated that that be the case. If there is some vagueness in the amendment, it should be modified to avoid that possibility.

* * *

Mr. MONDALE. Mr. President, I ask unanimous consent to modify my amendment to add in the second sentence of subsection (w) of my substitute amendment, following the word "Any prevailing party" the words "in any proceeding brought by or against the Commission or the United States under this title," and further to add in the first line of the second paragraph of subsection (w) after the words "Any prevailing party" the words "in such a proceeding."

The modification is designed to deal with a problem which the Senator from New York brought up; namely, a wholly private proceeding in which the Commission is not involved. I would hope that there would be no objection.

* * *

Mr. MONDALE. Mr. President, I hope that there is no misunderstanding on the desirability of bringing relief to the small businesses and small unions in legitimate cases where they are the prevailing party. What we have proposed by way of substitute here greatly liberalizes that relief. To the credit of the Senator from Georgia, it was his amendment which helped to make the need for such action apparent.

We do so in two ways.

First, we make fees available on a discretionary basis with respect to proceedings before the Commission, as well as to proceedings before the court.

Second, we make the provision of such costs mandatory for small businesses and for small unions when they are prevailing parties; these fees would not be discretionary for small unions and for small businesses.

To go beyond that is to bankroll resistance and to encourage baseless litigation. It would put the Government in the business of financing resistance to the very legislative objective we seek to obtain here.   * * *

Under the principle embodied in the amendment offered by the Senator from Georgia, we would be saying, "Never mind how baseless your law suit is and never mind how discriminatory you have been in your employment practices, you will

get your fees anyway, as long as you do not act in an unethical fashion, up to $5,500." We say, instead, "If you are the prevailing party, you will be entitled to part or all of the cost of this litigation."

That encourages litigation of responsible lawsuits. But to go beyond that, in my opinion, would be to encourage and to bankroll resistance to the objectives of this legislation. I, therefore, hope that my amendment in the nature of a substitute will be adopted.   * * *

The purpose of the amendments is to make it clear that the fees would be payable only in the event that the proceeding was brought by the Commission or the United States, and also to make it clear that fees would not be payable until after the Commission had made its determination in such proceeding.

I ask unanimous consent that the modifications be made.

Appendix F-17

Enforcement: Remedies—Back Pay

EDITORS' NOTE: *An amendment to the Dominick amendment, No. 611, introduced by Sen. Beall (R., Md.) and co-sponsored by Sen. Dominick (R., Colo.) provided that back-pay liability would not exceed that which accrues from a date not more than two years prior to the filing of a charge with EEOC. The proviso, adopted by a unanimous vote of 73 yeas, appears in the legislation enacted.*

Senate

1-25-72

p. 472

Mr. BEALL. Mr. President, I send an amendment to the desk and ask that it be stated.

The PRESIDING OFFICER. The amendment will be stated.

The assistant legislative clerk proceeded to read as follows:

On page 5, line 7 of the Dominick amendment, insert the following after "appropriate." Back pay liability shall not exceed that which accrues from a date more than two years prior to the filing of a charge with the Commission.   * * *

Mr. BEALL. Mr. President, in a brief explanation of this amendment, it is indicated in reading the amendment, that it goes to page 5, line 7, of the Dominick amendment No. 611. It includes a provi-

sion that was already in the original legislation. We are interested in being fair to all parties, whatever the outcome of the current controversy as to whether this particular Dominick amendment should be agreed to; but should there be a finding in favor of the plaintiff in one of these cases, we want to make sure that the penalty is within the balance of fairness.

In the committee, there was agreement that should there be a finding, any award of back pay liability should not go back further than 2 years prior to the time that the charges were brought before the Commission.

My amendment would amend the Dominick amendment so that were there to be an award by the court, the back pay liability would not extend more than 2 years back on which the charges were brought before the Commission again.

Mr. JAVITS. Mr. President, will the Senator from Maryland yeld?

Mr. BEALL. I yield.

Mr. JAVITS. Is it not a fact that the bill as we reported it on page 40, on lines 6 to 9, contains the same provision?

Mr. BEALL. That is correct.

Mr. JAVITS. This was fought out in committee. Those of us who wished to sustain the committee bill insofar as we could, in all fairness to what was given as well as what we received, would have to support this provision.

Mr. BEALL. Precisely. I agree with the Senator from New York on that.

Mr. President, this is a brief and I believe a sufficient explanation of my amendment.   * * *

Mr. DOMINICK. I will not take very long. I am very glad the Senator brought this matter up. That would be our intention, in the event my amendment is adopted, to offer this as a subsequent amendment to the bill because it was stricken in the amendment by inadvertence. It is eminently fair, and I am glad the Senator brought the matter up. I am happy to have it included in my amendment.

Appendix F-18

Enforcement: House Bill

EDITORS' NOTE: *An amendment identical to the House-passed bill, H.R. 1746, was introduced as a substitute by Senators Allen (D., Ala.) and Ervin (D., N.C.). The main object of the amendment was to place judicial functions in the hands of the federal district courts, rather than EEOC. The amendment was tabled by a vote of 45 to 32.*

Senate

1-27-72

pp. 635, 636

The assistant legislative clerk read as follows:

In lieu of the language proposed to be substituted for the original language of the bill by the committee substitute, as amended, substitute the following:

SEC. 2. (a) Paragraph (6) of subsection (g) of section 705 of the Civil Rights Act of 1964 (42 U.S.C. 2000e–4(f)(6)) is amended to read as follows:

"(6) to refer matters to the Attorney General with recommendations for intervention in a civil action brought by an aggrieved party under section 706, or for the institution of a civil action by the Attorney General under section 707, and to recommend institution of appellate proceedings in accordance with subsection (h) of this section, when in the opinion of the Commission such proceedings would be in the public interest, and to advise, consult, and assist the Attorney General in such matters.

(b) Subsection (h) of such section 705 is amended to read as follows:

"(h) Attorneys appointed under this section may, at the direction of the Commission, appear for and represent the Commission in any case in court, provided that the Attorney General shall conduct all litigation to which the Commission is a party in the Supreme Court or in the courts of appeals of the United States pursuant to this title. All other litigation affecting the Commission, or to which it is a party, shall be conducted by the Commission."

SEC. 3. (a) Subsection (a) of section 706 of the Civil Rights Act of 1964 (42 U.S.C. 2000e–5) is amended to read as follows:

"(a) Whenever it is charged in writing under oath by a person claiming to be aggrieved, or a written charge has been filed by a member of the Commission where he has reasonable cause to believe a violation of this title has occurred (and such charge sets forth the facts upon which it is based and the person or persons aggrieved) that an employer, employment agency or labor organization has engaged in an unlawful employment practice, the Commission, within five days thereafter, shall furnish such employer, employment agency, or labor organization (hereinafter referred to as the 'respondent') with a copy of such charge and shall make an investigation of such charge, provided that such charge shall not be made public by the Commission. If the Commission shall determine after such investigation, that there is reasonable cause to believe that the charge is true, the Commission shall endeavor to eliminate any such alleged unlawful employment practice by informal methods of conference, conciliation, and persuasion. Nothing said or done during and as a part of such endeavors may be made public by the Commission without the written consent of the parties, or used as evidence in a subsequent proceeding. Any officer or employee of the Commission who shall make public in any manner whatever any information in violation of this subsection shall be deemed guilty of a misdemeanor and upon conviction thereof shall be fined not more than $1,000 or imprisoned not more than one year."

(b) Subsection (d) of section 706 of the Civil Rights Act of 1964 (42 U.S.C. 2000e–5) is amended to read as follows:

"(d) A charge under subsection (a) shall be filed within one hundred and eighty days after the alleged unlawful employment practice occurred, except that in the case of an unlawful employment practice with respect to which the person aggrieved has followed the procedure set out in subsection (b), such charge shall be filed by the person aggrieved within two hundred and ten days after the alleged unlawful employment practice occurred, or within thirty days after receiving notice that the State or local agency has terminated the proceedings under the State or local law, whichever is earlier, and a copy of such charge shall be filed by the Commission with the State or local agency. Except as provided in subsections (a) through (d) of this section and in section 707 of this Act, a charge filed hereunder shall be the exclusive remedy of any person claiming to be aggrieved by an unlawful employment practice of an employer, employment agency, or labor organization."

(c) Subsection (e) of section 706 of the Civil Rights Act of 1964 (42 U.S.C. 2000e-5) is amended to read as follows:

"(e) If within thirty days after a charge is filed with the Commission or within thirty days after expiration of any period of reference under subsection (c), the Commission has been unable to obtain voluntary compliance with this Act, the Commission may bring a civil action against the respondent named in the charge: *Provided,* That if the Commission fails to obtain voluntary compliance and fails or refuses to institute a civil action against the respondent named in the charge within one hundred and eighty days from the date of the filing of the charge, a civil action may be brought after such failure or refusal within ninety days against the respondent named in the charge (1) by the person claiming to be aggrieved, or (2) if such charge was filed by a member of the Commission, by any person whom the charge alleges was aggrieved by the alleged unlawful employment practice. Upon application by the complainant and in such circumstances as the court may deem just, the court may appint an attorney for such complainant and may authorize the commencement of the action without the payment of fees, costs, or security Upon timely application, the court may, in its discretion, permit the Attorney General to intervene in such civil action if he certifies that the case is of general public importance. Upon request, the court may, in its discretion, stay further proceedings for not more than sixty days pending the termination of State or local proceedings described in subsection (b) or further efforts of the Commission to obtain voluntary compliance."

(d) Subsections (f) through (k) of section 706 of the Civil Rights Act of 1964 (42 U.S.C. 2000e-5) are redesignated as subsections (g) through (l), respectively, and, in newly designated subsection (k) the reference to subsection (i) is changed to subsection (j), and the following new section is added after setcion 706(e) thereof:

"(f) Whenever a charge is filed with the Commission and the Commission concludes on the basis of a preliminary investigation that prompt judicial action is necessary to carry out the purposes of this Act, the Commission may bring an action for appropriate temporary or preliminary relief pending final disposition of such charge the court having jurisdiction over such action shall have the authority to grant such temporary or preliminary relief as it deems just and proper: *Provided,* That no temporary restraining order or other preliminary or temporary relief shall be issued absent a showing that substantial and irreparable injury to the aggrieved party will be unavoidable. It shall be the duty of a court having jurisdiction over proceeding under this section to assign cases for hearing at the earliest practicable date and to cause such cases to be in every way expedited."

(e) Subsection (h) of section 706 of the Civil Rights Act of 1964 (42 U.S.C. 2000e-5) as redesignated by this section, is amended to read as follows:

"(h) If the court finds that the respondent has intentionally engaged in or is intentionally engaging in an unlawful employment practice charged in the complant, the court may enjoin the respondent from engaging in such unlawful employment practice, and order such affirmative action as may be appropriate, which may include reinstatement or hiring of employees, with or without back pay (payable by the employer, employment agency, or labor organization, as the case may be, responsible for the unlawful employment practice). Interim earnings or amounts earnable with reasonable diligence by the person or persons discriminated against shall operate to reduce the back pay otherwise allowable. No order of the court shall require the admission or reinstatement of an individual as a member of a union or the hiring, reinstatement, or promotion of an individual as an employee, or the payment to him of any back pay, if such individual, pursuant to section 706(a) and within the time required by section 706(d), neither filed a charge nor was named in a charge or amendment thereto, or was refused admission, suspended, or expelled or was refused employment or advancement or was suspended or discharged for any reason other than discrimination on account of race, color, religion, sex, or national origin or in violation of section 704(a). No order made hereunder shall include back pay or other liability which has accrued more than two years before the filing of a complaint with said court under this title."

* * *

Mr. ALLEN. Mr. President, the amendment which is at the desk and up for consideration seeks to substitute for the pending committee amendment the language of House bill H.R. 1746 entitled, "A bill to promote equal employment opportunities for American workers."

The bill, S. 2515, introduced in the Senate and referred to the Health and Education Subcommittees of the Committee on Labor and Public Welfare, was amended in the committee by the writing of an entirely new bill, and that is what was the pending business until the pending amendment was offered, which would substitute the House language for the language which the committee seeks to substitute for the bill as originally introduced.

Appendix F-19

Enforcement: Jury Trials

EDITORS' NOTE: *Litigants would have had the right to a jury trial under amendment No. 908 introduced by Sen. Ervin (D., N.C.). The proposal was defeated by a vote of 30 to 56.*

Senate

2-22-72

pp. 2277, 2278

The assistant legislative clerk read as follows:

On page 66, insert the following new section between lines 13 and 14:

"SEC. 13. Upon demand of any party, the issues of fact arising in any civil action brought under the provisions of this Act or the provisions of title VII of the Civil Rights Act of 1964 shall be determined by a jury."

Renumber "SEC. 13" as it appears on page 66, line 14, as "SEC. 14".

Mr. ERVIN.

The purpose of this amendment is just to make it certain that litigants who are summoned under this act to the Federal courts shall have the right to demand a trial by jury on the issues of fact, and to make it certain that there shall be citizen participation in the enforcement of the provisions of this bill.

Mr. JAVITS. I yield myself 2 minutes.

Mr. President, in the first place, this is an equity proceeding in the Federal courts; and even the other body, in passing this bill, did not include a requirement for a jury trial: It would be special and unusual, and available only for this particular kind of proceeding which would be carried out by the Commission. If it is valid for this, why is it not valid for all proceedings under the 14th amendment, which would include education, housing, and everything else in the Civil Rights Act of 1964?

The real objection to it is that it would simply proliferate the court delays which were the primary element in the struggle here, and we had the assurances of the Senator from Colorado in his amendment that there was expedited procedure, including the possibility of a three-judge Federal court. When the Senate adopted that approach, notwithstanding that a majority did not want it but finally had to yield to the fact that it wanted a bill, it was without any contemplation that we would simply pyramid the difficulties we already had in court delays running up to 40 months—3 years and 4 months in many jurisdictions—by now imposing what would be a special requirement in these cases, as distinguished from the antidiscrimination field generally, of jury trial.

I believe that the Senate, having decided that it is going to go the route of litigation, does not desire simply to stop the litigation dead in its tracks even further by clogged calendars. As there are many safeguards, with appeals and so forth, and as we have many cases in equity, including those dealing with environment and other matters fully as serious as this, if not more so, I see no justification for introducing the jury trial except to delay these cases further.

Appendix F-20

Enforcement: Pattern-or-Practice Actions

EDITORS' NOTE: *An amendment to the committee bill introduced by Sen. Hruska (R., Neb.) would have left unchanged the procedures of the Justice Department in "pattern or practice" cases. The amendment was defeated by a vote of 33 to 43.*

Senate

2-16-72

pp. 1891, 1892

Mr. HRUSKA. Mr. President, I rise in support of the amendment to the pending measure which seeks to delete section 5 from the bill. Section 5, as written, adds three new subsections to section 707 of the Civil Rights Act of 1964, thereby affecting the transfer of the functions and the jurisdiction and the authority of the Attorney General to prosecute "pattern and practice" cases over to the jurisdiction and the authority of the EEO Commission. * * *

Mr. President, section 707 of the Civil Rights Act deals with pattern and practice cases, cases in which a group or groups might engage in any practice or activity which would result in the denial of, or the resistance to the full exercise of the rights and the privileges that are contained in title VII of the Civil Rights Act of 1964 and those rights that have to do with assuring persons who are employees or who are applicants for employment of no discrimination, on account of the several grounds upon which discrimination might be exercised.

If a situation of that kind appears to exist, the Attorney General is authorized to investigate the case and then to prosecute a civil case. And the suit would be brought in the Federal district court. However, if the Attorney General certifies that it is of general public interests and requests a three-judge court, a three-judge court will be convened by the chief judge of the circuit and will hear the case on an expedited basis. Appeal would lie to the Supreme Court directly from that three-judge court. If there is no certificate of general public interest, the case is tried by a regular district court and goes through the regular routes of appeal that such cases normally take.

The suits that are involved in this pattern or practice category are a special kind of suits that partake in large measure of a class action bill that can involve a company with all of its branches, all of its divisions, and all of its affiliates, or they can take a labor union having a membership of tens of thousands of members. They can take employers and companies and unions in the same proceedings, or, as a matter of fact, they may take the form of affecting an entire industry, so that it would be a class action. * * *

Section 5 of the bill would take all of those functions that have heretofore been exercised by the Attorney General and assigned to him and transfer them over to the Equal Employment Opportunity Commission. The Commission would be directed to try those cases under procedures set out in section 706 of the Civil Rights Act.

Mr. President, it is the opinion of this Senator that this bill has been greatly improved by the adoption of the Dominick amendment. There are additional views as to how the matter might have been handled, but by assigning and adjudicating disputes and controversies in the proper place, namely, the courts, where trial of the case is had, where a decree is entered into, and where orders of compliance and postcompliance judgments may be taken, seems to me, in my judgment, a great improvement.

I do believe that the bill would be further improved by the adoption of the pending amendment, because there would be the concurrent judgment or at least a concurrent jurisdiction residing in the Department of Justice in the cases involving employment discrimination.

* * *

There are a number of reasons why this amendment is an improvement over the committee provision.

I might assign as the first reason the basic proposition that the Attorney General and the Department of Justice already have general jurisdiction and general enforcement authority over other types of civil rights acts and statutes, so that the Attorney General has jurisdiction and has authority and litigates in the field of discrimination in housing, education, voting, employment, and many others.

It would be a very singular development indeed if the Attorney General were to be deprived of his jurisdiction to prosecute civil rights cases, cases arising from the conferring of civil rights to people in the interests of employment. There is no justification for it that this Senator can see under the present conditions and the status of the bill S. 2515 together with the Dominick amendment.

So first of all we have the Attorney General having the general power of enforcing civil rights laws. Second, the Department of Justice is well equipped to handle such cases. They have the FBI to make investigation. They have the U.S. marshals to assist with the enforcement of the proceedings, and they have the appeals unit in Civil Rights Division of the Department of Justice which assures nationwide standards and uniformity. In addition they are a part of a great department with all of its resources. The employment section has a well trained corps of lawyers, some 35 in number, with great expertise in this special field.

They have gained a good deal of expertise in this particular kind of case, in addition to the experience that the Department of Justice has gained in the prosecution of other types of civil rights cases. And the Department has the 93 U.S. Attorneys' offices with their numerous staffs throughout the Nation to assist with these cases. The EEOC cannot duplicate these resources. To transfer 707 authority will be to guess that in 2 years the EEOC will be able to handle these cases in a professional and effective manner. We have no need to guess when we know Justice is doing the job very capably at present.

Section 5 provides that under this section there shall be transferred to the Commission "the function of the Attorney General," together with such personnel, property, records, and unexpended balances of appropriations, allocations and other funds available, held, or used in connection with the functions of section 707.

It cannot be done.

Notwithstanding that provision for transfer, it is not possible to transfer the FBI to the Commission. It would not go. It is impossible to transfer the investigators they have available. It is impossible to transfer the personnel, as much of the personnel, and especially the lawyers, are attached to the Department of Justice and have other duties and commitments. The section is an integral part of the Department and cannot be moved about like a chess piece together with supporting resources.

There is no way of forcing any of the attorneys or the personnel to go to another agency. Many of the attorneys there are willing to work for the Department of Justice but would not be willing to devote their efforts and their time to the work of the Commission.

That is not derogatory to the Commission. It is a matter of personal and professional discretion and judgment. It is true that the Commission may in due time develop a system of investigators; it is true that in time the Commission may develop and have an organization built up; but it will take time and moreover it would be a duplication of what is now taken care of in very good shape under the present system.

Another point which would argue in favor of the Department of Justice retaining this jurisdiction is that in the field of enforcement and compliance they have gained a good deal of valuable experience in other types of civil rights cases than those which involve only employment. There would be a continuity of litigation in this field if the Attorney General and the Department of Justice retain jurisdiction instead of abandoning and negating the past education and expertise. There would be a continuity of a very fine record to which I shall refer in a little while.

Not only has the Department done a very effective job of enforcing section 707, and I would point out that it has been successful in every single case brought to final judgment, but it has acted expeditiously as well. Of the past dozen or so cases filed by the Department pursuant to its "pattern and practice" authority, every one has been reduced to judgment within 11 months. That is a most excellent and enviable record which will be very difficult, if not impossible, for the EEOC to duplicate.

It may be 3 years before there would develop within the EEOC a pipeline of cases which would insure effective enforcement of section 707 because of the necessity of developing a new staff, personnel, and procedures for this particular kind of special case.

Furthermore, with the Department of Justice it is possible to develop in an orderly way and in a logical way case law which will serve as a valuable precedent. They can do that because they see the picture as a whole; they see civil rights, not consisting of separate segments, but consisting of many aspects, including voting, education, housing, and so on, which require a rounding out of precedents that can be logically developed in the litigation of pattern and practice cases.

It would take a long time to develop that machinery and it should not be engaged in when it would be a duplication and in some ways a useless procedure.

The record of the Department of Justice has been a good one. It is sometimes said, "Well, they have tried only about 70 or 75 cases." That is true, but there has been a great deal of progress in those 70 cases. Let us say for purposes of convenience that the number of cases is 70. Those lawsuits have affected over 275,-000 positions directly and many more indirectly because of the precedent set.

The case record of individual complaints before the EEOC is in the range of 30,000 a year. They can process only a very small percentage of them, they investigate some and are able to discard them or find them to be without merit, and so on. That volume of 30,000 cases is estimated to grow to 40,000 this year, according to Chairman William Brown of the Commission. When we consider that the Department has 70 lawsuits in the hard form of a court decree, with compliance and enforcement procedure, at the hands of the judge who issues the decree, then we know it is a very potent and a very effective piece of machinery toward achieving the goals of title VII of the Civil Rights Act.

Mr. President, the fact is that the Equal Opportunity Employment Commission does not want this new power, this new authority, to prosecute pattern and practice cases. Chairman Brown of the Commission testified on that subject and he pointed out that because of the heavy caseload which is now in the range of 30,000, and which probably will be 45,000 this coming year, they have more than enough to do.

The situation since he gave that testimony has become even greater and more burdensome by way of volume and proceedings because under this bill the Commission will have additional power to bring suits in court and to prosecute them. Heretofore that was not the case.

Chairman Brown testified along that line in the committee even when the caseload was not so burdensome. He said at one point:

> Mr. BROWN. Mr. Chairman, I certainly feel that the commission has the competency to handle these matters.
>
> I would question at this time whether it has the ability in terms of resources—that is, financial resources—or in terms of people.
>
> I would be very much against the transfer, as I have indicated in my prepared text, of the Office of Federal Contract Compliance responsibility at this time.
>
> I would be against the transfer of Attorney General's right in Title VII at this time and also the responsibility of the Civil Service Commission to the EEOC.

Chairman Brown went on to state:

> One of the problems, as I have mentioned, is the overwhelming backlog of cases.

He goes into the figures and then he states:

> As a matter of fact, in the budget which was submitted for fiscal year 1973 we anticipated some 45,000 new incoming charges of discrimination in fiscal year 1973.

He concludes his testimony on this aspect by stating:

> So, taking those figures into consideration—plus the fact that in some cases I question the advisability of putting some of the provisions in this Commission—as it relates to the Office of Federal Contract Compliance—my position would be that I am not in favor of those transfers.

When he says "those transfers" he includes that of title VII.

So we have a situation here, Mr. President, where the agency itself does not want the powers, and certainly, together with all the other reasons, that would be good ground for leaving the power and authority exactly where it is. It would subserve the right of the employees and the public in a more expeditious, more thoughtful, and more stable enforcement of the provisions of the bill and title VII.

Senate

2-16-72

pp. 1895-1897

Mr. WILLIAMS. Mr. President, the bill that is before the Senate was introduced on September 14 last year. The amendment now being debated, offered by the Senator from Nebraska, was introduced and printed on January 27 of this year. I mention this to point out that this amendment really contemplated the legislation in the form in which the bill was originally introduced back in September.

Since this measure has been before us, for the last 5 weeks—to some it might be longer—there have been some significant changes, and probably the most significant change was the amendment voted on yesterday, offered by the Senator from Colorado (Mr. DOMINICK), which dealt with the mechanism and the method of enforcement available to the Equal Employment Opportunities Commission.

Under the bill as introduced, as we all know, the method and mechanism was, as it is with other agencies, cease and desist with appropriate court review. We had three votes on that issue: two votes to retain cease and desist and one vote to delete it and establish court proceedings as the method of enforcement.

The significant thing is, of course, that out of the three votes, the last vote did change the jurisdiction or the method of enforcement from cease and desist orders through the Equal Employment Opportunity Commission and its general counsel to prosecuting the cases in court.

In view of yesterday's action, I had thought that in all logic the Senator from Nebraska might well not call up his amendment, because it seems to me that it was introduced under different circumstances. The present circumstances certainly would suggest to me that this amendment is unnecessary, because we now have an Equal Employment Opportunity Commission, assuming the enactment of the legislation, now must go to court. Therefore, this particular method of court enforcement presents certain great problems, including duplication of the possibility—to use a word that has been used here a great deal—of double jeopardy, in the sense that respondent can be approached from either side, from the Department of Justice or from the Equal Employment Opportunity Commission.

Whether it is double jeopardy or not—it is not in the criminal sense—harassment is certainly possible if this particular jurisdicton over patterns and practices is not transferred to the agency that I suggest in logic should control the subject matter with which we are dealing in this bill.

The matter is before us, and we will have to have a vote on it, although, without any order for the yeas and nays, there is still time to withdraw it even without unanimous consent, I suggest to the Senator.   * * *

Mr. HRUSKA. Would it be just as relevant and just as pertinent, in view of the totally different picture we now have in the bill since the adoption of the Dominick amendment, that the manager of the bill would withdraw section 5, because there is no duplication, in that the pattern and practice cases are of a different nature than the complaint procedures that are contained in section 706? Section 5 says that all the functions will be transferred to the commission, and the commission, in prosecuting pattern and practice cases, must follow the procedures set out in section 706. Section 706, I submit, is a complaint-oriented procedure and is not geared to the handling and the management of pattern and practice cases which are in the nature of class actions.

It seems to me that the manager of this bill would be well advised to eliminate that section, because it is wrong to put into the Commission's authority the prosecution of what amounts to class actions. They are not equipped to do it, and particularly are not equipped when they are going to be circumscribed, when they are going to be hemmed in, by a complaint-oriented procedure which is contained in section 706.

Mr. WILLIAMS.

I should like to back up and review just where we are and how we got here, with respect to patterns and practices in equal employment opportunity and this law that deals with discrimination in employment.

Mr. President, at the time title VII of the Civil Rights Act was enacted, it was felt that the enforcement of violations of that title could be accomplished through voluntary compliance and through conciliation. Many believed that compulsory enforcement powers would only be necessary in those rare instances where recalcitrant and persistent violations were encountered. Therefore, it was decided that enforcement powers in the Department of Justice, to be activated either by the Department on its own initiative

or through the recommendations of the EEOC; would be enough to cope with these more severe problems. This anticipation felt in 1964 has proven to be wrong.

We did not anticipate the extent of discrimination which existed at the time we enacted the legislation, nor did we fully understand its nature. We permitted a fatal flaw to be passed into law. But that was in 1964. We have now seen the effects and the extent of the problem. Employment discrimination represents a major widespread practice in the Nation. At the same time, the only Federal machinery available for the enforcement of the provisions of title VII; the Justice Department has not been able to keep up with the need for extensive litigation in this field. The Department itself has placed employment discrimination low on its list of priorities and, of course, its priority list is long and broad.

During the past 7 years, it has only brought 69 cases under its authority granted in section 707 of the act. This has produced a tremendous gap between the needs and the realities as illustrated by the fact that in fiscal 1970 alone, the EEOC, under the provisions of its recommending powers, recommended that the Justice Department bring actions in no less than 78 separate cases. That is, in 1 year, the EEOC, with the recommendation authority it now has, recommended 78 separate cases. The total 7-year history of the Department of Justice has been a history of bringing only 69 cases—less than the EEOC had recommended in 1 year. It is obvious from this figure that vast numbers of persons are not receiving the full measure of justice that we attempted to provide them when we enacted that landmark legislation, even with the inadequacies of that legislation as they have appeared since its enactment.

In providing for this transfer, the committee was nonetheless, very much aware of the outstanding contribution to the development of title VII that has been made by the Civil Rights Division of the Justice Department. The complaint is not at all with the quality of the actions brought—it has been excellent—but, rather, with the number of cases. Sixty-nine in 7 years is just not sufficient, in terms of the activity that is needed in bringing enforcement through the demands of law that there not be discrimination in employment.

However, we recognized the important reservoir of talent and expertise in the Justice Department and provided for a

2-year phase-out of the Attorney General's responsibility—a phase-out of this responsibility and a full phase-in to the Equal Employment Opportunity Commission.

The EEOC now will have—under the bill as it is at this moment—jurisdiction to bring discrimination cases before a Federal district court. There will be no difference between the cases that the Attorney General can bring under section 707 as a "pattern and practice" charge and those which the Commission will be able to bring as a result of yesterday's decision to give EEOC court enforcement powers. Frankly, the pattern and practice section becomes a redundancy in the law. We anticipate that the Justice Department and EEOC will cooperate during this period so that the Commission will have an opportunity to build up its ability to handle these cases.

I think the Senator from Nebraska is wise and correct in his observation that it might take 2 to 3 years for the Commission to be fully equipped. We have provided this 2-year transitional period, which does fit the time estimate of the distinguished Senator from Nebraska.

The Justice Department will be able to maintain the momentum it has established until such time as the Commission assumes sole responsibility.

The consolidation of the "pattern or practice" jurisdiction of the Justice Department into EEOC will benefit the complainants, the employers, and the courts.

It will benefit the employer by consolidating all authority and guidance for employment discrimination. This will eliminate the possibility of harassment from multiple investigations and will make the employer answerable only to the one agency. It will eliminate such instances as illustrated by the case of Crown Zellerbach Corp. against United States in 1969. In this case, the union and the employer negotiated a conciliation agreement with the EEOC, after intensive and lengthy investigation and negotiation. However, subsequently the Office of Federal Contract Compliance entered the picture, and then the Justice Department filed suit in the Federal court. These subsequent steps reopened an area that had already been investigated, and subjected the company to new investigations and, of course, subsequent suit. This duplication of effort is wasteful—most unnecessarily wasteful. It is not our aim to unnecessarily harass employers or to subject them to inconsistent demands from a variety of Federal agencies.

The complainant will also be benefited by the consolidation of the functions for title VII enforcement in one agency. He will now be able to bring his complaint to the one agency with the full knowledge that his grievance can be remedied through the procedures of the EEOC, and that this agency will investigate the situation, allow the parties to settle their differences, or will institute its own enforcement provisions to resolve the dispute. In this manner, the complainant is assured of a fair and speedy resolution of his problem, and as a general rule will not have to look elsewhere for his remedies.

In closing, Mr. President, I would like to emphasize that the transfer of the pattern-or-practice jurisdiction to the EEOC is an integral part of the basic goal which we are trying to achieve here—the giving of additional meaning to the Civil Rights Act. We cannot allow ourselves to make the same kinds of mistakes today that we made 7 years ago when we passed the Civil Rights Act. Employment discrimination robs the Nation of its full potential and undermines the national goals of social equality and economic stability. To make the mistake in 1964 was understandable. To continue to make the same mistakes in 1972, in my judgment, is unforgivable. We must provide the Nation with strong and uniform enforcement of those goals of equal employment which we so clearly established by that significant step that was taken back in 1964.

Mr. President, all the reasons I have cited marshal themselves against this amendment offered by the Senator from Nebraska.

I urge rejection of the amendment.

Mr. JAVITS.

The Department of Justice retains the right to sue in respect of State and municipal agencies. We understand there is a very good reason for that because we are dealing with governmental entities within the federal system. But here we are dealing not with those Government entities but with, as I say, simply another order of magnitude, from the order of magnitude of the individual suit, which by decision we have taken yesterday, it seems to me, should have absolutely sealed the fate of this amendment. By our decision yesterday we gave the EEOC the power to bring suit in big as well as small cases.

The committee was cognizant of the argument of readiness, that is, is the Commission ready to deal with litigation on a major scale. We dealt with that by delaying the transfer by 2 years.

So we have taken the real precaution, the sensible precaution of deferring the operative date of the transfer so as not to load onto the Commission any more immediacy than is necessary. Therefore, as the Department of Justice is set up for these litigations on the pattern or practice basis, let them go ahead with it.

We took an even further precaution in giving the President—and I think this is a critically important point—the power even to stop the transfer after the 2 years if, when he looked at the situation, he found it was desirable to continue to permit both EEOC and the Justice Department to bring these cases.

We did that by utilizing the reorganization plan technique which is found on page 51, lines 6 to 10 in the bill in which we provide that the transfer is to be made in 2 years of this jurisdiction, "unless the President submits, and neither House of Congress vetoes, a reorganization plan pursuant to chapter 9, of title 5, United States Code, inconsistent with the provisions of this subsection."

To wit—inconsistent with the transfer.

So, it seems to me that we have very carefully and very intelligently made this change.

One other point which it seems to me is absolutely decisive is that the EEOC, under the Dominick amendment, has the authority to institute exactly the same actions that the Department of Justice does under pattern and practice. These are essentially class actions, and if they can sue for an individual claimant, then they can sue for a group of claimants.

It seems to me that this is provided for by the rules of civil procedure in the Federal courts, and also it is inherent in the amendment which we adopted. Under those circumstances it seems to me that this amendment is conclusively dealt with, and whatever may have been the argument which might have obtained in respect of cease and desist orders and the desire to retain this jurisdiction in the Department of Justice when the Commission was going to proceed by cease and desist order rather than by suit, has now given way to the fact that the Commission can only proceed by suit. And if it proceeds by suit, then it can proceed by class suit. If it proceeds by class suit, it is in the position of doing exactly what the Department of Justice does in pattern and practice suits.

I have referred to the rules of civil procedure. I now refer specifically to rule 23 of those rules, which is entitled Class

Actions and which give the opportunity to engage in the Federal Court in class actions by properly suing parties. We ourselves have given permission to the EEOC to be a properly suing party.

Therefore, to sum up this argument, we have first the Commission with the authority to act in exactly the same type of case in which the Department of Justice acts. Second, we have taken away the cease and desist authority and substituted the power to sue which fully qualifies the Commission to take precisely the action now taken by the Department of Justice.

Third, we have delayed the transfer to deal with the possibility of overwork and have even given the President the opportunity to delay it further if he wishes to file a reorganization plan at the end of the 2-year period which we have provided.

Mr. President, in the area in which the Department of Justice will deal with Government entity, we leave the right to sue with them. So, to inhibit the transfer of pattern and practice suits is simply to create two agencies to do the work of one.

If we inhibit that, we risk complete confusion as both the Commission and the Attorney General can proceed in exactly the same kind of case.

There is really no reason for it in view of the legal staff and the other reasons which the Commission itself would develop.

There is one further point on which I draw again from my experience with respect to the Civil Rights Act of 1964. I have said on a number of occasions in this debate that that was a compromise and that much was given up, especially in respect of the right of seeking a remedy against discrimination in employment. And one of the things that was given up was any enforcement authority or the right to sue by the EEOC that we are trying to repeal now. That is why we felt we had to give the Attorney General the power to sue in big cases, in class action cases, and in cases where there was a constant pattern of discrimination directed at individuals with limited resoures whom we were relegating to the courts and who could hardly be expected to carry such a broad and deep case. We are now changing that and giving it back to the Commission.

It seems to me that the logical conclusion which follows from that is that the authority previously given to the Justice Department is no longer necessary.

For all of those reasons and with special emphasis upon the fact that we made the decision yesterday, which it seems to me is absolutely controlling on this amendment, I believe that the amendment should be rejected.

Appendix F-21

Enforcement: Filing of Charges

EDITORS' NOTE: *An amendment introduced by Sen. Hruska (R., Neb.) provided that, with certain exceptions, a charge filed with EEOC would be the exclusive remedy for anyone claiming to be aggrieved by a violation of the law. The amendment was defeated in a tie vote, 33 to 33. A motion to reconsider was rejected by a vote of 37 to 50.*

Senate

2-8-72

pp. 1458, 1459

Mr. HRUSKA. Mr. President, one of the more glaring defects of S. 2515 is that it permits a multiplicity of actions to be instituted against a respondent before a number of separate and distinct forums for the same alleged offense. A little later in my remarks I shall give a specific example of the unfairness and the burdens and harassment involved in this regard.

In addition to the unfairness, burden, and expense visited upon a respondent, there is the factor that such a multiplicity will have the inevitable and unfortunate effect of tending to inhibit respondent from entering into any voluntary settlement or conciliation agreement. This is so because any such voluntary agreement or conciliation will not eliminate the potential liability in actions brought in any of the other available forums.

To correct the defect described the amendment which I have introduced on this subject would provide that with certain named exceptions, a charge filed with the Commission shall be the exclusive remedy of any person claiming to be aggrieved by an unlawful employment practice.

The amendment would have the tendency also to remove the possibility that an individual can utilize the potential for litigating two or more of the multiple actions as to a single alleged offense now available under the bill as written, but based upon nonmeritorious claims, with a view of "blackmailing" the respondent into settlements.

MULTIPLICITY OF SEPARATE ACTIONS INVOLVING THE SAME ALLEGED OFFENSE

Mr. President, the best way to illustrate the severe inequity perpetuated by S. 2515 in this regard is to provide a typical example of a single incident of alleged employment discrimination which could result in the virtual bankruptcy of a small employer or labor organization required to defend itself before a multiplicity of forums.

Assume a situation where, for example, a black female employee is denied a pay raise and/or a promotion to a better position which she believes has resulted from her employer's bias against blacks and/or females. Let us also suppose that her job is covered by a collective bargaining agreement. After going to her union and presenting her evidence, the union files a grievance on her behalf, but after investigating her claim, the union refuses to insist on arbitration under the union contract because of its belief that the company's action was justified and not based upon unlawful considerations. Under S. 2515 as presently written, the employee could institute the following proceedings against the employer and her union:

First, she could file a charge against her employer and union with the State fair employment practices agency where her employer and union do business. Since most of these agencies possess subpena powers, the respondent's books and records will probably be subpenaed and they will be called upon to produce evidence concerning the employment actions taken with respect to the allegations of her charge. In the meantime, she could also file an identical charge with the Commission which, under S. 2515, would only be required to withhold investigation of her charge for a period of 60 days from the date the charge was filed with the State agency. Once this 60-day period elapsed, the Commission would be authorized to commence its own investigation and, like the State agency, could also demand the production of records and evidence from the company and union to determine whether or not the charge had merit. Moreover, even if the State subsequently dismissed the charge or even settled it, this would not preclude the Commission from accepting the State's findings or conclusions; but the Commission could, instead, issue its own complaint against either or both of the respondents.

Second. In the event the Commission dismisses her charge, she could still institute a suit under title VII alleging that her rights under title VII had been violated. She could do the same thing in the event that the Commission failed to issue its own complaint within 180 days after filing her charge with the Commission. She could also institute suit even if the respondent has entered into a settlement agreement which is acceptable to the Commission since, under the provisions of S. 2515, the aggrieved party can veto any such settlement by simply refusing to become a signator to it.

Third. While at the same time pursuing her charge before the State commission and the Federal Commission and/or Federal court under title VII, she could additionally file a charge with the National Labor Relations Board. Under recent Board and court rulings, the Board would not only have jurisdiction to investigate a claim based upon the union's refusal to demand arbitration—*Miranda Fuel Co.*, 1962, 51 LRRM 1585—but would also have jurisdiction to determine whether the employer violated the Taft-Hartley Act by adhering to a "policy and practice of invidious discrimination on account of race."

In the event the Board found merit to her charge, it would also issue a complaint and would not be precluded from doing so merely because an identical complaint was outstanding before the Commission—whether State or Federal— or before a Federal court in a title VII action.

Fourth. The employee could, in addition, and while the foregoing proceeding were pending, file a complaint in Federal of State court under section 301 of the National Labor Relations Act based upon the union's alleged breach of its duty of fair representation in the handling of her grievance and upon the employer's alleged contract breach in denying her a promotion (*Vaca* v. *Sipes*, U.S. Sup. Ct., 1967, 64 LRRM 2369).

Fifth. In addition to concurrently pursuing each of the foregoing remedies, the employee could completely bypass both the EEOC and the NLRB and file a complaint in Federal court under the provisions of the Civil Rights Act of 1866

against both the employer and union. In addition, she could also file a complaint with the Labor Department against her employer in the event she believed she was receiving less pay than that being received by male employees performing comparable work.

Sixth. Concurrently with the foregoing, the Attorney General could also be pursuing "a pattern and practice" investigation against the employer and union either on its own initiative or as a result of a referral from the Commission. At the same time, in the event the employer is a party to a government contract exceeding $50,000, the OFCC could be conducting its own investigation on its own initiative or, as a result of a complaint by the employee, to determine whether the employer or union's action violated their commitments under the appropriate executive order.

This Senator questions the fairness of permitting liability to be imposed upon a respondent in a multitude of different proceedings. The fact that under S. 2515 an individual is permitted to institute a multiplicity of suits will inevitably inhibit respondents from entering into any voluntary settlements, because any settlement effectuated before one forum will not eliminate the potential liability in actions brought before any of the other available forums.

It is to correct the foregoing defect in S. 2515 that my amendment thereto is directed. It provides that, with the exception of actions first filed by the Attorney General pursuant to the authority granted in section 707; second, arising out of the provisions of the Equal Pay Act of 1963; or third, brought before State agencies, a charge filed with the Commission shall be the exclusive remedy of any person claiming to be aggrieved by an unlawful employment practice.

This amendment will thereby prevent an individual from subjecting a respondent to the time-consuming and financial burdens incident to defending against a number of separate actions before a number of separate and distinct forums. The amendment also removes the possibility that an individual can utilize the potential for litigating inherent in S. 2515 as a means to blackmail respondents into monetary settlements based upon non-meritorious claims.

Senate

2-9-72

pp. 1522, 1523

Mr. JAVITS.   * * *

Mr. President, the amendment which has been proposed by the Senator from Nebraska involves an issue in which the Department of Justice stands directly opposed to the position taken by the Senator. I should like to refer, in that regard, to a hearing before the Committee on Labor and Public Welfare held October 4, 1971, in which we had the testimony of David Norman, an Assistant Attorney General, stating the Department's position.

I refer the Senate precisely to pages 162 and 163 of the hearings record, where Mr. Norman deals with the issue which has been brought up by the Senator from Nebraska, with an exception or two which I shall indicate, which do not interfere with the argument I shall make.

The amendment which the Senator from Nebraska seeks to insert into this measure is a sentence included in the bill as passed by the other body in a somewhat more restricted form; that is, as to the singleness of the remedy which is available to a complainant. The restriction in terms of its form was as follows: In the House bill, there is no exception made for individual suits if the Commission decided not to sue itself, and there is no exception made for the so-called Equal Pay Act, relating to equal pay as between men and women. These exceptions are contained in the amendment before us, but they do not affect the argument made against the substance of the amendment by the Department of Justice, and, referring to the House bill that I have just described, this is what the Department's representative, Mr. Norman, said with reference to the House bill provision that I have just described, beginning at page 162 of the hearings:

Section 3(b) of H.R. 1746 provides that charges filed with the EEOC and lawsuits brought, either by EEOC or by private individuals pursuant to Title VII "shall be the exclusive remedy of any person claiming to be aggrieved by an unlawful employment practice of an employer, employment agency, or labor organization." This could be interpreted as eliminating the use of provisions of federal law other than Title VII in the attack on employment discrimination.

We will be happy to work with the Committee staff in clarifying the language in both instances.

He continues, as shown at the top of page 163:

In sum, although we favor the granting of judicial enforcement authority to EEOC, we are concerned that at this point in time there be no elimination of any of the remedies which have achieved some success in the effort to end employment discrimination. In the field of civil rights, the Congress has regularly insured that there be a variety of enforcement devices to insure that all available resources are brought to bear on problems of discrimination. For example, housing discrimination may be the subject of suit by the Attorney General, a private suit by the party affected, or a conciliation effort by the Department of Housing and Urban Development. Again, in the field of education, remedies for discrimination are available to private persons, the Attorney General and the Department of Health, Education and Welfare.

At this juncture, when we are all agreed that some improvement in the enforcement of Title VII is needed, it would be, in our judgment, unwise to diminish in any way the variety of enforcement means available to deal with discrimination in employment. The problem is widespread and we suggest that all available resources should be used in the effort to correct it.

That is the entire quotation, Mr. President, showing the opposition of the Department of Justice to this type of provision. It is in the House bill, as I say, in an even more restricted form.

With the attitude of the Senate toward this legislation, we oppose including it in the Senate bill.

What is allowed by the present legal situation? For one, Mr. President, it permits a range of actions under the National Labor Relations Act and the Railway Labor Act and before the National Labor Relations Board where an unfair practice can be charged by a worker against discrimination in a union or even by an applicant to join a union. We consider this opportunity to test out these questions in that forum as an extremely important one, and obviously the Attorney General does as well.

It would permit, for example, the decertification of a union for engaging in discrimination which is contrary to the provisions of title VII of the Civil Rights Act of 1964.   * * *

One other aspect of the matter which is cut off is the possibility of using civil rights acts long antedating the Civil Rights Act of 1964 in a given situation which might fall, because of the statute of limitations or other provisions, in the interstices of the Civil Rights Act of 1964. This is rather infrequent, but it is a valuable protection. The Attorney General feels that it is desirable to maintain it, and we agree with him. The idea is to enforce the law and not let people drop between two stools where they are actually violating the law.

Therefore, we believe that this enforcement should not be hobbled in this way. It is bad enough that we have such very long backlogs and that it takes long enough to get a case considered. We should not cut off the range of remedies which is available.   * * *

Mr. HRUSKA.

Mr. President, the testimony of David Norman on behalf of the Department of Justice, to which reference has been made, is directed to very unyielding language in the House bill which is not at issue in the pending amendment. Three aspects are spelled out in the pending amendment which were not in the language considered by Mr. Norman, in that part of his testimony which was just read by the Senator from New York.

There is an exclusion in that pending amendment as to pattern and practice suits. There is an exception as to the Equal Pay Act of 1963. There is an exception for proceedings before State agencies. Any proceedings before State agencies could proceed, and this exclusion would not affect those three classes.

So that Mr. Norman was testifying on something totally different. He did say in his testimony, on page 162:

We will be happy to work with the committee staff in clarifying the language in both instances.

He had some doubts in his mind as to how far the availability of other actions would go.

The fact is that the amendment would not cut off class suits, because the amendment is directed to an individual. The language of the House amendment is that except as provided elsewhere, a charge filed hereunder shall be the exclusive remedy of any person claiming to be aggrieved by an unlawful employment practice of an employer, employment agency, or labor organization. Mr. David Norman was concerned with the cutting off of the class action, and he

said he would be willing to work with the committee to develop language which would clarify the situation in that regard.

It is the contention of this Senator that the language of the pending amendment does not cut off that class action. It would be a remedy pertaining to individuals only. Federal action on behalf of citizens would not be curtailed. It would not pertain to class actions that would affect a class. That removes it from the inhibitions of the amendment we are now considering.

I have every sympathy for varied approaches to enforcing one's employment rights as against discrimination. But the point of this amendment is, let us get them in one proceeding and not go to as many as a half dozen different forums and try simultaneously to confuse the proceedings and to make them more expensive, in terms of money as well as in terms of time and personnel.

Furthermore, it would be much more expeditious to do it this way, and that would be something in which every employee would be interested.

Mr. President, the Justice Department in Mr. David Norman's testimony, was objecting to the possible narrow interpretation that could attach to the House approved language. The amendment that has been proposed by this Senator takes into consideration the objections to the wording in H.R. 1746. It is much more narrow than the House provision and provides for certain exceptions not mentioned in the House bill.

It is a refinement over H.R. 1746 which takes into account the problems found therein. I believe the pending amendment should be approved.

The amendment is not designed to eliminate remedies for unfairly treated employees, but only to provide that they be litigated in one rather than a multitude of forums.

Appendix F-22

Enforcement: Charges Pending Before EEOC

EDITORS' NOTE: *An amendment introduced by Sen. Javits (R., N.Y.) and included in the final bill makes the amended Act applicable to charges pending before EEOC at the time of enactment.*

Senate

2-21-72

p. 2183

The assistant legislative clerk read as follows:

On page 66, line 15, beginning with the word "not" strike out through the word "Act" in line 17 and insert in lieu thereof the following: "be applicable with respect to charges pending with the Commission on the date of enactment of this Act and all charges filed thereafter".

Mr. JAVITS. Mr. President, this amendment would make whatever we do enact into law applicable to pending cases. The Department of Justice has requested it in a letter to the minority leader; that is my reason for offering it.

Mr. ERVIN. Mr. President, will the Senator yield?

Mr. JAVITS. I yield.

Mr. ERVIN. Did I understand the Senator from New York to say that this amendment merely provides that charges existing at the time the bill is passed shall remain in existence, and that the bill as amended shall be considered a part of the Civil Rights Act of 1964?

Mr. JAVITS. That is right.

Mr. ERVIN. In other words, it is just to keep pending charges alive, and make them subject to the amendment to the original act?

Mr. JAVITS. To this particular act, whatever it is, at the time it becomes law.

Appendix F-23

Enforcement: Preponderance of Evidence

EDITORS' NOTE: *Under an amendment introduced by Senators Ervin (D., N.C.) and Allen (D., Ala.), the courts would not be bound by EEOC's findings of fact unless they were supported by a preponderance of the evidence. The amendment was rejected by a vote of 22 to 43.*

Senate

1-28-72

p. 686-689

AMENDMENT NO. 811

Mr. ERVIN. Mr. President, I call up amendment No. 811, which has been proposed by the Senator from Alabama (Mr. ALLEN) and myself, and ask that it be stated in full, because that will explain what it does.

The PRESIDENT pro tempore. Is there objection to the proposal to vote on this amendment at 11:30? The Chair hears none, and it is so ordered.

The amendment will be stated.

The legislative clerk read as follows:

1. On page 42, lines 17, 18, and 19, strike out the words "if supported by substantial evidence on the record considered as a whole shall be conclusive," and insert in lieu thereof the words "shall be reviewed by the court, which shall reject them and make its own findings of fact on the evidence in the record in the event it concludes that the findings of fact of the Commission are not supported by the preponderance of the evidence in the record."

2. On page 43, lines 5 and 6, strike out the words "if supported by substantial evidence on the record considered as a whole shall be conclusive," and insert in lieu thereof. the words "shall be reviewed by the court under the rule hereinbefore specified governing its review of other findings of fact of the Commission."

3. On page 44, lines 17 and 18, strike out the words "if supported by substantial evidence on the record considered as a whole shall be conclusive," and insert in lieu thereof the words "shall be reviewed by the court, which shall reject them and make its own findings of facts on the evidence in the record in the event it concludes that the findings of fact of the Commission are not supported by the preponderance of the evidence in the record."

4. On page 45, lines 5, 6, and 7 strike out the words "if supported by substantial evidence on the record considered as a whole shall be conclusive," and insert in lieu thereof the words "shall be reviewed by the court under the rule hereinbefore specified governing its review of other findings of fact of the Commission." * * *

What is the definition of "preponderance"?

It is this: Superiority in weight, quantity, power, importance, or the like.

Under the law of every State in the United States, a party suing in a civil court to establish a complaint of any kind is required to establish the truth of his cause by the preponderance of the evidence, that is, by the evidence which outweighs the evidence in opposition and the evidence which shows that his allegations are probably true.

Not so with this bill. It disables the courts to search for the truth with respect to the facts by decreeing that the court, no matter how inconsistent the findings of the Commission may be with respect to questions of fact, is bound by its findings if they are supported by substantial evidence.

Now what is "substantial evidence"?

According to the definition of the courts, it is merely evidence which is more than a scintilla. It is merely evidence which is a percentage point beyond being purely imaginary. Five percent of the evidence is substantial evidence.

Thus, we have a situation here that, in their zeal to deny all Americans rights for the supposed benefit of one segment of our society—for which the pressure groups supporting this bill have appointed themselves guardians—we have a system under which the courts are denied the right to search for truth with respect to issues of fact, even if those issues of fact are supported by as little as 5 percent of the evidence and are shown to be false by at least 95 percent of the evidence.   * * *

Mr. President, I urge the Senate to adopt this amendment and thus enable the courts which review the findings of the Commission to search for truth in accordance with the evidence in the case and thus to set aside the findings of fact which are not supported by a preponderance of the evidence. In any case, under this amendment, where the findings of the Commission are supported by a preponderance of the evidence, the court would be bound by those findings.

But this amendment would merely provide, where the court finds the findings of the Commission are not supported by the greater weight of the evidence, or the more convincing evidence, or the preponderance of the evidence, that the court itself can make findings of fact.

* * *

Mr. WILLIAMS. Mr. President, I have heard an overwhelming weight of persuasion by the Senator from New York that this amendment should be defeated by a preponderance of the statements and by reason of all the precedents.

Mr. President, in the first place, I do not feel that the use of the term "preponderance of the evidence" is at all useful or necessary in the context of this bill. It neither clarifies the degree or nature of the evidence that we would be dealing with in these situations nor introduces any added benefit for the resolving of complaints under this bill in these situations.

In general, Mr. President, the courts have avoided using the term or applying it in to any significant number of cases. While it is generally termed to be the standard of persuasion in civil cases, its precise meaning or an understanding of its application has never been fully undertaken by the courts. The questions still remains. A widely accepted definition is that evidence preponderates when it is more convincing to the trier than the opposing evidence. While this kind of commonsense explanation has grown out of repeated use, its applicability has been restricted to jury-trial situations where the jury is led to believe, through proof by preponderance, that the existence of a contested fact is more probable than its nonexistence. However, this ceases to be applicable in appellate cases.

This nonapplicability of the term "preponderance of the evidence" can be best illustrated by reference to the experiences of the NLRB. While the National Labor Relations Act contains the requirement that the Board make its findings by a "preponderance of the testimony," a search of the labor board cases as reviewed by the courts discloses no reference to "preponderance". The courts rather refer repeatedly to "substantial" evidence.

Second, Mr. President, I feel that the amendment, as proposed by the distinguished Senator from North Carolina, seeks to introduce a new and unnecessary element in the courts' reviewing process of administrative decisions. If I understand the amendment correctly Mr. President, it would require the appellate courts to hold, in effect, a trial de novo in those cases where "it concludes that the findings of fact of the Commission are not supported by the preponderance of the evidence in the record."

Mr. President, it is one of the fundamental traditions of our system of courts that there is a gulf fixed between the trial court and the reviewing court. The reviewing court examines only questions of law, and is barred, except in a few exceptional situations like mandamus actions or disbarment proceedings, from examining issues of fact. This amendment, Mr. President, would specifically alter this separation of functions.

The traditional and long-standing procedure of administrative review in this country is that the courts of appeals review an agency decision by examining the record of the administrative proceeding to determine whether there is "substantial evidence on the record" to sustain the agency's finding. This process is guaranteed by the Administrative Procedure Act and by the provisions of S. 2515.

Appendix F-24

Administration: General Counsel of EEOC

EDITORS' NOTE: *Sen. Schweiker (R., Pa.) offered an amendment, drafted by Sen. Taft (R., Ohio), creating the post of EEOC General Counsel, to be appointed by the President with the advice and consent of the Senate. The amendment was adopted by a vote of 67 to 0.*

Senate

1-20-72

pp. 164-166

Mr. SCHWEIKER. Mr. President, I rise in support of the amendment offered by the distinguished Senator from Ohio (Mr. TAFT), the distinguished Senator from New York (Mr. JAVITS), the distinguished Senator from Maryland (Mr. BEALL), and myself. I am offering this amendment today in behalf of the distinguished Senator from Ohio, as one of its cosponsors, as a result of his inability to be here because of pressing business in his home State.

This amendment would establish the Office of General Counsel, under the EEOC, who would be appointed by the President, with the advice and consent of the Senate, for a 4-year term. Under existing law the EEOC has a General Counsel's office but that office is clearly subordinate to the Chairman and other Commissioners. We feel, however, that since this bill, S. 2515, is going to turn the EEOC into a body very much like a court, this court should not either exercise control over its prosecutors or provide its own prosecutors. Instead, the prosecuting arm of the EEOC should be separate and distinct from the judicial arm. Hence, the reason for our amendment.

Our amendment, by setting up an independent General Counsel's office, would accomplish this. Thus, the Commission would not be able to sit as prosecutor, judge, and jury combined. The prosecuting attorneys would serve under an independent, presidentially appointed general counsel not tied to the rest of the agency. This would free the Commission members to concentrate on their work of hearing cases brought before them, much as judges would do in a regular court. The General Counsel and his staff attorneys would issue complaints, prosecute those complaints before the Commission, and conduct litigation both on individual cases and the "pattern and practice"

type of suits. When we separate the prosecuting function from the EEOC's judicial function in this way, we are safeguarding due process of law before the EEOC for all parties concerned.

While the Administrative Procedure Act does require as a general policy that these functions shall be separate within a particular agency, our amendment underscores this in the case of the EEOC as a matter of congressional intent.

Under S. 2515, the EEOC would take on powers similar to those of the National Labor Relations Board. It is significant, Mr. President, that the National Labor Relations Board has since 1947 had an independent General Counsel's office as an entity separate from the Board itself. Congress decided, in the case of the NLRB, that that Board had sufficient power in its own right without also being in control of the prosecuting arm. This is the way I feel about the new EEOC that we are chartering in S. 2515. As we increase the powers of this agency, and with good reason for doing so, nevertheless we should clearly observe the traditional "separation of powers" doctrine that has always operated to protect all citizens from the abuse of Government power.

In order to explain in laymen's terms exactly what we are trying to do, I should say, first of all, that this bill, S. 2515, attempts to expedite the cases brought to the EEOC by citizens who feel they have been discriminated against for one reason or another in their search for employment.

The bill, S. 2515, as the distinguished Senator from New Jersey said yesterday and my colleague on this side of the aisle, the distinguished Senator from New York, said today, gives enforcement powers to the EEOC, namely the power to hear complaints and issue cease-and-desist orders. These orders are reviewable by the circuit courts of appeals, so we have in effect provided proceedings within the EEOC at the trial level, instead of holding these trials in the Federal district courts. After EEOC hears the case and issues an order, it is still subject to review by a court of appeals and then the Supreme Court. So we still have three distinct steps in resolving equal employment opportunities cases.

Because the bill is substituting the Equal Employment Opportunities Commission as a hearing body for the district court, our amendment is intended to provide the normal safeguards found in a court of law. Our amendment underscores that the EEOC prosecutor shall be separate and independent from the EEOC judge and the jury. The judge and the jury in this case will be the members of the Equal Employment Opportunities Commission.

But under our amendment, the prosecutor, a General Counsel will be appointed by the President, will be directly responsible to the President, and will be separate and independent from the judge and the jury, or the EEOC Commission. So that by the amendment we are offering today, we make it crystal clear that even though we are substituting what we believe is a fast, a fair, and a more efficient procedure—the EEOC hearing procedure—for the logjammed Federal courts, with their lengthy delays and great time consuming judicial processes, this will provide due process of law because the prosecutor and the judge are two distinct entities. So that this amendment, in a nutshell, would simply provide that the prosecutor and the judge shall not be the same person, shall not be in the same line of command, and shall not be responsible to the same people.

This amendment would give the President the right to name an independent EEOC General Counsel who would report solely to him. It would be his duty and his function to decide what cases to prosecute and what cases not to prosecute from the cases presented to him where injustice is alleged on the basis of race, color, creed, or sex. This would assure that once the prosecutor makes the decision to prosecute on the basis of discrimination, the judge and the jury in this case would be separate and distinct and will be, in effect, the new Equal Employment Opportunities Commission.

I can think of no better way to insure that the new and hopefully faster, more efficient system in S. 2515 will operate justly toward all Americans. Our amendment will protect the parties on both sides of the dispute and assure that the prosecutor and the judge come from two different appointment procedures and have two different responsibilities. In this case the prosecutor goes directly to the President himself for his appointment, and for advice and consent of the Senate.

This is a fair amendment. It is in keeping with our Nation's judicial history, judicial customs and our judicial system.

It makes crystal clear the fact that we are trying to achieve, by this bill, and this amendment, a fast, efficient, and fair way to determine where alleged injustices exist in our society and to provide a way whereby, once proven to exist, they can be decided expeditiously so that the people most involved will know they can get a quick and fair hearing, for "justice delayed is justice denied."

I urge, Mr. President, the adoption of this amendment giving to the Equal Employment Opportunities Commission under our bill a new, independent General Counsel's Office.   * * *

Mr. WILLIAMS. Mr. President, I first want to state that, as manager of the bill, I am in agreement with the amendment which has been offered by the Senator from Ohio and fully explained by the Senator from Pennsylvania. It will make a substantial contribution to the substance of this legislation. It certainly meets many of the anxieties felt about the bill as it now exists.

This amendment calls for the establishment of a General Counsel's Office in the Equal Employment Opportunity Commission, which, though a part of the Commission and empowered to act in its name, is to be independent of its control. The purpose of the amendment is to insure that the prosecutorial and decisional functions of the Commission will be firmly separated and to eliminate any lingering notion that the Commission would be involved in a conflict of acting as prosecutor and judge.

Under the scheme of the Civil Rights Act of 1964, the Commission was established as an investigative body to facilitate a statutory scheme emphasizing voluntary compliance through the processes of conference, conciliation, and persuasion. To this end the Commission was empowered, after investigation, to determine only whether reasonable cause existed to believe that an employer, employment agency, or labor organization had violated the act. In essence, then, the Commission's primary present function—deciding whether to proceed on charges filed by aggrieved persons or individual Commissioners—has been wholly prosecutorial in nature. Likewise, the Commission's function in administering the day-to-day work of its component sections has involved the Commissioners, particularly the chairman, deeply in investigation, conciliation, case handling, and even litigation in title VII cases before the district courts.

The bill under consideration vests the Commission with extensive quasi-judi-

..al powers similar to those possessed by many other administrative agencies, such as the Occupational Safety and Health Commission and the National Labor Relations Board. This amendment would reorganize the Commission along the lines of the NLRB which has an independent office of General Counsel created by Congress in the Taft-Hartley Act.

The Commission's present organization is devoted entirely to investigation and other prosecutorial functions. The preparation of reasonable cause decisions is closely tied to the work of investigative officials, who prepare draft decisions for the consideration of the Commission in many instances. It would be difficult for the Commission to abandon all its current practices and procedures immediately; to suddenly drop the reins of its present prosecutorial functions and withdraw to a purely decisional role .as the Administrative Procedure Act requires. Indeed, the several functions of the Commission have become so commingled under present law that exceptional measures are necessary to assure that a firm dividing line is drawn between the Commission's prosecutorial and decisional functions in the future.

While the Administrative Procedures Act would mandate the separation of functions in any event, one way to accomplish this goal is to draw upon the time-tested experience of the NLRB and establish an independent General Counsel to exercise authority, on behalf of the Commission, over the issuance of complaints, conciliation efforts, and prosecution of complaints before the Commission and litigation in the courts.

Moreover, vesting an independent General Counsel with these powers will free the Commission from many of its administrative chores, thus enabling it to devote its time to quasi-judicial duties. The task of formulating policy, of course, would be left to the Commission.

The amendment assures charging parties of expert representation before the Commission because the charge will be prosecuted by attorneys in the General Counsel's Office instead of by appointed counsel.

It should be noted that this amendment contains a significant check on the powers of the General Counsel in respect to the issuance of complaints. If he decides not to process a charge of its conclusion, the charging party may nonetheless file an action in the appropriate district court seeking relief on his own behalf.

Therefore, this amendment would accomplish the goal of insuring that separation of powers basic fairness requires. It would facilitate the Commission's work in eradicating employment discrimination by enhancing public confidence in the fairness of its procedures. It will also permit the Commission to devote its time to its quasi-judicial duties. At the same time the integrity of the Commission is protected by its retention of its central policymaking role. And, finally, minority group members are assured of competent representation by employees of the General Counsel's Office, yet they are also protected against an undue concentration of power over the complaint process in the General Counsel by the ability to seek judicial relief when he refuses to act.

SUMMARY OF AMENDMENT

The amendment provides for the appointment by the President of the Commission's General Counsel for a 4-year term. It gives the General Counsel responsibility over the Commission's main prosecutorial functions: Issuance of complaints, their prosecution before the Commission, and conduct of all litigation in the Federal courts as well as other duties the Commission prescribes or the law provides. It does not give the General Counsel authority over the investigation of charges, the efforts of the Commission to achieve voluntary conciliation with respondents, except after a complaint has been issued, and supervision over Commission personnel except for the appointment of Regional Attorneys and concurrence in the Chairman's appointment of Regional Directors.

Furthermore, it contains the key language of section 5(c) of the Administrative Procedure Act which prohibits the same agency personnel engaged in the prosecution of a case or any similar case from having anything to do with the decision in such case or cases. The amendment also provides for the continuation of the General Counsel or Acting General Counsel in that position after enactment of this bill until a new appointee can take over. This will maintain some continuity in this important position.

RATIONALE OF THE AMENDMENT

The purpose of this amendment is to ensure fundamental fairness for respondents, integrity of the Commission's decisions, and confidence in the eyes of the public regarding such decisions. This is accomplished by the separation of functions that I have here described.

The appointment of the General Counsel by the President guarantees that he will not be the pawn of the Commission in carrying out his prosecutorial responsibilities. Those functions which are strictly prosecutional are, accordingly, made the responsibility of the General Counsel. It must be remembered, however, that the evil to be guarded against is the contaimination of the judicial function by the prosecutorial one. This would occur only when the same persons are actually engaged in both functions.

It is also necessary to avoid the creation of a two-headed agency with dual authority to make policy. Therefore, supervision and authority of agency personnel remains under the Chairman, with the exception of the appointment of Regional Attorneys, so that Commission policy will be effectively carried out. The exception as well as the requirement that the General Counsel concur in the appointment of the Regional Directors is to better enable the General Counsel to carry out his prosecutorial responsibilities in the field. The Commission and not the General Counsel oversees the concilation endeavors under the bill. Since fundamental policy decisions may be made at this juncture, the Commission should be responsible for the conciliation endeavors. The General Counsel may, however, after a complaint has been issued, engage in conciliation attempts—like any lawyer—in performance of his prosecutorial duties. Any agreement he may reach must be approved by the Commission before it has any effect. In this way the Commission exercises control over the policy regarding conciliation agreements. Likewise, investigations are left under the supervision of the Comsion so that the Commission will be the responsible party for the initial contact made with a respondent in the field as well as for the manner, timing, and conduct of the investigation as well as of the investigators.

Mr. President, as I indicated at the outset, I am in agreement with the amendment. The proposed change in the bill, in my judgment, is an improvement in the bill as reported to the Senate by the committee.

Two years ago when basically the same measure was before the Senate, I stood in the same position. An amendment with reference to General Counsel was offered, and again I indicated support. That amendment was agreed to. And we are in just about the same situation as this bill is before the Senate this year.

Appendix F-25

Administration: Executive Pay Scale for Employees of EEOC

EDITORS' NOTE: *Under amendment No. 850, introduced by Sen. Javits (R., N.Y.), the chairman of EEOC was authorized to establish 10 additional supergrade positions, as needed to carry out the purposes of Title VII. The amendment was included in the final version of the Act.*

Senate

2-21-72

p. 2184

The amendment is as follows:
On page 66, between lines 13 and 14, insert the following new section:
"Sec. 13. Section 5108(c) of title 5, United States Code, is amended by—
"(1) striking out the word 'and' at the end of paragraph (9);

"(2) striking out the period at the end of paragraph (10) and inserting in lieu thereof a semicolon and the word 'and'; and
"(3) by adding immediately after paragraph (10) the last time it appears therein the following new paragraph:
"'(11) the Chairman of the Equal Employment Opportunity Commission, subject to the standards and procedures prescribed by this chapter, may place an additional ten positions in the Equal Employment Opportunity Commission in GS–16, GS–17, and GS–18 for the purposes of carrying out title VII of the Civil Rights Act of 1964.'."
On page 66, line 14, strike out "Sec. 13" and insert in lieu thereof "Sec. 14".

Mr. JAVITS. Mr. President, this amendment proposes to establish 10 supergrade jobs in the Equal Employment Opportunity Commission to deal with the added responsibilities which are vested in the Commission.   * * *

Appendix F-26

Administration: Dominick Amendment

EDITORS' NOTE: *Sen. Dominick (R., Colo.) offered amendment No. 611 to the committee bill. It would have struck all language vesting EEOC with cease-and-desist powers and substituted language giving the Commission authority to take certain employment discrimination disputes that couldn't be conciliated to the federal district courts for resolution. After a number of amendments to the amendment had been adopted, the modified amendment was rejected by a vote of 46 to 48.*

Senate

1-20-72

pp. 173-175

Amendments No. 611 are as follows:

On page 33, after line 24, insert the following:

"SEC. 4. (a) Paragraph (6) of subsection (g) of section 705 of the Civil Rights Act of 1964 (78 Stat. 258; 42 U.S.C. 2000e-4) is amended to read as follows:

"'(6) to refer matters to the Attorney General with recommendations for intervention in a civil action brought by an aggrieved party under section 706, or for the institution of a civil action by the Attorney General under section 707, and to recommend institution of appellate proceedings in accordance with subsection (j) of this section, as redesignated by section 4(d) of the Equal Employment Opportunities Enforcement Act of 1971, when in the opinion of the Commission such proceedings would be in the public interest, and to advise, consult, and assist the Attorney General in such matters.'

"(b) Subsection (h) of section 705 of such Act is amended to read as follows:

"'(h) Attorneys appointed under this section may, at the direction of the Commission, appear for and represent the Commission in any case in court, except that the Attorney General shall conduct all litigations to which the Commission is a party in the Supreme Court or in the courts of appeals of the United States pursuant to this title. All other litigation affecting the Commission, or to which it is a party, shall be conducted by the Commissioner.'"

On page 34, beginning with line 1, strike out through the end of the parenthetical in line 3 and insert in lieu thereof:

"(c) Subsections (a) through (e) of section 706 of such Act."

On page 38, beginning with line 7, strike all through line 7, page 50, and insert in lieu thereof the following:

"(f) If within thirty days after a charge is filed with the Commission or within thirty days after expiration of any period

of reference under subsection (c) or (d), the Commission has been unable to obtain voluntary compliance with this Act, the Commission may bring a civil action against the respondent named in the charge. If the Commission fails to obtain voluntary compliance and fails or refuses to institute a civil action against the respondent named in the charge within one hundred and eighty days from date of the filing of the charge, a civil action may be brought after such failure or refusal within ninety days against the respondent named in the charge (1) by the person named in the charge as claiming to be aggrieved or (2) if such charge was filed by an officer or employee of the Commission, by any person whom the charge alleges was aggrieved by the alleged unlawful employment practice. Upon application by the complainant and in such circumstances as the court may deem just, the court may appoint an attorney for such complainant and may authorize the commencement of the action without the payment of fees, costs, or security. Upon timely application, the court may, in its discretion, permit the Attorney General to intervene in such civil action if he certifies that the case is of general public importance. Upon request, the court may, in its discretion, stay further proceedings for not more than sixty days pending the termination of State or local proceedings described in subsection (c) of this section or further efforts of the Commission to obtain voluntary compliance."

On page 50, beginning with line 8, strike all through line 19, and insert in lieu thereof the following:

"(d) (1) Subsections (f), (h), (i), (j), and (k) of section 706 of such Act, and all references thereto, are redesignated as subsections (h), (j), (k), (l), and (m), respectively.

"(2) Subsection (g) of such section 706 is redesignated as subsection (i), and a new subsection (g) is inserted as follows:

"'(g) Whenever a charge is filed with the Commission and the Commission concludes on the basis of a preliminary investigation that prompt judicial action is necessary to carry out the purposes of this Act, the Commission may bring an action for appropriate temporary or preliminary relief pending final disposition of such charge. It shall be the duty of a court having jurisdiction over proceedings under this section to assign cases for hearing at the earliest practicable date and to cause such cases to be in every way expedited.'

"(e) Subsection (i) of section 706 of such Act, as redesignated by paragraph (2) of section 4(d) of this Act, is amended to read as follows:

"'(i) If the court finds that the respondent has engaged in or is engaging in an unlawful employment practice charged in the complaint, the court may enjoin the respondent from engaging in such unlawful employment practice, and order such affirmative action as may be appropriate, which may include, but is not limited to, reinstatement or hiring of employees, with or without back pay (payable by the employer, employment agency, or labor organization, as the case may be, responsible for the unlawful employment practice), or any other equitable relief as the court deems appropriate. Interim earnings or amounts earnable with reasonable diligence by the person or persons discriminated against shall operate to reduce the back pay otherwise allowable.' "

On page 56, beginning with line 7, strike all through line 19.

On page 56, line 20, strike out "SEC. 8" and insert in lieu thereof "SEC. 7".

On page 60, beginning with line 3, strike all through line 9, page 61.

On page 61, line 10, strike out "(h)" and insert in lieu thereof "(f)".

On page 61, line 13, strike out "SEC. 9" and insert in lieu thereof "SEC. 8".

On page 62, line 18, strike out "SEC. 11" and insert in lieu thereof "SEC. 10".

On page 65, line 21, strike out "(q)".

On page 65, strike out lines 23 and 24.

On page 65, line 25, strike out "(e)" and insert in lieu thereof "(d)".

On page 66, line 6, strike out "SEC. 12" and insert in lieu thereof "SEC. 11".

On page 66, line 14, strike out "SEC. 13" and insert in lieu thereof "SEC. 12".

* * *

Mr. DOMINICK.

Mr. President, as far as my colleagues are concerned, I should say that I am going to give just a brief explanation today, perhaps engage in a little colloquy with the Senator from New Jersey if he cares to, and then go into the matter at more length with a number of Senators who want to speak on this particular issue tomorrow. I say the matter needs some extended discussion, because I think we are dealing with perhaps the most important single issue in the complete bill. The issue really is whether we should put into one executive agency the powers to make rules, the powers to investigate whether or not those rules are being abided by, the powers to charge violations of those rules, and then the powers to decide whether or not the violations are in fact in existence, and if they are, to issue appropriate judicial orders.

We used to have a word for this in the old English common law. They used to call it a Star Chamber proceeding, where one person or one group would have the power to issue the rules, decide whether there has been a violation, and then impose the punishment. That is exactly what the cease-and-desist procedure would do.

It seems to me it is far more beneficial, from an overall governmental policy standpoint, to separate these functions just as we have them in the three branches of government under the federal system. Second, it also seems to me that, looking at it from the point of view of those who feel that they have been discriminated against, they are going to get a much more objective hearing before the courts than they would before this particular body, the EEOC, and that they will get a much more expeditious hearing. As I believe, has probably been pointed out already by the distinguished manager of the bill, the EEOC now, without cease-and-desist authority and without the additional coverage provided by this bill, is 32,000 cases behind, with over a 20-month backlog, in determining and resolving unlawful employment practices. I do not care who it may be, or how long they may have been claiming discrimination, if they have to wait 20 months before they even find out whether or not the Commission feels that the charge is valid, all one can say is that justice delayed is justice denied.

The average backlog of the Federal district courts at the present time is about 12 months. So my amendment would immediately speed the process of justice up by 8 months by transferring these matters to the Federal district courts, rather than keeping them within the Commission, even if there were no additional employees put within the jurisdiction of the Commission.

We have, however, greatly enlarged the Commission's jurisdiction. We are adding approximately 10.1 million State and local employees, 6.5 million private employees of small employers, and 4.3 million educational employees. Thus, we are talking about an expanded coverage of approximately 21 million potential aggrieved.

Interestingly enough, there has been a trend in recent EEOC investigations concerning alleged discriminatory cases involving sex discrimination. Are women being given unfair treatment or, conversely, are they being given preferential treatment? In either situation, the person who feels aggrieved has charged sex discrimination and is bringing these cases before the EEOC at the present time. Additionally, there will be the need, under cease-and-desist powers if they are left in the bill, for the training of hearing examiners who will have to set up special courts or special hearing rooms within the Commission. These hearing examiners will need to be trained in the subtleties of what is or is not discrimination. It will take almost 2 years to get the necessary number of trained people on board in order to accomplish these demands. Each one of these factors, as I see it, simply adds to the problems of discrimination in employment and frustrates the resolution thereof.

One thing that I think all of us in this body, regardless of who we are, would like to get rid of is discrimination, particularly when it involves something as essential as someone's livelihood. My feeling, which is concurred in by a great number of knowledgeable Senators, is that we can overcome employment discrimination much better by utilizing our existing Federal district courts, which are free from political patronage, which are free from the subtleties of political winds that occur when an administration changes course or a new administration comes in, and consequently can handle these matters on the same objective, fair basis that the Federal district courts have been handling cases before them of all kinds for a long period of time.

There is a kind of simplistic argument that has been given, a kind of sloganeering against this amendment, wherein it is alleged that my amendment is anticivil rights, and that it is anti the intents and purposes of the original EEOC bill, neither of which could be further from the truth.

What I am trying to do is to find a mechanism whereby the EEOC can initiate prompt enforcement in an impartial tribunal that guarantees the protection of all constitutional rights to all parties and to do it as soon as pssible after conciliation has not worked and where the charge seems legitimate.

I reiterate that my amendment is not contradictory to the independent general counsel amendment which has just been adopted unanimously by the Senate.

Senate

1-21-72

p. 221

Mr. DOMINICK.

What the amendment does do is to provide for trial in the U.S. district courts whenever the EEOC has investigated a charge, found reasonable cause to believe that an unlawful employment practice has occurred, and is unable to obtain voluntary compliance. The Commission would have complete authority to decide which cases to bring to Federal district court and those cases

would litigated by Commission attorneys. Once a Federal district court had issued a decision and order in a case, appeals litigation in a U.S. Court of Appeals or the U.S. Supreme Court would be conducted by the Attorney General's office. An aggrieved person would retain the right to commence his own action in Federal court if the EEOC dismissed his charge.

This amendment protects the rights of both respondents and aggrieved by providing a fair, effective, and expeditious resolution of the dispute.

I might point out here, Mr. President, that my amendment simply takes the enforcement procedure down one level in the court system and out of the hands of the executive agency. The enforcement procedure, as the bill proposes, puts adjudicatory power in the hands of the executive agency with appeal to the court of appeals. What we are doing is avoiding star chamber procedure in the executive agency system, which has not worked in the past and which we do not believe will work in this situation.

Whereas the court approach preserves the traditional separation of powers which we as a nation so highly cherish, the cease and desist procedure seriously threatens the respondent's due process rights in a star chamber procedure which joins the prosecutory function with the adjudicatory function. Under a cease and desist proceeding the EEOC would investigate the charge, issue the compaint, prosecute the complaint, adjudicate the merits of the case, and seek enforcement of its decisions in the U.S. circuit courts of appeals. Elemental concepts of fairness and due process require an impartiality in the adjudicatory function which could not be attained under S. 2515, but could be under my amendment if agreed to.

This amendment provides a combination of the expertise of the EEOC in investigating, processing, and conciliating unfair employment cases with the expertise and independence of the Federal courts. An expertise, which as I mentioned earlier had exhibited unusual understanding of the rights of minorities in areas of public accommodations, voting rights, education, housing and equal employment. The equal unemployment area is one which produces strong emotions among all parties—those discriminated against, those accused of discriminating, and even those charged with enforcing the law. I believe that these strong emotions should be tempered by restraint when the adjudication of personal rights is at issue. The Federal courts are best able to provide the tempering restraint which will allow for a rational resolution of the issues of any given case. * * *

As I pointed out, effective protection of the rights of both the employer and the employee demands a speedy resolution of the dispute. Facts in addition to the previously discussed backlog problems indicate that the court enforcement procedure is more expeditious as it involves a one-step enforcement procedure whereas the cease-and-desist order requires two steps. A district court order is immediately self-enforcing as it is backed by court contempt proceedings. A commission cease-and-desist order must be brought to the court of appeals before it achieves similar sanction power. Additionally, there is a definite practical advantage in having the judge who enters the original order be the person who will hear any subsequent enforcement proceedings. A judge who is enforcing his own orders rather than those of some commission will be determined that such orders are properly enforced.

Senate

1-24-72

pp. 372, 373

Mr. DOMINICK.

Not only does the independent General Counsel fail to remedy other cease defects, it fails to effectively accomplish its one avowed purpose—the separation of the prosecutory and adjudicatory functions, so as to accomplish a medium of impartiality. Consider the following facts, and then decide for yourself whether the General Counsel actually is an independent and separate body.

First, the amendment is not clear whether the General Counsel's office would be placed in the Commission offices, but it is assumed that it would be. Also, the amendment is silent as to who would pay the salaries of the Counsel, but once again, I assume that the Commission would. Although the amendment's silence on the above two topics is confusing, some of the things it does say are even more confusing. Language in the newly added section 705(b) expressly indicates that no employer or agent of the commission may engage in both the prosecution and adjudication of the same case—clearly an attempt to separate the two functions. Yet, the same section, 705(b) gives the chairman concurrance power in the appointing of re-

gional attorneys. Other language in the bill gives the General Counsel concurrance powers over the appointment of regional directors. I fail to see how a General Counsel can be independent from a Commission which has final say on whether or not he is to be hired. Conversely, I fail to see how regional directors can be impartial in hearing cases prosecuted by a General Counsel's office which ultimately hired him. With this overlapping hiring power it is impossible to have an impartial adjudication.

Whereas the independent General Counsel amendment attempts and fails to separate the adjudicatory function from the prosecutory function, it does not even attempt to separate the adjudicatory function from the investigatory function. Presumably, a respondent's due process rights are not violated if an officer or employee of the Commission files an unlawful employment practice charge, serves notice of the charge on the respondent, investigates the charge, determines that reasonable cause for the filing exists, attempts to conciliate the charge, and, that proving unsuccessful, recommends that the General Counsel file a complaint so the Commission can hear the case and make findings of fact and enter a cease-and-desist order thereon.

It is absurd to claim that the adjudicatory institution can be substantially and directly involved in the investigatory process right up through recommending the filing of the complaint and still be able to reach an impartial decision. The distinguished Senator from North Carolina (Mr. ERVIN) last Friday cited Justice Jackson's opinion in Wong Yang Sung against McGrath as requiring the separation of investigatory and adjudicatory functions to achieve a "genuinely impartial hearing conducted with critical detachment." The fact that field staff members did the actual investigatory work while different officials within the same organization conducted the hearings was not sufficient in Justice Jackson's mind to provide a "guarantee of insulation and independence of the presiding official." Justice Jackson went on to recommend that judges be confined "entirely to the duties customary for a judge."

Mr. President, I too, believe that judges be confined entirely to the duties customary for a judge; and, as we know, the forum where this is most expertly practiced is in the Federal district courts. I fail to see why so many of my colleagues continue to avoid the unavoidable logic of Federal court enforcement. It offers an existing network of forums staffed by competent, experienced judges known for their impartiality, yet famous for their protection of individual civil rights. Yet, many of my respected colleagues continue to advocate the establishment of a vast new and untested administrative apparatus which is contrary to our constitutional separation of powers concept, jeopardizes the aggrieved employee's rights with a potential administrative nightmare of unconscionable backlogs and ineffective enforcement orders and the respondent's due process rights with a star chamber proceeding. The importance of equal employment opportunity makes it inappropriate to desert our proven and respected Federal court system at this point. I urge my colleagues to support this amendment.

EDITORS' NOTE: *Sen. Javits (R., N.Y.) introduced an amendment to the Dominick amendment, No. 611, authorizing EEOC attorneys—rather than the Attorney General— to handle enforcement proceedings in the appeals courts. Under the Javits proposal, the Attorney General's authority was limited to the U.S. Supreme Court. The Javits amendment was agreed to by a vote of 40 to 37.*

Senate

1-24-72

pp. 396-398

Mr. JAVITS. Mr. President, I submit an amendment to the amendment.

The PRESIDING OFFICER. The amendment will be stated.

The legislative clerk read as follows:

On page 2, line 13 and 14, strike out the words "or in the Courts of Appeals."

* * *

Mr. DOMINICK. Mr. President, a point of inquiry, if the Senator from New York does not mind. I am just trying to find out if this is an amendment to my amendment, or an amendment to the bill.

Mr. JAVITS. It is an amendment to the Senator's amendment.   * * *

Mr. JAVITS. Mr. President, this amendment is directed only to the amendment by the Senator from Colorado, and it would propose to qualify the attorneys for the Commission to conduct litigations in the courts of appeals as well as the district courts.   * * *

Mr. JAVITS. Mr. President, this amendment would propose to allow the attorneys for the Commission to appear in the courts of appeals of the United States in respect of the scheme of enforcement which the amendment seeks to put into effect, rather than the Attorney General, and would limit the Attorney General's authority to the Supreme Court of the United States. It is my understanding that the authority of the commision in that case would pretty well go along with the authority given to the National Labor Relations Board, which is probably a fair model of this kind of cease and desist order enforcement or court enforcement which succeeds it, and would give the agency itself greater control over the litigations to which, in the final analysis, this amendment would confine it.

I might say, also, that I am advised that the Department of Labor, in the Fair Labor Standards Act, presents a direct analogy to this situation.

Mr. President, it is well known that I favor the cease and desist procedure which is contained in the basic measure before the Senate and which this amendment seeks to overturn, and which has now been reconsidered.

If we are going to go into the court proceedings, it strikes me that one thing is very interesting. The argument was made that the agency—to wit, the Equal Employment Opportunity Commission— would have to hire a hundred lawyers, or some such number, if it sought to do everything it is required to do under our bill. With the enormous amount of litigation which is going to descend upon the Federal courts of the United States, every word which is uttered about the backlog of the agency immediately proliferates the burden upon the courts; because if the recourse of the agency is going to be to the courts, then one must expect that if it is going to have any teeth, so that it can bring about conciliation and compromise in respect of the many complaints which might be brought in to the Commission, it would have to engage in an enormous number of litigations.

Talk about vexation. That has been the main argument made on this whole proposition. The vexation and the expense which respondents will go to in the thousands of cases which the Commission has will be absolutely unbelievable if this tremendous burden of literally thousands of cases is thrown upon the courts. As we argued earlier, the idea of getting conciliation because there is a stop sign, a terminal point, at the end of the road, so far as this particular commission's activities are concerned, will not be present, thereby, in my judgment, making the job more difficult for the Commission and more difficult for the respondents. Proceedings before the Commission in one place and under rules of procedure which even accommodate appearances in person will hardly be as costly as proceedings in the courts. Yet, this is the only recourse the Commission would have, under the amendment.

So far as the practice of the various commissions is concerned, there is a very good reason why the cease and desist authority has been granted to so many of these commissions, and that reason is precisely why we who feel as we do are resisting this particular amendment so strongly. These commissions, after all, are, in a sense, tribunals for administrative purposes, designed to do a particular job with a particular kind of expertise and with the great desirability of trying to curtail the difficulties surrounding that job by proceedings which are, as it were, in house. This does not mean any lack of protection so far as concerns equal opportunity to be heard and to have witnesses, and so forth—the due process which is required in these cases; but it does mean a far greater informality of procedure and a far less expensive procedure than is provided for by the courts.

I might point out, too, that under an amendment which I sponsored, we have the provision for the appointment of four additional commissions, in the discretion of the President, should the burden of work which is involved require it; and that also goes to facilitating and making it possible for the Commission to do its work within the cease and desist context.

So, in my judgment, if we are going to go to the court route—the Senate has not decided that yet, but it will, with respect to the amendment which is now again before the Senate—that court route should at least be within the control of lawyers, at least until it gets to the Supreme Court, where there are problems of basic policy on the part of the Solicitor General for all the courts of the United States, and certainly in the appellate courts it should continue to be within the control of the Commission's own lawyers, so that some unity of approach, some coordination of their efforts, in respect of all these cases may be effected.

The interesting thing about those who argue against the cease and desist power is that I really believe it is going to be to their very serious detriment. I believe

that by giving a power to the Commission with no alternative whatever to institute suits, they are going to make it much stiffer and much more expensive for themselves, with less certainty—and the businessman is always looking for certainty—in the way of decision, because of the great diversity of the views of judges, the very different constructions of the law which are received in various courts, with no settlement of the law in a final way until it actually is in the U.S. Supreme Court for final determination.

I cannot see how the path to efficiency, administrative decisiveness, or any of the other aspects of this matter will be easier if the recourse is to litigation instead of to the likelihood—because that has been the record of all these agencies—that the overwhelming majority of cases will be settled, compromised, conciliated, or agreed upon by cease and desist orders entered, as is very frequently the case. For example, we have the NLRB which has shown an extraordinary basis for that, all of which is designed to bring the procedure within manageable bounds in time and in due course. I hope very much, therefore, that the Senate—I shall have quite a few of these amendments which will go both to this amendment and to parts of the bill which is sought to be stricken itself—will look favorably on this amendment and at least——

The PRESIDING OFFICER (Mr. BEALL). The time of the Senator from New York has expired.   * * *

Mr. DOMINICK. Mr. President, I will not be very long. This is a very simple amendment. What the Senator from New York is saying is that the Attorney General and the Justice Department should not be entitled to appear on behalf of the Commission in the course of an appeal.

It strikes me that this is going pretty far when we put a provision in legislation that the Department of Justice is not entitled to appear on behalf of the Commission on an appeal. For that reason, I am opposed to it.

EDITORS' NOTE: *An amendment to the Dominick amendment, No. 611, proposed by Sen. Javits (R., N.Y.) provided Federal Government employees with court-appointed attorneys and payment of court costs in proceedings under the Act. The amendment was agreed to in a voice vote. The final legislation states that the court may allow the prevailing party a reasonable attorney's fee as part of the costs.*

Senate

1-24-72

p. 399

Mr. JAVITS. Mr. President, this is an amendment to the amendment. It would strike that part of the amendment of the Senator from Colorado which relates to pages 65, lines 23 and 24, of the bill.

If Senators will refer to that particular section, they will find that page 65, lines 23 and 24, applies the provisions of another section of the Equal Employment Opportunities Act, to wit, 706 (q) through (w), to civil actions brought by Federal Government employees under the equal employment opportunity protections of the law. The Senator from Colorado (Mr. DOMINICK) proposes to strike that out. Sections 706(q) through 706(w) will no longer apply if the amendment should pass unamended.

If you refer to those provisions, insofar as they are applicable, you find that the main point is that where the complainant is suing in court, you have arrived at the stage of the proceeding where he has that remedy, and in such circumstancs as the court may deem just, the court may appoint an attorney for the complainant and authorize the commencement of the action without the payment of fees, costs, or security.

Mr. President, that is a very important right for the individual, just as it is a very important right for a Government employee, for the individuals involved are not, in the main, high-salaried, in that those who would be likely to sue in these equal employment opportunity cases are fairly modest people.

So I see no reason, Mr. President, why in the one case, to wit, that of the normal complainant who is not a Government employee with a remedy in court, that complainant shall be the beneficiary of a court-appointed lawyer, and not have to pay these costs or securities, and why this provision should be stricken out when it comes to a Federal Government employee who has to sue and is also a person, because that is the generality of the cases, of modest means.

So the motion which I make is to strike out the provision of the Dominick amendment which would withdraw that opportunity from a Government employee. I do not see how we can very well make that distinction. * * *

Mr. JAVITS. Mr. President, again, this amendment goes to the effort to phase the Dominick amendment—and we will be doing that, I think, for a little while—

to whatever the Senate may wish to do in respect of exercising its will, but to fashion it so that at least when it is presented to the Senate finally, as it now will be, it will be a fair and balanced proposition. If the complainant is going to have nothing but a remedy in court, at least let us lock that up in the best way we can, and that is the point of this amendment, as it was of the preceding amendment.

Mr. President, one other thing which I think is important in this regard: We have now learned through hard experience the critical mass which is involved in the choice of a lawyer. It is interesting to me that one of the things we have learned about the poor is that they value dignity even over and above money and what one would think superficially would alleviate their immediate distress. We have found—this goes for Senator DOMINICK and myself, both of us are rather senior on the Committee on Labor and Public Welfare, as well as Senator WILLIAMS and others—that one of the most important aspects of our antipoverty program is the legal services program.

It is true that Members have various complaints about it, and we are trying to deal with those, but essentially the idea that a poor man can have a lawyer, too, is an extremely attractive proposition to him, and this amendment which I have offered is offered very much in that same spirit, that as we are going to what we, can to get legal service for the complainant who is not a Government employee, let us at least do our utmost to lay on with an even hand as far as the complainant who is a Government employee is concerned.

EDITORS' NOTE: *Sen. Javits (R., N.Y.) offered an amendment to Dominick's amendment, No. 611, giving a complainant the right to sue in his own name in a case in which EEOC entered into a conciliation agreement to which the complainant did not assent. The amendment also said that where a conciliation agreement was not reached, EEOC "shall" bring a civil action against the respondent named in the charge. The "shall" was changed to "may" at the request of Sen. Dominick (R., Colo.), and the amendment as modified was adopted by a voice vote. The stipulation was included in the final bill.*

Senate

1-25-72

pp. 468-470

The assistant legislative clerk read as follows:

On page 3, of the Dominick amendment strike lines 1 through 8 and insert in lieu thereof the following: "mission has been unable to secure from the respondent a conciliation agreement acceptable to the Commission, the Commission shall bring a civil action against the respondent named in the charge. If a charge filed with the Commission pursuant to subsection (b) is dismissed by the Commission, or if within one hundred and eighty days from the filing of such charge or the expiration of any period of reference under subsection (c) or (d), whichever is later, the Commission has not filed a civil action under this section, or the Commission has not entered into a conciliation agreement to which the person aggrieved is a party, the Commission shall so notify the person aggrieved and within ninety days after the giving of such notice a civil action may be brought against the respondent"

Mr. JAVITS. I yield myself 10 minutes.

Mr. President, as we go into the Dominick amendment, because of the very odd situation in which we found ourselves yesterday, we find things in it that even the author of the amendment himself would want to see changed—not that this is one of those, but, in any case, we do find that.

Yesterday, we were able to offer two amendments which really were essential and just, and very materially bear on the rights which would be affected should this amendment be adopted and become part of our bill. Similarly with the amendment I have now called up.

It will be noted that this amendment deals with the right of the complainant in a job discrimination charge to bring an action in his own name, and this would obtain if the Commission did not choose to sue under this amendment. The way in which that happens is that this amendment provides that if the Commission has been unable—I quote from the top of page 3—

to obtain voluntary compliance with this Act, the Commission may bring a civil action against the respondent named in the charge.

So far so good.

If the Commission fails to obtain voluntary compliance and fails or refuses to institute a civil action against the respondent named in the charge within 180 days from the date of filing the charge, a civil action may be brought after such failure or refusal, within 90 days, against the respondent.

That means by whom? Then we go on. I have read only the words affected by my amendment. By whom? To wit, the respondent named in the charge, either by the person claiming to be aggrieved or, if the charge was filed, by an officer or employee of the Commission, by any person who the charge alleges was aggrieved by the alleged unlawful employment practice.

The missing link is this: if a complainant is cut off by the fact that the Commission obtains voluntary compliance, then, what is voluntary compliance, and what does the complainant have to say about it? Remember that you are cutting off his right to sue, and if you cut off his right to sue, does he have no voice in the matter whatever, or is he simply foreclosed by whatever the Commission decides is voluntary compliance, whatever that means? No effort is made to define it, nor can it be defined; because if you deal with a negotiated settlement proposition or a consent proposition, you cannot very well define it into things.

One problem is that the words "voluntary compliance" are not words of art such as are used in this field. The words I have used in the amendment are "conciliation agreement." Those are words of art, and they also are executive words, in the sense that an agreement has to be entered into, signed, sealed, and delivered; whereas, "voluntary compliance" is a kind of amorphous proposition which may consist of a combination of acts, letters, telephone calls, and so forth. So, in the first place, the amendment is desirable in terms of precision.

Second, the amendment will require that the conciliation agreement be one to which the complainant has consented. In short, if he does not assent, he has a right to sue. If he does assent, he has no right to sue. It seems to me that that is the very least that should be provided.

You could go further, if you really wanted to establish a complicated procedure, and say that no agreement should be binding on the complainant unless a court proceeding was had in the absence of his consent and the court approved it as fair, because the party would not be a party to the agreement; whereas, the Commission would, having accepted it in lieu of a suit by it, under the Dominick amendment.

That is what is done, for example, in derivative stockholder suits, where you face a somewhat similar situation. Should this prove to be a change which Senator Dominick would accept, I would be willing to revise the amendment in the alternative—that is, to provide that the complainant may sue or that the Commission may submit the agreement to a court of suitable jurisdiction; and if the court found it fair and equitable, the complainant would be bound.

Obviously, some element of consent, or what is tantamount to it, is urgently necessary in terms of common equity if you are not to get into a situation where you cut off a complainant's right and the complainant cannot do anything about it and the agency which cuts off his right is a party to the settlement. That is the distinction.

I, myself, have argued for the cease-and-desist order practice on the part of the Commission. But there it is not a party to any settlement. It is acting in a judicial capacity. Here, it would be a party to a settlement, and therefore something more than the sheer settlement should be required before the complainant is cut off from his right to sue. That is the essence of the agreement, Mr. President.   * * *

Mr. DOMINICK. Under those circumstances, I yield myself 10 minutes in order to ask some questions on this matter and to raise some precautionary warning signals.

I say to the Senator from New York that I can understand that he wants to use perhaps some different wording—namely, "conciliation agreement" instead of "voluntary compliance." I have no objection to that.

However, I should like to point out that under the amendment as presently written it now says that if within 30 days after a charge is filed with the Commission within 30 days after the expiration of any period of reference under subsection (c) or (d), the Commission has been unable to obtain voluntary compliance, the Commission may bring a civil action.

Whereas the language of the present amendment gives the Commission the discretion to file an action, this language requires that the Commission "shall" bring a civil action.

Without trying to be too technical or too difficult about it, I believe that "shall" defeats the purpose of the 30-day delay which is simply designed to try to get, as they say in the delivery business, "a burr under the tail" of the parties. But I do not see why we should require them within 30 days to bring suit. They might be able to accomplish voluntary compliance within 40 days or it might take 32 days, but under the language of

this amendment what happens if they do not file suit within 30 days? Then what do we do?

In other words, I think that the word "shall" in the second line of the Senator's amendment should be changed back to the word "may," as is the case, if the Senator will look through his amendment, to the question of whether the person aggrieved is going to sue or not going to sue.

I would therefore ask the Senator whether he would be amenable to changing that?

Mr. JAVITS. May I point out that the reason we included "shall" is, in a sense, that it goes with the original bill. If the Senator will be kind enough to refer to page 38 of the bill, subsection (f), which deals with this particular matter, he will see that it says:

(f) If the Commission determines after attempting to secure voluntary compliance under subsection (b) that it is unable to secure from the respondent a conciliation agreement acceptable to the Commission, which determination shall not be reviewable in any court, the Commission shall issue and cause to be served upon any respondent not a government, governmental agency, or political subdivision a complaint stating the facts upon which the allegation of the unlawful employment practice is based, together with a notice of hearing before the Commission, or a member or agent thereof, at a place therein fixed not less than five days after the serving of such complaint. In the case of a respondent which is a government, governmental agency, or political subdivision, the Commission shall take no further action and shall refer the case to the Attorney General who may bring a civil action against such respondent in the appropriate United States district court.

In other words, having found reasonable cause, the Commission, according to the original bill, is required to serve a complaint, and so forth.

Mr. DOMINICK. May I continue to point out that what we are trying to do whenever we can is to have the unlawful employment practice charge solved by voluntary compliance. I think that all of us would prefer to see this rather than a commission filing a cease and desist order, or as in my amendment, having to go to court. I point out to the Senator that although the word "shall" is in subsection (f) on page 38 of the original bill, the difference between that situation and the one posed by the amendment which I have prepared is the fact that there is no time limit in subsection (f) in which the commission has to determine when voluntary compliance is or is not possible. So that there is no 30-day limit. All I am saying is that we are putting a 30-day limit where we are saying, "Okay. If you have not settled by that time, we have the right to go to court."

It would seem to me that in the interest of flexibility of the Commission's schedule, and in the interest of flexibility in working something out through voluntary compliance, it would be far better to put in the word "may."

If the Senator from New York will change that word "shall" to "may," I shall be happy to accept the amendment.

Mr. JAVITS. May I ask this of the Senator: If we do that, if we change the word "shall" to "may," do we not have to have some cutoff time as far as the Commission is concerned, with respect to its exercise of that discretion in bringing a civil action assuming, for example, if the Senator's amendment—if within 30 days after a charge is filed with the Commission or 30 days after a period of reference in subsection (c) or (d)—this relates to State and local governments references and the Commission has been unable to obtain compliance, the Commission may bring a civil action. Would not the Senator agree that if we are going to adopt that suggestion, that we leave it at "may," we have to put some termination date upon the Commission itself so that the complainant may sue without necessarily sitting around awaiting 6 months.

Mr. DOMINICK. I had thought that we then go on with the rest of the Senator's amendment. We can shorten the 180-day private filing restriction as far as I am concerned, but I think we should keep in mind that this is a Commission which has been appointed for the purpose of trying to solve any employment discrimination that there may be and, consequently, I do not think that we should assume they will not take action where there is a clear case. Problems will arise where there are gray areas, or where they are not sure whether they have substantial evidence to support a case. Under those circumstances, it would seem to me that we should give them more time. If we want to say 90 days from the filing of such a charge, or on the expiration of any period, instead of 180 or 120, that is all right with me. If the Senator would do that, then we are changing the timetable which the committee has already worked out in the process of trying to determine what should be done with enforcement procedures.   * * *

Mr. JAVITS. Mr. President, I modify my amendment by changing the word

"shall" in the second line to "may".

* * *

The PRESIDING OFFICER. The amendment is so modified.

Mr. JAVITS. Mr. President, the reason for the modification is that I do not feel, with an agency of this character, that the word "shall" would have any greater meaning than the word "may" and also because I feel the Commission should not, in view of its purpose, be under the kind of strict timetable within the parameters, of course, that the amendment sets out that it would otherwise be if we left the word "shall" which is mandatory. We assume that they must obey the law in the amendment.

We have retained the greater good for the interest of the person aggrieved the ability to sue, which is the main point. That is being retained in the amendment as modified and I think this is the desirable way in which to proceed.

* * *

Mr. DOMINICK. Mr. President, I yield myself 2 minutes.

I appreciate the courtesy of the Senator from New York. I think this change is very meritorious, as I pointed out in my first statement. I do not think the Commission should be mandated on what date an agency should bring suit when we are trying to work out matters the best we can by conciliation.

As a result, with the word "may' instead of "shall" and having preserved the right to the Commission to file suit, and the respondent if he does not feel the Commission acted properly, it would seem proper to proceed in this way. Therefore, I have no objection to the adoption of the amendment as modified.

EDITORS' NOTE: *Sen. Williams (D., N.J.) introduced an amendment to Dominick amendment, No. 611, giving the Attorney General, rather than EEOC, authority to bring civil actions in the federal district courts in cases where the respondent is a state or local governmental agency. The amendment was agreed to by voice vote and was included, with minor changes, in the bill as enacted.*

Senate

1-25-72

pp. 470-472

The legislative clerk read the amendment to the amendment of the Senator from Colorado (Mr. DOMINICK), as follows:

On page 3, line 3 of the Dominick amendment strike "the respondent named in the charge" and substitute in lieu thereof: "any respondent not a government, governmental agency, or political subdivision named in the charge. In the case of a respondent which is a government, governmental agency, or political subdivision, the Commission shall take no further action and shall refer the case to the Attorney General who may bring a civil action against such respondent in the appropriate United States District Court."

On page 3, line 7, insert after the word "section" the following: "the Commission or the Attorney General in a case involving a government, governmental agency or political subdivision."   * * *

The purpose of this amendment is to correct a very important oversight in the amendment offered by the distinguished Senator from Colorado. His amendment would substitute for the administrative hearing procedure permitting the commission, after it is unable to obtain voluntary compliance, authority to bring a civil action against a respondent named in the charge.

The amendment of the Senator from Colorado appears to treat all respondents in the same manner. During discussions of this issue in the committee there was a strong feeling that respondents which were governments or governmental agencies or political subdivisions should be given special consideration in the handling of charges brought by employees of such agencies.

Mr. President, the amendment that I am offering started as an amendment in the executive session for the writeup of this bill. It was offered by the Senator from Missouri (Mr. EAGLETON), and the Senator from Ohio (Mr. TAFT) and it prevailed there. It is in the bill that is before us. I am now offering an amendment to have the same provision apply to the Dominick amendment.

The procedure worked out by the committee was to permit actions brought against State and local government agencies to be brought by the Attorney General in the U.S. district courts.   * * *

Mr. WILLIAMS. Mr. President, the amendment of the Senator from Colorado would allow actions against State and local government agencies to be brought in Federal district courts but would require the Commission to file the complaint.

I believe that this discussion in the committee and the intent of the committee in providing that the Attorney General bring such actions was basically twofold.

First, there was the strong feeling that cases of discrimination by State and local

government agencies should be handled by the full force of the United States of America acting directly through the Attorney General. By placing the full weight of the U.S. district courts behind equal employment opportunity in State and local governments, the committee bill provided the necessary machinery to insure that State and local government agencies fulfill the promise of equal rights.

In addition, the special enforcement procedure when State and local government agencies are respondents provides the necessary power to achieve results without the needless friction that might be created by a Federal executive agency issuing administrative orders to States and localities.

I will say, Mr. President, as further background, that sitting on the Labor and Public Welfare Committee we have men who have had distinguished careers before coming to the United States Senate in State government, some as attorneys general of the States that they represent here. So we felt that they spoke with particular authority about the possibility of friction that might be created by a Federal executive agency issuing administrative orders to sovereign States and their subdivisions.

Mr. President, it is for these reasons that I believe the amendment of the Senator from Colorado should be amended to provide special treatment for respondents who are governments, governmental agencies, or political subdivisions. In those cases the Commission should be required, after failing to obtain voluntary compliance, to refer the case to the Attorney General who would then be empowered to bring a civil action against a respondent in the appropriate United States district court.

Mr. President, further amplification is included in the committee report, and I ask unanimous consent that excerpts from the report constituting a further discussion of the wisdom of this amendment be printed in the RECORD at this point.   * * *

Mr. WILLIAMS. I know that this amendment was supported when it was offered to the bill and supported in the committee by the Senator from Colorado, and I would hope that he might favorably consider it as an amendment to his amendment.

This again, Mr. President, is one of the amendments offered to the Dominick amendment now. It was not offered before the vote was taken yesterday. These amendments were discovered to be necessary when we were put to a more complete examination of the Dominick amendment, and we felt that it would be wise indeed to add those things that Senator JAVITS and I and other Senators felt would be constructive additions to the Dominick amendment. This is one of those amendments.   * * *

Mr. DOMINICK.   * * *

Mr. President, I think this is an excellent amendment and I am very happy that the Senator from New Jersey brought it up. I think it is only fair for the purposes of the RECORD to remark that it is ironic that just yesterday the Senator from New York, backed by the Senator from New Jersey, eliminated the Attorney General or any of his staff from taking any case before the U.S. Court of Appeals, thereby limiting the Attorney General's office to appeals before the U.S. Supreme Court. This language provides fair representation for alleged aggrieved State, county, or local government employees in district court.

I, of course, heartily support that idea. I think it is very good; and, as the Senator from New Jersey has so properly said, it just does not seem right, and did not seem right in committee, that any agency of the Federal Government, as such, should have the right to sue, whether it be a State, city, town, school district, sanitation district, or whatever it might be, alleging that their employment practices were illegal.

It would seem to me, if we are going to provide grievance procedures for these employees it ought to be within the Justice Department so that the respondent governmental unit is dealing with one of the Federal Government's most respected and objective departments.

As a result, I am happy to endorse this particular amendment, and to have it added on to mine.

EDITORS' NOTE: *Sen. Javits (R., N.Y.) summarized the changes made in the Dominick amendment, No. 611, following its introduction and summarized the arguments of the opponents of the amendment.*

Senate

1-26-72

pp. 559, 560

Mr. JAVITS.

Mr. President, the absence of Members from the Chamber is obviously attribut-

able to the fact that Members are pretty well determined how they are going to vote. We have had enough practice in the last few days in view of this amendment and the various stages of it, I believe, to know our own minds. So, in the time allotted to me, I shall do only two things. One is to note the changes which have been made in the Dominick amendment in terms of what will be finally voted on, as no further amendment is permitted. Second, I shall summarize the arguments and the side of the opponents to the Dominick amendment as I see it.

Mr. President, first, as to the changes, we have given authority to the commission to send its own lawyers into the courts in terms of litigation, should the Dominick amendment carry, up through the Court of Appeals, leaving only the Supreme Court to the Attorney General, and leaving also pattern and practice suits to the Attorney General as well as suits involving government employees at the State and local levels. Those are three items that relate to the Attorney General.

Second, we have assured a government employee who is a complainant of the same treatment in respect of counsel and counsel fees as we do nongovernmental employees.

Third, we have given the respondent who is denied the right to sue, because the commission sues, the right to agree or disagree to a conciliation agreement or a settlement of his particular case which the commission might make. If he is going to be cut off, he has to agree to the settlement.

Also, we have limited backpay recovery to 2 years, which was in the original bill and somehow or other it was left out of the pending amendment inadvertently, as the Senator from Colorado explained.

Now, Mr. President, those are all desirable changes. Obviously these are important changes in the amendment. I believe they improve the amendment, but I believe the amendment should be defeated notwithstanding the precautions that the Senator from New Jersey (Mr. WILLIAMS) and I, and others, have taken to "clean it up," which we had the opportunity to do in the last day and a half.

The reasons I believe the amendment should be rejected are six. I shall list them, and I do not list them necessarily in order of importance because I think they all rank equally in importance.

The first reason is that this is a usual power for Government agencies which we intend to have power. Most analogous, of course, to this situation is the National Labor Relations Act. I have submitted a long list of agencies, led off by the National Labor Relations Board, so both commissions and Government departments have cease-and-desist powers.

The second point is that 32 of the 50 States which give authority in respect of fair employment practice activities, led by my own State of New York, which passed the Ives-Quinn bill bearing the name of Irving Ives who served with distinction in this Chamber, have enforcement powers in the State agency or commission, or the local attorney general, to wit, a cease-and-desist order. So there is nothing unusual in granting the authority.

All the fears expressed by the Senator from Colorado (Mr. DOMINICK) and those who support him that the authority would be used in an inquisitorial way, or in an arrogant or arbitrary way, were voiced 26 years ago in New York. Those fears have all come to naught. It has been an entirely satisfactory statute where the cases going to court have been few and the conciliations have been many. It has kept the workload within reasonable bounds and that has been possible also in other States.

The third point is that the cease-and-desist power is important because it gives agencies some teeth—even a little teeth because any respondent can take a case into court. But it gives the agency some teeth because the agency can proceed with finality. It gives the agency a greater likelihood of getting a conciliation than would otherwise be possible.

* * *

The fourth point is that the backlog in the courts is extremely heavy. In the district courts, where under the Dominick amendment suits would have to be filed, it is the heaviest, being around a 20-month period in the major industrial States where most of these cases would be carried on. Again, to relieve that congestion, a minimization of cases flowing to the courts would go to the Circuit Courts of Appeal, which is of great importance in terms of the cease-and-desist power.

Fifth, we want the law enforced. We passed the law in terms of the Civil Rights Act of 1964 so we should want it enforced and it is not being adequately enforced as evidenced by the thousands of cases in the backlog.

The sixth point is that the best way to cut the workload is to give the cease and desist power: one, to encourage conciliation agreements, and that is the experience of Federal and State agencies; and second, and critically important because so few cases, and that is the experience, go from these cease and desist powered commissions or other agencies to the courts.

Appendix F-27

Administration: Oaths or Affirmations

EDITORS' NOTE: *Senators Allen (D., Ala.) and Ervin (D., N.C.) introduced an amendment restoring the requirement that charges under the Act be made in writing under oath or affirmation. The amendment was adopted and appeared in the final bill.*

Senate

2-21-72

pp. 2182, 2183

The assistant legislative clerk read as follows:

On page 50, between lines 19 and 20, to insert the following at the end of section 4 with a proper subsection designation:

As used in this act, the term "charge" shall mean an accusation of discrimination supported by oath or affirmation."   * * *

Mr. President, the purpose of this amendment is to require that charges of discrimination filed with the Commission shall be under oath or affirmation. For some reason unexplained, but apparently not intentional, the amendment as drafted and the committee substitute as reported, leave off the requirement that a charge be under oath.

The present law and the committee report containing a copy of the present law, at page 55, section 706(a) points out:

Whenever it is charged in writing under oath by a person claiming to be aggrieved—

So all this amendment would do would be to go back to the present law and make no change in the requirement, meaning charges are to be filed and made under oath in writing.

I am advised that the sponsors of the bill have no objection to the amendment. I trust that they will so state.

Mr. WILLIAMS. Mr. President, I gather that one copy has been taken from the Chamber. Does the Senator have another copy of the amendment?

Mr. ALLEN. No, sir. The amendment adds a new section at the end of section 4, and it is between lines 19 and 20 on page 50 of the bill. It merely states that the word "charge" as used in the act shall be a charge supported by oath or affirmation.

Mr. WILLIAMS. I wonder if the Senator would refer to the bill at page 34, and whether this would not be the place to make the bill conform to present law.

Mr. ALLEN. The only reason we did not put it there would have been because four or five subsections start off with reference to a charge, and it would have been necessary to amend the bill at about four or five places, whereas if we add one coverall, blanket statement it would cover the matter without trying to amend it as four or five different points, and possibly not covering every one.

Mr. WILLIAMS. The present law makes the requirement in one place, and it is in section 706.

Mr. ALLEN. Yes.

Mr. WILLIAMS. "Whenever it is charged in writing under oath." I do not know why it was taken out of the bill, but I would think that would be the place to put it back.

Mr. ALLEN. As I stated, if it were put back, it would also have to be put back

on page 35, subsection (c), where it refers to the case of a charge; it would also have to be put on page 36, subsection (d), where it refers to the case of a charge; it would also have to be put on page 37, subsection (e), where it refers to the case of a charge.

Mr. WILLIAMS. If the Senator will yield further, if it could be done in one place, it probably would be best to do it in section 706(b) where the requirement would be put at the very beginning: "Charges shall be in writing under oath or affirmation." That would be on line 21, page 34, of the bill before the Senate.

* * *

Mr. WILLIAMS. The Senator has accommodated this provision to those who, for one reason or another do not resist taking an oath, and suggests putting it "in writing under oath or affirmation."

Mr. ALLEN. That is the way we have worded it.

Mr. WILLIAMS. Certainly, in the liberal spirit of today—

Mr. ERVIN. Mr. President, if the Senator will yield, I would suggest to the distinguished Senator from Alabama that he modify his amendment so as to read, on page 34, line 21, insert the following between the word "writing" and the word "and": "under oath or affirmation."

Mr. ALLEN. Very well.

Mr. President, I offer a modification of my amendment in the manner suggested by the distinguished Senator from North Carolina.

The amendment, as modified was, on page 34, line 21, after the word "writing," insert "under oath or affirmation."

Appendix F-28

Administration: Affirmative Action Programs

EDITORS' NOTE: *Under an amendment introduced by Sen. Ervin (D., N.C.), OFCC, having approved an affirmative action plan, could not subsequently reject the plan without giving the employer an opportunity to be heard under the Administrative Procedure Act. After two provisions were added to the amendment, it was adopted by a vote of 77 to 0 and was included in the bill as enacted.*

Senate

1-26-72

pp. 578-580

Mr. ERVIN. Mr. President, I modify my amendment so that it will read as follows:

On page 61, after line 23, insert the following new section:

SEC. 10. No Government contract, or portion thereof, with any employer, shall be denied, withheld, terminated, or superseded, by any agency or officer of the United States under any equal employment opportunity law or order, where such employer has an affirmative action plan which has previously been accepted by the Government, without first according such employer full hearing and adjudication under the provisions of 5 U.S.C. section 554 and the following pertinent section: *Provided, however,* That if such employer shall deviate substantially from such previously agreed to affirmative action plan, this section shall not apply. * * *

Mr. ERVIN. I modify my amendment to read as I have stated, and send the amendment to the desk in that form.

I have had many complaints from employers seeking Government contracts that, after long negotiations with the Office of Contract Compliance of the Department of Labor, they have filed affirmative action plans in full compliance with all of the suggestions made by the Office of Contract Compliance and that such affirmative action plans have been approved by the Office of Contract Appliance, and that after all these procedures have been complied with, the Office of Contract Compliance, without any warning or any notice of any further opportunity to be heard, has refused to approve the contract sought by those employers.

This amendment would merely give some semblance to fair play in cases where employers had filed and had approved by the Office of Contract Compliance an affirmative action plan, and provide that after it had approved it the Office of Contract Compliance could not reject that plan without giving the employer an opportunity to be heard under the Administrative Procedure Act.

The amendment safeguards the Office of Contract Compliance by providing that if there is a substantial deviation from the approved affirmative action plan, this section, which gives the employer in such cases the right to a hearing and adjudication under the Administrative Procedure Act, does not apply.

It seems to me this is a fair amendment and that it ought to be supported by any Senator who believes in fair play under those circumstances. I sincerely hope the Senate will adopt it.

Mr. WILLIAMS. Mr. President, as I heard the amendment stated, I thought I heard the word "superseded," so that the amendment would read:

No Government contract, or portion thereof, with any employer, shall be denied, withheld, terminated, or superseded, by any agency . . .

I believe the word should be "suspended."

Mr. ERVIN. Suspended. I will modify the amendment and change the word from "superseded" to "suspended."

Mr. WILLIAMS. Then, as I understand the amendment, it brings the Administrative Procedure Act due process provisions to bear when there is an action to cancel a contract and an affirmative action plan is already in effect with that employer.

Mr. ERVIN. That is the objective.

Mr. WILLIAMS. That is the objective of the amendment.

Frankly, it strikes me as an eminently fair requirement where an employer is working under an agreement for affirmative action. This kind of suspension could sweep away his contract even though he thought he was complying.

Mr. ERVIN. That is correct. If affords an escape value for the Office of Contract Compliance by providing that this provision is not binding on the Office of Contract Compliance in the event the employer substantially departs from the agreed to affirmative action plan.

Mr. WILLIAMS. That is the objective—provided, however, that if such employer shall deviate substantially from such previously agreed to affirmative action plan, this section—which is the amendment—shall not apply.

It strikes me on its face as a fair procedure.

We had no testimony on it, I will say to the Senator from North Carolina, and no opinions from departments or agencies or otherwise. So it comes de novo, but as it comes de novo, it comes with some effect.

I know the Senator from New York, with the best of his good legal mind, is at work on this amendment at the moment, and so I will yield to the Senator from New York.

Mr. JAVITS. The Senator can practically see my wheels turning, as he can see the wheels of the Senator from North Carolina turning.

There are a few questions I would like to ask the author of the amendment, if he will indulge me. By the way, we are checking upon the question of whether this may not be attributable to the very same section I dealt with, but that will not matter. I will agree with the Senator about writing it so that it will conform to the amendment which was offered by me.

Mr. ERVIN. I tried to conform it. It may be that it deals with the same section. I think we can straighten that out by applying it to the same subsection.

Mr. JAVITS. We do not have any problem, but I wanted to ask the Senator a couple of questions.

There are two things which strike me at first impression, and again, as th Senator from New Jersey (Mr. WILLIAMS) said, it is new matter, first impression, so I hope the Senator will not feel I am just engaging in supererogation. I really do not know.

The Senator speaks, in line 5, of an affirmative action plan. It would seem to me that in order to have it appropriate, the words "in effect" should appear after the word "plan." I do not know whether these plans are limited in time or what is the situation, just off the top of my head, but I certainly believe that it would be necessary to have a plan ongoing at the time, rather than merely qualifying under this section because at one time there was an agreement.

Mr. ERVIN. If they have a plan that has been approved by the Office of Contract Compliance, it has been approved and there it is, it would be in effect.

Mr. JAVITS. Not necessarily, because if it had a time limit, and that time limit had expired, it would still be an affirmative plan which had been approved, but might not be in effect.

It just strikes me as a lawyer that we ought to include the fact that it has been an ongoing plan.

Mr. ERVIN. I think it is implied that it is in effect, but the trouble of it is, if we put that word in there, it may be construed to give them the right to repudiate, and get them back to the very position that the amendment is intended to safeguard the man against.

Mr. JAVITS. I do not see how that could happen, because the initiatory action is on the part of the employer; he can demand a hearing.

In other words, the Government is in a position where, if he gets a hearing, that operates this section. But all I am saying is, I think we ought to be protected against that situation.

Mr. ERVIN. Well, here is the difficulty: The Office of Contract Compliance has been approving plans, time after time they approve a plan and then, after approving the plan, they refuse to give a man a contract based on the plan that they have approved.

The objective of the plan is to prevent discrimination, and all this says is that after they have approved a plan, they cannot deny the man the contract as long as he is willing to comply with it,

and it gives the man the right to go into court and let the court decide whether the plan that has been approved by the Office of Contract Compliance, which they seek to repudiate, complies with the provisions of the Executive order or the provisions of the law outlawing discrimination.

The trouble is that under the present circumstances you cannot sue in the courts because when you offer to give a contract it is not approved; and this is an effort to give some legal remedy where the compliance contract has been approved by the agency, and then the agency seeks to repudiate it. It is to try to get out from that arbitrary practice which they now have.

I have many complaints about this. The trouble with the Office of Contract Compliance, so I have been informed by many employers, is that they will never put in writing what they require, but they make the employer come and put his plan in action, and then they either accept it or repudiate it. This ends repudiating it after they have accepted it, and gives him a legal remedy, and allows the court to say whether the contract complies with the Executive order and the law, instead of leaving that matter to be determined solely by the Office of Contract Compliance.

Mr. JAVITS. Well, Mr. President, there is nothing which the Senator has stated which, it seems to me, answers the point which I make, unless he says that by implication, though I do not know where it arises, it must be a plan, to wit an affirmative action plan, which is in effect; because if the contracting agency, in making and approving the plan, has limited the time of its approval—suppose, for example, that in making and accepting the plan and approving the plan, they said, "We approve it for 1 year" or "We approve it for 2 years," after the expiration of that time, certainly, I would expect that the mover of the amendment does not expect this section to be effective if the time of approval given to the plan has expired.

That is all I am asking. In other words, that it is an affirmative action plan that is in effect.

Mr. ERVIN. The trouble of it is, since the Office of Contract Compliance is the one that makes the contract, they can say, "We have decided that we have changed our mind, and although we have approved this in the past as a sufficient compliance, we now change our mind and demand that you submit another plan"; and if we have "in effect," it is implied that this whole arbitrary power of changing the rules for compliance will be perpetuated.

Mr. JAVITS. As I understand the Senator, then, he expects that government agencies will be forever bound, without any opportunity to change any kind of plan with any contractor, once they have acted. Under those circumstances, they would never approve a plan; they would be foolish if they did.

Mr. ERVIN. Well, they have to approve a plan.

Mr. JAVITS. If they would approve something more permanent than the Constitution of the United States, which is what the Senator is arguing for; if, once they approve the plan, that is the end of it forever and ever, I just cannot see that.

Mr. ERVIN. No; the amendment does not provide that. It says that once they have approved a plan, the Office of Contract Compliance cannot repudiate its approval, but, instead of having them repudiate it, once they have approved it, the matter is for the courts to decide.

Mr. JAVITS. I am glad to get that construction. Then the amendment says that once they have granted approval, it is approval forever and ever unless otherwise ordered by the courts. I could not approve it on that ground.

Second, Mr. President, I asked the Senator whether it is his intention, and I gather from the language that it is, that nothing may be done about the contract whatever under such a plan—which is, incidentally, a "forever plan"—without an extended court proceeding, or a court proceeding, no matter how long it takes, even if successful appeals to the U.S. Supreme Court may take years—no limitation whatever upon the time taken in respect to court adjudication and hearing, et cetera. Is that not true?

Mr. ERVIN. Yes; if you have a legal remedy afforded a man, I do not know how you can take it away.

Mr. JAVITS. That is all right. I understand.

Mr. ERVIN. I just do not believe in arbitrary action. Under the present circumstances, the Office of Contract Compliance has the arbitrary power to deny a man a Government contract, even though the man is complying fully with the executive order and the law. It denies access to the courts, and gives to the Office of Contract Compliance an arbitrary power which any absolute eastern potentate would envy.

Mr. JAVITS. Mr. President, I do not see that the amendment of the Senator gives the courts an opportunity to review an affirmative action plan, that is, make a judicial review of an affirmative action plan, at the time that such a plan takes effect, or at any time that it is effective.

What I see is that there is an absolute mandate, without any possibility of it even being changed by the court itself, that so long as there are legal proceedings pending, no matter how dilatory they maybe in the conduct of them, nothing may be done about that contract.

On that basis, Mr. President, I think the prejudice is very strongly against the enforcement of the law; it gives any contractor an opportunity just to make the claim, he need prove nothing else; then he goes into court, and just as long as he takes, he takes, and no penalty whatever ensues.

That is a pretty easy deal for anybody who wants to break his affirmative action plan, or has a disagreement about what it means, and there is no penalty whatever—to just take it to the courts and just keep it there. We certatinly have a great deal of experience with long court cases. If that is the construction of the amendment, I would feel, in conscience, that I would have to be very strongly against it. I would have no reason to be against an amendment to give judicial review.

To simply suspend any possibility of action of any kind during the conduct of legal proceedings—I cannot conceive of that as being conducive to fair enforcement of the law, and I shall oppose the amendment.

Mr. ERVIN. Mr. President, if this amendment is not adopted, the Office of Contract Compliance of the Department of Labor has arbitrary, tyrannical power that cannot be reviewed by any court on the face of the earth. If they can deny due process, they can deny hearing, and no power on the face of this earth can interfere with them, even though the affirmative action plan which the office has approved is in full compliance with the law and would be so adjudged by a court of law under the Administrative Procedure Act.

I think that every Member of the Senate who does not think the courthouse door should be totally nailed shut and the Office of Contract Compliance given power which nobody on earth can review, as to whether it is in compliance with the law, ought to vote for this amendment.

Mr. WILLIAMS. Mr. President, will the Senator yield for a question?

Mr. ERVIN. I yield.

Mr. WILLIAMS. On line 5 of the Senator's amendment, it reads "where such employer has an affirmative action plan." The word "has" suggests the present tense to me, and that suggests an affirmative action plan that is in effect.

Mr. ERVIN. That is right.

Mr. WILLIAMS. I thought that was one of the questions that the Senator from New York asked. I thought he was suggesting that there was a possibility that under this amendment there could have been a former affirmative action plan but one that was not in effect at the moment when a contract might have been denied or suspended.

Mr. ERVIN. I think the Senator's interpretation is absolutely correct. It must have been approved by the Office of Contract Compliance. It must be in existence.

Mr. WILLIAMS. That clarifies that part of it for me.

The other question I have is as to the impact of the words "under the provisions of title 5, United States Code, section 554, and the following sections thereto." The Senator from New York was developing the suggestion that action on a contract could be held up following long, long court procedures. Is this a procedure going to court or is this the hearing——

Mr. ERVIN. It would go to the court on the record already made in the Office of Contract Compliance.

Mr. WILLIAMS. These are the Administrative Procedure Act provisions of an administrative hearing?

Mr. ERVIN. Yes; all the court would have the power to consider would be the record already made in the Office of Contract Compliance.

Mr. WILLIAMS. On another matter, we were on other sides of an issue of the dignity of an administrative hearing, and I wanted to clarify that. But that refers to the Administrative Procedure Act agency hearing, with all its provisions.

Mr. ERVIN. Yes; so there cannot be anything very long about that. They already have in writing all the evidence that can be considered.

Mr. JAVITS. Mr. President, the section 554 hearing, which I have not even had a minute to check out, assuming even what the Senator says, which is set up in the appendix to our own report—I do not know whether it is complete or partial here—represents an adjudication which relates to an agency proceeding.

Those cases can take years, and there is no way, if we adopt this amendment and leave it this way, in which that process can be changed. A man might be able to go on violating as much as he likes, so long as he claims he is not.

Mr. President, I have just stood with leaving OFCC in the Department of Labor, and that is why it is my duty to question this amendment. I want to find out if it would nullify or put in the hands of any contractor the ability to nullify any effort to really get a remedy. One other thing: The proviso at the end says:

Provided, however, that if such employer shall deviate substantially from such previously agreed to affirmative action plan, this section shall not apply.

In other words, if the agency is trying to penalize him because he has deviated, then he is home free under this amendment, and the only time he can be dealt with is if he shall deviate after he says he did not deviate; and the previous transaction is completely overlooked, if you follow the words of this amendment.

So, Mr. President, under these circumstances, I respect the Senator from New Jersey—he has had this matter under first impression, as have I; but I could not be a party to accepting the amendment without further study, especially in view of the good faith involved in just having adopted an amendment which leaves the authority in the Department of Labor. I certainly could not see my way clear to, in my judgment, just emasculate it by this amendment.

Mr. ERVIN. Mr. President, I can understand the Senator from New York favoring nailing the courthouse door shut. But it would mean injustice because of nonreviewable arbitrary exercise of power by a public official. It is a very peculiar position for a lawyer of his distinguished record to take.

These contracts are referred to the Office of Contract Compliance for only one purpose. Otherwise, the contracts are worked out by the other agencies of the Federal Government. They are referred to the Office of Contract Compliance merely for the purpose of affording that office an opportunity to determine whether the affirmative action plan which is required is in compliance with the laws, the Executive order, and the regulations prohibiting discrimination in employment. That is the only function of the Office of Contract Compliance in the matter. Here they approve an affirmative action plan. They say it is in compliance with the laws, the Executive order, and the regulations. All this says is that after they have approved, they cannot repudiate the approval without affording the employer who has satisfied the other agencies of Government with the terms of the contract the opportunity to have the question determined, not by arbitrary action on the part of an executive office but by a court of justice.

With all due respect to my good friend from New York, the contention that there will be any protracted litigation in a case of this kind is absurd. That is so because that court hears the matter and determines whether there is sufficient compliance with the laws, the Executive order, and the regulations prohibiting discrimination. It has to hear it and determine it on the record. Otherwise the Office of Contract Compliance can dictate and lay down terms that are absolutely inconsistent with the laws, terms which are inconsistent with the Executive order, and inconsistent with their own regulations on the subject. American citizens who have supported this Government by their taxes are powerless and have no remedy this side of heaven.   * * *

Mr. JAVITS. Mr. President, in my judgment, the import of the amendment—and that is the reason I oppose it at this time and perhaps will propose a substitute to it—will not have the effect of fairly and equitably getting a judicial review of a contested situation where an individual government contractor feels that he is being imposed on notwithstanding the fact that he is complying with the affirmative action plan which is in effect.

Now the distinguished Senator from North Carolina (Mr. ERVIN) argued that the words which he used, "has an affirmative plan which has previously been accepted by the Government," complies in effect with what was told the distinguished Senator from New Jersey (Mr. WILLIAMS), but with me, he denied that. He says, once there had been affirmative action, then there was affirmative action forever. That is one of the things I cannot accept.

Second is the proviso which is tacked on at the end here which says that "if such employer shall deviate substantially from such previously agreed to affirmative action," thereby reiterating the point which the Senator certainly would not concede, in my judgment, but which I think has to be conceded in language, in view of the argument about it—to wit, that once the plan is previously agreed to, it remains forever, the plan to which the Government is bound, even though the Government may not wish further to be bound and the plan itself might have a definite time limitation on it which the

parties would have a perfect right to insert. The words "shall deviate" also may indicate that whatever has been the violation with which the contractor is charged is forgiven.

It only means that he shall not have the advantage of this section for any future violation. I certainly think that would vitiate the intent of fairness, especially if there is no limitation whatever in the power of any court to terminate this immunity which is granted to the individual contractor once he makes the claim—that is all he has to do. It seems to me that we can then completely nullify the whole enforcement scheme which is incorporated in the Executive order simply by making a complaint that the Government is penalizing us unduly in respect of the affirmative plan that was approved—God knows when—and whether it is still in effect, and then there is no penalty whatever on the contractor of any kind or character and he can get all the Government contracts he wants.

That certainly is making a real mockery of the whole idea that the Government will have any authority to enforce its Executive order. It is entirely possible—and I do not say that it is not—perhaps to put this particular proposition—although it is one of first impression—into shape, because we do not even know right now, and I do not know and I cannot represent to the Senate whether it is or is not—any right of judicial review in respect of this matter at this time. This is a very important question so that we may at least juxtapose the remedy which is sought here with the remedy now in effect. Therefore I really want a little while to have a good look at this. It may be possible to work out an amendment, or by amending the amendment, or by agreement with the Senator from North Carolina which will make a fair disposition of this matter. I have every desire to do so, but I am not going to be rushed into acting on this matter up or down without having some opportunity to see what should be done about it.

Senate

1-27-72

p. 632

Mr. JAVITS. Mr. President, if the Senator will yield, overnight my staff and that of Senator WILLIAMS and the staff of Senator ERVIN and the agencies concerned—to wit, the Equal Employment Opportunity Commission and Government procurement people—have been in touch with each other. That is, the agency of the Department of Labor dealing with Government contractors and equal employment opportunity have been in touch with each other, and they have now produced a draft of a revised Ervin amendment which takes account of the problems raised by the Senator, with which there was substantial agreement by the Senator from New Jersey (Mr. WILLIAMS) and myself, except that I could not see that the way in which the amendment had been drafted solved the problems. I now believe that it solves the problems equitably, technically, and appropriately and I am prepared, on a rollcall vote, to vote for the amendment.

* * *

Mr. ERVIN. I therefore ask unanimous consent that my amendment No. 597 be modified to conform to the draft agreed upon by the staff of the Senator from New Jersey, the staff of the Senator from New York, and my staff. I send to the desk a copy of the revised draft and ask the clerk to state it so that the Senate may know what modifications are being made.

The ACTING PRESIDENT pro tempore. The modification will be stated for the information of Senators and then the question will be put as to whether unanimous consent is granted for the modification.

The legislative clerk read the modified amendment as follows:

At the end of the bill add the following new section.

SEC. 14. No Government contract, or portion thereof, with any employer, shall be denied, withheld, terminated, or suspended, by any agency or officer of the United States under any equal employment opportunity law or order, where such employer has an affirmative action plan which has previously been accepted by the Government for the same facility within the past twelve months without first according such employer full hearing and adjudication under the pro-

visions of 5 U.S.C. § 554, and the following pertinent sections. *Provided, however,* That if such employer has deviated substantially from such previously agreed to affirmative action plan, this section shall not apply. *Provided further,* That for the purposes of this section an affirmative action plan shall be deemed to have been accepted by the government at the time the appropriate compliance agency has accepted such plan unless within 45 days thereafter the Office of Federal Contract Compliance has disapproved such plan.

Mr. ERVIN. Mr. President, perhaps I should clarify the remarks I made about the manner in which the compromise draft was reached. I stated that it was worked out by the staffs of the Senator from New York, the Senator from New Jersey, and myself. I might state that they did so under our direction. The staffs did a remarkable job in putting in understandable phraseology, the agreement which we had reached in respect to this very important matter.

Mr. WILLIAMS. Mr. President, I wanted to say that rather late last evening I was working with the Senators' staffs. I think that we can all be grateful for their faithfulness to the observations made by the Senator from North Carolina on the floor and after we left the floor. It represents, in my judgment, a solution to the question and some of the anxieties felt which prompted the Senator to offer the original amendment in the spirit in which I agreed with it yesterday with certain reservations. The reservations have now been removed. I think that this modification is necessary as part of this legislation to insure that the objectives are reached and the process of scrupulous fairness preserved.

Mr. ERVIN. I thank the Senator. I would suggest, so early in the session, with so few Senators in the Chamber, that it might be advisable to have a quorum call before we vote. So far as I am concerned, I am ready to vote.

Appendix F-29

Administration: Court Review of EEOC Determinations

EDITORS' NOTE: *Senators Allen (D., Ga.) and Ervin (D., N.C.) sought to strike from the bill language providing that an EEOC determination that the Commission cannot secure a conciliation agreement is not reviewable by the courts. The amendment was defeated 14 to 49.*

Senate

1-14-72

p. 1649

Mr. ALLEN. Mr. President, the amendment which I have just sent to the desk for myself and the distinguished senior Senator from North Carolina (Mr. ERVIN) would knock from the bill one phrase, as follows: On page 38, beginning on line 10, "which determination shall not be reviewable in any court."

This bill as introduced and as amended by the committee empowers this Commission to act as court, jury, investigator, and prosecutor all rolled into one. It provides that if the Commission at the outset of the complaint and its investigation determines it is unable to secure voluntary compliance from the respondent under a conciliation agreement acceptable to the Commission, which determination shall not be revealable in any court, then this would knock out that phrase "which determination shall not be reviewable in any court."

Senate

1-14-72

p. 1651

Mr. JAVITS. Mr. President, as we understand the amendment—we have sought to analyze it quickly in the time which has been made available—it seeks to provide a court review where the Commission rejects, or is unable to secure, a conciliation agreement from the respondent.

We can hardly conceive seeking to deprive the Commission of the opportunity to use its judgment, through court review, to endeavor to obtain a conciliation agreement or to substitute a court for it in deciding whether a conciliation agreement is acceptable. We come to the conclusion that that is what the amendment means when it says if the Commission determines—that is, the determination after attempting to secure voluntary compliance under subsection (b)—that it is unable to secure from the respondent a conciliation agreement acceptable to the Commission.

Therefore, it seems to us that if this amendment is adopted, the words "acceptable to the Commission" might just as well be stricken, because if the Commission is not permitted to determine that it is unable to secure a conciliation agreement, certainly one is not going to stultify the Commission and demand that it accept one which is not acceptable to it. Therefore, the determination beomes meaningless.

It seems to me that if we are going to give them the power of entering into a conciliation agreement at all, it has got to be one which they regard as acceptable, and not one mandated upon them by a court. So, if the amendment is to prevail, the whole clause ought to be stricken and the statement just ought to be that if the Commission determines, after attempting to secure voluntary compliance to subsection (b), that it cannot secure voluntary compliance, then it may go ahead and issue a complaint, or—if the Senate decides tomorrow to vote on the substantive matter—if it has got to sue, that it then can go ahead and sue.

I cannot see how one can expect the Commission to stultify itself by being subject to an order of the court that it is able rather than unable to secure a conciliation agreement acceptable to it. I emphasize that the amendment does not seek to strike those words. They remain in the clause.

So it seems to be that the words "which determination shall not be reviewable in any court," if we strike those out, now that they have occurred, it would simply stultify the Commission as well as the process. Our understanding of what is sought to be done here may be incorrect, but that is the way it seems to us, Mr. President.

For those reasons, as we wish to favor rather than frustrate conciliation with respect to activities of the Commission, and most of these cases, the overwhelming majority, are settled as a result of conciliation agreements, and since there is no compulsion on the respondent—he does not have to enter into the conciliation agreement in any way, shape or form—it seems to me that the determination which this amendment would carry out is quite inappropriate, and that the Senate should reject the amendment.

Appendix F-30

Administration: Reverse Discrimination

EDITORS' NOTE: *An amendment prohibiting the Federal Government from requiring an employer to practice discrimination in reverse— that is, requiring him to employ persons of particular race, religion, or national origin in either fixed or variable numbers—was introduced by Sen. Ervin (D., N.C.) and defeated by a vote of 22 to 44.*

Senate

1-28-72

pp. 691, 692

The assistant legislative clerk read as follows:

Add a new section at the end of the bill appropriately numbered and reading as follows: "No department, agency, or officer of the United States shall require an employer to practice discrimination in reverse by employing persons of a particular race, or a particular religion, or a particular national origin, or a particular sex in either fixed or variable numbers, proportions, percentages, quotas, goals, or ranges. If any department, agency, officer, or employee of the United States violates or attempts or threatens to violate the provisions of the preceding sentence, the employer or employee aggrieved by the violation, or attempted or threatened violation, may bring a civil action in the United States District Court in the District in which he resides or in which the violation occurred, or is attempted or threatened, or in which the enterprise affected is located, and the District Court shall grant him such relief by way of temporary interlocutory or permanent injunctions as may be necessary to redress the consequences of the violation, or to prevent the attempted or threatened violation. * * *

Mr. President, this amendment is very clear. It is in complete harmony with the other provisions of the Senate committee bill, strange to say.

All the other provisions of the Senate bill are avowedly included in the bill to prevent any employer, whether he is engaged in the work of Caesar or in the work of the Lord, who is touched by the bill, from practicing discrimination against applicants for employment or persons who desire to be promoted or persons who desire not to be discharged on account of their race, religion, national origin, or sex.

The amendment is in perfect harmony with that objective of the Senate committee bill because it forbids discrimination in reverse.

It gives access to the courts to prevent any department or agency or officer of the United States from requiring any employer to practice discrimination in reverse.

When Congress adopted the Civil Rights Act of 1964 it undertook to forbid discrimination in reverse.

It inserted in title VII of that act a provision which stated in about as plain words can be found in the English language that no employer should be required to hire employees on a quota system; that is, a system which required him to employ certain numbers or percentages of a particular race, or a particular religion, or a particular national origin, or a particular sex.

I thought that that provision of title VII of the Civil Rights Act of 1964 was so plain that he who runs might read it and not err in so doing.

But some officials who are charged by the Executive order relating to discrimination in employment—Executive Order 11246—and who are charged with enforcing the provisions of title VII of the Civil Rights Act of 1964 were apparently illiterate or educated way past their intelligences, and they could not understand the plain and the unambiguous words of Congress which were designed to prevent what is probably known as discrimination in reverse.

As a consequence of this lack of understanding of the plain and unambiguous words of the English language employed in title VII of the Civil Rights Act of 1964, the Office of Contract Compliance on virtually every occasion has required employers seeking Government contracts to practice discrimination in reverse. The EEOC, on less frequent occasions, has haled employers before its bar to practice discrimination in reverse.

It is to be noted that the Office of Federal Contract Compliance in the Department of Labor is charged with exactly the same duty in respect to employers seeking Government contracts that the EEOC is charged with in respect to employers generally. The sole function of the Office of Federal Contract Compliance under the Executive order is to review proposed contracts which various executive departments or agencies have made to obtain work or services for the Federal Government and to make sure that those contracts prohibit discrimination against employees or applicants for employment because of their race or religion or national origin or sex.

One of the strange things about Government is that it has an insatiable thirst for power and that if we give an executive department or an executive agency an inch of authority, it converts that inch of authority into a mile of authority. This has been true in respect to the Office of Federal Contract Compliance in the Department of Labor and it has been true in some instances in respect to the EEOC itself. The most notorious example of discrimination in reverse has been embodied in the concept set forth in what is popularly known as the Philadelphia plan.

The Office of Federal Contract Appliance adopted the Philadelphia plan and required building contractors who obtained contracts from the Federal Government of certain magnitude to deny the employment of members of the majority race until the employees belonging to the minority race reached certain percentages or certain proportions of their total employees.

Manifestly this requires discrimination in favor of the members of the minority race and discrimination against members of the majority race. In other words, it requires discrimination in reverse.

EDITORS' NOTE: *Amendment 907, introduced by Sen. Ervin (D., N.C.), would have made the prohibition on requiring preferential treatment applicable to all executive departments and agencies engaged in enforcing equal employment opportunity laws. The measure was defeated by a vote of 30 to 60.*

Senate

2-22-72

pp. 2275, 2276

Mr. ERVIN.   * * *
I ask unanimous consent that subsection (j) of section 703 of the Civil Rights Act of 1964 be printed in the RECORD at this point.

There being no objection, the statute was ordered to be printed in the RECORD, as follows:

PREFERENTIAL TREATMENT

(j) Nothing contained in this title shall be interpreted to require any employer, employment agency, labor organization, or joint labor-management committee subject to this title to grant preferential treatment to any individual or to any group because of the race, color, religion, sex, or national origin of such individual or group on account of an imbalance which may exist with respect to the total number or percentage of persons of any race, color, religon, sex, or national origin employed by any employer, referred or clas-

sified for employment by any employment agency or labor organization, admitted to membership or classified by any labor organization, or admitted to, or employed in, any apprenticeship or other training program, in comparison with the total number or percentage of persons of such race, color, religion, sex, or national origin in any community, State, section, or other area, or in the available work force in any community, State, section, or other area.

Mr. ERVIN. Any Senator who is desirous of understanding this amendment can read the amendment in the light of subsection (j) of section 703 of the Civil Rights Act of 1964 and understand what it would do.

It is designed to make the prohibition upon preferential treatment created by this subsection of the original act applicable not only to the EEOC, but also to the Office of Contract Compliance and to every other executive department or agency engaged, either under the statute or under any Presidential directive, in enforcing the so-called equal employment opportunity statutes.

Mr. JAVITS. Mr. President, I yield myself 1 minute in opposition to the amendment.

What is sought to be done here is to apply a particular provision of the Civil Rights Act of 1964 to the Executive order in order to make unlawful any affirmative action plan like the so-called Philadelphia Plan, and, by including the Executive order in this title, that would effectively be done, so that the Federal Government, as an employer, would be inhibited from putting into effect such a plan.

We have held that, because the Federal Government—we voted on that here; we debated it and we decided it—has an interest in maintaining constitutional guarantees, it has discretion as to whom it will contract with and will not contract with, to affirmatively encourage nondiscrimination and full utilization of minority group employees and women. So we—and the courts have sustained us—permitted the Federal Government to put into effect an affirmative-action plan.

This amendment, for practical purposes, would simply nullify that action. For those reasons, I oppose the amendment and hope it will be rejected.

Appendix F-31

Administration: Preponderance of Evidence

EDITORS' NOTE: *Sen. Ervin (D., N.C.) introduced an amendment making clear that EEOC should make its findings of fact conform to the preponderance of the evidence. The amendment was agreed to in a voice vote but eliminated in conference.*

Senate

1-28-72

p. 706

Mr. ERVIN. Mr. President, if I may have the attention of the distinguished manager of the bill for a moment, I will state that the amendment would merely make clear that in making findings of fact, the Commission should make the findings of fact conform to the preponderance of the evidence. I understand that there is a probability that the distinguished manager of the bill may be willing to accept the amendment.

Mr. WILLIAMS. Yes. We discussed the purport of the amendment during the debate on an earlier amendment. I recall that this amendment, dealing with the preponderance of evidence at the Commission level, was included in a bill passed by the Senate 2 years ago. The Senator from North Carolina offered the amendment then, it was agreed to, and was in the bill passed by the Senate at that time. It was not included in the bill reported by the Senate committee this year. It should be in the bill, in my judgment.

Appendix F-32

Administration: EEOC Acceptance of Voluntary Services

EDITORS' NOTE: *Sen. Allen (D., Ala.) proposed striking from the committee bill language permitting EEOC to accept voluntary and uncompensated services. The amendment was rejected by a vote of 26 to 53.*

Senate

1-26-72

pp. 581-583

Mr. ALLEN. Mr. President, the amendment seeks to strike from the bill words that were added by the committee to the bill as a proposed addition to the present law. These are the words which the committee seeks to enact and the amendment seeks to prevent from becoming law. The commission is given the authority—

And to accept voluntary and uncompensated services, notwithstanding the provisions of Section 3679(b) of the Revised Statutes (31 U.S.C. 665(b)).

What is that section of the code from which the committee substitute seeks to exempt the EEOC? The present law, going back to the year 1870, in the section cited:

No officer or employee of the United States shall accept voluntary service for the United States or employ personnel service in excess of that authorized by law, except in cases of emergency involving the safety of human life or the protection of property.

I was not on the committee which brought forth this substitute, but I have read some of the hearings, and I did not come across any testimony in the hearings. I am not saying that some testimony was not there that I did not see, but I would invite the manager of the bill to cite to me those pages. I do not see one single bit of testimony in favor of this language that seeks to give the Commission the authority to accept voluntary and uncompensated service from individuals.

What is the purpose of this language? Why should the EEOC come out from under the law that applies to every other Federal agency in the country? So far as the junior Senator from Alabama knows, no agency, no branch of the Government, is authorized to call in hordes of individuals off the streets and, in effect, to accept their services and give them the power, the authority, and the indicia of office as Federal employees. Obviously, there would be no volunteers unless the persons volunteering were biased or prejudiced or had some ax to grind. Why would they come forward and volunteer to work for the EEOC? There is no reason in the world, except that they would have an ax to grind. They would have a prejudice or a bias, or else they would not offer their services. They would not offer their services to any other branch of the Government, so far as the junior Senator from Alabama is concerned.

Furthermore, Congress is supposed to have the power to circumscribe or to limit the power, the authority, and the scope of the work of any agency of Government by controlling the amount of money appropriated to that department or agency. But in this instance the EEOC would have the authority, unless this amendment shall be adopted, to accept the voluntary and uncompensated services of hundreds of thousands of people— people with prejudices, people with biases, people subsidized by interested organizations, people subsidized by foundations which have an interest in carrying on this work.

So, Mr. President, the EEOC might have 1,000, 2,000, 3,000, or 4,000 Federal employees on the payroll, but there would be nothing whatsoever, in the absence of this amendment, to prevent the EEOC from availing itself of the services of tens of thousands of individuals who would be sent out over the country like a swarm of locusts to harass business and industry—small business, persons employing as few as eight people.

So since the year 1870, according to the footnote to this section, this provision of law has applied to the agencies of the Federal Government—that they shall not have the authority to reach out and get voluntary employees, uncompensated employees, and put them to work.

Does that make sense, Mr. President? Is it not necessary for a Federal employee to pass a civil service examination? Is it not necessary that some check be made as to his reputation, his loyalty to the Government, his educational qualifications, his personality, his fitness for Government employment?

But, under this committee substitute, Mr. President, which we are seeking to change by this amendment, no check need be made, and the agency could become a colossus, a Frankenstein, of volunteer and uncompensated employees, uncompensated so far as the Government is concerned.

Who would be paying these uncompensated employees and volunteer employees? Not the Federal Government, but someone having an interest in seeking harassment of business and industry and of employees and employers.

Mr. President, all the amendment seeks to do is to take out the language that has been added by the committee. I showed this language to a distinguished member of the committee just the other day. He said:

I was on that committee and heard the hearings. I did not know we had a section like that in the bill.

A very learned member of the committee, a very able Member of the Senate, said:

I had no idea such a section was in the bill.

I hope the manager of the bill will accept the amendment; that he will not insist on taking out the provisions of law which prohibit the use of uncompensated and voluntary employees with respect to this one agency of Government.

Why should it stand on any basis higher than the Justice Department? Do they accept volunteer employment? Can any zealous person come to the Justice Department and say, "I am interested in this activity of the Federal Government and I want to go out as a volunteer worker for the Government"? What would be the liability of the Government for the acts of such employees? Who would be responsible for what they did? Would the Government be liable or responsible for the act of such employees? What would it be?

There must be some reason—and I think we have suggested some of them— why for 100 years there has been a prohibition against the use of volunteer and uncompensated employees by any branch of the Federal Government, and the bill before the Senate would take the EEOC out from under this very fine safeguard against such a practice.

I would be interested in learning from the manager of the bill why this section was put in. Is not the EEOC going to be satisfied with the appropriations made by the Congress? Is it not going to be satisfied to limit its activity to the scope envisioned by the Congress in setting the appropriation? The machinery set up in the committee substitute would give the EEOC the authority to enlarge this department, to enlarge the scope of its activities, 50 percent, 100 percent, 200 percent—any amount of enlargement that it would care to have—through the use of volunteer employees, compensated by someone else, because you can rest assured that they are going to be compensated. They are not going to work for nothing.

* * *

Mr. WILLIAMS. Why is this necessary and whether there is enough money to hire the personnel needed? Was that the question?

Mr. ALLEN. No. I asked the Senator to respond to my inquiry as to why the committee put in the provision giving the EEOC the authority to use volunteer or uncompensated employees when no other branch of the Federal Government has that authority and when there is an express provision in the code prohibiting the use of such employees.

Mr. WILLIAMS. I am not sure whether that is accurate as to any other agency.

Mr. ALLEN. There is a law on it.

Mr. WILLIAMS. I know, but there are exceptions made for other agencies. My understanding is that title VII, when enacted in 1964, said that the Commission shall have power to cooperate with, and with their consent utilize, regional, State, local, and other agencies, both public and private, and individuals. Under this provision, individuals were used who were volunteers. Some question was raised and, in order to insure that volunteers could be used in limited circumstances, this provision was put in the bill, as we had it 2 years ago. It was preserved in this bill. It was in the bill that we voted on and which passed the Senate 2 years ago.

Mr. ERVIN. Is the Senator saying this is not new language?

Mr. WILLIAMS. It was in the bill as introduced.

Mr. ERVIN. The committee report shows otherwise, Senator. It is in italics, which indicates that it was inserted.

Mr. WILLIAMS. While this is being walked over to the Senator, I would say that the following is the situation: This could be called the Johnny Cash amendment in the bill. This provides that a Johnny Cash or a Bill Cosby who wants to use his talent to deal with the idea of equal opportunity in a song, or prose, or poetry, can do so however he wants to: "You fellows have an Equal Employment Opportunity Commission and, if you are being denied, that Commission is there on your side." That is what it is.

That is what it is. It is the Bill Cosby provision of the EEOC bill that is before us.

Mr. ALLEN. Well, now, if the Senator would allow me to engage in a little colloquy with him on this point, was there any testimony before the committee as to the desirability of putting this section or this language in? If so, I would like him to cite it to me.

Mr. WILLIAMS. I do not know that it was formalized in the hearing, but certainly the information reached us that a question had been raised about the procedure being used by the Commission, and to clarify it so there would be no mistaking the authority, this language had been put in, and it was put in when we drafted the bill, yes.

Mr. ALLEN. So the committee decided, then, that it would be necessary to take them out from under the provisions of the code forbidding that practice, is that correct?

Mr. WILLIAMS. To make it clear that volunteers could participate, yes.

Mr. ALLEN. Who pays these volunteers? Would the Senator enlighten the junior Senator from Alabama on that question? Do they have any volunteers from industry or business?

Mr. WILLIAMS. I cannot answer that. I would hope so. I would imagine that there are people from the ministry, from business, from entertainment, and just people who might——

Mr. ALLEN. Who think that discrimination exists throughout the country, and they want to cure that evil?

Mr. WILLIAMS. As I understand it, those who have been used have been helpful in publicizing the fact that this country has an Equal Employment Opportunity Commission.

Mr. ALLEN. Who pays those individuals?

Mr. WILLIAMS. That is it. This is to be noncompensated. These are volunteers.

Mr. ALLEN. I understand, but most of them have to eat, I suppose. Who pays them?

Mr. WILLIAMS. Well, now, there are as I understand it, 100 of the major companies, business organizations, which have been combined in the plans for progress organization, have volunteered their people, their names, themselves. Who pays them for this work? Nobody.

Mr. ALLEN. That is to go out and check other industries and businesses, is it?

Mr. WILLIAMS. No, it is not investigation. It is to publicize the fact of the existence of an Equal Employment Opportunity Commission.

Mr. ALLEN. There is nothing in here that would prevent them from doing some investigating, is there?

Mr. WILLIAMS. I beg the Senator's pardon.

Mr. ALLEN. There is nothing in the bill to prevent them from doing anything the commission wanted them to do, including investigation.

Mr. WILLIAMS. Well, there is nothing in there because it is so wholly unlikely. There are many things that are not in here that are obviously not needed.

Mr. ALLEN. Would the Senator feel that there would be a chance that, through the use of volunteer uncompensated-by-the-Commission employees, it would be possible for the commission to double its size without coming to Congress?

Mr. WILLIAMS. No.

Mr. ALLEN. Why not?

Mr. WILLIAMS. Because it would violate every reason known to man, that is why.

Mr. ALLEN. The Senator said 100 industries were turning their employees loose. How many from each industry?

Mr. WILLIAMS. As I have seen it work, a vice president may be assigned to this worthy, worthy activity, without major staff, but he, with his commitment and with the backing of his company, will come to the activity and publicize its support of the work of the Equal Employment Opportunity Commission.

Mr. ALLEN. How many employees does the EEOC have now, does the Senator know?

Mr. WILLIAMS. At this point?

Mr. ALLEN. Yes.

Mr. WILLIAMS. The last figure that reached me was just over 1,000 employees

Mr. ALLEN. Well, how many does the Senator feel it would take to carry on the expanded work, the expanded scope of the commission, if this bill passes as it now stands?

Mr. WILLIAMS. Well, we have a judgment on that out of the hearings—and I believe it is stated in the committee report. Page 32 shows the estimate of costs, and that could be, with the employees we have now, the increase could be, roughly estimated, it would be an increase over the years projected—1972, 1973, 1974, 1975, 1976—it would be an increase, over the next 4 years, doubling the number of employees. With the 1,000 now, it would be 2,000 then. That is an estimate.

Mr. ALLEN. The Senator would not feel it would be possible for the commission to utilize another 2,000 from the ranks of volunteer and uncompensated employees?

Mr. WILLIAMS. Well, I do not know where—I think it is most unreasonable to assume that there is any possibility of that. In fact, it is just plain unreasonable to think in those terms.

Mr. ALLEN. Could the Senator say how many volunteer employees the commission is using now, without the sanction of this section?

Mr. WILLIAMS. Well, the major—the area of greatest impact is one man and his talents: the entertainer, Bill Cosby.

Mr. ALLEN. I understood the Senator to say there were 100 industries.

Mr. WILLIAMS. One hundred businesses have been associated, and I think it is high-level executives; I have already estimated that at 100.

Mr. ALLEN. One hundred businesses, but how many from each business?

Mr. WILLIAMS. That is on a part-time basis. I would say, on a strictly part-time basis, as I have observed it, for every vice president of a regional telephone company, there may be three people working with him, and it is obviously not full time.

Mr. ALLEN. That would be about 300, then? Three for each one of the businesses?

Mr. WILLIAMS. If it were 100, and they each had a total of three, that would add up to 300.

Mr. ALLEN. Under the present law, though, they are not taken out from under this section of the United States Code, are they?

Mr. WILLIAMS. No.

Mr. ALLEN. Yes. Now, if it is 300 without any sanction of law, then, without any bill taking them out from under the Code section, there would be no limit to the number of voluntary employees that they could use. Is that correct, there would be no limit?

Mr. WILLIAMS. Well, there is not any limit in the bill as it applies itself, no.

Mr. ALLEN. No. What would these people be? Would they be Federal employees, or what would their status be?

Mr. WILLIAMS. I beg the Senator's pardon.

Mr. ALLEN. What would the status of these voluntary persons be? Would they be Federal employees?

Mr. WILLIAMS. No.

Mr. ALLEN. They would not be Federal employees?

Mr. WILLIAMS. If the President of United States Steel wanted to voluntarily make an announcement of his association or his company's association with the objectives of the Equal Employment Opportunity Commission, that would be permitted under this act.

Mr. ALLEN. Yes. Well, now, if the Southern Christian Leadership Conference wanted to furnish the EEOC with 200 or 300 volunteer employees to go out over the country working on this project——

Mr. WILLIAMS. Which project?

Mr. ALLEN (continuing). They could be accepted, could they not?

Mr. WILLIAMS. Well, what is the project? Which project?

Mr. ALLEN. Well, the matter of bringing equal economic opportunities to the people in the country. That is what the bill is for, is it not? That is what I understood.

Mr. WILLIAMS. Does the Senator mean to publicize and——

Mr. ALLEN. I do not know what they would do. They could investigate if they wanted to.

Mr. WILLIAMS. No, no, no, these are not investigators by any means.

Mr. ALLEN. Where does the bill say that?

Mr. WILLIAMS. These are not employees. The law provides for the employment of people, and the employment of people for all of the procedures of this commission. Volunteers are not to go to court or to investigate.

Mr. ALLEN. Where does the bill say that? The bill does not say that. They want to get 10 attorneys in the general counsel's office.

Mr. WILLIAMS. It is in the report, and that does not have the force of law. I would be happy if the Senator would want to offer another amendment to further define the volunteer.

Mr. ALLEN. No. I would rather eliminate the entire section.   * * *

Mr. ERVIN. Mr. President, I rise in support of the amendment.

I think it is repugnant to the first principle of sound government to allow volunteers to exercise governmental power. The provision which the amendment—which has been ably discussed by the distinguished Senator from Alabama—seeks to strike is found on the last three lines of page 59, lines 23, 24 and 25, and the first two lines of page 60. This provides that the Commission can accept voluntary and uncompensated services notwithstanding the provisions of section 3649(b) of the revised statutes.

I respectfully submit that it is extremely unwise for a commission, which is charged with the performance of a judicial function and which exercises the power of judges, to have the assistance of volunteers who are so biased in favor of the enforcement of the law that they are willing to work for nothing, provided they are allowed to exercise governmental functions and assist a commission that is supposed to sit as an impartial judge of a cause.

For these reasons, I think the amendment of the Senator from Alabama should be adopted and that the commission should not be accepting the services of biased people whose bias prompts them to volunteer their services. I think it is essentially incompatible with sound government for nongovernmental officials to be performing a governmental function. This provision should be stricken from the bill.

EDITORS' NOTE: *An amendment introduced by Sen. Chiles (C., Fla.) specified that EEOC could accept volunteer or uncompensated services for the limited purpose of publicizing in the media the Commission and its activities. The amendment was adopted by a vote of 67 to 3, but did not appear in the final bill.*

Senate

1-31-72

pp. 821, 822

Mr. CHILES. Mr. President, last week, the distinguished Senator from Alabama (Mr. ALLEN) offered an amendment to section 705, subsection (e), to strike that section, whereby the Commission could, contrary to present statutes, accept voluntary and uncompensated services. That amendment was rejected.

At that time, the distinguished chairman of the committee, the Senator from New Jersey (Mr. WILLIAMS), made statements in the RECORD to the extent that it was necessary or that they felt it was good for the Commission to be able to accept voluntary services solely to be able to publicize the work and activities of the Commission. I think the example was given that it was valid to have a provision whereby a personality like Bill Cosby could say on television, "If you don't think you have been treated fairly, there is a commission, and you can go to that commission and find out what your rights are."

Mr. President, I am not sure that it is necessary to have any language in the bill, regardless of our present statutes, for any person to be able to speak through any of the media to publicize anything that is the law of the United States.

The first amendment of the Constitution and the other provisions would certainly give to every citizen the right to speak but, at the same time, I was concerned that the amendment by the Senator from Alabama did fail, and the language now in the present law certainly is sufficiently broad which would lend itself to the Commission, regardless of what the present purpose is today, and regardless of what Congress is today. Certainly the language was there, and sufficiently broad, and would allow the Commission to accept any number of volunteers up into the thousands for anyone, regardless of what the motivation and the interest is, to go to the Commission and, the way the law is now framed, have the right not only to make findings of fact but also to issue cease and desist orders of those findings.

If that is not the purpose, and we say it is not, then we should narrow the scope of the law. That is what the amendment I have introduced proposes to do. In the language, where we seek to accept voluntary or uncompensated services, we would strike the express limitation or limiting language for the limited purpose of publicizing in the media the Commission and its activities. This would allow the Bill Cosby situation—it is allowable anyway—but if we strike the whole thing it is allowable, but certainly allowable under the language and, at the same time, we would narrow it, as I think the Senator from Alabama was attempting to do in his amendment; that is, to clarify that we would not have this open for any group of volunteers which felt it had to or expressed itself as wanting to come in and be clothed with authority to investigate and perhaps to prosecute activities of the Commission when we do not do this anyway in any agency of Government.

I first considered that we bring this to the attention of the Senate by way of drawing up an amendment which would say that any of these volunteers who were so accepted by the Commission would also be entitled to be volunteers with the FBI or the Internal Revenue Serv-

ice. I think, when we think in those terms, none of us would consider having volunteers for any purpose; and yet the express purpose of this, we are told, is not for that but only to publicize it. If that is so, then I would think this amendment would clarify and narrow it.

I urge adoption of my amendment.

Mr. WILLIAMS. Mr. President, there was an amendment offered to strike from the bill the provisions that permitted acceptance of volunteer services. It was an amendment which did not carry. This provision stayed, in. Notwithstanding that vote, there has been some discussion of just what services are contemplated under the provisions in the bill.

As I have listened to the Senator from Florida, it seemed to me that some of the anxieties expressed were expressed in extravagant terms as to what it really meant.

As I debated, in opposition to the original amendment, I indicated that it was the basic purpose of the provisions in the bill to permit the Commission to receive the services of volunteers who wanted to publicize the work of the Commission and what it was all about. I mentioned certain people who do work and are prominent in the media. I recall mentioning particularly Bill Cosby. It may be my impression but the limitations we were contemplating is that this is an amendment that clarifies in bill language the purpose that I thought were the intentions in the bill and, for that reason, it clarifies and pinpoints the activities that can be accepted publicizing in the media the Commission and its activities. It is certainly acceptable to me. The Senator from New York and I have discussed this and he shares my view. It is acceptable to him as well.

The Senator's clarification is in good order.

Appendix F-33

Administration: Transfer of OFCC Functions

EDITORS' NOTE: *Sen. Saxbe (R., Ohio) introduced an amendment to the committee bill striking those provisions under which the functions of OFCC would be transferred to EEOC. The amendment was agreed to by a vote of 49 to 37.*

Senate

1-26-72

pp. 563, 564

Mr. SAXBE. Mr. President, the amendment I offer concerns a most difficult legislative decision involving the area of equal employment opportunity, specifically the Executive order program of the Department of Labor, insuring equal employment by Federal contractors and subcontractors.

We shall soon be asked to vote upon S. 2515, which would provide, among other things, for the wholesale removal of the Department's Executive order program, which is now competently administered by the Office of Federal Contract Compliance, to the already overburdened EEOC. The amendment would strike section 10, which is the transfer section of the bill we are considering.

I believe that the significance of our decision in this matter warrants a brief explanation of the nature of the Executive order program administered by the Department's OFCC and how well the Department of Labor's OFCC has executed the President's mandate.

As Senators undoubtedly know, the "affirmative action" concept is the mainstay of the Executive order program, having had its importance first recognized by then Vice President Richard M. Nixon, who observed that "overt discrimination" was not the principal obstacle to achieving equal employment opportunity for today's generation of citizens. The affirmative action concept was thereafter adopted by President John F. Kennedy in 1961 by Executive Order 10925. It has since been reaffirmed by President Johnson in Executive Order 11246 and by President Nixon through several Executive orders, the numbers of which I shall supply.

The OFCC's affirmative action programs have tremendous impact and require that 260,000 Government contractors in all industries adopt positive programs to seek out minorities and women for new employment opportunities. To accomplish this objective, the OFCC has utilized the proven business technique of establishing "goals and timetables" to insure the success of the Executive order program. It has been the "goals and timetables" approach, which is unique to the OFCC's efforts in equal employment, coupled with extensive reporting and monitoring procedures that has given the promise of equal employment opportunity a new credibility.

The Executive order program should not be confused with the judicial remedies for proven discrimination which unfold on a limited and expensive case-by-case basis. Rather, affirmative action means that all Government contractors must develop programs to insure that all share equally in the jobs generated by the Federal Government's spending. Proof of overt discrimination is not required.

The success of the OFCC's affirmative action program is clearly evident among the Nation's leading industries. As a result of OFCC programs for the construction industry, 46 voluntary and imposed plans have been created to bring more than 30,000 minority workers into the skilled construction trades. Special efforts in the textile industry resulted in an increase of minority employment rate from 12.8 percent in 1968 to 18.4 percent of the total 1971.

In education, 101 monitored universities had established a goal of 10,784 new hires for minorities and women and actually hired 17,889, and in the banking industry, the 2,400 largest banks covered by the Executive order increased minority employment from 8 percent in 1966 to 14 percent in 1970.

The critical OFCC mission to insure equal employment opportunity can continue to register such successes only if performed within the executive branch, and within that branch, the Department of Labor is clearly the most appropriate agency to further that mission. This is so because, to be effective, the contract compliance program must be an integral part of the procurement process. The process of procuring goods and services, as I am sure you recognize, is peculiarly a function of the executive branch.

Equal employment opportunity, is of course, a workplace standard much like the many other employee protections which are now offered employees, as minimum wage and safety standard. The Department of Labor is the Government's expert administrator of workplace standards.

Moreover, occupational training programs are the keys to successful employment and the Department's Manpower Administration plays a critical role in the implementation of the Executive order program. Further and of particular moment, the Department has been a leader in developing programs designed to assist women in the workforce; namely, the Department's vigorous enforcement of the Equal Pay Act and the functioning of the Women's Bureau within the Department are examples of its total commitment to EEO for women. Cooperation between OFCC and the Women's Bureau was an essential aspect of OFCC's recent issuance of revised order No. 4 requiring Government contractors to develop goals for new hire and upgrading opportunities for women. Further, the presence of Cabinet-level direction has achieved the vital program coordination necessary to program success and funding and staffing of the OFCC through the Department of Labor enables the OFCC to draw upon the full range of staff and resources of a Cabinet agency.

The proposed transfer of functions under Executive Order 11246 from the OFCC to the EEOC would jeopardize the contract compliance program. The EEOC is ill-equipped to assume the responsibilities for the implementation of the Executive order program. Chairman Brown of the EEOC has stated that the assumption of Executive order responsibilities by the EEOC is administratively impracticable and has given four reasons: First, there is an ever increasing number of cases pending before the EEOC which has already resulted in a 2-year backlog; second, the incompatibility of agency functions: EEOC is a regulatory agency under title VII—OFCC is a procurement program manager under the Executive order; third, new and different responsibilities would disrupt coordination in title VII and its administration would suffer, and perhaps most importantly there might be serious problems of conflict in both the area of remedies and the area of investigation.

There is a great potential conflict in the assumption by EEOC of the Executive order program responsibility. For example, Chairman Brown described a situation where no violation of title VII might be found but where a violation of the contract compliance standards would be evident.

The affirmative action concept as innovatively and successfully employed by the OFCC has been challenged as a violation of title VII—the courts have responded by stating that the Executive order program is independent of title VII and not subject to some of its more restrictive provisions.

Section 10 of the proposed bill would place the entire Executive order program under title VII and might well result in renewed challenges to the many important programs established thereunder—for instance, the Philadelphia plan. Further, the proposed bill would endanger the survival of the contract compliance program by making its resources dependent upon the EEOC—an independent, hybid agency with limited manpower and economic resources.

For these reasons, I ask that you vote for the amendment to S. 2515 striking that provision of the bill—section 10—which would transfer the Office of Federal Contract Compliance to the EEOC.

Appendix F-34

Administration: EEO Coordinating Council

EDITORS' NOTE: *Creation of an Equal Employment Opportunity Coordinating Council, consisting of the Secretary of Labor, the chairman of EEOC, the Attorney General, and the chairman of the Civil Rights Commission was provided under an amendment offered by Sen. Javits (R., N.Y.). The amendment was agreed to, and the bill as enacted provided for the creation of a Coordinating Council.*

Senate

1-26-72

pp. 576, 577

The amendment reads as follows:

On page 61, after line 23 add the following:

SEC. 715. There shall be established an Equal Employment Opportunity Coordinating Council (hereinafter referred to in this paragraph as the Council) composed of the Secretary of Labor, the Chairman of the Equal Employment Opportunity Commission, and the Attorney General, and the Chairman of the United States Civil Rights Commission, or their respective delegates. The Council shall have the responsibility for developing and implementing agreements, policies and practices designed to maximize effort, promote efficiency, and eliminate conflict, competition, duplication and inconsistency among the operations, functions and jurisdictions of the various departments, agencies and branches of the Federal government responsible for the implementation and enforcement of equal employment opportunity legislation, orders, and policies. On or before July 1 of each year, the Council shall transmit to the President and to the Congress a report of its activities, together with such recommendations for legislative or administrative changes as it concludes are desirable to further promote the purposes of this section.   * * *

Mr. JAVITS.   * * *

Mr. President, this amendment proposes to establish an Equal Employment Opportunity Coordinating Council composed of the Secretary of Labor, the Chairman of the Equal Employment Opportunity Commission, the Attorney General of the United States, and the Chairman of the U.S. Civil Service Commission, or their respective delegates. The Council will have the responsibility of developing and implementing agreements, policies, and practices designed to maximize the efficiency and effectiveness of the whole equal employment opportunity program of the Federal Government, including, of course, the program covering Federal contractors under Executive Order 11246.

On or before July 1 of each year, the Council is required to report to the President and to the Congress.

Mr. President, when we were debating the amendment which was just agreed to, I said that I would submit an amendment. It seemed to me to be a balance of equity. I voted for the Saxbe amendment without any particular joy in my heart. I know how deeply how many people, including the civil rights organizations, felt about the transfer of OFCC, and I am all for the bill, as is well known. However, on this particular situation, I felt that the backlog was such that in decency to my own argument that cease and desist was necessary to break the backlog, I should not add to it. This is a totally new responsibility and would add to it. Therefore, as we can make this transfer at any time, I felt that in sustaining that point of view and in sustaining my own feeling——   * * *

Mr. JAVITS. Therefore, since we can make this transfer at any time, I felt that in sustaining that point of view and in sustaining my own feelings about the so-called Philadelphia plan, for which I fought and bled successfully on this floor, I felt consistently that we had to leave this particular office at this time where it was. But it was a legitimate point made by Father Hesburgh in the testimony and report which the Senator from New Jersey (Mr. WILLIAMS) so very properly called to our attention, that there is an inadequacy of coordination between this effort and the efforts of the Equal Employment Opportunity Commission. And in view of the fact that the Chairman of the Civil Rights Commission himself made this point, I thought that the best way to handle it if the amendment succeeded, as it has, was to create some kind of high-level agency,

not in a money sense or an institutional sense but as a body to ride herd on this particular proposition.

So I announced during the debate on the amendment of the Senator from Ohio (Mr. SAXBE) that I would make this proposal. I hope very much that under the circumstances of the amendment having been adopted it will be found acceptable to both sides. I do not feel that it is an oppositional thing at all; I think it will help both sides to deal with the situation.

Finally, all of us are, I think, agreed on the question whether the administration of this particular office by the Department of Labor has left very much to be desired. The Secretary of Labor himself recognizes that. I read into the Record the letter which he wrote to me, in which he proposes really to shake up this whole office. I think that may have been a matter of influence in respect of how Senators voted. I believe that the office of a high-level council, accountable to the country, will give us a greater sense of assurance that the deficiencies which the office has admittedly had may be more likely to be corrected by the composition of the council, because of the equal voice of the Secretary of Labor, in whose office it now is, as well as of the coordinating functions of the Chairman of the Equal Employment Opportunity Commission and the corrective functions of the Attorney General and of the Chairman of the U.S. Civil Rights Commission, who did recommend the transfer.

For all these reasons, I hope very much that the amendment, in view of the adoption of the previous amendment, will be adopted with the consent of both sides; I yield the floor.   * * *

Mr RANDOLPH. As I understand, the able Senator from New York is saying, in essence, that in no wise would this be a competitive approach; it would be an approach of coordination, with certain functions allotted to the several agencies mentioned.

Mr. JAVITS. I would take the first statement completely—that it is in no wise a competitive approach; it is a question of coordination. It is not even an allotment of functions. The functions will stay with the office in the Department of Labor. But at least we will have the security of knowing, first, that it is effectively tied into the Equal Employment Opportunity Commission; and second, that someone on a high level will be riding herd, to see to it that the office is really effective where it is.

Mr. RANDOLPH. I think the purpose of the amendment is excellent. As one who supported the Saxbe amendment, I certainly intended to support the effort of the distinguished Senator from New York.

It is critical that employers be in a position to rely on a coordinated government position on all matters, not the least of which is equal employment opportunity. It is just as vital to employees who feel that they have been subjected to discriminatory employment practices that the relevant agencies of government coordinate their efforts. It is also clear that the Government's effectiveness can be improved significantly. I believe the amendment offered by the distinguished Senator from New York (Mr. JAVITS) will help achieve these objectives.

* * *

Mr. WILLIAMS. The amendment would create an Equal Employment Opportunity Coordinating Council made up of the Secretary of Labor, the Chairman of the Equal Employment Opportunity Commission, the Attorney General, and the Chairman of the U.S. Civil Rights Commission.

Mr. JAVITS. The Senator is correct.

Mr. WILLIAMS. Or their respective delegates.

Mr. JAVITS. The Senator is correct.

Mr. WILLIAMS. I merely wanted to inquire about the term "their respective delegates." I am wondering whether we should name the agency or department and require that a delegate be the representative of the office. The delegation at this point somewhat disturbs me. I have the feeling, frankly, that I would rather not see someone outside of the Civil Rights Commission be the delegate of the Chairman of the U.S. Civil Rights Commission.

Mr. JAVITS. There are no hidden motives in the amendment. I would just as soon strike that part. My purpose was to use my best recollection, because I had to write the amendment rather quickly. I had no opportunity to use what we consider "boilerplate." If the Senator's assistant or mine can give us the usual "boilerplate" in this regard, I should be glad to use it. There is no desire to add another dimension to the amendment. We do not do it in other cases of high level interdepartmental committees.

The amendment will be in conference, and the Senator from New Jersey and I will be conferees. My suggestion is that

we work out there whatever is agreeable and convenient to the officials concerned. The purpose and intent of the amendment is to have attendance at the highest level. Unless the officials object very seriously, it would be fine with me if they are required to attend.

I am just concerned about doing this in the first instance, as I just do not know. But I would assure the Senator that I will join with him in conference in making it entirely agreeable to the officials, but making it on the highest level. If they are willing, we will strike out the reference to any delegation.

Mr. WILLIAMS. Of course, the Senator from New York has put his finger on my concern. It should be focused at the highest level.

Mr. JAVITS. I thoroughly agree, and I will join with the Senator in doing whatever is necessary for that purpose.

Mr. WILLIAMS. That is agreeable to me.

EDITORS' NOTE: *Sen. Javits (R., N.Y.) introduced amendment No. 848, which made the chairman of the Civil Service Commission a member of the Equal Employment Opportunity Coordinating Council. The amendment was included in the legislation as adopted.*

Senate

2-21-72

p. 2183

The assistant legislative clerk read as follows:

At the end of the bill add the following new section:

SEC. 14. The Chairman of the United States Civil Service Commission, or his delegate, shall be a member of the Equal Employment Opportunity Coordinating Council established by section 715 of the Civil Rights Act of 1964, as amended by this Act.

Mr. JAVITS. Mr. President, the purpose of this amendment is to make the Chairman of the U.S. Civil Service Commission a member of the Equal Employment Opportunity Coordinating Council, the idea being that, as we are introducing the Civil Service Commission into this legislation, the highest official of that Commission ought to be a member of the Coordinating Council which is established under this bill.

Appendix G

Amendments Adopted and Rejected by U. S. Senate

January 19, 1972—February 22, 1972

I. Amendments Adopted

	Sponsor	What Amendment Provided	Action Taken
1.	Schweiker (R., Pa.)	Provided for appointment by the President of a General Counsel for EEOC and gave such office responsibility over the Commission's main prosecutorial functions. (No. 797) Section 705(b) (1).	Offered, debated, and adopted. (1/20/72) Roll call vote, 67-0.
2.	Randolph (D., W.Va.)	Defined the term "religion" to include all aspects of religious observance and practice. Section 701(j).	Offered, debated, and adopted. (1/21/72) Roll call vote, 55-0.
3.	Javits (R., N.Y.)	Provided that all litigations in the federal appeals courts be conducted by EEOC, rather than the Attorney General. (Amendment to Dominick amendment No. 611; see No. 1 in Part II of this table.)	Offered, debated, and adopted. (1/24/72) Roll call vote, 40-37.
4.	Javits (R., N.Y.)	Struck those provisions of the Dominick amendment No. 611 (see No. 1 in Part II of this table) that withdrew legal services from federal employees.	Offered, debated, and adopted. (1/24/72) Voice vote.
5.	Javits (R., N.Y.)	Gave complainant the right to sue if EEOC entered into a conciliation agreement to which the complainant did not assent. (Amendment to Dominick amendment No. 611; see No. 1 in Part II of this table.)	Offered, debated, and adopted. (1/25/72) Voice vote.

	Sponsor	What Amendment Provided	Action Taken
6.	Williams (R., N.Y.)	Permitted actions against state and local government agencies to be brought in the federal district courts by the Attorney General, rather than EEOC. (Amendment to Dominick amendment No. 611; see No. 1 in Part II of this table.)	Offered, debated, and adopted. (1/25/72) Voice vote.
7.	Beall (R., Md.)	Provided that back pay liability shall not exceed that which accrues from a date more than two years prior to the filing of a charge with EEOC. Section 706(g).	Offered, debated, and adopted. (1/25/72) Roll call vote, 73-0.
8.	Saxbe (R., Ohio)	Struck that section of the bill transferring OFCC functions to EEOC. (No. 822)	Offered, debated, and adopted. (1/26/72) Roll call vote, 49-37.
9.	Javits (R., N.Y.)	Established the Equal Employment Opportunity Coordinating Council. Section 715.	Offered, debated, and adopted. (1/26/72) Voice vote.
10.	Ervin (D., N.C.)	Barred withholding or termination of a government contract with any employer without a full hearing and adjudication where the employer had an approved affirmative action plan. (No. 597) Section 718.	Offered, debated, and adopted. (1/27/72) Roll call vote, 77-0.
11.	Ervin (D., N.C.)	Made clear that EEOC's findings of fact should conform to the preponderance of the evidence. (No. 599)	Offered, debated, and adopted. (1/28/72) Voice vote.
12.	Gambrell (D., Ga.)	Provided for payment by the federal government of reasonable expenses and attorneys' fees of small businesses and small unions charged under the Act. (No. 833)	Offered, debated, and adopted. (1/31/72) Roll call vote, 72-2.
13.	Chiles (D., Fla.)	Specified that EEOC could accept volunteer or uncompensated services for the limited purpose of publicizing its activities. (No. 830)	Offered, debated, and adopted. (1/31/72) Roll call vote, 67-3.

14.	Ervin (D., N.C.)	Provided that Title VII cover employers of 25 or more and unions with 25 or more members. (No. 813) Modified by Williams-Javits amendment extending coverage to employers of 15 or more and unions with 15 or more members. Section 701(b).	Offered, debated, and adopted. (2/8/72) Roll call vote, 81-1.
15.	Dominick (R., Colo.)	Provided that where EEOC is unable to secure a conciliation agreement, it notifies the General Counsel, who may then bring a civil action in the appropriate federal district court against any respondent other than a government agency. (No. 884)	Offered, debated, and adopted. (2/15/72) Roll call vote, 45-39.
16.	Williams (D., N.J.) Javits (R., N.Y.)	Originally gave original jurisdiction to the federal district courts in issuing orders against discriminatory employment practices. (No. 878) It was amended by the Dominick substitute (see No. 15 above).	Offered, debated, and adopted. (2/15/72) Roll call vote, 81-3.
17.	Dominick (R., Colo.)	Amendments of a technical and conforming nature.	Adopted without debate. (2/15/72) Voice vote.
18.	Ervin (D., N.C.)	Provided that the term "employee" shall not include elected state officials or personal assistants chosen by such officials to render legal advice. (No. 888) Section 701(f).	Offered, debated, and adopted. (2/17/72) Roll call vote, 69-2.
19.	Ervin (D., N.C.)	Exempted religious organizations from application of the bill insofar as their right to employ people of any religion is concerned. (No. 809)	Offered, debated, and adopted. (2/21/72) Voice vote.
20.	Williams (D., N.J.)	Amendments of a technical or conforming nature. (Nos. 896, 897, and 899-902)	Adopted without debate. (2/21/72) Voice vote.
21.	Williams (D., N.J.)	Amendments of a technical nature.	Adopted without debate. (2/21/72) Voice vote.
22.	Allen (D., Ala.)	Required that charges of discrimination filed with EEOC be under oath or affirmation. Section 706(b).	Offered, debated, and adopted. (2/21/72) Voice vote.
23.	Javits (R., N.Y.)	Two amendments of a conforming nature.	Adopted without debate. (2/21/72) Voice vote.

Sponsor	What Amendment Provided	Action Taken
24. Javits (R., N.Y.)	Made provisions of bill applicable to pending cases. Section 14, P.L. 92-261.	Adopted without debate. (2/21/72) Voice vote.
25. Javits (R., N.Y.)	Made chairman of the Civil Service Commission a member of the Equal Employment Opportunity Coordinating Council. (No. 848)	Adopted without debate. (2/21/72) Voice vote.
26. Javits (R., N.Y.)	Established supergrade positions in EEOC. (No. 850) Section 12, P.L. 92-261.	Adopted without debate. (2/22/72) Voice vote.
27. Cranston (D., Calif.)	Brought Library of Congress under provisions of the bill relating to Government employees. Section 717.	Adopted without debate. (2/22/72) Voice vote.
28. Javits (R., N.Y.)	Provided that if designated judge hasn't assigned case for trial within 120 days after issue has been joined, he may appoint a master pursuant to rule 53 of federal rules of civil procedure. (No. 909) Section 706(f) (5).	Adopted without debate. (2/22/72) Voice vote.

II. Amendments Rejected (Title VII)

Sponsor	What Amendment Provided	Action Taken
1. Dominick (R., Colo.)	Would have permitted EEOC to take certain unlawful employment practice disputes that the Commission couldn't conciliate to the federal district courts for resolution. (No. 611)	Offered, debated, and rejected. (1/24/72) Roll call vote, 41-43. Motion to reconsider agreed to, 40-39. (1/24/72) Amendment rejected, 46-48. (1/26/72)
2. Allen (D., Ala.)	Would have deleted language permitting EEOC to accept voluntary and uncompensated services. (No. 819)	Offered, debated, and rejected. (1/26/72) Roll call vote, 26-53.
3. Allen (D., Ala.)	Would have substituted the House bill for the Senate version.	Offered, debated, and tabled. (1/27/72) Roll call vote, 45-32.

	Sponsor	Description	Disposition
4.	Ervin (D., N.C.)	Would have provided for court determination of a case in which the court concluded that EEOC's findings of fact weren't supported by the preponderance of the evidence in the record, rather than by substantial evidence. (No. 811)	Offered, debated, and rejected. (1/28/72) Roll call vote, 22-43.
5.	Ervin (D., N.C.)	Would have prohibited the federal government from requiring an employer to practice discrimination in reverse by employing persons of a particular race, religion, or national origin in either fixed or variable numbers, proportions, or percentages. (No. 829)	Offered, debated, and rejected. (1/28/72) Roll call vote, 22-44.
6.	Ervin (D., N.C.)	Would have removed provisions of the bill giving EEOC jurisdiction over employment practices of states or political subdivisions. (No. 812)	Offered, debated, and rejected. (1/31/72) Roll call vote, 16-59.
7.	Ervin (D., N.C.)	Would have exempted from the bill employers of individuals in educational or religious institutions. (No. 815)	Offered, debated, and rejected. (2/1/72) Roll call vote, 25-55.
8.	Hruska (R., Neb.)	Would have provided that, with certain exceptions, a charge filed with EEOC would be the exclusive remedy for any person claiming to be aggrieved by an unlawful employment practice. (No. 877)	Offered, debated, and rejected. (2/9/72) Roll call vote, 33-33. Motion to reconsider rejected. (2/15/72) Roll call vote, 37-50.
9.	Ervin (D., N.C.)	Would have exempted from coverage employment of physicians or surgeons by public or private hospitals. (No 858)	Offered, debated, and rejected. (2/14/72) Voice vote.
10.	Allen (D., Ala.)	Would have struck language providing that an EEOC determination that the Commission is unable to secure a conciliation agreement will not be reviewable by the courts.	Offered, debated, and rejected. (2/14/72) Roll call vote, 14-49.
11.	Hruska (R., Neb.)	Would have struck from the bill provisions transferring Attorney General's "pattern-and-practice" authority to EEOC. (No. 834)	Offered, debated, and rejected. (2/16/72) Roll call vote, 33-43.
12.	Allen (D., Ala.)	Would have provided that Title VII of Civil Rights Act not be applicable to state or local	Offered, debated, and rejected. (2/17/72) Roll call vote, 21-44.

	Sponsor	What Amendment Provided	Action Taken
13.	Ervin (D., N.C.)	government employees as long as Congressional employees are exempt therefrom. (No. 890)	
		Would have removed from the coverage of the bill employment of teachers or other faculty members of public schools. (No. 860)	Offered, debated, and rejected. (2/22/72) Voice vote.
14.	Ervin (D., N.C.)	Would have made prohibition on preferential treatment applicable to other executive agencies engaged in enforcing equal employment opportunity laws. (No. 907)	Offered, debated, and rejected. (2/22/72) Roll Call vote, 30-60.
15.	Ervin (D., N.C.)	Would have removed from coverage of the bill employment practices of all educational institutions. (No. 844)	Offered, debated, and rejected. (2/22/72) Roll call vote, 15-70.
16.	Ervin (D., N.C.)	Would have given litigants right to demand trial by jury of actions brought under this Act or Title VII of the Civil Rights Act. (No. 908)	Offered, debated, and rejected. (2/22/72) Roll call vote, 30-56.

Appendix H

Amendment Adopted by House of Representatives

September 16, 1971

Sponsor	What Amendment Provided	Action Taken
Erlenborn (R., Ill.)	Provided for court enforcement powers in lieu of "cease-and-desist" authority for EEOC; did not broaden EEOC's jurisdiction or transfer the functions of OFCC to EEOC. Sections 705, 706.	Offered, debated, and adopted. Teller vote, 200-194.

Topical Index